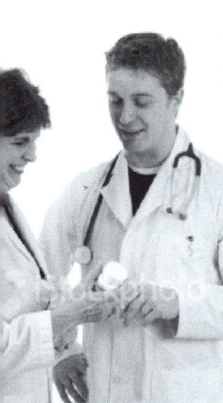

COMMUNITY AND CLINICAL PHARMACY SERVICES

A STEP-BY-STEP APPROACH

Notice

Medicine is an ever-changing science. As new research and clinical experience broaden our knowledge, changes in treatment and drug therapy are required. The authors and the publisher of this work have checked with sources believed to be reliable in their efforts to provide information that is complete and generally in accord with the standards accepted at the time of publication. However, in view of the possibility of human error or changes in medical sciences, neither the authors nor the publisher nor any other party who has been involved in the preparation or publication of this work warrants that the information contained herein is in every respect accurate or complete, and they disclaim all responsibility for any errors or omissions or for the results obtained from use of the information contained in this work. Readers are encouraged to confirm the information contained herein with other sources. For example and in particular, readers are advised to check the product information sheet included in the package of each drug they plan to administer to be certain that the information contained in this work is accurate and that changes have not been made in the recommended dose or in the contraindications for administration. This recommendation is of particular importance in connection with new or infrequently used drugs.

COMMUNITY AND CLINICAL PHARMACY SERVICES

A STEP-BY-STEP APPROACH

Editors

Ashley W. Ellis, PharmD, BCACP
Clinical Assistant Professor of Pharmacy
 Practice
University of Mississippi School of Pharmacy
Oxford, Mississippi

Justin J. Sherman, MCS, PharmD
Coordinator, Community Practice Residency
 Program
Associate Professor of Pharmacy Practice
University of Mississippi School of Pharmacy
Jackson, Mississippi

New York Chicago San Francisco Lisbon London Madrid Mexico City
Milan New Delhi San Juan Seoul Singapore Sydney Toronto

Community and Clinical Pharmacy Services: A Step-by-Step Approach

Copyright © 2013 by The McGraw-Hill Companies, Inc. All rights reserved. Printed in the United States of America. Except as permitted under the United States Copyright Act of 1976, no part of this publication may be reproduced or distributed in any form or by any means, or stored in a data base or retrieval system, without the prior written permission of the publisher.

1 2 3 4 5 6 7 8 9 0   DOC/DOC   18 17 16 15 14 13

ISBN 978-0-07-176375-2
MHID 0-07-176375-9

This book was set in Adobe Garamond by Aptara, Inc.
The editors were Michael Weitz and Robert Pancotti.
The production supervisor was Catherine H. Saggese.
Project management was provided by Amit Kashyap, Aptara, Inc.
The cover designer was LaShae V. Ortiz.
Cover photograph: istockphoto.com
RR Donnelley was the printer and binder.

This book is printed on acid-free paper.

Library of Congress Cataloging-in-Publication Data
Ellis, Ashley W., Sherman, Justin J.
Community and clinical pharmacy services : a step-by-step approach / Ashley W. Ellis, Justin J. Sherman
    p. ; cm.
    Community Pharmacy Services–organization & administration–United States
    Includes bibliographical references and index.
    ISBN 978-0-07-176375-2 (softcover : alk. paper)
        I. Pharmacies–organization & administration–United States.   II. Pharmacists–United States.
III. Professional Role–United States.   IV. Professional-Patient Relations–United States.   V. Program Development–United States.
    [DNLM: QV 737 AA1]

615.1068

2012047478

McGraw-Hill books are available at special quantity discounts to use as premiums and sales promotions, or for use in corporate training programs. To contact a representative, please e-mail us at bulksales@mcgraw-hill.com.

DEDICATION

This book is dedicated to my family. To Brent, my supportive husband. To Hadley, my adorable and future pharmacist little girl. And to John Ross, my baby boy who has literally been with me every step of the way while writing this book.

Ashley W. Ellis, PharmD, BCACP

This book is dedicated to my wonderful family: Sheila, my lovely wife, and Samantha, my talented daughter. Thank you for your unending love and support.

Justin J. Sherman, MCS, PharmD

CONTENTS

Contributors | ix

Reviewers | xi

Foreword | xiii

Preface | xv

Chapter 1	Practical Aspects of Service Implementation	1
Chapter 2	Documentation	15
Chapter 3	Counseling and Motivational Interviewing	29
Chapter 4	Medication Therapy Management	49
Chapter 5	Asthma	63
Chapter 6	Immunization Services	97
Chapter 7	Nonprescription and Self-Care	131
Chapter 8	Lipid Disorders	143
Chapter 9	Smoking Cessation	161
Chapter 10	Anticoagulation Services	197
Chapter 11	Diabetes	223
Chapter 12	Hypertension	253
Chapter 13	Osteoporosis	277
Chapter 14	Obesity—Weight Management Services	299

Answers and Explanations for Study Questions | 321

Index | 333

CONTRIBUTORS

LeAnn Causey Boyd, PharmD, BCPS, CDE
Causey's Pharmacy, Inc., Natchitoches, Louisiana

Liza G. Chapman, PharmD
Clinical Coordinator, The Kroger Company, Atlanta Division, Atlanta, Georgia

Meagan Brown, PharmD, BCACP
Clinical Assistant Professor of Pharmacy Practice and Coordinator of Community Pharmacy Development, University of Mississippi School of Pharmacy, Jackson, Mississippi

Courtney Davis, PharmD, BCACP
Clinical Assistant Professor of Pharmacy Practice, University of Mississippi School of Pharmacy, Jackson, Mississippi

Ashley W. Ellis, PharmD, BCACP
Clinical Assistant Professor of Pharmacy Practice, University of Mississippi School of Pharmacy, Oxford, Mississippi

Michelle Z. Farland, PharmD, BCPS, CDE
Associate Professor of Clinical Pharmacy, University of Tennessee Health Science Center College of Pharmacy, Knoxville, Tennessee

Stephanie S. Holliday, PharmD
Director, Clinical Program Development, Residency Program Director, AcariaHealth, Falls Church, Virginia

Sarah A. Parnapy Jawaid, PharmD
Associate Professor of Pharmacy Practice, Shenandoah University School of Pharmacy, Virginia

Lisa M. Lundquist, PharmD, BCPS
Assistant Dean for Administration and Clinical Associate Professor, Mercer University College of Pharmacy and Health Sciences, Atlanta, Georgia

Stephanie Harriman McGrath, PharmD
Clinical Community Pharmacist, Rite Aid Pharmacy, Assistant Professor, University of Pittsburgh School of Pharmacy, Pittsburgh, Pennsylvania

Brice L. Mohundro, PharmD, BCACP
Assistant Professor of Clinical and Administrative Sciences, University of Louisiana at Monroe College of Pharmacy, Louisiana

Katherine S. O'Neal, PharmD, MBA, BCACP, CDE, BC-ADM, AE-C
Clinical Assistant Professor, University of Oklahoma College of Pharmacy, Oklahoma

Shannon L. Reidt, PharmD, MPH
Assistant Professor, Department of Pharmaceutical Care and Health Systems, University of Minnesota College of Pharmacy, Minneapolis, Minnesota

Daniel Riche, PharmD, BCPS, CDE
Assistant Professor of Pharmacy Practice, University of Mississippi School of Pharmacy, Mississippi

Justin J. Sherman, MCS, PharmD
Associate Professor of Pharmacy Practice, Coordinator, Community Practice Residency Program, University of Mississippi School of Pharmacy, Jackson, Mississippi

Leah Snyder, PharmD
Community Pharmacy Resident, Causey's Pharmacy, Inc., Natchitoches, Louisiana

Todd D. Sorensen, PharmD, FAPhA
Professor and Associate Head, Department of Pharmaceutical Care and Health Systems, University of Minnesota College of Pharmacy, Minneapolis, Minnesota

Matthew Strum, PharmD, BCACP, CDE
Clinical Assistant Professor, Department of Pharmacy Practice, University of Mississippi School of Pharmacy, Oxford, Mississippi

Laurie Warrington, PharmD, BC-ADM, BCACP
Clinical Assistant Professor of Pharmacy Practice, University of Mississippi School of Pharmacy, Mississippi

Emily Weidman-Evans, PharmD, BC-ADM, CPE
Associate Professor of Clinical and Administrative Sciences, University of Louisiana at Monroe College of Pharmacy, Louisiana

Sarah M. Westberg, PharmD, BCPS
Associate Professor, Assistant Director, Ambulatory Care Residency Program, Pharmaceutical Care and Health Systems, University of Minnesota College of Pharmacy, Minneapolis, Minnesota

REVIEWERS

Lauren Bloodworth, PharmD, BCPS
Clinical Assistant Professor, Department of Pharmacy Practice
Director of Student Affairs
Coordinator of Student Services and Student Professional Development - UMMC
Administrator of Community-Based Research Program
University of Mississippi School of Pharmacy
Jackson, Mississippi
Reviewer: Asthma

Ashley W. Ellis, PharmD, BCACP
Clinical Assistant Professor, Department of Pharmacy Practice
University of Mississippi School of Pharmacy
Oxford, Mississippi
Reviewer: Documentation, Medication Therapy Management, and Osteoporosis

Stephen Foster, PharmD, FAPhA, FNAP
Professor and Vice Chair for Community Programs
University of Tennessee College of Pharmacy
Memphis, Tennessee
Reviewer: Immunization Services

Andrea Franks, PharmD, BCPS
Associate Professor, Clinical Pharmacy and Family Medicine
Assistant Dean, Assessment and Education
University of Tennessee College of Pharmacy
Knoxville, Tennessee
Reviewer: Hypertension

Jan Kavookjian, MBA, PhD
Associate Professor of Pharmacy Care Systems
Harrison School of Pharmacy
Auburn University
Auburn, Alabama
Reviewer: Counseling and Motivational Interviewing

Ann Reaves, PharmD, BCACP
Clinical Pharmacy Specialist-Ambulatory Care
PGY-1 Residency Coordinator
Methodist University Hospital
Memphis, Tennessee
Reviewer: Anticoagulation Services

Rachel Robinson, PharmD
Clinical Assistant Professor, Department of Pharmacy Practice
University of Mississippi School of Pharmacy
Oxford, Mississippi
Reviewer: Nonprescription and Self-Care

Jennifer Smith, PharmD
Associate Professor, Department of Pharmacy Practice
Campbell University, College of Pharmacy and Health Sciences
Buies Creek, North Carolina
Reviewer: Diabetes

Matthew W. Strum, PharmD, BCACP, CDE
Clinical Assistant Professor, Department of Pharmacy Practice
University of Mississippi School of Pharmacy
Oxford, Mississippi
Reviewer: Diabetes

Renee Ahrens Thomas, PharmD, MBA
President, RBT Consulting
Reston, Virginia
Reviewer: Obesity—Weight Management Services

Courtney Young, PharmD, BCPS
Clinical Pharmacy Specialist
Baptist Memorial Hospital-DeSoto
Southaven, Mississippi
Reviewer: Anticoagulation Services, Lipid Disorders

FOREWORD

What an exciting time to be a pharmacist! We chose pharmacy as a profession because we care about people and we want to help them. Growing up in a community pharmacy in a small town in Mississippi, I saw firsthand how accessible and trusted pharmacists were. I watched my father and other pharmacists in our community truly help people. As pharmacists today, we have the ability to help people in many different ways—whether it is working with the health-care team in a hospital to make sure a patient is prescribed the best medication at the correct dose and monitored appropriately or making sure that patients leave our community pharmacy with a medication that will address what "ails" them with an understanding of that medication and how to administer it for the best outcome. We are able to do this because, through the years, our profession has evolved to meet the changing health-care needs of the society that we serve. Once again, we find ourselves in an evolutionary process because our health-care system is changing. With the recent passage of health-care legislation and the implementation of its provisions, we are discovering new challenges and promising opportunities for pharmacy.

Because most pharmacists enter practice in the community setting and more and more opportunities become available for pharmacists to integrate into the health-care teams in clinic settings, the information provided in this book is timely and of utmost importance. At the University of Mississippi, we have had the unique opportunity to establish a Community-Based Research Program (CBRP) through which we worked with partners in 14 communities to implement medication therapy management (MTM) services in independent and chain pharmacies, in primary provider clinics, and in an employer-based worksite setting. This work is focused in the Mississippi Delta region, a medically underserved area that is disproportionately burdened with chronic disease and health disparities. Ask any member of our team and they will tell you that working directly with patients in these communities of need, in both clinic and pharmacy settings, is the most rewarding practice they can imagine. This experience is something that we all want to share with others.

Many of the contributing authors for this book have participated in this work or similar efforts at their institution and in their state. As we embrace the opportunities before us and embark on establishing more pharmacy services in clinic and community practice settings, let us learn from the experiences of those who have paved the way. This book provides pharmacists and other health-care professionals or administrators a step-by-step look at the implementation of pharmacy services. It identifies barriers, necessary skills, knowledge, issues related to preparation, types of interventions, anticipated patient outcomes, economic aspects, and marketing considerations for therapeutic areas commonly addressed in the outpatient setting. I hope that you find this guidance helpful as your practice evolves and I wish you every success as you work every day to help the patients in your community.

Leigh Ann Ross, PharmD
Associate Dean for Clinical Affairs
Chair and Associate Professor, Department of Pharmacy Practice
University of Mississippi School of Pharmacy, Jackson,
Mississippi

PREFACE

The idea for this book, *Community and Clinical Pharmacy Services: A Step-by-Step Approach*, was born from the core assertion that our profession is capable, well trained, and willing to fill a gap in health care for millions of Americans. Pharmacists are trained with exceptional clinical knowledge, but a gap still exists between our ability to help patients achieve health goals and the widespread creation of advanced pharmacy services in community and clinic settings. This book provides practical—not merely ideological—solutions to address this gap.

The structure of this book is unique. The first four chapters discuss practical general aspects for providing advanced pharmacy services, documentation skills, motivational interviewing of patients, and medication therapy management (MTM). These are essentially the "management" skills needed to implement and maintain advanced patient care services.

The subsequent chapters thoroughly discuss disease states that most likely would be amenable to development of pharmacy services. Each of these chapters begins with a short therapeutic refresher and quickly dives into the "how to" aspects of providing services for each disease state. Aspects such as equipment, pricing services, developing a business plan, securing outside stakeholder support, and marketing are discussed. In particular, the structure of these "disease state" chapters holds many pearls. As is the case with other books in this subject area, learning objectives and summary points are provided to enhance the reader's knowledge. In addition, many chapters contain an interview with a pharmacist who has implemented and maintained pharmacy services in that particular disease state, including a practical discussion of the "pearls of wisdom" that they gained and the barriers that they had to overcome. Furthermore, a simulated patient case integrates many of the therapeutic components covered in the first part of the chapter. Finally, a set of chapter-focused questions with answers and explanations and an online PowerPoint presentation are provided to ensure applicability of the content toward an academic setting.

Exceptional pharmacists across the country are successfully providing advanced pharmacy services with a sustainable business model. This book seeks to put the tools of those success stories into the reader's hands to help achieve a more widespread advancement of the profession as a whole and, most importantly, the health of our patients. This book is ideal for student pharmacist electives, resident and preceptor development, and as an enhancement of practice ideas and skills for pharmacists working in a community or clinic setting who seek to initiate MTM services or to diversify their current practice. Because both of us have developed services in multiple settings, we recognize that implementation and maintenance of such services requires knowledge, skills, and dedication. Likewise, we have sought authors for each chapter who we feel have been able to provide important pearls that they gained while building their services. *Community and Clinical Pharmacy Services: A Step-by-Step Approach* represents the accumulated wisdom and experience of many pharmacists, and we hope that this shared knowledge will enable pharmacy as a whole to reach new levels of implementing health-care services.

1

PRACTICAL ASPECTS OF SERVICE IMPLEMENTATION

LeAnn Causey Boyd and Leah Snyder

■ LEARNING OBJECTIVES

After reading this chapter, the pharmacy student, community practice resident, or pharmacist should be able to:

1. Identify the different players involved in MTM services.
2. Categorize potential payers of MTM services.
3. Evaluate variables to include in the business plan for MTM services.
4. Explain the difference between hard and soft dollar saving.
5. Recognize important components to evaluating documentation software.

INTRODUCTION

As pharmacists, most of us enter the profession because of a desire to help patients. This mission is exemplified through the practice of medication therapy management (MTM) services. There are a variety of services that pharmacists can offer to help patients better understand their medications and disease states. It is essential to realize that MTM services have different meanings in various health-care groups and can mean evaluation of patient-specific medications, disease-specific management, or a mixture of the two. Generally, reimbursement from insurance companies for MTM is only for face-to-face sessions and telephone consults. In the future, hopefully, reimbursement for telehealth services will emerge. To provide MTM services, one must be aware of the people involved, the barriers, and important financial considerations to grow a successful business.

IDENTIFY THE PLAYERS

In providing MTM services, there are many people involved, including the patient and/or caregiver, pharmacist, prescriber, support staff, pharmacy students, and payer. Through professional collaboration, everyone involved works together with the patient to achieve their personal health goals.

The Patient/Caregiver

The patient is the central focus of MTM services. Patients often are caught up in the traditional role of the pharmacist as a medication dispenser. MTM is a new concept to many patients and may initially require more education and persuasion to participate in the service. Patients are often overwhelmed with numerous medications, disease state, and dietary instructions. Patients must feel that you are a credible health-care professional qualified to review both medications and disease states with them. One way to increase patients' trust in your services would be to mention that you work collaboratively with their physician to share information to make the best therapeutic decisions. To begin, make sure that all information provided is individualized for that specific patient. Start the session with a few general open-ended questions to learn more about the patient and their current state of management. Then, use this information to customize your message specifically to the patient. For example, instead of saying "People with diabetes should be on a statin for cholesterol," you could say, "I see that Dr. Good has put you on simvastatin, which is a recommended drug for cholesterol in people with diabetes." Also, if there is a legal caregiver or a spouse present, involve them as much as possible to increase their awareness of how they can be a better support to their loved one. Patients do not respond well to health-care providers who "talk above their head." Make sure that all information is delivered in a way that is appropriate for the individual's age and literacy level.

The Pharmacist

Pharmacists should always have a positive attitude about the profession and the services they provide. The pharmacist is a crucial part of MTM services. MTM is a way for you to gain a more intimate relationship with your patients. It may be difficult at first to determine where the line is between patient counseling and providing MTM services. However, MTM focuses on the next level of patient care by addressing things like therapeutic goals, medication nonadherence, or efficacy issues.[1]

By developing a closer patient–pharmacist relationship, you are also helping to build patient loyalty to your pharmacy. In delivering your services, remember to start with general concepts about their medication or disease state and then move to more specific points. If you develop a basic foundation, your patients are much more likely to understand the information you present and to be able to apply it to their daily lives. Be sure to update all health-care professionals involved in a patient's care on your findings and education with the patient.

The pharmacist is the advocate for the necessity of MTM to both the patient and payer. To produce a successful MTM business, the pharmacist must take on many different roles, including clinician, marketer, business manager, and collaborator. By participating in medication management services, you are marketing yourself as a medication expert. Therefore, it is imperative to the success of your practice that you live up to the expectations of the patients and prescribers with which you work. Commit yourself to being a lifelong learner by keeping up with current medications, disease state guidelines, health-care issues, immunization recommendations, and professional opportunities. As you gather information from various sources, choose reference articles that are of specific interest to you and contact the author for more information. Pharmacists should be professional at all times when interacting with patients, support staff, and other health-care providers. It is up to the pharmacist to engineer a practice that revolves around patient care and improves the profession.[2]

The Prescriber

The prescriber is an integral part of MTM and must be included in therapy-altering decisions. Prescribers should also receive updates on your interventions with their patients. As you prepare to provide MTM services, let the prescribers with whom you will be working know what to expect and what services you will provide. As with patients, you must work with the prescriber to cultivate an acceptance of the clinical pharmacist's role. Keeping them informed about your services will increase their acceptance of your practice and recommendations.

Prescribers are similar to patients in that there is not one overall approach and each intervention must be individualized. Although there is a wide spectrum of collaboration, typically prescribers can be divided into three categories: The Physician Champions, The Participators, and The Nonresponders. The Physician Champions are those prescribers who go beyond merely following recommendations and often consult you on cases. They can also be influential in persuading others to accept your clinical role and recommendations. The Participators are those prescribers who participate in MTM by accepting recommendations, but may not be quite as involved as the Physician Champion. The Participators understand that you are trying to work synergistically for the best interest of the patient. The Participators may not always communicate directly with you. They may fail to include you in the communication loop or update you on the status of your recommendations. To determine the outcome, you must follow up directly with the patient. The Nonresponders are those who reply to your recommendation with comments such as "I don't need you to do this" or "These are my patients and I will make the therapy decisions." To these prescribers you politely respond that it is your job to assess the therapy and share therapy recommendations with the prescriber, who may choose not to accept the recommendation. Of course, there are prescribers who fit between categories, or may be best classified on a case-by-case basis.

Support Staff

Developing a solid support staff is key to a successful MTM service. Tasks such as scheduling patients, billing payers, filing documentation, and drawing labs are all great ways that a trained support staff member could lighten the load of the pharmacist. Also, these

	Nonresponders	Participators	Physician Champions
Their attitude	My patients are my business	Too busy to respond to recommendations, whether accepted or denied	Very thankful for your input and value your recommendations
Your approach	Make your recommendations and tell them you are just doing your job	Follow up with the patient to get the full picture and continue to make recommendations	Continue to make recommendations and use these prescribers as references for others

staff members can assist in marketing strategies and help to create and distribute promotional items. Staff members should be well trained and have sound patient interaction skills. By delegating these tasks, the pharmacist can focus on billable patient interaction time and documentation.

Pharmacy Students

Pharmacy schools are now more actively preparing students to pursue clinical roles. Pharmacy students are an excellent resource when providing MTM services. An instructional training module should be created to best represent the MTM process. Pharmacy students should also be familiar with current guidelines and recommendations for the management of different diseases. The most important point when utilizing a pharmacy student is that they should prepare interview questions ahead of the appointment for the preceptor to review. It is often intimidating for students to initiate patient interactions, and important points can be missed. Create a documentation guide that will ensure that the proper questions are asked. Before becoming the lead interviewer on an MTM case, have the student sit in with you for an appointment as an observer. Then, following the session, ask questions about the patient conversation and highlight pertinent points. The mission to expand MTM services is fulfilled through properly utilizing students and training the next generation of pharmacists.

■ IDENTIFY AND ENGAGE THE PLAYERS

There is no question that MTM services provided by pharmacists are a valuable asset to both the patient and the overall health-care system. However, to make this endeavor worth your time you must be compensated for your services. Unlike the dispensing role, there is no tangible product when billing for MTM services, and you are being paid solely for your expertise and time. For the greatest chance of financial stability, structure your practice so that there is a mixture of payer types. There are several different payer sources, which include self-funded employer groups, private insurance employer groups, Medicaid (for applicable states), Medicare Part D prescription drug plans, and self-pay patients.

Self-Funded Employer Groups

Self-funded employer groups are recommended as a target for services because they pay the health-care costs of their employees and greatly benefit from MTM services. Self-funded groups usually comprise greater than 500 employees, but could have as few as 200 employees. For the best outcome, try to aim for those employers who already have some sort of health or wellness initiative. An active wellness initiative shows that the company considers the health and welfare of their employees a priority. Use your networking skills to identify a key person in the organization to approach for brainstorming and to gather information on the services that would best benefit the employer to build your service plan.

There are a few different ways to approach payment for services, including per member per month, per employee per month, price per disease state case, hourly rate, daily rate, or percentage of health-care savings. For example, you could charge $X per member per month for 500 employees or $X per diabetes patient. There is a difference between per member per month and per employee because most plans allow the employee to have dependents who may also be eligible for your services. Whatever your structure, the cost of your services should not exceed the savings the service will generate. For the best participation, persuade the employer to provide some type of incentive for employees to participate. Incentives could be in the form of paid time to exercise, offering discounts on healthier food options for lunch or snack, gym membership discounts, and more. In your initial meetings with the employer to design your service, determine what is important to them. This will help you create reports that are the most meaningful to your client. Also, make sure that expectations and time lines are clear from the planning stages for a smooth transition to providing the services.

Medicare Part D Plans

The Medicare Modernization Act of 2003 developed requirements for MTM programs as a way to optimize therapeutic outcomes and control costs for patients. Each Part D plan must include an MTM program within the benefits package. To be included in the MTM program, the plans target members with multiple chronic disease states, multiple covered prescription medications, and incur annual costs that exceed a preset threshold. The Centers for Medicare and Medicaid Services (CMS) determines the range of parameters for inclusion.

> At a minimum, sponsors must target at least four of the following seven core chronic diseases: Hypertension, Heart Failure, Diabetes, Dyslipidemia, Respiratory Diseases (such as Asthma, Chronic Obstructive Pulmonary Disease or Chronic Lung disorders), Bone Disease-Arthritis (such as Osteoporosis, Osteoarthritis, or Rheumatoid Arthritis), and Mental Health Diseases (such as Depression, Schizophrenia, Bipolar Disorder, or chronic and disabling disorders).[3]

CMS has established that the plan must include beneficiaries receiving between two and eight Part D covered medications. However, the specific number and drug classifications included are left for each plan to select. For example, each plan can choose whether any Part D medication can be included, or each can include only those medications directly linked to the targeted disease states. The anticipated incurred medication costs are also a trigger for inclusion into the programs. However, the exact dollar amount of this requirement fluctuates with each CMS update (pharmacists should refer to the latest update for the most recent information). Each individual plan has variations on the different requirements. All plans are required to have person-to-person interaction that can be defined as in-person or telephone interventions. Although plan sponsors are only required to target beneficiaries for the MTM program enrollment quarterly, some plans identify beneficiaries monthly.[4]

Medicare plans have certain services that are required to be included in the MTM package. The CMS states that plans "must offer a comprehensive medication review (CMR) by a pharmacist or other qualified health-care provider at least annually and perform quarterly medication reviews with follow-up interventions when necessary." The comprehensive medication review is an interview where the pharmacist reviews all of the patient's prescriptions, herbal supplements, dietary foods, and over-the-counter (OTC) medication regimens to observe possible noncompliance, misuse, underuse, or therapeutic duplication. The pharmacist should provide patient education as necessary. Often the patient will learn something new during this encounter even about chronic prescriptions. The goal is to offer this person-to-person session as a time for patients to really focus on their therapy and ask questions about the medications they take. Pharmacists should also have patients demonstrate the use of medication devices to confirm proper usage. Plans also require that the patient be provided with some sort of written documentation to summarize the session. This is most commonly fulfilled through a personal medication record, medication action plan, and personalized education recommendations. An efficient platform collects data throughout the intervention and can populate the required documentation during the encounter. In the future, CMS may require a more standardized approach across all plans. Plans are also required to include physician interventions in their program structure.[3]

Consultations can be performed in a variety of ways including fax, telephone, or mailed communication. As you work with the physicians you will learn which methods of communication are most effective. Individualizing communications with each physician's preferred method will promote the pharmacist–physician relationship. The Medicare plans are operated through different platforms, providing the opportunity to experience diverse approaches to structuring MTM.

Self-Pay Patients

Patients are often unsure of their insurance coverage for medication management services. Many personal insurance plans currently do not have a benefit for MTM services, which leaves these patients with the bill. Performing a verification of benefits prior to your appointment with the patient will eliminate any surprises in billing. A menu of services with their costs is a helpful piece of information to include in the patient information packet. The most popular billing framework for self-pay patients is fee-for-service. For example, a flat rate would be charged for a 30-minute comprehensive medication review. In the self-pay scenario, the patient may be self-referred or referred to you by a prescriber. It is important to thoroughly explain the value of your services and anticipated positive outcomes from the services provided. This explanation will help the patient understand why your service is a valuable use of their financial resources. Rather than discussing return on investment with these patients, focus should be placed on personal improvements in their life that can result from gaining a better understanding of their medications and disease states. Engaging self-pay patients has a very strong tie to resourceful and specific marketing.

■ BUSINESS PEARLS

MTM is a value-added service for the patient. However, just as with any business venture you have to produce and follow a business model to assess whether or not the service will be beneficial to your company overall. By creating a business plan and services analysis, you can see which services are needed in your area and which could be the most profitable to add to your clinical service mix.

Legalities

Before you begin to see patients, you need to verify that both you and your pharmacy are covered by your professional insurance policy for the services you will be providing. Do not make the mistake to assume that your cognitive clinical services are covered under your standard umbrella or professional liability insurance. It is highly recommended when providing such services that you have your own professional liability insurance rather than depending solely on the insurance of your pharmacy or employer.

Service Mix

After you have determined who your primary population will be, develop a focus group from the population to help you determine what services are necessary. It is good to have a variety of services, but the theory of supply and demand still applies to cognitive pharmacy services. For instance, in a town or state where smoking has just been banned in public buildings and restaurants, it would be much easier to get a payer's buy-in for a smoking cessation program over a weight-loss program. Start with one or two services that are complementary to one another, and then you can gradually add services as your patients' needs evolve. You could start with a weight-loss program, then offer other screening such as cholesterol testing, which may later lead to a dyslipidemia clinic program.

During MTM sessions, the patient's immunization status and records should be reviewed. If immunization is needed and the patient agrees, the physician should be contacted to obtain a prescription (if necessary). If your MTM business is tied to a community pharmacy, this is a great way to serve your customers and create revenue for your pharmacy as well. This helps you to go beyond recognizing a need, but also meeting the patient's need within your facility. If your business model is not linked directly to an immunization provider, you should have a reference base for those patients eligible for vaccinations. Some payers are reimbursing for an MTM-based immunization review in addition to comprehensive reviews and other common MTM services.

Marketing

Persistence is key when starting any new business or adding new services. It is often difficult in the beginning to make patients and prescribers realize the value of your services. However, skeptical prescribers begin over time to not only accept your recommendations but also may become "Proactive prescribers" and enlist your help with additional patients. Be aware that frustration can occur as it takes time to gain credibility with patients and prescribers.

After you have set up your clinical space, invite local prescribers to come and tour the area. During their tour, you can give them a basic understanding of your actions and services while the patient is at your facility. Have patient documents such as educational handouts, videos, screening tests, and other devices out for display. Also, develop a standard reporting document that you can send to them for recommendations and progress reports. Get creative in ways to stay in touch with the prescribers in addition to your patient reports. For example, every week you could fax a short newsletter with a cartoon related to diabetes to local prescribers to promote your diabetes education services. The fax is a way to routinely remain in the prescribers' awareness without physically having to stop by their office.

In your marketing scheme, be sure to include information on the difference between drug utilization review (DUR) services provided by an insurance company's pharmacy benefit manager and the MTM services that you will provide. Many prescribers and employers may not realize the difference. While MTM can contain a cost savings component, the DUR is often solely cost associated. MTM is associated with a prescriber and patient relationship to manage a disease or drug regimen to help the patient get the best results from their medication.

Whether your services are tied into another institution or are part of a stand-alone business, you should develop a logo or icon to be associated with your services. For example, if your diabetes education services are provided at your local pharmacy, then use the same icon, photo, or slogan underneath your pharmacy's logo on all printed materials and documentation.

Distribute printed advertisements using your local pharmacies, prescriber offices, health centers, and hospitals to help advocate your services. Printed patient pamphlets can be used as bag stuffers or be placed at checkout registers. Also, use your local media outlets. As you begin to offer patients services, call your local news station or newspaper company to see if they would be interested in doing a story on your new services. You can purchase newspaper advertisements to attract your self-pay patients. Public services announcement participation or a radio advertisement is also a good medium to reach patients. Also, social media outlets and other Internet outlets have become a great way to reach your target audience. Do not be afraid to think outside of the ordinary to get your message to your target audience. Participating in local health fairs is often a low-cost way to advertise your services and is another way to get exposure in the community.

The best marketing tool that any business can have is word of mouth. As you are starting out your business, try to target influential peers and patients to participate in your services. A promotional 30-minute medication therapy review with the receptionist of a large prescriber group could be more beneficial than a newspaper advertisement. If your services are provided in a retail pharmacy, get cashiers involved in your marketing. For instance, if the cashier notices a patient checking out with a package of smoking cessation aids, they could recommend the patient join your smoking cessation classes, or mention other patient's successes with your smoking cessation services.

■ FINANCIAL MATTERS

MTM services are distinctly different than retail pharmacy services and should be billed as such. To get compensation for MTM services, pharmacists must continue to bill for them. Prior to an appointment, a verification of eligibility for services should be performed if the patient's insurance coverage is in question. Always be up front about the cost of your services, especially with self-pay patients.

Hard and Soft Dollar Savings

When presenting savings to your payer, it is essential to recognize that two general categories exist: hard dollar savings and soft dollar savings.[5]

Hard dollar savings are those tangible savings that are a direct result of an intervention by the pharmacist during an MTM assessment. A few examples are savings from the following: a reduced co-payment as a result of a medication regimen change, elimination of a duplicate therapy, changing from a nonpreferred to preferred formulary drug, changing from a prescription to an OTC medication, selecting generic rather than brand medications, and ensuring appropriate medication use. Hard dollar savings are easier to justify because there is evidence of the savings when comparing the cost prior to the intervention and after the intervention. If you can access claims data for your patients, especially in an employer paid setting, you will have concrete data as well as the opportunity to catch many cost savings opportunities. However, if you are not able to access claims data, get as much information as you can from your patients for your own documentation purposes. Ask your patients to bring in their insurance claims information, co-payment slips, receipts of OTC items, and any other information regarding the cost of their current medication regimen instead of just asking them approximately how much they spend. Usually patients will not be able to bring in these items and it may be easier to just ask for a pharmacy printout of medications including patient co-payment. It is much easier to justify MTM services when you can specify an exact amount saved versus an approximation. Also, when working with self-funded employer groups or prescription drug plans, you can show both individual and plan savings. Remember that for these groups your changes save the employer as well as the employees. For a medication change the co-payment difference for the patient may seem small or insignificant, but the savings for the plan is often substantial. Again, to be able to make these changes, you must have a thorough understanding of the plan's formulary and cost sharing principles.

Soft dollar savings are intangible savings that come from preventing a health-care cost as a result of an intervention. For example, by performing a screening and discovering a patient has an extremely elevated cholesterol level, you could say that you avoided an office visit for labs. There are several common soft dollar savings interventions that are routinely used such as the following avoided events: health-related employee absenteeism, outpatient physician visit, specialty office visit, emergency room or urgent care visit, hospital stay, laboratory costs, and home care or long-term care admission. Also, savings occur by keeping disease state measures at goal. There is less concrete information regarding soft dollar savings, which makes them much more difficult to keep track of if they are not included in your software platform. Through trying to achieve soft dollar savings, it may be necessary for a medication to be added to a patient's regimen to help avoid the negative outcome. For example, the patient with exceptionally high cholesterol levels, upon screening, may require the addition of a cholesterol lowering medication to avoid a heart attack or stroke. Keeping records of these savings requires persistence and diligence from the pharmacist. To help with tracking, choose a software program that has the ability to report these savings.

The savings report to the payer should include both hard dollar and soft dollar savings. Many employers realize the importance of the life-changing health events that are avoided with pharmacist intervention and appreciate the soft dollar savings reports. When reporting, include both individualized savings, as well as savings for your patient population as a whole. Reports must have de-identified data and not reveal any personal information about your participants. When reporting to an entity, you also want to include a return on investment calculation based on your hard dollar savings to give further credibility to the services provided. If reporting to a self-pay patient, the report should be very personal covering soft dollar savings and their importance as well as the tangible hard dollar savings.[5]

Billing for Services

Billing for services provided is essential to your bottom line. Accurate coding and promptly filing claims are essential to getting properly reimbursed for services rendered. Billing is the last step of the documentation process but should be viewed as the most important part of the process. No matter the payer, the requirement for documentation of services is critical to making sure that you get correctly compensated for services rendered.

From the beginning, create a system to follow up on filed claims and constantly update claims. Be proactive in discovering reasons for rejected or unpaid claims. While it is very efficient to employ additional staff to assist with billing, it is imperative that they remain up to date with billing procedures and understand the importance of filing each claim properly and promptly. Relevant ICD-9 codes should always be included in documentation and billing as appropriate.

Financial Issues

As mentioned earlier, any new business venture should be approached with a business plan. In the business plan, consideration must be given to both fixed and flexible expenses. If MTM services are to be provided in a community pharmacy setting, you must decide if an additional space and employees will be necessary and account for them separately in the financial planning. Also, service-specific marketing costs should be included in the services budget. Similarly, overhead costs should be calculated and accounted for in the business plan. Additional requirements such as laboratory supplies, equipment, space, document storage, and professional insurance should be considered. Opportunity costs should also be evaluated.

■ SOFTWARE

Technology plays an important role in making the most of your MTM services. Choosing your documentation platform is one of the most difficult tasks in setting up an MTM business. There are several different platforms and software licensing programs to choose from, or a custom documentation program can be designed.

When choosing software, there are several factors to consider such as disease states included, reporting features, documentation, data comparisons, data safety, capability to capture claims data, and efficiency. Be sure that the system that you choose has the capability to extract a comprehensive data file in the event that you no longer wish to use the system. Before choosing your software, you need to evaluate what data is important now as well as the ability to expand to other services in the future. For example, if you are currently targeting patients with diabetes, you may want to use software that is specifically designed for that disease state. Some MTM software is focused on a few key disease states only, whereas other software is more encompassing for multiple disease states and in-depth medication reviews.

There are several key reports that are vital to MTM services that should be built-in such as the personal medication record, patient medication action plan, and progress notes. These reports are required of many insurance companies for reimbursement and will greatly increase your efficiency if they are built into the system. When shopping for your software, ask if personalized reports can be added into the system. Some systems offer capability for personalized features to be created, but you have to pay for the time to develop the feature. The software should be easy to use and not add additional work for you to complete. For instance, if you have a system that populates a patient's medication record as you complete your progress note, you do not have to spend time to create a second document in addition to your charting. It is very beneficial to be able to quickly compare patient-specific data over a period of time. For instance, in monitoring hypertension you want to be able to see blood pressure trends or data values from each visit quickly rather than flipping through the text of several progress notes to identify change. Whether you are using a laptop or desktop computer, you must always think about data safety and backup. Investigate how your potential software stores patient-specific information to ensure that you will remain compliant with patient data protection regulations.

An internal scheduling function is a central feature of an efficiency-based documentation software. In disease state management patients, follow-up appointments are often months or years apart and can easily result in lost revenue due to lack of follow-up. Most scheduling features prompt you to contact the patient or have the patient appointments show up on your clinic calendar.

If you are performing prescription savings services, choose a software that has the capability to capture claims data. This becomes important if you are working with an employer group to show hard dollar savings.

There are some programs which have interfaces that are patient-accessible. This allows patients to access their personal medication record from home that may be especially appreciated if you have a patient base with a high prescription volume. This feature would also be a nice value-added service for retail pharmacy customers.

■ CONCLUSION

In order to initiate MTM services, the pharmacist must identify all potential stakeholders of their services. Services can be started in a certain area or disease state, depending on the maximum number of potential patients and other factors. Then, MTM services can be expanded after successful initial implementation. A business plan should be constructed, including factors such as identifying payers, service mix, marketing, and billing for services. Finally, the optimal software system would allow efficient documentation of both patient visits and claims data. After considering all of these factors, a pharmacist working in either a retail or clinic setting would be ready to implement their MTM services.

■ PATIENT CASE

LS is a 45-year-old Caucasian male who is visiting with the clinical pharmacist today for a health screening and medication review. LS works a 12-hour day shift and arrives at work at approximately 6:30 AM. Upon interview, we discover that LS has a very strong family history of heart disease and says that is his main health concern. He also has environmental allergies year-round and says he sneezes and suffers constantly. He found a new medication, Zyrtec®, that seemed to help, but says he had to stop taking it because he was tired and sluggish at work. LS states that he often forgets to take Simvastatin and generally only takes it about three times per week. LS stops at a local restaurant and eats a sausage and biscuit every morning and picks up fried chicken for lunch on his way to work.

Current Medications:

Simvastatin: 20 mg 1 po qhs
Metoprolol succinate: 50 mg 1 po qd
Zyrtec: 10 mg 1 po qd
Aspirin: 81 mg 1 po qd

Labs:

Weight: 240 lb
Blood pressure: 128/80
Height: 5′ 6″
Total cholesterol: 240 mg/dL
HDL: 32 mg/dL
TG: 280 mg/dL
LDL: 152 mg/dL

How could you help LS?

- Disease state education regarding dyslipidemia. LS stated that his main concern was heart disease; however, his risk is increased by having an LDL above goal. Often patients do not understand that there is a direct correlation between their lifestyle/medication compliance and their blood results. Patient education about the separate components of the total cholesterol value would be very beneficial here. Also, this is an opportunity to review healthy, cholesterol-friendly food choices and the importance of limiting fried and fatty foods.
- Provide disease state education about seasonal allergies. Review ways to identify and eliminate triggers. Also, LS is experiencing a side effect of the Zyrtec that might cause him to lose his job if he does not stop taking the medication. Upon further questioning, LS had never tried loratadine 10 mg, which has a lower incidence of drowsiness. Recommendation was to try

> loratadine on the weekend to see how it effects his cognition and function.
> - Savings
>   - Hard dollar savings
>   - Switch from brand Zyrtec to generic loratadine
>   - Soft dollar savings
>   - Savings from additional cholesterol medication when the problem was non-compliance with original medication
>
> Recommendation/Plan
> - LS has a smartphone and will set an alarm to remind him to take cholesterol medication daily.
> - LS will do a trial run of loratadine over the weekend, and then will begin taking daily.
> - LS also has a new meal plan and food options to help him make better choices to avoid extra cholesterol in his diet.
> - LS has also committed to walking 20 minutes at least four times weekly.

■ SUMMARY POINTS

- There are many different people involved in MTM.
- The patient or caregiver may not be fully aware of the benefits of MTM. Take time at the beginning of your session to provide an overview including possible benefits and outcomes of your encounter.
- The pharmacist is a valuable member of health-care services and has the opportunity to further help patients through MTM. However, if you participate in these services, you must be prepared to perform the services you market. Strengthening your communication skills is a great way to prepare to provide MTM services. Sessions should include personalized education and recommendations based on the patient's previous knowledge and goals.
- Pharmacists are the advocates for MTM and as such must be prepared to live up to the expectations of both your patients and prescribers through these services. Commit yourself to being a lifelong learner to provide your patients and prescribers with the most up-to-date therapy recommendations.
- Prescribers have varying levels of initial acceptance of the clinical pharmacist role. Find a Physician Champion and use them to help get other prescribers onboard.
- A strong support staff is an incredible asset to help your practice's efficiency. Learn to delegate tasks to help promote your business. Support staff is key to word-of-mouth promotion and ensuring that the patients have a pleasant encounter when scheduling, waiting for their appointment, and checking out.
- MTM is a great opportunity to involve pharmacy students. Students can gather hands-on experience in clinical pharmacy and expand their understanding of drugs and disease state management techniques. MTM is also a great way for pharmacy students to strengthen communication skills with patients and other health-care professionals.
- There are many different possible payers to fund MTM.
  - Self-funded employer groups
    - Self-funded employer groups are a good target for MTM services because they can save on the health-care costs that the company is paying through services such as increased medication adherence, cost savings searches, and better disease state education.
  - Medicare Part D plans
    - MTM is a requirement of the Medicare Part D plans. However, each individual plan can have a different method of providing these services. Some plans have pharmacists in house that provide MTM services, while others allow community pharmacists to perform the MTM reviews for their own patients. This is another way to provide a service to your patients and build the pharmacist–patient relationship.
  - Self-pay patients
    - As the personalized time patients get to spend with prescribers dwindle, they

are often left with unanswered questions about their medications. Comprehensive medication reviews and other components of MTM can be very beneficial to these patients.
- MTM must be thought of as a separate service provided to your patients. Creating a business plan for these services will help you determine the amount of time you can spend in clinical pharmacy and will allow you to compare opportunity costs and new overhead costs associated.
- Marketing is a key component to the success of your services. Whether you are creating a separate clinical pharmacy business, or just offering your retail customers a clinical option you must market to your target audience.
- Savings are the best way to prove to patients and payers the importance of the clinical pharmacist in MTM. Calculating hard dollar and soft dollar savings is very beneficial when providing a review of your services to you payer. Always remember that you can only share de-identified data that cannot be traced back to your patient.

■ STUDY QUESTIONS

1. Where is the best location for MTM to be performed?
   a. At the counseling counter of your retail pharmacy
   b. At the back of your pharmacy
   c. In a quiet partitioned room
   d. In a separate building from the main pharmacy

2. Which method would best help your patient understand MTM?
   a. A marketing advertisement with the definition in the pharmacy waiting area
   b. A pamphlet at the prescriber's office
   c. A brief overview at the beginning of the appointment
   d. A definition in an automated phone message with the appointment reminder

3. Which of the following would be the best information to start off with in an MTM session with a patient with type 2 diabetes?
   a. Ask for a demonstration of how to use insulin
   b. Ask for blood glucose logs
   c. Review the treatments of hypoglycemia
   d. Review the basis of type 2 diabetes

4. If a prescriber does not like your recommendations and does not act on them, you should:
   a. Stop sending recommendations to that prescriber
   b. Have the patient take the recommendation to the prescriber
   c. Continue to send your recommendations to the prescriber
   d. Send your recommendations to another prescriber in the same group

5. Which of the following ways could a support staff member assist the clinical pharmacist?
   a. Schedule patients
   b. Create medication charts
   c. Take initial measurements of blood pressure, weight, height, etc.
   d. All of the above

6. Which self-funded company would be the most likely candidate to participate in an MTM program?
   a. A company with 300 employees that has an annual health screening
   b. A company with 50 employees that pays for a smoking cessation program
   c. A company that has 1000 employees spread across 5 different cities
   d. A company that has 2000 employees between two different states

7. For a community pharmacy that wants to add MTM services, which would be the easiest payer to incorporate?
   a. Self-funded employer groups
   b. Medicare Part D plans
   c. Self-pay patients
   d. You cannot perform MTM at a community pharmacy

8. Which of the following chronic disease states would NOT be covered under the Medicare MTM requirements?
   a. Bipolar disorder
   b. Asthma
   c. Benign prostate hyperplasia
   d. Osteoporosis

9. How often must a pharmacist perform a comprehensive medication review in Medicare-related MTM?
   a. Quarterly
   b. Biannually
   c. Annually
   d. Monthly

10. Which of the following would represent soft dollar savings by saving a prescriber visit and costs associated with bad clinical outcomes?
    a. A patient was improperly taking a proton pump inhibitor three times daily and you recommended he take one pill daily plus an antacid if needed
    b. A patient who had been taking a brand medication was switched to a generic
    c. A patient who has not been taking his cholesterol medication due to a side effect, and you recommend a different medication
    d. A recommendation to stop a duplication of therapy

BIBLIOGRAPHY

1. McDonough, Randy. Targeted MTM interventions: don't get lost in the details. *Pharmacy Today.* July 2010: 38.
2. McDonough, Randy. DUR vs. MTM: it's not only about cost. *Pharmacy Today.* August 2010:48.
3. Centers for Medicare & Medicaid Services. 2010 Medicare Part D Medication Therapy Management (MTM) Program. 8 June 2010. https://www.cms.gov/PrescriptionDrugCovContra/Downloads/MTMFactSheet_2010_06–2010_final.pdf. Accessed September 2, 2011.
4. American Pharmacists Association. Medication Therapy Management Digest: Perspectives on MTM Service Implementation. March 2008. www.pharmacist.com. 2110 2011http://www.pharmacist.com/AM/Template.cfm? Section=Home2&TEMPLATE=/CM/ContentDisplay.cfm&CONTENTID=22666>.
5. Boyd S, Boyd L, Zillich A. Medication therapy management survey of the prescription drug plans. *J Am Pharm Assoc.* 2006:46(6):692-699.

2

DOCUMENTATION

Stephanie Harriman McGrath and Stephanie S. Holliday

■ LEARNING OBJECTIVES

After reading this chapter, the pharmacy student, community practice resident, or pharmacist should be able to:

1. Establish documentation practices that can be easily integrated into a community pharmacy's workflow.
2. Utilize the assistance of ancillary staff, student pharmacists, residents, and staff pharmacists in documenting clinical services within the community pharmacy setting.
3. Develop a method for documenting pharmacist interventions and patient outcomes within the community pharmacy setting that abide by state and federal law.
4. Report these outcomes to other members of the pharmacy team, other health-care providers, and third-party payers in support of the value of clinical pharmacist services within the community pharmacy setting.
5. Apply these outcomes to improve clinical practice within the community pharmacy setting.

INTRODUCTION

"If it isn't documented, it didn't happen," is a statement that resonates with many pharmacists and other health-care professionals. Whether it was during a pharmacy law class or during clinical rotations, the first time a pharmacist hears this quote marks the beginning of a dedication to documentation. From product verification to narcotic inventories, documentation is required for most activities performed by a pharmacist. For years, the act of documentation by pharmacists served as a means to assign ownership. Documenting that a bottle of Oxycontin® (oxycodone ER) was double counted or placing initials on a work log assigned liability and protects both the pharmacist and the patient in the event of unexpected adverse effects or achievement of optimal therapeutic response.

The livelihood of a pharmacist continues to rely largely on documentation practices as the profession expands clinical services in outpatient practice settings, namely community pharmacies. As pharmacists' authorities expand beyond providing vaccinations and therapeutic drug-level monitoring, documentation practices have become more intricate, most cases requiring more that just initials to not only establish ownership but payment for services as well.

Proper documentation is required by state and federal law for pharmacists to be reimbursed for the provision of clinical services, such as immunizations and medication therapy management (MTM) services. Documentation is mandatory to operate any patient care practice.

Cipolle, Strand, and Morley have defined documentation in the following manner: "Documentation refers to all patient-specific information, the clinical decisions, and the patient outcomes that are recorded for use in practice. This includes everything written down in long-hand, or entered into a computer program that becomes data and is used to facilitate the care of patients."[1] Pharmacy as a profession has come a great distance in terms of documentation of patient care services, but the profession lacks a uniform method of documentation and billing of clinical services.[2] Key stakeholders within the health-care system have recognized that as a limiting factor, and while this chapter will not solve the problem of a universal electronic health record (EHR), it will highlight the importance of documentation and describe key components that will be required for the documentation of patient care services.

WHY DOCUMENT?

Documentation is necessary for a spectrum of patient care services provided in a pharmacy, and the level and breadth of documentation will vary depending on the patient care service(s) provided. While not universally required by law, any intervention that a pharmacist makes during the process of dispensing should be documented accordingly for several reasons. Details of that intervention such as a statement of the problem, process to resolve, and a dated resolution will not only enhance the continuity of care and allow for compensation of services when contracted but also provide some level of protection for the pharmacist in the event of legal ramifications. For example, if a drug–drug interaction is identified during the dispensing process, the resolution of that problem (i.e., educating the patient) should be documented electronically in the dispensing system. Any communication with other health-care providers regarding a patient's care should be appropriately documented, such as accepted or rejected pharmacist recommendations for changes in the patient's medication regimen.

Continuity of Care

Proper documentation requires the pharmacist to capture information about a patient encounter. Whether the patient was being seen for an immunization or a comprehensive MTM session, the information shared through documentation establishes a record of that service. A pharmacist must be aware of the information essential to the continuity of that patient's care and include information necessary for the next health-care provider to further assist the patient in their health-care management.

Professional Liability

Documentation serves as official record of service provision and allows for maintenance of patient records according to legal standards. To this point, documented information must be accurate and consistent with practice and institution policies and standards. For example, if during a session, the pharmacist provides the patient with names of over-the-counter medications that can be used for a rash, the names of those agents must be documented. If those agents are listed and the pharmacist did not note that the patient was instructed on how to use and administer those agents, the pharmacist may be considered at risk for liability should the patient experience an adverse event.

Some state boards of pharmacy have established regulations to manage clinical services provided within community pharmacy settings. These regulations currently address documentation requirements for pharmacists providing vaccinations. However, as MTM services continue to establish a niche within the community setting, more states will look to require additional documentation standards.

Regulatory Policy

In addition to what is currently expected for clinical practice, documentation has legal implications as well. Thorough and consistent documentation practices protect the word and work of the pharmacist from liability when the presence or quality of services rendered is in question. Additionally, some third-party payers may require very specific pieces of information, and pharmacists must adhere to these requirements to prevent infractions upon an audit.

For example, in New York State, where a pilot program for MTM is being implemented, program guidelines state that each Medicaid MTM-designated pharmacy must retain a hard copy of the MTM Consultation Form, signed enrollee Consent for Release of Medicaid Information to Health-Care Providers form, and other documentation pertinent to the visit for a minimum of 6 years.[3]

Each patient must have his or her own "chart" or record of care. This record may be integrated in to the pharmacy's current dispensing software, or exist in a stand-alone capacity that is dedicated to the documentation of pharmaceutical care. The type of patient care service may dictate the extent of documentation. For example, state regulations very clearly dictate the patient-specific components required to be documented in a patient's chart when pharmacists administer vaccines. Such regulations vary from state to state, but may include information about the vaccine (i.e., lot number and expiration date) in addition to demographic information of the patient and details of the service provided. The Centers for Medicare and Medicaid Services (CMS) has established a standardized format for documentation for MTM programs to be enacted in January 2013.[4] Examples of these formats are provided in Figures 2-1 and 2-2. Providers of MTM must provide documentation in the format dictated by CMS, and must therefore stay abreast of evolving regulations and make the necessary changes to their documentation practices.

■ COMPONENTS OF DOCUMENTATION

In 2004, 11 associations, representing various practice niches within the profession of pharmacy, collaborated to establish a consensus definition of MTM. In this definition, entitled "Medication Therapy Management in Pharmacy Practice: Core Elements of an MTM Service Version 1.0," components essential to an MTM encounter were defined. In 2008, version 2.0 of this guidance document was released to further assist pharmacists in executing MTM services. The core elements described serve to facilitate patient understanding of appropriate drug use, improve adherence, and detect and/or prevent adverse drug events.[5]

While traditional patient counseling meets expectations of licensed pharmacists, MTM services exceed expectations of licensed pharmacists by focusing on the complete medication profile of each individual patient.[6,7]

MTM Practice Logo

January 1, 2013

<Patient Address>

<Dear Patient Name>:

Thank you for talking with me on <insert date of service> about your health and medications. <Name of Program> MTM (Medication Therapy Management) program helps you make sure that your medications are working. Along with this letter are an action plan (Medication Action Plan) and a medication list (Personal Medication List). The action plan has steps you should take to help you get the best results from your medications. The medication list will help you keep track of your medications and how to use them the right way.

- Have your action plan and medication list with you when you talk with your doctors, pharmacists, and other health-care providers.
- Ask your doctors, pharmacists, and other health-care providers to update them at every visit.
- Take your medication list with you if you go to the hospital or emergency room.
- Give a copy of the action plan and medication list to your family or caregivers.

If you want to talk about this letter or any of the papers with it, please call <insert contact information for MTM provider, phone number, days/times, TTY, etc.>. <I/We> look forward to working with you and your doctors to help you stay healthy through the <insert name of Part D Plan> MTM program.

<Insert closing, MTM provider signature, name, title, enclosure notations, etc.>

MEDICATION ACTION PLAN FOR <Insert Patient's name, DOB: mm/dd/yyyy>

This action plan will help you get the best results from your medications if you:

1. Read "What we talked about."
2. Take the steps listed in the "What I need to do" boxes.
3. Fill in "What I did and when I did it."
4. Fill in "My follow-up plan" and "Questions I want to ask."

Have this action plan with you when you talk with your doctors, pharmacists, and other health-care providers. Share this with your family or caregivers too.

DATE PREPARED: <Insert date>

What we talked about: <Insert description of topic>

What I need to do: <Insert recommendations for beneficiary activities>

What I did and when I did it: <Leave blank for beneficiary's notes>

What we talked about:_____

What I need to do:_____

What I did and when I did it:_____

What we talked about:_____

What I need to do:_____

What I did and when I did it:_____

My follow-up plan (add notes about next steps): <Leave blank for patient's notes>

Questions I want to ask (include topics about medications or therapy): <Leave blank for patient's notes>

If you have any questions about your action plan, call <insert MTM provider contact information, phone number, days/times, etc>.

Figure 2-1. Medication action plan (MAP) adapted to CMS requirements.[4]

MTM Practice Logo

PERSONAL MEDICATION LIST FOR <Insert Patient's name, DOB: mm/dd/yyyy>

This medication list was made for you after we talked. We also used information from <insert sources of information>.

- Use blank rows to add new medications. Then fill in the dates you started using them.
- Cross out medications when you no longer use them. Then write the date and why you stopped using them.
- Ask your doctors, pharmacists, and other health-care providers to update this list at every visit.

If you go to the hospital or emergency room, take this list with you. Share this with your family or caregivers too. Keep this list up-to-date with prescription medications, over the counter drugs, herbals, vitamins, and minerals.

DATE PREPARED: <Insert date>

Allergies or side effects: <Insert patient's allergies and adverse drug reactions including the medications and their effects>

Medication: <Insert generic name and brand name, strength, and dosage form for current/active medications.>

How I use it: <Insert regimen, including strength, dose, and frequency (e.g., 1 tablet [20 mg] by mouth daily), use of related devices and supplemental instructions as appropriate>

Why I use it: <Insert indication or intended medical use>

Prescriber: <Insert prescriber's name>

<**Insert other title(s) or delete this field**>: <Use for optional product-related information, such as additional instructions, product image/identifiers, goals of therapy, pharmacy, etc., and change field title accordingly. This field may be expanded or divided. Delete this field if not used.>

Date I started using it: <May be estimated by Plan or entered based upon patient-reported data, or leave blank for patient to enter start date>

Date I stopped using it: <Leave blank for patient to enter stop date>

Why I stopped using it: <Leave blank for patient's notes>

PERSONAL MEDICATION LIST FOR <Insert Patient's name, DOB: mm/dd/yyyy>

Medication: <Insert generic name and brand name, strength, and dosage form for current/active medications.>

How I use it: <Insert regimen, including strength, dose, and frequency (e.g., 1 tablet [20 mg] by mouth daily), use of related devices and supplemental instructions as appropriate>

Why I use it: <Insert indication or intended medical use>

Prescriber: <Insert prescriber's name>

<**Insert other title(s) or delete this field**>: <Use for optional product-related information, such as additional instructions, product image/identifiers, goals of therapy, pharmacy, etc., and change field title accordingly. This field may be expanded or divided. Delete this field if not used.>

Date I started using it: <May be estimated by Plan or entered based upon patient-reported data, or leave blank for patient to enter start date>

Date I stopped using it: <Leave blank for patient to enter stop date>

Why I stopped using it: <Leave blank for patient's notes>

Figure 2-2. (*Continued*)

Medication: <Insert generic name and brand name, strength, and dosage form for current/active medications.> (Continued)

How I use it: <Insert regimen, including strength, dose, and frequency (e.g., 1 tablet [20 mg] by mouth daily), use of related devices and supplemental instructions as appropriate>

Why I use it: <Insert indication or intended medical use>

Prescriber: <Insert prescriber's name>

<**Insert other title(s) or delete this field**>: <Use for optional product-related information, such as additional instructions, product image/identifiers, goals of therapy, pharmacy, etc., and change field title accordingly. This field may be expanded or divided. Delete this field if not used.>

Date I started using it: <May be estimated by Plan or entered based upon patient-reported data, or leave blank for patient to enter start date>

Date I stopped using it: <Leave blank for patient to enter stop date>

Why I stopped using it: <Leave blank for patient's notes>

Medication: <Insert generic name and brand name, strength, and dosage form for current/active medications.>

How I use it: <Insert regimen, including strength, dose, and frequency (e.g., 1 tablet [20 mg] by mouth daily), use of related devices and supplemental instructions as appropriate>

Why I use it: <Insert indication or intended medical use>

Prescriber: <Insert prescriber's name>

<**Insert other title(s) or delete this field**>: <Use for optional product-related information, such as additional instructions, product image/identifiers, goals of therapy, pharmacy, etc., and change field title accordingly. This field may be expanded or divided. Delete this field if not used.>

Date I started using it: <May be estimated by Plan or entered based upon patient-reported data, or leave blank for patient to enter start date>

Date I stopped using it: <Leave blank for patient to enter stop date>

Why I stopped using it: <Leave blank for patient's notes>

Other Information:
If you have any questions about your medication list, call <insert MTM provider contact information, phone numbers, days/times, etc.>.

Figure 2-2. Personal medication record (PMR) adapted to CMS requirements.[4]

The core elements of an MTM service model provide guidance for pharmacists to focus on the patient as a whole through five components of care (Table 2-1).[5]

Identifying Outcomes to Track Through Documentation

The pharmacist's role in patient care is through the identification and resolution of drug therapy problems.[1] Those drug therapy problems have been classified in four categories: indication, efficacy, safety, and compliance (Table 2-2).

Additionally, an estimated cost avoidance (ECA) may be assigned to the resolution of these drug therapy problems.[8,9] This ECA may range from improving the quality of a patient's care through educating them on the proper use of their medication, to avoiding a hospital admission by identifying and resolving an adverse

Table 2-1. Core Elements of MTM[4]

Core Element	Description
Medication therapy review	• Collection of patient-specific information • Assessment of medication therapies to identify medication-related problems • Development of a prioritized list of medication-related problems • Creation of a plan to resolve medication-related problems
Personal medication record (PMR)	• A medication record that accurately reflects the patient's medication regimen • Given to the patient to share with his or her health-care providers • Patients are encouraged to keep the PMR updated and bring it with them to every provider appointment.
Medication-related action plan (MAP)	• A "to-do" list for patients to track his or her progress of self-management of drug therapy problems • Specific, measurable, achievable, realistic, and time-bound • Agreed on by the patient and the pharmacist; the patient should be held accountable to it
Intervention and/or referral	• Pharmacist may refer to other health-care providers with relevant expertise for complex drug therapy problems or medical conditions • Aids the patient in maximizing his or her medication use
Documentation and follow-up	• Allows the pharmacist to follow the patient's progress and bill services • Allows for communication with other providers, maintenance of health-care records, protection against professional liability, justification of billing, and assessment of clinical and economic outcomes • Documentation should be provided to the patient, the patient's prescriber(s), and the patient's third-party payer (when applicable) • Frequency of follow-up is patient specific • All follow-up visits should be appropriately documented

drug event in its early stages. Another example that relates to reduced health-care costs is the documentation of successful brand to generic medication changes. In capturing this information through proper documentation, pharmacists may demonstrate their impact on the health-care system and further support their role in patient care.

When documenting patient care outcomes, the pharmacist must place focus on clinical information that can be tracked to assess improvement in and maintenance of health status over time. Information about physiologic assessments (i.e., blood pressure and lipid panel) and drug therapy problems must be tracked. If a direct patient care encounter is being submitted to a third-party payer for compensation, then payer will typically determine required outcomes for specific patient groups, and the pharmacist's documentation

Table 2-2. Classification of Drug Therapy Problems[1]

Indication	1. Unnecessary drug therapy 2. Needs additional drug therapy
Efficacy	3. Needs different drug product 4. Dosage too low
Safety	5. Adverse drug reaction 6. Dosage too high
Compliance	7. Noncompliance

process must allow for the capture of all required information.

The SOAP Note Revisited

In many outpatient settings other than community pharmacies, the SOAP (subjective, objective, assessment, plan) note format is an accepted method of documentation as it is used widely among the health-care profession. Subjective observations include pertinent patient reported information such as previous medical history, family history, social history, chief complaints, and allergies. Objective information includes known allergies, laboratory results, vital signs, physical exam results, and a review of symptoms. An assessment can be determined once analysis of the subjective and objective information has occurred. Also known as the problem list, the assessment establishes the medication-related problems that are present. The plan documents the actions that were taken during the encounter and any additional considerations that should be taken to resolve medication-related problems.

Considering the environment of a community pharmacy practice, prescriber letters should be accurate, concise, and specific to allow for quick interpretation and concerted efforts to resolve the most significant medication-related problems. Because of the documentation systems utilized in community pharmacies, the traditional SOAP note has largely been replaced by a physician consult letter. Keep in mind that unlike hospital systems, community pharmacies do not uniformly participate in EHRs, so most communication to the patient's prescriber is accomplished through fax and a letter format is more appropriate. In most cases, health-care professionals receiving a consultation note (Fig. 2-3) from the community pharmacy practice setting may have additional responsibilities that they must juggle while providing patient care services. Pharmacists in the community setting may also have dispensing responsibilities integrated throughout their shift and physicians and nurses may be reading the consultation note between patient cases. In cases like this, the provider will want to know the most urgent medication-related issues to address so that they can quickly act on these issues if needed and return to their other patient care activities. A concise note may allow that provider more time to focus on identifying and addresses new medication-related problems.

The "plan" section of a consultation note (Fig. 2-4) not only communicates a plan of action but also creates a forum to communicate any recommendations to the prescriber for alternations and additions to current therapies and treatment plans. To ensure efficiency, it is important to be specific and clear about recommendations. For example, when recommending the addition of an ACE inhibitor, the pharmacist must be specific with drug, dose, and directions for the prescriber to respond to. The addition of a "yes" or "no" check box next to a recommendation for a specific number of additional refills for a medication or a list of options to choose from for alternate therapies ensures for clear communication of intent for both providers.

Some documentation platforms do not require full SOAP note content, and may be an open documentation field. All health-care providers, including pharmacists, have the responsibility to document patient care activities completely, and this SOAP format may be applied to systems that allow for open documentation. For example, some documentation platforms do not require a full SOAP note, but rather ask for specific information about medications and ECA. Some platforms contain an open field for additional notes, and to promote continuity of care, it is recommended that complete documentation of the patient visit is added to that field.

Documentation Reminders

Efficiency and efficacy in health-care is necessary for any practice to succeed. Documentation should occur immediately during or following a patient visit to minimize data "lost" due to lack of memory over time. Remember that documentation must be concise but completely convey all necessary information. Consider that another pharmacist colleague may follow up with that patient and that he or she will need to quickly understand what was discussed during the initial visit and appreciate the patient's medication-related needs.

Patient Name: John Doe	DOB: 1/13/1981		
Pharmacist Name: Dr. Jones	Date: 2/1/12	Time: 10:00am	

Reason for Referral:	Boot Camp	**Medication Adherence**	Smoking Cessation (____/day)	Nutrition	Cholesterol Management	Other:

Medication allergies: NKDA	Chief Complaint: "I have a rash"

Subjective: JD is a 31 y/o male here today for a medication adherence check for his new medication, Atripla, which he started taking 2 weeks ago. He reports 100% adherence with his new regimen despite having experienced a handful of vivid dreams, which he does not mind. He also reports a rash that has developed since initiating therapy. He states that the rash is itchy and annoying and is mostly on his chest and back; he admits to taking 25 mg of Benadryl when it gets really bad. JD currently takes Advair once daily for prevention of asthma symptoms; he has not needed to use his albuterol inhaler within the past 6 months. He reports 100% adherence with his Bactrim and azithromycin; he uses a pill box.

Labs (ref.)	Value:	Date Collected:	ROS: (check if present)	Medication	Dose	Directions
CD4	20	1/1/11	___ no complaints	Atripla	300 mg/ 200 mg	1 tab PO daily
CD4%	2%	1/1/11	___ Appetite change			
VL (<75)	300,000	1/1/11	___ Chills	Azithromycin	500 mg	2 tabs PO weekly
SCr (0.78–1.34)	0.90	1/1/11	___ Cough	Advair	250/50	1 puff BID
eGFR (>60)	>60	1/1/11	___ Diarrhea	Albuterol HFA		2 puffs as needed for wheezing
AST (10–40)	30	1/1/11	___ Dizziness			
ALT (9–60)	45	1/1/11	___ Dysphagia	Bactrim	DS	1 tab PO daily
Trig (<150)	120	1/1/11	___ Fatigue			
LDL (<100)	70	1/1/11	_x_ Vivid dreams			
TChol (<200)	150	1/1/11	___ Myalgias			
HDL (>40)	45	1/1/11	___ Nausea/vomiting			
TBili (0.2–1.2)	0.8	1/1/11	___ Mental status change			
HgbA1C% (<6.5%)	5.5	1/1/11	___ Pain			
Glucose (70–130)	90	1/1/11	_x_ Rash			
			___ Sweats			
			___ Vision change			
			___ Weight loss			

Problem	**Assessment**	**Recommendation**	**Plan**
HIV+	Adverse Drug Event: LH is in good spirits with regards to his therapy. He expresses no concerns about his therapy with Atripla, except for the rash.	Patient should be seen for an urgent visit at this clinic for assessment of rash.	Patient referred to nurse practitioner so that rash can be assessed. Provider and pharmacist to discuss cause of rash and actions for resolution. Patient to return to see pharmacist in 4 weeks for follow-up and adherence check.
Asthma	Noncompliance: Patient is taking Advair incorrectly	Patient should be taking Advair twice daily	Counseled patient on twice daily administration. Follow-up with patient in 4 weeks to assess adherence.

Figure 2-3. Example of consultation note.

Patient Name: Jane Doe   DOB: 4/4/1944

☐ I agree with the following recommendation. This serves as a prescription and may be filled at the patient's pharmacy:
- Start: lisinopril 10 mg   Sig: Take 1 tablet by mouth once daily
  Quantity: 90   Refills: 3

☐ I agree with the above recommendation with the following changes:
- Start   Sig:
- Quantity: Refills:

☐ I do not agree with the recommendation.
☐ Please have the pharmacist contact me to address this.
☐ Please have the patient contact me to address this.

Figure 2-4. Example of "plan" section of a consultation note.

Subjective information must be concise, and all lab data or other objective measurements should be presented. The assessment and plan should be prioritized, specific, and clear. Lastly, the language used in documentation may depend on the intended audience. For example, very different health-related terms will be used when writing a physician consult letter and a patient MAP. All documentation should be proofread for error and should convey an appropriate level of professionalism.

■ DOCUMENTATION RESOURCES

Understanding Your Current Environment

Documenting patient care requires a collection of resources. An assessment of the practice site, through inventory, and the development of a process map will shed light on to the resources available and those that are lacking. When making this assessment, it is critical to understand which employees are responsible for each task, and how workflow is currently structured. Observe the current workflow from an objective perspective by creating a process map[7] (Fig. 2-5). To create a process map, start with an outlined diagram of the pharmacy setup. Include prescription drop off and pickup areas, workstations, phones, computers, and the location of patient charts. Next, add the employees involved with the pharmacy workflow such as cashiers, technicians, pharmacists, students, and residents. The process in which prescriptions get filled by following a new prescription and documenting on the map the order of steps and the people involved should then be mapped. This examination of the current environment will allow the pharmacist to propose a more successful mechanism to engage other pharmacy employees, utilizing everyone's time and skills appropriately.

Documentation System

Once the pharmacist has a better understanding of the current environment, the documentation system can begin to be defined. Some practices currently sustain on paper documentation, some are electronic only, and some may be a mix; however, with the move to the nationwide use of an EHR all new practice sites will eventually need to focus on the incorporation of an EHR into their practice rather than a paper charting system. By 2014, all health-care providers will need to transition to EHRs in order to meet CMS standards, and thus be compensated for services.

Electronic documentation systems should be housed in a HIPAA compliant computer system. This computer system may require extra storage capacity and Internet access, which all need to be accounted for when designing how the new service will be implemented. Pharmacists may have the ability or need to see patients off site, and therefore would require

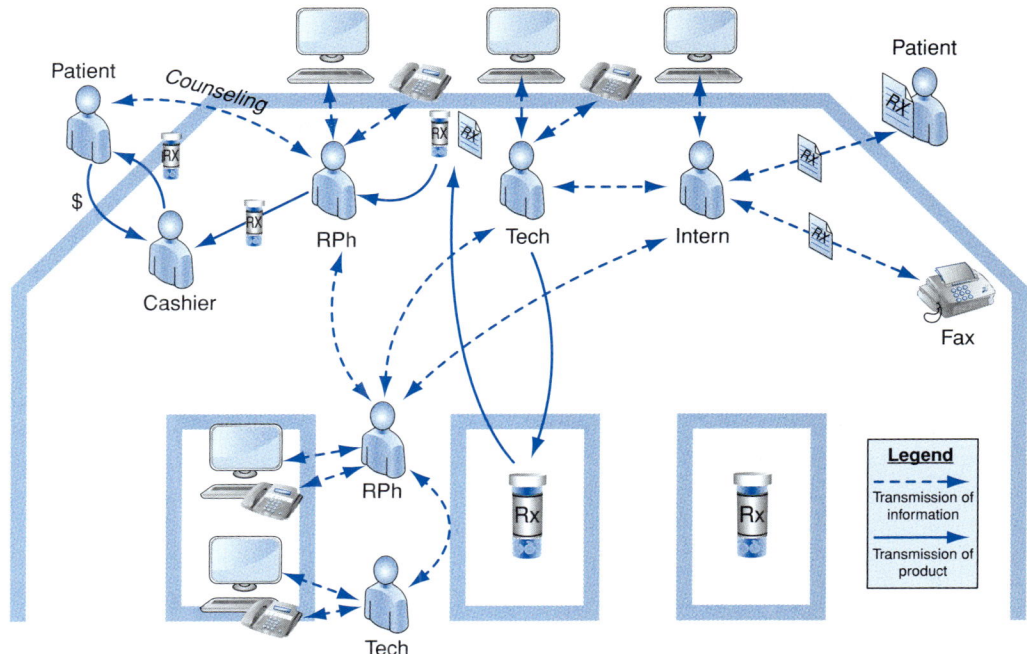

Figure 2-5. Process map.

a portable method of documentation using the same system established for the practice, such as a laptop or tablet, to adequately document patient care activities outside of the primary practice site. Reliable electric power sources and an Internet connection should be considered, and the ability to print documents for the patient, such as medication action plans (MAPs) and personal medication records (PMRs) are necessary to ensure continuity of care and ensure consistent follow-up activities.

In addition to hardware specifications that ensure reliable maintenance of information, it may be advantageous to assess a system's capability to interface with already existing EHRs specific to affiliated institutions or providers. This interface provides potential for collaboration with other health-care providers involved in the care of patients as well as allowing for efficient and accurate transmittal of patient health-care information.

The cost of an electronic documentation system is often the deciding factor for implementation. Costs related to customization, maintenance, hardware, user training, and technical support must be assessed prior to and throughout implementation of an electronic documentation system. Customization is a key element to documentation systems since it allows the user flexibility in the software's utility. Often times, reports must be transmitted to a third party to receive payment for services. It may also be advantageous to develop additional reports to furnish to providers or patients who track treatment outcomes relative to pharmacy-provided services. Without customization, pulling date from documentation systems can prove to be a tedious and inefficient task.

It is wise to get hands-on experience with a documentation system before investing the time and money for installation and utilization. Most software developers are willing to meet with potential clients for demonstrations and often provide trial subscriptions. If selecting to purchase an already existing documentation system, make sure that it meets all the needs of the business and enables the pharmacist to provide clinical services efficiently and effectively. An ideal documentation system will allow the pharmacist to fully document the SOAP components of an MTR; generate a PMR, MAP, and physician communication that abide by CMS regulations; and collect reportable outcomes (i.e., drug therapy problems identified).

Staff Training

Adequate staffing is essential to perform all components of documentation. Despite having a perfectly operating documentation system, if there are limitations to staff members or time, sufficient documentation will not be possible. Consider which elements of documentation need to be completed by a pharmacist, and which do not. Can student pharmacists input data into an electronic system? Can technicians help fax documents to patients' physicians or will the electronic system allow e-fax options? For example, the OutcomesMTM™ documentation and billing platform allow for technician access. Technicians can contribute to the documentation of MTM services through this platform and leave claims as "pending" until the pharmacist confirms them. Consider how each of these pharmacy team members may play a roll and engage them in the practice.

All assisting staff members will need to be trained to some degree. Adult learners learn by "doing" and therefore on the job training is most appropriate.[10] Through supervised hands-on experience, your staff members will gain the knowledge they need to assist you in documenting aspects of patient care that do not need to be completed by a pharmacist, which will ultimately make your practice more productive and efficient.

■ WHAT TO DO WITH THE DOCUMENTATION

Documentation systems can serve as incredible sources of data if there are mechanisms in place to mine this data. Individually, a well-documented patient care encounter provides a foundation for clinical or financial outcomes. When combined with all patient encounters for patients seen in a practice(s), this data is much more powerful. This data may ultimately establish the case for provision of and payment for pharmacist cognitive services.

Once an improvement in a patient's condition has been realized as a result of an encounter with a pharmacist through the identification and resolution of drug therapy problems, adequate documentation of relevant services provides pharmacists with an opportunity to demonstrate reductions in health-care costs. Data pulled from documentation systems is integral to a practice-based research. Published data from national patient care initiatives have demonstrated that pharmacist-provided care leads to decreases in hospitalizations and physician visits, and improvements in physiologic markers as a result of improved disease state management have led to a decrease in overall health-care costs.[10] These opportunities exist at the community and institutional level. However, as the most accessible health-care providers, community pharmacists are offered very apparent opportunities to create a shift in health-care expenditures.

Implications on the Pharmacy's Bottom Line

For every pharmacist that documents patient care services within the community setting, there is a pharmacy that can benefit from those services. The outcomes that can be reported to third-party payers to indicate a reduction in health-care costs can also be reported to pharmacy owners, patients, and prescribers. These outcomes speak to the value of patient care services available from that pharmacy. Pharmacies and pharmacists can use these outcomes to market MTM and other clinical services. For example, if a blood pressure screening service was to exist within a pharmacy, and patients were able to sign up for an assessment with every blood pressure medication refill, the outcomes of the screening service could be made available to providers. If, through outcomes analysis, a reduction in blood pressure readings was realized due to patient services available from that pharmacy, prescribers may be more likely to refer patients to that pharmacy for their blood pressure medications. Coupling dispensing services with clinical services also has the potential to reduce the burden of clinical monitoring on prescribers, allowing them more time to address more critical concerns. The potential for patient encounters that result from this shift in responsibility opens opportunities for pharmacists to have an even greater impact on patient outcomes. Pharmacists and pharmacies may also benefit from providing clinical services for medication classes with higher profit margins, such as specialty medications. Introduction of an adherence program for patients on these high yielding medications may prove of benefit to the pharmacy's bottom line. However, these services cannot be marketed as valuable without documentation. Additionally, reporting relevant outcomes for marketing purposes will require an initial baseline assessment in order to determine relevance and must be taken into account prior to the new service.

Continuous Quality Improvement

After beginning to utilize a new documentation system, it is important to evaluate its success as part of a Continuous Quality Improvement (CQI) initiative. All system participants should be involved in this evaluation, and the evaluation should be ongoing or "continuous" in a cyclical manner.[11] Improvements should be integrated and optimum quality is the ultimate goal as the process evolves. Some questions to consider: How could this system be easier to use? How could it allow the pharmacist to document in a more complete and efficient manner? Are the core elements of MTM easy to pull from the system, and in a format that is acceptable to the audience? Are outcome reports captured, and in the best manner to present to patients, other health-care providers, and third-party payers? The documentation system should be adaptable to meet the needs of each stakeholder, and through CQI the pharmacist will need to ensure that this is accomplished.

■ CONCLUSION

Documentation is necessary to a patient care practice, and must be consistently and thoroughly executed. Elements of documentation are essential to regulatory compliance, professional accountability, and continuity of care. Furthermore, documentation has aided and continues to establish the argument to justify compensation for pharmacist-provided services based on improvement in treatment outcomes and cost avoidance. To ensure reputable documentation practices, pharmacists must establish electronic methods of documentation that allow for timely and accurate transmission of information to patients, providers, and third parties. To support documentation practices, pharmacists may also employ the support of pharmacy technicians and other personnel capable of facilitating pharmacist documentation practices. Once a documentation system has been defined, pharmacists must consistently analyze documentation practices through cost analysis, efficacy, and efficiency to establish a case for the continued provision of services.

■ SUMMARY POINTS

- Documentation practices within the community pharmacy setting should be concise, incorporate components of SOAP note documentation, and allow for the identification of drug therapy problems.
- Documentation systems can be easily integrated into a community pharmacy's workflow by assessing technological and personnel resources essential to service provision.
- Documentation does not need to be executed in solidarity. Pharmacists should employ the assistance of student pharmacists, residents, and staff pharmacists in documenting clinical services.
- Well-documented patient care outcomes can be used to market MTM services and justify clinical pharmacist services within a pharmacy's business model.

STUDY QUESTIONS

1. The following are all examples of documentation in a community pharmacy EXCEPT:
   a. Logging the filling of a narcotic prescription in the perpetual inventory book
   b. Counseling a patient on a new medication
   c. Recording the lot number of a vaccine that was administered
   d. Asking the patient to sign his or her name at prescription pickup

2. The following are all reasons to appropriately document EXCEPT:
   a. Proper documentation is required by state and federal law
   b. Proper documentation enhances continuity of care
   c. Proper documentation aides in questions of professional liability
   d. All of the above

3. According to current MTM practice guidelines, the following core elements are provided to the patient at visit completion:
   a. Updated vaccination history
   b. Personal medication record (PMR)
   c. Medication action plan (MAP)
   d. Physician consult letter
   e. B and C

4. Documentation can serve as communication to the following parties EXCEPT:
   a. The patient who service was provided for
   b. The patient's other health-care provider(s)
   c. The patient's family members, without the patient's permission
   d. The patient's third-party payer

5. Create a CQI plan in regard to your current or proposed documentation system, including a proposed method of evaluation and resolution.

Bibliography

1. Cipolle RJ, Strand LM, Morely PC. *Pharmaceutical Care Practice: The Clinician's Guide*. 2nd ed. New York, NY: McGraw-Hill; 2004.
2. Millonig MK. Mapping the route to medication therapy management documentation and billing standardization and interoperability within the health care system: meeting proceedings. *J Am Pharm Assoc.* 2009;49(3):e41-e51.
3. New York State Medicaid Program: Provider manual. http://www.health.ny.gov/health_care/medicaid/program/mtm/docs/2009–2010_provider_manual.pdf. Accessed March 8, 2012.
4. Form CMS-10396 (01/12) Form Approved OMB No. 0938–1154.
5. American Pharmacists Association, National Association of Chain Drug Stores Foundation. Medication therapy management in pharmacy practice: core elements of an MTM service model (version 2.0). *J Am Pharm Assoc.* 2008;48:341-353.
6. McGiveny MS, Meyer SM, Duncan-Hewitt W, et al. Medication therapy management: it's relationship to patient counseling, disease management and pharmaceutical care. *J Am Pharm Assoc.* 2007;47:620-628.
7. Barnett MJ, Frank J, Wehring H, et al. Analysis of pharmacist-provided medication therapy management (MTM) services in community pharmacies over 7 years. *J Manag Care Pharm.* 2009;15(1):18-31.
8. Wilson DL, Kimberlin CL, Brushwood DB, et al. Constructs underlying community pharmacy dispensing functions relative to Florida pharmacy technicians. *J Am Pharm Assoc.* 2007;47:588-598.
9. Wick JY. *Supervision: A Pharmacy Perspective*. Washington, DC: APhA; 2003.
10. Cranor CW, Bunting BA, Cristensen DB. The Asheville Project: long-term clinical and economic outcomes of a community pharmacy diabetes care program. *J Am Pharm Assoc.* 2003;43(2):173-184.
11. Desselle SP, Zgarrick DP. *Pharmacy Management: Essentials for all Practice Settings*. 2nd ed. New York, NY: McGraw-Hill; 2009.

3

COUNSELING AND MOTIVATIONAL INTERVIEWING

Justin J. Sherman

■ LEARNING OBJECTIVES

After reading this chapter, the pharmacy student, community practice resident, or pharmacist should be able to:

1. Discuss the role of patient counseling techniques such as the three prime questions and behavioral change models.
2. Recognize pharmacist-centered, patient-centered, and environmental barriers to change and how to overcome them.
3. Explain how motivational interviewing is useful and effective as a style of counseling.
4. Discuss the role of the five core communication principles as they apply to motivational interviewing.
5. Assess a patient's readiness and self-efficacy to change their behaviors.

INTRODUCTION

Whether in a community or clinical setting, pharmacists usually do not have abundant time to fully discuss medication and behavior change issues with patients. In the case of many community settings, the environment and other factors may serve as barriers; however, evidence-based communication strategies are crucial to resolving barriers, to increasing patient adherence to medications, and to improving clinical outcomes. Even in environments conducive to optimal counseling and effective medication therapy management (MTM), the most effective medications can be rendered ineffective if patients struggle to make behavior changes in medication adherence and other disease management behaviors. Motivational interviewing (MI) has been shown to be an effective counseling method for ambivalent or resistant patients, as it is designed to resolve ambivalence and to help patients decide internally and on their own to make changes.

THE OMNIBUS RECONCILIATION ACT OF 1990 AND THE INDIAN HEALTH SERVICE MODEL

Patient counseling standards originally were set in the Omnibus Budget Reconciliation Act of 1990 (OBRA 1990), which is a law mandating that pharmacists offer counseling to patients regarding their prescriptions.[1] If the patient accepts this offer, pharmacists should discuss the following:

- Name of medication
- Intended use and expected action
- Route, dosage form, dosage, and administration schedule
- Proper storage
- Common adverse effects that may be encountered
- Techniques for self-monitoring of drug therapy
- Prescription refill information
- Action to take if a dose is missed
- Potential drug–drug or drug–food interactions or other therapeutic contraindications

Although the law was intended for Medicaid patients, individual states adopted rules to make counseling applicable to other patients, as well.[1] Thus, counseling is one of the tools that may be used to provide MTM services. One of the limitations of counseling, however, is that information generally is provided in a one-way, provider-centered manner (i.e., pharmacist to patient or pharmacist to caregiver). Instead, the pharmacist should ask questions to elicit needed information from the patient to fill the medication(s) in question and also to ensure that all of the patient's medications are providing optimal benefit. This can become a time-consuming process.

To streamline the process for discussing medications, the "three prime questions" of the Indian Health Service Model can help determine the patient's baseline understanding of a medication.[2] This method promotes a conversation with the patient during which the pharmacist elicits information that the patient already knows, with the intention to fill in any gaps of understanding. Thus, discussing medications does not consist of simply the pharmacist reciting everything about the medication. This is a time-efficient method of conversing with the patient and consists of asking the following prime questions:

1. What did your prescriber tell you this medication is for?
2. How did your prescriber tell you to take the medication?
3. What did your prescriber tell you to expect?

These questions stimulate a discussion of purpose for the medication, directions for use, all aspects of dosing and administering, and what the desired outcome should be. The questions are asked in a nonthreatening, non-judgmental manner to encourage the patient to seek more information for optimal medication use. The pharmacist should ask subsequent questions to provide information that will help the patient achieve his/her goals.² Subsequent questions for each may include:

- What problem or symptoms is this medication supposed to help? What is the medication supposed to do? (Prime question #1)
- How often and how long are you supposed to take it? How much are you supposed to take? What do the directions (e.g., two times a day) mean to you? (Prime question #2)
- What good and bad effects did your physician tell you to watch out for? How will you know if the medication is working? What are you supposed to do if it doesn't work? (Prime question #3)

■ DISCUSSING BEHAVIOR CHANGES WITH PATIENTS

The pharmacist may find that the patient requires change(s) in therapy, including a need to alter doses or to initiate or consolidate medications. However, many pharmacists discover when initiating conversations that the underlying problems often consist of patients not engaging in healthy behaviors (e.g., nonadherence to medications, not eating healthy, or not exercising regularly). Patients also engage in harmful behaviors/habits (e.g., smoking, drinking excessive alcohol, and others). Although medications and doses may be optimized for the patient's particular disease or condition, the aforementioned unhealthy behaviors can prevent goal achievement (e.g., for diabetes: HbA_{1c} (A_{1c}) <7%, blood pressure <140/80 mm Hg, and LDL <100 mg/dL). Moreover, maintaining healthy eating habits and regular physical activity comprise the cornerstone of therapy for many chronic diseases, including diabetes, hyperlipidemia, and hypertension. In many cases, the patient lacks the motivation needed to change these underlying behaviors that would optimize outcomes.³

The Transtheoretical Model of Behavior Change

A well-studied model that can be used to explain or predict behavior change is the Transtheoretical Model (TTM).⁴ This model does not explain behavior change as a single event in time; rather, it takes into account that change is a process for many patients that occurs over time. It includes five stages of motivational readiness for change, which concerns emotional, cognitive, and behavioral readiness.⁴ A wide variety of target health behaviors have been studied using the TTM paradigm, including smoking cessation, weight control, exercise, stress management, alcohol and drug abuse, screening recommendations adherence, and medication management.⁵ Patients cycle through the stages of change before being able to maintain long-term change, and the temporal association can be long or short. In other words, patients could be in one stage for years, or they could move rapidly through several stages in a matter of days or sometimes even hours—perhaps even during the course of a formal counseling session. Relapse is sometimes considered a stage in relation to the TTM concepts since it is common; in smoking cessation, for example, the average number of relapse episodes before a successful quit has been four to five. Upon relapse, patients may revert back several stages in the TTM readiness continuum as a result of the feelings of failure that a relapse can bring.

The utility of the TTM for the pharmacist is to recognize the stage of behavioral change the patient is currently in, and then use the associated stage-matched tools to help the patient move toward the next stage. Table 3-1 describes the five primary stages of change, including precontemplation, contemplation, preparation, action, and maintenance.⁴ After classifying a patient in one of these stages, pharmacists can develop appropriate interventions to assist the patient in moving toward the next stage. A patient often has ambivalence because the "cons" for moving toward the next stage outweigh the "pros." For example, perhaps the smoker discussing the need to set a quit date cannot commit to this because the person "enjoys smoking,"

Table 3-1. Five Stages of the Transtheoretical Model of Behavior Change as Applied to Smoking Cessation

Stage and Description	Examples of Assisting Movement to the Next Stage
1. Precontemplation Not intending cessation within the foreseeable future (e.g., next 6 months); patients unaware of consequences of smoking or demoralized from unsuccessful attempts to stop smoking; may be in denial	–Pharmacist simply should be supportive and state that they can be used as a resource if the patient would like to discuss how smoking harms and how stopping smoking is beneficial for health
2. Contemplation Smoker intending to stop in the next 6 months; more aware of pros for stopping but also aware of cons; can produce profound ambivalence and not move toward preparation	–Examining barriers to change and emphasizing pros for stopping may be helpful at this stage –Patients at this stage may be more receptive to health information, emphasizing individualized "pros" for stopping, and discussion of available cessation programs and medications. Remember to respect the patient's autonomy when giving information.
3. Preparation Smoker is intending to take action in the immediate future (e.g., within the next month)	– While some information could have been shared in Contemplation, these smokers need to enroll in cessation programs and develop an active quit plan; strategy should move from exploring motivation to developing behavioral change skills
4. Action Overt modification in the patient's lifestyle is taking or has taken place; the patient is abstinent from smoking and is trying to maintain that abstinence	–Implementing a well-developed quit plan is crucial during this stage, including the development of behavioral changes on a daily basis. A thorough action plan that can be individualized for patients can be found in the "Smoking Cessation" chapter of this book
5. Maintenance The recent quitter is trying to prevent relapse; as time progresses, the quitter becomes more confident that they can continue their cessation	–Attention should be given toward reinforcing the behavioral changes implemented in daily activities. Also, the patient should be aware of both physical and psychological dependence (e.g., tendency to relapse during stressful situations) and develop strategies to counter both

has a spouse who is also a smoker, has enough money to buy two packs per day, and has not yet experienced an adverse health problem because of this "habit." Perhaps the patient is aware of diseases and problems that could result from continuing to smoke and is intending a quit attempt within the next 6 months (contemplation stage). The problem may be that the listed "pros" for continuing to smoke outweigh the listed "cons" for quitting, such as the expense of smoking cessation medications, history of nicotine patches "not working", an adversity to experiencing intense cravings, and "missing" the daily routine of smoking. In this case, strategies would include interviewing in a way that the patient ends up countering self-identified barriers in an individualized way that should assist the patient in moving toward the preparation and action stages.

The Readiness Ruler

The willingness for patients to change their behavior in a meaningful and long-lasting way is highly individualized. Using a "readiness ruler" is another tool for discussing change in a positive manner.[6] The readiness ruler asks the patient to rate his/her level of readiness to change on a scale of 0 to 10, where "0" represents "absolutely not ready" and "10" represents "absolutely ready." Even if the patient scores himself or herself with a low number, such as a "4," the pharmacist should focus on the positive aspect by comparing the stated 4 with the minimum, saying, "why a 4 and not a 1?" Then, to infer an expectation for only incremental change for the patient, the pharmacist could say, "What would need to happen for you to choose a score of 5 or 6?" The pharmacist should not suggest a "10" because that suggests too much of a change all at once and also may shame the patient who may then perceive that the 10 he or she is "failing" to achieve is expected. This can create more resistance for the patient and can interfere with building a therapeutic, trusting relationship between patient and pharmacist.

BARRIERS TO COMMUNICATION

As opposed to traditional counseling, MI involves developing a partnership with a patient in order to exchange information and facilitate a shared, informed decision.[3] MI will be discussed as a framework for addressing barriers; thus, it is important to first note barriers to communication that may exist within the current pharmacist–patient relationship. Barriers to communication can be personal (or pharmacist-centered), patient-centered, and environmental.[7]

Personal (Pharmacist-Centered) Barriers

Some pharmacists think that good counseling skills are innate and that certain people are born with these skills. This is rarely true. Effective counseling skills, especially using MI, can be learned and developed if the pharmacist is willing. Consider that a significant component for entrance into most schools of pharmacy involves an interview. The interview is designed to target as potential pharmacists those who have adequate baseline communication skills. Although most pharmacists should have good baseline skills, confidence may be lacking that he or she can communicate at the level necessary to provide MTM and develop services.[7]

Pharmacists may not be aware that several factors, including poor body positioning, could lead a patient to feel that the pharmacist is not being attentive. The pharmacist should try to stay within 1&1/2 to 4 feet from the patient who is being counseled—not too close to invade "personal space," and not too far away either. Distracting body movements should also be avoided, such as folding arms across the chest, tapping a foot, clicking a pen, or "playing" with one's hair, for example. In general, any movement that could be construed by the patient as not having the pharmacist's full attention should be avoided. A very common position that pharmacists take is facing their computer terminal instead of the patient. Although this is conducive to using the computer to gather important information, the patient could perceive this as the pharmacist not being attentive.

Remember that nonverbal communication is as important as verbal. When counseling the patient, lean squarely toward the patient, maintain an open body posture and a reasonable amount of eye contact (50–75% of interaction time), and control any distracting mannerisms. If nonverbal communication is incongruent with what the pharmacist is saying, the patient is most likely to believe the nonverbal communication. The pharmacist always should use nonverbal behaviors that are nonjudgmental and nonthreatening. Maintaining good eye contact, using responsive body language (e.g., head nodding), and using a calm and conversational tone will go a long way in communicating a spirit of collaboration.

Regarding one's voice, the pharmacist should be vigilant and sensitive to tone, particularly in regard to a tone the patient may perceive as antagonistic, judgmental, or condescension. The result could be resentment and resistance to change, thus increasing barriers to good communication, and ultimately not being effective in an MTM encounter. An overarching point to remember is to be vigilant of how the message is being perceived by the patient and act accordingly.

Other personal barriers are less obvious. The pharmacist should monitor for internal conversations or judgments that could create barriers. For example, a pharmacist filling prescriptions in the back of the pharmacy may overhear a patient checking out and giving the pharmacy technician a difficult time over the price of a medication. The pharmacist may not "jump in" right away in order to think about how to deal with this particular situation. This is fine, of course, and prevents a rash action by the pharmacist. However, when in conversation with a patient, if that pharmacist's thoughts are wandering—or perhaps thinking about all of the tasks that must be completed after that conversation—those thoughts (i.e., internal conversations) are now overriding the ability to listen effectively.

Finally, one might want to be aware of using a "Righting Reflex" when discussing behavioral change with patients.[3] This comes into play when the pharmacist assumes the position of expert on medication and changing behaviors while not taking the patient's goals into account. The righting reflex will be discussed in more detail in the MI sections.

Patient-Centered Barriers

Barriers that are patient-centered are sometimes easy to detect but difficult to overcome.[7] Patients could have language barriers for which the pharmacist would need to use an interpreter. Specialized educational tools or other accommodations might have to be used for patients with visual, hearing, or physical challenges. For example, older patients may have trouble discerning higher-pitched voices, so communication may require using a lower pitch. Low literacy of the written or spoken word, as well as low health literacy may, be common in many locations, and can inhibit effective communication.[7] For example, written instructions should be composed at the fourth to sixth grade reading level for patients, and the pharmacist should use plain language rather than medical terminology. Verbal instructions should be direct, succinct, unambiguous, and followed-up to check for patient understanding.

Finally, a patient may not be reacting to the present experience in the pharmacy, but to past experiences. A bad experience with another pharmacist or staff person, or other health-care encounters, may have left emotions of fear and anger toward providers in general or pharmacists specifically. It is important to consider all of the cues, both verbal and nonverbal, that the patient is giving to try to understand the overall problem. MI is a method with tools for attempting to assess all cues together and responding in a patient-centered manner.

Environmental Barriers

This final barrier is the most obvious but is still very significant and difficult for many pharmacists to overcome. The prescription counter is positive from several standpoints: patients needing a prescription filled can identify this area quickly, it provides a private and secure area for pharmacy staff, and staff easily can watch over the prescription area from this vantage point. However, the prescription counter can be intimidating for patients. They may not be able to readily identify the pharmacist, and they may have the impression that the pharmacist is not accessible.[7] The process of dropping off prescriptions and picking them up in certain areas may not be well identified and can be confusing. Most pharmacies have a "patient counseling area," but the area should be reappraised on a regular basis for its ability to meet a variety of patient counseling needs. Many designated patient counseling areas have a lack of privacy due to space limitations. There are also other factors to examine regarding the designated patient counseling area. Is it accessible for the patient? Do pharmacy personnel immediately approach the patient when standing at the counseling area? Is the area itself blocked or cluttered by advertisements or displays? Does the patient have to "look up" to converse with pharmacy personnel? These considerations must be appraised and rectified, perhaps even reevaluating workflow issues, for effective counseling sessions to occur.

A good workflow system with attention to the patient could minimize environmental barriers. As the patient approaches the prescription area, the patient should be able to attain the pharmacist's attention quickly. Also, prescription areas are noisy and crowded, with plenty of chances to be interrupted by phone calls and questions from technicians and other patients. The pharmacist should train technicians how to triage calls well and not interrupt a counseling session unless it is absolutely necessary. Consider reorganizing the workflow, if necessary, to shift dispensing tasks more to the technicians and using support personnel. Making the pharmacy conducive for providing MTM services is an individualized process for every location. The pharmacist should be willing to make changes that will be more conducive to providing effective counseling – including privacy concerns. Finally, it is important to ensure that the flow is reasonable from the patient's perspective. The process for leaving prescriptions, picking up medications, and especially how to receive counseling should be unambiguous for the patient.

Non-pharmaceutical items could create confusion in the communication process about healthy behaviors. For MTM to be successful, patients should view the pharmacy as a place where health-care is deemed important. If the pharmacy sells alcohol or cigarettes, patients could perceive these items as being counterproductive to health. This could create an unintentional barrier to discussions about health behavior change regarding habits associated with these products. Also, tobacco cessation products should be in an area convenient and conducive for initiating therapeutic conversations. In addition, placement of herbals and vitamins is important. While the average person may understand the usefulness of a multivitamin, placing scientifically unproven products together in the same area as legitimate vitamins and herbals could lead the patient to assume all products in that area are useful; this could get in the way of an effective, trusted conversation about needed supplements (e.g., calcium for the patient with osteoporosis, versus unproven "remedies" that offer unfounded hope for cure or symptom relief).

While it is not absolutely essential for a pharmacy to have a private room dedicated for counseling, having one available would greatly decrease the environmental barriers.[7] A private consultation room is indeed the ideal environment for MTM sessions and is becoming more common in community pharmacy settings. Studies have shown that patients counseled in a private area in the pharmacy were more adherent with their medication regimens, retained more information, and were more satisfied with their care. A dedicated room could be stocked with equipment and education materials needed to provide MTM services (as discussed in the disease state management chapters), and patient files could be kept in a locked cabinet for easy reference. The pharmacist could schedule sessions to occur at specific times convenient for both patient and pharmacist rather than simply waiting for a spontaneous encounter when the patient comes to pick up monthly prescriptions.

The most important barrier for pharmacists who want to initiate MTM services is overcoming patient expectations regarding pharmacy flow. Based on their past experiences, patients have come to expect a certain flow to the services provided by their pharmacist. However, patients experiencing MTM services are more likely to expect these services in the future, particularly if barriers to receiving such services are minimized.

■ WHY THE NEED FOR MOTIVATIONAL INTERVIEWING?

Traditional pharmacist-centered counseling sessions have centered on giving information to the patient and advising on medications and diseases. Medication issues such as adverse effects, proper medication administration, and identification of efficacy are paramount points for patients to understand. Because of time constraints, pharmacists may ask directed questions to discern a patient's baseline knowledge and then give specific information to "fill the gaps." However, many patients have diseases where behavior changes like medication adherence and lifestyle change are critical to achieving optimal outcomes (e.g., diabetes, hypertension, and hyperlipidemia). Thus, increasing the patient knowledge regarding medications and diseases is a critical component to achieving optimal outcomes. However, knowledge alone is not the answer.[8]

MI is an effective communication strategy set that is designed to assess a patient's readiness to change, and to assist patients in deciding to change. One underlying principle of MI is the concept that while patients may know that changes need to be made, they are often ambivalent—or even actively resistant—in taking steps to actually make the changes.[3]

In the patient's view, obtaining a knowledgeable health-care provider who cares about them on a personal level is essential. Thus, developing a caring, therapeutic relationship with the patient is a prime component of MI. Pharmacists involved with patient care already understand the value of relationship development in achieving treatment adherence and good clinical outcomes. Using components that describe the spirit of MI can assist in developing this needed relationship. Components that describe the spirit of MI include the following: collaborate with and empower the patient, support and respect patient problem-solving capability, and develop internal motivation by eliciting change talk from the patient about the target behavior.[3] Strategies that convey the spirit of MI include, among others, using nonjudgmental open-ended questions, affirmation and self-efficacy support, reflective listening and empathic responding, and summary statements. These components are described in Table 3-2. This style of interviewing is designed to assist the patient in making an argument in favor of the changes.

In contrast to the spirit of MI, clinicians across health professions are often trained to take an advisory—perhaps even a parental-type—role when communicating with patients. Because pharmacists are experts regarding medications, this could be an inherent tendency when it comes to talking about adherence and other health behaviors needed for disease management. This tendency to advise and fix is described as the *righting reflex* in MI terminology and is counter to supporting patient autonomy and self-efficacy.[3] Pharmacists may have a natural inclination during counseling sessions to "fix" what is "wrong" with the patient, whether it is adherence, smoking, unhealthy eating, or remaining sedentary. Often the pharmacist gives advice to "fix" these behaviors. From the pharmacist's perspective, these are pearls of wisdom, grounded in evidence-based medicine. This represents a provider-centered approach rather than patient-centered. These strategies represent the pharmacist's decisions, not the patient's, about what is best for the patient. From the patient's perspective, these suggestions may be useful for someone else, but they may not fit within the patient's daily activities and may be impossible to implement. Also, the patient loses autonomy when excluded from participating in the process of thinking about changes that could be made. Rather than openly discussing reservations, the patient may simply listen to the advice without admitting that they will not implement it. Thus, the traditional counseling method could increase ambivalence and even resistance if the patient feels disrespected by the provider.[3]

For example, consider the following scenario: the pharmacist has been following a patient with type 2 diabetes for half a year. With guidance, the patient is now adherent with metformin and glyburide, both medications at maximum doses. Upon the fifth visit with the pharmacist, starting insulin therapy has been discussed but with considerable resistance. The patient states that an uncle started insulin several years ago and died soon afterward. The patient's physician previously initiated both oral medications because of resistance to starting insulin, but the patient's A_{1c} is still at 9.0%. Despite good medication adherence, the patient is not making any progress in the healthy eating and physical activity goals established by the pharmacist. Would frustration be kicking in for the pharmacist at this point? Should the pharmacist begin discussing in emphatic detail the microvascular complications that could occur, such as failing kidneys, blindness, and foot amputation?

Unfortunately, the tone of such "scare tactics," followed by instructions on how to make the changes, could cause the patient to become ashamed and resentful, losing autonomy in the process. This could result in increased ambivalence or resistance, exacerbating the medical concerns because the patient may feel judged by an "unhelpful" provider.

In contrast, the pharmacist using MI should *not* assume the role of health-care expert. Instead, the pharmacist employing this patient-centered communication style should interview the patient in a nonjudgmental way to gauge readiness to act on the target behavior. Then, the pharmacist should explore any ambivalence or resistance rather than arguing about it.[9] The pharmacist should explore the patient's

Table 3-2. Components of Motivational Interviewing

Component	Definition and Examples
Open-ended questions	–**Definition**—allow patients more complete answers to questions, encouraging better patient interaction and open responses –"What are some things that you might be able to do in order to remember your medications for diabetes better?" –"We have been discussing how high your blood pressure has been lately. What do you think we could do to help manage it better?" –"Since you continued to smoke through the quit date that you discussed with me previously, what have been the biggest obstacles in quitting?" –"What are your goals for losing weight over the next few months?" –"Which foods are you trying to eat more, and which foods are you trying to eat less in order to stay on the diet you discussed with me previously?"
Affirmations	–**Definition**—statement that the provider appreciates a patient's action –"I appreciate the fact that you have been checking your blood glucose as soon as you awaken each day. How many more times during the day would you be willing to try to check your blood sugar?" –"You've been doing a great job working in your garden at least once a week. Based on your goal of weight loss that you discussed with me, how often and for how long would you be willing to walk each week, too?" –"Even though you have been missing your mealtime insulin at times, I think it is great you have been consistently taking your long-acting insulin. How do you think you would best remember taking mealtime insulin?"
Reflective listening	–**Definition**—reflecting back statements from the patient, often restating thoughts or feelings with a different perspective or in a positive light –Patient—"I really don't like taking my medicine." –Pharmacist—"You really don't like taking your medicine." (Repeating) –Patient—"I am too sleepy at night and usually forget that medicine." –Pharmacist—"I'm hearing that although you fall asleep many nights, and this prevents you from taking medicine, you really want to take it." (Rephrasing) –Patient—"I'm a failure. I can't remember to take the mealtime insulin." –Pharmacist—"Even though you can't remember to take insulin at mealtimes, you are great about taking the long-acting insulin and may just need a little help to remember it at mealtime." (Reframing) –Patient—"I just don't understand why I can't control my sugar with one shot a day." –Pharmacist—"On one hand, you would like to control your sugar with only one shot a day. On the other hand, you have found high values after checking your blood sugars 2 hours after meals. Could we discuss how only taking a once daily long-acting insulin is not effective for those times your blood sugar is high?" (Double-sided reflection)
Summary statements	–**Definition**—the pharmacist provides a recap of instructions or other things that are discussed at strategic points to ensure understanding – "Some of the things that we have been discussing today are ..."

understanding of the disease and treatments in an open-ended manner and assist in developing an appropriate treatment plan, involving both medication and behavior changes. The pharmacist should discuss the patient's current interests and concerns with the treatment plan, respects the patient's autonomy to choose relevant steps to take in making changes, and assist the patient in overcoming ambivalence and/or resistance toward making those changes.[9]

This approach, in comparison to the more traditional counseling trends, has been effective in improving medication adherence for several disease states. During traditional counseling, the practitioner is the health-care expert, assumes the patient lacks knowledge, and provides information to the patient. The goal is to *motivate* by persuading the patient to change behavior. In contrast, in MI a collaborative partnership develops between practitioner and patient.[3] Information is exchanged in order to facilitate the patient's informed decision. The goal is to *assess the patient's internal motivation* and to facilitate a commitment to change behavior. Even when the patient ultimately may not change the behavior, the practitioner respects the patient's autonomous decision *not* to change. Thus, the trusting, respectful relationship is preserved, in hopes that the patient may approach the provider in the future when more information is needed to actually make the changes.[3]

The patient's readiness to act on the target behavior depends on the internalized decisional balance. The patient will weigh the relevant and perceived pros and cons prior to taking steps conducive to an overall behavior change. If the cons take precedence over the pros, changes will typically not be implemented.

For example, some smoking cessation programs have created an actual activity out of the "pro vs. con" thought process. Patients may be asked to draw a balance, with each side representing the pros and cons, respectively. Then, the patient is asked to fill in the relevant pros and cons, and a discussion can ensue regarding the value the smoker placed on each item on the scales. When this process is repeated later during a series of meetings with smokers, the list of pros may increase while the list of cons decrease as the smoker becomes more in touch with internal motivations for setting a quit date and actively engaging in the actual quit attempt (i.e., the preparation and action stages of the TTM).[10]

In the ways discussed herein, MI can be truly rewarding and empowering for the patient. During this process, not only will the plan developed for behavior change be patient-specific, autonomy in the decision-making process is also respected, and the relationship between patient and provider is truly being established. These are the foundations necessary for the patient to make successful and sustained health behavior changes.

■ HOW TO USE MOTIVATIONAL INTERVIEWING

Although algorithms exist for the management of chronic diseases, treatment must always be individualized. This individualized aspect is also true for MI. No one script or algorithm will be effective for every patient. A prepared script would make the conversation very provider-centered, which is contradictory to the spirit of MI.

Reviewing the Indian Health Services Model with the "three prime questions," it is important to begin a conversation about behavioral change by pinpointing the patient's knowledge level about a particular disease and its treatments, and then "filling in the gaps." The difference with MI, however, is that the pharmacist should respect the patient's autonomy (i.e., that the patient may *not* want the provider to give more information).[3] Prior to giving information or initiating a more lengthy discussion, the pharmacist should *ask for permission* from the patient to do so. An example of this is given in Case Study #1 and #2 regarding possible interaction/dialogue sequences between the pharmacist and the patient. Also, the pharmacist should lead the patient into tying behavior changes directly to avoidance of negative consequences the patient is at risk for if changes are not made.

The pharmacist preserves autonomy by allowing the patient to ask questions about behavior changes at the beginning of the conversation, and by giving choices about which behavior targets to talk about first.[3] If the pharmacist "sets the agenda" for the discussion, the patient may become anxious about their unanswered questions while the pharmacist is speaking about something that concerns them less. Addressing patient concerns first builds the relationship and initiates trust, important initial components for implementing long-standing behavior changes. One challenge to agenda setting occurs if the patient has many questions or has a lot to say while time allowance for the visit is limited. The topics most important to the patient still should be addressed during the visit. If topics remain unaddressed at the end of the encounter, the efficient pharmacist will give the patient literature on the topic (at the appropriate learning level). Then, the next visit will begin with the patient's ensuing questions. This also establishes continuity for the patient during subsequent visits and assures that the pharmacist is very interested in the patient as a person.[11]

One of the main facets of MI is assisting the patient to move toward behavior change (i.e., similar to the preparation and action stages of the TTM). The patient is closest to taking necessary actions to change behavior when the patient initiates *change talk*. Change talk is when the patient's statements can be interpreted as acceptance or steps taken toward behavior change.[12,13] These statements are more likely to incorporate the "pros" of change rather than the "cons." Thus, patients are expressing a decisional balance that is now more geared toward making changes. When patients engage in change talk, they could discuss the following: a plan for changing behavior, the importance of making changes, or verbalizing short-term goals. Miller and Rollnick, the originators of MI, suggest that change talk can be categorized as expression of desires ("I want" or "I wish"), ability ("I can" or "I could"), reasons, or need ("I should" or "I need to"), commitment ("I will" or "I promise"), and taking steps.[14] To help patients engage in change talk, pharmacists can focus on past successes or current small changes that have already been implemented.

The time frame for change talk is important, as many times a goal may be unattainable in the short term. For example, the pharmacist asks a sedentary patient with diabetes and a body mass index of 35 taking 20 units of long-acting insulin, "What is your goal?" The patient may state as a goal: to stop having to take insulin. This would be a great long-term goal but impossible to achieve without considerable weight loss, which takes time when done appropriately. Thus, the pharmacist would likely help the patient develop a reasonable weight-loss goal with increments of achievement over time, including an individualized diet and exercise plan. These goals should be small and achievable at first.

Achievement of each small goal should increase the patient's self-efficacy. Self-efficacy is the confidence that the patient has to make a specific behavior change.[3,8] As the patient accomplishes each of the smaller goals, internal motivation may increase to the point that a bigger goal could be tackled. For example, consider a 20 pack year smoker preparing for a quit attempt. After meeting with the pharmacist each week for the past 3 weeks, the patient is almost ready for the quit date. The patient has selected nicotine patches as the medication of choice, so the patches will need to be started on the quit date. With the pharmacist's help, the patient has been able to cut the consumption in half every week. Previously smoking a pack per day, the patient has cut down to two or three cigarettes per day. Although the patient was "not anywhere near ready" 3 weeks ago, the patient feels ready to approach the quit date at the end of the week! The important point is that the pharmacist has congratulated the patient through every small success, resulting in the smoker now being ready to take that huge step to totally quit.

In conclusion, pharmacists can use certain tools to help the MI process. These include individualizing conversations and goals, respecting the patient's autonomy (by asking for permission to give more in-depth information, using open-ended questions, and letting the patient set the agenda), engaging the patient in change talk, and helping the patient set and accomplish small goals on the way toward attaining the larger overall goal.[15,16]

■ CORE COMMUNICATION PRINCIPLES

In addition to the tools already described, MI consists of five main communication principles, sometimes described by the acronym READS: (1) *r*oll with resistance, (2) *e*xpress empathy, (3) *a*void argumentation, (4) *d*evelop discrepancy, and (5) *s*upport self-efficacy. While the acronym is helpful in understanding the principles, they will be discussed in an ordered manner conducive to better understanding.[3,6,15]

Expressing Empathy

Expressing empathy requires one to try to understand the meaning of another person's statement through reflective listening. It is nonjudgmental communication that respects the patient's feelings and shows support. The pharmacist could show attentiveness to the patient's underlying feelings in the following example: a patient with diabetes is being switched to insulin because goals are not being met with maximum doses of oral medications. The patient is resistant because an uncle who started on insulin a few years ago died soon after initiation. The patient says, "For me, starting insulin is a death sentence, and it means that I've failed to take control of my diabetes."

An MI-appropriate response might start with expressing empathy: "You seem worried that starting insulin is a death sentence and means somehow that you've failed. Some of my patients see insulin as a tool to take control and prevent complications and bad outcomes. What do you think about that?"

An important caveat with expressing empathy is for the pharmacist to avoid the tendency to be the focus. Many otherwise excellent communicators in the above situation would say, "I understand how you feel (that starting insulin equates with death)." Whether the patient verbalizes it or not, this phrase may seem to be a parental, patronizing statement. Also, countering in this manner only brings the emphasis back on the pharmacist. Instead, the emphasis should always be on the patient and the target behavior changes.[3]

Roll with Resistance and Avoid Argumentation

How the pharmacist reacts to patient resistance is key. The patient's resistance may be active (verbalized) or passive (not verbalized but the patient will not implement the behaviors discussed). When encountering resistance, the pharmacist should avoid arguing with the patient and recognize that resistance is information to be explored. The patient expects an argument in response to resistance; when the pharmacist does not argue or put the patient on the defensive, this can be thought provoking for a patient who has felt disrespected by others who have argued. The relationship will most likely endure when the pharmacist collaborates with the patient rather than placing oneself as the expert.[3]

Going back to the previous example regarding the patient with diabetes being switched to insulin, the patient showed resistance to the change. The patient stated, "For me, starting insulin is a death sentence, and it means that I've failed to take control of my diabetes." By not negating the patient's statement—that initiating insulin is not a death sentence—the pharmacist avoided being drawn into an argument. In fact, technically the pharmacist did not deny the patient's statement. The pharmacist simply avoided arguing with the patient and rolled with the resistance.

However, strong patient resistance can be difficult to deal with for even seasoned pharmacists. For example, perhaps the same patient with diabetes is supposed to try insulin and come back in a week for follow-up. The patient comes back instead 3 weeks later and admits to not starting insulin. The patient argues that the cons for starting insulin outweigh the benefits (pros). Developing discrepancy can be a very useful tool when strong resistance is encountered.

Developing Discrepancy

As a patient-centered approach MI is also a directive approach that allows for gentle, non-judgmental confrontation. This is *developing discrepancy*, which is sometimes warranted and appropriate. The pharmacist should be assertive when needed for a sincere and honest encounter. This strategy helps illustrate that what the patient is doing or not doing is incongruent with their own stated goals. For example, the patient can be asked what their own goal would be for treating diabetes. Then, the patient can be asked how being non-compliant with insulin injections does not support the patient's own stated goal.

Another way to develop discrepancy includes discussing the patient's stated pros and cons for the target behavior and/or desired outcomes. Thus, the patient should sense the discrepancy when verbalizing these. A patient should sense how their own actions, or lack of actions, are preventing goal achievement. Paramount to this principle, however, is that the pharmacist should keep a professional, caring, and nonjudgmental tone.[3]

Continuing with this example:

The pharmacist begins to develop discrepancy when the patient does not start insulin therapy. The patient adamantly refuses to start insulin despite knowing that this is not congruent with achieving previously stated goals. Still, the pharmacist should not argue. A more effective strategy would be to ask, "Mr. Smith, you sound as if you are not willing to start insulin at this time. May I tell you what concerns me about this?" Recognize that the patient's autonomy is still respected by asking permission to give more information. Then, the pharmacist could describe the complications that the patient may become at risk for and should then followup by asking what the patient's thoughts are about this.

Another strategy for the resistant patient would be to acknowledge that it is the patient's right to make a personal choice about whether to change or not. The pharmacist could state, "You know, we have discussed starting insulin, but it will always be your decision as to whether you will take insulin or not. All I can do is to discuss the advantages and disadvantages of taking insulin, but it is up to you to decide." The patient knows that their action is not what the pharmacist wants and expects an argument. Instead, the pharmacist has verbalized that the final decision is up to the patient. By using the two tools above, the pharmacist shows respect for the patient's autonomy, most likely preserves the relationship, and actually could plant the seed to assist the patient in starting insulin in the future.

Supporting Self-Efficacy

Self-efficacy, or the patient's own belief in being able to achieve their goal, previously has been discussed. This consists of giving sincere encouragement and positive feedback about behavior changes or even for statements that suggest the patient is thinking about the change. For example, a person sincerely trying to lose weight may not have implemented widespread behavior changes first. The patient is surprised when the pharmacist responds with the following: "That's fine! The important thing is that you want to lose weight and are trying to (achieved the small goal, such as walking for 10 minutes daily, etc.). And, you did not *gain* weight either, so that is important!" In addition, it is important to remember that the behavior itself should be praised, rather than the person.[3]

■ CASE STUDY #1: PATIENT CONVERSATION THAT IS NOT MI ADHERENT

Nicholas Anderson is a 56-year-old man with diabetes and hypertension who has had medications filled by Delta Don's Pharmacy for the past 10 years. According to pharmacy records, the patient has been taking metformin 1000 mg twice daily, glyburide 10 mg twice daily, and lisinopril 20 mg daily for the past 6 months. The patient is overweight, exercises little, and is not following a healthy diet. However, the patient has a history of obtaining timely refills. A note in the computer profile dated 2 months earlier provides the patient's laboratory results (including A_{1c} of 10.0%); these lab values were brought in by the patient at that time for discussion. Today, the patient brings the prescription for Lantus 10 units injected at night, which was dated 3 weeks ago.

Mr. Anderson: Instead of filling the insulin prescription, could you call my doctor to renew my other diabetes medications? I don't really want to start insulin and poke myself with a needle. It's bad enough I have to stick myself to check my sugar four times a day.

Pharmacist: I understand (the pharmacist states while staring at the prescription). Mr. Anderson, do you realize this prescription is dated for 3 weeks ago? What took you so long to get this filled?

Mr. Anderson: Can you just call Dr. Purdy like I asked? I've already explained why I haven't gotten the insulin filled yet.

Pharmacist: Mr. Anderson, we are really busy today. I'll call later if you really want me to. Are you afraid to stick yourself with a needle? Think it's going to be too painful?

Mr. Anderson: No (glaring at the pharmacist). I already told you I stick myself four times a day. I'm a retired bricklayer and have dropped tons of bricks on myself in my time. I'm not afraid of pain. Never mind (grabs the prescription back)! I have an appointment next week with the doc. I'll ask him myself (storms out of the pharmacy, leaving in his wake other patients confused and upset at the altercation they have just witnessed).

Pharmacist (muttering to nobody in particular): He'll be back.

■ CASE STUDY #2: PATIENT CONVERSATION THAT IS MI ADHERENT

Mr. Anderson: Instead of filling this insulin prescription, could you call my doctor to refill my other diabetes medications instead? I don't really want to start insulin and poke myself with a needle. It's bad enough I have to stick myself to check my sugar four times a day.

Pharmacist: Sure, we can call your doctor, Mr. Anderson. You are really doing a great job by checking your blood sugar four times a day. What did Dr. Purdy say about the insulin last time you met with him?

Instead of focusing on the patient having done something wrong (not filling his prescription for 3 weeks), the pharmacist takes the opportunity to praise an action (checking blood glucose four times daily). Note that the action, rather than the person, is praised.

Mr. Anderson: Thanks (smiling briefly). Well, he said, my A_{1c} was too high, and starting anything other than insulin would not be effective in reducing my risks of complications.

Pharmacist: Oh, yes. We have in our records your last A_{1c} was 10.0%. You told me before that you and Dr. Purdy discussed that it would be a good goal to get your A_{1c} less than 7.0%.

The focus is on the patient's goal, setting up the ability for the pharmacist to show that the patient's action (not starting insulin) is not congruent with his goal. This creates discrepancy.

Mr. Anderson: Yes, that's right (lowering his eyes toward the floor).

Pharmacist: Well, can I talk to you about increasing the doses of your oral medications as opposed to starting insulin?

The pharmacist respects the patient's autonomy by asking permission to give him more information before "filling in the gaps."

Mr. Anderson: Sure.

Pharmacist: You are currently taking the highest doses of your oral diabetes medications. They are helping, but because your A_{1c} is at 10.0%, you would need to get it down by at least 3 more percentage points to reach your goal. There isn't any other medication that can be taken by mouth that can do that for you. So, the next step toward reducing your risk of complications from diabetes would be to start insulin.

The reasoning behind starting insulin rather than increasing the dose of his oral medication is explained. Also, this is stated in a way that relates the action of taking insulin with achieving his goal. This reinforces the benefits (increasing the "pros") while providing the opportunity for the patient to make his own decision, preserving autonomy.

Mr. Anderson: I guess so (looking down again). The next step toward my grave.

Pharmacist: Oh, Mr. Anderson, you sound concerned. Tell me more.

Mr. Anderson: Well, my mom had diabetes years ago. We buried her 3 months after she started taking insulin. Starting insulin in my family is ... a death sentence.

Pharmacist: Mr. Anderson, I am so sorry to hear that about your mom! I want you to know that starting insulin can be a step in the *right* direction for reducing risks of complications that you don't want to experience. Insulin can bring down your A_{1c} a lot.

Genuine concern is shown for the patient, while the real problem is identified. The patient is not worried about injecting himself with a needle. Instead, he associates starting insulin with death based on a bad experience with insulin in his family.

Pharmacist: Mr. Anderson, there are also other things you can do on your own to help lower your A_{1c} and risks for complications. Tell me what you know about these other things.

Mr. Anderson: Well, I'm not sure what you mean.

Pharmacist: May I share some thoughts about this with you?

Mr. Anderson: Sure.

Pharmacist: We can talk about physical activity and eating habits; which of these would you like to talk about first?

Mr. Anderson: Well, how about physical activity.

Pharmacist: Tell me about how often you are able to get physical activity into your routine?

Mr. Anderson: Maybe once a month. My wife is always bugging me to go walking with her after dinner. She walks every day, but it has been so hot lately!

Pharmacist: What are your thoughts about asking her if she would be willing to walk with you first thing in the morning, when it is not so hot?

The pharmacist continues to identify resolutions to the "cons" of exercising.

Mr. Anderson: Yeah. She actually walks then, too. She really takes good care of herself.

Pharmacist: That's great that you're recognizing that walking is good for you and that you're thinking about getting her to include you in some of her walks. Consistent exercise is a key to reducing risk of diabetes complications.

Instead of dwelling on the patient's lack of exercise, the pharmacist emphasizes the positive while being assertive and gently confrontational.

Mr. Anderson: I guess you're right. Maybe I could walk with my wife three or four times a week.

Pharmacist: Hey, that's a good goal.

The pharmacist allows the patient to set his own goal. The patient is more likely to be compliant with a goal he has set for himself rather than one the pharmacist has set.

Mr. Anderson: Yeah, I could do that (smiling again). Oh, I have to run (looking at his watch). Could you fill the insulin, and I could pick it up this afternoon?

Pharmacist: Sure. I could show you how to use the insulin at that time, too.

■ USING MOTIVATIONAL INTERVIEWING IN PRACTICE

In Case Study #1, the pharmacist immediately focuses on the fact that the prescription is dated 3 weeks prior to the patient getting it filled. The pharmacist in this scenario uses responses that are more judgmental and paternalistic in nature and clearly contribute to the patient becoming defensive. The pharmacist keeps the focus on himself ("I understand" is not empathic) and on the fact that the patient's action (not filling the prescription for 3 weeks) was wrong. In response, the patient quickly escalates from ambivalence to being actively resistant and defensive. The pharmacist even "cuts off" the patient in mid-sentence to remind him that the pharmacy is busy, further conveying a lack of caring. He also assumes that the patient is "afraid of a needle stick" rather than exploring the real reason for the patient's reluctance in getting the prescription filled.

In contrast, Case Study #2 illustrates the effectiveness of using MI as a communication strategy. The patient is not ready to engage in the next step of therapy by starting insulin. The underlying problem is the fact that the patient associates starting insulin with progression toward death, rather than progression toward health. The pharmacist explores this and does not blame the patient, but rather exhibits genuine concern and respects the patient's autonomy. The pharmacist explores the resistance and asks permission to give information about other things the patient can do to reduce the risks for complications and mortality. Discrepancy is shown between the patient's present action (reluctance in getting the prescription for insulin filled) and the goals for therapy. Also, discrepancy is best when the patient comes to this conclusion rather than being told, although in this case the patient needed more information for this to occur. The pharmacist facilitates the patient in coming to the correct conclusion that the insulin prescription needed to be filled. Also, the pharmacist helps the patient develop further goals (exercising) in a gently assertive way. Toward the end of the conversation, the pharmacist helps the patient recognize that much progress has been made in a short time period and suggests further follow-up rather than overwhelming the patient with more information.

The patient in Case Study #2 is much more likely to begin behavior change on a long-term scale. The pharmacist did not need to apply every MI technique in this case. Rather, the pharmacist chose strategies that fit best with a natural style of conversing and with this particular patient. It is clear that even though the patient has been coming to the pharmacy for many years, this short conversation has resulted in a better relationship between the pharmacist and patient. A more patient-centered approach, paired with a good provider relationship, has been associated with increased adherence, patient satisfaction, and enhanced clinical outcomes. This interaction with the patient clearly took more time than in Case Study #1, but the opportunity for a long-standing relationship with the patient that may lead to behavior changes and better outcomes would be worth the slight extra time spent. Studies have shown that in practice there is a minimal time difference between patient-centered approaches and standard approaches of communication – in some cases as low as a 2-minute difference. However, most studies have focused on the physician–patient interaction, and more research needs to be done within the pharmacy setting. Despite the need for more research, MI is clearly a useful tool that has much potential in the pharmacy or clinical setting.

■ CONCLUSION

Counseling patients using the Indian Health Service Model and the TTM are useful for efficient counseling and for determining a patient's stage of readiness for behavior change, respectively. Also, the pharmacist should be aware that different types of communication barriers may exist during a counseling session, such as personal, patient-centered, and environmental barriers. MI is an evidence-based communication strategy set and way of being that helps assess a patient's readiness to change and address ambivalence or resistance for change. This patient-centered style of counseling is in contrast to the more traditional provider-centered model. The five core communication principles can be used as tools to implement MI and to assist patients in deciding to change.

■ SUMMARY POINTS

- The OBRA of 1990 is a law that mandated that pharmacists offer counseling to patients regarding their prescriptions, which individual states adopted to extend applicability to more than just Medicaid patients.
- The Indian Health Service Model includes three prime questions that promotes a philosophy that elicits patients' baseline knowledge in order for pharmacists to "fill in the gaps." This streamlines the conversation with the patient in an efficient manner.
- The TTM consists of five primary stages of motivational and behavioral readiness for change, including precontemplation, contemplation, preparation, action, and maintenance. Pharmacists can identify which stage patients are in and assist them in moving toward the next stage with stage-matched intervention strategies.
- Pharmacist-centered barriers include a lack of confidence in their abilities to counsel patients, poor nonverbal communication habits like body positioning and/or tone of voice, incongruent nonverbal cues, and an inability to stop judgmental or provider-centered internal conversations during counseling sessions.
- Patient-centered barriers include language barriers, visual or hearing deficits, negative past experiences, and others.
- Environmental barriers include staff and pharmacy services placement incongruent to good communication, items sold perceived to be counterproductive to health, and lack of a private room for counseling patients.

- MI is an effective style of counseling that is designed to assess a patient's readiness to change, and to assist patients in committing to change. This style addresses the ambivalence and, sometimes direct resistance, to making behavior changes.
- MI consists of five core communication principles but still must be individualized depending on the patient and other factors of the encounter. Important concepts of this communication style are to respect and preserve the patient's autonomy, to assist patients in beginning their own change talk, and to focus on achievement of incremental goals to enhance self-efficacy.
- The five main communication principles of MI include the following: (1) roll with resistance, (2) express empathy, (3) avoid argumentation, (4) develop discrepancy, and (5) support self-efficacy.
- MI strategies can be used as a tool within the scope of a pharmacist–patient interaction. With practice, and taking into account the individualized situation, the pharmacist can facilitate a patient in developing long-lasting behavioral changes.

Study Questions

1. Which of the following are subsequent follow-up questions directly related to prime question #2?
   a. How often and how long are you supposed to take the medication?
   b. What problem or symptoms is this medication supposed to help?
   c. How do you know if the medication is working?
   d. What good and bad effects did your physician tell you to watch out for?

2. If a smoker states that he is intending to quit within the next 6 months, he is most likely in the _____ stage of behavioral change.
   a. Precontemplation
   b. Contemplation
   c. Preparation
   d. Action

3. If the pharmacist exhibits a lack of confidence in his or her ability to communicate with patients, he or she is exhibiting a _____ communication barrier.
   a. Personal
   b. Patient-centered
   c. Environmental
   d. None of the above

4. When a pharmacist's nonverbal communication is incongruent with the verbal communication, the patient is most likely to . . .
   a. Become confused as to the message the pharmacist intends to send
   b. Use both nonverbal and verbal communication equally for interpretation
   c. Believe the nonverbal over the verbal communication
   d. Believe the verbal over the nonverbal communication

5. Motivation interviewing is . . .
   a. A provider-centered approach to patient counseling
   b. Respectful of a patient's autonomy even when behavior is not changed
   c. Helpful only if the patient is already willing to make behavioral changes
   d. An approach to counseling where the provider sets the agenda for discussion

6. Prior to giving more information to a patient, what should the provider using motivational interviewing do first?
   a. Research the data to ensure that he or she is giving the correct information
   b. Ask yes/no questions to elicit baseline information that the pharmacist desires
   c. Point the patient toward articles to research the information independently
   d. Ask the patient for permission before giving information or advice

7. When patients make statements that can be interpreted as acceptance or steps taken toward behavior change, this is known as _____.
   a. Patient-centered change
   b. Developing discrepancy
   c. Decisional balance
   d. Change talk

8. When the provider asks questions or makes statements that illustrate that what the patient is doing or not doing is incongruent with the target behavior, this is known as _____.
   a. Patient-centered change
   b. Developing discrepancy
   c. Decisional balance
   d. Change talk

9. "Rolling with resistance" means that the provider ...
   a. Acknowledges the patient's statement and remains focused on the main topic
   b. Agrees with the patient's statement and then changes the subject
   c. Shows attentiveness to the patient's feelings by expressing empathy
   d. Reminds the patient what his or her stated goals are for changing behavior

10. A 300-pound man with diabetes begins to walk 15 minutes every other day and loses 10 pounds. Which of the following statements is an example of supporting self-efficacy?
    a. "If you keep going at this rate of weight loss, you'll look like a stick!"
    b. "Great! Now you need to lose 20 pounds before your next visit."
    c. "It is great that you have started walking 15 minutes every other day!"
    d. "Since you lost that weight, you can reward yourself by eating some chocolate."

BIBLIOGRAPHY

1. Schatz R, Belloto RJ Jr, White DB, et al. Provision of drug information to patients by pharmacists: the impact of the Omnibus Budget Reconciliation Act of 1990 a decade later. *Am J Ther*. 2003;10(2):93-103.
2. Lewis RK, Lasack NL, Lambert BL, et al. Patient counseling-a focus on maintenance therapy. *Am J Health-Syst Pharm*. 1997;54:2084-2098.
3. Kavookjian J. Motivational interviewing. In: Richardson M, Chant C, Chessman KH, Finks SW, Hemstreet BA, Hume AL, et al., eds. *Pharmacotherapy Self-Assessment Program*. 7th ed. Lenexa, KS: American College of Clinical Pharmacy; 2011:1-18.
4. Prochaska JO, DiClemente C. Stages and processes of self-change of smoking: Toward an integrative model of change. *J Consult Clin Psychol*. 1983;51(3):390-395.
5. Norcross JC, Krebs PM, Prochaska JO. Stages of change. *J Clin Psychol*. 2011;67:143-154.
6. Berger BA, Felkey BG, Krueger KP. Applying motivational interviewing principles. *US Pharm*. 2005;3:38-47.
7. Beardsley RS, Kimberlin CL, Tindall WN. In: *Communication Skills in Pharmacy Practice*. 5th ed. Baltimore, MD: Lippincott Williams 2007:38-49.

8. Possidente CJ, Bucci KK, McClain WJ. Motivational interviewing: a tool to improve medication adherence? *Am J Health Syst Pharm*. 2005;62:1311-1314.
9. Miller W, Rollnick S. Ten things that motivational interviewing is not. *Behav Cogn Psychother*. 2009;37:129-140.
10. Collins SE, Eck S, Torchalla T, et al. Understanding treatment-seeking smokers' motivation to change: Content analysis of the decisional balance worksheet. *Addict Behav*. 2013;38:14721480.
11. Borrelli B, Riekert K, Weinstein A, et al. Brief motivational interviewing as a clinical strategy to promote asthma medication adherence. *J Allergy Clin Immunol*. 2007;120:1023-1030.
12. Miller W. Motivational interviewing in service to health promotion. *Am J Health Promot*. 2004;(suppl):1-10.
13. Miller WR, Rose GS. Toward a theory of motivational interviewing. *Am Psychol*. 2009;64:527-537.
14. Rollnick S, Miller W, Butler C. In: *Motivational Interviewing in Health Care*. New York, NY: Guilford Press; 2009.
15. Scales R, Miller J, Burden R. Why wrestle when you can dance? Optimizing outcomes with motivational interviewing. *J Am Pharm Assoc*. 2003;43(5, suppl 1):S46-47.
16. Britt E, Hudson SM, Blampied MV. Motivational interviewing in health care settings: a review. *Patient Educ Couns*. 2004;53:147-155.

4

MEDICATION THERAPY MANAGEMENT

Sarah M. Westberg, Shannon L. Reidt, and Todd D. Sorensen

> ### ■ LEARNING OBJECTIVES
>
> After reading this chapter, the pharmacy student, community practice resident, or pharmacist should be able to:
>
> 1. Explain how pharmacists are in a unique position to provide medication therapy management (MTM) services.
> 2. Recognize the differences between MTM and pharmaceutical care.
> 3. Explain how MTM services are implemented with the five core elements.
> 4. Discuss how innovative patient care programs have assisted in the development of MTM.
> 5. Recognize how implementation of MTM services is evolving into the overall health-care structure.

INTRODUCTION

Nearly half of all Americans have at least one chronic illness[1] resulting in millions of patients relying on prescription medications to help maintain their health. This prevalence of medication use creates a significant opportunity for both medical and monetary consequences if these agents are not managed safely and effectively. Unfortunately, evidence suggests that our health system is not performing well in this regard. It is estimated that 1.5 million preventable adverse drug events (ADEs) occur in our health system each year[2] and the Institute of Medicine (IOM) has declared that for every dollar spent on ambulatory medications, another dollar is spent to treat new health problems caused by the medication.[3] Despite the presence of these avoidable adverse events and costs, it has been determined that potentially up to half of patients on persistent medication receive no drug monitoring in 1 year.[4-5] The IOM predicts that with these trends, the number and costs of outpatient ADEs will increase unless effective interventions to improve health-care system delivery and outpatient safety are implemented.

There are multiple factors that contribute to the medication use problems and their negative outcomes. These include patient-centered factors, therapy-related factors, social and economic factors, and disease factors.[6] Health literacy, cost, concern about adverse effects, lack of urgency about the disease, and an impaired perception of the efficacy of the medications are just a few specific patient-centered examples. Societal issues like poverty, cultural differences, and a lack of a social support structure create obstacles for treating the population as a whole. Lastly, problems with the health-care system such as lack of accessibility, long waiting times, difficulties filling prescriptions, or unpleasant interactions with health-care professionals also affect patient's medication use experience and may result in medication-related problems.

Pharmacists are in an excellent position to address these problems due to their focused training, unique perspective, and unparalleled access. Pharmacists have the most specific training in drug therapy of all health-care professionals, which creates an opportunity to evaluate a patient's medication needs in a manner that is unique to the health-care team. In the ambulatory care environment, pharmacists are the most accessible health-care professionals. While most health-care professionals require an appointment or emergency situation to be accessible to patients, the ease of access to community pharmacists allows them to often serve as the first and/or the most frequent point of contact between a patient and their health-care team.

However, to take advantage of these differentiating characteristics and fully meet the medication-related needs of individual patients and society, the profession must actively engage the health-care reform principles that are underway in the United States. The services that pharmacists deliver must align with "the Triple Aim" of achieving better patient health, improved quality of care, and lower costs. In order to accomplish this, new practice models must be adopted.

The adoption of new practice models more focused on ensuring that patients achieve desired drug therapy outcomes has been occurring over the past 20 years; however, large-scale adoption of this type of practice remains elusive. Despite over two decades of debate and development, there still remains ambiguity and inconsistency in defining the core role of pharmacists and the services through which this role serves patients.

MEDICATION THERAPY MANAGEMENT AND PHARMACEUTICAL CARE—SAME PRACTICE WITH DIFFERENT NAMES?

Pharmaceutical Care: A Definition

In 1990, Hepler and Strand defined pharmaceutical care as "the responsible provision of drug therapy for the purpose of achieving definite outcomes that improve a patient's quality of life."[7] This definition served as a foundation for Strand, Cipolle, and Morley to define responsibilities of a pharmaceutical care practitioner. These include (1) to assure that all of a patient's drug therapy is appropriate, effective, safe, and convenient to take as indicated and (2) to identify, resolve, and prevent any drug therapy problems.[8] As a pharmaceutical care practitioner, the pharmacist takes responsibility for a patient's drug-related needs and is held accountable for this commitment.[9] Pharmaceutical care is a patient-centered practice with three components: philosophy of practice, patient care process, and a management system.[10]

Philosophy of Practice

All pharmaceutical care practitioners share a set of values that guide behaviors, clinical decisions, and professional standards. It is this set of values that unites practitioners and provides the foundation for the other two components of pharmaceutical care: patient care process and a management system. The philosophy of pharmaceutical care practice calls for the practitioner to accept the social responsibility to reduce medication-related morbidity and mortality. This responsibility is met by assessing a patient's medication-related needs, bringing the necessary resources to meet those needs, and follow up with the patient to determine that these needs have been met. The core element of this philosophy is the patient-centered approach taken to meet a patient's needs. In other words, the patient remains at the center of attention at all times despite a practitioner's preferences.[11]

Patient Care Process

Although each practitioner may carry out the patient care process differently, pharmaceutical care has only one patient care process. This is essential to provide consistent quality care to patients across care settings and to educate future practitioners. As the name implies, the patient care process is patient centered and driven by an individual patient's needs. However, in order to maintain quality and consistency, the process is practiced systematically. Three steps comprise the process: assessment, care plan, and evaluation. These steps occur continuously to meet a patient's medication-related needs. During the assessment, the pharmacist determines the patient's medication-related problems. Drug therapy is evaluated for indication, effectiveness, safety, and convenience. Problems related to medications are identified, including those problems that have potential to cause harm. Before medication-related problems can be solved, a therapeutic relationship must exist between the pharmacist and the patient to ensure that medications are assessed comprehensively. The second step of the patient care process is the care plan. The care plan is created to define goals, determine interventions, and agree upon responsibilities for the practitioner and the patient to meet goals of therapy. The objective of the patient-centered care plan is to identify, resolve, and prevent medication-related problems. The care plan is complete when goals have been set, interventions agreed upon, and responsibilities of the patient and practitioner accepted. The final step of the patient care process is the follow-up evaluation. During the follow-up evaluation, the practitioner collects information from the patient to determine if interventions have been successful in meeting goals set during the assessment and care plan. The follow-up evaluation is also an opportunity to determine if any new medication-related problems have developed. Patients with chronic diseases will require a series of follow-up evaluations.[10]

Management System

The third component of pharmaceutical care is a practice management system. In order to have a financially successful practice, new patients must be added to the practice. As described, a systematic approach exists to providing pharmaceutical care to individual patients; likewise, a systematic approach exists for managing a pharmaceutical care practice. A practice management system includes the following: mission statement; physical, financial, and human resources to support the practice; means by which to evaluate the practice; documentation system; and the means by which to reward the practitioner and financially support the practice. The long-term success of the practice relies on a supportive practice management system.[10]

■ MEDICATION THERAPY MANAGEMENT: A DEFINITION

After the Medicare Prescription Drug Improvement and Modernization Act passage in 2003, the pharmacy profession needed to define MTM. In 2004, 11 national pharmacy organizations developed a consensus definition of MTM. The American Pharmacists

Association (APhA) facilitated the group's work and had three objectives for the process. The definition had to be inclusive of services and programs provided in diverse pharmacy practice settings and had to document examples of services that could be implemented by a majority of practitioners. Lastly, APhA wanted to create a consensus that all involved organizations could support and utilize as they worked for regulatory changes. The consensus definition states that MTM is a "distinct service or group of services that optimize therapeutic outcomes for individual patients. MTM services are independent of, but can occur in conjunction with, the provision of a medication product."[6]

APhA/NACDS Core Elements

In 2004, the APhA and the National Association of Chain Drug Stores (NACDS) created a framework within which MTM could be provided in a community setting. This model framework of MTM in community pharmacies was created to improve care, enhance communication among providers, improve collaboration among providers, and optimize medication use leading to improved patient outcomes. In 2004, the framework defined five core elements comprising MTM in the community.[12,13] In 2008, the framework was revised; however, the core elements remained the same. The features of the updated framework include a broad focus on patients in diverse care settings and patients transitioning through health-care settings, collaborating with physicians, and empowering patients. The five core elements of an MTM service model in pharmacy practice include medication therapy review (MTR), personal medication record (PMR), medication-related action plan (MAP), intervention and/or referral, and documentation and follow-up. All elements are essential to provide MTM; however, elements may be modified to meet a patient's needs.[14]

An MTR is defined as "systematic process of collecting patient-specific information, assessing medication therapies to identify medication-related problems, developing a prioritized list of medication-related problems, and creating a plan to resolve them." The purpose of the MTR is to educate patients about their medications, address medication-related problems, and motivate patients to manage their medications and conditions. An MTR may be a comprehensive assessment of all medications or it may be targeted at one particular disease state. In addition to obtaining a medication history, a pharmacist conducting an MTR may assess the following of the patient: physical and overall health, preferences and values, goals of therapy, cultural or socioeconomic issues, and laboratory values. A pharmacist will also identify and prioritize medication-related problems related to clinical appropriateness, safety, efficacy, and accessibility to the patient. A plan to resolve medication-related problems will be devised that may include patient education, monitoring of therapy, and communication to other providers. Ideally, a patient would receive one comprehensive MTR annually and additional, more focused MTRs throughout the year to address specific problems.[14] A PMR is defined as "a comprehensive record of the patient's medications (prescription and nonprescription medications, herbal products, and other dietary supplements)." The PMR may be generated manually or electronically; however, it should be written at a literacy level that can be understood by the patient. Information that should be a part of the PMR includes primary care physician, pharmacy/pharmacist, allergies, adverse drug reactions, date last updated and reviewed, and medications. The purpose of the PMR is to give the patient a tool to manage his/her medications. If a medication or any other information related to the PMR changes, the patient should update the PMR; however, the maintenance of the PMR may be seen as a collaborative effort among the patient and his/her pharmacist and physicians. By sharing the PMR with all health-care providers, continuity of care may be facilitated.[14] A MAP is a patient-centered document that lists interventions the patient may employ to self-manage medications. A MAP contains only the actions that the patient will do; however, these actions do not include anything that is outside of a pharmacist's scope of practice or has not been approved by an appropriate health-care team member. The MAP is an important core element as it promotes patient-centered care and patient self-management of health.[14]

Intervention and/or referral represents the fourth core element of MTM. While providing MTM, the pharmacist may need to intervene to resolve medication-related problems. Examples of interventions include collaborating with the patient's other health-care providers or providing education to a patient. In some instances, the resolution of medication-related problems requires a referral to another provider. For example, a pharmacist may discover a medical problem, a patient is experiencing that needs further evaluation. Resolution of all medication-related problems requires collaboration among health-care providers and self-management by the patient. The final element of MTM is documentation and follow-up. Documentation is essential to MTM delivery because documents provide reports of patient progress and support billing for services. Additionally, documentation has purposes in communication, quality improvement, and continuity of care. Documentation may be paper or electronic, but a consistent format should be used. The PMR and MAP should be included in documentation. Follow-up care is also documented and should be scheduled according to a patient's medication-related needs.[14]

Are Pharmaceutical Care and Medication Therapy Management Interchangeable?

Although pharmaceutical care and MTM may be used interchangeably, it is important not to lose sight of their differences. As previously described, pharmaceutical care is a patient-centered approach taken by a pharmacist who accepts responsibility for a patient's medication-related needs. Pharmaceutical care has three components, including a philosophy. The philosophy is the foundation of pharmaceutical care and forms the basis for the process and the practice management system. In contrast, MTM lacks a philosophy and relates to a practice management system by way of requiring a documentation system. Components of the patient care process of pharmaceutical care and the five core elements of MTM are similar. Both require an assessment of medication-related needs, development of a care plan, and appropriate follow-up. However, the pharmaceutical care process recommends that the assessment be done in-person, while core elements of MTM suggest that patients may be assessed via telephone. MTM may be aptly described as the strategy to care out the philosophy of pharmaceutical care into everyday practice.[14,15] Patients with medication-related problems may exist in all care settings, including community pharmacies, ambulatory care clinics, hospitals, nursing homes, and within home care agencies. More importantly, patients may experience medication-related problems as they transition across settings of care. Although settings may differ where MTM is delivered, a consistent approach should be used. The core elements of MTM were developed with the consideration that MTM could be delivered in many health-care settings. In 2006, the American College of Clinical Pharmacy (ACCP) released a commentary recommending how core elements could be implemented in the ambulatory care setting. Their major recommendations included expanding the elements to include more guidance on collecting patient information, assessing this information, monitoring and evaluating drug therapy, and documenting services. ACCP recommended that the core elements place greater emphasis on collaboration among health-care providers.[16]

■ RESEARCH SUPPORTING PHARMACISTS AS MTM PROVIDERS

MTM provides many opportunities for pharmacists to improve medication use. Organizations such as the US Department of Veterans Affairs and Kaiser Permanente Colorado have utilized clinical pharmacists for decades to manage pharmacotherapy related to dyslipidemia, smoking cessation, anticoagulation, and solid organ transplant. Both organizations have reported data illustrating positive health outcomes and cost savings. Estimates from a Veterans Affairs pharmacist-run smoking cessation clinic included an annual savings of $691,200 and a net cost benefit to the Veterans Affairs of $551,200.[17] Pharmacists may play a pivotal role in the management of chronic diseases by monitoring and modifying drug therapy and by educating patients.

Because pharmacists are present in acute care, community, ambulatory, and home care settings, they are positioned to be a valuable member of the health-care team. A 2008 systematic review evaluated 21 clinical trials to determine the effect of pharmacists' interventions on diabetes management. Interventions included medication and lifestyle counseling and medication management through in-person visits or telephone follow-up. The primary outcome of interest was change in hemoglobin A_{1c} (HbA_{1c}). Measurements of HbA_{1c} improved by 0.1–2.1 across all trials with greatest improvement shown when pharmacists were given prescriptive authority.[18] Pharmacists' impact is not limited to the management of diabetes. Evidence supports pharmacists' interventions as a means to improve medication adherence, blood pressure control, and other cardiovascular risk factors in ambulatory care patients. In an analysis of 30 randomized controlled trials involving approximately 12,000 patients, pharmacists' interventions were associated with significant reductions in systolic and diastolic blood pressures with a reduction of 8 mm Hg in systolic blood pressure. Significant reduction in low-density lipoprotein cholesterol (–13 mg/L) and tobacco use was also demonstrated. A review of 15 studies involving almost 3500 hypertensive patients illustrated significantly improved medication adherence in 43.8% of patients.[19,20] MTM involves the identification, resolution, and prevention of medication-related problems. Pharmacists' interventions made as a part of an MTM encounter can improve clinical outcomes; however, MTM interventions can also result in cost savings. As part of a demonstration project in Connecticut, 9 pharmacists worked closely with 88 Medicaid patients providing MTM. Over 10 months, the pharmacists identified 917 drug therapy problems and resolved nearly 80% of them after four encounters. The project resulted in an estimated annual savings of $1123 per patient on medication claims and $472 per patient on medical, hospital, and emergency department expenses.[21] Similarly, positive outcomes were shown by an analysis of 10 years of experience implementing pharmaceutical care services in a large integrated health-care system. Data from MTM services provided to 9068 patients over 10 years were retrospectively analyzed for economic, clinical, and humanistic outcomes. During the 10-year period, there were 33,706 documented encounters (mean 3.7 per per patient). In the clinical status assessment of the 12,851 medical conditions in 4849 patients who were not at goal when they enrolled in the program, 55% of the conditions improved, 23% were unchanged, and 22% worsened during the course of MTM services. Pharmacist-estimated cost savings to the health system over the 10-year period were $2,913,850 ($86 per encounter) and the total cost of MTM was $2,258,302 ($67 per encounter), for an estimated return of investment of $1.29 per $1 in MTM administrative costs.[22] Evidence supporting pharmacists as MTM providers is further demonstrated by a systematic review and meta-analysis done by Chisolm-Burns and colleagues in 2010.[23] The objective of the review was to examine the effects of pharmacist-provided direct patient care on therapeutic, safety, and humanistic outcomes. Nearly 300 articles were included in the analysis with a majority, 65%, conducted in an outpatient setting. Favorable results were found in therapeutic and safety outcomes, and meta-analyses conducted for HbA_{1c}, LDL cholesterol, blood pressure, and ADEs were significant ($p < 0.05$), favoring pharmacists' direct patient care over comparative services. Likewise, medication adherence, patient knowledge, and quality of life-general health meta-analyses were significant ($p < 0.05$), favoring pharmacists' direct patient care. As discussed, there is a body of evidence supporting pharmacists' contributions to clinical, economic, and humanistic outcomes. However, several noteworthy initiatives involving pharmaceutical care and MTM merit discussion.

■ NOTEWORTHY INITIATIVES IN THE EVOLUTION OF MTM SERVICES

Over the past two decades, MTM services have been implemented in a variety of care models across the country, and the evidence shows that MTM services have positive clinical and economic outcomes on patient care. Over this time frame, a variety of noteworthy initiatives, including payment models, have been explored. In this section, how these noteworthy initiatives have created an evolutionary time line in MTM services is described.

Minnesota Pharmaceutical Care Project

An early example of multi-site research in community pharmacy: The Minnesota Pharmaceutical Care Project was conducted between June 1992 and November 1995 through the University of Minnesota. This implementation project included 54 pharmacists from 20 community pharmacy practice sites in Minnesota. The study was designed to implement the pharmaceutical care philosophy in the community pharmacy setting. After 3 years, a total of 9000 patients representing approximately 25,000 encounters were cared for in this project. A subanalysis of the patients seen in the last year of the program identified 5480 patients, seen for 12,376 encounters, with a total of 7223 drug therapy problems identified. The collective experience of the researchers in this project and their data analysis helped to shape the pharmaceutical care practice defined by Cipolle, Strand, and Morley. As described earlier, this pharmaceutical care practice definition became the basis for defining MTM. The Minnesota Pharmaceutical Care Project proved that this care process can be successfully integrated into community pharmacies across chain, independent, rural, and urban settings.[24]

Mississippi Medicaid Disease Management Program

An early state program paying for pharmacist services: Mississippi Medicaid program was the first state to offer payment to pharmacists for cognitive services in 1998 through a disease management program.[25] The Mississippi Medicaid program has credentialed pharmacists in specific chronic disease states of asthma, diabetes, hyperlipidemia, or others. In order to be credentialed, pharmacists complete specific educational programs for each of the disease states available. Physicians order a written referral to pharmacy disease management to a credentialed pharmacist provider. The primary components of this service, as defined by Mississippi Medicaid include patient evaluation, compliance assessment, drug therapy review, and disease state management according to clinical practice guidelines, patient/caregiver education.[26]

This program did not achieve rapid uptake from the Mississippi pharmacy community. In a preliminary report in 2003, only 25 pharmacists in the state were submitting claims for caring for Medicaid patients under this model. The challenges of this model include the necessity to be credentialed in each disease state, and the financial gain for pharmacists was felt to not meet costs for some pharmacies.[27]

HRSA Clinical Pharmacy Demonstration Grant Program—An early federal initiative supporting clinical pharmacy services: The first federal initiative to recognize MTM services was launched through the Health Resources and Services Administration in the form of Clinical Pharmacy Demonstration Projects (CPDP). This initiative began in 2000, and funded 18 demonstration projects across the country. A final report of the initial projects was released in 2004.[28] These projects included Disease Management and Other Clinical Pharmacy Services, Expanding Access to Pharmaceuticals, Efficiency Activities, and Training. The disease management programs in these demonstration projects were focused primarily on diabetes. The clinical results illustrated statistically and clinically significant improvements in diabetes control in the patient groups who received care from the pharmacist (A_{1c}'s decreased from 9.1% to 7.7%; Percent of patients at optimal glucose control increased from 18% to 37%). Although this was an early demonstration project only, the successful results were critical in launching HRSA's commitment to support and develop clinical pharmacy services in community health centers across the country. Additional programming through HRSA developed into the Patient Safety and Clinical Pharmacy Services Collaborative (PSPC). The PSPC is described by HRSA as "a breakthrough effort to improve the quality of health-care across America by integrating evidence-based clinical pharmacy services into the care and management of high-risk, high-cost, complex patients."[29] The PSPC works with healthcare teams in community-based clinics to integrate evidence-based clinical pharmacy services to improve patient health outcomes. This initiative is responsible for significant growth of clinical pharmacy services, including MTM, in underserved populations across the country.

Medicare Part D

First Federal Payment Program: In 2003, the Medicare Prescription Drug Improvement and Modernization Act was put into law. As part of this act, MTM services were defined at the federal level for the first time, and it opened an opportunity for pharmacists across the country to receive payment for MTM services. General requirements for MTM services provided for Medicare Part D are developed and updated regularly from CMS. Third-party insurers apply to be included as a Part D provider and must offer an MTM services program, which meets the documented requirements. Since Medicare Part D was first offered in 2004, CMS has revised the requirements of the Part D Plan sponsors. Most notably, in 2010, the Part D Plans were required to implement an "opt-out" model of MTM delivery rather than "opt-in." Plans are required to identify targeted beneficiaries at least quarterly. In addition, CMS has more clearly defined the MTM services in 2010. Each beneficiary will receive a comprehensive medication review and a quarterly medication review. These reviews can be done over the phone or face-to-face. In 2010, approximately 25% of the medication reviews were completed face-to-face. As CMS continues to evaluate the results of this program, it is expected that the requirements of the Part D plans will continue to change.[30] Although Part D MTM coverage has opened significant opportunities for pharmacists to provide MTM services to elderly patients, it is still challenging for a single pharmacy and/or pharmacist to participate in all Part D Plans. Many of the Part D plan sponsors will provide MTM internally through their own employees, which limit the ability of community or clinic-based pharmacists to receive reimbursement to care for these patients in their own environments.

North Carolina and New Mexico Certified Pharmacy Practitioners

Evolution of pharmacy practitioner recognition and credentialing: In New Mexico, a category of pharmacist clinician was established in 1993 under the Pharmacist Prescriptive Authority Act.[31] Once certified as a pharmacist clinician, the pharmacist is granted prescriptive authority under a collaborative practice agreement through a supervising clinician, similar to other mid-level practitioners. This prescriptive authority includes controlled substances, if appropriate DEA registration is obtained. A major requirement to become a certified pharmacist clinician includes completion of approved training in physical assessment skills.[32] North Carolina has a similar program, started in 2000,[33] in which a clinical pharmacist practitioner (CPP) is a licensed pharmacist approved to provide drug therapy management, including controlled substances, under the direction of, or under the supervision of, a licensed physician.[34] Only a pharmacist approved by the Pharmacy Board and the Medical Board may legally identify himself/herself as a CPP. In order to be approved as a CPP, the pharmacist must complete a certificate program approved by the NC Board of Pharmacy.

The movement to recognize pharmacists as mid-level providers with prescriptive authority is unique to these two states, although most states grant pharmacists the authority to prescribe under collaborative practice agreements, with the details varying from state to state. Unfortunately, even in these progressive states, the additional credential does not guarantee payment for services.

Medicaid Programs

Expansion of state programs reimbursing for MTM: In 2008, ASHP published a policy analysis detailing the pharmacist provider status in 11-state health programs in the country. The states included as currently providing some form of reimbursement for MTM services for the Medicaid population were Iowa, Florida, Minnesota, Mississippi, Montana, North Carolina, Ohio, Vermont, and Wyoming. Each of these states has followed a different methodology in setting up payment for medical assistance patients to receive MTM services. Each state has a different set of eligibility criteria, different mechanisms for billing, and varying amounts of reimbursement.[35]

Employer-Based Programs

Expansion of payment for MTM by self-insured employer groups: One of the most often cited examples of MTM is the Asheville Project. The Asheville Project was initiated in Asheville, North Carolina with two self-insured employer groups: the City of Asheville and the Mission-St. Joseph's Health System. The employer groups began offering to pay for pharmacist's pharmaceutical care services to care for members with diabetes. Patients received consultation with a community pharmacist, and also received waivers on co-pays for diabetes medications and supplies as an incentive to participate.[36]

The clinical and economic benefits of the initial diabetes study were convincing enough for the employers to expand the benefit to include asthma, dyslipidemia, and hypertension.[37,38] In addition, this model for self-insured employers to offer pharmaceutical care as a benefit grew across the country. Through the support of the American Pharmacists Association Foundation, the Ten City Challenge was initiated. The Ten City Challenge replicated the care model and reimbursement model developed in Asheville across 10 other cities. The results of the Ten City Challenge were able to replicate the positive impact seen in the initial Asheville studies.[39]

The successful implementation of these employer-based programs has had a significant impact on the pharmacy community across the country. It has served as the impetus for many other self-insured employers to consider offering a pharmaceutical care benefit to their employees. In the state of Minnesota alone, MTM service is a covered benefit by 12 major self-insured employers.

The pharmacy profession has evolved significantly over the last two decades to be recognized as providers of MTM service. Many pharmacists across the country are dedicating their careers to providing this service. However, the challenge continues to exist that widespread payment of MTM service across majority of payer groups does not yet exist. Therefore, except in unusual circumstances, it is not yet possible for a pharmacist to bring in enough financial revenue to fully support a full-time, independently economically sustainable model of pharmacist-provided, face-to-face MTM. Given this present reality, pharmacists continue to create MTM services successfully and to integrate themselves with other members of the health-care team in creative ways for patient care endeavors.

■ INTEGRATING MTM INTO AN EVOLVING HEALTH SYSTEM—FUTURE DIRECTIONS

The Affordable Care Act of 2010 created unprecedented changes for the manner in which health-care services would be delivered and health-care providers and systems would be compensated. As the programs established within this act are implemented, it is critical that pharmacists seek to understand the changes that will evolve from this law and seek to align medication management services with the systems that are created. Two models that are currently being developed rapidly and are highlighted briefly are the patient-centered medical home (PCMH) and accountable care organizations (ACO).

Patient-Centered Medical Home

The "medical home" is a phrase originally used in the 1960s and described a model of primary care that is patient-centered, comprehensive, team-based, coordinated, accessible, and focused on quality and safety. The concepts embedded in this model have gained a renewed and widespread interest in the early 2000s. In 2007, the leading primary care associations endorsed a set of principles that define the PCMH in the context of the current health system.[40]

Many states Medicaid programs as well as several national organizations have established programs or criteria for recognizing health-care provider organizations as PCMHs. For example, the National Committee on Quality Assurance (NCQA) and URAC (formerly the Utilization Review Accreditation Commission) have established programs that recognize organizations for achieving a set of standards and processes consistent with PCMH principles.

Currently, the degree to which PCMH recognition programs have clear criteria for medication management within its overall criteria is quite limited.

As a result, recognized PCMHs may not have a specific process for effectively coordinating and managing medication use by patients on complicated medication regimens as they transition from various systems and providers within their course of medical care. The presence of direct pharmacist involvement in the services provided by a recognized PCMH is rarely required or expected. As a result, engagement of pharmacists in the PCMH environment is a significant opportunity to facilitate team-based care and significantly impact the quality of patient care services.[41] One outlet for this effort, on a national scale, is the Patient Centered Primary Care Collaborative (PCPCC), which has recognized the importance of integrated medication management services into a PCMH.[42]

Accountable Care Organizations

ACOs are a form of integrated care and payment model that bring together providers across care settings in a "risk-sharing" arrangement. These care settings include hospitals, primary care clinics, long-term care facilities, or other organizations as deemed appropriate by the founding entities. A key element of ACOs is the expectation that health-care provider performance and patient outcomes are tied to compensation opportunities.

As a result, quality metrics like hospital readmission rates and ADEs will influence compensation within ACOs. This model has the potential to increase opportunities for pharmacists as fee-for-service payment will become less of a focus, and services that achieve improved outcomes and cost savings will increase in value. Medication management services in ACOs may occur through integration of employed pharmacists with the various service centers of large health systems that serve as the hub of an ACO or through contractual relationships between health systems and local pharmacy organizations. At the time of writing this chapter, both of these models are evolving.

■ CONCLUSION

Pharmacists are in a position to address medication-use problems due to their unique training, perspective, and access to patients. MTM was embraced by the pharmacy profession after passage of the Medicare Prescription Drug Improvement and Modernization Act in 2003. Consisting of five core elements that are essential for patient care, MTM services provided by pharmacists have been well documented. The present use of MTM services has developed roots from a variety of patient care models implemented in the past and is being integrated into the evolving overall health-care system.

■ SUMMARY POINTS

- Pharmacists are in a unique position to address medication-use problems due to their unique training, perspective, and regular access to patients.
- Pharmaceutical care is defined as "the responsible provision of drug therapy for the purpose of achieving definite outcomes that improve a patient's quality of life" and contains three components: (1) philosophy of practice, (2) patient care process, and (3) a management system.
- MTM, which consists of five core elements that are essential for patient care, was embraced by the pharmacy profession after passage of the Medicare Prescription Drug Improvement and Modernization Act in 2003.
- Although the terms pharmaceutical care and MTM may be used interchangeably, there are differences. MTM does not have a philosophy, and the management system involves documentation.
- Much research has been completed documenting the effectiveness of pharmacists as MTM providers for economic, clinical, and humanistic outcomes for a variety of disease states.
- In the evolution of MTM services, early initiatives that had a significant impact include the Minnesota Pharmaceutical Care Project, Mississippi Medicaid Disease Management Program, and the HRSA Clinical Pharmacy Demonstration Grant Program.
- As MTM is integrated into an evolving health-care system, future directions may include PCMHs and ACOs.

STUDY QUESTIONS

1. Patient-centered factors that contribute to medication-use problems and their negative outcomes include all of the following *except*:
   a. Lack of urgency about the disease
   b. Concern about adverse effects
   c. Long waiting times
   d. Health literacy

2. Which of the following statements accurately describe the concept of pharmaceutical care?
   a. Practitioners accept the responsibility to reduce medication-related morbidity and mortality.
   b. Multiple patient care processes are involved, with each practitioner carrying out the processes differently.
   c. The long-term success of an established practice relies on establishing a pharmacist-centered care plan.
   d. The management system and patient care process require an intuitive approach rather than a systematic approach.

3. The five core elements of MTM service model include:
   a. PMR, provider referral, personnel review, payment plan, and documentation
   b. MTR, PMR, action plan, intervention, and documentation
   c. Intervention, MTR, adverse event monitoring, intervention, and provider referral
   d. Documentation, systematic provider contact, MTR, PMR, and payment plan

4. Which of the following outcomes have been demonstrated through pharmacists' use of MTM services?
   a. Economic
   b. Humanistic
   c. Clinical
   d. All of the above

5. In which of the following states can a pharmacist become certified as a pharmacist clinician in order to have prescriptive authority?
   a. Mississippi
   b. Minnesota
   c. New Mexico
   d. All of the above

6. A project in which state was designed to prove that the pharmaceutical care process could be implemented in community pharmacies?
   a. Mississippi
   b. Minnesota
   c. New Mexico
   d. All of the above

7. The Ten City Challenge replicated the patient care model of which of the following projects?
   a. Pharmacy Demonstration Projects
   b. Ashville Project in North Carolina
   c. Mississippi Disease State Management Project
   d. Minnesota Pharmaceutical Care Project

8. Clinical pharmacist practitioners . . .
   a. Are licensed practitioners with prescriptive authority in Ohio
   b. Can prescribe any medication except for narcotics
   c. Must complete a certificate program with the Board of Medicine
   d. Legally must be approved by the Boards of Pharmacy and Medicine

9. A patient care model that centers on one personal physician taking care of all aspects of a patient's health is _____.
   a. An ACO
   b. A PCMH
   c. A Primary Care Initiated Service
   d. An Evidence-Based Medicine Approach

10. A performance-based model of reimbursement . . .
  a. Encourages providers to work in a collaborative care environment
  b. Provides incentives to offer care that may not be in the patient's best interest
  c. Ensures an increased payment system because a patient undergoes many tests
  d. Encourages patients to seek higher-cost services to increase provider revenue

BIBLIOGRAPHY

1. Centers for Disease Control and Prevention National Center for Chronic Disease Prevention and Health Promotion. http://www.cdc.gov/nccdphp. Accessed January 25, 2013.
2. Wilson IR, Schoen C, Neuman P, et al. Physician-patient communication about prescription medication nonadherence: a 50-state study of America's seniors. *J Gen Intern Med.* 2007;22(1):6-12.
3. Kohn LT, Corrigan JM, Donaldson MS. (eds.). *To Err Is Human: Building a Safer Health System.* Washington, DC: National Academy Press.; 2000.
4. Stelfox HT, Ahmed SB, Fiskio J, Bates DW. An evaluation of the adequacy of outpatient monitoring of thyroid replacement therapy. *J Eval Clin Pract.* 2004;10(4):525-530.
5. Raebel MA, Carroll NM, Andreade SE, et al. Monitoring of drugs with a narrow therapeutic range in ambulatory care. *Am J Manag Care.* 2006;12(5):268-274.
6. Jin J, Sklar GE, Min Sen Oh V, Chuen Li S. Factors affecting therapeutic compliance: a review from the patient's perspective. *Ther Clin Risk Manag.* 2008;4(1):269-286.
7. Hepler CD, Strand L.M. Opportunities and responsibilities in pharmaceutical care. *Am J Pharm Ed.* 1990;53(winter suppl):75-155.
8. Strand LM, Morley PC, Cipolle RJ, et al. Drug-related problems: their structure and function. *DICP Ann Pharmacother.* 1990;24:1093-1097.
9. Strand LM. Re-visioning the professions. *J AM Pharm Assoc.* 1997;NS37(4):474-478.
10. Cipolle RJ, Strand LM, Morley PC. *Pharmaceutical Care Practice.* New York, NY: McGraw-Hill; 1998.
11. Cipolle RJ, Strand LM, Morley PC. *Pharmaceutical Care Practice.* New York, NY: McGraw-Hill; 2004.
12. Bluml B. Definition of medication therapy management: development of profession wide consensus. *J Am Pharm Assoc.* 2005;45:566-572.
13. American Pharmacists Association and National Association of Chain Drug Stores Foundation. Medication therapy management in community pharmacy practice: core elements of an MTM service (Version 1.0). *J Am Pharm Assoc.* 2005;45:573-579.
14. American Pharmacists Association and National Association of Chain Drug Stores Foundation. Medication therapy management in community pharmacy practice: core elements of an MTM service (Version 2.0). *J Am Pharm Assoc.* 2008;48:341-353.
15. McGivney MS, Meyer SM, Duncan-Hewett W, Hall DL, Goode JR, Smith RB. Medication therapy management: its relationship to patient counseling, disease management, and pharmaceutical care. *J Am Pharm Assoc.* 2007;47:620-628.
16. American College of Clinical Pharmacy. ACCP Commentary. Medication therapy management services: application of the core elements in ambulatory care settings. 2006. http://www.accp.com/govt/positionPapers.aspx. Accessed January 14, 2013.
17. Manolakis PG, Skelton JB. Pharmacists' contributions to primary care in the U.S.—collaborating to address unmet patient care needs. AACP Issue Brief, July 2009.
18. Wubben DP, Vivian EM. Effects of pharmacist outpatient interventions on adults with diabetes mellitus: a systematic review. *Pharmacotherapy.* 2008;28(4):421-436.
19. Santschi V, Chioler A, Burnand B, Colosimo AL, Paradis G. Impact of pharmacist care in the management of cardiovascular disease risk factors. *Arch Intern Med.* 2011;171(16):1441-1453.
20. Morgando MP, Morgado SR, Mendes LC, Pereira LJ, Castelo-Branco M. Pharmacist interventions to enhance blood pressure control and adherence to antihypertensive therapy: review and meta-analysis. *Am J Health-Syst Pharm.* 2011;68:241-253.

21. Smith M, Giuliano MR, Starkowski MP. In Connecticut: improving patient medication management in primary care. *Health Aff.* 2011;4:646-654.
22. Ramalho de Oliveira D, Brummel AR, Miller DB. Medication therapy management: 10 years of experience in a large integrated health care system. *J Manag Care Pharm.* 2010;16(3):185-195.
23. Chisolm-Burns MA, Lee JK, Spivey CA, et al. US pharmacists' effect as team members on patient care: systematic review and meta-analyses. *Med Care.* 2010;48:923-933.
24. Cipolle RJ, Strand LM, Morley PC. Outcomes of pharmaceutical care practice. In: *Pharmaceutical Care Practice.* New York, NY: McGraw-Hill; 1998:205-235, chap 6.
25. Carlson B. Others await promise of Mississippi's experiment with pharmaceutical care. Managed Care. March 1999. http://www.managedcaremag.com/archives/9903/9903.states.html. Accessed January 11, 2013.
26. Division of Medicaid State of Mississippi Provider Policy Manual. Pharmacy. Pharmacy Disease Management. http://www.medicaid.ms.gov/Manuals/Section%2031%20-%20Pharmacy/Section%2031.19%20-%20Pharmacy%20Disease%20Management.pdf. Accessed January 11, 2013.
27. Young D. Promising results revealed in Mississippi disease management program. But program has low pharmacist participation. *Am J Health-Syst Pharm.* 2003; 60(17):1720, 1722, 1724.
28. Felt-Lisk S, Mays G, Harris L, et al. Evaluation of HRSA's Clinical Pharmacy Demonstration Projects. Final Report. Submitted to Department of Health and Human Services by Mathematica Policy Research, Inc., November 30, 2004.
29. Patient Safety and Clinical Pharmacy Services Collaborative. Health Resources and Services Administration. U.S. Department of Health and Human Services. http://www.hrsa.gov/publichealth/clinical/patientsafety/index.html. Accessed January 11, 2013.
30. Center for Medicare and Medicaid Services. 2011 Medicare Part D Medication Therapy Management Programs Fact Sheet. https://www.cms.gov/PrescriptionDrugCovContra/Downloads/MTMFactSheet2011063011Final.pdf. Accessed January 11, 2013.
31. Dole EJ, Murawski MM, Adolphe AB, et al. Provision of pain management by a pharmacist with prescribing authority. *Am J Health-Syst Pharm.* 2007;64:85-89.
32. New Mexico Board of Pharmacy. Pharmacist Clinician Certification. http://www.rld.state.nm.us/uploads/files/PC%20Log%20Instructions.pdf. Accessed January 14, 2013.
33. Dennis BH. An overview of clinical pharmacist practitioner in North Carolina. North Carolina Association of Pharmacists. http://www.ncpharmacists.org/displaycommon.cfm?an=13. Accessed January 14, 2013.
34. North Carolina Board of Pharmacy. Clinical Pharmacists Practitioners. http://www.ncbop.org/pharmacists_cpp.htm. Accessed January 11, 2013.
35. Daigle LA, Chen D. Pharmacist Provider Status in 11 State Health Programs. American Society of Health Systems Pharmacists Policy Analysis. September 2008. http://www.ashp.org/DocLibrary/Advocacy/ProviderStatusPrograms.aspx. Accessed January 11, 2013.
36. Cranor CW, Bunting BA, Christensen DB. The Asheville Project: long-term clinical and economic outcomes of a community pharmacy diabetes care program. *J Am Pharm Assoc.* 2003;43:173-184.
37. Bunting BA, Cranor CW. The Asheville Project: long-term clinical, humanistic, and economic outcomes of a community-based medication therapy management program for asthma. *J Am Pharm Assoc.* 2006;46:133-147.
38. Bunting BA, Smith BH, Sutherland SE. The Asheville Project: clinical and economic outcomes of a community-based long-term medication therapy management for hypertension and dyslipidemia. *J Am Pharm Assoc.* 2008;48:23-31.
39. Fera T, Bluml BM, Ellis WM. Diabetes Ten City Challenge: final economic and clinical results. *J Am Pharm Assoc.* 2009; 49e52-e60.
40. Joint Principles of the Patient-Centered Medical Home. Patient-Centered Primary Care Collaborative. http://www.pcpcc.net/content/joint-principles-patient-centered-medical-home. Accessed January 27, 2013.
41. Berdine H, Dougherty T, Ference J, et al. The pharmacist's role in the patient-centered medical home. *Ann Pharmacother.* 2012;46. doi: 10.1345/aph.1R189.
42. Integrating Comprehensive Medication Management to Optimize Patient Outcomes—A Resource Guide. 2nd ed. The Patient-Centered Primary Care Collaborative. June 2012. http://www.pcpcc.net/files/medmanagement.pdf

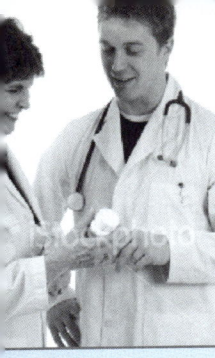

5

ASTHMA

Ashley W. Ellis

■ LEARNING OBJECTIVES

After reading this chapter, the pharmacy student, community practice resident, or pharmacist should be able to:

1. Describe the economic and clinical impact of uncontrolled asthma.
2. List the four components of asthma management.
3. Synthesize a business plan for asthma clinic development in community pharmacies including successful marketing and pricing strategies.
4. Describe the structure of patient visits required in an asthma clinic in a community pharmacy setting.
5. Develop appropriate documentation for prescriber communication, internal documentation, and third-party documentation requirements.

INTRODUCTION

According to the National Health Interview Survey conducted by the Centers for Disease Control and Prevention (CDC), 13.3% of the population in the United States has been diagnosed with asthma.[1] The Asthma and Allergy Foundation of America reports the following associated costs of asthma to patients, society, and the health-care system. They state that every day in America:

- 40,000 people miss work or school.
- 30,000 people have an asthma attack.
- 5,000 people visit the emergency room (ER).
- 1,000 people are admitted to the hospital.
- 11 people die.[2]

Uncontrolled asthma has negative effects on clinical, humanistic, and economic outcomes. The Task Force on Community Preventative Services, a volunteer group of preventative and public health-care experts appointed by the director of the CDC, has recommended an educational and interventional approach to asthma care that has demonstrated an increase in symptom-free days and in cost avoidance. Evidence-based interventions for patients with asthma include proper inhaler technique and trigger identification and avoidance.[3]

Community pharmacists are uniquely positioned to identify asthma patients with uncontrolled asthma through simple observation such as early or frequent refills of rescue inhalers. A recent study found that community pharmacists were able to identify patients at risk for poorly controlled asthma using assessment tools to determine patient symptoms and medication records to determine appropriate fill history of asthma medications and devices.[4]

Patient counseling for meter dose inhalers (MDI) and dry powder inhalers (DPI) is an opportunity community pharmacists experience every day that can make a measurable impact on the control of symptoms for patients with asthma. New prescriptions for spacers and peak flow meters also give pharmacists an opportunity to speak with a patient not only regarding the use of a new device but also regarding the reasoning behind the new prescription. An educational intervention may uncover a patient suffering from asthma that is not as well controlled as it could be. Incorrect inhaler technique has been reported frequently in the literature and is estimated to be present in 28–68% of patients.[5] Incorrect inhaler technique has been linked to decreased control of asthma symptoms and an increase in ER visits.[6] Further research has determined that repeated instruction and demonstration of correct inhaler technique can help to decrease intentional nonadherence to asthma medications.[7]

One of the most common interventions community pharmacists can utilize is the discovery of underutilization of inhaled corticosteroid (ICS) inhalers. Sometimes patients may use multiple pharmacies to fill their asthma prescriptions; however, when rescue inhalers are dispensed, simply questioning a patient about maintenance therapy may be the key to discovering undertreated asthma and suboptimal outcomes for that particular patient.

ASTHMA MANAGEMENT

Definition of Asthma

The National Institutes of Health, National Asthma Education, and Prevention Program Expert Panel Report 3 (EPR3) defines asthma as the following:

> Asthma is a chronic inflammatory disorder of the airways in which many cells and cellular elements play a role: in particular, mast cells, eosinophils, T-lymphocytes, macrophages, neutrophils, and epithelial cells. In susceptible individuals, this inflammation causes recurrent episodes of wheezing, breathlessness, chest tightness, and coughing, particularly at night or in the early morning. These episodes are usually associated with widespread but variable airflow obstruction that is often reversible either spontaneously or with treatment. The inflammation also causes an associated increase in the existing bronchial hyperresponsiveness (BHR) to a variety of stimuli. Reversibility of airflow

limitation may be incomplete in some patients with asthma.[8]

Clinical Presentation of Asthma Symptoms

The majority of asthma symptoms occur due to airway constriction, BHR, and inflammation of the airways.[9] The symptoms of asthma are highly variable and can even vary within a single person's lifetime. Exacerbation and remission of symptoms is common. Symptoms can include wheezing (a high-pitched whistling noise resulting from bronchoconstriction), coughing, chest tightness, chest pain, and/or dyspnea.[8] During periods of remission, these symptoms may be absent but patients at all stages of asthma have demonstrated airway inflammation, the degree of which can contribute to the severity of the presenting symptoms.[10] Persistently inflamed airways can lead to airway remodeling and more permanent decline in lung function.[8]

Four Components of Asthma Management

The National Institutes of Health, National Asthma Education, and Prevention Program EPR3 recommends four components for effective asthma management.

1. Objective testing, assessment, monitoring, and physical examination to determine asthma control
2. Asthma care education
3. Control of environmental factors and comorbid conditions
4. Pharmacologic therapy[8]

Pharmacists are well positioned to provide several of these components and to partner with practitioners to ensure patients are not receiving fractionated care for their asthma and to increase the effectiveness of the therapy they are receiving.

Objective Testing

The purpose of assessment and monitoring of asthma is to quantify severity of the disease, control of functional impairment, and responsiveness to treatment. Impairment that symptoms may cause and the risk of asthma exacerbations or decline in lung function help practitioners to determine the patient's current state of control and set goals for the future.[8] Pharmacists and other health-care professionals can assess severity of patient symptoms via validated patient completed questionnaires. Several of these exist and have been used in clinical research to assess and measure changes in control. The Asthma Control Questionnaire (ACQ©)[11], Asthma Therapy Assessment Questionnaire (ATAQ©)[12], and the Asthma Control Test (ACT™)[13] ask similar questions regarding need and use of rescue inhalers, timing of symptoms, and interruption of activities of daily living caused by asthma symptoms. Each provides a score with interpretation giving the clinician an indication of asthma control and each offers different advantages. For example, the ACQ© includes a section for the clinician to include pulmonary function testing, and the ACT™ includes a version that can be used for children (see Table 5-1 for a comparison of these three questionnaires). Despite the validity of the questionnaires, some patients may be poor perceivers of their lung function, which can be due to many factors such as age, obesity, lack of fitness, or accommodation to symptoms over time.[8] In these cases, spirometry and lung function testing become even more important.

Spirometry should be used to determine pulmonary function. It is widely available in the clinical setting, and handheld devices are available for purchase in a community pharmacy setting. Spirometry reports pulmonary function by plotting flow of air versus time. Important outcomes for determining asthma control are the forced vital capacity (FVC) and forced expiratory volume in the first second of expiration (FEV_1). FVC is the total amount of air that can be exhaled. FVC is often expressed as the FEV_1. It is important to note that FEV_1 can be falsely lowered due to a lack of effort on the part of the patient.[14] Values for FEV_1 can be predicted based on age and height. Increases in $FEV_1 \geq 12\%$ after inhalation of a bronchodilator from baseline or $\geq 10\%$ from predicted value objectively indicate treatment effectiveness.[8]

Spirometry does have a better predictive value of asthma control than peak flow meters, but peak flow meters are affordable, valuable tools for patients to

Table 5-1. Validated Asthma Symptoms Assessment Questionnaires

Name	Question Type	Interpretation of Results
Asthma Control Test (ACT™)[13]	Frequency of symptoms or use of rescue medications with an assigned lower score for poorer control	If the score is ≤19, asthma may not be optimally controlled
Asthma Control Questionnaire (ACQ©)[11]	Seven questions about symptoms, FEV_1% predicted and daily rescue inhaler use with higher scores for more impairment	Questions are equally averaged and a the mean corresponds to the impairment 0 (totally controlled) and 6 (severely uncontrolled)
Asthma Therapy Assessment Questionnaire (ATAQ©)[12]	Assesses asthma symptom control, interference with daily activities, and rescue inhaler use; patients may answer yes, no or unsure to each question	0 = asthma is well controlled 1–2 = asthma is not well controlled 3–4 = asthma is poorly controlled

assess their own control. Peak flow meters measure peak expiratory flow rate (PEFR) and are recommended for patients with moderate-to-severe asthma. As with spirometry, peak flow monitoring can be highly dependent on patient effort and training is required for their proper use by patients.[8]

Asthma Care Education

Asthma care education should be collaborative and begin with patients and care givers at the time of diagnosis and continue through follow-up care. The National Institutes of Health, National Asthma Education, and Prevention Program EPR3 recommends components of asthma education that include the level of asthma control the patient can expect, self-monitoring techniques, proper inhaler use, and a written asthma action plan.[8] Written asthma action plans explain specific treatment actions taken by the patient in response to changes in symptoms (Fig. 5-4). Pharmacists are particularly helpful in this area of asthma management because it involves helping the patient understand the purpose of his or her medications. In general, asthma medications can be categorized as controllers or rescue medications, and a patient's ability to distinguish between the two can be of vital importance in exacerbations. Asthma action plans should be updated as needed at follow-up visits and pharmacists should encourage patients to have several copies. For instance, parents should provide a copy to school nurses and teachers for children with asthma or other adults if the child is planning to be away from home for overnight visits.[8,15]

Asthma education programs are available at many community pharmacies that may include medication therapy management (MTM targeted to patients with asthma. Recognizing the costs of uncontrolled asthma to patients and the health-care system, many states offer reimbursement to community pharmacists for asthma education. The Asheville Project was a monumental achievement for community pharmacists interested in asthma education. The Asheville Project provided education and long-term follow-up to patients with asthma covered by two self-insured third-party payers. Over a 12-month period, pharmacists were able to demonstrate a decrease in emergency department visits, health-care costs related to asthma, and a decrease in missed days of work.[16]

Control of Environmental Factors and Comorbid Conditions

Pharmacists can use targeted questions and a comprehensive patient history to help determine individualized asthma triggers.[8] Pharmacists may find some of the following questions helpful for this assessment:

- During which season do you find your asthma symptoms the most severe? Least severe?
- Do you have any pets living inside your home?
- Have you noticed shortness of breath after eating any foods?

Determining the answer to these and other questions can help the patient avoid known triggers. Solutions may be as simple as having the family pet live outside or avoiding fur or feathers in the bedroom. Each of these may help improve asthma symptoms. Additional allergy testing may be required for patients unsure of his or her triggers or unable to identify the cause of escalating symptoms.[8]

A thorough social history should also include the patient's occupation. A patient's occupational exposure to inhaled irritants or tobacco smoke may require the patient to develop a plan with his or her employer to avoid these triggers or, if at all possible, seek employment elsewhere.[8]

Medication histories should again be continually examined to determine if worsening symptoms could be due to the addition of a new agent, the continuation of an agent such as a nonselective beta-blocker for hypertension or even performance anxiety. Again, this is a vital area in which pharmacists bring their expert medication knowledge to the collaborative health-care team and recommend alternative agents that would avoid worsening asthma symptoms. For each trigger identified, the pharmacist should help the patient devise a plan to decrease exposure to minimize the impact on asthma control.[8]

Management of comorbid conditions such as gastroesophageal reflux disorder (GERD) or obesity should again require the input of the collaborative team managing the patient's asthma. Nonpharmacologic approaches such as eating smaller meals, elevating the head of the bed, and avoiding food and drink 3 hours before bedtime can help to minimize many GERD symptoms and better help the patient to distinguish between asthma and GERD symptoms. Also, planned careful reduction in caloric intake and increase in exercise, as determined by the health-care team, can help reduce asthma severity in obese patients.[8]

Medications

Medication management is the area of asthma management in which the pharmacist brings his or her expertise to the collaborative team. An analysis of pharmaceutical care interventions for patients with asthma in community pharmacies, performed by McLean and McKeigan, found improved outcomes, which were demonstrated in programs that provided pharmacists with asthma certification training opportunities, utilized detailed protocols that indicated expectations of the program, and targeted patients with uncontrolled asthma.[17]

MTM is a separate and distinct service from community pharmacy dispensing activities. During an MTM encounter, a pharmacist spends more focused time with the patient determining the state of current asthma control and specific therapeutic strategies to improve it.

As mentioned earlier, asthma medications are broadly categorized as long-term controller medications and quick-relief medications (Table 5-2). Pharmacists educate patients about which category their medications are classified, the proper use of those medications, potential side effects and strategies to avoid them, and when self-initiation or self-adjustment of

Table 5-2. Asthma Medication Classification[8]

Long-Term Control Medications	Quick-Relief Medications
Corticosteroids	Anticholinergics
Cromolyn sodium	Short-acting beta-agonists (SABAs)
Immunomodulators	Systemic corticosteroids
Leukotriene modifiers	
Long-acting beta-agonists (LABAs)	
Methylxanthines	
Nedocromil	

Allergy & Asthma Network
Mothers of Asthmatics
800.878.4403
www.aanma.org

ASTHMA ACTION PLAN

Date: ____________
Name: ____________
Doctor: ____________
Doctor's Phone Number: ____________
Hospital/Emergency Department Phone Number: ____________

ROUTINE ZONE

Doing Well

- No cough, wheeze, chest tightness, or shortness of breath during the day or night
- Can do usual activities

Target Peak Expiratory Flow Rate (PEFR) should be between

________ and ________

If prescribed, use a daily inhaled corticosteroid or other medication to prevent airway inflammation:

Medication ____________

How much to take ____________

When to take it ____________

At first sign of symptoms or 5–15 minutes before exercise: ❒ Take: ____________ ❒ 2 or ❒ 4 puffs

CAUTION ZONE

Symptoms Present

- Cough, wheeze, chest tightness, or shortness of breath, or
- Waking at night due to asthma, or
- Can do some, but not all, usual activities

-Or-

PEFR: ________ to ________

1 FIRST **Use albuterol or levalbuterol—and keep taking your GREEN ZONE medication.**
____________ ❒ 2 or ❒ 4 puffs, every 20 minutes for up to 1 hour

2 Second **If your symptoms or PEFR return to GREEN ZONE after 1 hour:**
❒ Continue monitoring to be sure you stay in the green zone.
-Or-
If your symptoms or PEFR do not return to GREEN ZONE after 1 hour:
❒ Take: ____________ ❒ 2 or ❒ 4 puffs or ❒ nebulizer
❒ Add: ____________ (oral corticosteroid) mg per day for ________ (3–10) days
❒ Call the doctor ❒ before/ ❒ within ________ hours after taking the oral steroid.

EMERGENCY ZONE

Medical Alert!

- Very short of breath, or
- YELLOW ZONE medications have not helped, or
- Trouble walking and talking
- Lips or fingernails turn blue or discolored due to lack of oxygen
- Symptoms are same or get worse

-Or-

PEFR: less than ________

Take this medication:
❒ ____________ ❒ 2 or ❒ 6 puffs or ❒ nebulizer
❒ ____________ mg
(oral corticosteroid)

Call your doctor NOW. Go to the hospital or call an ambulance if:
❒ You are still in the red zone after 15 minutes AND
❒ You have not reached your doctor.

Exercise

- Prevent or reduce allergic reactions through allergen avoidance, medication, or immunotherapy.
- Pre-medicate before exercise.
- Warm up and cool down 10 minutes pre- and post exercise.
- Tailor exercise intensity until symptom-free.

- No physical activity until in yellow or green zone.

Adapted from Asthma Action Plan © 2010 by Allergy & Asthma Network Mothers of Asthmatics, sponsored by TEVA Respiratory, LLC and used with permission.

Figure 5-1. Asthma action plan.

doses is appropriate. The written asthma action plan (Fig. 5-1) should be used during these discussions with patients. As will be discussed further, MTM by pharmacists can include patient counseling, device training, adherence monitoring, and recommendations to prescribers or even direct management via collaborative practice agreements (CPAs).

A key aspect of asthma medication management is the classification of the patient's asthma both by symptoms and pulmonary function testing. As mentioned earlier, validated questionnaires and patient interviews help pharmacists assess symptom control, and spirometry can help confirm these results or help the practitioner become aware of changes in lung function if the patient does not perceive the change. A complete review of the classifications of asthma severity can be found in the National Institutes of Health, National Asthma Education, and Prevention Program EPR 3, but a summary of classifications in patients ≥12 years old can be found in Figure 5-2.[8] The guidelines recommend a stepwise approach to therapy depending on severity of the disease (see Fig. 5-3[8]). An individual patient may change classifications over the course of their own disease. It is also recommended that before any

Asthma 69

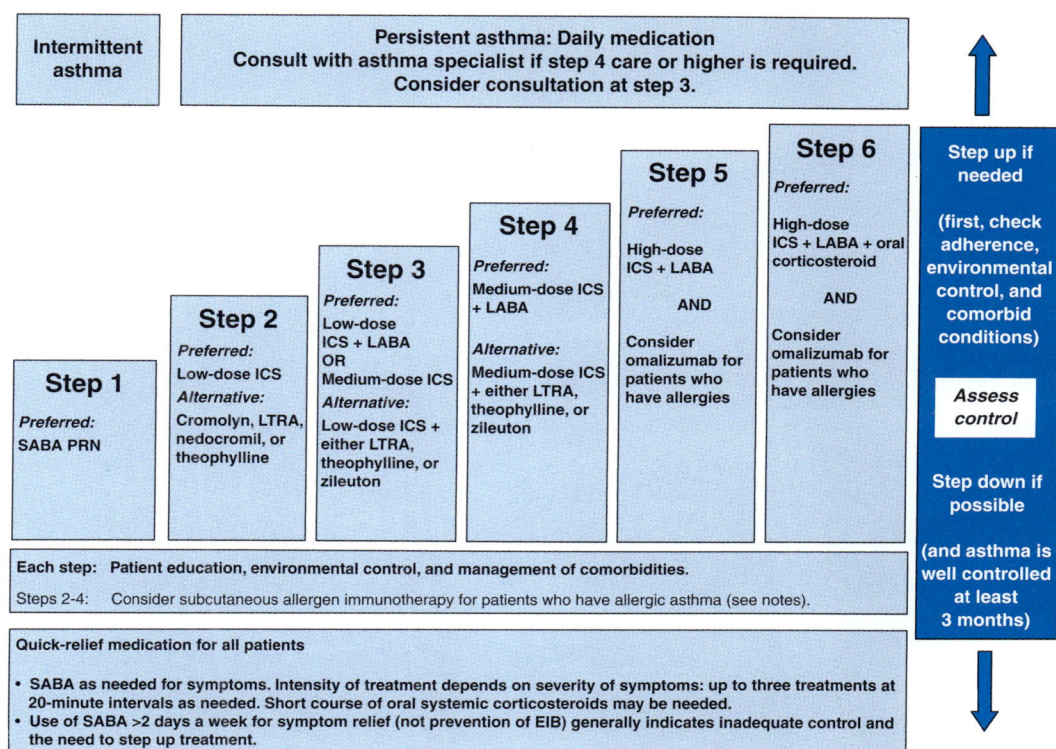

— Key: Alphabetical order is used when more than one treatment option is listed within either preferred or alternative therapy. EIB, exercise-induced bronchospasm; ICS, inhaled corticosteroid; LABA, long-acting inhaled beta$_2$-agonist; LTRA, leukotriene receptor antagonist; SABA, inhaled short-acting beta$_2$-agonist

Notes:

- The stepwise approach is meant to assist, not replace, the clinical decision making required to meet individual patient needs.
- If alternative treatment is used and response is inadequate, discontinue it and use the preferred treatment before stepping up.
- Zileuton is a less desirable alternative due to limited studies as adjunctive therapy and the need to monitor liver function. Theophylline requires monitoring of serum concentration levels.
- In step 6, before oral systemic corticosteroids are introduced, a trial of high-dose ICS + LABA + either LTRA, theophylline, or zileuton may be considered, although this approach has not been studied in clinical trials.
- Step 1, 2, and 3 preferred therapies are based on Evidence A; step 3 alternative therapy is based on Evidence A for LTRA, Evidence B for theophylline, and Evidence D for zileuton. Step 4 preferred therapy is based on Evidence B, and alternative therapy is based on Evidence B for LTRA and theophylline and Evidence D for zileuton. Step 5 preferred therapy is based on Evidence B. Step 6 preferred therapy is based on (EPR—2 1997) and Evidence B for omalizumab.
- Immunotherapy for steps 2-4 is based on Evidence B for house-dust mites, animal danders, and pollens; evidence is weak or lacking for molds and cockroaches. Evidence is strongest for immunotherapy with single allergens. The role of allergy in asthma is greater in children than in adults.
- Clinicians who administer immunotherapy or omalizumab should be prepared and equipped to identify and treat anaphylaxis that may occur.

Figure 5-2. Stepwise approach for managing asthma in youths ≥12 years of age and adults.

— **Assessing severity and initiating treatment for patients who are not currently taking long-term control medications**

Components of severity		Classification of asthma severity ≥12 years of age			
			Persistent		
		Intermittent	Mild	Moderate	Severe
Impairment Normal FEV$_1$/FVC: 8-19 year 85% 20-39 year 80% 40-59 year 75% 60-80 year 70%	Symptoms	≤2 days/week	>2 days/week but not daily	Daily	Throughout the day
	Nighttime awakenings	≤2x/month	3-4x/month	>1x/week but not nightly	Often 7x/week
	Short-acting beta$_2$-agonist use for symptom control (not prevention of EIB)	≤2 days/week	>2 days/week but not daily, and not more than 1x on any day	Daily	Several times per day
	Interference with normal activity	None	Minor limitation	Some limitation	Extremely limited
	Lung function	• Normal FEV$_1$ between exacerbations • FEV$_1$ >80% predicted • FEV$_1$/FVC normal	• FEV$_1$ >80% predicted • FEV$_1$/FVC normal	• FEV$_1$ >60% but <80% predicted • FEV$_1$/FVC reduced 5%	• FEV$_1$ <60% predicted • FEV$_1$/FVC reduced >5%
Risk	Exacerbations requiring oral systemic corticosteroids	0-1/Year (See note)	≥2/Year (See note) →→→→→→→→→→→→→→→→→→→→→→		
		←←←←←← Consider severity and interval since last exacerbation. →→→→→→ Frequency and severity may fluctuate over time for patients in any severity category. Relative annual risk of exacerbations may be related to FEV$_1$.			
Recommended step for initiating treatment (See Figure 5-2 for treatment steps)		Step 1	Step 2	Step 3 and consider short course of oral systemic corticosteroids	Step 4 or 5 and consider short course of oral systemic corticosteroids
		In 2-6 weeks, evaluate level of asthma control that is achieved and adjust therapy accordingly.			

Key: FEV$_1$, forced expiratory volume in 1 second; FVC, forced vital capacity; ICU, intensive care unit

Notes:

- The stepwise approach is meant to assist, not replace, the clinical decision making required to meet individual patient needs.
- Level of severity is determined by assessment of both impairment and risk. Assess impairment domain by patient's/caregiver's recall of previous 2-4 weeks and spirometry. Assign severity to the most severe category in which any feature occurs.
- At present, there are inadequate data to correspond frequencies of exacerbations with different levels of asthma severity. In general, more frequent and intense exacerbations (e.g., requiring urgent, unscheduled care, hospitalization, or ICU admission) indicate greater underlying disease severity. For treatment purposes, patients who had ≥2 exacerbations requiring oral systemic corticosteroids in the past year may be considered the same as patients who have persistent asthma, even in the absence of impairment levels consistent with persistent asthma.

Figure 5-3. Classifying asthma severity and initiating treatment in youths ≥12 years of age and adults.

changes in therapy be considered, adherence and environmental factors be assessed as possible factors for loss of symptom control or pulmonary function (Fig. 5-2).[8] Examples of a stepwise approach to therapy include starting with a short-acting beta-agonist (SABA) for mild asthma. If a patient's symptoms worsen and the patient needs to use the SABA 2 or more times per week, excluding use prior to exercise, or is awakened by nighttime symptoms, initiating a low or medium-dose ICS would be appropriate. If the patient contracted influenza or pneumonia with severe asthma symptoms, it would be appropriate to increase the ICS to a high dose and add oral corticosteroids.[8]

■ CLINIC INITIATION

Preparing Yourself for Clinic Initiation

As the results of the Asheville Project demonstrate, pharmacist preparedness has an impact on the quality of the pharmacy asthma program. Pharmacists interested in beginning an asthma clinic should hone their clinical skills and become familiar with the latest guidelines available, the medications used, and the assessment techniques.[16] The National Asthma Educator Certification Board is an organization that maintains the competencies required of a certified asthma educator (AE-C) through an exam process. Reviews for the Asthma Educator Exam are often provided by local American Lung Association chapters. Pharmacists are eligible to sit for this exam and become credentialed.[18] Community pharmacy residencies or pharmacy practice residencies are excellent opportunities to develop not only clinical skills but also marketing and entrepreneurial aspects of implementing an asthma clinic. When pharmacists can demonstrate achievements such as these additional education offerings, it often increases acceptance of new asthma services by both prescribers and patients.

Developing a Business Plan

Environmental Scan

After a pharmacist has established the clinical background necessary to be a competent asthma care provider, a complete scan of the environment should be conducted to ensure that an asthma clinic is feasible, acceptable to stakeholders, and sustainable. If the pharmacist is not the pharmacy manager or owner, he or she must start with garnering support from all decision makers concerning initiating asthma services. This can be accomplished through demonstrating a need. The interested pharmacist should determine the percentage of patient's refilling rescue inhalers and review the pharmacy's inventory for use and turnover of asthma-related products. Next, build support from external stakeholders. Physicians or practitioners who are familiar with other services in the pharmacy are the best place to start. For example, if the pharmacy already offers influenza immunizations through a CPA with a provider, he or she would be more likely to support expansion of clinical services than a provider only familiar with dispensing services. Relationships with nurses or clinical support staff are key to the success of any new clinical service. Nurses can identify patients seen at the provider's office who can be targeted by the new service. If value can be demonstrated to nurses, they can often help overcome any objections or questions raised by prescribers and often ensure referrals to the service that are sent to you with complete information.

Writing the Business Plan

As mentioned earlier in several chapters of this book, a business plan is necessary for the success of any new business venture. Pharmacy services are no exception. Pharmacists should determine if asthma education or MTM services are offered at other institutions in close proximity. For instance, if a local hospital offers free asthma education services and area prescribers are satisfied with the program, it would be difficult to persuade them to refer patients to the pharmacy to pay for the same level of service. If this is the case, pharmacists should survey his or her own business and determine what will set this new service apart. If the service is an expansion from education to disease state management, using any collected data for marketing and justifying the service would help garner buy-in from stakeholders.

Performing a SWOT Analysis A SWOT (Strengths, Weaknesses, Opportunities, Threats) analysis should also be performed. Strengths could include having a residency-trained pharmacist or one who has recently become an AE-C. Other strengths could include a high volume of inhalers dispensed and strong relationships with area providers for other clinic offerings or immunizations. Weaknesses could include a lack of clinical confidence by the pharmacists, a busy workflow making scheduling appointments difficult, or patients who are unaware of the need for the service. Opportunities could include expanding already successful immunization services for patients who have asthma as a natural referral to asthma services within the pharmacy, engaging practitioners with heavy patient load and lack of time for chronic disease education, and capturing available payment for pharmacist-provided services such as with several state Medicaid programs or third-party payers. Threats to the new service could include competitors offering similar services, unwillingness of patients to pay for services if they are not covered through insurance, and the high cost of most asthma medications and devices. A thoughtful business plan will allow the pharmacist to think through each potential threat and develop a plan to avoid or overcome them.

Pricing and Payment for Services When determining pricing strategies, several factors must be considered. First, the cost of administrative materials needed. Whether the pharmacy chooses paper charts or electronic software, this cost, as well as other minimal office supplies, should be considered. If a private patient care area is available, the investment for asthma services would be minimal. However, if a new area is to be constructed, a table, chairs, file cabinet, and asthma handouts should be obtained. Partnering with an area pharmaceutical sales representative can be invaluable in the beginning because he or she can often provide handouts, models, coupons, and demonstration inhalers. Second, at a minimum, a peak flow meter with disposable mouthpieces will be needed for patients to demonstrate its use and to assess peak flow rates at visits. Handheld spirometry is optional equipment that would help to solidify recommendations and assessment of lung function, but it can be expensive. Pharmacies or clinics may consider initially investing in this equipment or could consider investing in it after the service begins generating revenue.

Before methods of payment for services are determined, correct pricing of services must be considered. Pricing can be determined by including the salary of all personnel involved (SAL), materials and supplies (MAT), non-salary direct fixed costs (NDC) such as glucometer strips if diabetes services were offered, and rent or non-rent overhead costs (OHC).

$$Cost = SAL + MAT + NDC + OHC^{19}$$

For example, Our Family Pharmacy is interested in starting asthma disease state management services. It is an independent pharmacy open Monday through Friday from 9 AM to 6 PM. The weekly rent for the 2,100 square foot store is $1,000 and pharmacists are paid $45 per hour. How much should it charge for 30-minute asthma MTM appointment?

Our Family Pharmacy has a 150 square foot patient care office and is estimating 10 appointments per week after beginning the asthma service. The pharmacist will be the only personnel seeing patients and scheduling appointments. Our Family Pharmacy has decided to utilize paper charts and estimate nominal office supplies to be about $50.00. A pharmaceutical sales representative donated a peak flow meter, mouthpieces, and demonstration inhalers. Marketing plans include practitioner calls totaling about 30 minutes (Table 5-3).[19]

Knowing that a 30-minute MTM appointment will cost the pharmacy $26.43, how much should the pharmacy charge for the asthma pharmacy services appointments?

Several components must be considered in order to determine the best price. Demand for services is a critical consideration. If a pharmacy has already built a strong patient base with considerable trust in the pharmacists and has patients who need better manage-

Table 5-3. Total Service Cost

Cost Component	Calculation	Total
Salary (SAL)	($45 × 0.5 hours marketing calls per week/10 appointments per week) + ($45 × 0.5 per appointment)	$24.75 per appointment
Materials (MAT)	$50/40 appointments per month	$1.25 per appointment
Non-salary direct fixed costs (NDC)	N/A	$0.00
Overhead costs (OHC)	(150 sq ft/2,100 sq ft) × (5 hours/49 hours) × $1,000 per week = $7.29 per week $7.29/10 appointments per week	$0.73 per appointment
Total service cost		$26.73 per appointment

ment of asthma, prices can be set higher. Competition from other institutions or pharmacies is important to consider. Pricing lower than competition may initially draw in patients, but differentiating the service from the competition will demonstrate the need to new patients. Pricing higher than the competition can be considered especially if MTM services are of higher quality, the expertise of the pharmacist is better, and the value the patient could expect. The image of the pharmacy is also very important in pricing and marketing new and expanded services. If the pharmacy has been a long-standing presence in the community, a positive image has likely been built over the years since the pharmacy has been in business. If the pharmacists and staff have consistently provided exceptional customer service, including going above and beyond the normal expectations of business, patients will be more likely to try a new service and a accept a higher price for service. Lastly, standard rates are important to consider when pricing services. For example, if other pharmacies in town offer a similar service at $30 per hour, Our Family Pharmacy would not likely attract many new patients by charging $30 for a half hour visit because this would drive the demand for the business to competitors.[19]

Payment for services can be generated by several methods or a combination of several options. Fee-for-service is an option pharmacists, other health-care professionals, and professionals in health-related fields (i.e., trainers, nutritionists, and dietary supplement counseling) have used to obtain payment directly from the patient. The benefits of the fee-for-service option include payment that is collected at the time of service without paperwork, risk of audit, or rejection from a third-party payer. Disadvantages include the perception by practitioners or patients that the service is not needed if it not covered by an insurance plan to which they pay monthly premiums. Pharmacists must work to overcome this objection by discussing demonstration of success such as decreased hospital or ER visits or asthma exacerbations by patients within the pharmacy's services or by using other successful projects such as the Asheville Project.[16] Pharmacists must become aware that while exacerbations, quality of life, or hospitalization rates may be improved, it may not be possible to reduce medication co-pays because underutilization of inhalers is a common intervention. Most currently marketed asthma medications do not have generics and are generally costly investments for patients. Therefore, adding an ICS may increase monthly medication co-payments; however, the likely decrease in symptoms and exacerbations can lead to decreased office, emergency department visits, or missed days of work. It is important to note, though, that some MTM sessions with patients with asthma may simply reveal incorrect inhaler technique, such as exhaling into a DPI or inhaling too slowly, which actually results in decreased benefit to the patient. This is an important educational component that may not involve the addition of a new product or inhaler.

Similar to fee-for-service, group education classes can provide an economical alternative for patients who need asthma education as opposed to disease state management. Group classes can be priced affordably for participants and having 5–10 patients attend at the same time can provide a reasonable return on investment for the pharmacist's time. Other benefits of group classes include the development of trust among the participants leading to a support system for them. Often participants can learn techniques or glean pearls from each other that result in improvement of asthma.

MTM benefits through Medicare Part D are another opportunity for pharmacists to bill for asthma services. Asthma has been a high-cost disease state for Medicare since older patients are at greater risk for adverse events or asthma complications than younger patients. Often through the utilization of the Medicare Part D formulary, pharmacists can offer therapeutic interchange of inhalers or other asthma medications and help patients save money on co-pays. Patients who overuse rescue inhalers may reach their "donut hole" earlier in the year leading to increased out-of-pocket expenses. Giving specific examples of the savings achieved within the program can help market these services. Pharmacies can contract with Medicare Part D or MTM providers to receive referrals based on the location of dispensing pharmacy customers and can provide asthma services to them.

Some third-party payers include a provision of asthma education through pharmacy services. To find out if this is an option, one must contact the insurance company and ask about benefits or the need to set up a contract for services offered. As more pharmacists and patients demand this from insurance companies, they may become more likely to pay for these services especially once demonstrable outcomes are collected and reported for their covered entities.

As in the case of the Asheville Project, self-insured employers are the prime target for asthma pharmacy services. Since the employer and pool of premiums paid shoulder the cost of all insurance benefits, it is advantageous to the employer to provide optimal services, especially if they can decrease health expenditures.[16] Employers are also very interested in decreased absenteeism, which can be very common in patients with asthma. Marketing and negotiating contracts with one or two self-insured employers can provide a steady stream of referrals and a sustainable revenue stream.

Finally, grant opportunities for innovative pharmacy services are available through granting agencies often interested in start-up projects or those with a proven track record of success. Partnering with a college or school of pharmacy can provide resources for increasing the likelihood of success with grant applications. Community pharmacy residents are also required to complete a residency project that often needs start-up funds in order to be successful. This would be another opportunity for applying for grant funds.

Marketing Services Practitioner buy-in is crucial for the success of any advanced pharmacy service and is best attained either before a new service is implemented or early in its development. Make appointments with practitioners who commonly prescribe other medications or refer patients to your dispensing pharmacy. Sometimes taking breakfast or lunch can help you gain more of the practitioner's time to speak about your services. When discussing the implementation or expansion of pharmacy services, emphasis should always be placed on improving teamwork, coordination of care, and complementing what the practitioner currently does. It is important to communicate that MTM services, disease state management, and asthma education will not undermine the relationship with the patient but instead strengthen it. Whether your service includes a CPA or simply recommendations, the patient must be followed by a practitioner for exams and laboratory follow-up. Many community pharmacy clinics have found it helpful to design a simple referral form for the practitioner to refer patients to the asthma service (see Figure 5-4 for an example). The form can be faxed to the pharmacy so that the pharmacist or pharmacy staff can make arrangements with

Our Family Pharmacy

REFERRAL FORM

Patient Name:_____ DOB:_____

Patient Phone Number:_____

Please check all that apply:

Disease State Management Program:

    Asthma:

    _____ Asthma Disease State Management Protocol with PharmD

Medication Therapy Management:

    Asthma:

    _____Asthma Medication Therapy Management with PharmD

    General MTM:

    _____Medication Therapy Management of two or more chronic conditions

    Specify Conditions:_____
    _____

Group Classes:

    Asthma:

    _____4 week series of 1 hour group asthma classes led by PharmD

- Thank you for the referral. If there is anything else we can help you with, please call us at 555-555-5555 (Our Family Pharmacy).

- When completed, please fax form to 555-555-5501, and the patient will be contacted to set up an appointment.

- Please attach any recent lab activities or notes.

Practitioner Name (please print):_____

Practitioner Signature:_____Date:_____

Figure 5-4. Referral form.

the patient for an appointment or class session. Practitioner referrals help to communicate the importance of the pharmacy service to the patient and often help in improving show rates for appointments. Depending on state regulations, individual patient practitioner referral to disease state management protocols may be needed for CPAs. Many practitioners also appreciate feedback on patients who do not present for services or refuse appointments after referral.

When patients self-refer or when the primary care provider has a less familiar relationship with the pharmacy, recommendations can often be perceived as undermining the level of care provided or implying that the practitioner has overlooked a needed medication or reaction. Denied pharmacist recommendations can often be avoided by a visit or phone call to the provider or a well-communicated cover letter. For several reasons, some practitioners may be more difficult to win over than others, but focusing on the successful collaborations is key to building a strong asthma pharmacy service. Often gaining the respect and collaboration of one partner within a group can be a strategy that influences others. Also, gauging the interests of each practitioner during face-to-face meetings can be greatly beneficial. For instance if a physician is extremely interested in research, partner with him or her for a demonstration project or apply for a research grant together. If a nurse practitioner has a strong interest in urgent care or a heavy patient load, discuss how chronic management of asthma can help ease patient load for avoidable asthma exacerbations.

Clinical Service Design
As mentioned earlier, an asthma pharmaceutical care service can take many forms including group classes, adherence interventions, patient counseling, MTM, or disease state management. Pharmacists can also consider offering a variety of these; however, it is often best to target one to two areas and demonstrate the effectiveness of the service before expanding into newer areas.

Curriculum Design   Whether group classes or individual appointments are selected as the target service, a curriculum should be designed to make all stakeholders aware of the value that can be expected from the new service. The American Lung Association offers both an adult and pediatric curriculum and train-the-trainer programs through local chapters that can be utilized for group classes. They also offer programs at elementary schools or summer camps.[20] Pharmacists can develop their own curriculum incorporating evidence-based education techniques recommended by the Association of Asthma Educators that publishes the *Journal of Asthma and Allergy Educators* and features new, innovative research regarding asthma and allergy education.[21] *The Asthma Educator Handbook* can serve not only as a refresher for pharmacists studying for the Asthma Educator Certification Exam but also as guiding principles to developing one's own asthma curriculum.[22] Conversation Maps® by Healthy Interactions have been proven to be an effective method for learner-led group diabetes education, and Respiratory Health Conversation Maps® are currently in development.[23]

Collaborative Practice Agreements   CPAs can be a great addition to or the basis for asthma pharmacy services if they are within the regulations of each state's pharmacy practice act. CPAs often help to improve continuity of care by providing the option of receiving asthma education, prescription products, and patient counseling in one location. Each state has different regulations regarding CPAs, but pharmacists can increase efficiency by utilizing one which eliminates the need to fax recommendation and receipts back, receipt of practitioner agreement to a recommendation, informing the patient of a new prescription product and the receiving product. At times without a CPA, this process can take days to a week or longer. If you have scheduled the patient's follow-up appointment for 1 month after an ICS is recommended and 2 weeks pass before the patient receives the medication, the anticipated benefit at the follow-up appointment will most likely not be achieved and the patient may have to reschedule the appointment or make additional appointments. An example of an asthma management CPA is available through the Minnesota Pharmacists Association website and is available as Appendix 5A.[24]

Table 5-4.	Our Family Pharmacy Personal Peak Flow Diary				
Date/Time	1st Attempt	2nd Attempt	3rd Attempt	Personal Best	Notes

Any CPA must be updated as new therapeutic options become available and as required by state regulations.

Despite the level of service offered, referring practitioners and patients will most likely need an explanation of the benefits that can be expected from the service. Many patients have never received advanced pharmacy services before, and stating the expectations at the beginning can be helpful. At each visit, pharmacists should check the patient's blood pressure and weight, and obtain a thorough medication history. While taking the medication history, it is an ideal time to ask the patient to demonstrate the use of each inhaler and to document refill history, if available, for other medications. Symptoms should be assessed by using a validated questionnaire or patient interview. After a classification of symptoms is assessed, it should be compared with previous visits, if available.

A PEFR should be obtained and proper technique should be demonstrated. If the patient does not have a personal peak flow meter, the pharmacist can recommend this product to the prescriber and provide the patient with a peak flow diary. Patients should be instructed to check peak flow at different times of the day with at least two attempts. Pharmacists can provide a peak flow diary for patients to use and bring to all for follow-up appointments. This helps establish the most accurate asthma action plan based on personal best PEFR (see Table 5-4 for an example). After the frequency of asthma exacerbations is established, management of these exacerbations should be discussed in detail.

Discovery and discussion of personal asthma triggers should be included in every visit. The pharmacist can work with the patient to develop a plan for each identified trigger. Nonpharmacologic interventions such as plastic covers for pillows or mattresses, smoking cessation or avoidance of secondhand smoke, and frequent vacuuming of carpet should be included when developing trigger avoidance plans.

Finally, a written asthma action plan is the cornerstone of asthma education. Every patient should receive a detailed explanation for managing his or her condition, and the asthma action plan should be

PHARMACIST REQUEST

Patient Name: KM   **DOB:** 12/03/1934
Patient Address: 100 Main Street, Anywhere, USA 50000

Medication Problem(s) Identified:
6/8/2012
S: 76 y/o female visiting clinic today for asthma education class. Feels asthma is under control but would like more education. Last documented Pneumovax 10 years ago.
O: BP 151/78, Peak flow personal best 200, Asthma Control Test (ACT) score 25
A: (1) Patient demonstrated slow inhalation of Advair dry powder inhaler that is most likely resulting in subtherapeutic dose. (2) Patient's ACT score and symptoms place patient in green zone/intermittent asthma and well controlled. Patient uses albuterol bid scheduled instead of prn. (3) Patient would like Peak flow meter to monitor asthma control at home. (4) Documented Pneumovax >5 years ago and new Pneumovax is indicated. (5) Patient's blood pressure is elevated but reports white coat HTN.
P: (1) Counseled patient on proper quick inhalation DPI technique. Patient stated and demonstrated understanding. (2) Recommend stepping down albuterol to two puffs qd for 1 month while monitoring with peak flow and return to pharmacy in 1 month for re-evaluation of dose with patient's peak flow diary. (3) Recommend peak flow meter. (4) Recommend Pneumovax. (5) Recommend at home blood pressure monitoring 3-4× per week and at pharmacy a few times per month and will reassess at next visit.

Amy Pharm, PharmD

Proposed Recommendations:
Peak flow meter UAD at least one time daily
Albuterol UAD prn
Pneumovax injection as directed at pharmacy

PRESCRIBER RESPONSE
(What would you like the pharmacist to do?)

_____Please implement the proposed recommendation as described above:

   ***#30 ___ refills
   *** #60 ___ refills

_____No, do not implement the above recommendations. Instead, please implement the following change(s):
_____
_____

_____Please have patient schedule an appointment with my office.

_____ Other:_____

PRESCRIBER'S SIGNATURE:
_____
Prescriber's Address and DEA number:_____

FROM: Amy Pharm, PharmD, working with Our Family Pharmacy
(555) 555-5555 phone   555-555-5501 fax
Thank you for your attention to this matter.
Information on this form is protected health information and subject to all privacy and security regulations under HIPAA.

Figure 5-5. Pharmacists request.

updated and reviewed at each visit.²² Because patients with asthma risk exacerbation if they contract influenza or pneumonia and current guidelines recommend routine immunization, a referral to the pharmacy's immunization service would be beneficial for the patient or could be included in the asthma visit.⁸

Documentation   Documentation is very important as discussed in detail in Chapter 2. Particularly in MTM visits or those including CPAs, regular communication with providers is necessary to facilitate a collaborative asthma management team. Documentation can be accomplished through SOAP notes or other progress notes but should specifically contain information obtained from the patient, any assessments of condition, any problems identified, and the plan or recommendation for resolution or monitoring of the plan. All recommendations should be specific and check boxes or closed-ended questions are generally best and prevent the pharmacist from having to call for clarification of information. For instance, if the pharmacist faxes a recommendation to ask for a "low-dose ICS" and the referring nurse practitioner responds by saying "please initiate," the pharmacist then would have to contact the clinic to verify which ICS, dose, interval, and how many refills. Instead, a specific recommendation of a suggested medication, dose, and dosing interval should be provided. For an example of a faxed communication form, see Figure 5-5.

All faxed communication should include a cover sheet explaining the service and reinforcing that the recommendations serve to strengthen the collaborative practitioner–patient relationship. As mentioned, it is generally best to call or send information to the provider if he or she is unfamiliar with the service before sending recommendations to help ensure the best chances for successful implementation.

Verbal communication is also an option for recommendations. It is best to communicate with each provider to determine his or her preferred method of communication for recommendations.

Follow-Up   Once the recommendation is returned, it is the pharmacist's responsibility to follow up with the patient concerning the new or modified prescription, the need to make an appointment with the provider, or any alternative plan the provider recommends.

Documentation at follow-up visits is equally important as initial visits. Follow-up documentation communicates to providers that you are establishing a relationship with the patient and that all members of the health-care team have the same goal of optimal health outcomes for the patient in mind.

■ PUTTING IT ALL TOGETHER: PATIENT CASE

NS is a 58-year-old female who reports to the clinic for initial individual asthma education visit. Patient is complaining of nighttime/early morning asthma symptoms causing awakening 2-3 times per week. She reports using her rescue inhaler 3-6 times per week due to asthma exacerbations excluding use before exercise. Patient exercises over 5 hours per week. She also has some allergy symptoms, but the use of a neti pot and occasional cetirizine 10 mg therapy control most symptoms. Patient reports receiving the flu vaccine yearly and no history of pneumococcal vaccine.

Medications include:

- *Albuterol HFA inhaler 1 puff q4-6 hours prn*
- *Cetirizine 1 po qd prn*
- *Atorvastatin 10 mg 1 po qd*
- *One daily essential vitamin 1 po qd*
- *Losartan/HCTZ 50/12.5 mg 1 po qd*

Lab data:

- *BP: 122/88*
- *ACT score: 15*
- *Peak flow reading: 350 L/min*
- *BMI: 28.3*
- **How is NS's asthma classified?**
  Moderate persistent.

- **Why?**
  Patient's nighttime awakenings require NS's asthma to be classified as moderate persistent despite not necessarily using her rescue inhaler daily.
- **Should any changes be made to NS's asthma therapy based on her classification?**
  Yes, preferred treatment is low- or medium-dose ICS and pneumococcal vaccine is recommended.
- **NS returns to the clinic with a peak flow diary indicating a personal best of 400.0 L/min. Calculate her green, yellow and red zones for her asthma action plan.**
  - *Green zone:* **320–400** *L/min*
  - *Yellow zone:* **200–319** *L/min*
  - *Red zone:* **<199** *L/min*

■ SUMMARY POINTS

- Pharmacists are well positioned to be vital members of a collaborative asthma management team.
- Evidence-based asthma management requires objective testing, asthma care education, control of environmental factors and comorbid conditions, and medication management.
- Support should be attained by internal and external stakeholders early in the clinic building process.
- Patients, practitioners, and pharmacists should have clear expectations of pharmacy asthma service offerings.
- Documentation and follow-up are necessary for all asthma-based pharmacy services.

■ EXPERT INTERVIEW

Lauren Bloodworth, PharmD
Clinical Assistant Professor of Pharmacy Practice
Coordinator of Student Services and Student
  Professional Development - UMMC
Administrator of the UM Delta Pharmacy Patient
  Care Management Services Project
The University of Mississippi School of
  Pharmacy, MS

- **Why should pharmacists be involved in asthma care?**
  Pharmacists are uniquely qualified and highly accessible in a variety of health-care settings (community pharmacies, hospitals, clinics) to assist in the overall management of asthma. Pharmacists can provide much needed medication and disease state education including proper asthma device technique, reinforce, and answer any questions pertaining to a patient's individual treatment plan, and closely monitor a patient's medication use and refill records. All of which can be shared among members of the health-care team to improve the patient's health outcomes.

- **As the administrator of the UM Delta Pharmacy Patient Care Management Services Project and former director of the UMMC Adult Asthma Clinic, what barriers did you experience in implementing asthma services? How did you overcome them?**
  One barrier in the community pharmacy setting was in provider education about the capabilities of a pharmacist with regard to asthma medication therapy management. Asthma services were implemented in rural Mississippi where it was not commonplace for collaborative practice agreements to exist. With this, it took more provider education about how the pharmacist and the provider could collaboratively work to improve the patient's asthma management. A clinical barrier that was frequently encountered was in the lack of long-term controller medication use in patients experiencing persistent asthma. Upon further questioning, several common themes became apparent. Some were found not to have been prescribed a controller medication; some were prescribed one but could not afford the medication; and others actually had a long-term controller medication but did not understand the difference between his/her reliever and controller medications. Several approaches were implemented to overcome these barriers. Provider communication recommending appropriate medications was provided in cases where a patient lacked a long-term controller medication like an inhaled corticosteroid. Patient assistance programs were utilized in situations where patients could not afford the medications. Finally, continuous patient education about the differences in asthma medications was emphasized at each patient visit including personal medication records often with pictures of the differing medications on it.

- **What would be the best way a pharmacist could prepare himself or herself to implement asthma services in a community setting?**
  I think that having a well thought out business plan as well as ensuring that you are as knowledgeable as you can be regarding asthma education and the treatment options available. An easy way to be clinically ready is by reading the most up-to-date national asthma guidelines and by becoming a certified asthma educator. Many states' local American Lung Association chapters offer prep courses for the exam that can be extremely helpful in broadening or refreshing your understanding of the asthma disease process, education pearls, and medication and treatment plans. Another good idea is to review the prescription records of your patients with asthma and discover which prescribers are writing the majority of your asthma medications. Then, targeted outreach to those prescribers to gain their buy-in and preferably a collaborative practice agreement in place for asthma management in your pharmacy setting.

- **What are the most common interventions you provided to your patients with asthma?**
  The most commonly encountered intervention in this population was in ensuring that patient's were prescribed and taking a long-term controller medication if he/she had persistent asthma. This might require contacting the patient's provider and recommending one or prescribing one if a collaborative practice agreement existed. Often times this required helping a patient complete a patient assistance form for an inhaled corticosteroids and making sure that the provider completed his or her portion and then helping the patient understand how to acquire the medication and refills if approved. Another common intervention was in patient education about the types and purposes of each of the patient's asthma medication and in demonstrating and having the patient's demonstrate proper technique for those inhalers and peak flow meters.

- **How do you measure success in patient's asthma control?**
  Asthma is a disease state in which success can be achieved very quickly through adequate education and proper medication management. Patient success with asthma control is monitored subjectively through patient interviews at follow-up visits and objectively through pulmonary function testing. Success can be seen by symptom control, frequency (or lack thereof) of short-acting beta$_2$-agonist, ability to maintain or improve activities of daily living including physical activity, pulmonary function stability, frequency of asthma exacerbations requiring emergency department visits, and optimal medication management.

- **Has it been difficult to get buy-in from the local physicians in town? How do you overcome any challenges you may have faced?**
  Provider outreach prior to implementing services is of utmost importance. I would suggest running a report of asthma medications from your practice management system to reveal which prescribers are writing the majority of those prescriptions. Then, target your outreach to those prescribers to gain their buy-in and preferably a collaborative practice agreement in place for asthma management in your pharmacy setting. Frequent communication with these providers will also help. Faxing or mailing a brief description of the encounter with the plan is appreciated too. The service will often "sell itself" through patient testimonials to providers.

■ STUDY QUESTIONS

1. GB is a 42-year-old male with asthma, GERD, and hypertension. He states that he has increased the use of his albuterol inhaler before bedtime and notices it mostly after he eats later and larger meals than usual for business dinners. What should the pharmacist do?
   a. Increase his albuterol to scheduled nighttime use.
   b. Increase his maintenance ICS to high dose.
   c. Assess GERD symptoms and suggest nonpharmacologic or over-the-counter therapy.
   d. Immediately refer to asthma specialist since GB's asthma is no longer controlled.

2. The pharmacist's important contributions to the asthma management team include all of the following except:
   a. Gathering complete, updated medication histories.
   b. Performing comprehensive physical exams.
   c. Inhaler and device training.
   d. Environmental trigger education.

3. Good Friend Pharmacy has decided to offer asthma services. It employs an RN who currently markets all of the pharmacy's advanced services twice per week by visiting practitioner clinics. The pharmacy manager decides the RN will make appointments from referrals and make reminder calls the day before the appointments. They estimate she will spend 45 minutes per week making these calls and her current salary is $35 per hour. When pricing the asthma services, in which category would this expense be categorized?
   a. SAL.
   b. MAT.
   c. NDC.
   d. OHC.

4. Which of the following is the best asthma medication management recommendation?
   a. NS's asthma is SEVERELY uncontrolled. She needs ICS yesterday!!!!
   b. NS's asthma is classified as moderate persistent based on spirometry and patient reported symptoms. Consider increasing her ICS to high dose.
   c. NS is not doing well today. Please send prescription for Pulmicort®.
   d. NS's asthma classified as moderate persistent based on changes in spirometry, limitation of activities, and 3 times weekly nighttime awakenings. Consider changing QVAR® 80 μg 2 puffs bid to Advair Diskus® 250/50 μg 1 puff bid. Patient will return to pharmacy for follow-up in 1 month.

5. Which of the following statements best describes peak flow monitoring and spirometry?
   a. Peak flow monitoring is less reliable so spirometry should be the only method for assessing pulmonary function in asthmatic patients.
   b. Peak flow monitors produce PEFR and spirometry produces a plot of airflow versus time that indicates pulmonary function and provides FEV_1.
   c. Peak flow meters highly rely on patient effort while spirometry does not.
   d. Peak flow meters and spirometry essentially measure the same information; therefore, if a patient has one, the other is not necessary.

BIBLIOGRAPHY

1. National Health Interview Study. Centers for Disease Control and Prevention. 10 Jan 2012. http://www.cdc.gov/asthma/nhis/default.htm. Accessed July 2, 2012.
2. Cost of Asthma. Allergy and Asthma Foundation. http://aafa.org. Accessed July 3, 2012.
3. Asthma Control. Home-Based Multi-Trigger, Multicomponent Environmental Interventions. The Guide to Community Preventative Services. 27 June 2011. http://www.thecommunity guide.org /asthma/multicomponent.html. Accessed July 2, 2012.
4. Armour CL, Lemay K, Saini B, et al. Using the community pharmacy to identify patients at risk of poor asthma control and factors which contribute to this poor control. *J Asthma*. 2011;48(9):914-922.
5. Fink JB, Rubin BK. Problems with inhaler use: a call for improved clinician and patient education. *Respir Care*. 2005;50:1360-1374.
6. Giraud V, Roche N. Misuse of corticosteroid metered-dose inhaler is associated with decreased asthma stability. *Eur Respir J*. 2002;19:246-251.
7. Takemura M, Kobayashi M, Kimura K, et al. Repeated instruction on inhalation technique improves adherence to therapeutic regimen in asthma. *J Asthma*. 2010;47(2):202-208.
8. National Institutes of Health, National Heart, Lung, and Blood Institute. National Asthma Education and Prevention Program. Full Report of the Expert Panel: Guidelines for the Diagnosis and Management of Asthma (EPR-3); July 2007. *http://www.nhlbi.nih.gov/guidelines/asthma*. Accessed July 2, 2012.
9. Kelly HW, Sorkness CA. Asthma. In: Talbert RL, DiPiro JT, Matzke GR, Posey LM, Wells BG, Yee GC, eds. *Pharmacotherapy: A Pathophysiologic Approach*. 8th ed. New York, NY: McGraw-Hill; 2011:chap 33. http://www.accesspharmacy.com/content.aspx?aID=7975293. Accessed July 2 2012.

10. Busse WW, Lemanske RF Jr. Asthma. *N Engl J Med.* 2001;344:350-362.
11. Juniper EF, O'Byrne PM, Guyatt GH, et al. Development and validation of a questionnaire to measure asthma control. *Eur Respir J.* 1999b;14(4):902-907.
12. Vollmer WM, Markson LE, O'Connor E, et al. Association of asthma control with health care utilization and quality of life. *Am J Respir Crit Care Med.* 1999;160(5 Pt 1):1647-1652.
13. Nathan RA, Sorkness CA, Kosinski M, et al. Development of the Asthma Control Test: a survey for assessing asthma control. *J Allergy Clin Immunol.* 2004;113:817-825.
14. Peters JI, Levine SM. Introduction to pulmonary function testing. In: Talbert RL, DiPiro JT, Matzke GR, Posey LM, Wells BG, Yee GC, eds. *Pharmacotherapy: A Pathophysiologic Approach.* 8th ed. New York, NY: McGraw-Hill; 2011:chap 32. http://www.accesspharmacy.com/content.aspx?aID=7975195. Accessed July 2, 2012.
15. Jones MA. Asthma self-management patient education. *Respir Care.* 2008;53(6):778-784.
16. Bunting BA, Cranor CW. The Asheville Project: long-term clinical, humanistic, and economic outcomes of a community-based medication therapy management program for asthma. *J Am Pharm Assoc.* 2006; 46(2):133-147.
17. McLean WM, MacKeigan LD. When does pharmaceutical care impact health outcomes? A comparison of community pharmacy-based studies of pharmaceutical care for patients with asthma. *Ann Pharmacother.* 2005;39(4):625-631.
18. National Asthma Educator Certification Board Certified Asthma Educator (AE-C) Candidate Handbook. 2012. http://naecb.com/pdf/NAECBhandbook.pdf. Accessed July 2, 2012.
19. Rupp MT. Analyzing the cost of delivering value added pharmacy services. https://www.pharmaccount.com/pdf-bin/analyzing_cos.pdf. Accessed July 2, 2012.
20. American Lung Association. http://www.lung.org. Accessed July 3, 2012.
21. George M. You haven't taught until they have learned: adult learning and asthma self-management. *J Asthma Allergy Educ.* 2012;3(3):98.
22. Fanta CH, Carter EL, Stieb ES, Haver KE. *The Asthma Educator's Handbook.* New York: NY: McGraw-Hill; 1998.
23. Asthma and COPD. Healthy Interactions. Available at: http://www.healthyinteractions.com/conversation-map-programs/helping-manage-chronic-disease/asthma. Accessed July 3, 2012.
24. Sample Collaborative Practice Agreement-Asthma. Minnesota Pharmacists Association. http://www.mpha.org/displaycommon.cfm?an=1&subarticlenbr=7. Accessed July 3, 2012

APPENDIX 5A. ASTHMA MANAGEMENT PROTOCOL

(*clinic/pharmacy name here*)

Effective Date: (date)
Approved By: (prescribers listed here)
Supersedes: (if appropriate))
Review Date: (recommended yearly))

Patient Population

Patients referred by a provider with a diagnosis of asthma who are not adequately controlled will be co-managed by the clinical pharmacist or pharmacy resident following this protocol.

Medication Ordering

Clinical pharmacist or pharmacy resident may make changes in inhaled short/long-acting beta-agonists, ICS, and combination therapy of these inhaled agents (Appendix 5A-1). The clinical pharmacist and pharmacy resident, under this protocol, are authorized to initiate therapy, adjust dosages, change medication, and authorize refills to the listed agents. All modifications to therapy must follow the detailed protocol and will be documented in the medical record.

Lab Monitoring

Under this protocol, the clinical pharmacist or pharmacy resident will have the authority to order labs to assess treatment and to monitor for adverse events from the drug therapy.

What This Protocol Does Not Cover

- Nebulizer solutions, systemic beta-agonists and corticosteroids, methylxanthines, and leukotriene modifiers.
- Conditions other than asthma.
- If patient exhibits signs of respiratory distress with PEFs, or if the patient symptoms are felt to be severe (acute exacerbation requiring nebulizer treatment and/or prednisone), or less than 18 years of age.
- Smoking cessation counseling (patients will be referred to smoking cessation programs as necessary).

Clinical Pharmacist and Pharmacy Resident Responsibilities for Patients Who Fall Outside This Protocol

- If only labs are needed prior to a treatment decision, the pharmacist may order the labs.
- The referring or primary provider will be consulted before making changes to the medications.
- The clinical pharmacist or pharmacy resident will make medication changes as directed by provider and follow up with the patient as necessary until patient is stable or at goal for at least 6 months.
- The clinical pharmacist or pharmacy resident will refer patient back to primary physician with recommendation for specialist referral.
- The patient will see the primary provider at least yearly and more frequently if other acute problems arise.

INITIAL VISIT PROTOCOL

The patient's chart will be reviewed and the following information will be gathered and discussed (using the form in Appendix 5A-2) during the initial visit:

- Blood pressure and pulse.
- Complete medication history regarding asthma therapy and any medications that could affect asthma (e.g., beta-blockers).
- Asthma history: treatments, hospitalizations, ER/urgent care visits, and intubations secondary to asthma in the past year.
- Assess asthma symptoms (cough, wheeze, SOB, chest tightness), frequency of daytime symptoms and nighttime symptoms, early morning symptoms that do not respond within 15 minutes of short-acting beta-2 agonist, symptoms with exertion.
- Review or order spirometry if not done at diagnosis.
- Assess and classify severity of asthma (Appendix 5A-3).
- Asthma medications will be initiated, discontinued, or adjusted as needed according NHLBI guidelines (Appendix 5A-4, 5A-5, 5A-6, and 5A-7).
- Social history, characteristics of home, work/environmental exposure, functional status.

- Identify asthma triggers and educate on avoidance.
- Assess and educate MDI technique and compliance.
- Provide patients with moderate persistent and severe persistent asthma and those with a history of severe exacerbations with PEFM/diary (or a prescription for a PEFM) to determine personal best.
  - Personal best = best value from 2 weeks of PEF values when symptoms controlled, excluding outliers.
  - Once the personal best has been established, the patient will be instructed to monitor every morning.
    - If the patient PEFs are typically <80% personal best, they will be instructed to monitor more frequently.
  - If the patient is not compliant with PEF monitoring to determine personal best, the population average for their age and height will be used.
- Develop an individualized asthma action plan for those patients with moderate persistent and severe persistent asthma or those with a history of severe exacerbations, with written instructions for patients (follow protocol in Appendix 5A-1 and complete asthma action plan on epic-related link).
- Provide patient with patient education.
- Follow up within 1–4 weeks following initial visit.
- General guidelines to refer patient back to primary physician and asthma certified educator are as follows:
  - Patient exhibits signs of respiratory distress with PEFs or symptoms are felt to be severe (acute exacerbation requiring nebulizer treatment and/or prednisone).
  - Patient presents to appointment with a recent life-threatening exacerbation.
  - Patient is not meeting goals after 3–6 months of therapy or sooner if deemed necessary.
  - Asthma complicated by other medical or psychosocial conditions.

■ FOLLOW-UP VISIT PROTOCOL

Follow-up visits will be jointly established between primary care physician and clinical pharmacist or pharmacy resident. Follow-up appointments will be scheduled approximately every 1-6 months depending on severity of symptoms. The number of follow-up visits will be determined by the clinical pharmacist and pharmacy resident. Appendix 5A-8 will be used to gather information for follow-up visits.

Severity	Regular follow-up visit
Intermittent	6–12 months
Mild persistent	6 months
Moderate persistent	3 months
Severe persistent	1–2 months and as often as needed to establish control

Assess at follow-up:

- Obtain an updated medication history, including both asthma and nonasthma medications.
- Frequency of signs and symptoms of asthma, daytime, nighttime, morning, and symptoms not responsive in 15 minutes to beta-agonist.
- History of asthma exacerbations.
- Pharmacotherapy: effectiveness, adverse effects, compliance
  - Asthma medications will be initiated, discontinued, or adjusted as needed according to NHLBI guidelines (Appendix 5A-4, 5A-5, 5A-6, and 5A-7).
- Review and reinforce environment control strategies/trigger avoidance.
- MDI/spacer/peak flow meter technique.
- Obtain PEF in clinic and review PEF record from patient, if available, for personal best, and set up patient's zones based on PEF values taken for 2–3 weeks to create an asthma action plan.
- If the patient fails to bring in the PEF record, then an action plan will be created using the population average for their age and height.
- If the patient's asthma is never under good control and personal best cannot be determined, then an action plan will be created using the population average for their age and height.
- When developing action plans, home treatment with oral steroids will not be included unless discussed with and agreed upon by the patient's primary physician.

- General guidelines to refer patient back to primary physician and asthma certified educator are as follows:
  - Patient exhibits signs of respiratory distress with PEFs or symptoms are felt to be severe (acute exacerbation requiring nebulizer treatment and/or prednisone).
  - Patient presents to appointment with a recent life-threatening exacerbation.
  - Patient is not meeting goals after 3–6 months of therapy or sooner if deemed necessary.
  - Asthma complicated by other medical or psychosocial conditions.

■ APPENDIX 5A-1. MANAGEMENT OF ASTHMA EXACERBATIONS: HOME TREATMENT PROTOCOL

(Give patients the Asthma Action Plan) Figure 5-6

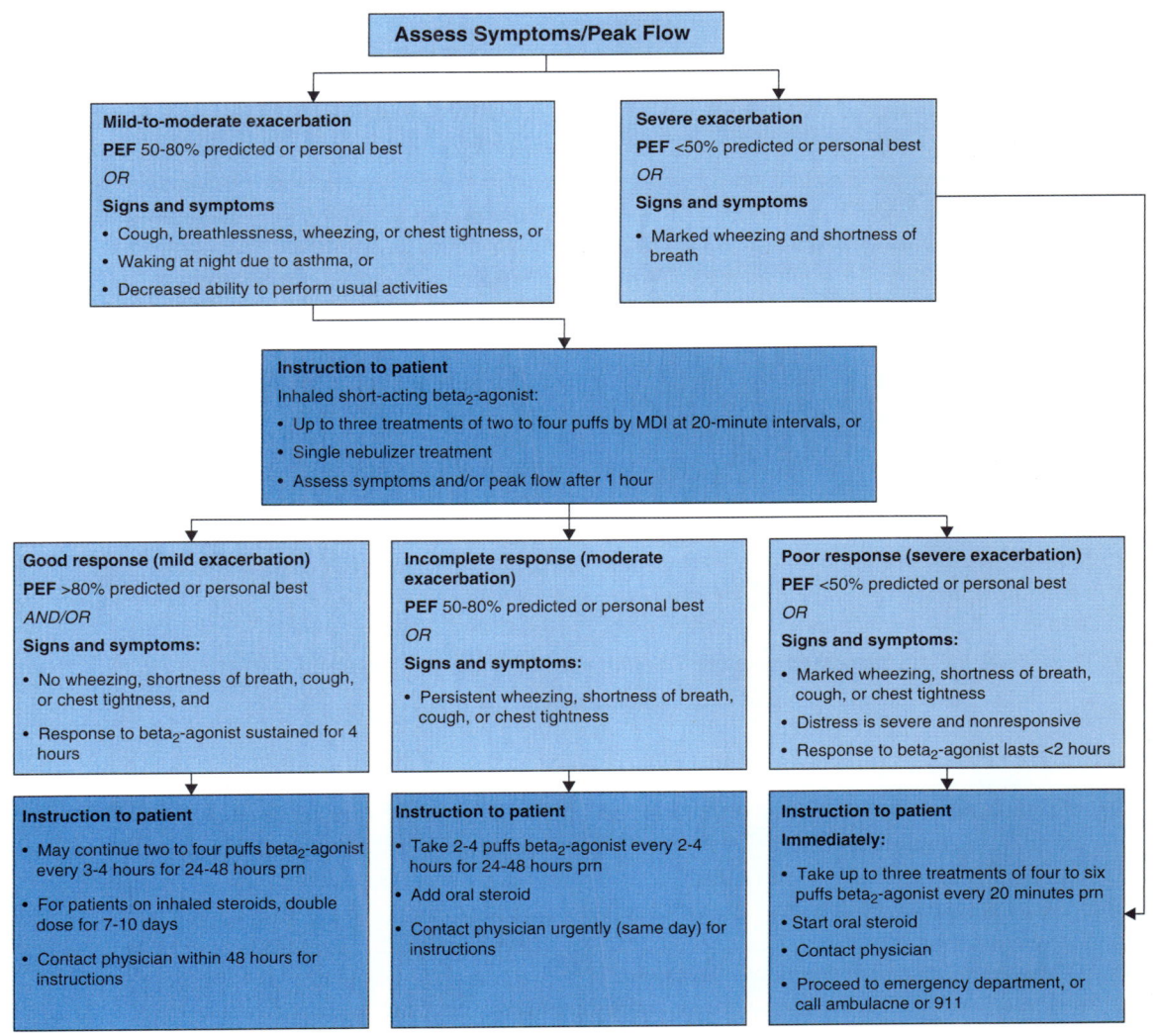

Figure 5-6. Home treatment protocol.

Adapted from NHLBI EPR3 guidelines.

[a]Patients at high risk for asthma-related death should receive immediate clinical attention after initial treatment. More intensive therapy may be required.

[b]Oral steroid dosages: 40-60 mg, single or 2 divided doses for 3-10 days (this medication falls outside of this protocol, see p. 1)

Date protocol begins: _____

Date protocol ends: _____

The undersigned hereby certify approval of and agreement with this written protocol:

_____ Date _____

_____

(list prescribers here)

_____ Date _____

_____

■ APPENDIX 5A-2. ASTHMA HISTORY WORKUP

1. Symptoms: Cough, wheezing, shortness of breath, and chest tightness
   - Frequency (past 2–4 weeks):

Daytime:	≤2×/week	>2×/week but <1×/day	Daily	Continuously
Nighttime:	≤2×/month	>2×/month	<1×/week	Frequent

2. Morning symptoms that don't respond to rescue inhaler within 15 minutes? YES/NO
   - Pattern: Spring, summer, fall, winter, and anytime of year
   - Triggers (circle all that apply):

   Outdoors (i.e., pollen)   Indoors (i.e., dust mites and mold)
   Cold air   Emotions (i.e., fear, anger, frustration, hard crying, or laughing)
   Strong odors   Occupation (weekday only symptoms, not on weekends)
   Animals (cat/dog)   Exercise/physical activity
   Smoke   Drugs (beta-blockers, ASA, NSAIDs)
   Foods (i.e., sulfites-processed potatoes, shrimp beer wine, and dried fruit)
   Others _____

3. Characteristics of home (circle all that apply):

   Carpeting   Old home/mold   A lot of upholstery/stuffed furniture
   Humidifier   Wood-burning stove/fireplace Stuffed animals on sleeping area

4. Does anyone smoke in the home (tobacco, other inhaled substances that produce fumes)? YES/NO
5. Do you smoke? YES/NO
   - If yes, how much per day? _____
6. Are you willing to quit at this time? YES/NO
7. Workplace characteristics that may interfere with compliance? _____

8. Have you ever gone to the emergency department for an asthma attack? YES/NO
   - If yes, how many times in the last 6 months? _____
9. Have you ever been hospitalized for asthma? YES/NO
   - How many times? _____ Intubated? YES/NO
10. How many days of work have you missed in the past 3 months due to asthma? _____
11. Does your asthma limit your activities? YES/NO
    - If yes, how? _____
12. Have you used any medications that help you breathe better? YES/NO
    - Name of medication (inhalers/pills, prescriptions/OTC): _____
13. What other medication have you used for asthma? _____
14. On average, how many times a day do you need to use your "quick-relief" inhaler (albuterol, Ventolin, Proventil, or Xopenex)? _____
    - How many puffs do you use each time? 1, 2, and >2
    - How many inhalers (canisters) of this medicine have you gone through in the past month? _____
15. Has your asthma medicine caused you any problems? YES/NO
    - If yes, what problems? Shakiness, nervousness, bad taste, sore throat, cough, upset stomach, fast heartbeat, or other _____
    - Which medication caused this problem? _____
16. Are there any other factors that may affect your ability or desire to take your medications as directed?
    _____
    _____
17. What worries you most about your asthma? _____
18. What do you want to accomplish at the visit? _____
19. What do you expect from treatment? _____
    _____

For staff use:

Asthma Severity Classification (circle)

Intermittent   **Mild Persistent**   **Moderate Persistent**   **Severe Persistent**

☐ Peak flow technique
☐ MDI technique
☐ Reviewed action plan: ☐ Daily medication ☐ Emergency medication

APPENDIX 5A-3. ASTHMA CLASSIFICATION SCHEME: BASED ON CLINICAL FEATURES BEFORE TREATMENT[a]

	Symptoms[b]	Nighttime Symptoms	Lung Function[c]
Step 4: Severe Persistent	• Continual symptoms • Limited physical activity • Frequent exacerbations	Frequent	• FEV_1 or PEFR $\leq 60\%$ of personal best • PEFR variability $\geq 30\%$
Step 3: Moderate Persistent	• Daily symptoms • Daily use of short-acting inhaled beta-agonist • Exacerbations affect activity • Exacerbations $\geq 2\times$/week; may last days	$>1\times$/week	• FEV_1 or PEFR 60–80% of personal best • PEFR variability $\geq 30\%$
Step 2: Mild Persistent	• Symptoms $>2\times$/week but $<1\times$/day • Exacerbations may affect activity	$>2\times$/month	• FEV_1 or PEFR $\geq 80\%$ of personal best • PEFR variability 20–30%
Step 1: Intermittent	• Symptoms $\leq 2\times$/week • Asymptomatic and normal PEF between exacerbations • Exacerbations brief (from a few hours to a few days); intensity may vary	$\leq 2\times$/month	• FEV_1 or PEFR $\geq 80\%$ of personal best • PEFR variability $\leq 20\%$

Adapted from the NHLBI EPR3 guidelines.

[a] The presence of one of the features of severity is sufficient to place a patient in that category. An individual should be assigned to the most severe grade in which any feature occurs. The characteristics noted in this figure are general and may overlap because asthma is highly variable. Furthermore, an individual's classification may change over time.

[b] Patients at any level of severity can have mild, moderate, or severe exacerbations. Some patients with intermittent asthma experience severe and life-threatening exacerbations separated by long periods of normal lung function and no symptoms.

[c] PEF is % of personal best. FEV_1 is % of predicted.

APPENDIX 5A-4. STEPWISE APPROACH FOR MANAGING ASTHMA IN ADULTS

Step 6	**Refer to Primary Care Provider**
Step 5	**Refer to Primary Care Provider**
Step 4: Severe Persistent	**Preferred Treatment:** • Medium- or high-dose ICS **AND/OR** • Leukotriene modifier[a] or theophylline[a] • Long-acting inhaled beta-2 agonist (should only be used if inhaled steroids alone do not control asthma) Recommended for uncontrolled asthma: oral corticosteroids[a]
Step 3: Moderate Persistent	**Preferred Treatment:** • Low- or medium-dose ICS **Alternatives:** • Medium-dose ICS and either leukotriene modifier,[a] theophylline,[a] or oral long-acting beta-2 agonist (should only be used if inhaled steroids alone do not control asthma) • Long-acting inhaled beta-2 agonist (should only be used if inhaled steroids alone do not control asthma)
Step 2: Mild Persistent	**Preferred Treatment:** • Low-dose ICS **Alternatives:** • Cromolyn, nedocromil, leukotriene modifier,[a] OR sustained release theophylline[a] (5–15 μg/mL)
Step 1: Intermittent	• No daily medications needed
All Patients	• Short-acting inhaled beta-2 agonist 2–4 puffs prn symptoms. • Depending on severity of exacerbation, up to 3 treatments at 20-minute intervals.

Step Down: Review treatment every 1–6 months. If control is sustained for ≥3 months, a gradual step reduction in treatment may be attempted.

Step Up: If control not achieved, consider step up in treatment. First review medication technique, adherence, and environmental control (avoidance of allergens or other factors that contribute to asthma severity). Use of short-acting bronchodilators >2 times/week (mild intermittent) or daily/increasing use (persistent asthma) may indicate the need for step-up therapy or initiate maintenance therapy.

Education:

Step 1:
- Teach basic facts about asthma
- Teach inhaler/spacer/holding chamber techniques
- Discuss role of medications

(Continued)

(Continued)

- Develop self-management plan
- Develop action plan for when and how to take rescue actions, especially for patients with a history of severe exacerbations
- Discuss appropriate environmental control measures to avoid exposure to known allergens and irritants

Step 2:
- Teach self-monitoring
- Refer to group education
- Review and update self-management plan

Step 3:
- Refer to individual education/training

Adapted from the NHLBI EPR3 guidelines.
[a]The clinical pharmacist and pharmacy resident will carry out any asthma treatment order the physician makes based on the recommendation(s) made.

■ APPENDIX 5A-5. COMPARATIVE DAILY DOSAGES OF INHALED CORTICOSTEROIDS

Drug	Low Dose	Medium Dose	High Dose
Beclomethasone CFC	168–504 μg	504–840 μg	>840 μg
42 μg/puff	(4–12 puffs)	(12–20 puffs)	(>20 puffs)
84 μg/puff	(2–6 puffs)	(6–10 puffs)	(>10 puffs)
Beclomethasone HFA	80–240 μg	240–640 μg	>480 μg
40 μg/puff	(2–6 puffs)	(6–12 puffs)	(>12 puffs)
80 μg/puff	(1–3 puffs)	(3–6 puffs)	(>6 puffs)
Budesonide DPI	200–600 μg	600–1,200 μg	>1,200 μg
200 μg/puff	(1–3 puffs)	(3–6 puffs)	(>6 puffs)
Flunisolide	500–1,000 μg	1,000–2,000 μg	>2,000 μg
250 μg/puff	(2–4 puffs)	(4–8 puffs)	(>8 puffs)
Fluticasone			
MDI	88–264 μg	264–660 μg	>660 μg
44 μg/puff	(2–6 puffs)	(6–15 puffs)	(>15 puffs)
110 μg/puff	(2 puffs)	(2–6 puffs)	(>6 puffs)
220 μg/puff	100–300 μg	(2–3 puffs)	(>3 puffs)
DPI	(2–6 puffs)	300–600 μg	>600 μg
50 μg/puff		(3–6 puffs)	(>6 puffs)
100 μg/puff			(>2 puffs)
250 μg/puff			

(Continued)

(Continued)

Drug	Low Dose	Medium Dose	High Dose
Mometasone Furoate **DPI** 220 µg/puff	220 µg (1 puff)	220–440 µg (1–2 puffs)	440–880 µg (2–4 puffs)
Combination Product **Fluticasone/Salmeterol** **DPI**	100/50 µg (1 puff q12 hours)	250/50 µg (1 puff q12 hours)	500/50 µg (1 puff q12 hours)
Combination Product **Budesonide/Formoterol** **MDI**	80/4.5 µg (1–2 puffs q12 hours)	160/4.5 µg (1–2 puffs q12 hours)	

Adapted from the NHLBI EPR3 guidelines.

Notes:
- The most important determinant of appropriate dosing is the clinical pharmacist's and pharmacy resident's judgment of the patient's response to therapy.
- The clinical pharmacist and pharmacy resident will monitor the patient's response on several clinical parameters and adjust the dose accordingly.
- The stepwise approach to therapy emphasizes that once control of asthma is achieved, the dose of medication should be carefully titrated to the minimum dose required to maintain control, thus reducing the potential for adverse effect.

■ APPENDIX 5A-6. USUAL ADULT DOSAGES FOR QUICK-RELIEF MEDICATIONS

Drug	Dose	Comments
Albuterol **MDI** 90 µg/puff **DPI** 200 µg/puff **For Nebulization**[a] 5 mg/mL (0.5%)	2 puffs 5 minutes before exercise 1–2 capsules q4–6 hours PRN and before exercise 1.25–5 mg (0.25–1 mL) in 2–3 mL of saline q4–8 hours)	*May double dose for mild exacerbations* *May mix with cromolyn or ipratropium nebulizer solutions*
Albuterol HFA 90 µg/puff	2 puffs 5 minutes before exercise	*May double dose for mild exacerbations*
Bitolterol **MDI** 370 µg/puff **For Nebulization**[a] 2 mg/mL (0.2%)	2 puffs tid-qid prn 0.5–3.5 mg (0.25–1 mL) in 2–3 cc of saline q4–8 hours	*May not mix with other nebulizer solutions*

(Continued)

(Continued)

Drug	Dose	Comments
Levalbuterol Nebulization[a] 0.63 mg/3 mL 11.25 mg/3 mL	0.63–1.25 mg tid	Routine dosing should not exceed 0.63 mg tid
Anticholinergics		
Ipratropium **MDI** 18 µg/puff **For Nebulization**[a] 0.25 mg/mL (0.025%)	2–3 puffs q6 hours, max dose of 12 puffs per 24 hours 0.25–0.5 mg q6 hours	Evidence is lacking for anticholinergic producing added benefit to beta-2 agonists in long-term asthma therapy
Tiotropium 18 µg/capsule	Inhale 1 capsule qd	
Systemic Corticosteroids[a]		
Methylprednisolone 2, 4, 8, 16, 32 mg	Short course "burst": 40–60 mg/day as single or 2 divided doses for 3–10 days	Short course or "burst" are effective for establishing control when initiating therapy or during a period of gradual deterioration
Prednisolone 5 mg tab, 5 mg/5 mL, 15 mg/5 mL		
Prednisone 1, 2.5, 5, 10, 20, 25 mg tabs; 5 mg/mL; 5 mg/5 mL		

Adapted from the NHLBI EPR3 guidelines.

[a] The clinical pharmacist and pharmacy resident will carry out any asthma treatment order the physician makes based on the recommendation(s) made.

APPENDIX 5A-7. USUAL ADULT DOSAGES FOR LONG-TERM MEDICATIONS

Drug	Dose	Comments
Long-Acting Beta-2 Agonists[a]		
Salmeterol DPI 50 μg/blister	1 blister q12 hours	
Formoterol Fumarate DPI 12 μg/dose (single-use capsule by inhalation)	1 capsule by inhalation bid	
Fluticasone/Salmeterol DPI 100/50 μg, 250/50μg, 500/50μg	1 puff bid	FDA approved for children 12 years of age and older
Sustained-Release Albuterol Tablet 4 mg/tablet	4 mg q12 hours	
Methylxanthines[a]		
Theophylline Liquid, sustain-release tablets, capsules	Starting dose 10 mg/kg/day up to 300 mg max; usual max 800 mg/day	Adjust dosage to achieve serum concentration of 5-15 μg/mL at a steady state (at least 48 hours on same dosage).
Leukotriene Modifiers[a]		
Montelukast 4 mg granules, 10 mg tablet 4 mg, 5 mg chewable tablet	10 mg qhs	
Zafirlukast 10 mg, 20 mg tablet	40 mg daily (20 mg bid)	Administration with meals decreases bioavailability; take at least 1 hour before or 2 hours after meals.
Zileuton 600 mg tablet	2,400 mg daily (one 600 mg table, qid)	Monitor hepatic enzymes (ALT)

Adapted from the NHLBI EPR3 guidelines.

[a]The clinical pharmacist and pharmacy resident will carry out any asthma treatment order the physician makes based on the recommendation(s) made.

APPENDIX 5A-8. ASTHMA FOLLOW-UP WORKUP

1. Since your last visit:
   - Has your asthma been any worse? YES/NO
   - Any changes in home or work environment? YES/NO (i.e., smoke and new pet)
   - Any exacerbations? YES/NO
     - ER visits? YES/NO
     - Hospitalized? YES/NO
     - Intubated? YES/NO
   - Missed work due to asthma? YES/NO
     - If yes, how much? _____
   - Have you missed any doses of your medications? YES/NO
     - If yes, how much? _____
     - How often? _____
     - Why? _____
   - How and when are you taking your asthma medications?
     _____
     _____
     _____
   - Has your asthma medicine caused you any problems? YES/NO
     - If yes, (circle) Shakiness, nervousness, bad taste, sore throat, cough, upset stomach, fast heartbeat, or other_____
     - Which medication caused this problem? _____
   - What questions do you have about the action plan? _____
2. In the past 2 weeks:
   - Has your peak flow value gone below 80% of your personal best? YES/NO
   - How many days have you used your quick-relief medicine? _____
   - Has your asthma limited your activities? YES/NO
     - If yes, how? _____
3. Describe for me how you know when to call your doctor or go to the hospital for asthma care?
   _____
   _____

For staff use:
☐ Peak flow technique
☐ MDI technique
☐ Reviewed action plan: ☐ Daily medication ☐ Emergency medication

6

IMMUNIZATION SERVICES

Emily Weidman-Evans and Brice L. Mohundro

> ### ■ LEARNING OBJECTIVES
>
> After reading this chapter, the pharmacy student, community practice resident, or pharmacist should be able to:
>
> 1. Describe the rationale for offering immunizations in a pharmacy setting.
> 2. Evaluate an individual patient's need for vaccines, based on his or her specific history.
> 3. Analyze the business management aspects needed to create and maintain immunization services in a community pharmacy setting, including the initial development of the service, marketing, documentation, and reimbursement.

INTRODUCTION

The advent and routine administration of vaccines are perhaps the biggest advancement ever experienced in public health. In the 20th century, the average number of reported cases of measles in the United States exceeded 530,000 annually.[1] This disease leads to many complications, including diarrhea, otitis media, and pneumonia. It can also result in encephalitis, seizures, and death in a small proportion of patients.[2] The vaccine for measles was licensed in 1963. In 2010, there were 61 cases reported.[1] Cases of mumps decreased from an annual average of over 162,000 cases through the 20th century to 2,528 in 2010. Similar decreases are seen in nearly all vaccine-preventable diseases after the advent of vaccines and widespread immunization. There were zero reported cases of smallpox, diphtheria, and paralytic polio in 2010. Newer vaccines have also led to significant decreases in annual cases since becoming routine. In comparison with the pre-vaccine era, varicella cases decreased by 89%, hepatitis B by 83%, hepatitis A by 91%, and invasive peumococcal disease in children (5 years of age) by 74% in 2008. Hospitalizations and ER visits due to rotavirus decreased by 88%, resulting in an estimated cost savings to the healthcare system of $278 million in 2008-2009 alone.[3]

Clearly, immunizations are vital for improving public health and decreasing healthcare costs. They work by provoking an immune response after vaccination similar to having the actual infection, and greatly minimize the possible complications.[4] The different characteristics of vaccines (such as live versus inactivated, route of administration, and presence of adjuvant ingredients, to name a few) determine how they are used and dosed, but their underlying mechanisms are the same: provoke active immunity against the natural disease, allowing the recipient to fight it off when exposed later.

The details of vaccine science or all vaccine-preventable diseases are beyond the scope of this chapter. Rather, this chapter will focus on the pharmacist's role in vaccine delivery and the establishment of a community pharmacy-based immunization service. There are many resources and references for more detailed information on the actual vaccines and diseases, some of which are listed at the end of the chapter.

Pharmacists and Immunizations

Pharmacists have served varying roles related to vaccines dating as far back as the 1800s.[5] In 1993, DHHS officially recognized that pharmacists were able to assist in the areas of immunization education, distribution, access/administration, and registries/tracking systems. In 1994, the first organized formal immunization training for pharmacists took place in Seattle, Washington. A year later, about nine states allowed pharmacists to administer vaccines under a protocol or collaborative practice agreement. In 2006, that was up to 44 states[6], and today pharmacists have the authority to administer vaccines in all 50 states and the District of Columbia.[7] When pharmacists are in the role of vaccine administrator, the impact on vaccination rates has been shown to increase, although studies truly quantifying the impact are hard to conduct. Between 1995 and 1999, patients aged 65 years and greater living in states where pharmacists could provide vaccines had significantly higher rates of influenza vaccines than those living in states where pharmacists could not.[8] One study of a large pharmacy database showed that high-risk patients receiving an influenza vaccine by a pharmacist were more likely to also receive their pneumococcal vaccine than in "usual care" settings.[9]

Even when not administering vaccines, pharmacists' direct involvement in promoting immunizations has been proven beneficial. Patients encouraged in a mailing from their community pharmacist to be immunized were 74% more likely to do so than those who were not.[10] Furthermore, influenza vaccination rates of high-risk patients nearly doubled when pharmacists in a rural clinic performed chart reviews and made recommendations regarding influenza vaccine.[11] While the impact on vaccination rates has not been studied, 30% of pharmacists responding to a 2001 survey also reported facilitating nurse-administered vaccines in their community pharmacies.[12] Pharmacists can also help to educate patients on the importance of receiving vaccinations and in dispelling many of the concerns surrounding vaccines that may dissuade people from getting them (Table 6-1).

Table 6-1. Common Concerns About Vaccines

The Concern	The Facts
Vaccines cause autism	The incidence of autism spectrum disorder has been steadily increasing in recent decades. However, several large studies have concluded that there is no relationship between vaccines (including those containing thimerosal) and autism. Unfortunately, autism rates have continued to increase since 2001 (when thimerosal was removed from childhood vaccines).[13,14]
Vaccines cause sudden infant death syndrome (SIDS)	Several large studies have concluded that there is no relationship between any vaccines and SIDS. Since the 1992 recommendations to place infants to sleep on their backs, the incidence of SIDS has actually decreased dramatically, even though the number of infant vaccines has increased.[15,16]
Vaccnes contain many ingredients that can be harmful, especially in children	Vaccines contain the antigen (inactivated or weakened form of the virus or bacteria) plus several additives, some of which sound scary:[17] • Aluminum (gels or salts) IS used in many vaccines to increase the body's immune response and allows for smaller amounts of the antigen to be used. There is no evidence of harm from this adjuvant. • Formaldehyde is used to detoxify or inactivate certain toxins or viruses, and a small amount IS left in the vaccine. This amount is safe, though, and is generally no more than what is contained in other household products (paper towels, mascara, carpeting). • Antibiotics ARE used to prevent contamination of many vaccines. Trace amounts may cause allergic reactions in those who are allergic, but this rarely occurs. • Antifreeze (ethylene glycol) is NOT contained in any vaccine. This is often confused with propylene glycol, which is used to inactivate the virus or bacteria. Propylene glycol is also found in many cosmetic and health items, such as toothpaste and lotions (including baby lotion). • Mercury is a component of thimerosal, a preservative. Thimerosal is no longer contained in ANY childhood vaccines, EXCEPT some influenza that comes from a multidose vial.
Too many vaccines are given at the same time to children	The CDC recommends vaccination against 16 diseases for children, all of which require 2 or more doses. While the discomfort of multiple and frequent injections is stressful for children and parents alike, there is no evidence that this can "overload" the immune system or cause any long-term effects. The immune system handles many hundreds of bacteria and viruses each day.[15,16]

(Continued)

Table 6-1.	Common Concerns About Vaccines (*Continued*)
The Concern	**The Facts**
Vaccines cause neurological conditions, including seizures	• Febrile seizures are fairly common in young children, and vaccines actually prevent many of the conditions that lead to high enough fevers to cause them. However, it is believed that certain vaccines (specifically, influenza and pneumococcal conjugate simultaneously) may very slightly increase the risk (by 1 additional seizure per 2,225 children vaccinated with the combination).[16] • Currently available data suggests a small increased risk of Guillain-Barre syndrome following immunization with meningococcal vaccine. As of 2008, there had been 26 cases reported within 6 weeks of receiving the vaccine (of the 15 million doses distributed), indicating this is a very rare adverse effect, if there is any association at all.[16] • Several large epidemiological studies suggest no relationship between hepatitis B vaccine and multiple sclerosis.[15,16]
Vaccines are derived from aborted fetuses	Some vaccines (varicella, rubella, hepatitis A) involve growing viruses in human cell culture. The cell cultures are derived from two human cell lines that came from two (legally) aborted fetuses in the 1960s. The cell lines have an indefinite life span, but no additional fetal tissue has been added or used since the original. No further abortions are necessary to maintain the culture of these vaccine products.[18]

VACCINE OVERVIEW

Tables 6-2, 6-3, and 6-4 contain information related to the specific vaccines that a pharmacist may be administering, and contains the information necessary to help a patient determine which vaccines they need. Note that the "Schedule" information assumes that they have not missed any doses and are currently on-schedule. If not, there are catch-up schedules available at the Centers for Disease Control and Prevention (CDC) Web site, to allow patients to get the optimal doses in minimal time. Also of importance is the fact that recommended vaccines schedules and indications are subject to change, so the official vaccine schedules should be consulted.

TIP: There are minimum intervals in between doses of most vaccines. Doses given inside of that interval do not count, and must be given again!

In order to know which vaccines a patient should receive, they must know what they have already had. Encourage patients to keep a vaccine record with them, especially if your state does not have a mandated central documentation database. If you are helping a patient determine what vaccines are needed and they do not have any record of receiving the vaccine (after checking multiple times), the rule of thumb is, "When in doubt, vaccinate."

TIP: Live injectable vaccines must be separated from blood products (interval varies by type). Live vaccines (but NOT inactivated) must also be separated from each other by at least 28 days. However, they can be given simultaneously (on the same day).

PLANNING YOUR SERVICE

Legal Issues

Prior to developing an immunization service in the community pharmacy, it is imperative to research the current legislation in your state to determine what a

Table 6-2. Adult Immunizations[19,20,21]

Vaccine	Signs/Symptoms	Scheduling	Contraindications/Precautions	Components	Administration	Adverse Reactions	Availability	Storage
Influenza (TIV or LAIV)	Sudden fever (ordinarily 101°–102°F), myalgia (typically affecting back muscles), sore throat, nonproductive cough, and headache	Annually for all persons over the age of six months	*TIV* Severe allergic reaction (anaphylaxis) to a component of the vaccine Severe allergic reaction following a prior dose Moderate/Severe acute illness History of Guillain Barre' syndrome within six weeks following previous dose *LAIV* Children <2 yo Persons ≥50 yo Persons with chronic medical conditions Children and adolescents receiving long-term aspirin therapy	Influenza type A (H1N1), type A (H3N2), and type B Residual egg protein	*TIV* 0.5 mL IM 0.1 mL intradermal *LAIV* 0.2 mL intranasal	*TIV* Local reactions Fever/malaise Immediate hypersensitivity (rare) *LAIV* Cough, runny nose, nasal congestion, sore throat, and chills	*TIV* Suspensions for IM injection: Afluria Fluarix FluLaval Fluvirin Fluzone ªFluzone High-dose Suspensions for intradermal injection: Fluzone Intradermal *LAIV* FluMist Intranasal Spray	*TIV* Do not freeze Store in refrigerator temperature (35°–46°F [2°–8°C]) *LAIV* Store in refrigerator Accidental freezing: place in refrigerator and use as soon as possible
Tetanus, Diptheria, Pertussis (Tdap)	**Tetanus** Trismus (lockjaw), neck stiffness, difficulty swallowing, and abdominal muscle rigidity	One time dose of Tdap and then Td booster every ten years	Severe allergic reaction to vaccine component or following a previous dose Moderate or severe illness	Tetanus toxoid, diphtheria toxoid, acellular pertussis	*TdapandTd* 0.5 mL per IM dose	Local reactions (erythema, tenderness, and injection site induration)	*Tdap* Adacel Boostrix *Td* Decavac Diphtheria & Tetanus Toxoids, Adult	Do not freeze (discard if frozen) Store in refrigerator temperature (35°–46°F [2°–8°C])
Tetanus, diphteria (Td)								

(Continued)

Table 6-2. Adult Immunizations (Continued)

Vaccine	Signs/Symptoms	Scheduling	Contraindications/ Precautions	Components	Administration	Adverse Reactions	Availability	Storage
	Diphtheria Exudative pharyngitis, exudate spreads within 2–3 days and may form bluish-white, adherent membrane possibly leading to respiratory obstruction, fever not high but exhaustion, pallor, rapid pulse, stupor, and coma may occur **Pertussis** Runny nose, sneezing, low-grade fever, and a mild, occasional cough (similar to a cold), cough gradually becomes more severe, numerous, rapid coughs, with a long inspiratory effort usually with a high-pitched whoop, cyanosis may occur							
Zoster	Vesicular eruptions in unilaterally distribution of a sensory nerve, usually involving the trunk or fifth cranial nerve Two to four days before eruption, pain and paresthesia may occur	Single dose for adults ≥60 yo with or without prior episode of herpes zoster	Severe allergic reaction to vaccine component or following a prior dose Immunosuppression from any cause (high does steroid) Pregnancy or planned pregnancy within 4 weeks Moderate or severe acute illness Current treatment with acyclovir, famciclovir, or valacyclovir	Varicella Neomycin Hydrolyzed gelatin	0.65 mL SQ	Local reactions (erythema, pain or tenderness, and swelling)	Herpes zoster vaccine (Zostavax)	Freeze at an average temperature of −15°C (5°F) or colder until reconstituted May be stored and/or transported at refrigerator temperature between 2°C and 8°C (36°F and 46°F) for up to 72 continuous hours prior to reconstitution

Vaccine	Disease/Symptoms	Indications	Contraindications/Precautions	Dose/Route	Adverse Reactions	Brand	Storage
Human papilloma virus (HPV)	Viruses associated with cervical, anal and genital cancers as well as genital warts and laryngeal papillomas	*Females:* Recommended for 13–26 yo if not vaccinated previously or who have not completed the series. May be administered after age 26 to complete series. *Males:* 3-dose series of quadravalent HPV vaccine may be given to ages 9–26. Doses should be given at 0, 2, and 6 months	Anaphylaxis to vaccine component or following a prior dose. Pregnancy. Vaccination should be deferred in those with moderate or severe acute illness until symptoms of acute illness improve	0.5 mL IM	Local reactions, fever	Cervarix (HPV 2) Gardasil (HPV 4)	Do not freeze (discard if frozen). Store in refrigerator: temperature (35°–46°F [2°–8°C])
						HPV4 Types 6, 11, 16, and 18 sodium chloride, L-histidine, polysorbate 80, and sodium borate *HPV2* Types 16 and 18, 3-O-desacyl-4′-monophosphoryl lipid A (MPL), and aluminum hydroxide, sodium chloride, and sodium dihydrogen phosphate dihydrate			
Pneumococcal polysaccharide (PPSV)	Sudden onset of fever, rigors, pleuritic chest pain, productive cough, dyspnea, tachypnea, and hypoxia	≥65 yo. ≥2 yo with chronic illness[b]. >2 yo immunocompromised at increased risk of pneumococcal disease or complications. >19 yo with asthma or who are smokers. Revaccination: Persons ≥65 yo if they received the vaccine more than 5 years previously, and were younger than 65 yo at time of first dose. Persons at high risk of severe infection (5 years after 1st dose)	Anaphylaxis to vaccine component or following a prior dose. Vaccination should be deferred in those with moderate or severe acute illness until symptoms of acute illness improve	0.5 mL IM or SQ injection	Pain, swelling, or erythema at the site of injection	Pneumovax 23	Store in refrigerator: temperature (35°–46°F [2°–8°C])
						Purified preparations of 23 types of pneumococcal capsular polysaccharide Phenol			

(Continued)

Table 6-2. Adult Immunizations (Continued)

Vaccine	Signs/Symptoms	Scheduling	Contraindications/Precautions	Components	Administration	Adverse Reactions	Availability	Storage
Pneumococcal Conjugate (PCV)	See above.	Adults ≥19 years with immunocompromising conditions, functional or anatomic asplenia, cerebrospinal fluid (CSF) leaks, or cochlear implants Ideally, give 8 weeks BEFORE first dose of PPSV, or at least one year after.	See above.	Purified preparation of 13 types of pneumococcal capsular polysaccharide conjugated to a nontoxic variant of diphtheria toxin Phenol	0.5 mL IM or SQ injection	Pain, swelling, or redness at injection site Decreased appetite or irritability	Prevnar 13	Do not freeze(discard if frozen) Store in refrigerator: temperature (35°–46°F [2°–8°C])
Meningococcal conjugate (MCV4)/ Meningococcal Polysaccharide (MPSV4)	Sudden onset of fever, headache, and stiff neck. Sometimes along with nausea, vomiting and photophobia, and altered mental status	Recommended for all unvaccinated adults at risk for meningococcal disease^c	Anaphylaxis to vaccine component or following a prior dose Moderate or severe acute illness	**Menactra(MCV4)** *N. meningitidis* serogroups A, C, Y and W-135 capsular polysaccharide antigens conjugated to diphtheria toxoid protein Sodium phosphate buffered isotonic sodium chloride **Menveo(MCV4)** Meningococcal serogroup A capsular polysaccharide conjugated to CRM197 (MenA) capsular polysaccharide of serogroup C, Y, and W135 conjugated to CRM197 Phosphate buffered saline **Menomune(MPSV4)** Meningococcal serogroup A, C, Y & W-135	Healthy persons ≥16 yo receiving their first dose do not need a booster dose **Revaccinate every 5 years if person remains at increased risk	Pain and redness at injection site Headache, malaise	Menactra Menveo Menomune (reserved for >55 yo)	Menactra/Menveo Do not freeze (discard if frozen) Store in refrigerator: temperature (35°–46°F [2°–8°C])

Disease	Symptoms	Recommended for	Contraindications	Vaccine components	Dose	Side effects	Brand names	Storage
Hepatitis B Virus (HBV)	Sudden onset of malaise, anorexia, nausea, vomiting, right upper quadrant abdominal pain, fever, headache, myalgia, skin rashes, arthralgia and arthritis, and dark urine followed by jaundice one to two days later	Recommended for all unvaccinated adults at risk for HBV infection[d] and those requesting protection from HBV infection Two doses 4 weeks apart and a third dose 4 to 6 months after the second dose	Anaphylaxis to vaccine component or following a prior dose Moderate or severe acute illness	Recombinant HBsAg Aluminum hydroxyphosphate sulfate (Recombivax HB) Aluminum hydroxide, trace thimerosal (Engerix-B)	**Recombivax HB** 1 mL (10 mcg) IM **Engerix-B** 1 mL (20 mcg) IM	Injection site reaction Mild systemic complaints	Recombivax HB (adult formulation) Engerix-B (adult formulation)	Do not freeze (discard if frozen) Store in refrigerator: temperature (35°–46°F [2°–8°C]) Freezing may decrease potency
Hepatitis A	Sudden onset of fever, malaise, anorexia, nausea, abdominal discomfort, dark urine, jaundice	Adults ≥19 years First dose and then booster 6 to 12 months later	Anaphylaxis to vaccine component or following a prior dose Hypersensitivity to alum or 2-phenoxyethanol	Inactivated whole-virus hepatitis A 2-phenoxyethanol (Havrix) Vaqta has no preservative	1 mL dose given IM	Injection site reaction Mild systemic complaints	Havrix Vaqta	Do not freeze (discard if frozen) Store in refrigerator: temperature (35°–46°F [2°–8°C]) Freezing may decrease potency

Abbreviations: TIV = trivalent influenza vaccine (inactive) LAIV = live, attenuated influenza vaccine yo = years old HBsAg = Hepatitis B surface antigen IM = intramuscularSQ=subcutaneous

[a]More potent formulation indicated for patients ≥65 yo. Data does not support increased efficacy with this formulation when compared with regular potency Fluzone.
[b]Cardiovascular disease, pulmonary disease, diabetes, alcoholism, cirrhosis, cerebrospinal fluid leak, or a cochlear implant; asplenic (functional or anatomic).
[c]Microbiologist exposed to isolates, military recruits, persons traveling to countries that are hyper endemic or epidemic (specifically sub-Saharan Africa), asplenia (functional or anatomic); complement deficiency.
[d]High-risk sexual exposure and/or percutaneous or mucosal exposure to blood, international travelers to region with HBsAg prevalence ≥2%, person with HIV.

Table 6-3. Pediatric Immunizations[19,20]

Vaccine	Signs/Symptoms	Scheduling	Contraindications/Precautions	Components	Administration	Adverse Reactions	Availability	Storage
Influenza (TIV or LAIV)	Sudden fever (ordinarily 101–102F), myalgia (typically back muscles), sore throat, nonproductive cough, and headache	Annually for all persons over the age of 6 m	*TIV* Severe allergic reaction (anaphylaxis) to a component of the vaccine Severe allergic reaction following a prior dose Moderate/severe acute illness History of Guillain-Barré syndrome within 6 weeks following previous dose *LAIV* Children <2 yo Children and adolescents receiving long-term aspirin therapy	Influenza type A (H1N1), type A (H3N2), and type B Residual egg protein	*TIV* ≥3 yo: 0.5 mL IM 6–35 m: 0.25 mL IM *LAIV* 0.2 mL intranasal	*TIV* Local reactions Fever/malaise Immediate hypersensitivity *LAIV* Cough, runny nose, nasal congestion, sore throat, and chills	*TIV* Suspensions for IM injection: Afluria (≥6 m), Fluarix (≥3 yo), Fluvirin (≥4 yo), Fluzone (≥6 m) *LAIV* FluMist Intranasal Spray (≥2 yo)	*TIV* Do not freeze Store in refrigerator: temperature (35–46°F [2–8°C]) *LAIV* Store in refrigerator Accidental freezing: place in refrigerator and use as soon as possible
Tetanus, diphtheria, pertussis (DTaP) Tetanus, diphtheria (DT)	*Tetanus* Trismus (lockjaw), neck stiffness, difficulty swallowing, and abdominal muscle rigidity *Diphtheria* Exudative pharyngitis, exudate spreads within 2–3 days and may form bluish-white, adherent membrane possibly leading to respiratory obstruction, fever not high but exhaustion, pallor, rapid pulse, stupor and coma may occur	DTaP: Four doses at 2, 4, 6, and 15–18 m First, second, and third doses should be separated by >4 weeks Fourth dose should follow third dose by no less than 6 m and should not be administered before 12 m	Severe allergic reaction to vaccine component or following a previous dose Moderate or severe illness	Tetanus toxoid, diphtheria toxoid, acellular pertussis	0.5 mL IM	Local reactions (erythema, tenderness and injection site induration)	*TDaP* Daptacel Infanrix Tripedia *DT* Diphtheria and tetanus Toxoids, Pediatric	Do not freeze (discard if frozen) Store in refrigerator: temperature (35–46°F [2–8°])

	Pertussis Runny nose, sneezing, low-grade fever, and a mild, occasional cough (similar to a cold), cough gradually becomes more severe, numerous, rapid coughs, with a long inspiratory effort usually with a high-pitched whoop, cyanosis may occur				
Varicella	Generalized and pruritic macules, papules, and vesicular lesions generally first on the head, then trunk, followed by extremities	All children without contraindications at 12–15 m May be given at any age regardless of prior varicella history Second dose at 4–6 yo, with second dose of MMR May be given early if at least 3 m have elapsed since first dose If second dose administered ≥28 days following the first, second dose does not need to be repeated Second dose recommended ≥4 through 6 yo who have received only one dose Doses in those ≥13 yo should be separated by 4–8 weeks	Severe allergic reaction to vaccine component or following a prior dose Immunosuppression Pregnancy Moderate or severe acute illness Recent blood product	Varicella Neomycin Hydrolyzed gelatin	0.5 mL SQ

Local reactions (pain, soreness, erythema, swelling) Generalized rash Systemic reactions uncommon	Varicella vaccine (Varivax) Combination MMR-varicella vaccine (ProQuad)	Frost-free freezer with an average temperature of −15°C (5°F) or colder May store for up to 72 continuous hours at refrigerator temperature (2–8°C; 36–46°F)

(*Continued*)

Table 6-3. Pediatric Immunizations (Continued)

Vaccine	Signs/Symptoms	Scheduling	Contraindications/Precautions	Components	Administration	Adverse Reactions	Availability	Storage
HPV	Viruses associated with cervical, anal, and genital cancers as well as genital warts and laryngeal papillomas	Females: Routine vaccination at age 11 or 12 with 3 doses of either HPV2 or HPV4 Recommended for ages 13–26 if not vaccinated previously or who have not completed series May be administered after age 26 to complete series Males: Three-dose series of HPV4 may be given to ages 9–26 Doses should be given at 0, 2, and 6 m	Anaphylaxis to vaccine component or following a prior dose Pregnancy Vaccination should be deferred in those with moderate or severe acute until symptoms of acute illness improve	HPV4: types 6, 11, 16, and 18 sodium chloride, L-histidine, polysorbate 80, and sodium borate HPV2: types 16 and 18, 3-O-desacyl-4'-monophosphoryl lipid A (MPL), and aluminum hydroxide, sodium chloride, and sodium dihydrogen phosphate dihydrate	0.5 mL IM	Local reactions, fever	Cervarix (HPV 2) Gardasil (HPV 4)	Do not freeze (discard if frozen) Store in refrigerator: temperature (35–46°F [2–8°C])
Pneumococcal conjugate (PCV)	Sudden onset of fever, rigors, pleuritic chest pain, productive cough, dyspnea, tachypnea, and hypoxia	All children 2–59 m given at 2, 4, and 6 m First dose can be administered as early as 6 weeks of age Booster dose recommended at 12–15 m	Anaphylaxis to vaccine component or following a prior dose Moderate or severe acute illness	Purified preparations of 7 or 13 types of pneumococcal capsular polysaccharide conjugated to a nontoxic variant of diphtheria toxin Phenol	0.5 mL IM or SQ injection	Pain, swelling, or redness at injection site (more common with the fourth dose) Decreased appetite or irritability	Prevnar Prevnar 13	Do not freeze (discard if frozen) Store in refrigerator: temperature (35–46°F [2–8°C])

	Single dose PCV13 may be administered to children 6–18 yo who have not received PCV13 and are at increased risk for invasive pneumococcal disease
Revaccination recommended for persons 2 yo at highest risk for serious pneumococcal infection or likely to have rapid decline in pneumococcal antibody levels
One PPSV23 revaccination dose is recommended for high-risk persons, to be administered ≥5 yo after first dose				
Meningococcal conjugate	Sudden onset of fever, headache, and stiff neck
Sometimes along with nausea, vomiting and photophobia, and altered mental status	11 or 12 yo, with a booster dose at 16 yo	Anaphylaxis to vaccine component or following a prior dose
Moderate or severe acute illness	*Menactra (MCV4)*
Neisseria meningitidis serogroups A, C, Y, and W-135 capsular polysaccharide antigens conjugated to diphtheria toxoid protein
Sodium phosphate buffered isotonic sodium chloride
Menveo (MCV4)	Healthy persons ≥16 yo receiving their first dose do not need a booster dose
**Revaccinate every 5 years if person remains at increased risk	Pain and redness at injection site
Headache, malaise	Menactra
Menveo
Menomune (use when MCV4 unavailable)	*Menactra/Menveo*
Do not freeze (discard if frozen)
Store in refrigerator: temperature (35–46°F [2–8°C])
Menomune
Store in refrigerator: temperature (35–46°F [2–8°C])

(Continued)

Table 6-3. Pediatric Immunizations (*Continued*)

Vaccine	Signs/Symptoms	Scheduling	Contraindications/Precautions	Components	Administration	Adverse Reactions	Availability	Storage
				Meningococcal serogroup A capsular polysaccharide conjugated to CRM197 (MenA) capsular polysaccharide of serogroup C, Y, and W135 conjugated to CRM197 Phosphate buffered saline *Menomune (MPSV4)* Meningococcal serogroup A, C, Y, and W-135				
HBV	Sudden onset of malaise, anorexia, nausea, vomiting, right upper quadrant abdominal pain, fever, headache, myalgia, skin rashes, arthralgia and arthritis, and dark urine followed by jaundice 1–2 days later	All infants before discharge from the hospital and then at 1 to 2 m and 6 to 18 m	Anaphylaxis to vaccine component or following a prior dose Moderate or severe acute illness	Recombinant HBsAg Aluminum hydroxyphosphate sulfate (Recombivax HB) Aluminum hydroxide, trace thimerosal (Engerix-B)	Recombivax HB: 1 mL (10 μg) IM Engerix-B: 1 mL (20 μg) IM	Injection site reaction Mild systemic complaints	Recombivax HB (pediatric formulation) Engerix-B (pediatric formulation)	Do not freeze (discard if frozen) Store in refrigerator: temperature (35–46°F [2–8°C]) Freezing may decrease potency
Hepatitis A	Sudden onset of fever, malaise, anorexia, nausea, abdominal discomfort, dark urine, jaundice	All children 12–23 m Second dose 6–12 m later	Anaphylaxis to vaccine component or following a prior dose Hypersensitivity to alum or 2-phenoxyethanol	Inactivated whole-virus hepatitis A 2-phenoxyethanol (Havrix) Vaqta has no preservative	0.5 mL IM	Injection site reaction Mild systemic complaints	Havrix Vaqta	Do not freeze (discard if frozen) Store in refrigerator: temperature (35–46°F [2–8°C]) Freezing may decrease potency

Vaccine	Disease	Schedule	Contraindications	Contents	Dose	Adverse reactions	Brand names	Storage
Haemophilus influenza type b (Hib)	Invasive disease can lead to meningitis, epiglottitis, pneumonia, arthritis, and cellulitis	All children at 2 m, 4 m, 6 m (if PRP-T used), and booster at 12–15 m	Anaphylaxis to vaccine component or following a prior dose Moderate or severe acute illness Age <6 weeks	Hib conjugated with tetanus toxoid (PRP-T) or meningococcal group B outer membrane protein (PRP-OMP)	0.5 mL IM	Swelling, redness, or pain Systemic reactions are infrequent Serious adverse reaction are rare	ActHIB Hiberix (booster only) Liquid PedvaxHIB	Do not freeze (discard if frozen) Store in refrigerator: temperature (35–46°F [2–8°C]) Protect from light
Rotavirus	Asymptomatic, self-limited watery diarrhea, or severe dehydrating diarrhea with fever and vomiting	All children at 2 m RV1: two-dose series RV5: three-dose series Separate doses by 1–2 m Maximum age for any dose is 8 m	Anaphylaxis to vaccine component or following a prior dose Severe allergy to latex Precaution in those with acute, moderate or severe gastroenteritis, or other acute illness until the condition improves, altered immunocompetence, history of intussusception	RV1: rotavirus human 89–12 strain (G1P[8] type) Dextran, D-glucose, sorbitol, and sucrose RV5: rotavirus outer capsid protein G1, G2, G3, G4, and rotavirus attachment protein P1A[8] Sucrose Latex rubber in RV1 oral applicator	RV1 1 mL PO RV5 2 mL PO	Fever, irritability, vomiting, diarrhea No serious adverse reactions	Rotarix RotaTeq (pentavalent)	Do not freeze (discard if frozen) Store in refrigerator: temperature (35–46°F [2–8°C]) Protect from light
MMR	*Measles* Increasing fever often peaking as high as 103–105°F, Koplik spots (mucous membrane rash appearing as punctate blue-white spots on buccal mucosa, maculopapular rash eruption beginning at hairline that then proceeds downward and outward *Mumps*	All children 12–15 m followed by a dose at 4–6 yo CDC recommends first dose of MMR and varicella vaccine be administered separately	Anaphylaxis to vaccine component (including gelatin or neomycin) or following a prior dose Moderate or severe acute illness Pregnancy Immunosuppression Recent blood product	Measles Mumps Rubella Neomycin	0.5 mL SQ	Arthralgias, fever, rash	MMR II ProQuad (contains MMR and varicella) Personal or family history of any seizure: vaccinate with MMR vaccine and varicella vaccine separately (increased risk of febrile seizure with MMRV)	Store between −50°C and −15°C (−58°F and 5°F) Protect from light

(*Continued*)

Table 6-3. Pediatric Immunizations (Continued)

Vaccine	Signs/Symptoms	Scheduling	Contraindications/Precautions	Components	Administration	Adverse Reactions	Availability	Storage
	Myalgia, anorexia, malaise, headache, low-grade fever and infection of the salivary glands often first realized as earache and jaw tenderness							
	Rubella							
	Low-grade fever, malaise, lymphadenopathy, and upper respiratory symptoms followed by maculopapular rash initially on face that spreads from head to foot							
Inactivated poliovirus vaccine (IPV)	Asymptomatic Nonparalytic aseptic meningitis: stiffness of the neck, back, and/or legs Minor non CNS illness: sore throat and fever, gastrointestinal disturbances, and influenza-like illness Paralytic: Most commonly affects spine causing asymmetric paralysis usually involving legs	Primary series is three doses at 2 m, 4 m, and 6–18 m Final dose at ≥4 yo	Anaphylaxis to vaccine component (including streptomycin, neomycin, polymyxin B) or following a prior dose Moderate or severe acute illness	Poliovirus	0.5 mL IM	Rare local reactions (redness, pain)	Ipol	Do not freeze Store in refrigerator: temperature (35–46°F [2–8°C])

Abbreviations:
m, months; MMR, mumps, measles, rubella

Table 6-4. Travel Vaccines[19–22]

Vaccine	Indications for Use	Scheduling	Contraindications/ Precautions	Components	Administration	Adverse Reactions	Availability	Storage
Hepatitis A	Susceptible people traveling to countries with high or intermediate hepatitis A endemicity	All children: First dose at 12–23 m and then second dose 6–12 m later Adults ≥19 years: First dose and then booster 6–12 m later	Anaphylaxis to vaccine component or following a prior dose Hypersensitivity to alum or 2-phenoxyethanol	Inactivated whole-virus hepatitis A 2-phenoxyethanol (Havrix) Vaqta has no preservative	Children: 0.5 mL IM Adults: 1 mL IM	Injection site reaction Mild systemic complaints	Havrix Vaqta	Do not freeze (discard if frozen) Store in refrigerator: temperature (35–46°F [2–8°C]) Freezing may decrease potency
Hepatitis B	Recommended for all unvaccinated adults traveling to region with HBsAg prevalence ≥2%, or who may engage in practices increasing risk for HBV infection	Children: All infants before discharge from the hospital and then at 1–2 m and 6–18 m Adults: Two doses 4 weeks apart and a third dose 4–6 m after the second dose	Anaphylaxis to vaccine component or following a prior dose Moderate or severe acute illness	Recombinant HBsAg Aluminum hydroxyphosphate sulfate (Recombivax HB) Aluminum hydroxide, trace thimerosal (Engerix-B)	Recombivax HB: Children: 0.5 mL IM Adults: 1 mL IM Engerix-B: Children: 0.5 mL IM Adults: 1 mL IM	Injection site reaction Mild systemic complaints	Recombivax HB (adult formulation) Engerix-B (adult formulation)	Do not freeze (discard if frozen) Store in refrigerator: temperature (35–46°F [2–8°C]) Freezing may decrease potency
Japanese encephalitis	Short-term travelers to endemic areas (Asia) during transmission season if traveling in nonurban areas and participating in outdoor activities or staying in places with no air conditioning, screens or bed nets	Three-dose series given on days 0, 7, and 30 Last dose should be given 10 days before travel Booster dose can be given in 2 years	Anaphylaxis to vaccine component (including protamine sulfate) or following a prior dose	Purified inactivated Japanese encephalitis Protamine sulfate	≥17 yo: 1 mL IM	Pain and tenderness Headache, myalgia, fatigue, and an influenzalike illness	Ixiaro (≥16 yo)	Do not freeze (discard if frozen) Store in refrigerator: temperature (35–46°F [2–8°C])

(Continued)

Table 6-4. Travel Vaccines (Continued)

Vaccine	Indications for Use	Scheduling	Contraindications/ Precautions	Components	Administration	Adverse Reactions	Availability	Storage
Meningococcal	Recommended for all unvaccinated adults traveling to countries that are hyper endemic or epidemic (specifically sub-Saharan Africa) Required for pilgrims to Mecca	11 or 12 yo, with a booster dose at 16 yo	Anaphylaxis to vaccine component or following a prior dose Moderate or severe acute illness	*Menactra (MCV4)* Neisseria meningitidis serogroups A, C, Y, and W-135 capsular polysaccharide antigens conjugated to diphtheria toxoid protein Sodium phosphate buffered isotonic sodium chloride *Menveo (MCV4)* Meningococcal serogroup A capsular polysaccharide conjugated to CRM197 (MenA) capsular polysaccharide of serogroup C, Y, and W135 conjugated to CRM197 Phosphate buffered saline *Menomune (MPSV4)* Meningococcal serogroup A, C, Y, and W-135	Healthy persons ≥16 yo receiving their first dose do not need a booster dose **Revaccinate every 5 years if person remains at increased risk	Pain and redness at injection site Headache, malaise	Menactra Menveo Menveo (>55 yo unless MCV4 unavailable can use <55 yo)	Menactra/Menveo: Do not freeze (discard if frozen) Store in refrigerator: temperature (35–46°F [2–8°C])
Polio (adult booster)	Travel to areas where poliomyelitis cases are still occurring	Adults who have received routine series during childhood should receive a booster b	Anaphylaxis to vaccine component (including streptomycin, neomycin, polymyxin B) or following a prior dose Moderate or severe acute illness	Poliovirus	0.5 mL IM	Rare local reactions (redness, pain)	Ipol	Do not freeze Store in refrigerator: temperature (35–46°F [2–8°C])

Disease	Indication	Schedule	Contraindications	Antigen	Dose/Route	Adverse reactions	Trade name	Storage
Rabies	May be recommended for veterinarians, animal handlers, field biologists, cavers, missionaries, and certain laboratory workers	Series of three doses at 0, 7, and 21–28 days		Rabies virus	1 mL IM	Local reactions (pain, erythema, swelling, or itching at the injection site) Mild systemic reactions (headache, nausea, abdominal pain, muscle aches, and dizziness)	Imovax (human diploid cell vaccine) RabAvert (purified chick embryo cell)	Imovax: Do not freeze Store in refrigerator: temperature (35–46°F [2–8°C]) RabAvert: Store between 2°C and 8°C (36°F and 46°F) Protect from light
Typhoid fever	Areas (Central and South America, India, Africa) where there is an increased risk of exposure to *Salmonella enterica* serotype typhi	*Oral live, attenuated vaccine* Four doses completed 1 week before exposure with booster every 5 years *Vi capsular polysaccharide vaccine (ViCPS)* One dose with booster every 2 years given >2 weeks before exposure	Anaphylaxis to vaccine or vaccine component *Oral* Acute febrile illness or acute GI illness *ViCPS* Acute respiratory or other active infection or intense physical activity during high temperatures	Viable *Salmonella typhi* Ty21a and nonviable *S. typhi* Ty21a *ViCPS* Purified Vi capsular polysaccharide	*Oral* One capsule every other day for four doses *ViCPS* 0.5 mL IM	*Oral* Abdominal discomfort, nausea, vomiting, and rash *ViCPS* Headache and injection site reactions	Typhim VI (ViCPS) Vivotif Berna Vaccine (oral)	Oral: Store between 2°C and 8°C (36–46°F) If frozen, thaw capsules before use Can tolerate 8 hours at 25°C (77°F) ViCPS: Do not freeze Store in refrigerator: temperature (35–46°F [2–8°C])
Yellow fever virus (YFV)[a]	Recommended for those ≥9 m traveling to or living in areas at risk for YFV transmission (tropical South America and sub-Saharan Africa) Only vaccinate people at risk of exposure or who require proof of vaccination to enter a country	One dose with booster every 10 years if at continued risk of exposure	Anaphylaxis to vaccine or vaccine component Age <6 m Immunosuppressed	Yellow fever	0.5 mL SQ	Low-grade fever, headache, and myalgias	YF-Vax	Shipped frozen dry ice; do not use unless dry ice present upon arrival Must be maintained continuously at 0–5°C (32–41°F) Do not refreeze

[a] Only designated YFV vaccination centers authorized to issue certificates of YFV vaccination can administer YFV vaccine.

pharmacist can and cannot offer, the requisite training and/or credentialing, what documentation is required, and how billing can occur. Many states allow pharmacists to administer any available vaccine, but only to adults, while others limit which vaccines can be offered. Some allow administration under a collaborative protocol, while others require an individual prescription for each vaccine administered. Table 6-5 reviews the laws regarding pharmacist administration of vaccines, by state. Please note that this table is current as of June 2012, and it is necessary for a pharmacist to confirm this information prior to offering vaccines.

All immunizing pharmacists must receive Occupational Safety and Health Administration (OSHA) training prior to administering immunizations and update it every year. Employers must offer and document this training. You also must develop an exposure control plan, document the evaluation of which type of safety needle you will be using as you administer vaccines, keep a sharps injury log, and offer all employees who may come into contact with blood products hepatitis B vaccination AT NO CHARGE.

Any pharmacist involved in administering vaccines must ensure that his or her liability insurance specifically covers this activity. Many policies have nebulous wording, so a clarification may be necessary. Most companies offer "riders" to standard policies covering activities outside of the normal scope of practice, as they define it.

TIP: The time to purchase appropriate liability coverage is before the first vaccine is ever given, during the planning stages for the service.

Evaluate Facilities and Resources

A list of necessary resources for implementing an immunization service is included in Table 6-6. Staffing requirements will vary, depending on the type of flow that will be used (discussed below) and also which tasks can be performed by whom in your state. While space is obviously needed to implement immunization services, a complete renovation of pharmacy space is not necessary (although offering them in an office is a nice, professional touch). These services can be offered with as few changes as a portable partition and a chair in a corner, away from the general flow of the pharmacy business, or even off-site, with a rolling cart or other means or transporting supplies with you.

TIP: One individual should be responsible for a continuous inventory of vaccine product and other supplies, to ensure proper storage and that they do not run out.

Once the legality of pharmacist-administered vaccines for your state has been researched and a list of necessary resources compiled, the next step is to determine which vaccines should be offered. Many pharmacists choose to start their immunization practices by offering influenza vaccines. This is due to the need for annual vaccines for nearly all patients, the ability to identify many of those at highest risk from the disease by prescription records, the ability to bill Medicare Part B and other third parties, and the general acceptance of this limited role by other healthcare providers and patients. Should you choose to offer others, however, the choice of which one(s) will be based on several factors, including the needs of the patient population being served, the support from healthcare providers in the community, and the expected workload changes with the projected volume of vaccines offered. Of course, the immunizations offered can change as demand and pharmacist motivation change as well.

Current patients can provide information regarding which necessary vaccines they have not received, as well as their perceptions of the value of being able to obtain those vaccines in a pharmacy setting, or by a pharmacist in another less traditional setting, like the patient's place of employment or another retail setting. Patient-specific factors such as age and socioeconomic status will play a large role in which vaccines you will offer. If your pharmacy serves a large proportion of senior citizens, then offering the pneumococcal polysaccharide vaccine (PPSV) would be a wise choice initially. If you are in a location that is near a college or university, focusing on vaccines that are often required for college admission, such as meningococcal or hepatitis B, may be a good place to start. If your patient base is made of affluent retirees, then perhaps offering travel vaccines would be a good choice.

TIP: To obtain information from patients regarding vaccines in the pharmacy, question those you know well,

Table 6-5. Vaccine Laws, by State[23]

State	Types of Vaccine	By Standing Order/Protocol	By Individual Prescription	Patient Age Limits
Alabama	Any (by individual prescription only)		✓	Any
Alaska	Any (some by individual prescription only)	✓	✓	Any[a]
Arizona	Any (some by individual prescription only)	✓	✓	≥6 years[a]
Arkansas	Any (some by individual prescription only)	✓	✓	≥7 years[a]
California	Any	✓		Any
Colorado	Any	✓		Any
Connecticut	Influenza, pneumococcal, zoster	✓		≥18 years
Delaware	Any (some by individual prescription only)	✓	✓	≥9 years
District of Columbia	Any (some by individual prescription only)	✓	✓	≥18 years
Florida	Influenza, pneumococcal	✓		≥18 years
Georgia	Any (some by individual prescription only)	✓	✓	≥13 years
Hawaii	Any (some by individual prescription only)	✓	✓	≥18 years
Idaho	Any	✓		≥12 years
Illinois	Any	✓	✓	≥14 years
Indiana	Any (some by individual prescription only)	✓	✓	≥14 years
Iowa	Any (some by individual prescription only)	✓	✓	≥18 years
Kansas	Any	✓		≥6 years
Kentucky	Any	✓		≥9 years
Louisiana	Any (some by individual prescription only)	✓	✓	≥7 years[a]
Maine	Any	✓	✓	≥9 years[a]
Maryland	Influenza, pneumococcal, zoster	✓	✓	≥9 years[a]
Massachusetts	Any (some by individual prescription only)	✓	✓	≥18 years
Michigan	Any (some by individual prescription only)	✓	✓	Any
Minnesota	Any	✓		≥10 years
Mississippi	Any	✓		Any
Missouri	Influenza, pneumococcal, zoster	✓	✓	≥12 years

(Continued)

Table 6-5. Vaccine Laws, by State (*Continued*)

State	Types of Vaccine	By Standing Order/Protocol	By Individual Prescription	Patient Age Limits
Montana	Any	✓		≥12 years
Nebraska	Any	✓	✓	Any
Nevada	Any	✓		≥14 years
New Hampshire	Influenza, pneumococcal, zoster	✓		≥18 years
New Jersey	Any (some by individual prescription only)	✓	✓	≥18 years
New Mexico	Any	✓		Any
New York	Influenza and pneumococcal only	✓		≥18 years
North Carolina	Influenza, pneumococcal, zoster	✓	✓	≥18 years
North Dakota	Any	✓		≥5 years
Ohio	Influenza, hepatitis A & B, HPV, meningitis, pneumococcal, Td/Tdap, zoster	✓	✓	≥14 years[a]
Oklahoma	Any	✓		Any
Oregon	Any	✓		≥11 years
Pennsylvania	Any	✓	✓	≥18 years
Puerto Rico	Influenza only	✓	✓	≥18 years
Rhode Island	Any	✓	✓	≥9 years
South Carolina	Any (some by individual prescription only)	✓	✓	≥18 years
South Dakota	Influenza, zoster	✓	✓	≥18 years
Tennessee	Any	✓	✓	Any
Texas	Any	✓	✓	Any
Utah	Influenza, hepatitis A & B, HPV, meningococcal, MMR, pneumococcal, Td/Tdap, varicella, zoster	✓		≥13 years
Vermont	Any	✓	✓	≥18 years
Virginia	Any (some by individual prescription only)	✓	✓	Any[a]
Washington	Any	✓	✓	Any
West Virginia	Influenza, pneumococcal, zoster	✓	✓	≥18 years
Wisconsin	Any	✓		≥6 years
Wyoming	Influenza, hepatitis A & B, HPV, meningococcal, MMR, pneumococcal, Td/Tdap, varicella, zoster	✓	✓	≥19 years

[a]Varies (for different vaccines, practice settings, etc.)
Data from reference 23.

Table 6-6. Necessary Resources

Space/Facilities	Supplies	Other Needs
Private area to: • Screen patient • Administer vaccine • Allow patient to wait Storage space for supplies	*Initial* • Refrigerator • Software (billing and/or documentation) • Office supplies (for paper charting, if applicable, and other needs) • Container(s) for immunization supplies • Emergency supply box *Ongoing* • Vaccines • Syringes • Cotton balls • Alcohol swabs • Bandages Contents of emergency supply box (Epi-pens, diphenhydramine)	Waste disposal services Staff training Marketing materials Hepatitis B vaccine for all employees OSHA training for employees

when they are not in a hurry and can take the time to discuss it with you at length, or develop a survey that patients can complete and drop in a box as they wait for their prescriptions to be prepared.

To determine the need for specific vaccines in your geographic area, it is also wise to talk with nearby healthcare providers. Healthcare providers in private practice, large healthcare systems, and at local public health institutions can tell you which vaccines they see "slipping through the cracks" in vulnerable patient populations. Are too few people receiving their boosters? Has there been an outbreak of hepatitis A recently? Are smokers receiving their pneumococcal vaccine? By approaching this from a, "How can we help?" standpoint and requesting the input of other healthcare providers, you may also be more likely to get their support and referrals as you begin to offer the vaccines in the pharmacy.

Determine Workflow

The legal requirements for pharmacist-administered immunizations and the resources available will, in part, dictate workflow, as will the type and anticipated number of immunizations offered. There are several options, with benefits and drawbacks to each one:

- *Point-of-service.* Patient requests one or more immunizations. That request is put into the prescription que, as if it were a new prescription to process. The patient is told how long they will have to wait, and the vaccine(s) is/are administered. The biggest benefit of this workflow includes minimal interruption to the normal procedure, and it works well when there is no extra or overlap pharmacist to assist in processing and administering the vaccine. It is also useful when the expected demand for immunizations is low, so that pharmacist time is not "dedicated" to only administering vaccines. In addition, it allows the technician to be involved in the "technical" aspects of the service (as allowed by state law): entering the prescription/order, drawing up the syringe, labeling appropriately, and collecting payment. The main drawback is that patients may not want to wait for the vaccine, especially if there is a long wait time. It also pulls pharmacists away from the normal workflow, so problems related to other prescriptions that arise may take longer to resolve.

- *By appointment.* Immunizations can be given on an appointment-only basis in most pharmacies. This will allow patients to be scheduled during times of lower prescription volume or when there are more personnel in the pharmacy. Whoever schedules the appointment can ask the general patient screening questions when the appointment is made, and document the responses. This also allows for adequate planning, so the prescription may be entered into the computer system (but not verified) and all other documentation (as discussed below) prepared prior to administering the vaccine. The downside is that this is not as convenient as a walk-in service for many patients, so could decrease the demand somewhat.
- *Vaccine clinics.* Dedicated blocks of time, possibly away from the actual pharmacy department, can be devoted to administering vaccines. This method is especially useful if a large number of patients are anticipated, such as during influenza season. It allows for adequate scheduling of staff for as short a time period as possible, so does not waste personnel resources. Vaccines can be prebatched (based on manufacturer's recommendations), and technicians can, again, be involved in much of the process, allowing the pharmacist to administer many vaccines. However, a vaccine clinic is ideally scheduled during times of high traffic in the pharmacy, which may not always be the most convenient time for staff.
  - *Off-site vaccine clinics.* An alternative to vaccine clinics held within the physical pharmacy involves the pharmacist and possibly technician or clerk traveling to a place of business (banks, daycares, dental offices, insurance agencies, etc.) to administer immunizations to employees and family members at a predetermined time. Note that all documentation and safety requirements are the same, regardless of site.

Develop a Business Plan

The purpose of any business plan is to encourage others to invest in your service. That investment may include money, time, and resources, or even professional trust. Whatever the purpose, a thorough and well-documented plan is essential. However, the focus may differ, depending on your intended audience. Standard components of a business plan may include:

- Executive summary
- Description of the business/setting
  - Type of pharmacy, physical structure/space, services offered, staff
- Description of the proposed service
  - Small amount of clinical background (to establish need), what vaccines will be offered, process to be used, workflow changes, how documentation will occur
- Credentials/training of pharmacist(s) and other staff
- Mission statement
- Sales and marketing
  - Environmental (SWOT) analysis, projected demand, competition, marketing objectives, marketing strategies, action plan
- Pro forma financial statements
  - Costs (initial costs, supplies, pharmacist/staff time), pricing, profits (including time line)
- Funding

Note that this list may not be all-inclusive, and not all of these areas may need to be covered for all audiences. If you are presenting your plan to (purely) financial investors, in the hopes of obtaining the capital to start and/or maintain such a service, then focusing on potential (monetary) profits would be wise. This audience will be less interested in the workflow and clinical aspects of the service, although they will still want to see that you have planned for these components.

Oftentimes, however, the financial investors are also involved in the day-to-day running of the pharmacy (such as an owner or regional manager), and these people will be more interested in how the service will impact the environment of the pharmacy. In addition to profits, workflow and staffing/resource requirements should take precedence in these presentations.

Occasionally, the audience for your business plan will be other healthcare providers or businesses, who you are hoping will invest their trust in your service and refer patients/employees. Focus these presentations on the clinical benefits of the immunization service, and how your process will comply with generally accepted best practices.

Identify Physician Collaborator(s) and Other Partners

It is only after you have a strong plan in place that you should approach a practitioner with whom you wish to collaborate. (This physician should also be looked on as an "investor.") The best means of identifying practitioner willing to collaborate is to consider those with whom you already have a good relationship through normal pharmacy business, such as those who routinely contact you with questions or requests. Other sources include public health departments, medical practices that are geographically near the pharmacy, or community organizations or nonprofit organizations (American Diabetes Association, American Heart Association, American Lung Association, county immunization coalitions, health disparity committees, etc.)

If you are in a state or area where pharmacists have been offering immunizations for some time, then your collaborating physician may not need any convincing, and may even already be collaborating with other pharmacists (if state law allows it). However, if this is a relatively new idea in your area, then you must be prepared to answer questions regarding liability, scope of practice, and the role of the physician(s). Draft or example protocols that conform to the laws in your state to present should be presented to any practitioner collaborators, as it should cover all of these issues and answer many of the questions he or she might have. Note that your protocol should (and must, in some states) include an "Emergency Plan," for cases of syncope, anaphylaxis, or other serious adverse events.

■ MARKETING

There are currently more than 175,000 pharmacists in the United States trained to give immunizations.[24] This is a generally well-accepted role for pharmacists. The American College of Physicians–American Society of Internal Medicine released a statement in 2002 that they "support the use of the pharmacist as immunization information source, host of immunization sites, and immunizer, as appropriate and allowed by state law,"[25] and 90% of healthcare providers responding to one survey stated that they felt comfortable with pharmacists providing immunization and thought it was appropriate for them to do so.[26] Results from patient surveys indicate moderately high levels of satisfaction with and support for immunization services offered by pharmacists.[5,27]

Your business plan will include a plan detailing to whom you will market your service and how. A 2001 report indicated how patients being immunized in a pharmacy came to learn about the service: 37% saw someone else being vaccinated, 20% learned of the service through family or friends, 5% from physicians, 1% from employers, and 30% from an advertisement.[28] These numbers, while possibly somewhat outdated, suggest that word-of-mouth and making the service highly visible are the most effective means of marketing.

Advertisements do not have to be expensive to reach a large number of patients, and will vary depending on your target population. In-store signage, "bag stuffers," and buttons on the staff are excellent ways to let regular patients know of immunization services being offered in the pharmacy. Other options to entice patients who are not regular customers include paid radio or television spots, ads on social media Web sites, and outdoor signage/billboards. Letters and/or flyers to physicians' offices and large businesses may also be effective at increasing interest in the service.

■ DOCUMENTATION

Once you are actually administering immunizations, you must document these services. The federal Vaccine Injury Compensation Program (VICP) offers no-fault compensation to a patient if injury occurs after most currently available vaccines (diphtheria, tetanus, pertussis, measles, mumps, rubella, polio, hepatitis B,

Haemophilus influenzae type b, varicella, rotavirus, and pneumococcal conjugate, influenza, and human papillomavirus). The VICP requires documentation of the following information, at a minimum:[29]

- Date vaccine administered
- Vaccine manufacturer
- Vaccine lot number
- Name, address, and title of person administering the vaccine
- Date printed on the Vaccine Information Sheet (VIS)
- Date the VIS is given to the patient or the patients legal representative

It is also wise to document the site of the vaccine (especially if more than one is to be given). While a signature/signed consent is not required by federal law, it is a good idea to obtain some form of acknowledgment that they received the VIS and asked any questions they had. This can be on the prescription (if one is generated by your software for immunizations) or in a separate file.

All of this information can be documented directly into the pharmacy software you are currently using (in the "sig" field), or a separate database or spreadsheet can be maintained for all vaccines given in the pharmacy. It is important that this information is readily retrievable, though, in case of adverse effects, patient requests for documentation, or if your state requires additional reporting for pharmacist-administered vaccines. Many states now also have an Internet-based statewide database where this information should be entered, so that all patient vaccine information is contained centrally.

TIP: Reporting to statewide immunization databases is almost always mandatory for children, but not for adults. Document adult vaccines there, anyway, whenever possible!

■ REIMBURSEMENT

While it would be commendable to offer immunizations simply to improve the public health, without regards for profit, this is unrealistic. Every minute that a pharmacist spends away from the dispensing area is potential money lost. Fortunately, there are several mechanisms for receiving reimbursement for immunizations administered, and this is a "non-traditional" area of practice that can be quite profitable.

The first, and possibly most common, is through simple self-pay or "cash." The patient receives the vaccine(s), and pays a flat price (which incorporates the cost of the vaccine, as well as an administration fee). Many patients are willing to pay up front, provided they receive a prescription receipt stating that they got the vaccine to submit to their insurance company. An alternative to this method is to split the price, and bill the vaccine itself to a third-party payer (and charge the patient the co-pay, if applicable), while charging the patient for the administration fee, since most insurers will not cover this.

Another common means of obtaining reimbursement is by billing Medicare Part B. It will pay pharmacies for influenza, pneumococcal polysaccharide, and hepatitis B (for select high-risk patients). Patients have no out-of-pocket expense in this case. Each year, CMS publishes reimbursement rates for these vaccines per dose, which are generally favorable. For example, in 2009-2010, a dose of trivalent influenza vaccine (TIV) costs the pharmacy about $13 per dose. Medicare reimbursed about $15 for the vaccine, plus an administration fee of about $19. (This varies by state and region.) Clearly, the profit margin is large, when compared with a typical prescription drug. (Medicare Part D will reimburse for zoster, but reimbursement rates vary by plan.)

Prior to billing Medicare Part B for immunizations, you must first get your National Provider Identification (NPI) number and a mass immunizer number from the local carrier (CMS form 855). Payment from Medicare Part B can then be obtained in one of several ways:

- Individual "paper" bill (CMS Form 1500)
- Roster "paper" bill (CMS Form 1500; preferred if billing for >5 patients; not allowed for hepatitis B)
- Electronic (through various software packages)

Table 6-7. Medicare Part B Reimbursement Codes[30,31]

Description	Diagnosis Code (ICD-9)	Product (CPT or Q-Code)	Administration (HCPCS Code)
Influenza vaccine (TIV) 6–35 m ≥3 years (LAIV)	V04.8 V04.81	90657 Temporary, product-specific Q-codes[a] 90660	G0008
Pneumococcal 23-valent (polysaccharide)	V03.82	90732	G0009
Hepatitis B	V05.3	90746	G0010

[a] These codes are active after January 2011, and will remain so until permanent codes are assigned: Q2035 (Afluria); Q2036 (Flulaval); Q2037 (Fluvirin); Q2038 (Fluzone); Q2039 (Not otherwise specified).

Table 6-7 lists the diagnosis, product, and administration codes that must be used when billing Medicare Part B, in order to receive reimbursement.

TIP: Do NOT advertise any immunizations as being "free" to Medicare Part B recipients. Rather, make it clear that there is no out-of-pocket expense to them, but their plan will be billed.

Another potential means for reimbursement is through contracting with local businesses and/or employer groups to offer vaccines to their employees. This often requires some "face time" to explain how covering or subsidizing the vaccines for their employees can decrease absenteeism or overall healthcare costs. The business may pay the entire agreed upon fee, or they may pay part, and the patient pays the rest. The patient may come to the pharmacy, or the pharmacist (with or without a technician) may travel to the place of business, as mentioned previously. If the pharmacist travels, *insurance claims can be processed at the pharmacy after the fact, or invoices can be sent to the employer or individuals, based on the contracts negotiated.*

There are also government-sponsored programs for reimbursement, such as Vaccines for Children (VFC). Anyone authorized by their state to administer immunizations can participate in VFC. In this program, the state will provide you with government-purchased vaccine to administer to eligible children, and you can charge an administrative fee, as determined by the Centers for Medicare and Medicaid Services (CMS).[32] Pharmacist participation in this program is not common, due to many states' limitations on them administering vaccines to children. However, a link for more information on this program is included in the Resources List at the end of the chapter.

■ CONCLUSION

Vaccine administration is a relatively well-accepted "non-traditional" role that a pharmacist in a community setting can take. Once dedicated to developing an immunization service, pharmacists must prepare before they can offer the first vaccines, and adequate vaccine knowledge and service planning is imperative. The potential benefits, though, are large, both in patient care and financially.

■ RESOURCE LIST

General

- *Pharmacy-Based Immunization Delivery* Certificate Program (American Pharmacist Association). http://www.pharmacist.com/pharmacy-based-immunization-delivery

- The materials from this course go into much more detail about all of the facets covered in this chapter. Completing this course prior to offering immunizations is highly recommended by the authors, and is also required in many states.
- Immunization Action Coalition. www.immunize.org
    - This Web site is expansive and contains many resources that can prove to be useful under the "For Health Professionals" tab: handouts for patients and staff, vaccine information statements (VIS), information on diseases and vaccines, and talking points about vaccines. Especially useful is the "Clinic Resources" section, which includes information and tools for billing and coding, documentation, scheduling, screening patients, and storage and handling of vaccine products.
- Centers for Disease Control and Prevention. http://www.cdc.gov/vaccines/
    - The most up-to-date immunization news and recommendations can be found at this Web site. Contains similar information to Immunization Action Coalition Web site, but is organized differently.
- Epidemiology and Prevention of Vaccine Preventable Diseases ("The Pink Book") (Centers for Disease Control and Prevention). http://www.cdc.gov/vaccines/pubs/pinkbook/pink-chapters.htm
    - Updated annually, this reference includes extensive information on the diseases being prevented by vaccines, as well as vaccine information such as efficacy, indications and scheduling, dosing, adverse effects, and handling requirements. It can be ordered as a hard copy, or each individual chapter downloaded as an Adobe Acrobat™ file.
- Pharmacist Immunization Center (American Pharmacist Association; membership required). http://www.pharmacist.com/imz
    - This Web site contains links to news, clinical vaccine information, including schedules, practice resources, and links to other useful sources. You can also sign up to receive the "Immunizing Pharmacist" newsletter and join the e-community.

Billing and Reimbursement

- Immunizations: Provider Resources (Centers for Medicare and Medicaid Services). https://www.cms.gov/Immunizations/
    - This Web site includes general information about what vaccines Medicare will cover, with links to documents with the most recent reimbursement rates and codes, as well as the most recent "Immunizers' Guide."
- Coding for Vaccines and Administration (American Academy of Family Physicians). http://www.aafp.org/online/en/home/practicemgt/codingresources/immunizations.html
    - This Web site contains important general information on the codes (diagnosis, administration, and products) and how and when to use them, with specific reference to Medicare patients.
- Vaccines for Children (VFC). http://www.cdc.gov/vaccines/programs/vfc/providers/default.htm
    - See this Web site for information on enrolling as a provider, documentation requirements, reimbursement, etc.

■ PRACTICAL PATIENT CASE

ES is a 34-year-old white male who last year was in an automobile accident and had to have his spleen removed. He has since been deemed disabled, and now has Medicare (parts A, B, and D).

He immigrated from Eastern Europe when he was 11 years old, and has records of receiving complete courses of the following vaccines: DTaP, PCV, Hib, IPV, and MMR. He has not had any vaccines since those. His medication profile shows the following prescription and over-the-counter drugs:

HCTZ 25 mg once daily
Multivitamin (men's) once daily

He confirms that he has hypertension, which is controlled with his medication. He tries to exercise daily and eats a low-carb, high-protein diet.

You have a standing order for any and all adult vaccines, and ES would like to have everything he needs done as soon as possible. Utilize the information contained in this chapter and the CDC vaccine schedules to design a plan for ES.

1. What vaccines does ES need to receive?
2. How will they be scheduled?
3. What information will you document for each vaccine?
4. For which of these vaccines can you bill Medicare?

■ SUMMARY POINTS

- The advent and routine administration of vaccines have led to a significant decrease in mortality and morbidity due to many common illnesses.
- Pharmacists can take several roles in immunizations, including vaccine administrator, in all 50 states, and in a variety of practice settings. It has been shown that when pharmacists become involved in immunizations, vaccine rates increase.
- There is a large amount of information necessary to assist patients in determining which vaccines they need. Pharmacists offering vaccines or serving as vaccine advocates must be familiar with this information.
- Prior to developing an immunization service, pharmacists must be aware of the legislation addressing this issue in their state. They should obtain all necessary training (including yearly OSHA training), and ensure that their liability insurance will cover them administering vaccines.
- There are many resources and supplies necessary to initiate and maintain an immunization service in a pharmacy setting. A marketing plan must also be developed. However, the costs for these resources do not have to be prohibitive.
- Pharmacists can choose to offer only one vaccine, or several. Which vaccines are offered will depend on patient and local provider demand. It is the pharmacist's responsibility to determine this need.
- Pharmacy workflow will be impacted by the development of an immunization service. How vaccines are handled will depend on the number and type of vaccines being offered, the amount of staff, and the anticipated demand.
- A business plan should be prepared to entice investors for an immunization service. "Investors," however, does not only mean those who will be contributing financially. Other stakeholders (such as store owner/manager, other staff, and potential collaborating physicians) and their goals and desires must be considered when developing the business plan.
- There is certain information that is required, by law, to be documented by vaccines administrators. This includes date vaccine administered; vaccine manufacturer; vaccine lot number; name, address, and title of person administering the vaccine; date printed on the VIS; and date the VIS is given to the patient or the patients legal representative. This documentation can be on paper or electronic, but should always be easily retrievable.
- The most common way of obtaining reimbursement is self-pay. Many pharmacists also choose to bill Medicare Part B for select vaccines. There is significant profit that can be made through administering vaccines in the pharmacy.

EXPERT INTERVIEW

Kathleen Wise, PharmD
Clinical Staff Pharmacist, St. Francis Hospital, Tulsa, Oklahoma

1. What was the setting of the service(s) you developed?

   Our services were offered in a local chain of supermarkets. Most of these supermarkets had pharmacies, but some did not. We also provided flu shots for certain businesses. In these instances, we would take our supplies to the business and immunize their employees on site.

2. How did you identify the provider(s) with whom you partnered for the service(s)?

   Having a connection with the provider who is chosen is helpful and close physical proximity is a bonus. One of the pharmacies in our chain had a good relationship with a physician who was located across the street from the supermarket. He agreed to be our provider. He was easily accessible and always willing to accommodate our requests.

3. What vaccines did you offer when you first developed your service(s)? Why did you choose these vaccines over others? How did this change as the service developed over time?

   Initially the flu and pneumonia vaccines were offered primarily due to demand. We decided to limit our vaccine administration to people 12 years of age and older. We had a large demand for these two vaccines from the senior citizen population. As more of our pharmacist staff became certified to give immunizations, we had more ability to offer additional vaccines. We chose the additional vaccines for the population we served.

4. What was the flow of your service(s)? How did this impact the overall workflow of the pharmacy?

   Each pharmacy had a drop-off window, and this window was ideal for administering vaccines. We had a cart with all of our supplies, and a pharmacist would review the customer's consent form, retrieve the vaccine, and administer it at the drop-off window. Some pharmacies had an office that could be used for giving immunizations, and during flu season tables would be set up in front of the pharmacy and designated staff would provide immunizations during flu shot clinic times. This allowed for minimal disruption of the pharmacy workflow.

5. What modifications, if any, had to be made to the physical space in which you were offering the service?

   Very little modifications were made to the physical space. Having a designated place for immunization supplies to be stored reduces the need for modifications. Chairs were readily available for customers who preferred to sit down while receiving their immunization.

6. How did you market your service to patients? To providers? What do you feel was the most effective means of marketing?

   Initially all marketing was done via fliers posted at the pharmacy. These fliers announced immunization clinic dates and times along with the cost of the immunizations. As our services grew, our marketing department began to advertise our services in the supermarket ad found in the local newspaper. Larger signs were made for better visibility inside the stores. Letters were sent to providers announcing the availability of our services, but continued marketing to providers was not necessary. Large employers in town were contacted to offer flu shot clinics for their employees. We went to many businesses to provide flu shots for employees. We also marketed to a local technical school and immunized many nursing students who attended there. Our best marketing efforts were to individual businesses and to students at the technical school.

7. How did you obtain reimbursement for your immunization services?

   All immunizations were paid for by the individual at first. Eventually I was able to obtain a Medicare provider number for the whole company. This allowed us to bill Medicare for vaccines given to senior citizens. Immunizations written as a prescription by a physician were billed to the patient's insurance. All other services were done on a cash pay basis.

8. What do you think is/are the biggest challenge(s) in developing and maintaining an immunization service in the pharmacy setting? What tips do you have for overcoming that/those challenges(s)?

One challenge is maintaining staff enthusiasm for the service. If the staff gets tired of dealing with immunization customers, it can cause problems. Getting the staff on board with the service from the beginning is a way to prevent this challenge from developing. It is also important to try to prevent one or two individuals from doing all of the immunizations. This ensures little possibility of burnout.

Another challenge is in reimbursement for immunization services. It is often necessary to acquire an immunization provider number with multiple insurance carriers. This is a time consuming, but worthwhile endeavor. Having the ability to bill insurance carriers for your services increases the likelihood that customers will come to you when they need immunizations.

■ STUDY QUESTIONS

1. Which of the following is a true statement?
   a. Diphtheria-containing vaccines cause sudden infant death syndrome
   b. Vaccines cause autism
   c. Meningococcal vaccine MAY be associated with Guillain–Barre syndrome
   d. Vaccines contain antifreeze
   e. Hepatitis B vaccine leads to multiple sclerosis

2. Pharmacists are authorized to administer vaccinations in all 50 US states.
   a. True
   b. False

3. Which of the following states only allows pharmacists to administer immunizations by individual prescription?
   a. Alabama
   b. California
   c. North Carolina
   d. Utah
   e. Washington

4. Which of the following is a true contraindication for TIV (inactivated)?
   a. Children <2 years old
   b. Chronic medical conditions
   c. History of seizures
   d. Minor illness
   e. History of severe allergic reaction to egg protein

5. How many doses of Tdap does a healthy 22-year-old black female need to receive?
   a. None
   b. 1
   c. 2
   d. 3
   e. Every 10 years

6. How many doses of HPV does a healthy, previously unvaccinated 22-year-old black female need to receive?
   a. None
   b. 1
   c. 2
   d. 3
   e. 4

7. Which of the following patients should receive a dose of PPSV at this time?
   a. An 18-month-old Hispanic boy who has never received the vaccine
   b. A 17-year-old Asian man who is entering college as a freshman who has never received the vaccine
   c. A 66-year-old black woman with type 1 diabetes mellitus who was vaccinated at the age of 55 years old
   d. A 63-year-old white woman with chronic heart failure who was vaccinated 2 years ago
   e. A 72-year-old white man with COPD who was vaccinated 5 years ago

8. Which of the following vaccines should not be given a week after a patient receives fresh frozen plasma?
   a. Hepatitis B
   b. Hib
   c. MMR
   d. Rotavirus
   e. Tdap

9. Which of the following should be documented after administering a vaccine?
   a. Lot number
   b. Patient co-payment
   c. Site of injection
   d. Both a & c
   e. All of the above

10. Medicare Part D reimburses pharmacies for which of the following vaccines?
    a. Hepatitis B
    b. Influenza
    c. Meningococcal conjugate vaccine (MCV)
    d. PPSV
    e. Zoster

BIBLIOGRAPHY

1. CDC. Data and statistics: Impact of vaccines in the 20th & 21st centuries. In: Atkinson WWS, Hamborsky J, eds. *Epidemiology and Prevention of Vaccine-Preventable Diseases.* 12th ed. Washington, DC: Public Health Foundation; 2011.
2. CDC. Measles. In: Atkinson WWS, Hamborsky J, eds. *Epidemiology and Prevention of Vaccine Preventable Diseases.* 12th ed. Washington, DC: Public Health Foundation; 2011.
3. Cortes JE, Curns A, Tate JE, et al. Rotavirus vaccine and health care utilization for diarrhea in U.S. children. *N Engl J Med.* 2011;265:1108-1117.
4. CDC. Principles of vaccination. In: Atkinson WWS, Hamborsky J, eds. *Epidemiology and Prevention of Vaccine Preventable Diseases.* 12th ed. Washington, DC: Public Health Foundation; 2011.
5. Hogue MD, Grabenstein J, Foster SL, Rothholz MC. Pharmacist involvement in immunizations: a decade of professional advancement. *J Am Pharm Assoc.* 2006;46:168-182.
6. Fact Sheet. States where pharmacists have the authority to immunize patients. http://www.pharmacist.com/AM/Template.cfm?Section=Home2&TEMPLATE=/CM/ContentDisplay.cfm&CONTENTID=6256. Accessed October 5, 2011.
7. APhA. Pharmacists play a vital role in providing immunizations in their communities. http://www.pharmacist.com/AM/Template.cfm?Section=News_Releases2&template=/CM/ContentDisplay.cfm&ContentID=23001. Accessed October 5, 2011.
8. Steyer TE, Ragucci KR, Pearson WS, Mainous AG 3rd. The role of pharmacists in the delivery of influenza vaccinations. *Vaccine.* 2004;22:1001-1006.
9. Taitel M, Cohen E, Duncan I, Pegus C. Pharmacists as providers: targeting pneumococcal vaccinations to high risk populations. *Vaccine.* 2011;29:8073-8076.
10. Grabenstein JD, Hartzema AG, Guess HA, Johnston WP. Community pharmacists as immunization advocates: a clinical pharmacoepidemiological experiment. *Int J Pharm Pract.* 1993;2:5-10.
11. Van Amburgh JA, Waite NM, Hobson EH, Migden H. Improved influenza vaccination rates in a rural

population as a result of a pharmacist-managed immunization campaign. *Pharmacotherapy.* 2001;21:1115-1122.
12. Kamal KM, Madhavan S, Maine LL. Pharmacy and immunization services: pharmacists' participation and impact. *J Am Pharm Assoc.* 2003;43:470-482.
13. IAC. Evidence shows vaccines unrelated to autism. http://www.immunize.org/catg.d/p4028.pdf. Accessed October 5, 2011.
14. CDC. Concerns about autism: CDC statement on autism and thimerosal. http://www.cdc.gov/vaccinesafety/Concerns/Autism/Index.html. Accessed October 5, 2011.
15. Quackwatch. Misconceptions about immunization. http://www.quackwatch.com/03HealthPromotion/immu/immu00.html. Accessed October 5, 2011.
16. CDC. Addressing common concerns. http://www.cdc.gov/vaccinesafety/Concerns/Index.html. Accessed October 5, 2011.
17. AAP. Questions and answers about vaccine ingredients. http://www.cdc.gov/vaccinesafety/Concerns/Index.html. Accessed October 5, 2011.
18. IAC. Ask the experts: miscellaneous. http://www.immunize.org/askexperts/experts_general.aspmiscellaneous. Accessed October 5, 2011.
19. CDC. Disease-specific chapters. In: Atkinson WWS, Hamborsky J, eds. *Epidemiology and Prevention of Vaccine-Preventable Diseases.* 12th ed. Washington, DC: Centers for Disease Control and Prevention; 2011.
20. Comparisons. DFa. Agents for active immunization. Facts & Comparisons eAnswers [online]: St. Louis, MO: Wolters Luwer Health, Inc; 2012. Accessed January 2, 2013.
21. CDC. Use of 13-valent pneumococcal conjugate vaccine and 23-valuent pneumococcal polysaccharide vaccine for adults with immunocompromising conditions: Recommenations of the Advisory Committee on Immunization Practices (ACIP). *MMWR.* 2012; 61: 816-819.
22. CDC. *CDC Health Information for International Travel 2012.* New York, NY: Oxford University Press; 2012.
23. APhA. Pharmacist Administered Vaccines. http://www.pharmacist.com/AM/Template.cfm?Section=Pharmacist_Immunization_Center1&Template=/CM/ContentDisplay.cfm&ContentID=26931. Accessed June 28, 2012.
24. APhA. Number of states authorizing pharmacists to administer influenza vaccine & number of pharmacists trained to administer vaccines. http://www.pharmacist.com/AM/Template.cfm?Section=Home2&ContentID=26925&Template=/CM/ContentDisplay.cfm. Accessed June 28, 2012.
25. Keely JL. Pharmacist scope of practice. *Ann Intern Med.* 2002;136(1):79-85.
26. Blake EW, Blair N, Couchenour RL. Perceptions of pharmacists as providers of immunizations for adult patients. *Pharmacotherapy.* 2003;23:248-254.
27. Bounthavong M, Christopher M, Mendes MA, et al. Measuring patient satisfaction in the pharmacy specialty immunization clinic: a pharmacist-run immunization clinic at the Veterans Affairs San Diego Healthcare System. *Int J Pharm Pract.* 2010;18:100-107.
28. Grabenstein JD, Guess HA, Hartzema AG. People vaccinated by pharmacists: descriptive epidemiology. *J Am Pharm Assoc (Wash).* 2001;41(1):46-52.
29. HRSA. National Vaccine Injury Compensation Program. http://www.in.gov/isdh/files/VICP.pdf. Accessed October 5, 2011.
30. CMS. Seasonal influenza vaccines pricing. http://www.cms.gov/McrPartBDrugAvgSalesPrice/10_VaccinesPricing.asp. Accessed October 5, 2011.
31. CMS. 2011–2012 Immunizers' Question & Answer Guide to Medicare Part B & Medicaid Coverage of Seasonal Influenza and Pneumococcal Vaccinations. https://www.cms.gov/Immunizations/Downloads/20112012ImmunizersGuide.pdf. Accessed October 5, 2011.
32. CDC. VFC federal register: Current fee table. http://www.cdc.gov/vaccines/programs/vfc/fee-fedreg.htmtable

7

NONPRESCRIPTION AND SELF-CARE

Sarah A. Parnapy Jawaid

■ LEARNING OBJECTIVES

After reading this chapter, the student pharmacist, community practice resident, or pharmacist should be able to:

1. Understand the importance of self-care and over-the-counter (OTC) products and how to integrate into daily workflow.
2. Describe the key components of obtaining a medication history for an OTC consult.
3. Assess and counsel a self-care patient using a structured process.
4. Be familiar with advanced services that are provided in a community pharmacy setting and how OTC products can be incorporated into these services.

INTRODUCTION

Self-care is defined as "the independent act of preventing, diagnosing, and treating one's own illnesses without seeking professional advice."[1] Self-care includes dietary interventions, dietary supplements, nonprescription or OTC products, home diagnostics, and monitoring and lifestyle modifications.[1] Self-care plays a vital role in health-care, and pharmacists are in a key position to assist patients with these interventions. Two of the most rewarding aspects of a community pharmacist's responsibilities are assisting patients in the selection of OTC medications and counseling patients on the proper use of these products.

OTC medicines are important to America's health-care, providing $102 billion annually in value to the U.S. healthcare system.[2] There are more than 300,000 marketed OTC medications in the market in 80 different therapeutic classes.[3,4] OTC medicines are available in the following categories: pain and fever, gastrointestinal, respiratory, ophthalmic, otic, reproductive, and genital and dermatologic disorders.[1]

OTC product sales in 2010 were estimated at $17 billion dollars compared with $2 billion dollar in 1965.[5] As more products come to market and as brand-extension products expand, pharmacists must be proactive when talking with consumers about these medications. Since OTC products are readily available to consumers, they need to be able to identify the problem and be able to identify exclusion for self-treatment and select the correct product for treatment. An incorrect diagnosis by a consumer, such as mistaking heartburn for symptoms of a heart attack, or improper product selection, such as selecting the incorrect dose of a pediatric analgesic, may lead to an adverse event or hospitalization.[6]

According to the 2010 American Pharmacists Association (APhA) Annual Survey, pharmacists make an average of 29 OTC recommendations each week, approximately 81% of consumers purchase an OTC product that their pharmacists recommended and the average time for an OTC consultation was about 3 minutes.[7] Convenience is cited as a primary reason patients choose OTC medications. In a 2008 National Council on Patient Information and Education (NCPIE) survey of 1005 Americans, 78% of participants stated they self-medicate because it saves a trip to the doctor's office, 78% of participants stated that their illness was not serious enough to warrant a doctor's visit, and 77% of participants stated that it saves time.[8] In addition to convenience and time, OTC medicines also save consumers money.[8]

A study conducted in 2010 shows that "90% of both consumers and physicians recognize that there are safe and effective OTC medicines for the first-line treatment of minor, repetitive and sometimes chronic conditions."[9] This study also showed that greater self-management of health-care and increased use of OTC medicines would save consumers and taxpayers approximately $5.2 billion annually.[9] Consumer demand for OTC products and physicians acknowledgement of the need for proper use of OTC medicines require student pharmacists and pharmacists to be proactive in assisting patients with the proper selection of these products.

In addition to patients using OTC products and pharmacists and providers recommending OTC products, many treatment guidelines include OTC product recommendations. For example, the American College of Chest Physicians recommends using dextromethorphan for short-term relief of a cough.[10] Some guidelines include OTC products as first-line therapies. For example, some of the first-line medications for tobacco cessation include nicotine gum, nicotine lozenge, and nicotine patch, which are all available OTC.[11]

OTC products can be purchased in a variety of retail outlets, including nonpharmacy locations, such as vending machines and gas stations. Therefore, the availability of pharmacists to assist with product selection and to assess patients and counsel on how to use the appropriate OTC medication can be a vital marketing tool to consumers when making the choice of where to purchase OTC products. Since these products are readily available and there are a variety of active ingredients in various combinations, it is important that patients use these products safely and effectively.[4] According to the FDA, each product's Drug Facts Label must include the following information: active ingredient and dose in each unit, purpose and use for the product, warnings for this product, and instructions for use and inactive ingredients.[12] It is imperative that pharmacists educate patients on the importance of reading the Drug Facts Label so they are aware of the information that is available to them to assist in product selection.

The Affordable Care Act (ACA) increases the role of the pharmacists in many settings where self-care is involved, including medical homes, transitions of care, medication reconciliation, continuity of care, and medication therapy management (MTM) opportunities.[13] Self-care and OTC medications are included in all aspects of MTM, including medication therapy review, personal medication record, medication-related action plan, intervention and/or referral, and documentation and follow-up.[14] Some examples how OTCs can be incorporated into MTM include, but not limited to, a review of all medications (including nonprescription, herbals, and dietary supplements), lifestyle modifications (nutrition and physical activity), and wellness support (weight management and tobacco cessation). You may be performing an MTM session for a patient who has hypertension, hyperlipidemia, diabetes, and COPD. When reviewing the patients' social history, they tell you that they smoke one pack per day. You can counsel and educate the patient on the importance of tobacco cessation and how it will affect and improve their other disease states that they currently have and are being treated for with prescription medications.

■ OBTAINING A MEDICATION HISTORY

It is crucial to obtain a thorough medication history when recommending an OTC product. Pharmacists are in a unique position to assess patients' medication history. Pharmacists need to be proactive when asking patients what medications they are currently taking including prescription, nonprescription, and complementary and alternative therapies. When patients utilize multiple healthcare providers, including pharmacists, accurate information and communication with other healthcare providers becomes vital. When asking about medications, the patient's adherence and compliance should be assessed. Patients may get their refills on time, but may not take their medications as directed. In addition to collecting a thorough medication history, patients disease states, economic status, dietary intake, and social support need to be collected.[15] When interviewing a consumer, keep in mind that the purchaser is not always the patient for whom the OTC product is intended.

During a medication history interview, the following information needs to be obtained[15]:

- Demographic information
- Dietary information
- Social habits
- Current and past prescription medications
- Current and past nonprescription medications
- Current and past complementary and alternatives therapies
- Allergies
- Adverse drug reactions
- Compliance and adherence

It is important to use open-ended questions when asking about medication history and listen to the patient's response. Effective listening is as important as effective questioning and the pharmacist needs to stay focused on the patient. A good statement to start the interview with is, "Tell me about your medications that you take on a regular basis." As the interview progresses, closed-ended questions may need to be used to get more information out of the patient. Remember, do not use leading or multiple questions.

After an appropriate history is collected from the patient, you have three options to provide to the patient[1]:

1. No product recommendation and non-pharmacological options are discussed (e.g., proper sleep hygiene rather than an antihistamine)
2. Self-care product recommendation
3. Refer to physician or other healthcare provider

■ ASSESSMENT OF PATIENT SYMPTOMS

When asking patients about their ailment or condition, it is important to ask all of the appropriate questions. There are two mnemonics that are utilized by self-care practitioners: QuEST/SCHOLAR or SCHOLAR-MAC and PQRSTA.[1,16]

QUEST/SCHOLAR OR SCHOLAR-MAC[1,16]

- **Qu**ickly and accurately assess the patient by asking about the following:
    - **S**ymptoms
    - **C**haracteristics
    - **H**istory
    - **O**nset
    - **L**ocation
    - **A**ggravating factors
    - **R**emitting factors
    - **M**edication use (including prescription and nonprescription products)
    - **A**llergic reactions
    - **C**oexisting conditions
- **E**stablish that the patient is able to use a self-care product
- **S**uggest an appropriate self-care product
- **T**alk with the patient about the product

PQRST Mnemonic for Symptom Analysis[1,16]

- **P**alliation (What caused the condition?)
- **Q**uality (describe the condition)
- **R**egion (What has helped the condition?)
- **S**igns and symptoms (Where is the problem?/How severe is it?)
- **T**emporal factors (When did the problem begin?/How often does it occur?)

■ INCORPORATE OTCs INTO PHARMACIST-PROVIDED CLINICS

As the number of patients that community pharmacists and student pharmacists see on a daily basis increases, it is important that we assist patients in proper OTC selection of products based on their symptoms, current disease states, and medications. In addition to the dispensing role, many community pharmacists are offering advanced pharmacy services and patient care clinics, including MTM, heart health clinics, osteoporosis clinics, diabetes support and education, and smoking cessation. These advanced services can also assist with appropriate OTC selection based on disease states and medications. While these services can lead to an OTC sale, adherence to both prescription and nonprescription medicines should be emphasized.

In a heart health clinic, pharmacists can provide blood pressure and cholesterol screenings. Pharmacists may recommend patients to take a low-dose daily aspirin depending on their risk factors, past medical history, family history, and current medications.[17] As cough and cold season approaches, it is important to emphasize to patients with a heart condition to use caution with OTC cough and cold product selection since some active ingredients (e.g., pseudoephedrine) may lead to an increase in blood pressure or heart rate.[18] If patients are looking for a pain reliever, the Drug Facts Label should be read carefully since heart-related warnings are included on certain products. Pharmacists could create a list of approved or unapproved OTC products for patients who have heart conditions to assist those patients in selecting the correct OTC medications. In addition to providing heart health education, pharmacists may focus specifically on cholesterol for some patients. Pharmacists can provide patients with therapeutic lifestyle changes (TLC), including reduced intake of saturated fat and cholesterol, increase intake of dietary soluble fiber, increased physical activity, and weight reduction.[19] In addition to TLC, pharmacists can make OTC product recommendations based on lipid panel values. Some OTC products that would be appropriate to help with the cholesterol panel could include niacin, omega-3 fatty acids, fiber, plant sterols and stanols, red yeast rice, and CoQ10.[20,21] When selecting appropriate supplements, it is important to select a product that is USP-verified.[22]

If a pharmacist is working in an osteoporosis clinic, patients can be provided with lifestyle changes to assist with bone health, which include eating foods that are high in dietary calcium and vitamin D and incorporating weight-bearing exercises into their daily routine.[23] It may be recommended for patients to get a calcium and vitamin D supplement to further help with bone health.[23] It is important that patients understand only 500–600 mg of calcium is absorbed at one time. So, if you have patient who is taking a multivitamin that contains calcium and a calcium supplement, they should separate the doses to maximize the absorption and benefits of the calcium.[23] It is important to ask patients if they take a medication for acid suppression, since they would need to take a calcium citrate product for better absorption.[24]

Many pharmacists offer diabetes support services at their pharmacy.[25,26] Pharmacists can provide diabetes education, including glucometer training, insulin injection technique, sick day management, proper foot care, and nutrition counseling. Products for blood glucose and A_{1c} testing are available to help patients monitor and manage their condition. In addition, products for skin care, oral hygiene, identification bracelets, sugar-free cough and cold products, glucose tablets, and diabetic foot lotion can be provided to patients.

Tobacco cessation is a well-established service that is available in many pharmacies.[27] Pharmacists can offer and lead support group sessions and provide various education venues to help with tobacco cessation. There are several products to assist with tobacco cessation, including nicotine replacement lozenges, gum, and patches. Pharmacists may also assist in lifestyle and behavioral modification techniques to assist with tobacco cessation.

Pharmacists who are working in a weight management clinic can provide healthy lifestyle counseling, including nutrition and physical activity, body mass index (BMI) calculations, and action plans to assist in maintaining a healthy weight.[28] Decreasing weight can be beneficial to overall health and specific disease states such as diabetes or heart health. alli© is the only FDA-approved product available OTC to assist with weight reduction.[29] If a patient is an appropriate candidate for this product, pharmacists can provide the proper counseling that is required, including the selection of an appropriate vitamin to use with this product.

Pharmacists can assist patients with proper selection of heartburn medications, depending on the severity and duration of symptoms. A pharmacist could recommend non-pharmacological therapy to assist with heartburn symptoms. In addition to non-pharmacological therapy, pharmacists can recommend proper use of antacids, regular use of a H2 receptor antagonist, or use of a proton pump inhibitor.

Pharmacists working in warmer climates or beach and outdoor tourist areas can incorporate proper sun health counseling. It is important to emphasize to patients the need for sunscreen including the proper amount to apply and when to apply/reapply. If patients present with a sunburn, pharmacists can provide treatment advice including adequate hydration, moisturizer, and pain relief.

It is imperative for pharmacists considering new advanced pharmacy services to offer to understand their patient population. For example, a pharmacist working in an area that has a high pediatric population may want to consider asthma or a healthy living service (versus an osteoporosis clinic). The goal in developing these services is financial viability and profitability as well as advancement of the practice of pharmacy. It is also important to advertise these services to local practitioners, so they are aware of what pharmacists can offer to their patients and to current pharmacy patrons. A way to advertise these services is to offer special discounts during the specific month (e.g., diabetes-related OTC and consultations during the month of November). Pharmacists can feature the selected OTC products during specific times of year (e.g., sunscreen during the summer months). Providing advanced services allows pharmacists to enhance their counseling skills and improve communication with their patients.

When developing specific services, a business plan along with a SWOT analysis should be conducted. A business plan can help develop a service or expand an existing service to help the pharmacy grow and provide advanced patient care.[30] A SWOT analysis includes analyzing the strengths, weakness, opportunities, and threats of a service.[30] An example of a SWOT analysis for providing a heart health education/screening is listed in Table 7-1.

Table 7-1. SWOT Analysis for Nonprescription Services

Strengths	Weakness
No pharmacy within 50 miles offers blood pressure and cholesterol screening	Staffing limitation
Opportunities	**Threats**
Increase patient satisfaction and increase OTC sales and payment for services. Appropriate patient population to market these services	Physicians may not support the service

■ DOCUMENTING OTC CONSULTATIONS

It is important to document OTC consults and recommendations. Pharmacists can document their OTC recommendations within the medication action plan, intervention/referral, and follow-up sections.[14] These interventions can be documented on paper or in a computer system in an organized and legible fashion. These consults can be documented via the SOAP note format.[15] A SOAP note includes the subjective, objective, assessment, and plan for the patient.[15]

■ PAYMENT FOR SERVICES

Pharmacists can provide services through various payment options, including Medicare (Part B and D), state Medicaid programs, third-party payers, and fee-for-service.[31,32] Under Medicare Part B, pharmacists are recognized to provide immunizations, durable medical equipment (including supplies for diabetes), and diabetes education.[31,33] In order for pharmacists to obtain reimbursement for diabetes education, the pharmacy must be an American Diabetes Association recognized site and provided by a team, including a certified diabetes educator (may be a pharmacist) and a dietician.[31,33]

Medicare Part D pays for MTM services, which may include a pharmacist providing this service.[34] The ACA recognizes pharmacists as providers of MTM.[13] Medicare Part D provides opportunities to receive payment for MTM. Current Procedural Terminology (CPT) codes were created for pharmacists to use and bill for these services.[34,35] In addition to providing revenue for the pharmacy, pharmacists are provided

Table 7-2. Example of Lower Cost RX to OTC Switches

Product Class	Prescription Product	OTC Product Options
Antihistamines	Xyzal® (levocetirizine), Clarinex® (desloratadine), Zyrtec® (cetirizine), Allegra® (fexofenadine), Claritin® (loratadine)	Zyrtec® (cetirizine), Allegra (fexofenadine), Claritin® (loratadine)
Proton pump inhibitors	Aciphex® (rabeprazole), Prilosec® (omeprazole), Prevacid® (lansoprazole), Protonix® (pantoprazole), Nexium® (esomeprazole), Dexilant™ (dexlansoprazole)	Prevacid® 24HR (lansoprazole), Prilosec OTC® (omeprazole)

advanced patient care services, improving patient outcomes, and decreasing hospitalizations.

OTC AS COST SAVINGS FOR PATIENTS

Patients may bring in prescriptions and ask for an OTC product alternative in order to save money. This substitution may help with insurance co-payments and could prevent people from falling into the donut hole with Medicare Part D.[36] Recommending a patient to use an OTC product in place of a prescribed product requires communication with the prescriber of this medication. Table 7-2 provides some examples of oral antihistamine and proton pump inhibitor prescription products that could be substituted for OTC products.

PATIENT CASE

KA is a 26 y/o WF who presents to the pharmacy with a "burning" feeling in her chest. Below is her history based on your pharmacy records.

Current medications: Advair 250/50, 1 inhalation twice a day, ProAir HFA inhaler 2 puffs as needed, Singulair 10 mg daily. No OTC or herbal products.

Medical conditions: Asthma

Family history: Father and mother alive and healthy, brother and sister alive and healthy

Social history: No tobacco, 1-2 glasses of wine weekly, 1-2 caffeinated beverages weekly, limited income.

Allergies: None

You use the PQRSTA mnemonic to assess the patient symptoms. After reviewing the responses, what would be the best treatment for this patient?

- **P**recipitating: "It seems like this feeling occurs after I eat spicy foods."
- **Q**uality: "It is a burning feeling in my chest."
- **R**elief: "I haven't really tried anything, so I am not sure what would help."
- **S**ite/severity: "The burning is just located in my chest, it isn't too severe, just more annoying than anything."
- **T**emporal factors: "It began about 2 hours after I ate some spicy foods, I did notice it last week after I ate spicy food as well, but I just thought that it was something that didn't agree with me."
- **A**ssociated symptoms: "Nothing"

A. Is the patient eligible to be treated with an OTC product? If so, what are the options for this patient?

Yes, she is a candidate for self-care.

1. The pharmacist should review non-pharmacological (including lifestyle and dietary) options for episodic heartburn with this patient. Non-pharmacological options for this patient specifically include avoid foods that aggravate her symptoms (spicy foods).
2. Antacids (example of active ingredients include magnesium hydroxide, magnesium carbonate, magnesium trisilicate, aluminum hydroxide, aluminum phosphate, calcium carbonate, and sodium bicarbonate)
3. OTC low-dose H_2RA (example of active ingredients include cimetidine, nizatidine, famotidine, and ranitidine)
4. OTC H_2RA and antacid

B. How long should this patient use the recommended therapy before she contacts her physician?

The patient should use therapy for up to 2 weeks. If her symptoms continue, then she should be referred to a physician.

C. What non-pharmacological options would you provide to this patient?

Since her symptoms are episodic and related to diet, recommend calcium carbonate 500 mg, chew 2-4 tablets as needed for symptoms with a maximum of 15 tablets/day. A recommendation to avoid spicy foods should be provided to KA.[37]

■ EXPERT INTERVIEW

Keith Guy, RPh
Owner of Guy's Innovative Pharmacy
Guy's Medical Center Pharmacy both located in McComb, MS

Guy's Innovative Pharmacy provided customers with the following services: bioidentical hormones, nutritional consults, compounding (sterile and nonsterile), home infusion (TPN, hydration therapy), and hospice consultation.

Keith offers OTC and self-care consultation services for patients by providing integrative or functional medicine, where he incorporated homeopathic recommendations along with OTC product selections.

When he is working with patients, he looks at the whole picture and not just the ailment that they are presenting for; he will ask about family history and make appropriate recommendations for patients to maintain a healthy lifestyle.

Keith has developed a respect within the community in which he serves. He is in a rural location in Mississippi, and being a leader within this innovative practice he always looks at the evidence and science behind recommendations when providing customer care. One of his biggest barriers to providing these services is the resistance to change within the medical community.

In addition to Keith providing these services, his staff, pharmacists, and two nurses employed by the pharmacy assist in these services. He charges patients a consultation fee for patients who take 30 minutes or more of his time, so he can provide the most value to the patient. When a patient comes to the pharmacy asking a question, which may be more complex to answer in the OTC aisles or at the pharmacy counter within 5–10 minutes, Keith will sit down with him/her to review his/her questions and assess the patient. Keith will review his consultation fee with the patient. Depending on the patient's needs and questions, Keith will review medication, order lab test, etc.

He has enjoyed his experience with these customers and the satisfaction that he has received in providing these services.

■ SUMMARY POINTS

1. Self-care and OTC products are used by many people and are valuable in treating ailments.
2. There are a variety of OTC products available to patients.
3. It is important to incorporate self-care and OTC recommendations into daily practice as a pharmacist.
4. Make sure to ask appropriate questions about current and past medication use prior to recommending an OTC product.
5. It is important to have a systematic approach to patients who approach for a self-care or OTC recommendation.
6. There are various OTC that can be incorporated into clinics that pharmacists can participate in.
7. Be familiar with the Drug Facts Label for OTC products.
8. When recommending an OTC product, make sure that the physician is aware of the product that is being recommended.

STUDY QUESTIONS

1. Self-care includes all of the following *except*:
   a. Dietary interventions
   b. Dietary supplements
   c. Nonprescription medications
   d. Home diagnostics and monitoring devices
   e. Pharmacist prescribed prescription medications via collaborative practice agreements

2. According to the 2010 APhA Annual Survey, a pharmacist's recommendation has little impact on consumer behavior regarding purchase of recommended OTC products.
   a. True
   b. False

3. Pharmacists should use which of the following methods to obtain accurate and complete medication histories?
   a. Validated survey tools
   b. Open-ended questions
   c. Effective listening
   d. Directed and leading questions
   e. All of the above
   f. B and C only

4. A patient describes foot pain as burning, tingling, and like "pins and needles." Which part of the PQRSTA mnemonic for symptom analysis would best describe this information?
   a. Precipitating
   b. Quality
   c. Relief
   d. Temporal factors

5. Documentation of OTC consultations is not necessary since OTC products are widely available at nonpharmacy retail outlets.
   a. True
   b. False

6. A patient asks about nonprescription alternatives to his/her expensive prescription for Xyzal®. Which of the following would be the most appropriate recommendation?
   a. Cetirizine
   b. Diphenhydramine
   c. Ranitidine
   d. Chlorpheniramine

BIBLIOGRAPHY

1. Krinsky DL, Berardi RR, Ferreri SP, et al. *Handbook of Nonprescription Drugs: An Interactive Approach to Self-Care*. 17th ed. Washington, DC: American Pharmacists Association; 2012.
2. Consumer Healthcare Products Association and Booz & Co. The Value of OTC Medicine to the United States, January 2012. http://www.yourhealthathand.org/. Accessed May 22, 2012.
3. U. S. Food and Drug Administration. Drug Applications for Over-the-Counter Drugs. http://www.fda.gov/drugs/developmentapprovalprocess/howdrugsaredevelopedandapproved/approvalapplications/over-the-counterdrugs/default.htm. Accessed September 29, 2011.
4. Report of the Consumer Healthcare Products Association's Clinical/Medical Committee. White paper on the benefits of OTC medications in the United States. *Pharmacy Today*. October 2010:68-79.
5. Consumer Healthcare Products Association. OTC Retail Sales – 1964–2010. http://www.chpa-info.org/pressroom/Retail_Sales.aspx. Accessed on May 21, 2012.
6. A Call to Action. *Protecting U.S. Citizens from Inappropriate Medication Use: A White Paper on Medication Safety in the U.S. and the Role of Community Pharmacists*. Horsham, PA: Institute for Safe Medication Practices; 2007.
7. American Pharmacists Association. Pharmacists' pick of the top OTCs. *Pharmacy Today*. February 2011:Suppl 1.

8. National Council on Patient Information and Education. Self-medication and allergies survey. www.bemedwise.org/survey/ExecutiveSummary/pdf. January 2008. Accessed July 1, 2011.
9. London PA and Associates. Your Health and Hand Survey. Potential Reduction in Unnecessary Visits to Doctors from Safe and Appropriate Use of OTC Medicines Could Save Consumers and Taxpayers Billions Annually. June 2011. www.yourhealthandhand.org. Accessed July 15, 2011.
10. Bolser DC. Cough suppressant and pharmacological protussive therapy: ACCP evidence-based clinical practice guidelines. *Chest.* 2006;129(Suppl 1):238S-249S.
11. Fiore MC, Jaen CR, Baker TB, et al. *Treating Tobacco Use and Dependence: 2008 Update. Clinical Practice Guideline.* Rockville, MD: U.S. Department of Health and Human Services, Public Health Service; 2008.
12. U.S. Food and Drug Administration. OTC Drug Facts Label. http://www.fda.gov/Drugs/ResourcesForYou/Consumers/ucm143551.htm. Accessed July 15, 2011.
13. American Pharmacists Association. Patient Protection and Affordable Care Act and Health Care Education and Reconciliation act of 2010: summary of pharmacy provisions. www.pharmacist.com/AM/Template.cfm?Section=Home2&TEMPLATE=/CM/ContentDisplay.cfm&CONTENTID=24358. Accessed September 2, 2011.
14. American Pharmacists Association, National Association of Chain Drug Stores Foundation. Medication therapy management in pharmacy practice: core elements of an MTM service model (version 2.0). *J Am Pharm Assoc.* 2008;48:341-353.
15. Tietze KJ. *Clinical Skills for Pharmacists: A Patient-Focused Approach.* 2nd ed. St. Louis: Mosby; 2004.
16. Buring SM, Kirby J, Conrad WF. A structured approach for teaching students to counsel self-care patients. *Am J Pharm Educ.* 2007;71(1):1-7, Article 8.
17. U.S. Preventative Services Task Force. *Aspirin for the Prevention of Cardiovascular Disease: Recommendation Statement. AHRQ Publication No. 09–051290EF-2, March 2009.* Rockville, MD: Agency for Healthcare Research and Quality. http://www.uspreventiveservicestaskforce.org/uspstf/uspsasmi.htm. Accessed September 6, 2011.
18. Salerno SM, Jasckson JL, Berbano EP. Effect of oral pseudoephedrine on blood pressure and heart rate. *Arch Intern Med.* 2005;165:1686-1694.
19. National Cholesterol Education Program. National Heart Lung and Blood Institute. National Institutes of Health. Third Report of the Expert Panel on Detection, Evaluation, and Treatment of High Blood Cholesterol in Adults (ATP III) Final report. September 2002. National Institutes of Health, Bethesda, MD: NIH Publication No. 02–5215.
20. *Omega-6 and omega-9 fatty acids.* Pharmacist's Letter/Prescriber's Letter; 2010;26(12):261214.
21. *Supplements for lowering cholesterol: an update.* Pharmacist's Letter/Prescriber's Letter; 2008;24(9):240909.
22. U. S. Pharmacopeia. The USP Dietary Supplement Verification Program. http://www.usp.org/USPVerified/dietarySupplements/ Accessed September 10, 2011.
23. National Osteoporosis Foundation. *Clinician's Guide to Prevention and Treatment of Osteoporosis.* Washington, DC: National Osteoporosis Foundation, 2010. http://www.nof.org/professionals/clinical-guidelines. Accessed August 22, 2011.
24. Straub DA. Calcium supplementation in clinical practice: a review of forms, doses, and indications. *Nutr Clin Pract.* 2007;22:286-296.
25. Johnson CL, Nicholas A, Divine H, Perrier DG, Blumenschein K, Steinke DT. Outcomes from diabetes CARE: a pharmacist-provided diabetes management service. *J Am Pharm Assoc.* 2008;48:722-730.
26. Sisson E, Kuhn C. Pharmacist roles in the management of patients with type 2 diabetes. *J Am Pharm Assoc.* 2009;49(suppl 1):S41-S45.
27. Kennedy D, Small R. Development and implementation of a smoking cessation clinic in community pharmacy practice. *J Am Pharm Assoc.* 2002;42:83-92.
28. Ahrens RA, Hower M, Best AM. Effects of weight reduction interventions by community pharmacists. *J Am Pharm Assoc.* 2003;43:583-589.
29. GlaxoSmithKline. alli. http://www.myalli.com/. Accessed September 10, 2011.
30. Hagel HR, Rovers JP. *Managing the Patient-Centered Pharmacy.* Washington, DC: American Pharmacists Association; 2002.
31. Stubbings J, Nutescu E, Durley SF, Bauman JF. Payment for clinical pharmacy services revisited. *Pharmacotherapy.* 2011;31(1):1-8.
32. Snella KA, Trewyn RR, Hansen LB, Bradberry JC. Pharmacist compensation for cognitive services: focus on the physician office and community pharmacy. *Pharmacotherapy.* 2004;24(3):372-388.
33. Centers for Medicare and Medicaid Services. Pharmacist Center. http://www.cms.gov. Accessed on June 4, 2012.

34. U.S. Department of Health and human Services. Centers for Medicare and Medicaid Services. Medicare prescription drug improvement and modernization act of 2003. http://www.cms.gov. Accessed June 4, 2012.
35. American Medical Association. *CPT 2012: Current Procedural Terminology*. Chicago: American Medical Association; 2012.
36. Proctor and Gamble. Money Saving Advisor Mary Hunt Teams Up With Timothy Tucker, Pharmacist and Medicare Expert, to Help Members Make the Most out of Part D Coverage. http://phx.corporate-ir.net/phoenix.zhtml?c=104574&p=irol-newsArticle&ID=1055791&highlight=. Accessed September 10, 2011.
37. Zweber A, Berardi RR. Heartburn and dyspepsia. In: Krinsky DL, Berardi RR, Ferreri SP, et al., eds. *Handbook of Nonprescription Drugs: An Interactive Approach to Self-Care*. 17th ed. Washington, DC: American Pharmacists Association; 2012:219-235.

8

LIPID DISORDERS

Daniel Riche and Laurie Warrington

> ### ■ LEARNING OBJECTIVES
>
> After reading this chapter, the pharmacy student, community practice resident, or pharmacist should be able to:
>
> 1. Describe lipids and lipoproteins and their associated disorders.
> 2. Identify the risk factors associated with the development of lipoprotein disorders.
> 3. Review prescription and over-the-counter (OTC) pharmacotherapy treatment options for lipoprotein disorders.
> 4. Apply patient case and pharmacist interviews to overcome barriers to implementation of lipid management services within the community pharmacy setting.
> 5. Analyze the business management aspects needed to create lipid management services in a community pharmacy.

Table 8-1. Definition, Classification, Characteristics, and General Treatment of Lipid Disorders

Name	Fredrickson Classification[a]	TC	LDL	TG	HDL	Medication Treatment
Hypercholesterolemia	IIa	↑	↑↑	–	–	1st Line: Statin 2nd Line: BAS and/or CAI, then niacin
Hyperlipidemia	IIb	↑	↑	↑	↑	1st Line: Statin 2nd Line: TG = Fish oil, fibrate LDL = BAS, CAI
Mixed dyslipidemia	IIb	↑	↑	↑	↓	1st Line: Statin 2nd Line: Fibrate, niacin, CAI, or BAS
Atherogenic dyslipidemia	III	–	–	↑↑	↓↓	1st Line: Niacin, fibrate If LDL ↑, then statin
Hypertriglyceridemia/ dysbetalipoproteinemia	III or IV or V	↑	↓	↑↑	–/↓	1st Line: Fibrate, niacin (if HDL ↓), or fish oil (if TG >400 mg/dL)

BAS, bile acid sequestrant; CAI, cholesterol absorption inhibitor
Obtained from Riche DM, Wooten JM. Hypolipidemic drugs. In: Smith KM, Riche DM, Henyan NN, eds. Clinical Drug Data. 11th ed. New York, NY: The McGraw-Hill Companies, Inc; 2010:484
[a]Fredrickson classifications do not directly account for HDL. Thus, the Fredrickson classifications are approximated into suitable categories.

■ INTRODUCTION TO LIPID DISORDERS

Description of Lipids and Lipoproteins

Cholesterol, triglycerides, and phospholipids are transported through the blood in particles made up of lipids and proteins (lipoprotein complexes). Low-density lipoprotein (LDL), high-density lipoprotein (HDL), and very low-density lipoprotein (VLDL) are the three main types of lipoprotein complexes present in serum. Intermediate-density lipoprotein (IDL) is included in the LDL measurement in clinical practice but is located between VLDL and LDL. Chylomicrons are lipoproteins that are formed in the intestine and carry triglycerides from dietary fat.

LDL (60–70% of total cholesterol) contains the apolipoprotein (apo), apo B-100, and is the primary target of cholesterol-lowering agents due to its atherogenic properties, while HDL (20–30% of total cholesterol) carries cholesterol from lipid-rich foam cells to the liver and may protect against atherosclerosis. HDL contains apo A-I and apo A-II. VLDL (10–15% of total cholesterol) is rich in triglycerides and contains apo B-100, C-I, C-II, C-III, and E. Chylomicrons not only contain apo C-I, C-II, C-III, and E but contains B-48 in the place of B-100.

Overview of Lipid Disorders

Lipoprotein disorders are classified based on the specific lipoproteins involved resulting from primary or genetic defects (see Table 8-1). There are also many secondary causes of lipoprotein disorders that must be considered when suggesting, initiating, or modifying therapy (see Table 8-2).

Table 8-2. Secondary Causes of Lipid Disorders

Hypercholesterolemia	Hypothyroidism
	Obstructive liver disease
	Nephrotic syndrome
	Anorexia nervosa
	Acute intermittent porphyria
	Drugs: Progestins, thiazide diuretics, glucocorticoids, β-blockers, isotretinoin, protease inhibitors, cyclosporine, mirtazapine, sirolimus
Hypertriglyceridemia	Obesity
	Diabetes mellitus
	Lipodystrophy
	Glycogen storage disease
	Ileal bypass surgery
	Sepsis
	Pregnancy
	Acute hepatitis
	Systemic lupus erythematous
	Monoclonal gammopathy: Multiple myeloma, lymphoma
	Drugs: Alcohol, estrogens, isotretinoin, β-blockers, glucocorticoids, bile acid resins, thiazides; asparaginase, interferons, azole antifungals, mirtazapine, anabolic steroids, sirolimus, bexarotene
Hypocholesterolemia	Malnutrition
	Malabsorption
	Myeloproliferative diseases
	Chronic infectious diseases: AIDS, tuberculosis
	Monoclonal gammopathy
	Chronic liver disease
Low HDL	Malnutrition
	Obesity
	Drugs: Non-ISA β-blockers, anabolic steroids, probucol, isotretinoin, progestins

Obtained from Talbert RL. Dyslipidemia. In: DiPiro JT, Talbert RL, Yee GC, Matzke GR, Wells BG, Posey LM, eds. *Pharmacotherapy: A Pathophysiologic Approach*. 8th ed. New York, NY: McGraw-Hill; 2011:Chap. 28. http://www.accesspharmacy.com/content.aspx?aID=7974214. Accessed February 14, 2012. Table 28-5.

PATIENT EVALUATION

Classification of Lipoprotein Levels

A lipid panel (after a 12-hour or longer fast) should be drawn every 5 years for all adults 20 years of age or older. The panel should include total cholesterol, LDL, HDL, and triglycerides. Since LDL is a calculated value, only total cholesterol and HDL are accurate if the patient is in a non-fasting state. Triglycerides may be falsely elevated when drawn non-fasting, resulting in the appearance of lowered LDL.

Identification of Risk

During lipid screenings or lipid management, the pharmacist should complete a detailed patient history. This history must assess traditional cardiovascular risk factors (see Table 8-3), as well as an assessment of emerging risk factors. Identification of physical manifestations of lipid disorders (e.g., xanthomas, abdominal pain, or pancreatitis history) should be considered.

Other than coronary heart disease (CHD) itself, several risk equivalents convey a high chance of CHD development. Based on the ATP III, the most widely accepted risk equivalents include diabetes mellitus (DM), peripheral artery disease (PAD), abdominal aortic aneurysm, cerebral vascular disease (CVD), or a Framingham score >20%. By stratifying patients based on their personal cardiovascular risk factors, pharmacists are able to determine individualized cholesterol goals (see Table 8-4).

Emerging Risk Factors

Many emerging risk factors have been identified over the past several decades to assist in the predication

Table 8-3. Traditional Cardiovascular Risk Factors

Age: Men ≥45 years; women ≥55 years or premature menopause without estrogen replacement therapy
Family history of premature CVD (myocardial infarction or sudden death before 55 years of age in father or other male first-degree relative, or before 65 years of age in mother or other female first-degree relative)
Cigarette smoking
Hypertension (≥140/90 mm Hg or on antihypertensive medication)
Low HDL cholesterol (<40 mg/dL)[a]

[a]HDL cholesterol (≥60 mg/dL counts as a "negative" risk factor; its presence removes 1 risk factor from the total count).

Obtained from Talbert RL. Dyslipidemia. In: DiPiro JT, Talbert RL, Yee GC, Matzke GR, Wells BG, Posey LM, eds. *Pharmacotherapy: A Pathophysiologic Approach.* 8th ed. New York, NY: McGraw-Hill; 2011:Chap. 28. http://www.accesspharmacy.com/content.aspx?aID=7974214. Accessed February 14, 2012. Table 28-7.

Table 8-4. Risk Stratification

Risk Category	LDL Goal	LDL Level at Which to Initiate Therapeutic Lifestyle Changes (TLC)	LDL Level at Which to Consider Drug Therapy
CHD or CHD risk equivalents (10-year risk >20%)[a]	<100 mg/dL[b]	≥100 mg/dL	≥130 mg/dL (100–129 mg/dL: drug therapy optional)
2+ risk factors (10-year risk ≤20%)[a]	<130 mg/dL	≥130 mg/dL	10-year risk 10–20%: ≥130 mg/dL; 10-year risk <10%: ≥160 mg/dL
0–1 risk factor	<160 mg/dL	≥160 mg/dL	≥190 mg/dL (160–189 mg/dL: LDL-lowering drug is optional)

[a]10-year risk based on Framingham risk score.
[b]If a patient has preexisting CHD and an additional CHD risk equivalent, an LDL goal <70 mg/dL should be considered.
Obtained from Riche DM, Wooten JM. Hypolipidemic drugs. In: Smith KM, Riche DM, Henyan NN, eds. Clinical Drug Data. 11th ed. New York, NY: The McGraw-Hill Companies, Inc; 2010:489.

of CHD development. Ideally, emerging risk factors with the highest risk of CHD development could be considered for individualization of cholesterol goals and treatment. Considering the extended duration of time since the last ATP III update, the concept of emerging risk factors relating to lipid disorders has increased in popularity. In fact, the Emerging Risk Factor Collaboration (EFRC) has been established to improve the predictive value of emerging risk factors based on evidence.

The EFRC has clearly identified lipoprotein (a) as an independent predictor of CHD. C-reactive protein (CRP) has also demonstrated a continuous association with CHD, but CRP is also a general marker of inflammation that could indicate less specific predictive potential. A large, randomized, placebo-controlled trial investigated the potential of lipid-lowering therapy (rosuvastatin 20 mg/day) in patients without preexisting dyslipidemia but with elevated CRP. Results demonstrated significant benefit of lipid-lowering therapy, possibly confirming the role of CRP as an independent CHD risk factor.

Coronary artery calcium (CAC) scores have been evaluated as an adjunct to traditional Framingham risk methods. Higher CAC scores (particularly >400) have been significantly associated with progressive stenosis independent of traditional risk factors. The most promising use of CAC scores may be in the moderate classification (Framingham risk 10-20%) to help determine aggressiveness of medication therapy. Two concomitant disease states have also been identified as potential risk factors for CHD: obstructive sleep apnea (OSA) and human immunodeficiency virus (HIV).

Emerging risk equivalents are also under investigation. Chronic kidney disease (CKD), defined as a glomerular filtration rate <60 mL/min/1.73 m^2, has been identified by the National Kidney Foundation Kidney Disease Outcomes Quality Initiative (NKF KDOQI) as a CHD risk equivalent. This stance is commonly implemented in clinical practice and is further substantiated by the Study of Heart and Renal Protection. The increased awareness of metabolic syndrome has impacted the field of lipid management over the past decade. Metabolic syndrome is a constellation of at least three metabolic characteristics including low HDL, elevated TG, glucose intolerance, hypertension, and increased waist circumference. The presence of metabolic syndrome confers similar CHD risk to its individual components and provides little additional predictive potential.

Other emerging risk factors mentioned in the ATP III have an unclear impact on CHD development or prevention. Particularly, carotid intimal medial thickening (CIMT), apolipoproteins, cholesterol ratios, and thrombogenic factors have not been consistently targeted as mechanisms of CHD prevention and treatment.

Therapeutic Lifestyle Changes

Vital to the management of lipid disorders is therapeutic lifestyle changes (TLC), a synergistic element with pharmacological therapy. The key components related to TLC are dietary intervention and increased physical activity. Similar to goal-based strategies for cholesterol, TLC goals should be set at an initial visit and evaluated at each subsequent visit. Exercise goals should consist of 30–60 minutes of moderate intensity continuous aerobic physical activity (based on tolerance) including intermittent resistance training on 5–7 days weekly. Dietary interventions are summarized in Table 8-5. Body weight should be reduced up to 10% in 12 months and continued until a body mass index (BMI) below 25 kg/m^2 is reached. Waist circumference goals (<40 inches in men; <35 inches in women) can also be considered. Other beneficial lifestyle modifications to cardiovascular risk should be emphasized including smoking cessation, salt-restricted diets for patients with hypertension, and supplemental soluble fiber. Strict compliance with TLC goals can lead to LDL reductions up to 30%. There are several Internet-based resources related to dietary intervention (see http://www.heart.org/HEARTORG/GettingHealthy/NutritionCenter/Nutrition-Center_UCM_001188_SubHomePage.jsp; http://www.nhlbi.nih.gov/health/index.htm).

Table 8-5. Therapeutic Dietary Recommendations

Component[a]	Recommended Intake
Total fat	25-35% of total calories
Saturated fat	Less than 7% of total calories
Polyunsaturated fat	Up to 10% of total calories
Monounsaturated fat	Up to 20% of total calories
Carbohydrates[b]	50–60% of total calories
Cholesterol	<200 mg/day
Dietary fiber	20–30 g/day
Plant sterols	2 g/day
Protein	Approximately 15% of total calories
Total calories	To achieve and maintain desirable body weight

[a]Calories from alcohol not included.
[b]Carbohydrates should be derived from foods rich in complex carbohydrates such as whole grains, fruits, and vegetables.
Obtained from Talbert RL. Dyslipidemia. In: DiPiro JT, Talbert RL, Yee GC, Matzke GR, Wells BG, Posey LM, eds. *Pharmacotherapy: A Pathophysiologic Approach.* 8th ed. New York, NY: McGraw-Hill; 2011:Chap. 28. http://www.accesspharmacy.com/content.aspx?aID=7974214. Accessed February 14, 2012. Table 28-9.

■ MEDICATION MANAGEMENT

LDL-Lowering Agents

HMG CoA Reductase Inhibitors (Statins)

Hydroxymethylglutaryl-CoA (HMG-CoA) reductase inhibitors (atorvastatin, fluvastatin, lovastatin, pravastatin, pitavastatin, rosuvastatin, simvastatin) are the most effective medication class in lowering LDL levels with the potential for decreasing LDL 18-55%, triglycerides 7-30%, and increasing HDL 5-15% (see Table 8-6). Statins have been shown in clinical trials to have favorable outcomes in CHD and CVD due to their beneficial effects on the atherosclerotic process. Statins are generally indicated for the treatment of type IIa and IIb hyperlipoproteinemias.

Statins work by inhibiting HMG-CoA reductase, which is the rate-limiting step in the synthesis of cholesterol. Statins are usually administered in the evening and have a high first-pass clearance by the liver and a short half-life, except atorvastatin and rosuvastatin that can be administered any time of the day due to longer half-lives.

Statins are generally well tolerated. Elevated hepatic transaminases rarely occur, but liver function tests must be monitored. Statins are contraindicated in active or chronic liver disease. Statin-induced myopathy can develop, and changes in creatinine phosphokinase (CPK) should be assessed. Myopathy is more common when statins are used in combination with medications metabolized by cytochrome P450-3A4, including cyclosporine, fibrates, macrolide antibiotics, certain antifungals, and nicotinic acid. Patients should report muscle pain or weakness and the presence of dark red/brown urine. Myopathy can be characterized by myalgia (lacking CPK elevation), myositis (CPK 2-3 times the upper limit of normal), and rhabdomyolysis (CPK 10 times the upper limit of normal). If rhabdomyolysis is suspected, the statin should be promptly discontinued and the patient should seek immediate care.

Ezetimibe

Ezetimibe selectively inhibits the sterol transporter at the brush border of the small intestine, which results in the reduced absorption of dietary and biliary cholesterol. Synergistic lowering of LDL occurs when ezetimibe is combined with statin therapy and ezetimibe is primarily utilized in this manner (See Table 8-7). Because less cholesterol is delivered to the liver, LDL receptors are upregulated and blood cholesterol is reduced.

Ezetimibe is relatively well tolerated with myalgias, diarrhea, and upper respiratory tract infections being the most common side effects. Hepatitis, elevated transaminases, arthralgia, and rhabdomyolysis can occur.

Bile Acid Sequestrants

Bile acid sequestrants (cholestyramine, colesevelam, colestipol) decrease LDL 15-30%, increase HDL 3–5%, and have either no effect on triglycerides or

Table 8-6. Approximate Dose Equivalence of Statins Based on LDL

LDL Reduction (%)	Lovastatin (Mevacor®, Altoprev®)	Simvastatin (Zocor®)	Pitavastatin (Livalo®)	Fluvastatin (Lescol®)	Pravastatin (Pravachol®)	Atorvastatin (Lipitor®)	Rosuvastatin (Crestor®)
17–22	–	–	–	20 mg	10 mg	–	–
23–29	20 mg (M/A)	10 mg	1 mg	40 mg	20 mg	–	–
30–38	40 mg[a] (M/A)	20 mg[b]	2 mg	80 mg[d,e]	40/80 mg[d]	10 mg	–
39–46	40 mg BID[c] 60 mg (A)	40 mg[a]	4 mg	–	–	20 mg[c]	5 mg[d]
46–48	–	80 mg	–	–	–	40 mg	10 mg[c]
51–52	–	–	–	–	–	80 mg	20 mg[c]
55	–	–	–	–	–	–	40 mg[c]

[a]Inferior to corresponding dose of atorvastatin.
[b]Inferior to corresponding dose of pitavastatin.
[c]Possible "next level" LDL reduction.
[d]Not evaluated (based on product information).
[e]XL daily or IR BID.
Adapted from Riche DM, Wooten JM. Hypolipidemic drugs. In: Smith KM, Riche DM, Henyan NN, eds. Clinical Drug Data. 11th ed. New York, NY: The McGraw-Hill Companies, Inc; 2010:490.

Table 8-7. Cholesterol Effects of Medications for Lipid Disorders When Combined with a Statin

Class	Cholesterol Absorption Inhibitor *Ezetimibe*	Bile Acid Sequestrants *Colesevelam* *Cholestyramine* *Colestipol HCl*	Niacin *Niacin ER*	Fish Oil *Omega-3 FA*	Fibrate *Fenofibrate* *Gemfibrozil*
LDL	↓ 24%	↓ 8–16%	↓ 10%[a]	↑ 4%	–/↑ 5%
TG	–/↓ 10%	–/↑	↓ 22–24%[a]	↓ 23%[b]	↓ 15–25%
HDL	↑ 2%	–/↑ 7%	↑ 21–24%[a]	↑ 5%	↑ 6–20%

[a]At higher doses.
[b]TG <500 mg/dL.
Obtained from Riche DM, Wooten JM. Hypolipidemic drugs. In: Smith KM, Riche DM, Henyan NN, eds. Clinical Drug Data. 11th ed. New York, NY: The McGraw-Hill Companies, Inc; 2010:484.

result in a slight increase. Their LDL-lowering effect is additive when combined with other agents, and beneficial outcomes have been demonstrated in clinical trials. Sequestrants are indicated for the treatment of primary hypercholesterolemia (types IIa and IIb) in patients whose triglycerides are below 400 mg/dL.

Sequestrants work by binding bile acids in the intestine via anion exchange and reduce their enterohepatic recirculation. In turn, cholesterol is oxidized to form new bile acids. LDL-receptor expression is enhanced in response to less cholesterol being produced. LDL is therefore decreased in the serum. Hepatic production of VLDL may increase in some people and lead to an increase in triglycerides.

Bile acid sequestrants pass through the intestine with systemic absorption or toxicity. Sequestrants can interfere with the absorption of other medications, which should be taken at least 4 hours prior to the sequestrant. Gastrointestinal symptoms, including constipation, bloating, abdominal pain, bloating, fullness, nausea, and flatulence, are common.

Nicotinic Acid (niacin)

Nicotinic acid lowers LDL 5–25%, triglycerides 20–50%, and increases HDL 20-50%. Niacin, in combination with other lipid-lowering therapy, has been shown to slow atherosclerotic progression, reduce the risk of recurrent myocardial infarction, and decrease total mortality in clinical trials. Niacin is indicated for the treatment of type IIa, IIb, III, IV, and V hyperlipoproteinemias.

Niacin is thought to inhibit lipoprotein synthesis in the liver and decreases the production of VLDL particles. Nicotinic acid also inhibits the peripheral mobilization of free fatty acids, which results in a decrease in the secretion of VLDL from the liver. It is the most effective agent at increasing HDL.

Niacin therapy commonly causes skin flushing that is more common with the crystalline formulation. Most people develop a tolerance to this side effect with extended use, but it can be minimized by taking niacin with meals, consuming an aspirin before taking the medication, and gradually increasing the dosage. Gastrointestinal symptoms, including nausea, dyspepsia, flatulence, vomiting, diarrhea, or activation of peptic ulcer, are possible. Hepatotoxicity, hyperuricemia, gout, and hyperglycemia may occur but are more common at higher doses.

Herbals

Red yeast rice products are available OTC and contain lovastatin. The Food and Drug Administration (FDA) issued a warning in 2007 that these products may interact with other medications and have similar toxicities to statins that may not be recognized by consumers. The LDL reduction is minimal. Other OTC products that have demonstrated potential for hyperlipidemia are plant sterols/stanols, supplementary fiber, and immediate-release niacin. Of note, OTC niacin products labeled as "flush-free" contain inositol hexaniacinate, which has not demonstrated significant absorption of nicotinic acid, the active ingredient in niacin products. Therefore, "flush-free" niacin products are generally void of cholesterol benefit.

Triglyceride-Lowering Agents

Fibrates

Fibric acid derivatives or fibrates are indicated for the treatment of type II, IV, and V hyperlipidemia (see Table 8-1). Fibrates decrease TG and increase HDL with variable effects on LDL (see Table 8-7). The primary mechanism of action is peroxisome proliferator-activated receptors or PPAR-α agonism. There also may be subsequent mechanisms (e.g., enhancing lipoprotein lipase activity, inhibiting VLDL synthesis, and reducing cholesterol synthesis). Commercially available fibrates include gemfibrozil (Lopid®), fenofibrate (TriCor®), and fenofibric acid (Trilipix®).

Gemfibrozil is given 600 mg twice daily with meals, while fenofibrate and fenofibric acid are administered once daily, usually with meals. Dose adjustments for any fibrate should be considered in renal impairment ($\downarrow$ ~50% or next lowest available dose). Fenofibrate has numerous branded generic preparations available (e.g., Antara®, Fenoglide®, Lofibra®, Lipofen®, and Triglide®) and each preparation has a different lowest and highest available dose. Fibrates are well known for potentiating statin-induced myopathy. In fact, many experts recommend avoiding the combination of gemfibrozil and any HMG-CoA reductase inhibitor, but avoidance of the combination with simvastatin and lovastatin is particularly emphasized. Fenofibric acid, the active metabolite of fenofibrate, is the first fibrate to be approved for use co-administered with a statin as it avoids hepatic conversion to an active metabolite and decreases potential for hepatic drug interactions.

The most common adverse effects are dyspepsia, abdominal pain, diarrhea, myalgia, rash, and xerostomia. More serious adverse effects, for example, acute appendicitis and rhabdomyolysis, may also occur, particularly when combined with a statin. Elevations in liver function tests and cholelithiasis can occur; therefore, fibrates are contraindicated in patient with primary biliary cirrhosis or preexisting gallbladder disease. Fibrates can enhance the bleeding risk of oral anticoagulants and hypoglycemia risk of oral antidiabetic agents, particularly warfarin and sulfonylureas, respectively.

While older trials (VA-HIT study) demonstrate significant improvements in major cardiovascular events in patients with CHD using fibrates (i.e., gemfibrozil) to target HDL, newer studies (FIELD, ACCORD) have shown less favorable results with fenofibrate in patients with diabetes. The best place in therapy for these medications is for patients with atherogenic dyslipidemia (elevated TG and low HDL) when LDL lowering is not required.

n-3 Polyunsaturated Fatty Acids (PUFA)

n-3 Polyunsaturated fatty acids (PUFA) or omega-3 fatty acids, commonly referred to as fish oil, transcend pharmacological and non-pharmacological lipid management. Dietary intake of PUFA, especially from cold water fish, can improve saturated to unsaturated dietary fat intake (see Table 8-5). Interestingly, supplementation of PUFA has also demonstrated significant cholesterol benefit (see Table 8-7). The mechanism of this effect is thought to be due to the ability of the omega-3 fatty acids to inhibit the release of triglycerides from the liver, thus reducing the number of VLDL components and by stimulating lipoprotein lipase, which increases the clearance of triglycerides from the plasma.

The most important concept regarding PUFA is the composition of two essential fatty acids, eicosapentaenoic acid (EPA) and docosahexaenoic acid (DHA) in a 46%/38% ratio, respectively. The remaining percentage of PUFA can be compromised of other omega-3 fatty acids, omega-6 fatty acids, or inactive ingredients. Regardless of the preparation (cod liver oil, omega-3 concentrate, krill oil, etc . . .), EPA/DHA ratios at the daily amount mentioned below should be considered. The recommended daily amount of PUFA varies by indication. A patient without CHD or a lipid disorder does not require supplemental PUFA, but should have a biweekly dietary intake of cold water or fatty fish. If CHD is present but there is no specific need for TG reduction, a minimum of 1 g/day of EPA/DHA in dietary or supplemental intake should be recommended. For TG reduction, 2–4 g/day of EPA/DHA should be recommended.

PUFA is available by prescription as Lovaza®, which is given as two-1 gram purified capsules by mouth twice daily. Unfortunately, the exact content of nonprescription supplemental PUFA is not guaranteed by a regulatory body, nevertheless the nutrition facts label should be evaluated. EPA and DHA content can vary substantially in nonprescription preparations, containing as little as 30% EPA and DHA per 1-gram capsule. Due to this variance, the proposed therapeutic dose of nonprescription PUFA is between 6 and 12 capsules per day for TG reduction.

Adverse effects are infrequent, but can contribute to noncompliance. They include gastrointestinal upset, an increase in LDL cholesterol (by as much as 40% in some studies), belching, distaste, diarrhea, and body odor. Elevations in liver function tests and bleeding time have also been reported and require monitoring. High-dose (>10 g daily) omega-3 fatty acids have also been used to treat psoriasis and rheumatoid arthritis with varying results. Omega-3 fatty acids can be administered with statins (instead of fibric acid derivatives) without an increased risk of rhabdomyolysis. This triglyceride reduction also seems to display diminished returns, that is, the higher the triglycerides upon initiation, the larger the percent reduction demonstrated and vice versa.

Special Considerations

Familial
Genetic contribution to hyperlipidemia is well established. In some situations, a patient will present with LDL concentrations exceeding 250 mg/dL. These patients can be defined as homozygous (HoFH) or heterozygous familial hypercholesterolemia (HeFH). The primary treatment of these patients is multiple medication therapies targeting LDL reduction to a concentration as low as possible. In most cases of HoFH and occasionally HeFH, LDL apheresis is required. This patient population is notorious for noncompliance with both medications and apheresis; therefore frequent and consistent monitoring and counseling is necessary.

Pregnancy
Medications for hyperlipidemia are difficult to manage in pregnancy. Other than in cases of HoFH or HeFH, the benefit of tightly controlled lipids during pregnancy is questionable. The most common class of medications (statins) is strictly contraindicated in pregnancy. The only medication that is currently pregnancy category B according to the FDA is colesevelam. All other prescription medications are pregnancy category C. Though prescription PUFA is labeled as pregnancy category C, PUFA are frequently used in low doses for maternal-fetal health. The International Society for the Study of Fatty Acids and Lipids recommends that pregnant and lactating women take 200 mg of DHA daily. In breast-feeding, it is generally best to avoid hypolipidemic medications.

Pediatrics
Prior to the obesity epidemic, the predominant use of cholesterol medications in children was related to HoFH and HeFH. Bile acid sequestrants were the drug of choice in this high-risk patient population. While bile acid sequestrants are still used, both statins (e.g., rosuvastatin, atorvastatin, simvastatin, pravastatin, lovastatin, and fluvastatin) and ezetimibe are FDA-approved in familial lipid disorders. The maximum daily dose of statins is typically 50% lower than the maximum adult dosage. Prescription niacin, fibrates, and PUFA are not used in children.

It is becoming more common to identify children with hyperlipidemia in the absence of a genetic abnormality. The obesity epidemic has led to the use of several cholesterol medications in the pediatric population. Generally, there is a lack of long-term safety or efficacy outcomes in children using cholesterol medications. Atorvastatin and ezetimibe are FDA-approved for use in children as young as 10 years including in combination.

Combination Therapy
Combination therapy is commonly implemented in patients with hyperlipidemia. Combining medications can be complex. Reasonable stepwise progression of

therapy is detailed in Table 8-1. Efficacy in combination with statins is outlined in Table 8-7. Particular consideration should be given to drug–drug interactions that occur in combination with statins. Some medication classes have significant adverse statin drug–drug interactions (e.g., fibrates), while others can be synergistic (e.g., bile acid sequestrants).

■ ESTABLISHING LIPID MANAGEMENT SERVICES IN THE COMMUNITY PHARMACY

Developing the Business Plan

Pharmacists are the most accessible health-care professionals and can provide the ideal environment to meet one-on-one with patients to provide education, monitor treatment goals, and address medication adherence. Lipid management services can valuable to patients by increasing their understanding of their medications and improving adherence. Patients may also save money by identifying more cost-effective regimens. Lipid management is a good way to expand services for patients in your community pharmacy. The Asheville Project demonstrated a $2,704 decrease in mean insurance cost per patient per year with ongoing community-based pharmaceutical care for patient with diabetes. This can be a selling point for employers to encourage participation in these programs.

The first step in the planning process for establishing lipid management services should be to develop a business plan that details your pharmacy's goals, operating plan, internal and external environments, and any potential opportunities and threats. The business plan should be developed at least 6 months before initiating any new service so that potential barriers can be identified. The earlier that research and planning is commenced, the more likely the new services are to be successful.

The business plan should include a mission statement for your pharmacy as well as for each new service to be established. Essential elements of the mission statement include the customers you wish to reach, as well as your values, goals, and image. The core components of the plan itself are a description of the business and services to be offered, a marketing and financial plan, a description of the management team (including who will provide the services and how roles will change), and equipment needs and plan for operation. Initial investment will require the purchase of a point-of-care lipid analyzer and its appropriate cartridges. A comparison study between the CardioChek PA and Cholestech LDX was conducted at the Colorado Prevention Center. Results demonstrated better reproducibility with the Cholestech LDX than the CardioChek PA analyzer when compared with laboratory gold standard analysis. More accurate categorization for a Framingham risk score was achieved. The Cholestech LDX Analyzer System costs approximately $2200, and supplies for the first 50 encounters will be approximately $700, including labels for the device printer, capillary tubes, plungers, control solution, lancets, and cartridges. These prices will vary among suppliers. In addition, the pharmacist's time and facility spacing requirements need to be taken into account when calculating planned fees for services.

Collaborative Practice Agreement

The collaborative practice agreement (CPA) is established between a physician(s) in the community and the pharmacist and defines the scope of services to be provided by the pharmacist under the physician(s)' supervision. Always contact your state board of pharmacy for regulations specific to your location. The physician(s) you choose to work with should be someone with whom you have already established a good rapport.

The CPA for lipid disorders should include the physical examinations that you may conduct (blood pressure, pulse), laboratory tests that you will perform (point-of-care cholesterol), and specifics about the medications you have authority to adjust. Define any processes for potential urgent medical situations that could develop during a patient encounter.

Recruiting Patients

Potential patients can be recruited at the point of dispensing lipid medications, especially if nonadherence or drug-related problems are identified. Patients can also be referred to you from physicians or other health-care professionals in your community, so build relationships via face-to-face meetings and express your mutual goal for improved patient care outcomes. A patient or caregiver may also self-refer after learning about your pharmacy's new services.

Patient Visits

Pharmacists should have a designated private area for meeting with patients. The encounter should include an explanation of the services to be provided, what the patient can expect, and a detailed review of patient and medication history.

Documentation, Communication, and Reimbursement

Documentation is the most important part of the patient visit to record details of the encounter, issues identified, follow-up plans, and to serve as evidence of the services. Information can either be documented on paper or electronically. It should include the patient's demographics, visit details, assessment and plan, interventions and recommendations, and the plan for follow-up. The SOAP format is familiar to other health-care providers. A letter should be sent to the patient's physician or other health-care provider by standard mail, fax, or secured electronic method to detail the findings of the visit.

Documentation is also essential for billing for services. Reimbursement structures can include fee-for-service billing with private insurers, incident-to-billing with Medicare, payment for MTM with Medicare part D, and payment from state Medicare programs.

■ PUTTING IT ALL TOGETHER: PATIENT CASE

A 52-year-old man comes to the pharmacy for his Zetia prescription. He had a myocardial infarction last year. The patient is also taking NPH insulin 15 units twice daily and HCTZ 25 mg daily. The patient has no complaints today. He has cut down from two to one pack per day of cigarettes.

Vital Signs: BP 125/78, HR 85, RR 20, Height 72, Weight 240 lbs
Total cholesterol 246 mg/dL
Triglycerides 295 mg/dL
HDL 27 mg/dL
ALT 28/AST 31

- What is the patient's calculated LDL? (160 mg/dL; TC − HDL − TG/5)
- What is patient's LDL goal? (<70 mg/dL due to coronary artery disease and diabetes)
- What would be the percent reduction necessary to reach his LDL goal? (~57% reduction; [160−70]/160)
- What cholesterol medication would you recommend for this patient? (With diabetes and coronary artery disease, a statin is emphasized. Crestor 40 mg/day is the only cholesterol medication with the potential to consistently reach this patient's LDL goal.)

■ SUMMARY POINTS

- LDL, HDL, and VLDL are the three main types of lipoprotein complexes present in serum.
- A lipid panel (after a 12-hour or longer fast) should be drawn every 5 years for all adults 20 years of age or older.
- During lipid screenings or lipid management, the pharmacist should complete a detailed patient history.
- Many emerging risk factors have been identified over the past several decades to assist in the predication of CHD development.
- Vital to the management of lipid disorders is TLC, a synergistic element with pharmacological therapy.
- Statins, ezetimibe, bile acid sequestrants, and niacin are LDL-lowering agents.
- Fibrates, niacin, and PUFA are triglyceride-lowering agents.
- MTM is a feasible option in the identification and management lipid disorders.

EXPERT INTERVIEW: LIPID MANAGEMENT SERVICES IN COMMUNITY PHARMACIES

Two local Mississippi pharmacists who have been successful in establishing lipid management services in traditional independent and chain pharmacies were interviewed about their unique experiences.

Stephanie Kile, PharmD
Retail Chain Community Clinical Pharmacist

1. **What prompted you to begin providing dyslipidemia management services to your customers?**

    As a community pharmacist, I enjoy making a positive impact on the lives of my patients. Providing services like dyslipidemia management along with generalized medication therapy management allows community pharmacists, like myself, to provide nondisruptive health-care to patients based on the trust that is already established within our profession. I enjoy the transition that community pharmacists are making, not only in utilizing the dispensing functions of pharmacy to better manage patient medication use but also in being a readily available clinical resource for disease state management and medication therapy management.

2. **Were there any special equipment/software requirements to get these services started?**

    As part of a commitment by my employer to provide these services, programs such as OUTCOMES Pharmaceutical Health-Care® and Mirixa® are already available. Clinical guidelines are also accessible online. Continuing education and certificate programs are also offered.

3. **What were the biggest barriers that you have had to overcome to initiate these services in your pharmacy?**

    Providing these services is a paradigm shift in the practice of pharmacy for community pharmacists in our area. In years past, the community pharmacy was a place to receive dispensed medications. Though we still provide that service, we have transitioned into a valuable health-care resource for our patients. A barrier to this process has been empowering pharmacists to provide this service while balancing the needs of a functioning retail pharmacy. Awareness of this program and communicating to patients the value of this service for them has also been a challenge, especially when communicating over the phone.

4. **What does each patient encounter involve? How much time is required? How does your staff assist you?**

    Each patient encounter involves a one-on-one 30-minute session with their pharmacist. It is an opportunity for the patient to discuss freely with their pharmacist any medication therapy problems that they are experiencing. Any other issue that they may be experiencing can be discussed that could have an impact on positive medication outcomes such as access to transportation, fixed income restrictions, and insurance requirements. Trained technicians can assist the pharmacist, interns, and residents with scheduling appointments and identifying opportunities for interventions.

5. **How do you document your encounters/interventions?**

    Encounters are documented online by way of notes in the patient profile, drug profile, or patient chart. Using medication therapy management vendors such as OUTCOMES Pharmaceutical Health-Care® and Mirixa® provides another opportunity to document and provide a source for reimbursement for these services.

6. **What benefits do these services provide, both for your store and your customers? What feedback have you received?**

    The professional satisfaction gained from providing these services is immense and immeasurable. The impact that can and has been made by this program is the reason why I wanted to be a pharmacist. With the drug knowledge and clinical skills that I have attained, providing medication therapy management is the natural transition for community pharmacists. The feedback that we receive from our patients has been overwhelmingly positive.

Lorelei Farr, PharmD
Independent Community Clinical Pharmacist

1. **What prompted you to begin providing dyslipidemia management services to your customers?**
   I recognized an opportunity to educate the public and provide an easily accessible service applicable to most of my patients. My patient population includes many with diabetes and heart medications, markers for high-risk conditions that may benefit from the services. In addition, knowing that a fasting lipid profile should be obtained at least once every 5 years for all adults 20 years of age and older, I realized that it could be beneficial for most of my patients, especially those who would ordinarily not take the time to get recommended screenings.

2. **Were there any special equipment/software requirements for get these services started?**
   Documentation equipment is required, whether it be paper forms or electronic. We use the electronic Assurance™ system MTM software to record data and outcomes and the Cholestech™ LDX system for point-of-care lipid testing. To provide point-of-care testing, the equipment-specific supplies needed are test cassettes and capillary tubes with plungers.

3. **What were the biggest barriers that you have had to overcome to initiate these services in your pharmacy?**
   The biggest barrier was myself, doubting that I would have adequate knowledge or skills to provide such services. I quickly found that my education trained me to be able to deliver clinical services and employ methods to fine-tune my clinical skills and knowledge base, even after being out-of-practice for a while. Other barriers the pharmacy faced in delivering services included adequate physical space, time, and compensation. The physical pharmacy site had to be rearranged to allow for a comfortable private area for meeting with the patients, but it was less than anticipated, due to the small size of point-of-care equipment and the use of electronic records. To address the time issue, tech duties were reassigned to allow the pharmacist(s) more clinical time. Outside pharmacists were allowed to come deliver the services, with a small percent of compensation going to the pharmacy for providing space and equipment. There are still third-party payers who do not compensate for the services, but for patients on these plans or with no insurance, an overwhelming amount are more than willing to pay out-of-pocket (see benefits, below). Lastly, kinks in interprofessional relationships were initially a barrier. It was important to stress to other health-care providers in the area that the services are meant to be an asset to, and not replace them, and that patients are encouraged to keep their provider appointments. In many cases, forwarding point-of-care testing results to the providers helped prevent unpaid lab bills at the clinics.

4. **What does each patient encounter involve? How much time is required? How does your staff assist you?**
   The staff assists by complying with reassignment of tasks to free up pharmacist time for clinical duties. In addition, they help with appointment scheduling and advertising, by stuffing medication bags with fliers regarding services and answering general inquiries regarding services.

5. **How do you document your encounters/interventions?**
   I make thorough notes during the encounter with the patient and spend 10–15 minutes transcribing these into formal notes on an electronic documentation system, which allows for easily organized storage. I document my findings, assessment, recommendations, and plans for monitoring and follow-up. In addition, I give the patient a "to do" list with a copy of his or her relevant labs and keep a copy for my records.

6. **What benefits do these services provide, both for your store and your customers? What feedback have you received?**
   For the customers, the fast turnaround time for affordable point-of-care testing gives them immediate access to objective information to gauge his or her response to therapy. Because of this, there has

been a noticeable improvement in medication compliance, attitude toward therapy, and likelihood of lower-fat diets. The customers have expressed their appreciation over explanations of their lab values, therapeutic goals, and medications. They also appreciate when our work has resulted in more cost-effective medication for them.

Because of the above benefits to the customers, these services set the pharmacy apart from others in the area, resulting in increased business. Point-of-care testing is an additional source of revenue, and the clinical aspect of the services has improved job satisfaction, especially as a pharmacist, and patient satisfaction.

STUDY QUESTIONS

1. Of the following agents, which statin produces the greatest percentage change in LDL levels?
   a. Pravastatin
   b. Atorvastatin
   c. Simvastatin
   d. Rosuvastatin

2. By establishing dyslipidemia management services in the community pharmacy, pharmacists are well positioned to address which of the following patient barriers to treatment success?
   a. Medication nonadherence
   b. Drug interactions
   c. Adverse drug reactions
   d. All of the above

3. According to the NCEP ATP III guidelines, which of the following is/are considered a risk equivalent when calculating a patient's LDL goal?
   I. Abdominal aortic aneurysm
   II. Hemorrhagic stroke
   III. PAD

   a. I only
   b. III only
   c. I and III only
   d. All of the above

4. What member of the class of fibric acid derivatives has an FDA-labeled indication for co-administration with statins?
   a. Antara®
   b. Lopid®
   c. TriCor®
   d. Triglide®
   e. Trilipix®

5. If checked when a patient is NOT fasting, triglycerides are generally falsely lowered.
   a. True
   b. False

BIBLIOGRAPHY

1. American Heart Association; National Heart, Lung, and Blood Institute. Diagnosis and management of the metabolic syndrome. An American Heart Association/National Heart, Lung, and Blood Institute Scientific Statement. Executive summary. *Cardiol Rev.* 2005; 13(6):322-327.

2. Baigent C, Landray MJ, Reith C, et al. The effects of lowering LDL cholesterol with simvastatin plus ezetimibe in patients with chronic kidney disease (Study of Heart and Renal Protection): A randomised placebo-controlled trial. *Lancet.* 2011;377(9784):2181-2192.

3. Malloy MJ, Kane JP. Chapter 35. Agents used in dyslipidemia. In: Katzung BG, Trevor AJ, eds. Basic and

Clinical Pharmacology. 12th ed. New York, NY: The McGraw-Hill Companies, Inc; 2012:619-34.
4. Budinski D, Arneson V, Hounslow N, Gratsiansky N. Pitavastatin compared with atorvastatin in primary hypercholesterolemia or combined dyslipidemia. *Clin Lipidol.* 2009;4(3):291-302.
5. Colhoun HM. Lipid goals in metabolic syndrome and diabetes. *Curr Atheroscler Rep.* 2007;9(4):286-295.
6. Dale RA, Jensen LH, Krantz MJ. Comparison of two point-of-care lipid analyzers for use in global cardiovascular risk assessments. *Ann Pharmacother.* 2008; 42(5):633-639.
7. Drager LF, Polotsky VY, Lorenzi-Filho G. Obstructive sleep apnea: an emerging risk factor for atherosclerosis. *Chest.* 2011;140(2):534-542.
8. Emerging Risk Factors Collaboration. C-reactive protein concentration and risk of coronary heart disease, stroke, and mortality: an individual participant meta-analysis. *Lancet.* 2010;375(9709):132-140.
9. Emerging Risk Factors Collaboration. Lipoprotein(a) concentration and the risk of coronary heart disease, stroke, and nonvascular mortality. *JAMA.* 2009;302(4): 412-423.
10. Emerging Risk Factors Collaboration. The Emerging Risk Factors Collaboration: analysis of individual data on lipid, inflammatory and other markers in over 1.1 million participants in 104 prospective studies of cardiovascular diseases. *Eur J Epidemiol.* 2007;22(12):839-869.
11. Grundy SM, Cleeman JI, Bariey Merz CN, et al. Implications of recent clinical trials for the National Cholesterol Education Program Adult Treatment Panel III guidelines. *Circulation.* 2004;110:227-239.
12. Harris IM, Baker E, Berry TM, et al. Developing a business-practice model for pharmacy services in ambulatory settings. *Pharmacotherapy.* 2008;28(2):7e-34e.
13. Ho JS, Fitzgerald SJ, Stolfus LL, et al. Relation of a coronary artery calcium score higher than 400 to coronary stenoses detected using multidetector computed tomography and to traditional cardiovascular risk factors. *Am J Cardiol.* 2008;101(10):1444-1447.
14. Keating GM. Fenofibrate: a review of its lipid-modifying effects in dyslipidemia and its vascular effects in type 2 diabetes mellitus. *Am J Cardiovasc Drugs.* 2011;11(4):227-247.
15. Koletzko B, Cetin I, Brenna JT, et al. Dietary fat intakes for pregnant and lactating women. *Br J Nutr.* 2007; 98(5):873-877. Epub 2007 Aug 10.
16. Kris-Etherton PM, Harris WS, Appel LJ; American Heart Association. Nutrition Committee. Fish consumption, fish oil, omega-3 fatty acids, and cardiovascular disease. *Circulation.* 2002;106(21):2747-2757.
17. McKenney JM, Sica D. Role of prescription omega-3 fatty acids in the treatment of hypertriglyceridemia. *Pharmacotherapy.* 2007;27(5):715-728.
18. National Cholesterol Education Program (NCEP) Expert Panel on Detection, Evaluation, and Treatment of High Blood Cholesterol in Adults (Adult Treatment Panel III). Third Report of the National Cholesterol Education Program (NCEP) Expert Panel on Detection, Evaluation, and Treatment of High Blood Cholesterol in Adults (Adult Treatment Panel III) final report. *Circulation.* 2002;106:3121-3143.
19. Norris RB. Flush-free niacin: dietary supplement may be benefit-free. *Prev Cardiol.* 2006;9(1):64-65.
20. Ose L, Budinski D, Hounslow N, Arneson V. Comparison of pitavastatin with simvastatin in primary hypercholesterolaemia or combined dyslipidaemia. *Curr Med Res Opin.* 2009;25(11):2755-2764.
21. Preis SR, Hwang SJ, Fox CS, et al. Eligibility of individuals with subclinical coronary artery calcium and intermediate coronary heart disease risk for reclassification (from the Framingham Heart Study). *Am J Cardiol.* 2009;103(12):1710-1715.
22. Riche DM, Wooten JM. Hypolipidemic drugs. In: Smith KM, Riche DM, Henyan NN, eds. *Clinical Drug Data.* 11th ed. New York, NY: The McGraw-Hill Companies, Inc; 2010:471-493.
23. Ridker PM, Danielson E, Fonseca FA, et al. Rosuvastatin to prevent vascular events in men and women with elevated C-reactive protein. *N Engl J Med.* 2008;359(21):2195-2207.
24. Salvo CS, Nigro SN. Cardiometabolic disease: (part 1) The pharmacist's tools for managing dyslipidemia and hypertension. *Drug Topics.* 2012:36-45.
25. Stender S, Budinski D, Hounslow N. Pitavastatin demonstrates long-term efficacy, safety and tolerability in elderly patients with primary hypercholesterolaemia or combined (mixed) dyslipidaemia. *Eur J Prev Cardiolog.* 2012;20(1):29-39.
26. Talbert RL. Dyslipidemia. In: DiPiro JT, Talbert RL, Yee GC, Matzke GR, Wells BG, Posey LM, eds. *Pharmacotherapy: A Pathophysiologic Approach.* 8th ed. New York, NY: McGraw-Hill; 2011:Chap. 28. http://www.accesspharmacy.com/content.aspx?aID=7974214. Accessed February 14, 2012.
27. Weiner DE, Sarnak MJ. Managing dyslipidemia in chronic kidney disease. *J Gen Intern Med.* 2004;19(10): 1045-1052.

28. Williams MA, Haskell WL, Ades PA, et al. Resistance exercise in individuals with and without cardiovascular disease: 2007 update: a scientific statement from the American Heart Association Council on Clinical Cardiology and Council on Nutrition, Physical Activity, and Metabolism. *Circulation.* 2007;116:572-584.
29. Wohl DA, McComsey G, Tebas P, et al. Current concepts in the diagnosis and management of metabolic complications of HIV infection and its therapy. *Clin Infect Dis.* 2006;43(5):645-653.
30. Writing a business plan for a new pharmacy service. Monograph 23. The dynamics of pharmaceutical care: enriching patients' health. http://www.pharmacist.com/sites/default/files/files/mtm_writing_business_plan.pdf. Accessed February 13, 2013.

9

SMOKING CESSATION

Justin J. Sherman

> ### ■ LEARNING OBJECTIVES
>
> After reading this chapter, the pharmacy student, community practice resident, or pharmacist should be able to:
>
> 1. Evaluate the individualized benefits and barriers for smokers who want to participate in a formalized smoking cessation program.
> 2. Assess OTC and prescription pharmacotherapy treatments that would be most successful for a particular smoker in his or her cessation attempt.
> 3. Develop individualized strategies for a smoking cessation attempt, including behavioral change, stress management, and pharmacotherapeutic factors.
> 4. Evaluate and overcome barriers in order to implement smoking cessation services within a community pharmacy or clinic.
> 5. Analyze the business management aspects needed to create and maintain smoking cessation services, such as recruitment, developing interdisciplinary support systems, and reimbursement issues.

INTRODUCTION

Current estimates in 2012 show that approximately 45.3 million adults (19.3%) were smokers in the United States, including 21.5% men and 17.3% women.[1] The prevalence has decreased slightly over the past several years. However, nicotine use still represents the single most preventable cause of premature death in the United States at over 440,000 people dying per year from smoking-related causes.[1] This is one out of every five deaths due to smoking. Every year, smoking results in 5.6 million years of life lost prematurely and approximately 92 billion dollars of lost productivity. The amount of annual death in the United States resulting from smoking is more than that resulting from alcohol-related deaths, motor vehicle and gun accidents, homicides, and suicides combined. Indeed, the statistics are staggering!

The statistics regarding who in the population is most likely to smoke is interesting as well.[1] Adults living below the poverty line are more likely to smoke than those living at or above the poverty line (28.9% versus 18.3% are smokers, respectively). Those with a GED diploma are more likely to smoke (45.2%), with 33.8% of those who have less than a high school education to consider themselves as "current" smokers. The most likely ages for smoking are adults between 25 and 44 years of age (22%), and American Indians and Alaskan Natives are the most likely ethnic groups who smoke (31.4%). Of interest, the 19.3% of Americans who smoke can be described as "regular" smokers, and greater than 80% of these smoke daily. Approximately 70% of polled smokers stated that they wanted to quit and have had at least one quit attempt in the past year.

BACKGROUND

The Impact of Nicotine Use

Approximately 8.6 million people in the United States have at least one serious smoking-related illness.[2] Smokers most often die from lung cancer, but the second and third most likely cause of death for smokers is chronic obstructive pulmonary disease (COPD) and coronary artery disease (CAD), respectively. Smokers should be aware of the variety of cancers that can be caused by smoking. For example, cancer of the larynx, lip, tongue, esophagus, bladder, pancreas, kidney, cervix, and uterus are all associated with smoking.[2] Smoking increases the risk of death from COPD and is dependent on the number of cigarettes smoked daily. Fifteen percent and 25% of one and two pack per day smokers, respectively, are likely to be diagnosed with COPD. Smokers also should be aware of cardiovascular ramifications. Smoking increases the risk of death by three times for people with CAD.[3] The blood pressure is raised for several hours after each cigarette. Smokers also die significantly earlier than nonsmokers—13.2 years for men and 14.5 years for women.[2]

Unfortunately, smoking-related mortality affects nonsmokers. Approximately 3000 nonsmokers die each year due to lung cancer. Secondhand smoke is associated with coronary heart disease as well. Kids and infants of smokers are the most affected by secondhand smoke. Secondhand smoke causes more than an estimated 202,000 asthma episodes, 790,000 cases of otitis media, and 430 sudden infant death syndrome (SIDS) cases each year.[2]

How Nicotine Is Harmful?

Smokers know that it is harmful for them to continue, but specific knowledge about nicotine use is important. Cigarettes are full of harmful chemicals, including over 4000 chemical compounds and at least 40 known carcinogens.[4] Some of these include ammonia, arsenic, carbon monoxide, hydrogen cyanide, toluene, tar, and polycyclic aromatic hydrocarbons.[4] Nicotine from smoking can reach the brain within 11 seconds and stimulates receptors in the ventral tegmental area.[5] Next, dopamine is released in the nucleus accumbens and prefrontal cortex. Dopamine, as can be explained to patients, releases feelings of euphoria and pleasure and is often described as the "pleasure neurotransmitters."[6] Thus, the dopamine reward pathway is stimulated by "rewarding" experiences such as food, sex, and smoking, and these experiences become associated with increased dopamine release. Dopamine leaves the system rapidly as well, within minutes. The combination of rapid stimulation and exit with the dopamine reward pathway stimulates the need for repeat administration until tolerance develops.[6]

In addition to activation of dopamine receptors, nicotine results in the release of other neurotransmitters such as norepinephrine and acetylcholine. Increased norepinephrine release results in elevated heart rate, blood pressure, stroke volume, and cardiac output. This can lead to the cardiovascular problems mentioned. The polycyclic aromatic hydrocarbons can stimulate cytochrome P450 metabolism in the liver. This can expedite insulin metabolism and lead to increased insulin requirements for patients with diabetes. Smoking is especially harmful for patients with diabetes. Carbon monoxide of cigarettes also can interfere with the carbon dioxide/oxygen transmission in the alveoli of the lungs, leading to decreased oxygenation in the tissues of the lower extremities. Decreased peripheral vascular blood flow and increased risk of neuropathy can result. Also, high-density lipoproteins are decreased, while low-density lipoproteins are increased. Smoking can also lead to reduced estrogen levels, which can increase the risk of osteoporosis over time. Smokers know that "smoking is harmful"; however, a more thorough conversation regarding details by the health-care professional is often needed and appreciated.

Benefits of Cessation

Unfortunately, many smokers think that they will reap the benefits of cessation immediately. This is not the case for many of the consequences of smoking, so the time-course of experiencing benefits should be part of the discussion with them. After their quit date, many experience nicotine withdrawal in varying severity. If withdrawal is severe, they are likely to feel that the "cons" of quitting outweigh the "pros" (i.e., because they do not "feel better" immediately). For example, after 10 years of quitting, the risk of developing lung cancer has decreased to 50% of those continuing to smoke.[7]

In contrast, some benefits can be experienced more rapidly. For example, circulation improves and walking becomes easier within 2 weeks to 3 months after quitting. Lung function will increase up to 30%, and within 1–9 months lung cilia will begin to function normally again.[7] Coughing, shortness of breath, and fatigue begin to decrease within this time period as well. Patients tend to not have to be hospitalized for minor infections as much. After 1 year, the risk of developing CAD decreases to half that of someone who has continued to smoke. The risk of being diagnosed with COPD decreases incrementally by year, and after 5 years the risk of stroke is reduced to the same as one who had never smoked. Smokers should also be reminded of other cessation benefits as well. They will feel better, look better, have more energy, and will have saved substantial money from quitting.

One particular drawback is weight gain after cessation. Most former smokers tend to gain a mean increase of 4 to 5 kg after 12 months of abstinence, with most weight gain within 3 months of quitting.[8] Food begins to taste better and it is natural that their appetite increases. Former smokers would have to gain a substantial amount of weight—some sources discuss a 100-pound gain—before the benefits of smoking cessation would be offset by the weight gain.

Another common barrier for many older smokers is the preconceived idea that quitting would not benefit them. A study in the *British Medical Journal* examined the survival benefits of quitting.[9] In this study, three different groups of physicians were followed between the years 1951 and 2001. The groups consisted of those who had never smoked, those who never stopped smoking over the course of their lifetime, and those who stopped at certain ages. The investigators found that if smokers stopped at age 30, they added 10 years to their lives and had a life expectancy similar to those who had never smoked. If they stopped at age 40, they lived an average of 9 years longer than the group who continued to smoke. If they stopped at ages 50 and 60, they lived an average of 6 and 3 years longer, respectively.[9] A discussion of this study can address patients' longevity questions, but the increased quality of life that they are likely to experience should also be stressed.

The Impact of Health-Care Providers

The *Treating Tobacco Use and Dependence Clinical Practice Guideline* states that all clinicians should ask about tobacco use during every visit with patients.[4] Smokers who receive assistance from physician clinicians are 2.2 times as likely to quit successfully for 5 or more months. Smokers are 1.7 times as likely to quit when receiving assistance from nonphysician clinicians in comparison to not receiving any assistance.[4] Of interest, self-help material is no more effective for a smoker to quit and achieve abstinence for 5 or more months versus no other methods of assistance. Thus, the following methods of assisting smokers are not very effective by themselves: handing the smoker reading material about cessation, sending them to a Web site, and giving them a package insert for cessation medications without personally getting involved in the smoker's quit attempt. The message is clear: smokers need assistance from health-care professionals through active methods of counseling.

Personal assistance given to the smoker for the quit attempt is important. The number of clinicians involved in the patient's care is important as well. When smokers receive assistance in their quit attempt from two or more clinicians, they are 2.5 times as likely to quit for a sustained period of at least 5 months in comparison to smokers who receive no help from a clinician.[4] Thus, the patient's physician, nurse, and pharmacist should all be giving the smoker the same firm smoking cessation message.

While the smoker may not be interested in cessation during one particular visit to the pharmacy, patients tend to cycle through various stages of willingness to change their behavior. This will be explained in more detail later, but the pharmacist will have the perfect opportunity to effect this change at some point. Pharmacists can have a powerful role in smoking cessation. They are the most easily accessible health-care professionals, and over-the-counter (OTC) cessation products are very effective. Because the patient visits the pharmacy for refills either every month or every 3 months, the pharmacist could encounter the patient multiple times before another physician appointment.

Brief Clinical Interventions

Pharmacists should make brief clinical interventions for the following: (1) those who are willing to quit, (2) those who are unwilling to quit at the time of the discussion, and (3) smokers who have already quit.[4] For those willing to quit, the pharmacist should be prepared to intervene effectively with the "Five A's":

- Ask—Systematically identify smokers at each visit, such as with new prescriptions. Also, the computer system could flag smokers when a prescription is picked up from the pharmacy.
- Advise—A clear, strong, personalized message should be given to the smoker that cessation is the most important action to improve health. If the patient has asthma or COPD, the message should be tied in to these disease states. For example, one message given to the smoker picking up an inhaler for COPD could be this: "Mr. Smith, I see that you are picking up your inhaler refills. The inhalers can help you breathe better, but did you know that the only action that will extend your lifespan is to quit smoking?"
- Assess—The pharmacist can ask, "Have you given any consideration to quitting smoking?" If the response is "yes," the pharmacist could ask, "What time frame did you have in mind for quitting?" This assesses the smoker's readiness to quit. If the patient responds, "within the next 6 months," then the patient is likely in the contemplation stage of behavioral change (explained in the next section). If the patient responds, "within the next month," the patient is considered to be in the preparation stage.
- Assist and Arrange—This chapter should adequately prepare the pharmacist to provide individualized counseling and assistance in a single or group setting. The pharmacist should arrange for follow-up within 1 week for the patient wanting to quit smoking.

Smokers who are unwilling to quit at the time it is first approached should not be "pushed" hard at first. At this point the patient usually is not ready to quit or even to begin talking about quitting. The best approach would be to state: "As your pharmacist, I would be glad to discuss smoking cessation with you at a later time when you are more ready." The smoker will appreciate this straightforward approach and will be more likely to seek advice at a later date.

Finally, for those former smokers who have quit, the pharmacist should be supportive. Former smokers are proud that they were able to quit. Many even remember the exact date and time they smoked their last cigarette! Applaud the patient's accomplishment, and be prepared if the patient gives any indication of relapse. If the patient is likely to relapse, information helpful for relapse prevention can be found later in this chapter.

■ IDENTIFYING STAGES OF BEHAVIORAL CHANGE AND LEVEL OF DEPENDENCE

Health-care providers of all types have been successful in helping smokers in the short term. Pharmacists are effective in asking, advising, and assessing smokers regarding a quit attempt. However, the health-care professions largely have not been as successful in the latter two components—assist and arrange. Smokers should be assisted with an individualized quit plan, and continuous follow up should be arranged. These are labor-intensive but essential for long-term success.

Transtheoretical Model of Behavioral Change

Smokers tend to cycle through stages ranging from "not considering quitting" to a "relapse" stage. This cycle has been linked to the Transtheoretical Model of Behavior Change.[10] At any time, a smoker could be in one of the following components of this cycle: (1) not thinking about quitting and not ready to quit (precontemplation); (2) thinking about quitting and ready to quit, usually within the next 6 months (contemplation); (3) taking action to prepare for quitting, usually within the next month (preparation); (4) currently making a quit attempt (action); and (5) recently quit (maintenance). Unfortunately, many smokers experience relapse. Reasons include susceptibility to lingering psychologic dependence on nicotine and failure to implement permanent behavior changes. It is useful to identify in which stage of the Transtheoretical Model the smoker is in. Then, the pharmacist can gently urge the smoker toward the next stage. The Transtheoretical Model was discussed in the Motivational Interviewing chapter; thus, readers are referred to that chapter to review the stages as they apply to nicotine cessation and actions to take in each stage.

The Fagerstrom Test of Nicotine Dependence

A powerful tool can be used to determine the level of nicotine dependence—the Fagerstrom Test.[11] The test consists of six questions (Table 9-1), with an overall score of 0–10 to gauge the level of nicotine dependence. A common misconception is that the level of nicotine dependence is only correlated with the number of cigarettes that a smoker uses daily. A few may rate "high dependence" on this scale despite using relatively lower amounts of daily nicotine. The prudent pharmacist will consider all factors of the Fagerstrom Test when developing an individualized plan to quit.

The Fagerstrom Test can also be used to discuss the differences between "habits" and "addiction". Many smokers are steadfast that smoking is a "habit" and nicotine use can be stopped "anytime". Higher scores on the Fagerstrom Test can be discussed in terms of the relationship between dependence and addiction. Patients tend to feel more comfortable when smoking is viewed as a "habit" rather than what it is—an addiction. By viewing nicotine use as an addiction, it may be easier for patients to implement the daily behavior changes needed for long-term success.

■ INITIAL COMPONENTS OF ASSISTING WITH A QUIT ATTEMPT

Several components to implement during a quit attempt include: establishing a quit date, an initial plan, practical counseling (past experience of tobacco use, quit attempts, and triggers), recommendation of pharmacotherapy, and discussion of social support.[4]

Table 9-1. Fagerstrom Test for Nicotine Dependence

Question	Score
1. How soon after you awaken in the morning do you smoke your first cigarette?	
a. After 60 minutes	0
b. 31–60 minutes	1
c. 6–30 minutes	2
d. Within 5 minutes	3
2. Do you find that it is difficult to refrain from smoking in places where it is forbidden to smoke (e.g., church and movie theater)?	
a. No	0
b. Yes	1
3. Which cigarette would you hate most to give up?	
a. The first one in the morning after awakening	1
b. Any other cigarette	0
4. How many cigarettes per day do you smoke?	
a. 10 or less	0
b. 11–20	1
c. 21–30	2
d. 31 or more	3
5. Do you smoke more frequently during the first few hours after awakening than during the rest of the day?	
a. No	0
b. Yes	1
6. Do you smoke even if you are so ill that you are in bed most of the day?	
a. No	0
b. Yes	1
Level of dependence on nicotine is:	
Very low	0–2
Low	3–4
Medium	5
High	6–7
Very high	8–10

Further discussion should include behavioral modification, cognitive, and stress management strategies.

Basic Components

Many who try to stop smoking will not have a definitive strategy in place. Some will cut down on nicotine consumption until it "feels ready" to quit. With such a high recidivism rate associated with smoking, this is not a good plan. Patients should develop a definitive cessation plan and stick with it (with the pharmacist to assist them in developing the plan).

The Quit Date

The basic plan should begin with a decision regarding the "quit date." This will be the first date that the patient will not smoke for the entire day. Some may try to link it to an important date, such as the patient's birthday or the Great American Smokeout

Day (sponsored by the American Cancer Society). It is best for the patient to choose the date, rather than have the whole class (if counseling in a group setting) stop on a specific date. The quit date should be a specific event. Encourage the smoker to circle it on the calendar and tell family and friends in anticipation of it. Of importance, the smoker should begin behavior modification strategies prior to the quit date. If the smoker does not follow through with this quit date, encourage the patient to set another as soon as possible before motivation is entirely lost. Each smoker's journey to long-term cessation is unique, but it has to start somewhere!

Quitting By The START Plan

One good quit plan can be described as *START*: *S*et a quit date within the next couple of weeks, *T*ell everyone about the upcoming quit attempt, *A*nticipate problems, *R*emove tobacco products from the environment, and *T*ake action. As *setting a quit date* has been discussed, smokers need to *tell the spouse, family, friends, and coworkers*, as appropriate, of this upcoming event. The smoker needs full cooperation from all for several weeks after the quit date. The patient needs to know that anyone who smokes will need to stay away during this crucial time period. A spouse will need to be especially understanding. A spouse who continues to smoke will need to go outside to smoke during this period. Having clean ashtrays and no access to cigarettes is important for the quit attempt as well. Any temptation during a "craving" due to nicotine withdrawal could lead one back to smoking. The spouse and family also will need to understand that mood changes could be experienced. A good way to enlist the help of the spouse would be to invite the spouse to join the smoker during cessation education.

Obtaining a thorough history of nicotine use is essential prior to the quit attempt in order to *anticipate problems*. A thorough history of nicotine use would include obtaining the following: current daily use of nicotine, how many cigarettes (or cigars, etc.) have they smoked daily at the highest amount (and least amount) of nicotine use, total time length of nicotine use, brand(s) used, how many quit attempts have been tried (and success of attempts), past use of cessation medications, support systems in place, and triggers. An example documentation of nicotine use history can be found in Table 9-2. A frank discussion, in particular, of any previous quit attempts is important. Any problems that the smoker had with previous quit attempts will need to be resolved (or at least something different should be tried) to ensure success with the current quit attempt. For example, the pharmacist could discover that the previous quit attempt was unsuccessful because nicotine gum was not used appropriately. Also, this would be a good opportunity to discuss with the smoker that most people who are ultimately successful try to quit multiple times. The pharmacist could also add, "And for this quit attempt you are putting a plan into place before the actual quit date, so you are already way more likely to succeed."

Removing tobacco products from the smoker's environment is important to limit quick access during the quit attempt. A few smokers balk at this idea, pointing out that a new pack of cigarettes could be purchased on the way home from work. Removing nicotine from the environment is strongly suggested due to the intensity and quick onset of cravings. Especially if it is the first attempt, the smoker may not be aware of how strong and fast a craving can occur. Also, if the patient does not have easy access, it would be a *conscious decision* for the patient to purchase a pack of cigarettes. The person hit with a craving on the way home from work would have to *decide* to stop at the store to purchase the cigarettes—and the patient is more likely to make the correct decision. Finally, the smoker preparing for the quit attempt should make sure that everything—ashtrays, lighters, and matches—associated with smoking is removed from the immediate environment.

Finally, the smoker must be willing to *take action*. Of all the most unhelpful behaviors, inaction is the worst. The smoker must be willing to put the individualized quit plan into action. In order to have the most success, the patient should be willing to begin making daily adjustments in behavior and thinking. If the smoker has not begun to take action after a couple of counseling sessions, the prudent pharmacist will focus on why—and perhaps use motivational

Table 9-2.	Smoking History

Name: _____ **Date:** _____ **Age:** _____ **Sex: M/F**

Favored method of tobacco use (check all that apply):
Cigarettes _____   Chew tobacco _____
Cigars _____   Other _____
Pipe _____   _____

Are you planning to make a quit attempt in the next: ___30 days ___ 6 months ___ never
Current # of cigarettes per day: _____
How long have you used nicotine? _____ months _____ years
What is the most amount of nicotine you have used per day, and what is the least?
_____

Previous quit attempts: # of attempts: _____
Length you have not smoked after: First attempt to stop:_____
                                     Reason for resuming smoking:
_____
                                     Second attempt to stop:_____
                                     Reason for resuming smoking:
_____
                                     Latest attempt to stop: _____
                                     Reason for resuming smoking:
_____

What type of medication was used during any of your previous quit attempts? (Circle all that apply)

Cold turkey (no medication)   patches   gum   lozenges   Other_____

Nicotine nasal spray   nicotine inhaler   bupropion (Zyban®)   varenicline (Chantix®)

What problems (if any) were encountered with any of the medications above?
_____

Your smoking habits and identifying possible "triggers":
When do you tend to smoke (Circle all answers that apply)?

When first awakening   with coffee   at home   when stressed   bedtime
With or after meals   with alcohol   at work/breaks morning   other:
While driving   on the phone   when relaxing   afternoon   _____

Smoking habits of other family members, friends, or coworkers:
Total # of household members who smoke: _____ # of friends/coworkers who smoke: ____
Any of these people willing to stop smoking at this time?   yes   no   not asked
Any of these people agreed to assist you to quit?   yes   no   not asked
Name who you can count as your "support system" at this time: _____
_____

On a scale from 0 to 10, how confident are you to be able to quit during this attempt?
0   1   2   3   4   5   6   7   8   9   10
No Confidence   **Extremely Confident**
|_____|_____|_____|_____|_____|_____|_____|_____|_____|_____|

interviewing techniques as a tool to explore the patient's lack of motivation. The actions that the smoker can take, the small steps, prior to the quit attempt will pay dividends down the road.

Behavioral Modification Strategies

Recognizing and Preventing Triggers

Behavioral modification strategies should begin prior to the quit date. This point cannot be overemphasized, because many unsuccessful quit attempts are initiated without implementing changes in daily behavior. Patients should recognize "triggers" and should be prepared to combat them during the quit attempt.[4] Although triggers are highly individualized, common ones include the tendency to smoke first thing in the morning after awakening, while drinking coffee or alcohol, after meals, while "relaxing" in front of the television, and while traveling in a vehicle.

The pharmacist should help the smoker initiate daily substitutes for smoking triggers—often called *stimulus control methods*. These substitutes can include taking long walks when the triggers occur, getting busy with projects such as washing dishes or doing other chores around the house, or working on long-term projects such as painting a room. Deep breathing and visualization are good stress management techniques that will be explained in more detail later.

Self-Observation

Self-observation is another useful tool prior to the quit attempt. For example, patients with diabetes or hypertension keep daily records of blood glucose or blood pressure levels, respectively. Record keeping is helpful for both the patient and the clinician. The smoker should keep a daily record, including what time of the day each cigarette was smoked, what (if anything) triggered the event, and the patient's mood (e.g., stressed or depressed). Many smokers who record nicotine use are surprised at the actual amount smoked. A "one-pack-per-day" smoker may in reality be smoking two packs per day! This recording gives the patient great insight into what triggers nicotine use, when the triggers occur, and what time of day most nicotine use occurs. The pharmacist should help the patient develop a plan to combat each of those times. Those will be the times when the strongest nicotine withdrawal (i.e., cravings) will be experienced.

Practical Changes to Implement

Self-observation can give the smoker insight as to what practical behavior changes need to be implemented prior to the quit date. Fewer than 5% of people who quit without assistance are successful for longer than a year. This underscores the fact that few smokers adequately prepare and plan for the quit attempt. The pharmacist should discuss that this is a process that starts weeks prior to the quit attempt, when the patient starts forming better habits to last through the attempt and beyond.

One of the first steps in changing behavior is to recognize the times one smokes "automatically." Many smoke during times of stress without even being aware of the nicotine use. Stress management techniques will be discussed in the next section, but patients smoke "automatically" at other times, too. If the patient smokes while drinking coffee, driving, or at a bar with friends, some suggestions for combating these triggers are given in Table 9-3.

The changes discussed in Table 9-3 to combat triggers should be made *prior* to the quit date. As some of these points involve "switching" suggest that the smoker switches the brand of cigarette. Many smokers balk at this because it is likely that one brand is prized above all others. When switching brands, the patient could try one with less nicotine (but remember: there is no such thing as a "safe" level of nicotine) or "light" cigarettes. Switching brands makes it a little easier for some because the patient has already "given up" a particular brand.

When preparing for the quit date, the smoker should be aware of each time nicotine is used. For example, the smoker should never buy another carton of cigarettes. Buying cigarettes by the carton makes it tougher to quit. The patient should begin purchasing only single packs weeks before the quit date. That way, every time another pack of cigarettes is purchased, the patient is making a conscious decision to continue smoking until the pre-set quit date.

Table 9-3. Suggestions for Combating Triggers and Making Behavioral Changes

- Drinking coffee—Ask the patient to change to a different brand of coffee, to decaffeinated coffee, to "half and half," or to a different drink altogether such as tea. Few smokers tend to have a difficult time with this one, but it should be encouraged. For example, coffee could be served during a cessation class. When a smoker makes the comment, "Coffee and smoking just seem to go together," it could be pointed out that he is enjoying coffee without smoking—so it can be done!
- Relaxing after meals—Ask the patient not to allow himself to relax after eating. Remind him that he has "trained himself" to smoke after he eats to "signal" that the meal is done. Instead, the patient should develop a new "signal" for the end of the meal. He should push away from the table and get busy doing something else, like taking a long walk, washing dishes, or going for a bike ride or jog.
- Enjoying the company of friends or relatives who smoke—Ask the patient whether these people would be willing to join him in his quit attempt. Especially if the other smoker is the spouse, having them both quit at the same time can benefit them both—a natural support system. If these other people are not ready to quit, the patient should ask them to be respectful of his quit attempt and to not smoke around him. This is very important for a spouse! The spouse should be willing to smoke outside for the next couple of months while the patient quits—and to keep cigarettes away from the person trying to quit as well! If the "friends" are not willing to quit or to stay away, caution the patient to avoid these people as much as possible for the next couple of months.
(One note here: This is an especially difficult situation. Someone in the house or close to the patient trying to quit who continues to smoke makes cessation extremely difficult. Beware, also, if the patient complains that the "friend" or relative *deliberately* smokes around him, and offers cigarettes during the quit attempt! For whatever reason, it is interesting that people close to the one trying to quit may try to sabotage the quit attempt!)
- On break at work—Ask the patient to stay inside during breaks if smoking is not allowed inside—or to turn the "smoke" break into a "coffee" break.
- At a bar with friends—Ask the patient to stay away from these situations at least for a couple of months until their physiologic dependence dissipates. Ask him to do something else with his free time.
- Driving in the car—Ask the patient to not carry cigarettes in the car with him anymore! If he has to have that "hand-to-mouth" feeling, have the patient take a straw with him while driving. One interesting alternative could be for the patient to tape the cigarettes up with duct tape if he does decide to keep them in the car. Then, he will have to unwrap the tape to obtain the cigarettes. Not only would this be difficult but also the patient will have to *make a conscious decision to smoke* if he unwraps the tape.
- They are bored or talking on the telephone—Ask the patient to have carrots, celery, or another healthy snack handy when this craving/association occurs. This will also provide that "hand-to-mouth" feeling. Also, "getting busy" doing something instead of allowing himself to be bored will help. This would be the perfect time to complete overdue long-term projects, such as painting the house, organizing the house, building a shed, planting a garden, or landscaping the entire yard.

Many smokers view smoking as an enjoyable activity, so this should be reversed. The smoker should no longer smoke when watching television, relaxing, or doing any enjoyable activity. Suggest that the patient only go outside to smoke, or smoke in a dark room (preferably a closet) or while facing a corner of the house. The patient should smoke the cigarette and then return to an enjoyable activity. To expand on this idea, have the smoker *not* clean up the ashtrays in the house for several weeks. As an alternative, cigarette butts could be placed into an empty milk container. Later, during the quit date and beyond, whenever the cravings are strong, the patient could pull out this foul-smelling milk container, uncap it, and take a whiff.

The patient also should attempt to taper nicotine use. A good general goal for tapering would be to decrease the nicotine use by one-half each week prior to the quit date. For example, a two-pack per day smoker could start a month prior to the quit date, and cut down to one pack per day. The next week, the patient could start at one-half pack, and so forth. Thus, even a two-pack per day smoker could have decreased the nicotine use from 40 cigarettes per day (two packs) to 2 or 3 cigarettes per day prior to the quit date. The only caveat to this is that the patient should have set the quit date beforehand.

■ THE QUIT DATE AND BEYOND

The quit date is the patient's pre-determined date for smoking cessation. For those using nicotine replacement therapy (NRT), the medications should be started on this date. If using bupropion or varenicline, those medicines should have been started 1–2 weeks prior to the quit date.[4] The behavior changes previously implemented should still be followed. The patient should be prepared for intense cravings, usually experienced at heightened times of nicotine use throughout the day. An especially strong craving may be experienced upon awakening. Some "hints" to assist the patient during the first day of the quit date can be found in Table 9-4. In addition, the patient should have a plan in place to handle the effects of nicotine withdrawal.

Nicotine Withdrawal Symptoms

Abstinence from nicotine use will lead to withdrawal symptoms on the quit date.[4] Medications will "take the edge away" from the withdrawal symptoms, but it is likely that they will still be experienced. Symptoms include anxiety, depression, irritability, frustration, anger, insomnia (but sometimes increased drowsiness), increased appetite, weight gain, difficulty concentrating, and restlessness. Patients can also experience increased coughing and other constitutional symptoms. Although not considered a withdrawal symptom according to the Diagnostic and Statistical Manual of Mental Disorders (DSM IV), most patients experience "cravings." The intensity with which patients experience cravings is inversely correlated with long term abstinence. Withdrawal symptoms tend to peak within 24–48 hours (at least within the first 3 days) after quitting and usually subside within 2–4 weeks.

Using Medications for Cravings

Many patients will want to manage cravings with medication therapy. If the patient is already using long-acting medications such as bupropion, varenicline, or nicotine patches, adding short-acting NRT is a reasonable way to combat "breakthrough" cravings. However, if NRT is the only medication used, it should not be used as needed. Rather, the patient should be counseled to "schedule" each dose of NRT. Medication use will be discussed more thoroughly in the next section.

Stress Management and Cognitive Techniques

Many smokers believe that nicotine helps to manage stress. In contrast, nicotine stimulates the nervous system and results in increased pulse and blood pressures. Stress is normal in everyday life, so it is one's *response* to stress that makes all the difference. Stress can be "good" when it motivates positive changes, but it can be "bad" when the response is inappropriate to the nature of the stressful situation. Because many smoke in response to stress, how to respond to stressful situations post-quit date must be addressed. While making a quit attempt, patients should be cognizant of usual life events that may cause stress and anticipate how to respond. Cognitive techniques are often very useful tools to assist with stressful situations.

Cognitive techniques involve changing the internal state.[4] They focus on retraining the way a person thinks (Table 9-5). If the patient is constantly "thinking about cigarettes," this can lead to relapse. The way

Table 9-4. Suggestions for the Quit Date

- Remember that by the time you wake up the morning of your quit date, you have already gotten around an 8-hour start for being a nonsmoker!
- Do not focus on "forever." Focus on getting through this first day only without smoking. Even years later, some former smokers still see themselves as "delaying my smoking for just one more day."
- Think about "scrambling" on that first day. Sleep with your feet at the headboard so that when you wake up, your first thought will be, "Today I will not smoke!" Then, if you used to smoke your first cigarette while drinking coffee, instead take a shower or walk the dog first. Then, drink your coffee (of a different brand, or temporarily switch to tea). If you used to smoke after breakfast, take a walk or find another morning chore to do instead. In other words, "scramble" your routines!
- If you are using nicotine replacement therapy, do not forget to start today!
- Get up and keep active all day long doing things. You should have already planned ahead of time activities that will keep you occupied throughout the day. Today is a great day for starting a large project that will keep both mind and body busy, like building a shed, starting a garden, painting a room or the whole house, or landscaping the whole yard.
- Schedule a dentist visit today and get the works done for your mouth. Clean the entire house and remove the smoky smell. If you used to smoke in the car, get the car detailed and smelling good.
- Drink plenty of fluids. This is good for combating some of the withdrawal symptoms, like increased cough and hunger.
- Continue attending the smoking cessation class and following your personalized quit plan. If the class developed a "buddy system" prior to the quit date, call your buddy if you are experiencing serious cravings.
- Avoid any high-risk situations that you have already identified as "triggers" for smoking.
- Accept that you will think about smoking today and you will have cravings. But having a craving and thinking about smoking is NOT smoking. Cravings tend to last for only a couple of minutes and WILL PASS. Get busy doing something and/or use cognitive thinking skills to ride out the craving.
- Read over your list of reasons why you want to quit smoking. Really think about these reasons and how **they** are what make up who **you** are, not the cigarette!
- Put your first money that you would have spent on cigarettes that day into the "ciggy bank." It is time to watch that money grow.
- Snack on healthy, crunchy snacks, like carrots and celery. Alternatively, many former smokers say that peppermint sticks are good, as well, to provide that "hand-to-mouth" feeling.
- Watch for **HALT**—Do not get too **H**ungry, **A**ngry, **L**onely, or **T**ired.
- Reduce or avoid alcohol—Especially on the quit date! Alcohol clouds judgment and can make it easier to slip. It can also be linked to smoking for many people.
- When you get a craving, take out your milk container of cigarette butts (as described in the chapter) and take a big whiff.
- Do not forget your family support. Let them congratulate you today, and let yourself feel good about this choice you have made!

Table 9-5. Cognitive Techniques

Use Positive Thinking
- Once the smoker has reached the quit date, it is amazing how negative, self-defeating thoughts can lead to relapse. If these thoughts occur, immediately take charge of the thought itself. Renew a commitment to quit smoking. Sometimes it even helps to say out loud, "I am a nonsmoker, and this temptation to smoke will pass. I can make it through one more day without smoking!"

Distractive (Thought Control) Techniques
- Also called "urge tamers," these techniques rely on recognition that you are thinking about smoking and distracting yourself for a few minutes until the craving is resolved.
- **"Now" Awareness**—Either think silently or aloud, "Now I am aware of _____ ." Then, take several minutes to repeat the sentence while filling in the blank with whatever you see. For example, you can say, "Now I am aware of the computer screen I am staring at. Now I am aware of the desk I am sitting in. Now I am aware of the window and what is going on outside."
- **Stopping a Thought**—This technique also could be called "startling a thought" because whenever you find yourself thinking about a cigarette, shout the word "STOP" as loud as possible. If yelling would be inappropriate in a certain situation, you could imagine yelling "STOP" while visualizing a large stop sign or flashing stop light.
- **Thought Zapper**—This is similar to "stopping a thought," but with this aversive technique you stop thinking about a cigarette by pairing this thought with an unpleasant stimulus. For example, the unpleasant stimulus could be snapping a rubber band around your wrist, and repeating this as often as necessary.

Relaxation and Stretching Exercises
- These exercises are helpful during cravings for the person who wants to "actively do something" until the craving subsides. Some examples include:
- **The Rag-Doll Dangle**—Stand with legs apart and bend at the waist; then, shake your hands and arms loosely; let your head hang, and then sway side-to-side; shrug your shoulders, then hang loosely to relax completely.
- **Head Tilt**—Keeping the shoulders down, tilt the right ear to the right shoulder slowly several times. Then, repeat with the left ear to the left shoulder several times.
- **Full Body Stretch**—Stand with the right arm raised, fingers stretching up as close to the ceiling as possible. Visualize yourself plucking $100 bills from the ceiling. After feeling the stretch in your right side from the tips of the fingers to the right foot, repeat with the left arm raised to the ceiling.

The Abdominal Breath
- Sit comfortably back in the chair with your feet flat on the floor. Put one hand on your abdomen and close your eyes.
- Inhale slowly and deeply through your nose, feeling your abdomen rise with your hand.
- Hold your breath while you silently count 2 seconds. Exhale slowly through your nose while feeling your abdomen fall again. Focus on the sensations of inhaling and exhaling, and your hand rising and falling.
- Repeat this for at least 5 minutes, twice daily, and repeat when you feel stress.

Visualization Technique
- This uses "creative imagination" to work through situations where cravings might be strong ahead of time in order to be better prepared to deal with it when it occurs. This can be done in combination with the abdominal breath as well.
- While sitting, let all of the muscles in your body relax. Use your imagination to picture yourself doing things you used to do with a cigarette in your hand, but now you are doing these things as a nonsmoker. For example, imagine driving, drinking coffee, relaxing, or waking up in the morning without smoking. The key is to let a "movie" play in your mind, with as many details as possible (sights, sounds, and objects in the imagined "movie").
- Repeat this for at least 5 minutes, twice daily, and repeat when you feel stress.

each patient experiences cravings is individualized, in number and in intensity. Cravings can be very uncomfortable and concerning. However, even "one puff" can lead back to recidivism. The old adage can be used here: "Cravings never killed anyone, but smoking to relieve the cravings has killed many who otherwise could have been successful."

Two other caveats regarding cravings should be discussed. Discussing cravings will not initiate a craving. It is important to discuss with the patient how to individually deal with cravings. Also, some patients may experience very little cravings initially, but then more intensely a few weeks after the quit date. Patients who do not experience strong cravings initially should be advised not to discontinue cessation medications prematurely. Patients who have "an easy time" in the first few days or weeks may become overconfident regarding long-term success and think that cessation medications can be discontinued early. The prudent pharmacist will be aware of the optimal length of therapy for each medication and advise the patient appropriately.

Slips Versus Slides

After the quit date, patients may "slip" and smoke a cigarette. They should be reminded to try not to "feel bad about themselves." They have not failed in their quit attempt and still have a chance for long-term success. The patient should be encouraged strongly to reset a quit date as soon as possible. Stress the progress made in comparison to where the patient was in this process just a short time ago. Cessation is a *process*, and a "slip" is not a "slide." Perhaps the patient experienced intense cravings and tried to smoke a cigarette for relief. However, the patient likely discovered that the cravings returned—perhaps even more quickly.

Beginning Relapse Prevention

After the quit date, the pharmacist should be diligent in providing relapse prevention. Due to the high recidivism rate, this diligence should be maintained from the quit date, through the full course of therapy with cessation medications, and beyond. Relapse prevention counseling is essential for the patient to have ultimate long-term success. Some helpful tips can be found in Table 9-6. A combination of overconfidence and unexpected cravings can be enough for the patient to begin smoking again. Maintaining behavior modifications and taking the full course of medications are helpful in this regard.[12]

New nonsmokers must be aware that smoking causes both physical and psychological dependence. After the physical cravings have decreased significantly, there may still be stressful situations during which cravings—strong ones—can catch the unwary off-guard. It surprises patients that cravings due to psychologic dependence to nicotine can occur months, even years, after the quit date. Maintaining constant diligence, especially during stressful situations, is the best way for former smokers to experience long-term success in cessation.

■ MEDICATION MANAGEMENT

The three classes of smoking cessation therapies approved by the Food and Drug Administration (FDA) are NRTs, psychotropics, and nicotine agonists. According to the U.S. Public Health Service Clinical Practice Guidelines for Treating Tobacco Use and Dependence, every patient undergoing a quit attempt—with the exception of special circumstances—should be encouraged to use pharmacotherapy.[4] Only patients who are pregnant or breast-feeding, smoking fewer than 10 cigarettes per day, have medical contraindications, or adolescents should not be offered pharmacotherapy during their quit attempt.[4]

The patients with special circumstances listed above should be the only smokers allowed to undergo a quit attempt "cold turkey." This is the terminology used for smokers who try to quit without the aid of pharmacotherapy. Many smokers, prior to seeking the assistance of a health-care professional, will attempt unsuccessfully to quit "cold turkey." Many patients will attempt to self-taper their tobacco use as well. Other nonpharmacologic methods include aversion therapy, acupuncture, hypnotherapy, massage therapy, and

Table 9-6. Tips to Prevent Relapse

Pay Attention to the Cardinal Rule: There is no such thing as *just one cigarette*!
- Most people who return to smoking will do so within the first few weeks after quitting. Thus, over the next few weeks, the ability to resist "just that one cigarette" will be the difference between success and failure.

Avoid Triggers and Other Urges
- Change the brand of coffee, or switch to half-and-half or decaffeinated brands.
- Limit alcohol use, especially in places where smoking and drinking are intertwined.
- Avoid stressful situations; if a stressful situation leads to thoughts of smoking, think about what it is you "really want"; most likely, you want to resolve the stressful situation rather than the cigarette.
- Make sure you have a "substitute," like a straw, carrots, or sugarless gum, while driving.
- After meals, make sure you push away from the table and get busy with an after-meal walk or washing the dishes rather than allowing a cigarette to "signal" the end of the meal. Remember to "scramble" your daily routines.
- Stick with your overall pre-quit plan of avoiding triggers. If the first way you had planned to avoid a trigger does not work, be resourceful and find another way to avoid them!

Overcome Urges When They Hit
- Nicotine gum or lozenges are great ways to control nicotine urges. As an alternative, you could chew sugarless gum or mints.
- Take a walk, go to the gym, drive around the block, or get busy on a "big" project.
- Brush your teeth, or eat an apple or celery (healthy foods that take a long time to chew).
- Go to a movie, volunteer at your church, or go to the library or bookstore (spend time at places where smoking is not allowed).
- Use cognitive coping skills, as discussed earlier.

Find Ways to Pamper Yourself
- Soak in a long hot bath for an hour or more, or let yourself relax with a good book.
- Go on a mini-shopping spree, or treat yourself to a pedicure and/or manicure.
- Splurge on a trip to the local yogurt shop.
- Buy a "fun" gift for yourself specifically with the money you've saved on cigarettes so far.
- Spend time thinking about what you will do with the thousand or more dollars you will save in your first year from not smoking.
- Find ways to reward yourself without cigarettes (develop a new reward system)!

Watch For Key Thoughts That May Lead You Astray
- Watch for self-pity. Just because others still smoke and you do not, you now have perspective. Think about all the times before you quit that you wanted to be that "guy who did not smoke." Now you are because you are successfully stopping the addiction!
- Watch for impatience. Even if it has been several weeks, and you are still craving cigarettes, remember that each person's quit journey is different. Quitting for good is a process, and it will take how long it takes. Be patient!
- Watch for self-deprecation. It is amazing how the self-defeating thoughts really start to swarm when you quit! "You cannot do it. You're not strong enough to quit. Something will always hold you back." Do not let these thoughts take away your positive momentum! Stay smoke-free for one more day, and watch how you begin to string these days together. Tell yourself that you *can* quit for good and be that person you've wanted to be!
- Watch for overconfidence. These thoughts are the polar opposite of the self-deprecating ones. These are the thoughts that are telling you, "Stop taking the cessation medicine. You're not having urges anymore. You don't need it." Or worse: "Go ahead and smoke one cigarette. You can quit again in the morning. You're good at quitting." Make no mistake: Dependence and addiction to tobacco is always waiting around the corner. All it will take is to stop the cessation medication prematurely and let that "horrible" craving finally hit. Smoking just one cigarette doesn't relieve the cravings—it just stimulates the next craving.

(Continued)

Table 9-6. Tips to Prevent Relapse (*Continued*)

Renew Your Dedication
- Reward yourself. Many who are trying to quit forget to do this, but quitting is a huge accomplishment. If you were to get a promotion at work, would not you celebrate? This is no less important. A week after you quit, go to a movie by yourself or with your spouse. A month after you quit, treat your family to a meal at an expensive restaurant. You can afford it since you are no longer paying for cigarettes, and the money saved will add up quickly! A year later, you may be able to buy something extravagant, go on a trip somewhere you have always wanted to go but could never afford, or you could really sock it away for a great retirement.
- Collect compliments from your support system. Periodically, announce to your family how long it has been since you smoked. Call relatives, friends, coworkers, and your quit buddy.
- Above all, keep going to your smoking cessation class or support group—especially after you have quit! Others will compliment you on your accomplishment, and you can be an encouragement to others who have slipped or have not yet quit.

Know When You Are Rationalizing
- You may say to yourself, "It is too hard to quit and just not worth it!" Remember that quitting is difficult, but it is *not* impossible. Get out your list of reasons why you wanted to quit and read them thoroughly. What are they? Better health, staying alive to see grandchildren graduate from school and get married, feeling better, breathing better, or avoiding major health issues. Say to yourself instead, "Quitting is the best thing that I can do for my health now and in the future!"
- You may say to yourself, "I need the cigarettes to cope with all of my stress." You may feel that your body is more calm and relaxed when smoking, but the opposite is true. Nicotine is a stimulant, so it actually increases your heart rate and blood pressure. During stressful situations, most smokers use the action of smoking to "allow themselves to calm down." However, the "calmness" that ensues is caused by actively allowing yourself to relax. See the exercises on deep breathing and relaxation techniques.
- You may say to yourself, "All I need is one smoke, and I'll feel better." However, that is all it takes to become addicted to nicotine again. Remember the Cardinal Rule above.

Active Exercises When Overcome With Urges
- Making a chart of the urges is often helpful. When the urges come, rank the strength from 1 to 10 (easiest to hardest to overcome). Chart what time of day they came, and what you did to make the urge go away.
- Take out that list of reasons why you are quitting. If you have not made a list of reasons yet, make such a list. Really think about these reasons. Put the list in a visible place, such as on your refrigerator or by your alarm clock if the morning urges are really bad.
- Write down a list of 10 good things about being a nonsmoker. Then, write down a list of 10 bad things about smoking.
- Make a list of all the great things that you could buy when your money begins to accumulate from not having to buy cigarettes.
- Think about potential situations in the future during which you may have urges, and write down how you will resolve this situation. For example, the next Christmas party may involve alcohol and smoking, so decide now how you will handle the situation. Write about bad news that you could get in the next year, and how you could respond. This is part of preparing for stressful situations in the future that could lead to relapse. Even those who have been smoke free for a year or more have certain situations that, due to stress, could lead to relapse due to the psychological dependence they have on nicotine.

using social support networks, which are available via the Internet and through state-sponsored phone services. Aversion therapy is a form of conditioning that exposes the smoker to an unpleasant stimulus while smoking. Tapering tobacco use while preparing for the impending quit attempt is useful but not generally effective by itself. The tendency is to eventually slide back into the previous level of smoking, or an increased level. All of the nonpharmacologic methods have been studied with varying degrees of success.

In contrast, studies have shown convincingly that all FDA-approved cessation medications are at least twice as effective as placebo and are considered first-line therapies.[4] Thus, smoking cessation should be highly individualized. Pharmacists should take into account many different factors when making a recommendation for pharmacotherapy. From the person's smoking history, the pharmacist should investigate which cessation medications have already been tried in previous quit attempts. The effectiveness and/or adverse effects of each medication should be explored in detail. Other factors include smoking triggers, concurrent medical conditions, cost of the medication, the need for stress management, patient desire for OTC therapy versus prescription, and other patient preferences. An example of how to individualize therapy for a quit attempt will be discussed in the *Putting It All Together* section, after an overview of available pharmacotherapy.

Nicotine Replacement Therapy

NRT includes both OTC and prescription-only products. The main OTC products available include nicotine gum, lozenges, and patches. Nicotine nasal sprays and inhalers are available only through a prescription. Patients may be wary of NRT because either they feel that OTC medications are not as effective as prescription-only therapy or they are concerned that nicotine will still "be in their system" during the quit attempt. However, all forms of cessation medications are twice as effective as placebo. Patients are far less likely to develop dependence on OTC medication in comparison to the present tobacco use. The ultimate goal for a successful quit attempt is for the patient to neither be smoking nor using cessation medication after a certain time period. The patient should be counseled that NRT is a *tool* toward that goal.

In addition, all NRT formulations deliver nicotine more slowly and at lower concentrations, with transdermal therapies having the slowest absorption. In contrast, nasal spray is delivered with the fastest absorption. Still, the concentrations delivered are not as high as with a cigarette but remains prescription-only. The nicotine inhaler is prescription-only due to the "hand-to-mouth" nature that imitates that of cigarettes and cigars.

If patients have certain conditions, NRT should be used with caution. For example, caution should be taken for smokers with underlying cardiovascular disease, such as a recent myocardial infarction (within 2 weeks), life-threatening arrhythmias, or severe angina. However, smokers recently recovering from hospitalization with a myocardial infarction may be more likely to try a quit attempt. Also, in comparison to the overall impact of continued tobacco use, the risk of using NRT in patients with cardiovascular disease is small. Other precautions include pregnant or lactating women. Nicotine is considered pregnancy category D, as there is evidence of risk to the human fetus.

OTC Medications

Nicotine Gum

Approved by the FDA in 1984 and receiving OTC status in 1996, nicotine gum was the first available NRT.[13] The product is nicotine polacrilex, a sugar-free chewing gum base consisting of a complex of nicotine and polacrilin. Many flavors are available, and two strengths: a 4 mg-strength if the smoker uses ≥ 25 cigarettes per day and a 2 mg-strength for ≥ 25 cigarettes per day.[4]

Several common mistakes may reduce patient success with nicotine gum. If used as monotherapy, the gum should be chewed on a fixed schedule and tapered appropriately. The suggested schedule includes one piece every 1–2 hours for the first 6 weeks. For the next 3 weeks, one piece should be chewed every 2–4 hours. For the final 3 weeks, one piece should be chewed every 4–8 hours. The gum should not be chewed in response to cravings alone. Also, many unsuccessful users do not chew enough gum daily. At least nine pieces per day are recommended.

Nicotine gum should not be chewed like ordinary gum, as rapid release of nicotine results in gastrointestinal upset. It should be chewed slowly. After 15–30 chews, a peppery, citrus, or minty taste (alternatively, a "tingling sensation") begins. At this time, the gum should be parked between the cheek and gum for buccal absorption of nicotine. When the taste or tingle fades, the gum should be chewed again. Most of the nicotine in the gum is gone within 30 minutes. In addition to specific counseling about chewing, patients should not to eat or drink for 15 minutes before or while using nicotine gum—especially coffee, soft drinks, or juices. These acidic beverages can lower the pH of the saliva, reducing the efficacy of buccal absorption.

Nicotine Lozenge

The nicotine lozenge is similar to the gum because it is available in 2-mg and 4-mg dosage forms and a variety of flavors. If the patient smokes within 30 minutes of waking up in the morning, the 4-mg dose should be used. The 2-mg dose should be used if the patient smokes after the first 30 minutes of awakening. The lozenge has a similar dosing schedule to the gum and is buccally absorbed. However, it should not be chewed or swallowed; rather, it should be relocated in different areas of the mouth over a 30-minute period to reduce mucosal irritation.[4,14]

Nicotine Patch

The nicotine patch was FDA approved in 1991 and available in OTC status in 1996. It delivers transdermal nicotine in a steady concentration over a 24-hour period. The 21-mg, 14-mg, and 7 mg-strengths are usually labeled as Step 1, Step 2, and Step 3, respectively. Patients who smoke ≤10 cigarettes per day are suggested to start with Step 2, while all other smokers should start with Step 1. After using the 21-mg strength daily for 6 weeks, patients should use the 14-mg strength for 2 weeks, then 7 mg for the final 2 weeks.[4,14]

Up to half of all patients experience skin irritation. Itching and tingling can occur within the first hour of use but normally resolves quickly. The strength may be reduced, but skin irritation may be due to the adhesive specific to the manufacturer of a particular OTC patch. Changing the medication brand used can help, along with using hydrocortisone cream for the irritation and relocating the next patch in another area of the body.

Prescription Medications

Nicotine Nasal Spray

This product is an aqueous formulation of nicotine delivered across the nasal mucosa through a metered spray inhaler. One dose is two sprays, each delivered to one nostril for a total of 1 mg nicotine. One to two doses should be delivered each hour for 6–8 weeks. This should not exceed five doses per hour, but patients who are successful with this medication use at least eight doses per day. Patients should prime the pump about six to eight times, then tilt the head back and give one spray to each nostril. They should breathe through their mouth and wait about 3 minutes before blowing their nose, if needed, while doing this procedure.

Side effects can be intense within the first week, including sneezing, coughing, watery eyes, runny nose, and a hot peppery feeling. Also, there is not a singular tapering strategy proven to be most effective. Some suggestions include using only one spray or skipping doses after the first 6–8 weeks of use. Caution should be used with both the nicotine nasal spray and inhaler, as they can lead to dependence.

Nicotine Inhaler

The nicotine inhaler may be useful for patients who really have a need to satisfy the "hand-to-mouth" ritual from smoking. However, other materials such as straws, toothpicks, or mints could suffice during the quitting process. The inhaler consists of a mouthpiece and a cartridge, which delivers 4 mg of nicotine from inhaled vapor. It is suggested that 6–12 cartridges should be used daily for the best chance of success, with a maximum of 16 cartridges per day. Treatment should last for a minimum of 3 weeks and maximum of 12 weeks. A gradual dose reduction can occur over the next 6-week period.

Each cartridge is inserted firmly onto the mouthpiece, puncturing the foil covering and releasing nicotine vapor following inhalation. The inhaler should be "puffed" as if lighting a pipe rather than inhaling deeply. Each cartridge is depleted of nicotine in about 20 minutes. Mild irritation of the mouth and throat can occur over the first week. Also, as with the nicotine gum, patients should not eat or drink for 15 minutes before or while using the inhaler because buccal absorption can be reduced with acidic drinks.

For both the nicotine nasal spray and the inhaler, patients should be followed closely with frequent follow-up to ensure dependence has not developed. It is also helpful to provide a specific titration schedule. An adequate trial should be given, but the medication should be stopped if the patient has not been able to quit by a certain time period. If patients are unable to stop smoking by the 4th week of therapy, these medications should be discontinued.

Bupropion

First FDA approved as an atypical antidepressant, bupropion is a non-nicotine oral tablet effective for smoking cessation. The mechanism of action is suggested to be due to blocking dopamine or norepinephrine reuptake in the central nervous system. The initial treatment is 150 mg of the extended release formulation once daily for 3 days, then 150 mg twice daily for 7–12 weeks. If patients need further treatment with this medication, it can be extended for another 12 weeks. The quit date should be set for 1–2 weeks after starting bupropion, as it takes at least 1 week to achieve steady-state levels.[4,15]

Bupropion can interact with other medications, as it undergoes extensive hepatic metabolism by cytochrome P450 2B6 enzymes. The concentrations of tricyclic antidepressants, antipsychotics, and selective serotonin reuptake inhibitors can be increased while taking bupropion. Levodopa, monoamine oxidase inhibitors, and ritonavir may increase bupropion concentration, while carbamazepine may decrease the concentration.

Bupropion is contraindicated for people with a history of seizures, anorexia, or bulimia. The potential to cause seizures is increased with the bupropion dose and should not be prescribed in daily doses exceeding 300 mg. Also, medications that could decrease the seizure threshold, such as theophylline, phenobarbital, and some antidepressants, should be avoided. Abrupt discontinuation of alcohol for a regular user could result in lowering the seizure threshold. Thus, abrupt discontinuation of alcohol while taking this medication is not encouraged. Side effects include tremor and insomnia, and taking one dose daily for the first 3 days helps to avoid this. If the patient has not made significant progress toward stopping completely after the 7th week of taking bupropion, it should be discontinued.

Varenicline

Varenicline is a partial agonist of the $\alpha 4\beta 2$ neuronal nicotinic acetylcholine receptor subunit. It stimulates dopamine release and decreases nicotine cravings while reducing the intensity of nicotine withdrawal. Similar to bupropion, varenicline should be titrated and started 1–2 weeks prior to the quit date. From day 1 to day 3, 0.5 mg should be taken daily; then, from day 4 to day 7, it should be taken twice daily; finally at day 8 and beyond the 1-mg strength should be taken twice daily. A "starter pack" may be prescribed for the first month to facilitate this titration. Although varenicline should be taken for 12 weeks, an additional 12 weeks of therapy can be continued if needed.[4,16]

Side effects are fairly mild for most people taking varenicline. Nausea, headache, insomnia, abnormal dreams, and dyspepsia are the common side effects. Although it does not increase the seizure risk or have the drug interactions as bupropion does, it can increase suicide ideation. It should be stopped immediately and the patient referred to medical attention if there is a significant increase in agitation, hostility, depression, suicidality, or worsening of preexisting psychiatric illness.[16]

Choosing the Best Therapy

All seven of the FDA-approved medications for treating tobacco use are recommended as first-line therapies.[4] As stated previously, all are at least twice as efficacious as placebo. Well-accepted algorithms to guide optimal selection among these medications do not exist. Therapy should be individualized. Factors to consider include medications used for prior quit attempts, potential side effects, the smoker's level of dependence, cost issues, whether OTC or prescription-only treatment is desired, and other factors in patient preference.

Regarding medications used for previous quit attempts, side effects or reduced efficacy could have been experienced due to inappropriate use. For example, tremor with bupropion could have been due to starting at the full 150 mg twice daily dose instead of titrating. Alternatively, a heavy smoker could have experienced decreased efficacy from a nicotine patch if too low of a dose was used (e.g., 7-mg patch used by a two-pack per day smoker). If a particular medication was ineffective or caused side effects due to inappropriate use, a re-trial using the medication correctly could be effective. However, if the medication was used for an adequate trial and was not effective, it would be prudent to use an alternative medication.

Whether the patient has insurance coverage or the likelihood of experiencing side effects could influence medication choice. For example, patients with depression may not be appropriate for varenicline, while bupropion may be a better choice. Patients with severe dermatitis should use nicotine patches only with caution, and those with severe reactive airway disease should not use nicotine nasal sprays or inhalers.

Weight gain may also be a concern. Patients concerned with weight gain could use bupropion or NRT—in particular nicotine gum or lozenges—in order to delay weight gain. However, these medications do not necessarily prevent weight gain in the long term, and individual effects may vary, of course.

Combination Therapy

Smokers who are heavy users or highly dependent on nicotine, have tried multiple quit attempts, or have comorbid disease states such as diabetes, combination therapy may be a good choice. There is evidence that combination therapy with the higher FDA-approved doses may be more effective than monotherapy.[4] A "long-acting" therapy may be appropriate in combination with as needed NRT. For example, bupropion or varenicline used twice daily combined with as needed nicotine gum or lozenges could be effective. Alternatively, daily nicotine patches could be substituted for oral therapy. Also, patients may need longer therapy, such as 6-month use in order to be fully effective.

■ INITIATION OF CLINIC AND/OR INDIVIDUAL SERVICES

Pharmacists in the community, either in retail environments or clinics, are in the ideal positions to develop smoking cessation programs. In the retail setting, pharmacists are the most easily accessible health-care provider, and most pharmacies sell nonprescription NRTs. Many cities and communities have laws and regulations to prevent smoking in public places. Smoking cessation has a tremendous potential for improving outcomes for patients—especially those with cardiovascular-related disease states. Thus, conducting such services would provide a tremendous opportunity to improve the health of the pharmacist's overall community.[17,18,19]

Pharmacists in clinics associated with hospitals have a great opportunity to initiate smoking cessation services as well.[20] The Joint Commission on Accreditation of Healthcare Organizations (JCAHO) requires core performance measures to be kept on several disease states, and measures addressing smoking cessation are included. Additionally, large companies who employ hundreds of workers have begun to realize the benefit of smoking cessation and other health-care services on decreasing unproductive days due to illness. These companies have begun to work with pharmacists to provide MTM services such as smoking cessation.

Initial Decisions and Overcoming Barriers

One of the first decisions that the pharmacist should make is whether smoking cessation services will be in-person, by phone, or through a referral service. As discussed previously, health-care providers are successful in providing the first three of the "Five A's": Ask, Assess, and Advise.[4] A wide network of quit programs exist by phone, online, or in-person, maintained through federal, state, or private programs. An example listing of these programs and additional resources can be found in Table 9-7. In general, cessation programs via phone services are not as successful as face-to-face efforts. Alternatively, many programs that initially meet in-person for the first two to four visits may elect to conduct follow-up visits by phone.

If MTM will be provided in-person, services could be one-on-one, in a group setting, or as a combination of both.[17,18] Individual services may require less workflow adjustment, as long as the counseling area is secluded enough to ensure adequate patient confidentiality. This would allow pharmacists to return to dispensing workflow when necessary. However, the pharmacist should consider *scheduling* such visits, especially with a longer initial visit, in order to allow consultation when the dispensing workflow is less intense. Also, pharmacy technicians may perform most of the dispensing tasks during scheduled visits.

Workflow issues may be a more significant consideration for group counseling, as attention should be paid solely to the participants during the session. This may require the pharmacist to not participate in most dispensing activities during the time of the sessions. Provisions will have to be made prior to each session, such as scheduling another pharmacist to cover the dispensing duties during that time. Alternatively, the sessions could be scheduled when no dispensing activities will occur. If scheduled later in the evening, this may increase participant enrollment for those who work during the day.[21] In exchange for the initial difficulty in providing group counseling sessions, there are benefits. Participants in a group will develop a rapport with each other over time that simply cannot be found with single-person cessation services. Patients in a group tend to hold each other accountable, and roadblocks and ideas that help one person can be shared with everyone.[21]

Pharmacist should find ways to overcome any anticipated barriers. In one study, pharmacists' confidence in providing public health services, including smoking cessation, was average to low.[22] They identified a need for further training to improve pharmacists' confidence levels. Other common barriers were lack of time and adequate counseling space. Some also reported an expectation of a negative reaction from clients. How to overcome these barriers, and other items to consider, will be discussed in the next few sections.

Physical Facilities and Providing Supplies and Medications

Physical facilities and supplies that would be needed are fairly minimal for smoking cessation services.[17,19,21] For group counseling sessions, a room with adequate chairs separate from the dispensing area (if during normal working hours) would be needed. If room does not allow for a group session, consider partnering with a physician and using that facility after hours. Dentists also support nicotine cessation efforts and may also be approachable for collaboration. If these outlets are not feasible, consider using a community center, church facilities, or the library. There is an abundance of low or no-cost places where services can be conducted—just make sure that such places are reserved well in advance of the sessions.

Regardless of whether individual or group counseling will be conducted, supplies would include a file cabinet for informational and patient counseling folders, supplies (e.g., "fake" cigarettes for providing the "hand-to-mouth" action during the quit process), an adequate documentation system (either paper or electronic), and a sphygmomanometer and stethoscope for checking blood pressure.[21,23] It is useful to provide a folder for each participant with photocopied handouts emphasizing the education and activities at every smoking cessation session. Participants will appreciate the items discussed from the handouts and the ability to review important points at greater depth later. This will also improve success for behavior modifications prior to the quit date.[21,22]

In addition to supplies, consider finding a way to provide cessation medications—even if in a limited supply—for participants in a smoking cessation group. One of the largest roadblocks for most smokers during

Table 9-7. Smoking Cessation Resources

Resources	Web sites or Other Contact Information
National Organizations/Agencies	
American Cancer Society	www.cancer.org
American Heart Association	www.americanheart.org
American Lung Association	www.lungusa.org
National Cancer Institute	www.nci.nih.gov
Smokefree.gov	www.smokefree.gov
Smoke-Free Women	http://women.smokefree.gov/
Smoker's Risk Web site	http://smokefree.gov/smokersrisk/
Quitting Smoking - How to Get Help	www.cancer.gov/cancertopics/factsheet/Tobacco/cessation
A Guide for Quitting Spit Tobacco	http://nidcr.nih.gov/OralHealth/Topics/SmokelessTobacco/SmokelessTobaccoAGuideforQuitting.htm
Centers of Disease Control and Prevention	
Office on Smoking and Health	www.cdc.gov/tobacco
Useful Resources on Quitting Smoking	www.cdc.gov/tobacco/how2quit.htm
The Department of Health and Human Services	www.smokefree.gov
Agency for Healthcare Research and Quality	www.ahrq.gov/consumer/tobacco/helpsmokers.htm
U.S. Surgeon General Tobacco Cessation	www.surgeongeneral.gov/tobacco/index.html
U.S. Department of Defense	www.ucanquit2.org/
National Institute on Aging	www.nia.nih.gov/HealthInformation/Publications/smoking.htm
National Partnership for Smoke-Free Families	http://smokefreefamilies.tobacco-cessation.org
Web site Support Groups and Pharmaceutical Resources	
Quitnet Support Group	www.quitnet.com/qnhomepage.aspx
American Legacy Foundation	www.becomeanex.org/
American Cancer Society - Yes You Can	www.yesquit.com/
GlaxoSmithKline's Way 2 Quit	www.way2quit.com/
GlaxoSmithKline's Committed Quitters	www.committedquitters.com/
Pfizer's My Time to Quit	www.mytimetoquit.com/
Resources for Health-Care Professionals	
Coverage for Cessation Treatments	www.cdc.gov/tobacco/quit_smoking/cessation/coverage/index.htm
A Practical Guide to Working with Health-Care Systems on Tobacco-Use Treatment	www.cdc.gov/tobacco/quit_smoking/cessation/practical_guide/index.htm
Telephone Quitlines	
National Quitline Number	(800) QUIT NOW or (800) 784-8669
American Cancer Society	(800) 227-2345
American Lung Association	(800) LUNG-USA (586-4872)
American Legacy Foundation	(866) 66-START (667-8278)
National Cancer Institute	(877) 44U-QUIT (448-7848)
Listing of State-Based Quitlines	www.naquitline.org/

a cessation attempt is the expense of cessation medications. Of course, it is optimal for smokers to view the expense in context of the overall lifetime course of paying for cigarettes. When the consequences from more adverse health are factored in, paying for cessation medications for a relatively short period of time is much less. However, it is difficult to coerce smokers to view the expense in these terms. Offering to provide some assistance with medication therapy, even NRT, is beneficial in maximizing participation. Some fee-for-service programs offer NRT as part of the overall package.[23,24] If cessation medications are offered, participants should commit to a certain number of sessions prior to receiving medication. For example, nicotine patches would not have to be distributed until just prior to the quit date, and by this time the participant should have completed two or more weekly sessions.[23,24]

Enrolling Participants

Although phone referral services, Web sites, and other programs are available, still almost one in five adults smoke. It remains the single most preventable cause of death in the United States. The high recidivism rate prevents long-term success for many. Thus, in many communities the need for this service, even if other alternatives are available, could still be very high.

Inquiring at various community clinics where relationships with health-care personnel have already been established may be helpful. One might ask the nurses, especially, if smokers could be referred to the pharmacist-run cessation services. Nurses tend to obtain smoking status along with other vital signs when prepping patients for the physician. The physicians could also be asked to provide the smokers with a prescription medicine (and make it clear that the smoker could fill the medicine at *any* pharmacy), if deemed necessary, after referral to the cessation clinic.

When enrolling potential participants, it would be prudent to enroll smokers in the preparation stage, according to the Transtheoretical Model of Behavior Change. Participants in an earlier stage may not be as likely to benefit from the more extensive counseling and education as offered in a formal smoking cessation program.[4] For new patients to the pharmacy, all pharmacy personnel should be trained to ask about smoking status and whether smokers are interested in stopping within the next 30 days.[23,24,25,26] Potential participants should be informed that the pharmacy is committed to assisting any smoker's quit attempt. Thus, referrals for this service could come from many avenues. Do not forget to place fliers for the service strategically throughout the pharmacy, and cessation medications should be in a prominent place. A standing smoking cessation class on a certain day and time of the week should be advertised as well. The message should be clear that the pharmacy is dedicated to helping smokers quit. Word of mouth is the best advertisement in communities, and there will be clients for such a service if the message is consistent.

Clinical Service Design

Individual services should be offered to accommodate smokers who do not feel comfortable in a group situation. However, due to the level of educational preparation necessary to provide such services properly, offering services for a group would be of significant benefit. Within a group setting, individualization of behavior changes and medication therapy can still occur while providing a "built-in" support system.[25,26]

While it can be daunting to conduct a group counseling session for the first time, it can also be extremely rewarding. Tips for providing counseling in a group setting can be found in Table 9-8. A feasible small group session usually consists of about five to eight participants. More can be enrolled, depending upon the pharmacist's comfort level with this counseling format. However, it would be prudent to call twice this number (e.g., 10–16 participants), as smoking cessation classes can have a significant no-show rate.[21] This number can decrease over time as well, as smokers may not truly "feel ready" for a quit attempt. A running list of potential participants to call can be kept if the total

Table 9-8. Preparing for and Conducting a Tobacco-Cessation Group Meeting

Timing	Actions
Weeks prior	• Choose a date and time that suits the audience (e.g., working adults like early evenings, seniors like mid-afternoon, and Saturday mornings may work for some groups)
	• Develop a recruitment plan, reserve space with a backup, recruit with definite starting and ending times, define the agenda, and prepare handouts and presentation materials
Days prior	• Call participants with a reminder of the meeting time, date, and place
	• Make sure all materials are ready, including refreshments, if served
Meeting day	• Lay out the meeting room how you want it (e.g., "horseshoe" shape is conducive to good participant interaction); consider refreshment table (e.g., coffee, light snack) and signs to direct participants to room
	• Ensure there are copies of all handouts for everyone (or folders, if preferred); give each participant a name tag to write first name, copy of agenda, and folder with handouts
	• Have pencils/pens on hand and any other supplies for counseling needed
Conducting the Visit (1 hour)	
Do:	• Start on time, greeting them with a sincere welcome, introducing them to yourself and any staff, discussing briefly any rules and the agenda (5–10 minutes)
	• Let them introduce themselves by first name to others and give a brief overview of their history of smoking and why they want to quit (15 minutes)
	• Give your prepared presentation for that meeting, going over all educational points, and allowing for questions from the group (30 minutes)
	• Be engaging, but be yourself; encourage questions and interaction from everyone, especially for the quiet members of the group; encourage others to answer questions
	• Stop briefly during the presentation and summarize points made, and then at the end; quizzing group members helps with retention; prepare items for active participation
	• Be wary of challenging group participants (listed below)
	• Wrap-up, thanking them for coming, briefly inform them what will be discussed at the next visit, and state, "stopping smoking is the best thing you can do for your health for now and in the future" (5 to 10 minutes)
Don't:	• Be judgmental in any way! Review the Motivational Interviewing chapter in the book
	• Be discourteous to anyone, but handle any problems immediately
	• Go way over on time (try not to go over at all); respect the time of the participants

(Continued)

Table 9-8. Preparing for and Conducting a Tobacco-Cessation Group Meeting (Continued)

Timing	Actions
Challenging Group Participants	
Style	*Moderator's Possible Responses*
Too-talkative	• Go back to the rules and agenda; emphasize time limitations but praise for enthusiasm
	• Assign a helpful task to get him involved and busy. Do not make eye contact with him
	• Establish as part of the group rules: each participant will have the right to speak twice regarding each issue, but the second comment cannot be made until all have spoken once
Shy/Reserved	• Pick an easy topic to comment on; ask a question requiring an open-ended response
	• When others share ideas about how to stop smoking ask, "So, ____, will you share how that may or may not work for you?"
Know-it-all or Arguer	• Try not to call on person; if it is unavoidable, limit to yes/no responses
	• Thank the person for comments and ask for the source of their information
	• Always be cautious of your reaction and that of the overall group; if they argue with others in the group state, "We need to move on for the sake of time," and switch topics
	• Offer to discuss any of the participant's concerns after the group session
Angry or Hostile	• Do not fight with the person! Control your responses by speaking low, quietly, and clear
	• Actively listen. Ask him, "What would you like us to do?" Use motivational interviewing
Questioner	• Redirect by asking what others in the group think about the comments
	• Do not bluff if you do not know the answer. Offer to research it and report later

group number drops significantly before the majority of the participants reach the quit date.

The literature discusses many different formats for conducting group classes for cessation, and they all have varying degrees of success.[4] However, one consistent finding is that when more classes can be offered to assist with an attempt, there is a proportionally better chance of long-term success. The number of classes that a pharmacist can feasibly offer may be limited by other factors. However, conducting weekly classes for at least 4–8 consecutive weeks may give smokers the best chance to succeed. The "support system" that inherently develops, as discussed, takes several weeks to blossom—usually solidifying about the time the majority approaches the quit dates. Also, conducting a class for several weeks allows a smoker who has to reset a quit date after "slipping" to still benefit from group support. Finally, setting several meetings before the quit date emphasizes the behavior changes smokers must implement for long-term success.

If eight sessions are conducted, the following can be used as a feasible outline for three stages: (1) for

Table 9-9. Example Implementation of an Eight-Session Smoking Cessation Class

1. **Conduction of the clinic: first session—introduction for the patients; initiation of the group and initial group dynamics**
   - Introduction of the clinic facilitators
     - Whether former use of nicotine by the facilitators is important, and how to get around this "rule" to ensure authority in the class
   - Define ground rules for patients attending the class
     - Mandatory attendance for as many classes as possible and advance notification for missing classes
     - Must have a willingness to at least try the techniques offered in class and to be courteous to all facilitators and classmates
     - No one may monopolize the conversation in the group, although all patients are encouraged to participate for the benefit of the overall group dynamics
   - Relaxing minute
     - It is important to open and close each session officially, and the relaxing minute is a good exercise with which to do this
     - The relaxing minute is a one-minute exercise on breathing; introduction of this as the first technique not only shows that the facilitator has a variety of helpful information, but that the techniques will be useful right away
   - Icebreaker: "Balloon-blowing"
     - Each patient is allowed to pick a balloon and, on a signal, all patients attempt to blow up their balloon. This exercise is done to reveal patients who are extremely short of breath
     - Even when a patient can blow up their balloon fast with minimal effort, the facilitator can emphasize how their faces turned red with the effort and use this to emphasize their need to stop smoking
     - To further emphasize this point, the facilitator can elect to take a pulse Ox and blood pressure for each patient. These also can be records that are kept for future follow-up and evaluation of clinic success
   - "Round-the-room" discussion
     - Experience with smoking cessation clinics shows that an opportunity at the beginning of the class for patients to interact with facilitators and each other is important
     - This discussion can be manipulated for two purposes: (1) each patient can respond individually about the successes they have had the previous week and (2) the facilitators can ask each patient to comment on a certain topic that will be discussed in more detail later on in the group counseling session
     - Patients have responded that throughout the week until they meet at this time, they do attempt to use the techniques learned; thus, the "round-the-room" discussion becomes a motivational tool for the patients because they know they will be accountable to their peers at this time
     - For this first meeting, everyone is encouraged to share with the class regarding their smoking history. They are asked to give a synopsis of:
       - How long they have used tobacco
       - Their choice of tobacco
       - How many packs per day they have smoked at their time of most use and how many they currently smoke
       - Whether they have tried to quit in the past and what led to their successes or failures in the past
       - Who they can count on as their support system in their cessation attempt

(Continued)

Table 9-9. Example Implementation of an Eight-Session Smoking Cessation Class (*Continued*)

- Facilitator-led presentation: "How smoking harms; how stopping helps"
  - Introduces hard facts regarding the overall impact of smoking
  - Impact of smoking on different types of cancer, chronic obstructive pulmonary disease, and coronary heart disease
  - Impact of smoking on other disease states, such as diabetes and hypertension
  - The addictive properties of nicotine and reinforcing properties of certain catecholamines (norepinephrine, dopamine)
  - How stopping helps physically, emotionally, and economically
  - Introduction on how behavioral, cognitive, and stress-management techniques help
  - Introduction on smoking cessation medications
  - Introduce the START mnemonic (Set a quit date within the next couple of weeks; Tell everyone you know that will support your effort; Anticipate problems with your current quit attempt; Remove all tobacco products from the environment; and Take action!)
- Relaxing minute

2. **Conduction of the clinic: second session—medication treatment**
- Relaxing minute
- "Round-the-room" discussion
  - Discuss progress made toward the quit date, decisions regarding medications, questions regarding the class or smoking cessation in general
- Explanation of medication choices for treatment
  - OTC medications: nicotine patch, nicotine gum, or lozenge
  - Prescription medications: nicotine nasal spray, nicotine inhaler, bupropion SR (Zyban®), varenicline (Chantix®)
  - Discussion of all pertinent items related to medication use for smoking cessation, including the following: dose, application, titration (if needed), possible adverse effects and how to overcome them, when to expect results, how to correlate medication use with the quit date, when and how to use combination therapy, and when to stop therapy
- Urge the patients to "Declare a Quit Date"
  - This topic should be a priority for discussion during the second session
  - Patients should be told reasons against declaring a quit date "too soon" versus procrastination of declaring the quit date
  - By announcing when their quit date is to the class, it becomes a real and tangible upcoming event for them and makes them accountable to this date by the rest of their classmates (with whom they are developing a group-type support system)
  - The quit date should be an important date to the patient individually, as soon as possible, and marked on a group calendar to take steps preparing for it
- Introduction of stress management techniques
- Take the Fagerstrom test for nicotine dependence
  - The patients may have never actually thought about the situations and times throughout the day during which they smoke; this is different for each individual smoker, but they should be aware of these times and situations
  - Once the person stops smoking, they will most likely experience cravings during those times, so they will need to prepare to defeat these cravings in advance
- Relaxing minute

(*Continued*)

Table 9-9. Example Implementation of an Eight-Session Smoking Cessation Class (*Continued*)

3. **Conduction of the clinic: third session—preparing for the quit date**
   - Relaxing minute
   - "Round-the-room" discussion
     - Discuss progress that everyone has made toward their quit date, any adverse effects with medications, whether they have practiced their breathing techniques, and any behavioral changes that they have begun
     - Discuss all accomplishments (e.g., patients that wish to work toward their quit date by cutting down the number of cigarettes per day should report on their progress)
   - Increasing lifespan by smoking cessation
     - Further discussion of studies that have been done regarding smoking cessation
   - Discuss how behaviors associated with smoking need to be changed as the quit date approaches
   - Stress management techniques
     - Understand stress and the relaxation response
     - Other stress management techniques
   - Discuss how much money can be saved over a lifetime by smoking cessation
   - Relaxing minute
4. **Conduction of the clinic: fourth session—the quit date and the first week**
   - Relaxing minute
   - "Round-the-room" discussion
     - Discuss the following with the group:
       - Has everyone set a quit date, and what progress are they making toward it?
       - What behavioral changes did they make during their last quit attempt? Why did or did not they work? Did they try to change their behavior at all prior to their last quit attempt?
   - Discuss "Physiologic Changes After Your Final Cigarette"
     - Patients should know that some physiologic changes begin early in the post-smoking cessation period
     - Also, it initiates a discussion regarding the nicotine withdrawal symptoms patients may experience, in order to let them know that problems related to smoking cessation can occur and to help them prepare for these
   - Behavioral changes
     - Introduce with a slide show presentation
     - Use the handout on "Behavioral Strategies"
       - Discuss ways to implement changes in each common situation
   - Cognitive changes
     - Introduce the principle of cognitive strategies—ways to control what you are thinking about in order to not give in to cravings each time they occur
     - Examples of "Thought Empowering Techniques"
       - Heightened awareness
       - Abrupt thought-stopping
   - Stress management techniques
   - Relaxing minute

(*Continued*)

Table 9-9. Example Implementation of an Eight-Session Smoking Cessation Class (*Continued*)

5. **Conduction of the clinic: fifth to seventh session—preventing physiologic and psychologic relapse**
   - Introduction to the fifth through seventh sessions—Facilitators are encouraged to be extremely flexible with material during this time, because each patient in the group may be at a different stage of smoking cessation success. The overall objectives of the facilitator at this time include:
     - For relapsed patients—Find out what caused them to relapse, whether it was lack of using techniques, nicotine withdrawal (including cravings), or even motivation; then, push for the patient declaring another quit date and revising their quit plans
     - For successful patients—Continue demonstrating techniques and talking about ways to prevent physiologic and psychologic relapse
   - Relaxing minute
   - "Round-the-room" discussion
     - For relapsed patients
       - Discuss that resetting a quit date is of utmost importance
       - Find out what, in particular, caused the relapse, and devise strategies to improve their chances for their next quit attempt
       - Use smaller successes, such as the patient stopping for a few hours, days, or weeks, to give them courage to translate into a more prolonged successful attempt
     - For successful patients
       - Discuss nicotine withdrawal symptoms (besides cravings) to make them aware that stopping is a process that is not without consequences on a temporary basis
       - Discuss all successes with behavioral, cognitive, and stress management changes implemented
       - Use the HALT mnemonic ("don't get too Hungry, Angry, Lonely, Tired") to prevent triggers associated with relapse
   - Discuss preventing relapse and reaffirming motivation
   - Behavioral techniques
     - Successful patients at this point tend to become helpful with giving the relapsed patients ideas that worked for them
     - Introduce former patient(s) who have had success to discuss how he or she made behavioral changes
   - Cognitive technique—Visualization
     - Introduce the concept of positive versus negative visualization
     - Take patients through a visualization exercise
   - Stress management
     - Relaxation exercises
     - Self-hypnosis exercises
   - Discuss the concept that there are two types of addiction to nicotine
     - Physical addiction—Cravings that are attenuated after the first couple of weeks
     - Psychologic addiction—Former smokers be aware that smoking was an adaptive behavior that will last for many years and may materialize during "first-time" situations in the future
   - Relaxing minute

(*Continued*)

Table 9-9. Example Implementation of an Eight-Session Smoking Cessation Class (*Continued*)

6. **Conduction of the clinic: eighth session—staying the course**
   - Relaxing minute
   - "Round-the-room" discussion
     - CELEBRATE!
       - Former smokers should acknowledge that for many of them giving up smoking might have been the most difficult thing they have done in recent years
       - Facilitators should set time aside to celebrate the accomplishment of their patients, and patients should be encouraged to continue rewarding themselves for smoking cessation
   - Create a "buddy list"
   - Go through the "Discussion topics for nonsmokers" handout
   - Invitation for successful nonsmokers to serve as speakers at a future smoking cessation group
   - Invitation for unsuccessful patients to give a group effort another try
   - Relaxing minute

the first two classes, orientation of the services can be discussed along with behavior changes and medication therapy. A quit date could also be set. (2) The third and fourth sessions could be reserved for preparing for the quit dates and the first subsequent week. (3) The fifth through eighth sessions could be reserved for resetting the quit date, if needed, and relapse prevention. An example of such a class can be found in Table 9-9.

Pharmacists who cannot conduct four to eight consecutive classes, however, should still provide some assistance. Telephone counseling is beneficial, as even brief interventions increase quit rates versus no assistance at all.[4] Thus, increasing the number of pharmacists committed to providing smoking cessation services in any format should have a positive impact on helping smokers quit and remain smoke-free in the long term.

Does the Leader of the Services Have to be a Former Smoker?

Smokers will ask whether the pharmacist conducting the group is a former smoker. Some will feel that a group leader who has never smoked before has never "experienced what it takes to stop smoking." While this is true, the pharmacist could point out the possible advantage with never having smoked: all the tools available to help with a quit attempt can be discussed, unbiased by "this worked for me, and this did not." Cessation is a highly *individualized* process. More important factors to successfully lead a smoking cessation group are to sincerely desire to help and to remain nonjudgmental at all times. Smokers appreciate a sincere nonjudgmental attitude and respond well to a leader that displays this, regardless of whether the leader is a former smoker or not.

CONCLUSIONS

In 2012, 19.3% of the US population was smokers, and smoking-related illnesses account for over 440,000 deaths yearly. Pharmacists in both community and clinic practice settings are ideally suited to assist and arrange a cessation attempt with either individualized or group counseling services. While seven medications have proven efficacious in cessation, long-term success is predicated upon making behavioral changes in daily activities to overcome physiologic and psychologic dependence. Cognitive and stress management strategies must also be considered. Although barriers exist in implementing cessation classes, helping patients to quit smoking through MTM services can be a rewarding endeavor.

PUTTING IT ALL TOGETHER: PATIENT CASE

TW is a 45-year-old man who has been smoking two packs per day for 20 years. He has tried to quit several times over the past year. His last attempt ended after 2 days of complete cessation because the 7-mg patch he was using caused his skin to become itchy, red, and swollen, and he was still experiencing significant cravings. In addition, TW has hypertension, diabetes, and depression, for which he is on the following medications: lisinopril 20 mg daily, metformin 1000 mg twice daily, glargine 30 units daily, and sertraline 50 mg daily. He drinks two glasses of wine per day and two cups of coffee each morning. He knows that smoking is "bad" for him; however, he states that when he has tried to quit in the past, he experiences a greatly increased appetite. He is afraid that quitting smoking will make him gain "too much weight." He has a recently measured BMI of 28. He asks, "Are there any nonprescription medications that don't have nicotine in them? My father passed away of a heart attack a couple of years ago. He was using those patches, too, and smoking with the patches on. I think too much nicotine caused him to have a heart attack!" TW has come to his local community pharmacist for advice, and he states that he is committed to quitting this time if he can find the right medication to help him do so.

- Should TW try to quit using the patch again? If so, what advice could the pharmacist give to avoid subsequent pruritus and erythema?

If TW does try the patch again, several issues will need to be discussed with him. He has lingering concerns that he may have a myocardial infarction like his father because he has hypertension and would be starting an NRT. This may be why he used a 7-mg patch in the past, which would be ineffective for a smoker with a 40-pack-year history (two packs per day × 20 years). If the nicotine patch were used with the present quit attempt, he would need to start with Step 1 (21-mg strength patch) for this to be effective. Because he was having significant epidermal irritation, he should be encouraged to use a different brand of patch. Different manufacturers use varied types of adhesive for the patches, so it is most likely the adhesive causing the irritation rather than the strength of the patch. He could be counseled that if irritation does develop, give it a 3–4-day trial and alternate each daily patch on a different site and treat the irritation and erythema with 1% hydrocortisone.

- What alternative medications could be used for TW to assist in his quit attempt? What counseling should be provided?

An effective alternative medication for TW may be bupropion ER 150 mg bid, rather than using the nicotine patch. Although there are no oral nonprescription medications for smoking cessation (as per his request), bupropion may be a more appropriate choice for him due to the depression. He should be counseled appropriately. He should be monitored for increased depression while attempting to stop smoking; if he has any experience of seizures, bupropion should be stopped immediately, and he should be referred to medical attention. Of note, he should be counseled not to abruptly stop drinking while starting bupropion, as this can decrease the seizure threshold. Given that he is a "heavy smoker" and has tried multiple quit attempts unsuccessfully, TW may be a candidate for dual smoking cessation therapy. He could start bupropion plus an OTC NRT, such as nicotine gum or lozenge. The NRT could be prn for breakthrough nicotine withdrawal symptoms while he is in the quitting process.

- What behavioral modification strategies would be helpful in TW's smoking cessation attempt? How could group counseling help?

TW should start with identifying when he has the most significant cravings throughout the day and prepare to counter those with specific behavioral change methods. For example, he should identify if he has significant cravings at first awakening, with coffee, while driving, relaxing in the evenings, etc. The encouragement to stop for "his health" should be as specific as possible. In TW's case, he could be told that his insulin may actually be more effective if he were to stop smoking due to smoke initiating the liver metabolizing system. Specifics regarding the decreased oxygenation at the extremities, possibly leading to increased neuropathy, could be discussed. He should also be told that most patients gain on average between 5 and 10 pounds when stopping smoking; however, there are things that he could be doing to prepare for this including: beginning an exercise program an eating healthy snacks such as carrot sticks, which could also be helpful for the habitual "hand-to-mouth" with smoking. Also, he should be counseled regarding the START method to begin his quit attempt. Group counseling is very effective and would give TW the opportunity to discover that many of his barriers in smoking cessation are also shared by others.

■ SUMMARY POINTS

- In 2009, approximately 45.4 million adults (21.6%) were smokers, including 24.1% men and 19.2% women. Although the prevalence has decreased slightly over the past several years, nicotine use still represents the single most preventable cause of premature death in the United States at approximately 450,000 people dying per year from smoking-related causes.
- At least one in five deaths in the United States is smoking related. Smokers most often die from lung cancer, but the second and third most likely cause of death for smokers is COPD and coronary artery disease (CAD), respectively. Smoking increases the risk of death from COPD ten times and from CAD three times. Smokers also die an average of 7 years earlier in comparison to nonsmokers.
- Approximately 70% of smokers who have been polled stated that they wanted to quit, and almost all who have indicated that they wanted to quit have had at least one quit attempt in the past year.
- Nicotine is harmful because it activates neurotransmitters in the central nervous system and leads to increases in epinephrine, norepinephrine, and dopamine. Dopamine is responsible for reinforcing addiction, while the other neurotransmitters increase blood pressure and heart rate. Smoking exacerbates complications of other disease states, including diabetes and hyperlipidemia. Cigarettes also contain more than 40 known carcinogens.
- All health-care providers should intervene with the "five A's" when a smoker indicates he or she wants to quit. The "five A's" are Ask, Advise, Assess, Assist, and Arrange.
- The Tobacco Use and Dependence Clinical Practice Guidelines from 2009 state that all smokers attempting to quit should be offered effective pharmacotherapy with the exception of the presence of special circumstances.
- Pharmacotherapy for smoking cessation includes NRT, psychotropics, and nicotine agonists. NRT that is available OTC includes nicotine patches, nicotine gum, and nicotine lozenges. All pharmacotherapy has been shown to be at least twice as effective as placebo for smoking cessation over a long period of time.
- Initiation of smoking cessation services in a community setting involves setting up a business plan, developing a strong referral plan, protocol, and documentation system, and finding a way to overcome any potential barriers.
- Counseling services should be implemented with behavioral, cognitive, and stress management techniques and provided in conjunction with cessation pharmacotherapy. Significant counseling should occur for individualizing a strategy for the smoker to quit, setting a quit date, planning for a quit date, and preventing relapse in the short- and long term.

STUDY QUESTIONS

1. Nicotine is a harmful substance because . . .
   a. It causes somatotropin to be released in the brain, which activates the reward pathway and helps to reinforce the addiction of smoking.
   b. Its slow penetration of brain tissues allows the substance to accumulate in the brain in order to exert its addictive effects.
   c. Diabetic neuropathy is more likely for patients with diabetes who smoke because tar builds up in the lungs and allows more oxygen to get to the tissues.
   d. It causes an increase in all of the following: blood pressure, stroke volume, and cardiac output.

2. How can pharmacists help smokers quit?
   a. For all patients willing to quit, follow the "five A's": ask, advise, assess, assist, and arrange.
   b. For the patient unwilling to quit, insist that they set a quit date within the next 2 weeks in order to make them quit.
   c. For patients willing to quit, recommend pharmacotherapy for all patients regardless of age.
   d. For patients willing to quit, implement the "R" part of the START plan: Resist the urge to smoke except at designated times.

3. Using the 4-mg strength nicotine gum would be most appropriate for which of the following patients?
   a. An adult male smoker who smokes his first cigarette within 30 minutes after waking up in the morning.
   b. A pregnant mother of two young children who smokes one and a half packs of cigarettes per day.
   c. An adult female smoker who smokes one and a half packs of cigarettes per day and agrees to schedule the use of at least nine pieces of gum daily.
   d. A 62-year-old cigar smoker with multiple cessation attempts with nonprescription medications in the past and only wants prescription therapy.

4. Which of the following is a TRUE statement regarding prescription therapy for smoking cessation?
   a. Bupropion is a partial nicotine agonist that should not be used by patients with a history of seizures.
   b. Varenicline should be started at 150 mg once daily and titrated up to 150 mg twice daily after the first 3 days of starting therapy.
   c. When smokers start therapy with Bupropion, the patient should be told to set their quit date for the exact day they start oral therapy.
   d. Nicotine inhalers have the most addiction potential because their plasma nicotine levels mimic that of cigarettes, and a clear method of tapering does not exist.

5. Which of the following is the most efficacious smoking cessation medication for all smokers?
   a. Nicotine gum
   b. Nicotine patches
   c. Bupropion
   d. Varenicline
   e. None of the above

6. An independent pharmacist has been practicing within a small community for the past 20 years and has developed good relationships with most of the local physicians. Most of his customers are cash-pay. He would like to implement group-counseling sessions to help smokers quit. Which of the following would serve as a significant barrier that he could not easily overcome?

a. Establishing a good referral system for his services
b. Developing an adequate reimbursement system
c. Obtaining approval from local city officials
d. Developing the knowledge needed to assist smokers in quitting
e. None of the above should serve as significant barriers

7. A patient comes into the pharmacy for follow-up on smoking cessation counseling. The patient failed Chantix previously but on this attempt has been using nicotine lozenges. He has been successful in smoking cessation; however, he has recently developed indigestion and heartburn for the last 2 weeks. What would be the most appropriate action for this patient?
    a. Continue lozenge and add proton pump inhibitor
    b. Switch patient to the nicotine patch
    c. Initiate therapy with Chantix
    d. Use lozenge as needed and add nicotine gum

8. Appropriate counseling for a patient using nicotine gum for smoking cessation would include which of the following statements?
    a. Nicotine gum should be chewed continuously for 30 minutes.
    b. Continue eating and drinking normally while using nicotine gum.
    c. Nicotine gum should be used only as needed for cravings.
    d. You may experience upset stomach while using nicotine gum.

9. A pregnant woman asks for a recommendation to help her stop smoking. She found out she was pregnant 1 week ago and continues to smoke a pack per day. What would be the most appropriate recommendation?
    a. Bupropion is prescription-only but would be the most appropriate choice.
    b. Nicotine patches are the most effective nicotine replacement for pregnant women.
    c. She should use a prescription-only nicotine inhaler because of the very low levels of nicotine absorption.
    d. She should try to quit "cold turkey" without using any medications for cessation.

10. Patients beginning smoking cessation treatment with Chantix or bupropion should be advised of which of the following statements?
    a. Begin taking your medication 1 or 2 weeks before your quit date.
    b. Start taking your medication on your quit date.
    c. You should begin taking your medication after not smoking for 1 full week.
    d. Stop taking your medication should you begin smoking again.

11. A pregnant woman asks for a recommendation to help her stop smoking. She found out she was pregnant 1 week ago and continues to smoke a pack per day. What would be the most appropriate recommendation?
    a. Bupropion is prescription-only but would be the most appropriate choice.
    b. Nicotine patches are the most effective nicotine replacement for pregnant women.
    c. She should use a prescription-only nicotine inhaler because of the very low levels of nicotine absorption.
    d. She should try to quit "cold turkey" without using any medications for cessation.

12. Chantix contains a black box warning for which of the following?
    a. Severe skin reactions
    b. Depressed mood
    c. Angioedema
    d. Nausea

BIBLIOGRAPHY

1. Centers for Disease Control Fact Sheet. http://www.cdc.gov/tobacco/data_statistics/fact_sheets/adult_data/cig_smoking/index.htm. Accessed July, 2012.
2. American Lung Association. http://www.lung.org/stop-smoking/about-smoking/facts-figures/general-smoking-facts.html. Accessed July, 2012
3. American Heart Association. http://www.heart.org/HEARTORG/Getting-Healthy/QuitSmoking/QuittingResources/Smoking-Cardiovascular-Disease_UCM_305187_Article.jsp. Accessed July, 2012
4. U.S. Department of Health and Human Services. *Treating Tobacco Use and Dependence: 2008 Update*. Washington, DC: Public Health Service; 2008.
5. Henningfield JE, Stapleton JM, Benoqitz NL, Grayson RF, London ED. Higher levels of nicotine in arterial than in venous blood after cigarette smoking. *Drug Alcohol Depend*. 1993;33(1):23-29.
6. Leshner AL, Koob GF. Drugs of abuse and the brain. *Proc Assoc Am Physicians*. 1999;111(2):99-108.
7. U.S. Department of Health and Human Services (USDHHS). *The Health Benefits of Smoking Cessation. A Report of the Surgeon General* (Publication No. CDC 90–8416). USDHS, Public Health Service, Centers for Disease Control and Prevention and Health Promotion, Office on Smoking and Health. Atlanta, GA; 1990.
8. Aubin H, Farley A, Lycett D, Aveyard P. Weight gain in smokers after quitting cigarettes: meta-analysis. *BMJ*. 2012;345:e4439.
9. Doll R, Peto R, Boreham J, Sutherland I. Mortality in relation to smoking: 50 years' observations on male British doctors. *BMJ*. 2004;22:1-9.
10. Prochaska JO. *Systems of Psychotherapy: A Transtheoretical Analysis*. Homewood, IL: Dorsey; 1979.
11. Fagerstrom KO. A comparison of psychological and pharmacological treatment in smoking cessation. *J Behav Med*. 1982;5(3):343-351.
12. Agboola S, McNeill A, Coleman T, Leonardi B. A systematic review of the effectiveness of smoking relapse prevention interventions for abstinent smokers. *Addiction*. 2010;105(8):1362-1380.
13. Nicorette gum package insert. Johnson and Johnson New Brunswick, NJ. *Nicorette*. 2011.
14. Moore D, Averyard P, Connock M, Wang D, Fry-Smith A, Barton P. Effectiveness and safety of nicotine replacement therapy assisted reduction to stop smoking: systematic review and meta-analysis. *BMJ*. 2009;338:1024-1033.
15. Johnson TS. A brief overview of pharmacotherapeutic treatment options in smoking cessation: bupropion versus varenicline. *J Am Acad Nurse Pract*. 2010;22(10):557-563.
16. Jorenby DE, Hays JT, Rigotti NA, et al. Efficacy of varenicline, an alpha4beta2 nicotinic acetylcholine receptor partial agonist, vs placebo or sustained-release bupropion for smoking cessation. *JAMA*. 2006;296(1):56-63.
17. Kennedy DT, Small RE. Development and implementation of a smoking cessation clinic in community pharmacy practice. *J Am Pharm Assoc*. 2002;42:83-92.
18. Dent LA, Harris KJ, Noonan CW. Randomized trial assessing the effectiveness of a pharmacist-delivered program for smoking cessation. *Ann Pharmacother*. 2009;43:194-201.
19. Dent LA, Harris KJ, Noonan CW. Tobacco interventions delivered by pharmacists: a summary and systematic review. *Pharmacotherapy*. 2007;27(7):1040-1051.
20. Robinson MD, Laurent SL, Little JM. Including smoking status as a new vital sign. *J Fam Pract*. 1995;40(6):556-561.
21. American Academy of Family Physicians. *A Guide to Tobacco Cessation Group Visits*. Washington, DC: AAFP; 2012.
22. Eades CE, Ferguson JS, O'Carroll RE. Public health in community pharmacy: a systematic review of pharmacist and consumer views. *BMC Public Health*. 2011;11:582-595.
23. Sinclair HK, Bond CM, Stead LF. Community pharmacy personnel interventions for smoking cessation. *Cochrane Database Syst Rev*. 2004;(1):CD003698.
24. Martin BA, Bruskiewitz RH, Chewning BA. Effect of a tobacco cessation continuing professional education program on pharmacists' confidence, skills, and practice-change behaviors. *J Am Pharm Assoc*. 2010;50(1):9-16.
25. Patwardhan PD, Chewning BA. Ask, advise, and refer: hypothesis generation to promote a brief tobacco-cessation intervention in community pharmacies. *Int J Pharm Pract*. 2009;17(4):221-229.
26. Williams DM. Preparing pharmacy students and pharmacists to provide tobacco cessation counseling. *Drug Alcohol Rev*. 2009;28(5):533-540.

10

ANTICOAGULATION SERVICES

Matthew Strum

> ### ■ LEARNING OBJECTIVES
>
> After completion of this chapter, the reader should be able to:
>
> 1. Identify common disease states that require anticoagulation.
> 2. Understand the value of an anticoagulation therapy service.
> 3. Evaluate the risks involved in providing anticoagulation therapy management services.
> 4. Evaluate the internal needs of the service including staffing and clerical support, space to assess patients, and laboratory services.
> 5. Develop a communication system with local health-care providers for patient referrals and patient report follow-up.
> 6. Understand the importance of the development of standard operating procedures for improved efficiency and effectiveness.
> 7. Identify potential training opportunities to ensure the delivery of optimized anticoagulant therapy.

Community pharmacies continue to expand their practice by offering innovative patient care services, specifically medication therapy management (MTM) services. The role of anticoagulation services may have a positive outcome in patients, when compared with "usual care" (i.e., personal physician) with potentials for decreases in bleeding and thromboembolism.[1] An anticoagulation service in a community pharmacy is a prime example of a MTM service that can be offered. Pharmacists providing anticoagulation services can improve patient outcomes and reduce the risk of adverse events.[2,3,4,5] New anticoagulants (i.e., Pradaxa®/Xarelto®) that do not require continuous international normalized ratio (INR) monitoring have recently been introduced but do not preclude the need for pharmacist-provided anticoagulation services. Warfarin is still the treatment of choice for many patients requiring anticoagulation (e.g., prosthetic valve [PV] replacement).[6] Managing oral anticoagulation with warfarin requires comprehensive, individualized attention to interactions with a patient's dietary patterns, OTC (over-the-counter) medications, prescription medications, and even lifestyle changes.

Warfarin is a product discovered over 60 years ago by scientists studying why cattle were spontaneously hemorrhaging and dying. The funding for much of this research came from the *Wisconsin Alumni Research Foundation* thus forming the first part of the name, warfarin, with the second part of the name due to it being a coum*arin* derivative.[7] Clinical application later developed in 1955 when then President Dwight Eisenhower was given warfarin after suffering a myocardial infarction. Due to the narrow therapeutic window of warfarin, additional developments in monitoring were needed. Prothrombin time monitoring was initially developed and in 1982, the INR by the World Health Organization (WHO) became the standard system of anticoagulation control worldwide.[8]

■ DISEASE STATES REQUIRING ORAL ANTICOAGULATION

Multiple disease states necessitate the need for oral anticoagulation to prevent many adverse sequela. While a review of all of the necessary situations in which anticoagulation could be indicated is beyond the scope of this chapter, the most common clinical situations that result in oral anticoagulation management with vitamin K antagonists (e.g., warfarin) are reviewed.

Stroke prevention secondary to atrial fibrillation is one of the most common reasons patients require anticoagulation. Atrial fibrillation is a major risk factor for ischemic stroke. It is estimated that approximately 2.3 million Americans have sustained or paroxysmal atrial fibrillation. Atrial appendage embolism thrombi secondary to atrial fibrillation has been estimated to account for approximately 10% of all ischemic strokes, and a higher average in the very elderly in the United States.[9] A valuable validated assessment tool that can be utilized to determine stroke risk in patients with atrial fibrillation is the $CHADS_2$ assessment.[9,10,11,12] Table 10-1 summarizes how to use the assessment tool and Table 10-2 provides the stroke risk based on the $CHADS_2$ score.

Venous thromboembolism (VTE) is a disease that includes both deep vein thrombosis (DVT) and pulmonary embolism (PE).[13] No national VTE surveillance system is currently in place, but US estimates put the overall annual rate at 900,000 cases of clinically evident VTE, which could result in as many as 300,000 deaths annually from PE.[14] There are age, race, and gender differences; however, due to variations in administrative reporting, true incidences are not known and may be significantly underreported.[15,16] Thus, patients may be treated for acute VTE or prophylaxis of VTE secondary to some comorbid condition. Importantly, VTE is preventable when appropriate prophylaxis is implemented (Table 10-3).

Table 10-1. $CHADS_2$ Scoring[10]	
Risk Factor	**Points**
Congestive heart failure	= 1
Hypertension	= 1
Age ≥75 years	= 1
Diabetes	= 1
Previous **S**troke/transient ischemic attack/systemic embolus	= 2

Table 10-2. CHADS₂ Stroke Risk[10]

CHADS$_2$ Score	Stroke Rate (%/year)	Recommended Therapy
0	1.9 (1.2–3.0)	Daily aspirin
1	2.8 (2.0–3.8)	Anticoagulation optional: warfarin (INR 2–3) or daily aspirin
2	4.0 (3.1–5.1)	
3	5.9 (4.6–7.3)	
4	8.5 (6.3–11.1)	Anticoagulation warranted: warfarin (INR 2–3)
5	12.5 (8.2–17.5)	
6	18.2 (10.5–27.4)	

Systemic embolism prophylaxis secondary to PV replacement is another clinical example that necessitates oral anticoagulation with warfarin. Between 1993 and 2007, 623,039 patients underwent cardiac valve surgery in North America (excluding pulmonary valves).[20] Current estimates put annual PV replacement rates in the United States at 90,000 and worldwide at 280,000.[21] With approximately half of the PV replacements being mechanical valves and half being bioprosthetic, oral anticoagulation with warfarin continues to be needed, since newly approved therapies do not carry indications for prophylaxis in patients with PV replacement. Patients may have atrial valve replacement (AVR), mitral valve replacement (MVR), or another heart valve, or even multiple heart valves replaced, all which would require anticoagulation of some type to prevent secondary embolism.[6]

WARFARIN

Warfarin continues to play a vital role in the management of VTE prophylaxis and stroke prophylaxis.[1,9,13] It is currently indicated for:[22]

1. The prophylaxis and/or treatment of venous thrombosis and its extension, and PE.
2. The prophylaxis and/or treatment of the thromboembolic complications associated with atrial fibrillation and/or cardiac valve replacement.
3. To reduce the risk of death, recurrent myocardial infarction, and thromboembolic events such as stroke or systemic embolization after myocardial infarction.

Warfarin is rapidly absorbed after oral administration; however, its resultant effect on increasing INR is delayed. To understand this delay, it is important to understand the clotting factors that warfarin inhibits and their concurrent half-lives (Table 10-4).[23] It is also important to understand that certain vitamin K-dependent products are the "natural" anticoagulants of the body (i.e., protein C and protein S). Realizing that protein C having the shortest half-life will be depleted first could potentially induce a hypercoagulable state. It is clinically important to cross-cover with a more rapid acting anticoagulant (i.e., low

Table 10-3. Risk Factors for VTE[17,18,19]

- Increasing age
- Previous history of DVT or PE
- Trauma (fractures of pelvis, hip, or leg)
- Metastatic malignancy
- Vein disease (such as varicose veins)
- Smoking
- Estrogen usage or current pregnancy
- Obesity
- Genetic factors (inherited thrombophilic syndromes)
  - Antithrombin deficiency
  - Protein C/S deficiency
  - Factor V Leiden mutation
  - Prothrombin G20210A mutation

Table 10-4. Clotting Factor Half-Lives[22]

Clotting Factor/Protein	Half-Life (hours)
Factor II	60
Factor VII	4–6
Factor IX	24
Factor X	48–72
Protein C	8
Protein S	30

molecular weight heparin [LMWH]), due to the delay in anticoagulant effect that is associated with warfarin.

Warfarin is a racemic mixture of warfarin-R and warfarin-S. The importance of this relates to the different routes of metabolism for each enantiomer, as well as the anticoagulation potency of each. Metabolism occurs via CYP pathways and thus allows for potential drug interactions with multiple medications.[1] Understanding these interactions is vitally important when doing an MTM assessment, and potentially preventing significant adverse reactions.

■ VALUE OF PHARMACIST-PROVIDED ANTICOAGULATION SERVICES

Individual prescribing physicians have traditionally managed oral anticoagulation therapy in the community setting. Patients have their blood drawn either at the physician's office, hospital, or local laboratory. The results of the INR are then transmitted to the physician's office where the physician or a delegate will interpret the results and then contact the patient with any recommendations that need to occur. In some instances, this could be 2–3 days after the blood draw. With this method of follow-up, very little patient interaction or evaluation can effectively occur. Some of these services result in physicians being unable to bill when the follow-up is via telephone. Many patients have been lost to follow-up in this setting, either by the office not being able to contact the patient or the patient fails to obtain their blood work on a consistent basis. This has resulted in many physicians being reluctant to prescribe oral anticoagulation therapy.[24] These problems associated with physician monitoring of anticoagulation provide an opportunity for pharmacists to provide an anticoagulation service that benefits both patients and physicians.

Pharmacists have established anticoagulation services in community pharmacies, ambulatory clinics, and in hospitals.[25,26] Physicians have collaborated with pharmacists in caring for anticoagulation patients to ensure better monitoring and patient outcomes. Studies have shown that pharmacist-managed anticoagulation services improve clinical and economic outcomes when compared with usual care.[2,3,4,5,27,28,29,30] Additionally, it has been shown that both patients and physicians have a high level of satisfaction with pharmacist-managed anticoagulation services.[31]

Pharmacists wanting to implement anticoagulation services should be prepared to provide documentation of the positive benefits of these services to primary care providers, payers, and other stakeholders. Equally important will be understanding the medical–legal issues associated with anticoagulation. Anticoagulation therapy involves understanding two equally serious clinical features—over- and under-anticoagulation—as both can have life-threatening consequences.[32] Thus, developing a systematic approach to the delivery of anticoagulation services can decrease the likelihood of adverse events.[33]

■ DECIDING TO DEVELOP ANTICOAGULATION SERVICE—BUSINESS PLAN

When deciding to implement an anticoagulation service in a community pharmacy, it is important to plan. This should include strategic planning and business planning. First, the pharmacist needs to consider whether the implementation of MTM services related to oral anticoagulation relates to the overall mission of the pharmacy or clinic. Second, the need for this service in the community must be determined. How many patients are prescribed warfarin? Is there an anticoagulation monitoring service available to providers and patients in the area? Is there at least one provider willing to refer patients to an anticoagulation monitoring service? Writing a business plan for the service will help determine the need and feasibility of developing and implementing the service. A business plan should include an environmental analysis, goals for the service, a description of the service to be offered, a description of the physical facilities used to offer the service, a target market description, a pricing plan, and a promotion strategy. During the business planning of the anticoagulation service, it is important for the pharmacy management to determine if the necessary resources are available and the expected time line for financial sustainability (or profitability) of the clinic.[34,35,36]

An environmental analysis, which could include a SWOT (Strengths, Weaknesses, Opportunities, Threats) analysis, should be performed, prior to any serious planning. The strengths and weaknesses of the SWOT analysis are focused on the internal aspects of developing the service. What are the strengths of the pharmacy for developing and implementing an anticoagulation service? And alternatively, what are the weaknesses? Examples of strengths may be, location, a well-trained pharmacist with experience in anticoagulation monitoring, private counseling area in pharmacy, pharmacy management supportive of development of patient care services, and already established relationships with providers. The opportunities and threats are the external factors influencing the development of the service. Examples of opportunities include a documented need in the community, overwhelmed or overly busy providers, and availability of third-party reimbursement or payment structure. It is extremely important to evaluate the potential use of the clinic by the local providers, the expected workload within the clinic, and the current structural layout of the clinic (e.g., do you have a private counseling area to perform lab work). Obtaining provider support for the clinic is important since they will be the source of your referrals. It is also important to assess the potential threats to the new service. Evaluating all these factors will provide insight into whether the service should be developed and if so, how the service should be developed.[37,38]

Initiating a clinical service from scratch can be a daunting task; therefore, during your initial assessment consider reviewing the current literature for examples of services similar to what you desire to develop. What are some of the issues faced when the authors initiated their services? How were they able to overcome the various obstacles they encountered in the beginning? Identifying these issues will assist in preparing the overall business plan. A good resource for assistance is a publication by Ansell et al: *Managing Oral Anticoagulant Therapy* (2nd Edition).[39] It is important to realize that every clinic has its own specific issues and problems that will develop, but identifying potential ones, and having a plan in place to overcome them, will put you a step ahead in development. Contacting professionals who have started a service similar to the one being developed is also beneficial. A list of registered anticoagulation services with contact information can be found at www.acforum.org. Professional organizations and schools of pharmacy may assist with implementation strategies as well.[40,41,42] A one-on-one discussion can facilitate the steps necessary to start a service. Ask the pointed questions as to the different challenges faced when establishing a clinical service. Utilize their experience to assist you in shaping the focus of your service and overcome the potential barriers. Additionally, some professional organizations will have workshops and seminars related to the implementation of patient care services and/or anticoagulation services.[40,42] These workshops often will provide helpful hints and networking opportunities that will be invaluable.

Once it is decided that it is feasible and desirable to develop and implement an anticoagulation service, the target market must be considered and the 4Ps of marketing evaluated: the product, the place, the price, and the promotion of the service. With your marketing strategy, you want to be able to differentiate yourself from other pharmacies in the area. The fact that you are implementing clinical services is a significant differentiator. You are creating a different service level within your market and trying to improve the overall quality of patient care. With this, you are creating higher expectations of your pharmacy and the overall services that are delivered.[43]

TARGET MARKET

Identify patients:

- Who will your patient be?
- Where will they come from?
- How many could there be?
- How many can you handle?

In the case of the target market, consider the referring provider. The pharmacist can look at their prescription records to see how many warfarin patients already patronize the pharmacy and who prescribes the warfarin. Identifying a provider with multiple patients already utilizing your pharmacy may be an optimal starting point for your service. Starting small and growing with this subset of patients could assist you in identifying a provider champion for your services.

Provider Referral

Obtaining provider support is vital to any pharmacy service. Identify advocates who will refer to you. Consider the various providers in your area who may prescribe warfarin as well as hospital discharge referrals. It is a good idea to start small, working with one or two providers initially and then begin branching out. Starting small also allows you to evaluate your procedures and make any necessary changes early on to assist in streamlining your clinic. It is recommended to develop a referral form so that providers can quickly refer a patient to the anticoagulation service and provide the necessary information needed (see Appendix 10-A for sample referral form).

Once a patient is referred, communication with the referring provider must be maintained, informing the referring provider of current anticoagulation status and changes made via protocol are crucial. Whether this communication should occur through electronic means, facsimile, or verbally should be decided between you and each provider. When you establish your collaborative practice agreements, it is important to remember to have all communication with various providers the same. This will assist you with standardizing your procedures.

Upon receiving a referral, a process in the pharmacy will need to be in place to ensure an appointment is made. This can be accomplished by having a standard policy in place that all referrals are responded to within one business day. This is crucial, as new anticoagulation patients need prompt follow-up to ensure appropriate anticoagulation is achieved and overanticoagulation does not occur. This could be an opportunity to utilize pharmacy technicians or clerks to schedule new patients upon referral.

ANTICOAGULATION SERVICE—GOALS AND SCOPE OF SERVICE

At the patient's initial visit, plan on spending between 30 and 45 minutes to provide adequate time for history and medication review. A patient history and medication form should be used to collect and document information needed to properly provide MTM and anticoagulation monitoring services (refer to Chapter 4 for more detail related to MTM services). Also during the initial visit, the patient needs to sign a HIPAA form, and if one has not been previously signed, a release of information form. This will allow you to obtain vital information from health-care providers as necessary and to payers as needed. Once patients are seen at the pharmacy, follow-up appointments need to be scheduled. An operational calendar for when the clinic will be in session should be maintained. This type of work could be delegated to a pharmacy technician or clerk. Additional items that can be managed by a pharmacy staff member other than a pharmacist could include missed appointment tracking, appointment reminder phone calls, and quality assurance reporting.

Protocol Development

Probably the most important aspect of the establishment of clinical services related to oral anticoagulation is the development of a protocol.[37,40] It is important to realize that the protocol should contain what the clinic can do, but also what the clinic cannot do. If anticoagulation services and diabetes management services are offered within the same pharmacy, separate protocols are required for each. It will be important to evaluate the regulations that your state would require prior to protocol development.

Within the protocol, the goals and the scope of service provided should be clearly defined. A process of care should be integrated that (1) uses time efficiently, (2) maintains low overhead costs by simplifying patient management, (3) improves patient adherence, and (4) most importantly improves patient outcomes. During protocol development, take the time to review literature resources and attempt to identify what has worked and what has failed.

The protocol should spell out specific procedures and patient flow during their entire time in your care. The initial visit should be detailed so that collaborating providers will be aware of exactly what will occur during patient visits. By mapping this initial visit, it also gives you the template needed to ensure that all the pertinent information is completely covered. Due to the amount of education required for correctly utilizing warfarin, pharmacists may want to develop personalized education materials and include these within the protocol.

Within the protocol you should reference the accepted INR goals as published in *Antithrombotic and Thrombolytic Therapy: American College of Chest Physicians Evidenced-Based Clinical Practice Guidelines* (9th Edition), published as a supplement to *Chest* journal in February 2012. This evidence-based guideline will assist you in providing the most up-to-date evidence for practical INR goals. It is important to recognize that these guidelines are periodically updated, thus protocol updates would need to take place when guideline updates are published. Also, there will be situations in which a provider may want to deviate from the recommended goals, and this should be documented within a specific patient referral.

Management of INR elevations should also be documented within the protocol. It is important to understand that the evidence changes with regard to the most appropriate way to manage patients who are experiencing overanticoagulation, thus maintaining up-to-date evidence-based guidelines is crucial.[44]

A sample anticoagulation protocol is available for review in Appendix 10-B.

Quality Control/Quality Assurance

Continuous quality control and assurance is necessary to ensure that appropriate outcomes are seen with anticoagulation services. Evaluating the overall incidence of adverse events (bleeding or thrombotic episodes) is the optimal way to evaluate quality; however, in a small anticoagulation service, patient numbers would not be sufficient to statistically validate the outcomes. Thus, an intermediate way to measure outcomes and thus quality is needed.[45] One of the ways to evaluate quality of anticoagulation is to measure "Time in Therapeutic Range" (TTR).[46,47] Another simpler measure of quality is calculating the percentage of patients within therapeutic range over a period of time.[45] This type of data can be presented to referring healthcare providers as a means to show the value you provide to patients. Quality does not start or stop with INR control; it also needs to be assessed with how laboratory values are obtained. Continuous assessment of how blood samples are obtained, how point-of-care (POC) monitors are maintained, and storage of all essential laboratory materials are needed including refrigerator temperature logs. Quality improvement is a continuous process that requires due diligence in its development.[22,24,47,48,49,50,51,52]

Resources Needed

Staff

Ensuring the pharmacist(s) and support staff who are adequately trained in anticoagulation monitoring is essential. Residency training in an ambulatory care setting that is involved in anticoagulation therapy could be beneficial. Otherwise, a systematic review of the current anticoagulation guidelines would need to be undertaken to ensure the best outcome for the patients referred to your service.

Pharmacy Design

Workflow design will need to be considered when developing the service. When a pharmacist is providing anticoagulation services, appropriate pharmacist coverage for your other pharmacy services will be needed. Thus, decisions about when the anticoagulation service is offered and staffing concerns will need to be considered. Likewise if a clinic patient comes without an appointment because of a concern, how this will be handled should be discussed and established.

Point-of-Care Monitors and Supplies

POC monitors are a significant capital investment, thus it is important to evaluate which monitor is the most optimal for your service. Other considerations that need to be reviewed are: storage for strips as many of them will require refrigeration and security for monitors. Other supplies that need to be available include sharps containers, alcohol pads, cotton balls, gloves, and bandages. A biohazard waste removal service will also be needed to dispose of medical waste that is inherently involved with managing an anticoagulation service.

When using POC monitors, it is important to understand the Clinical Laboratory Improvement Amendments (CLIA) of 1988.[30,53] These were enacted to ensure that all medical laboratories are meeting quality standards. CLIA is administered by the Centers for Medicare and Medicaid Services (CMS) and each individual site is responsible for registration. It is important to choose a POC device that is CLIA waived. Your pharmacy/clinic has to complete a certificate of waiver if interested in performing a waived test. Once you have completed the registration, CMS will assign the pharmacy/clinic a CLIA number and send a CLIA fee-remittance coupon.[54] A biannual fee of $150–$200 is required to receive a CLIA waiver certificate. By doing this, the pharmacist providing the waived tests agree to follow manufacturer instructions, perform quality control procedures, and store and monitor reagents properly. For more information see https://www.cms.gov/CLIA/downloads/HowObtainCertificateofWaiver.pdf[54]

OR

https://www.cms.gov/clia/05_CLIA_Brochures.aspTopOfPage[53]

Educational Materials

Personalized patient education material that contains your service name or logo is an easy way to distinguish your involvement in MTM services (see, e.g., Appendix 10-C) This can also assist you with marketing your pharmacy services in the community. Patients can take the education materials with them to subsequent physician visits to help identify your service as being an integral part of patient care. These materials can be warfarin dosage reminder cards, pamphlets related to foods high in vitamin K, or drug interaction wallet cards that patients can carry with them anytime another health-care provider will be seen who might prescribe a medication. Standardization of education materials will also benefit the service, as all patients will be educated similarly. This could help improve the overall quality of the education provided.[55]

Documentation System

Documentation is the process for gathering and integrating the information from a patient visit for future reference and specific managerial needs. Because documentation is critical to the success of the service, one should consider purchasing a software system to support MTM, anticoagulation service documentation, and all anticipated expansions of clinic services offered. There are various systems available. It is also recommended to use the software system for appointment scheduling.

In regard to anticoagulation services, complete and accurate documentation is necessary for several reasons, simply put, if it is not documented, it did not happen.

1. When caring for patients on oral anticoagulation, *documentation of the INR over several visits will allow you to see any trends in the intensity of anticoagulation*. For example, Jane Smith has been a patient in the anticoagulation clinic for over a year and she has been consistent with warfarin 5 mg daily. Her INR has always been between 2.1 and 2.8.

Suddenly she has an INR of 3.9. You diligently question her to identify the cause of the elevated INR, at which point she remembers that she was prescribed Bactrim™ 2 days ago for a UTI. If you had not appropriately documented the INR results for the past year, you may consider decreasing the patients' warfarin dosage without identifying a potential cause (i.e., the patient was started on an interacting antibiotic for a UTI). This could have subsequently resulted in a subtherapeutic INR yielding an embolic event.

2. *Documentation is also crucial for information exchange with other health-care professionals.* For example, Joe Smith is a patient you have been following for 2 years. He was recently in an automobile accident requiring hospitalization and multiple surgeries. The physicians were informed that he was followed in your clinic for oral anticoagulation and they wish to restart his warfarin. They want to know his previous 4 months INRs and what his warfarin dose was prior to the accident in order to discharge him on the same dose. If you had not documented, you would be unable to provide the needed information.

3. *Documentation is imperative if you desire to obtain reimbursement for your services.* You may need to convince third-party payers/employers of the value. To support your claims, you will need to show documentation of your services. Quality of services, cost-savings, and prevention of adverse events will be necessary to obtain payment from any payer. This should be discussed with any software vendor when considering purchase to ensure that data reporting is easily accessible.

4. *Documenting is important for legal reasons.* Pharmacists should always document completely and accurately to reduce their personal and professional liability. Excellent clinical results are sometimes not possible even with the best clinical services. For example, a patient who has been chronically subtherapeutic on multiple visits. You document a history of nonadherence to the prescribed therapy, including the unwillingness of the patient to maintain a diet that is consistent in vitamin K intake. This nonadherence to recommended therapy resulted in the patient having a stroke secondary to their subtherapeutic INR. The documentation you provide pertaining to the nonadherent behaviors could prevent liability.

LOCATION

During the initial stages of clinic development, identify an appropriate area within your pharmacy to see and evaluate patients. Are you going to need to expand or remodel to have a semiprivate room? If doing so, you may want to consider having the area somewhat open for promotion purposes (i.e., have a windowed room with blinds to close while seeing patients). Other patients may walk in and ask what you do with your clinic room. This gives you an opportunity to advertise verbally to potential MTM patients. This semiprivate setting helps distinguish your pharmacy and develops true patient care relationships.

In addition to the physical attributes of the pharmacy, pharmacy management must decide if the anticoagulation service needs to be offered everyday or select days as well as for all day or only for a few hours per day, with consideration for the amount of time per patient. With a limited number of patients in the beginning, it is advised to select a few hours on a couple of days and schedule most patients during this time. As your service grows, then decide on how to expand. It is important to keep in mind that expansion may also include adding employees to distribute the workload appropriately. As you see more patients, you also become more efficient at the patient visits, which could allow you to decrease the amount of time per patient. An anticoagulation service might be an ideal setting to incorporate a community pharmacy resident to assist with the clinical aspects of the pharmacy's growth.

PROMOTION PLAN

For the anticoagulation service to be successful, it is critical that people in the community are aware of the service. There are multiple ways to promote your service[56,57] but most importantly its benefits must be communicated to hospitals, physicians, patients, payers, and other stakeholders in the area. Money should be budgeted for promotion. Pharmacists can promote the service themselves as well as hire a promotion company to assist with promotional efforts.

It is important for the pharmacy itself to promote the service. Signs in the pharmacy should inform people who enter the pharmacy that additional patient care services are provided beyond dispensing. Business cards that promote the service should be available. Flyers pertaining the service could be stuffed in bags. Pharmacy staff training to inform patients of your anticoagulation service can be effective, especially for patients who are picking up anticoagulation medications.

Promotion of anticoagulation services often consists of advertising, personal selling, public relations, and direct mail. Pharmacies should consider advertising their anticoagulation services via the local newspapers, the yellow pages, and the local radio/TV. If the pharmacy has a Web site, the Web site should communicate the availability of all patient care services offered by the pharmacy. Direct mail can also be used. Physicians in the area may be mailed a flyer or brochure about the service.

Personal selling is a cost-effective initial marketing method. The pharmacist will need to develop or strengthen relationships with health-care providers in the area who can refer patients. One strategy might be to provide lunch or dinner to a medical clinic and provide a formal presentation about the anticoagulation service. Suggest to them that the service can decrease their "hassle factor" while improving patient outcomes. Inviting physicians and nurses to your pharmacy after-hours to show them the service is another strategy.

Public relation is another approach used to promote the service. Writing a column in the local newspaper about anticoagulation and the importance of monitoring will increase awareness of the anticoagulation services in your pharmacy. Furthermore, having the newspaper or television station develop a story about your anticoagulation service is effective in increasing awareness. Attending health fairs and other events in the community will also generate awareness of your pharmacy and its services.

■ BILLING STRATEGY

Developing and implementing an anticoagulation service requires an initial investment; therefore, to provide the service, pharmacies need to develop a billing strategy.[58] The pharmacy can bill the patient's medical provider or the patient directly. Considering the patient referred will provide insight into the best billing strategy. It is best to designate one person in the pharmacy responsible for billing and reimbursement issues. Having one person responsible will allow that person to learn about the billing process and to work with payers to ensure appropriate reimbursement. Another option is to hire a billing firm.

Fee schedules should be established based on the services you render as listed in the Current Procedural Terminology (CPT) coding system. Often payers will have a maximum payment amount for anticoagulation services, thus implementation costs compared with reimbursement rates should be analyzed. If the cost to provide the service is far greater than any reimbursement, the service would not be sustainable. When billing third-party payers is being considered, establishing contact before services are provided will help ensure maximum familiarity with each company's policies and procedures for reimbursement, ultimately saving time, frustration, and risking rejected claims due to incomplete or faulty claims.

■ PUTTING IT ALL TOGETHER: PATIENT CASE

JS is a 58-year-old male who presents with a new prescription for warfarin. Upon questioning you are informed that he was recently diagnosed with atrial fibrillation and was initiated on warfarin to decrease his risk of stroke. Past medical history includes dyslipidemia, hypertension, and diabetes. He states that he has to go to the hospital laboratory in 2 days to have his "blood thinner level" checked, since his nurse practitioner (NP) does not draw labs "in house."

Current Medications:

Simvastatin 40 mg daily at bedtime

Lisinopril/HCTZ 20/25 mg once daily every morning

Metoprolol succinate 50 mg once daily every morning

Metformin 1000 mg twice daily with meals

Linagliptin 5 mg once daily in the morning

Aspirin EC 81 mg once daily with food

Current prescription is for warfarin 5 mg once daily that you fill and counsel the patient. During counseling, you talk with the patient about your newly initiated anticoagulation service. He agrees to follow up in your pharmacy if his NP is alright with the pharmacy managing. Upon consultation with his NP, you establish a collaborative practice to manage anticoagulation.

What are major counseling points that need to be covered with the initiation of warfarin?

Ideally you would cover the following: Current dose of warfarin, indication for which he is receiving warfarin, potential drug–drug, drug–food, and drug–disease state interactions. Maintaining a consistent intake of foods high in vitamin K. Very important to cover the signs and symptoms of bleeding associated with elevated INR: hematuria, hemoptysis, GI bleeds, melena, and easy bruising, and what steps to take if any of these events occur.

What is JS's CHADS$_2$ score?

2 (1 point for hypertension and 1 point for diabetes)

Hospital Lab Data: (2 days after warfarin initiation)

INR: 1.3
CBC: within normal limits (WNL)
LFT's: WNL

You are able to have JS return to your pharmacy for management of his warfarin therapy 3 days after his hospital labs were reported.

Finger stick INR: 1.6 on warfarin 5 mg daily.

Secondary to the patient having a subtherapeutic INR, you recommend increasing to warfarin 6 mg daily (15–20% increase). Based on your collaborative practice agreement, you give JS enough warfarin 1 mg tablets until his follow-up in 3 days.

Finger stick INR: 2.4 on warfarin 6 mg daily.

Can JS now schedule a follow-up appointment in 4 weeks?

No, he needs to have another INR in 2–3 days to verify that his warfarin dose is stable.

You follow up with JS in 5 days and his INR is now 2.7, can he have a 4-week-follow-up?

No, ideally you would want to see him back in 1–2 weeks. If his INR is still within therapeutic range at that time, then he could be scheduled for follow-up in 4 weeks.

What would you recommend JS do if he brought in a prescription for "Bactrim DS" that he obtained for an infection?

He would need to hold his warfarin dose and come in the following day to have his INR checked. Despite holding his warfarin, JS might have a precipitous increase in his INR as this is significant drug–drug interaction. Then you would closely monitor his INR every 2–3 days to ensure appropriate anticoagulation.

JS informs you that he is starting a new "diabetes diet" that requires him to only eat salads? Would any changes in warfarin be indicated?

JS would need to be reminded that a consistent weekly intake of vitamin K in his diet is vital. If he chooses to initiate this diet, then he would need to have his INR monitored closely for about 2 weeks to determine the effect it would have on his anticoagulation therapy.

ANTICOAGULATION QUESTIONS FOR PHARMACY EXPERT

Jeremy Thomas, PharmD, CDE
Assistant Professor
Department of Pharmacy Practice
Phone: (501) 686-8709
Fax: (501) 296-1168
Office: Education II Bldg 6/132H
Email: jlthomas2@uams.edu

- **Why should pharmacists be involved in anticoagulation management?**

Pharmacists often offer specialized services for medications requiring monitoring due to a narrow therapeutic window. Warfarin with its many drug–drug interactions, drug–food interactions, adherence requirements, and adverse event profile requires a level of pharmacokinetic and pharmacotherapeutic knowledge that a pharmacist can provide.

In addition, the community pharmacist can provide a level of access that few health-care professionals can match. Patients requiring monitoring on a frequent and consistent basis for a medication such as warfarin can benefit from a greater level of access to their health-care provider not only for monitoring but also for recommendations and advice on interacting medications and reducing the risk of adverse events.

While increased revenues from additional services are also a benefit to the pharmacist, the professional satisfaction of practicing to the highest level of our degree and training to ensure patients receive the most from their drug therapy goes beyond any monetary compensation.

- **What are the major barriers to implementing an anticoagulation management services? How did you overcome them?**

The pharmacist wishing to engage in anticoagulation services needs to be aware of several barriers they may face. The first being the scope of practice allowed by the state's Pharmacy Practice Act. Many states now allow pharmacist prescriptive authority under protocols or collaborative practice agreements with physicians. Each state may differ slightly in the allowed scope of practice for such advanced pharmacy services. A thorough understanding of the state's Pharmacy Practice Act is the first step in determining the feasibility of such a service.

With significant up front costs, the return on investment (ROI) needs to be determined. Many factors will affect the ROI. The most significant is the patient referral base that requires physician support. A strong physician champion is needed in many cases.

The development of a sound fee structure is also crucial in overcoming difficulties with ROI. Partnering with local employers to provide reimbursement for these services many times will aid in developing a sustainable service.

- **What would be the best way for a pharmacist to prepare himself or herself to implement anticoagulation management services in a community setting?**

Apart from a solid business plan, the pharmacist would be well advised to reach out to other pharmacists who have implemented such services to discover the pearls and pitfalls of creating a successful anticoagulation service in a community setting. Networking with pharmacists who have similar services at professional meetings such as the annual American Pharmacists Association meeting and the annual American College of Clinical Pharmacy meeting is a good first step.

For the pharmacist who might benefit from more advanced clinical training in anticoagulation management there are numerous opportunities for training and/or certification courses. The most popular and nationally recognized Certified Anticoagulation Care Providers Exam (CACP) offered by the National Certification Board for Anticoagulation Providers (NCBAP) is a certification course that requires previous experience in anticoagulation.

A Web site, www.clotcare.com, was created in 2000 by a pharmacist to serve as a resource for health-care professionals who provide anticoagulation services. In addition to many helpful articles, discussions and information about anticoagulation, a list of certification, and training courses can be found there.

- **With the increase in the number of medications approved for anticoagulation in the past 2 years, have you seen a decrease in the number of patients you care for with your anticoagulation service?**

We have not experienced a decline in the number of patients referred to our service. The new anticoagulants on the market do not have as comprehensive of an indication list as warfarin currently does. There are also subsets of patients in which warfarin will be a better choice. While these medications may gain market share in the near future, there will still be a need for warfarin-focused anticoagulation services. Many patients and physicians prefer a medication with a known track record. The emergence of newer anticoagulants with less monitoring requirements and fewer drug interactions provides an even greater reason for specialized anticoagulation services for patients on warfarin as other health-care providers become less familiar with the complexities of warfarin management.

- **What, if any, knowledge did you feel that you lacked in order to adequately manage patients requiring anticoagulation?**

Through my residency experiences, I felt adequately trained clinically to manage anticoagulation therapy according to the latest CHEST guidelines and evidence-based medicine. However, over the years I have found the diversity of patients and their personal experiences and needs is what provides the greatest challenge in managing anticoagulation. A strategy that works for one patient may not be the best for the next patient. While anticoagulation management may seem straightforward according to protocols and guidelines, the patients are what make this a very rewarding and challenging service.

- **What are the most common interventions you provided to your patients who are on anticoagulants?**

Education. While a dose adjustment may seem like the logical solution, patient education resolves many issues in anticoagulant therapy. Many times a dose adjustment is an easy fix, while patient education will provide a longer lasting, more stable, and effective intervention. Patient education is essential at all phases of anticoagulant therapy including those patients who have been on an anticoagulant for many years.

- **How do you measure success in a patient on anticoagulant therapy?**

In the individual patient, overall success is measured by the absence of events, thrombotic events, or adverse events due to anticoagulant therapy. Individual patient satisfaction with the services is another measure of success.

- **How do you measure success in your anticoagulation management program?**

For the program as a whole, a more quantitative approach is necessary where we will examine time in the therapeutic range, patient satisfaction on a population-based scale, and revenue generation from the service.

- **Is it difficult to get buy-in from the local physicians when you tell them you are a pharmacist who manages anticoagulation?**

In my specific setting, physician support is a principal driver of our service. Once exposed to the benefits of pharmacist-managed anticoagulation, they demand those types of services. However, having experienced physician pushback from other types of services, there are common themes pharmacists may face. The first and easiest to overcome is that pharmacists are not qualified to provide such services. The wealth of information from published studies easily refutes this notion and supports the advantages of such pharmacist-provided services. In addition to the literature, certifications and additional training are solutions for the individual pharmacist who may face this type of pushback.

The more difficult issue is that of taking away a potential revenue stream from the physician. Careful needs assessment and identifying the target population such as those with difficulty accessing anticoagulant care are potential solutions to this issue. Also, by managing anticoagulant patients the pharmacist may shift patient-contact time so that physicians can focus on more critically ill patients without losing revenue.

SUMMARY

As you can see, the development of an anticoagulation service may take some time and capital investment, but the rewards can be significant. If providing other MTM services, it can be a way to provide additional income to your pharmacy. Ensuring that you have taken the time to optimally develop your protocol can ease the initiation of services. Important points to remember:

- Perform an *environmental analysis* prior to initiating your service.
- *Develop a business plan* to incorporate your current practices.
- Education for yourself, clinic staff, referring providers, and most importantly—patients.
- *Communicate* with the health-care providers referring patients to your service.
- *Maintain* an up-to-date protocol by ensuring that recent guidelines and medications are included.
- Continuous *quality control* and *quality improvement* are vital to the success of your service.
- *Document*, document, and document more.
- Do not forget to *bill* for your services for sustainability.

These simple points can help you maintain a successful anticoagulation service and most importantly improve the overall quality of care to the patients you serve.

STUDY QUESTIONS

1. When developing an anticoagulation service, which of the following needs to be obtained prior to utilizing POC devices to monitor a patient's INR?
   a. CLIA waiver certificate
   b. HCFA form 1500
   c. HIPAA form
   d. Personal provider certification

2. In order to obtain personal information related to a patient's medical history, which of the following does a patient need to sign prior to a request being forwarded to a provider or hospital?
   a. CLIA waiver certificate
   b. HCFA form 1500
   c. HIPPA form
   d. Personal provider certification

3. When developing your service protocol, which of the following would be the best resource to utilize for establishing evidence-based INR goals to be utilized in your clinic?
   a. Antithrombotic and Thrombolytic Therapy: American College of Chest Physicians Evidenced-Based Clinical Practice Guidelines (9th Edition)
   b. Deep-Vein Thrombosis: Advancing Awareness to Protect Patient Lives. White Paper. American Public Health Association; Public Health Leadership Conference
   c. Guideline for the Primary Prevention of Stroke: A Guideline for Health-care Professionals From the American Heart Association/American Stroke Association
   d. Surveillance for Deep Vein Thrombosis and Pulmonary Embolism: Recommendations from a National Workshop

4. Which of the following best describes a quality process that can be easily evaluated.
   a. Growth of Provider Referrals (GPR)
   b. Days till Goal INR Achieved (DGIA)
   c. Percent Time in Therapeutic Range (PTTR)
   d. Time in Therapeutic Range (TTR)

5. Which of the following best describes a validated tool to access the stroke risk of a patient who presents with atrial fibrillation.
   a. AFIB-Assess
   b. CHA2DS2-VASc
   c. CHADS$_2$
   d. CVA-Fib

BIBLIOGRAPHY

1. Ageno W, Gallus AS, Wittkowsky A, Crowther M, Hylek EM, Palareti G. Oral anticoagulant therapy: antithrombotic therapy and prevention of thrombosis, 9th ed: ACCP evidence-based clinical practice guidelines. *Chest.* 2012;141(Suppl. 2):e44S-e88S.
2. Bond CA, Raehl CL. Pharmacists-provided anticoagulation management in United States hospitals: death rates, length of stay, Medicare charges, bleeding complications, and transfusions. *Pharmacotherapy.* 2004;24:953-963.
3. Chiquette E, Amato MG, Bussey HI. Comparison of an anticoagulation clinic with usual medical care: anticoagulation control, patient outcomes, and health care costs. *Arch Intern Med.* 1998;158:1640-1647.
4. Ellis RF, Stephens MA, Sharp GB. Evaluation of a pharmacy-managed warfarin-monitoring service to coordinate inpatient and outpatient therapy. *Am J Hosp Pharm.* 1992;49:387-394.
5. Ernst ME, Brandt KB. Evaluation of 4 years of clinical pharmacist anticoagulation case management in a rural, private physician office. *J Am Pharm Assoc.* 2003;43:630-636.
6. Whitlock RP, Sun JC, Fremes SE, Rubens FD, Teoh KH. Antithrombotic and thrombolytic therapy for valvular disease: antithrombotic therapy and prevention of thrombosis, 9th ed: ACCP evidence-based clinical practice guidelines. *Chest.* 2012;141(Suppl. 2):e576S-e600S.
7. McAlister V. Control of coagulation: a gift of Canadian agriculture. *Clin Invest Med.* 2006;29:373-377.
8. Wardrop D, Keeling D. The story of the discovery of heparin and warfarin. *Br J Haematol.* 2008;141:757-763.
9. Goldstein LB, Bushnell CD, Adams BJ, et al. Guidelines for the primary prevention of stroke: a guideline for healthcare professionals from the American Heart Association/American Stroke Association. *Stroke.* 2011;42:517-584.
10. Gage BF, Waterman AD, Shannon W, et al. Validation of clinical classification schemes for predicting stroke: results from the National Registry of Atrial Fibrillation. *JAMA.* 2001;285:2864-2870.
11. Gage BF, van Walraven C, Pearce L, et al. Selecting patient with atrial fibrillation for anticoagulation: stroke risk stratification in patients taking aspirin. *Circulation.* 2004;110:2287-2292.
12. You JJ, Singer DE, Howard PA, et al. Antithrombotic therapy for atrial fibrillation: antithrombotic therapy and prevention of thrombosis, 9th ed: ACCP evidence-based clinical practice guidelines. *Chest.* 2012;141(Suppl. 2):e531S-e575S.
13. Kearon C, Akl EA, Comerota AJ, et al. Antithrombotic therapy for VTE disease: antithrombotic therapy and prevention of thrombosis, 9th ed: ACCP evidence-based clinical practice guidelines. *Chest.* 2012;141(Suppl. 2): e419S-e494S.
14. Raskob GE, Silverstein R, Bratzler DW, Heit JA, White RH. Surveillance for deep vein thrombosis and pulmonary embolism: recommendations from a national workshop. *Am J Prev Med.* 2010;38(4S):S502-S509.
15. Beckman MG, Hooper WC, Critchley SE, Ortel TL. Venous thromboembolism: a public health concern. *Am J Prev Med.* 2010;38(4S):S495-S501.
16. White RH. The epidemiology of venous thromboembolism. *Circulation.* 2003;107:I-4-I-8.
17. Anderson FA, Spencer FA. Risk factors for venous thromboembolism. *Circulation.* 2003;107: I-9-I-16.
18. Goldhaber SZ. Deep-vein thrombosis: advancing awareness to protect patient lives. White Paper. American Public Health Association; Public Health Leadership Conference: Washington, D.C. February 26, 2003.
19. Holst AG, Jensen G, Prescott E. Risk factors for venous thromboembolism: results from the Copenhagen City Heart Study. *Circulation.* 2010;121:1896-1903.
20. Lee R, Li S, Rankin JS, et al. Fifteen-year outcome trends for valve surgery in North America. *Ann Thor Surg.* 2011;91:677-684.
21. Pibarot P, Dumesnil JG. Prosthetic heart valves: selection of the optimal prosthesis and long-term management. *Circulation.* 2009;119:1034-1048.
22. Coumadin® Prescribing Information. Bristol Myers Squibb Company. *Princeton NJ*; 2011. http://www.accessdata.fda.gov/drugsatfda_docs/label/2011/009218s107lbl.pdf. Accessed June 8, 2012.
23. Crowther MA, Ginsberg JS, Hirsh J. Practical aspects of anticoagulant therapy. In: Colman RW, Hirsh J, Marder VJ, Clowes AW, George JN, eds. *Hemostasis and Thrombosis: Basic Principles & Clinical Practice.* 4th ed. Philadelphia, PA: Lippincott Williams & Wilkins; 2001:1497-1516.
24. Ryan F, Byrne S, O'Shea S. Managing oral anticoagulation therapy: improving clinical outcomes: a review. *J Clin Pharm Therap.* 2008;33:581-590.
25. Foss MT, Schoch PH, Sintek CD. Efficient operation of a high-volume anticoagulation clinic. *Am J Health Syst Pharm.* 1999;56:443-449.

26. Wilson Norton JL, Gibson DL. Establishing an outpatient anticoagulation clinic in a community hospital. *Am J Health Syst Pharm.* 1996;53:1151-1157.
27. Dager WE, Branch JM, King JH, et al. Optimization of inpatient warfarin therapy: impact of daily consultation by a pharmacist-managed anticoagulation service. *Ann Pharmacother.* 2000;34:567-572.
28. Hall D, Buchanan J, Helms B, et al. Health care expenditures and therapeutic outcomes of a pharmacist-managed anticoagulation service versus usual medical care. *Pharmacotherapy.* 2011;31:686-694.
29. Witt DM, Tillman DF. Clinical pharmacy anticoagulation services in a group Model Health Maintenance Organization. *Pharm Pract Manag Q.* 1998;18:34-55.
30. Wilt VM, Gums JG, Ahmed OI, Moore LM. Outcome analysis of a pharmacist-managed anticoagulation service. *Pharmacotherapy.* 1995;15:732-739.
31. Lodwick AD, Sajbel TA. Patient and physician satisfaction with a pharmacist-managed anticoagulation clinic: implications for managed care organizations. *Manag Care.* 2000:47-50.
32. McCormick WP. Medical-legal implications of anticoagulation. *J Thromb Thromb.* 2001;12:95-97.
33. Garcia DA, Witt DM, Hylek E, et al. Delivery of optimized anticoagulation therapy: consensus statement from the anticoagulation forum. *Ann Pharmacother.* 2008;42:979-988.
34. Schumock GT, Wong G. Strategic planning in pharmacy operations. In: Villarreal F, Desselle SP, eds. *Pharmacy Management: Essentials for All Practice Settings.* 2nd ed. New York, NY: McGraw-Hill; 2009:Chap. 3. http://www.accesspharmacy.com/content.aspx?aID=5002799. Accessed June 21, 2012.
35. Schumock GT, Wong G. Business planning for pharmacy programs. In: Villarreal F, Desselle SP, eds. *Pharmacy Management: Essentials for All Practice Settings.* 2nd ed. New York, NY: McGraw-Hill; 2009:Chap. 4. http://www.accesspharmacy.com/content.aspx?aID=5003538. Accessed July 5, 2012.
36. Brushwood D, Spivey-Miller S, Henry HW. Clinical, business, and legal issues in warfarin therapy. *America's Pharmacist.* 1997;(Suppl):29-36.
37. Kuo GM, Buckley TE, Fitzsimmons DS, Steinbauer JR. Collaborative drug therapy management services and reimbursement in a family medicine clinic. *Am J Health Syst Pharm.* 2004;61:343-354.
38. Wilkin NE. General operations management. In: Villarreal F, Desselle SP, eds. *Pharmacy Management: Essentials for All Practice Settings.* 2nd ed. New York, NY: McGraw-Hill; 2009:Chap. 5. http://www.accesspharmacy.com/content.aspx?aID=5003659. Accessed June 21, 2012.
39. Ansell JE, Oertel LB, Wittkowsky AK. Managing oral anticoagulation therapy: Clinical and operational guidelines. 2nd ed. St. Louis, MO:Wolters Kluwer Health, 2005.
40. Harris IM, Baker E, Berry TM, et al. ACCP White Paper: developing a business-practice model for pharmacy services in ambulatory settings. *Pharmacotherapy.* 2008;38(2):7e-34e.
41. Crader MF, Chelette CT, Steffenson MB. Creating a pharmacist-managed anticoagulation clinic: an example of a joint endeavor between a community hospital and a college of pharmacy. *Hosp Pharm.* 2010;f45:618-623, 633.
42. Snella KA, Sachdev GP. A primer for developing pharmacist-managed clinics in the outpatient setting. *Pharmacotherapy.* 2003;23:1153-1166.
43. Doucette W. Marketing applications. In: Villarreal F, Desselle SP, eds. *Pharmacy Management: Essentials for All Practice Settings.* 2nd ed. New York, NY: McGraw-Hill; 2009:Chap. 21. http://www.accesspharmacy.com/content.aspx?aID=5001631. Accessed July 5, 2012.
44. Holbrook A, Schulman S, Witt DM, et al. Evidence-based management of anticoagulant therapy: antithrombotic therapy and prevention of thrombosis, 9th ed: ACCP evidence-based clinical practice guidelines. *Chest.* 2012;141(Suppl. 2):e152S-e184S.
45. Witt DM. Quality measures and benchmarking for warfarin therapy. *J Thromb Thromb.* 2011;31:242-248.
46. Schmitt L, Speckman J, Ansell J. Quality assessment of anticoagulation dose management: comparative evaluation of measures of time-in-therapeutic range. *J Thromb Thromb.* 2003;15:213-216.
47. Melamed OC, Horowitz G, Elhayany A, Vinker S. Quality of anticoagulation control among patients with atrial fibrillation. *Am J Manag Care.* 2011;17(3):232-237.
48. Menzin J, Boulanger L, Hauch O, et al. Quality of anticoagulation control and costs of monitoring warfarin therapy among patients with atrial fibrillation in clinic setting: a multi-site managed-care study. *Ann Pharmacother.* 2005;39:446-451.
49. Phillips KW, Ansell J. Outpatient management of oral vitamin K antagonist therapy: defining and measuring high-quality management. *Expert Rev Cardiovasc Ther.* 2008;6:57-70.
50. Rose AJ, Berlowitz DR, Frayne SM, Hylek EM. Measuring quality of oral anticoagulation care: extending

quality measurement to a new field. *Jt Comm J Qual Patient Saf.* 2009;35:146-155.
51. Rose AJ, Hylek EM, Ozonoff A, Ash AS, Reisman JI, Berlowitz DR. Risk-adjusted percent time in therapeutic range as a quality indicator for outpatient oral anticoagulation: results of the veterans affairs study to improve anticoagulation (VARIA). *Circ Cardiovasc Qual Outcomes.* 2011;4:22-29.
52. Warholak TL. Ensuring quality in pharmacy operations. In: Villarreal F, Desselle SP, eds. *Pharmacy Management: Essentials for All Practice Settings.* 2nd ed. New York, NY: McGraw-Hill; 2009. http://www.accesspharmacy.com/content.aspx?aID=5003890. Accessed July 9, 2012.
53. Centers for Medicare and Medicaid Services. Clinical Laboratory Improvement Amendments (CLIA). CMS.gov. https://www.cms.gov/Outreach-and-Education/Medicare-Learning-Network-MLN/MLNProducts/Downloads/CLIABrochure.pdf. Accessed June 8, 2012.
54. U.S. Department of Health and Human Services. *Centers for Medicare and Madicaid Services - CLIA Brochures.* https://www.cms.gov/CLIA/downloads/HowObtainCertificateofWaiver.pdf. Published March 2006. Accessed August 22, 2011.
55. Wofford JL, Wells MD, Singh S. Best strategies for patient education about anticoagulation with warfarin: a systematic review. *BMC Health Serv Res.* 2008;40. doi:10.1186/1472–6963-8–40.
56. Doucette WR, McDonough RP. Beyond the 4Ps: using relationship marketing to build value and demand for pharmacy services. *J Am Pharm Assoc (Wash).* 2002;42:183-194.
57. Garcia GM, Snyder ME, McGrath SH, Smith RB, McGivney MS. Generating demand for pharmacist-provided medication therapy management: identifying patient-preferred marketing strategies. *J Am Pharm Assoc (Wash).* 2009;49:611-616.
58. Snella K. Compensation for value-added pharmacy services. In: Villarreal F, Desselle SP, eds. *Pharmacy Management: Essentials for All Practice Settings.* 2nd ed. New York, NY: McGraw-Hill; 2009:Chap. 26. http://www.accesspharmacy.com/content.aspx?aID=5002287. Accessed July 9, 2012.

APPENDIX 10A. SAMPLE REFERRAL FORM

**Pharmacy XYZ
Anticoagulation Service
Referral Form**
Phone: 555-555-2345

Patient Name:_____
Phone Number:_____
PLEASE PRINT

FAX TO: 555-555-1234

Referring Physician/Clinic Information

Name:_____

Service:_____

Phone:_____

Patient Information Address & Phone Number:_____
_____

Current Medications:_____
_____

Past Medical History:_____
_____

Indication for Anticoagulation:_____

Goal INR: 2.0–3.0   2.5–3.5
       Other:_____ (*Please provide evidence to support*)

Date Anticoagulation Initiated:_____

Initial Warfarin Dose:_____

If hospitalized; INR at Discharge:_____

Was Patient Discharged on Heparin/Low Molecular Weight heparin? **Y/N**
If Yes, Drug/Dosage/Duration: _____

Duration of Therapy: Ambulatory   Chronic   3 Months   6 Months

                             Other:_____

(Referring provider will be consulted prior to discontinuation of warfarin therapy)
Patients managed by the Pharmacy XYZ Service should be followed every 6 months by the referring physician to assess the continued need for anticoagulation therapy and primary medical problems.

Physician (Printed):_____ (*phone*):_____

Signature:_____

APPENDIX 10B. PHARMACY XYZ ANTICOAGULATION SERVICE PROTOCOL

Pharmacy Practice Protocol
Latest update
August 2012
PROTOCOL—ANTICOAGULATION CLINIC
Pharmacy XYZ, Anywhere USA
July 2012

I. OBJECTIVE

To achieve consistent management and surveillance of therapy, provide continuity of care and promote maximum effectiveness for patients receiving warfarin, with minimal risk from adverse effects and overdosage.

II. RATIONALE

Close supervision of warfarin therapy is considered necessary for the following reasons:
A. Warfarin exhibits pronounced interindividual kinetics. This variation is primarily ascribed to differences in the amount of free fraction of the drug in the serum.
B. Many medications, both prescription and over-the-counter preparations, as well as dietary supplements, can produce clinically significant interactions with warfarin.
C. Many disease states can alter the pharmacological response to warfarin.
D. Hemorrhage, the major adverse effect of warfarin, may cause significant morbidity and mortality.
E. Elderly patients are particularly at risk for complications associated with warfarin therapy. They are more likely to suffer from the common comorbid conditions that may alter warfarin kinetics and often require multiple medications due to multiple medical problems.

III. GOALS AND FUNCTIONS

Goals:
A. Provide a consultative service to physicians and health-care practitioners (HCP's) initiating and maintaining warfarin therapy and/or low molecular weight heparins (LMWHs).
B. Assist HCP's in both short- and long-term management of patients maintained on warfarin and/or LMWHs.
C. Provide continuity-of-care for patients receiving warfarin and/or LMWHs so they receive the maximum benefits of therapy.
D. Reduce untoward effects in the patient resulting from warfarin or LMWH therapy.
E. Educate medical, nursing, and pharmacy staffs, as well as patients, regarding various aspects of anticoagulation and to serve as an educational site for pharmacy residents and students.

Functions:
A. Pharmacists from the Pharmacy XYZ Anticoagulation Service (AS) will be available for consultation on both an inpatient and outpatient basis.
B. Consultative services should include, but not be limited to:
 1. Assist in stabilizing the patient's warfarin dose.
 2. Educating patients about appropriate use and side effects associated with warfarin and/or LMWHs.
 3. Screen for drug–drug, drug–food, and drug–disease state interactions.

4. Evidence-based advice concerning the recommended target therapeutic prothrombin times (PT) and international normalized ratio (INR) goals, and duration of therapy for various thromboembolic complications.

C. It is essential that each patient be educated thoroughly about the safe and appropriate use of anticoagulants and other medications in relation to their anticoagulation. This education should be started prior to the patient's hospital discharge, if possible. Education should be reinforced at each clinic visit, which will include precise written and verbal instructions regarding dosage regimens and precautions. Pharmacy XYZ staff will also provide educational materials to each patient. Each patient will be assessed periodically to ensure that he/she has an adequate understanding of anticoagulation therapy and his/her role in its success.

D. Documentation of the patient's progress will be done at each clinic visit by charting the notes accurately in the patient's medical record as well as the patient's AS profile.

E. The AS pharmacists will screen for drug–drug, drug–food, and drug–disease state interactions, as well as adverse drug effects and compliance problems at each AS visit.

F. Dosage will be adjusted when indicated. Pharmacodynamic principles will be utilized to maintain the patient at a safe and effective level of anticoagulation.

G. Assessment of medication-related problems and communication of findings to the HCP will be carried out so that the patient receives appropriate medical attention.

H. The AS pharmacist will attempt to ensure that a physician reevaluates each patient, at least once every 6 months, or more often as needed, to ascertain the need for continued anticoagulation.

I. The AS will provide educational programs upon request for medical, nursing, and pharmacists regarding basic principles of anticoagulation and new developments in the field of anticoagulation.

IV. DESIGN

A. Consultation and referral.
1. All patients will be seen at the Pharmacy XYZ AS on a consult basis only. HCP's referring to the AS will need to establish a collaborative practice agreement with Pharmacy XYZ.
2. When possible, patients discharged from the hospital or clinic on warfarin need to be seen within 4 days of warfarin initiation. It may be appropriate for the discharging physician to call the AS Coordinator to establish the initial visit for a patient.
3. Patients may be referred to the AS at any stage of therapy. Consults must include the following information:
   a. Therapeutic indication for anticoagulation
   b. Current medication list
   c. Associated past medical history
   d. Desired therapeutic or target range for PT/INR
   e. Expected duration of anticoagulation therapy
   f. Service/physician responsible for periodic assessment of medical problems and the continued need for anticoagulation
   g. Date anticoagulation with warfarin was initiated
   h. Phone number if the AS is to contact the patient secondary to nonadherence to initial clinic appointment
4. EACH PATIENT REFERRED MUST HAVE A PRIMARY PHYSICIAN WHO ASSUMES RESPONSIBILITY FOR PERIODICALLY ASSESSING THE CONTINUED NEED FOR

ANTICOAGULATION AND MANAGEMENT OF THE PATIENT'S CONCURRENT MEDICAL OR SURGICAL PROBLEMS.

5. In the event of difficulties, lack of cooperation, etc., the patient will be referred back to the primary physician for reevaluation and may be discharged from the clinic to be followed only by the primary HCP.
6. If a patient misses three consecutive AS appointments without contacting the AS staff, the patient will be discharged from the AS and referred back to the primary service/physician. A certified letter will be mailed to the last known address for the patient in an attempt to inform them of discharge from the AS. The letter will inform them to contact their primary care physician for follow-up and to obtain new prescriptions for warfarin. A copy will be placed in the patient's medical record.

B. Patient interview.
1. During the first visit to the AS, the pharmacist will interview the patient in order to supplement information gained by review original referral. In addition, the pharmacist will ascertain the patient's level of understanding of his/her indication for anticoagulation therapy, and assess their ability or willingness to comply with therapy and clinic visits. The patient will receive education and instruction regarding the importance of the PT/INR in monitoring therapy, importance of regular and frequent follow-up, drug–drug, drug–food and drug–disease interactions, and signs and symptoms of bleeding, and what steps to take if excessive bleeding occurs (i.e., go to emergency department). The basic organization of the clinic will be described.
2. Education of the patient concerning the use of warfarin will be a major component of the patient's clinic visits.
3. Special instructions will be given to a competent caregiver if the patient is unable to understand or comply with therapy.

C. Clinic procedure.
1. Patients will have scheduled appointments in the AS that could include outpatient laboratory service.
2. Patients will come to the Pharmacy XYZ for their appointments. Patients who arrive early will be seen as soon as space is available between regularly scheduled appointments.
3. Patients will have their INR evaluated using the POC monitor ABC. Blood samples will be obtained by finger stick to evaluate patient's INR. If the INR obtained by the ABC monitor is ≥ 4.5, the patient will also be sent to an outpatient lab to have a venipuncture to obtain a second INR. The patient will then be instructed to wait until the lab INR value is reported and therapeutic decisions will be made from the lab INR.
4. Unscheduled patients will be seen as soon as space permits in the clinic schedule for that day.
5. If deemed appropriate by the pharmacist, patients may have PT/INR monitoring on nonclinic days. This is to accommodate patients with transportation difficulties. These patients may also have a PT/INR obtained by an outpatient lab. These patients will be phoned with PT/INR results and dosage instructions.
6. During interviews, the clinic pharmacist will record all objective and subjective findings in the patient's medical record using the SOAP format. Important information (adverse effects, personal comments, PT/INR results, dosage adjustment and scheduled return appointments) will also be recorded in the patient's clinic profile.
7. On the basis of objective and subjective findings, the pharmacist will be authorized to adjust the warfarin dose to maintain the patient's INR in the target range (± 0.2) or as specified by the

referring physician in the original consult or by the HCP providing primary care to the patient. Currently, the suggested therapeutic guidelines are as follows:
   a. Prophylaxis of DVT (deep vein thrombosis)
      Treatment of DVT/PE (pulmonary embolism)
      Atrial fibrillation INR = 2.0–3.0
   b. Acute MI (myocardial infarction) INR = 2.5–3.5
   c. Peripheral arterial disease INR = 2.5–3.0
   d. Cardiac valve replacements:

Factor	Target INR	Aspirin (mg)
Aortic valves		
• St. Jude bileaflet valves	• 2.5	• 81
• All other mechanical valves	• 3.0	• 81
• Bioprosthetic valves	• 2.5 for 3 months	• 325 indefinitely
○ Thromboembolic risk factors	○ 2.5 indefinitely	○ 81
Mitral valves		
• First-generation tilting-disk valves	• 3.5	• 81
• All other mechanical valves	• 3.0	• 81
• Bioprosthetic valves	• 2.5 indefinitely	• 81
○ Low thromboembolic risk and high bleeding risk	○ 2.5 for 3–6 months	○ 325 indefinitely
• Mitral valve repair	• 2.5 for 3 months	• 325 indefinitely
○ Thromboembolic risk factors	○ 2.5 indefinitely	○ 81

Adapted from Mayo Clin Proc. July 1998, Vol 73:671.
[1]Hirsh J. et al. Oral anticoagulants: mechanism of action, clinical effectiveness, and optimal therapeutic range. *Chest.* 2001;119:8s-21s.
[2]Tiede DJ, Nishimura RA, Gastineau DA, et al. Modern management of prosthetic valve anticoagulation. *Mayo Clin Proc.* 1998;73:665-680.

8. For patients initiated on warfarin therapy as an outpatient, the PT/INR should be evaluated daily until the therapeutic range has been achieved and maintained for at least 2 consecutive days. Then PT/INR evaluation should be performed one to three times weekly for 1–2 weeks, then less often, depending on the stability of the PT/INR results.
9. Patients will be referred to a physician when:
   a. The patient requests consultation with a physician.
   b. The pharmacist notes a history or findings suggestive of increasing congestive heart failure, bouts of arrhythmia, increased angina, or another worsening medical problem.
   c. Evidence suggestive of gross hematuria, melena, or serious bleeding is obtained.
   d. Evidence suggestive of worsening thromboembolic disease is obtained.
   e. The expected duration of warfarin therapy has been reached. The patient should be reevaluated for further need of the medication.
   f. There is suggestive evidence of a new or worsening medical condition.
10. Dosages will be changed based on patient history and a dosage change protocol *and/or* at the discretion of the AS pharmacist.

V. DOCUMENTATION
   A. Initial patient interview.
      1. During the initial interview, a clinic profile will be completed and be kept for reference by the AS staff. All information will be verified by reviewing the patient's medical record. The pharmacists will review all current medications and consider how each medication affects or is affected by warfarin. Any potential problems arising from warfarin therapy will be noted.
      2. During the initial interview, appropriate education about warfarin therapy will be conducted and documented in the patient's medical record. Problems/information will also be documented. These problems include but are not limited to:
         a. Inability of the patient to comply with anticoagulant therapy.
         b. Questionable reason for anticoagulant therapy, including a risk/benefit analysis of anticoagulation indication (i.e., $CHADS_2$ scoring for patients with atrial fibrillation).
         c. Significant predisposition to bleeding.
         d. History of severe, chronic or intermittent alcohol abuse.
         e. Significant drug–warfarin interaction.
         f. Disease history that could affect anticoagulation therapy.
      3. Women of childbearing age or pregnant will be advised of the adverse effects of warfarin therapy to the developing fetus (warfarin fetal syndrome).
   B. Subsequent patient interviews.
      1. Following the initial visit, each visit will be documented in the patient's medical record and the clinic profile.
      2. Adverse effects of warfarin, as well as other medication therapies, will be evaluated.

VI. MONITORING AND EVALUATION
   A. Assessment.
      1. Patients will be evaluated both on the basis of INR evaluation via ABC monitor and personal interviews. All patients will be questioned using the same basic criteria regardless of PT/INR, with special emphasis on current or potential problems identified. These criteria include:
         a. Current dose of warfarin
         b. Signs and symptoms of excessive over/under-anticoagulation
         c. Recent alteration in diet, medication, or alcohol intake
         d. Changes in lifestyle or health status
         e. Compliance to medication regimen
         f. Status of the particular medical problem necessitating warfarin therapy and other problems unrelated to warfarin
      2. With the addition of new medications that present potential therapeutic incompatibilities or drug interactions, the pharmacist will attempt to contact the prescribing HCP and recommend a suitable substitute of a noninteracting medication based on the clinical significance of the problem.
      3. Patients will be scheduled for return INR checks every 4 weeks *when possible*, except in special circumstances (i.e., when a dosage adjustment is made following a high INR or a subtherapeutic INR).
      4. Discharge from the AS will occur when:
         a. The patient's warfarin therapy is discontinued.
         b. The patient is to be followed in another clinic.

c. The patient misses more than three consecutive appointments without contacting the clinic personnel.
d. The patient is abusive toward clinic staff or personnel.

5. DISCONTINUATION OF WARFARIN THERAPY WILL BE ACCOMPLISHED ONLY AT THE DISCRETION OF A PHYSICIAN OR OTHER HCP. When the patient has been on warfarin therapy for the appropriate length of time (as noted in the original referral), the AS pharmacist will refer the patient to the appropriate HCP for reevaluation of continued need for warfarin.
6. Every patient should be seen by his/her primary care physician at least once every 6–12 months.

B. Therapeutic adjustments.
1. The therapeutic goal of warfarin therapy is to maintain the patient's PT/INR in an acceptable range as determined by the patient's physician. This range must be established for each patient individually and at the discretion of the referring physician.
2. If the therapeutic range established by referring physician is determined to be inappropriate by an AS pharmacist, the AS pharmacist will contact the prescribing HCP for appropriate evidence-based adjustment of goal INR range.
3. Patients previously maintained in good control who present with an INR outside the therapeutic range will be intensely questioned in an attempt to identify precipitating factors that, if controlled, would eliminate the need for dose adjustment.
   a. If the most recent INR is lower than the therapeutic range, compliance will be first suspected. Other variants commonly implicated in decreased response to be considered include drug–drug interactions, dietary alterations, and increased alcohol intake.
   b. If the most recent INR is higher than desired, patients will fall into two categories:
      i. Those without evidence of excessive anticoagulation who require a downward adjustment in dose and careful monitoring to regain therapeutic control.
      ii. Those with actual or suspected signs and symptoms of bleeding whose dose should be adjusted downward. These patients will be referred to his/her physician for evaluation, or sent directly to the emergency department for care.
4. IF NO REASONABLE FACTOR CAN BE IDENTIFIED, WARFARIN WILL BE ADJUSTED BY THE PHARMACIST IN ACCORDANCE WITH PAST DOSE-RESPONSE DATA AND WARFARIN PHARMACODYNAMIC PRINCIPLES. A RETURN VISIT WILL BE SCHEDULED FOR PREFERABLY NO LATER THAN 2 WEEKS.
5. Patients will be given a written schedule of his/her drug regimen when dosage adjustments are made.

VII. APPOINTMENT SCHEDULING

A. Every effort should be made to schedule the patients' appointments on regular clinic days to ensure adequate follow-up and the availability of appropriately trained AS staff. Patients who are being admitted to the clinic following hospital discharge should be scheduled *preferably within 4 days of discharge*. After a patient has had two consecutive INR values within his/her target range and has had no adverse reactions during that period, the follow-up visits may be scheduled at 4-week intervals.
B. If a patient does not attend a scheduled clinic visit, adequate follow-up will be attempted by mailing the patient a letter with a follow-up appointment. If this is unsuccessful, the pharmacist will attempt to notify the patient's physician of the problem.

VIII. EDUCATION
   A. Patient education.
   Education is the most important aspect of successful anticoagulant control. Each patient will be given instructions during his/her first visit to AS. The educational process will be individualized depending on the patient's ability to comprehend the subject. The patient will be given the following information:
      1. Name, description, and purpose of the medication.
      2. How it works.
      3. Time, strength, and method of administration.
      4. Interacting drugs, foods, and diseases.
      5. Signs and symptoms of over- or under-anticoagulation and procedures to follow in case of bleeding, heavy bruising, or anticipated dental work.
      6. Importance of regular follow-up and description of PT/INR and what the goal INR will be.
      7. Importance of compliance with medication regimen and appointments.
      8. Appropriate counseling of women of childbearing age and/or pregnant.
   B. Health-care provider education.
   The AS staff will offer presentations on various aspects of anticoagulation therapy to medical, nursing, pharmacy, and other HCPs on request. The AS personnel will offer periodic updates on new monitoring methods and therapies as necessary.

IX. PHARMACY XYZ ANTICOAGULATION SERVICE STAFF
   A. Each pharmacist working in the Pharmacy XYZ AS must have clinical privileges as listed:
      1. The ability to interview a patient to obtain and record, in the patients' medical records, pertinent information required for dosing determination and medication histories.
      2. Orders appropriate laboratory tests for monitoring medication therapy and adverse effects associated with medication therapy.
      3. Evaluates patients' responses to pharmacologic therapy according to an established therapeutic endpoint and adjusts dosages as necessary.
      4. Renews or rewrites prescriptions for continuing medication therapy per collaborative agreement.
      5. Identifies and makes verbal or written recommendations for specific corrective action for drug-induced problems.
      6. Identifies and makes verbal or written recommendations to assist in the selection of the most cost-effective therapy for an individual patient.
      7. Performs physical measurements as necessary to assess the patients' responses to drug therapy.
      8. Provides and documents in the medical records patient education and information regarding side effects of pharmacologic therapy or treatment rationale.
      9. Provides highly specialized education, training, and information to other professional services.
   B. Each pharmacist working in the Pharmacy XYZ AS must complete the requirements for special training. These requirements include but are not limited to the following activities:
      1. Review the pharmacotherapeutics related to thromboembolism and its treatment.
      2. Complete an annual competency evaluation.
      3. Observe and conduct actual clinic visits under direct supervision of an AS pharmacist and be cosigned by an AS pharmacist for at least 4 weeks.

4. Complete annual competency training for the ABC point-of-care monitor and demonstrate satisfactory levels of competence and complete an annual competency evaluation.

Pharmacy XYZ Anticoagulation Service Coordinator
_____
Name:
Pharmacy XYZ
Medical Directors:
_____
_____

■ APPENDIX 10C. PHARMACY XYZ ANTICOAGULATION SERVICE COUMADIN® (WARFARIN) DOSAGE REMINDER CARD

Patient Name: _____   Date: _____

Daily Dose	Sunday	Monday	Tuesday	Wednesday	Thursday	Friday	Saturday

XYZ Logo

Pharmacy XYZ Anticoagulation Service is located in ….

Name: Clinic Coordinator
(555)555-2345
Fax: (555)555-1234
MTMpharmacist@pharmacyXYZ.com

Anticoagulation Service days of operation:
Monday from 1:00 P.M. to 4:00 P.M.
Tuesday from 1:00 P.M. to 4:00 P.M.
Wednesday from 8:30 A.M. to 11:30 A.M.
Thursday from 8:30 A.M. to 11:30 A.M.

11

DIABETES

Ashley W. Ellis, Courtney Davis, Meagan Brown, and Justin J. Sherman

> ### ■ LEARNING OBJECTIVES
>
> After reading this chapter, the pharmacy student, community practice resident, or pharmacist should be able to:
>
> 1. Recognize the role of pharmacists in diabetes management services.
> 2. Define diabetes.
> 3. Review the goals of diabetes management.
> 4. Identify key concepts in diabetes management.
> 5. Discuss ways to prepare for clinic initiation.
> 6. Identify aspects to consider when developing a business plan.
> 7. Discuss clinic design.

INTRODUCTION

Diabetes is a devastating disease affecting nearly 25.8 million people, which corresponds to roughly 8.3% of the U.S. population.[1] Of the 25.8 million affected, it is estimated that nearly 7 million are undiagnosed.[1] In 2007, diabetes was labeled the 7th leading cause of death based on death certificates, which was likely underreported as a primary cause of death.[1] Overall, the risk of death is doubled for patients with diabetes compared with those without.[1] Complications resulting from diabetes may include heart disease, stroke, blindness, kidney disease, amputations, dental disease, and pregnancy complications.[1] Notably, diabetes is the leading cause of new cases of blindness in adults 20–74 years of age, accounts for 44% of all new cases of kidney failure, and is the cause of >60% of nontraumatic lower-extremity amputations.[1] According to a national survey in 2007–2009, Puerto Ricans, Mexican Americans, non-Hispanic blacks, and Hispanic/Latinos age 20 years or older comprised the highest percentage of the population with diabetes (13.8%, 13.3%, 12.6%, and 11.8%, respectively).[1] Non-Hispanic whites made up 7.1%, while Cuban Americans and Central and South Americans each made up 7.6% of the population of patients over 20 years of age with diabetes.[1] The increased prevalence in minority populations may be due to genetic factors, lower income status, or lack of access to health-care. Community pharmacist-delivered pharmaceutical care is one way to help address this disparity and increase access to care for some of these patients.

The total cost of diabetes was estimated in 2007 to be at least $174 billion, with $27 billion used to treat diabetes directly, $58 billion to treat chronic complications related to diabetes, $31 billion in excess medical costs, and $58 billion accounting for reduced national productivity.[2] On average about $1 in $5 health-care dollars was spent caring for someone with diabetes, while $1 in $10 health-care dollars was attributed directly to diabetes.[2] The average annual expenditures attributed to the disease were estimated at $6649 in 2007.[2]

When diabetes is uncontrolled there is a greater likelihood of a rise in complications, which in turn can lead to increases in costs. The United Kingdom Prospective Diabetes Study (UKPDS 35), which was reported in 2000, found a reduced incidence of microvascular complications (including neuropathy, nephropathy, and retinopathy) in patients with type 2 diabetes that achieved intensive glycemic control.[3] For every 1% decrease in mean hemoglobin A1C (A1C), there was an associated 37% reduction in risk of microvascular complications, 14% reduction in risk of myocardial infarction, and 21% reduction in risk of any end point related to diabetes.[3] Additionally, the Diabetes Control and Complications Trial (DCCT) concluded that intensive diabetes therapy successfully slows the progression and onset of diabetic retinopathy, nephropathy, and neuropathy in patients with type 1 diabetes.[4] In 1997, Gilmer and colleagues looked at medical care charges for 3017 adults with diabetes over 4 years and found that charges increased for every 1% increase above A1C of 7%.[5] As the A1C increased, the increase in charges also escalated.[5] It is evident from these findings that glycemic control helps reduce both complications and costs associated with diabetes.

With the steady rise in diabetes over the past decade, it is projected that by 2050 the prevalence of diabetes will increase from 14% to between 21% and 33% of the adult population.[6] This rise is expected to be at least partially due to the increasing size of high-risk minority populations and the aging of the population.[6] The burden of diabetes is rapidly growing and placing a significant impact on the health-care system as well as the quality of life for these individuals.

Pharmacists in a variety of practice settings can be an integral part of managing patients with diabetes or identifying those patients at a high risk of developing diabetes. Pharmacists are exposed to rigorous curriculums that prepare them not only to be medication experts but also to effectively manage patients with chronic disease states, such as diabetes. With the increasing number of patients affected by diabetes and amount of education and attention needed to properly manage these patients, combined with shortage of primary care providers, patients may not be receiving adequate diabetes education or management. Pharmacists are well positioned and qualified to help fill this gap in care experienced by many patients. Having a pharmacist as part of the diabetes care team allows the practitioner to see more patients with acute problems while still having the large number of patients with chronic conditions managed. The Asheville Project is a prime example of how community pharmacists have positively impacted the health of employees with diabetes. In this study, pharmacists provided community-based pharmaceutical care services for self-insured employees of the City of Asheville, NC.[7] Average A1C decreased overall in these patients and total direct medical costs decreased by $1200 to $1872 per patient per year when compared with baseline.[7] The City of Asheville also noted an increase in productivity valued at $18,000.[7] Another study showing positive results from pharmacist interventions in patients with diabetes compared 87 men with diabetes who were managed by physician-supervised pharmacists to 85 similar patients who did not receive pharmacist care, but were managed in the same health-care system between October 1997 and June 2000.[8] The relative risk of achieving an A1C of $\leq$7% was significantly higher in the pharmacist-managed group versus the control group (RR 5.19, 95% confidence interval [CI] 2.62–10.26).[8] The average frequency of unscheduled diabetes-related visits/patient/year was also significantly higher in the nonpharmacist managed group when compared with the pharmacist-managed cohort (1.33 +/– 3.74, 0.11 +/– 0.46, $p + 0.003$).[8] The evidence clearly demonstrates the positive impact of pharmacists' contributions to diabetes management. Many opportunities exist for pharmacists to provide innovative diabetes management services.

THERAPEUTIC MANAGEMENT OF DIABETES

Categories and Goals of Diabetes Mellitus and Concomitant Disease States

The American Diabetes Association (ADA) classifies diabetes mellitus into four separate categories, including (1) type 1 diabetes, resulting from β cell destruction; (2) type 2 diabetes, resulting from progressive insulin resistance and reduced insulin secretion; (3) diabetes due to other causes, such as genetic defects in β cell function or insulin action; or (4) gestational diabetes, diagnosed during pregnancy. Because approximately 90% of all patients with diabetes in the United States have type 2, this chapter will focus on the care and management of patients in this category. However, the goal and management of patients with type 1 diabetes is the same as those with type 2. Both are chronic illnesses that require continuous medication therapy management (MTM) and medical care, along with intensive counseling and patient self-management to decrease the risk of long-term complications.[9]

Diagnosis

Although pharmacists are not diagnosticians, pharmacists should be aware of the diagnostic criteria for diabetes. Test results of one of the following would be diagnostic for diabetes, after a repeat test is completed for verification: (1) A1C $\geq$6.5%; (2) fasting plasma glucose $\geq$126 mg/dL; (3) oral glucose tolerance test $\geq$200 mg/dL; or (4) a random plasma glucose $\geq$200 mg/dL (in a patient with classic symptoms of hyperglycemia). Point-of-care (POC) A1C assays are widely available, but the ADA cautions that these assays are not sufficiently accurate for diagnosing diabetes. However, POC can be used for diabetes screenings or to determine treatment changes.[9]

Overall Goals

The major goal for most patients with diabetes is to decrease A1C to <7%. This has been shown consistently in many studies to decrease microvascular complications, including retinopathy, nephropathy, and neuropathy.[9] If achieved soon after diagnosis, this goal has been associated with long-term reduction in macrovascular complications as well. Macrovascular complications include cardiovascular disease (CVD), stroke, and peripheral vascular disease. However, a more stringent goal of <6.5% is reasonable for selected patients, usually younger with a short duration of diabetes, long life expectancy, and no significant CVD. Hypoglycemia has been associated with an increased risk of death; thus, clinicians should be cognizant of hypoglycemia in certain populations. These are generally older patients with long-standing diabetes and/or a history of severe hypoglycemia, limited life expectancy, comorbidities, and advanced micro- or macrovascular complications. For these latter patients, a less stringent goal of A1C <8% would be reasonable. Patient attitude and expected treatment outcomes are also important determining factors for the approach to hyperglycemia management. Those who are highly motivated, adherent, with excellent ability to perform self-care management and a good support system should be able to achieve more stringent goals.[10]

Concomitant Disease State Goals

CVD associated with macrovascular complications is a major cause of morbidity and mortality for patients with type 2 diabetes. However, controlling the concomitant disease states of hypertension and hyperlipidemia is as important as achieving the goal A1C. Both are independent risk factors for CVD in the patient with diabetes, each with their own separate goals. In particular, the American Association of Clinical Endocrinologists (AACE) suggests that by preventing the micro- and macrovascular complications associated with diabetes, control of hypertension has the most significant impact on morbidity and mortality.[11]

According to ADA recommendations, blood pressure for patients with diabetes should be measured at each visit. A goal blood pressure of <140/80 mm Hg is appropriate for most patients with diabetes and concomitant hypertension. Lower goal targets (<130/80 mm Hg) may be appropriate for some, such as younger patients, if this can be achieved without significant adverse events. Lifestyle changes should be suggested if the blood pressure is > 120/80 mm Hg. If patients have a blood pressure ≥140/80 mm Hg, prompt initiation of medication along with lifestyle therapy should occur. Multiple agents may be needed to achieve significant blood pressure reduction. Angiotensin-converting enzyme (ACE) inhibitors or angiotensin II receptor blockers (ARBs) may be used as first-line agents for controlling hypertension due to the high CVD risk associated in patients with diabetes. Also, many patients with hypertension require multiple-drug therapy to reach treatment goals. A variety of antihypertensive agents are valuable in reducing cardiovascular effects, including ACE inhibitors, ARBs, diuretics, β-blockers, and calcium channel blockers. Selection could be based on other comorbidities (e.g., CVD, heart failure, and post-myocardial infarctions), presence of albuminuria, potential metabolic adverse effects, pill burden, adherence, and cost.[9]

Fasting lipid profiles should be measured at least annually with the following goals for patients with diabetes: low-density lipoprotein (LDL) <100 mg/dL, high-density lipoprotein (HDL) >40 mg/dL in men and >50 mg/dL in women, and triglycerides (TG) <150 mg/dL.[9] To improve the lipid profile, lifestyle modifications should be recommended as the cornerstone of therapy. In addition, for individuals under 40 years of age and without overt CVD, therapy with a statin should be started if the LDL is >100 mg/dL. A statin should be started, regardless of baseline lipid levels, for any patient with diabetes who has overt CVD.[12]

If the individual without overt CVD is under 40 years of age (i.e., lower risk patients), LDL cholesterol >100 mg/dL could require implementation of a statin in addition to lifestyle therapy. In patients with overt CVD, attempting to attain a more stringent LDL goal of <70 mg/dL is an option. While it is reasonable to strive for the goals of all fasting lipid profile components, LDL-targeted therapy using a statin is preferred. If target goals of therapy are not achieved with maximum statin therapy (or maximum doses cannot be tolerated), a 30 to 40% reduction in baseline LDL goal is reasonable. Combination therapy with a statin has not been shown to provide additional cardiovascular benefit in comparison to a statin alone, and is not recommended.[9]

Other recommendations for patients with diabetes include the use of antiplatelet agents and smoking cessation. Daily therapy with an 81 mg strength aspirin is recommended as secondary prevention for all patients with diabetes and a history of CVD. For those without CVD, primary prevention is not as clear-cut. If patients with type 1 or 2 diabetes are at increased cardiovascular risk (i.e., 10-year risk is >10%), daily aspirin therapy is recommended. These patients would include men 50 years of age or older and women 60 years of age or older with at least one other major risk factor including: hypertension, family history of CVD, smoking, dyslipidemia, or albuminuria. For younger patients without additional risk factors, the risk of bleeding will outweigh the benefits of daily aspirin therapy. For those with an allergy to aspirin, clopidogrel may be used as an alternative.[9]

Smoking cessation is encouraged for all patients with diabetes. Tobacco users with diabetes have an increased risk of CVD and mortality rates, and a quicker propensity to develop microvascular complications. Neuropathy, in particular, is problematic in smokers with diabetes. Smoking also may be correlated to development of type 2 diabetes. Of interest, blood glucose levels can increase in the short-term post-cessation, while reductions in A1C and mortality are benefits in the long-term.[9] Smoking cessation may be particularly difficult, as patients with diabetes may view tobacco use as part of a weight-control tool. However, these patients must be assured that the long-term benefits of A1C and mortality reduction strongly favor cessation. Smoking also increases insulin metabolism, possibly increasing insulin doses required for control. Smokers with diabetes should be offered cessation medications along with support counseling, as both together are more effective than either alone. Also, combination cessation therapy may be needed in this special population. Using cessation medications that do not cause weight gain, such as bupropion SR, may also be considered.[9]

Primary Counseling Concepts

Hypoglycemia and Hyperglycemia

Patients with diabetes should know the signs and symptoms of hypoglycemia and hyperglycemia, and the resultant action to take, as either condition can be life-threatening.

Hypoglycemia can be a significant barrier in achieving A1C goals. When titrating insulin, sulfonylureas, or meglitinides, or when patients do not manage meals or exercise regimens properly, hypoglycemia can result. These symptoms can be especially unnerving during a first-time experience. Hypoglycemia should be discussed during an initial visit because medications will be titrated to achieve the A1C goal. Hypoglycemia is an acute circumstance that must be addressed immediately. The symptoms of hypoglycemia include shakiness, nervousness, hunger, sweating, dizziness, confusion, anxiety, or weakness. For many patients, hypoglycemia may be experienced when blood glucose levels drop <70 mg/dL, with symptoms if blood glucose is <60 mg/dL.[9,10]

When symptoms occur, patients should promptly check the blood glucose. The preferred form of treatment is 15 g of glucose, usually three or four tablets, depending on the brand. Other options for treatment include four ounces of juice or sugar-sweetened soda or eight ounces of low-fat milk. If the blood glucose has not increased to an acceptable level after 15 minutes, the treatment regimen should be repeated. Once blood glucose has normalized, the patient can then eat a small meal or snack containing protein and carbohydrate to prevent any recurrence. For the patient at risk for severe hypoglycemia, a glucagon kit should be prescribed and administration instructions taught to family members and caregivers. Glucagon should be administered when patients are unable to swallow or are unconscious due to hypoglycemia. Also, the pharmacist should monitor for medications that could cause hypoglycemia unawareness, such as β-blockers. This class of antihypertensives is not contraindicated for patients with diabetes, but sweating may be the only indication of hypoglycemia when a β-blocker is used. The pharmacist should ensure that such patients maintain awareness when the blood glucose runs low. If the patient has hypoglycemia unawareness, short-term allowance of higher glycemic targets is in order. After several weeks of higher blood glucose levels, counter-regulation and awareness of hypoglycemic symptoms may be improved.[9]

Hypoglycemia may be experienced at relatively higher blood glucose levels when A1C is greatly elevated at baseline. These patients may "just feel better" when their blood glucose levels are elevated and may be more reluctant to titrating medications. Titration may be "uncomfortable" for these patients at first, but they should be counseled to treat for hypoglycemia only when blood glucose levels are less than 70 mg/dL. They should be reassured that they will become more accustomed to this lower "set point" for hypoglycemia, and that hyperglycemic complications could occur if the medications are not titrated. Until the patients become accustomed to lower blood glucose levels, half of a usual treatment dose for hypoglycemia (e.g., two ounces of orange juice rather than four ounces) could be recommended.[9,10]

Another common mistake concerning hypoglycemia is when a patient withholds insulin inappropriately. Patients are often uncomfortable giving insulin injections when the blood glucose is below a certain level. This results in withholding long-acting insulin, with later glucose levels in the day being greatly elevated. Patients should be counseled to administer long-acting insulin to prevent elevated blood glucose levels later in the day—unless blood glucose levels are low (e.g., less than 50 or 60 mg/dL) and the patient is having difficulty increasing the blood glucose levels. Short-acting insulin doses should be withheld if hypoglycemia is occurring, and the hypoglycemia should be treated. Then, as the hypoglycemia is resolved, a normal schedule of insulin injections can be implemented along with a normalized meal schedule.

A patient experiencing hyperglycemia should be counseled to contact the provider. Hyperglycemia is not necessarily an acute event, unless associated with hyperosmolar hyperglycemic nonketotic syndrome (HHNS) or ketoacidosis. The classic symptoms of hyperglycemia are polyuria (excessive urination), polyphagia (excessive hunger/eating), and polydipsia (excessive thirst/drinking). Other symptoms may include blurred vision, weight loss, fatigue, dry mouth, pruritus, frequent urinary tract infections, and poor wound healing. The patient should have a plan in place with their medical provider if they begin to experience these symptoms along with elevated blood glucose levels.[9,10]

Lifestyle Modifications— Medical Nutrition Therapy (MNT) and Exercise

Lifestyle modifications are the cornerstone of management for all patients with diabetes. This is often the most difficult aspect of MTM for patients with diabetes because most are overweight and will need significant behavioral modification. Achieving weight loss is an important goal; even a modest weight loss of 5–10% is associated with improved glycemic control and reduced insulin resistance. Many patients believe that this goal should be much higher and may become discouraged when the weight does not immediately respond to initial efforts. A sustained 1% weight loss per week is the most achievable goal in the long term. However, to achieve and maintain weight loss goals, patients should implement both components of lifestyle modification—MNT and exercise.[9,10]

For MNT, diets low in carbohydrates and fats, restricted in calories, or Mediterranean diets may be efficacious in the short term. Although a "fad" diet may be tempting, the long-term effectiveness is poor. Moreover, the long-term health effect of very-low-carbohydrate diets is unclear. Instead, dietary improvements should become a way of life. The best mix of the macronutrients carbohydrate, protein, and fat will vary according to the individual. An individualized meal plan based on population-wide dietary recommendations and the patient's culture and preferences should be recommended. High-fiber foods (vegetables, some fruits, whole grains, and legumes) and lean meats should be a large part of the diet. Conversely, foods high in saturated fats and sugar-sweetened drinks, desserts, and snacks should be greatly minimized. Attention should be given to total carbohydrate intake, whether by counting carbohydrates, calculating carbohydrate choices, or another method. Clinical studies have documented that effective MNT programs can reduce the A1C from 0.25% to 2.9% in even short periods of time.[9,10]

Two common problems that many people have upon first starting lifestyle modifications are that they consume sugar-sweetened beverages and eat fewer, but larger, meals throughout the day. Many mistakenly believe that "healthy" beverages include fruit juices and sports-type drinks. Removing these completely can achieve better glycemic control. Consuming these drinks usually results from inability to read a nutrition label, so it is helpful to discuss how to read and determine the following: serving size, total carbohydrates, total number of calories, amount of sugar, and alternative forms of sugar. Helping the patient switch solely to drinks with artificial sweeteners—and optimally, water—often produces quick results. Also, patients should consume smaller, more frequent meals at specific times throughout the day. An optimal number of meals would be four to six small meals, eliminating snacks altogether. The patient should also check postprandial blood glucose levels before and after changing to a four to six small meal per day regimen to learn the effect of certain foods on glycemic control.[9,10]

Simple carbohydrate counting may also be effective. The patient could be counseled that women need 45–60 g of carbohydrate (or 3 to 4 choices, as 1 carbohydrate choice = 15 g carbohydrate) at each of three meals and 15 g (1 choice) for snacks. Men need 60–75 g (4 to 5 choices) at each of three meals and 15–30 g (1 to 2 choices) for snacks. Patients should calculate the total carbohydrate per serving size and divide that total number by 15. The resulting number is the number of carbohydrate choices in that particular serving size of the food item. However, these carbohydrate choice recommendations are for the average patient. If the patient is consuming many more daily carbohydrate choices at baseline, the pharmacist should recommend "small steps" to achieve the goals, as recommended above.[9,10]

Other helpful information for MNT includes having the patient keep up with all meals and portion sizes for a week. Then, the pharmacist can discuss how to make better food choices throughout the day. Using a sample meal plan and providing a food list for that meal plan is also effective. Other discussions could include the plate method of planning meals and estimating portion sizes based on the palm, fist, thumb, and thumb tip. The plate method involves limiting a quarter of the plate to each of the following: fruit, nonstarchy vegetables, lean meat, and starches.[13] Portion sizes can be estimated according to the following: the palm equals three ounces of cooked meat, the fist equals 1 cup (30 g) of carbohydrates, the thumb equals one tablespoon or serving of salad dressing or reduced-fat mayonnaise, and the thumb tip is about one teaspoon or serving of margarine. The ADA Web site (www.diabetes.org) provides other useful tips regarding MNT.[14]

If time allows, the MNT discussion should be coupled with tips on increasing physical activities and exercise. Patients with diabetes should spend at least 150 minutes per week engaging in aerobic exercise of moderate intensity, designed to increase the heart rate to 50–75% of the maximum. If patients spent 30 minutes per day for 5 days a week, they would be able to adhere to this recommendation. Ideally, no more than two consecutive days should pass without increased activity in this manner. This standard recommendation, in practice, must be highly individualized to implement. The most important thing to remember is for the patient to start implementing small increments of exercise into a daily routine to work toward this goal. Many patients become frustrated with this recommendation. They feel that they are "active," but upon further questioning the pharmacist may discover that the activity is not aerobic. Instead, patients consider "puttering in the garden" as being active. It should be emphasized that the 30 minutes (alternatively, exercise can be two separate 15-minute activities) should be a *continuous* activity with the goal of increasing the resting heart rate to at least half of its maximum rate. Also, many patients (e.g., patients with arthritis) have limitations for weight-bearing exercise. These patients should be encouraged to participate in activities such as swimming or swim aerobics. Even walking in place for 30 minutes can be helpful for some patients. Patients should be encouraged at each visit to increase their level of activity in order to realistically achieve their weight loss goal.[9,10]

Other Counseling Points for Initial Visits

In addition to the other topics of discussion, the pharmacist should be prepared to discuss the following:

- Proper education on medications
- Insulin injection technique and proper storage (if applicable)
- Diabetes self-management education (DSME)
- Sick day management
- Foot care
- Importance of adherence

Medication Therapy and Principles of Management

The overall aims for MTM of diabetes are to achieve individualized A1C goals and to prevent microvascular complications of diabetes while avoiding hypoglycemia, blood glucose instability, and significant quality-of-life reduction. As tools to accomplish these aims, several new classes of medications have received approval by the Food and Drug Administration (FDA) for treatment of diabetes over the past decade. Treatment guidelines and principles of medication management have changed in response to new studies and medication approvals. Although guidelines by several organizations recently have been published, all agree that treatment for patients with diabetes must be individualized.[15–21]

General Principles of Using Oral Agents

As stated earlier, reduction in A1C to <7% has been associated with significant reductions in microvascular complications and, if achieved early in the course of type 2 diabetes, possibly macrovascular complications as well. Thus, a main principle to consider prior to starting therapy is the baseline A1C. Patients with a high baseline A1C are not likely to achieve sufficient A1C reduction with oral therapy—even with dual or triple combination therapy.[9] A recent position statement from the ADA and the European Association for the Study of Diabetes (EASD) suggests that insulin therapy should be started if the baseline A1C is ≥10%. If baseline A1C is below this level, it may be reasonable to begin oral therapy according to this position statement.[22] Alternatively, the most recent guideline from the AACE suggests that if the patient is symptomatic for hyperglycemia and the A1C is >9%, insulin could be started.

Most guidelines suggest that metformin, a biguanide, should be initiated for treatment of type 2 diabetes along with lifestyle interventions at the time of diagnosis. Metformin should be initiated unless (1) contraindications exist, (2) the A1C level indicates the need for insulin (at which time both insulin and metformin could be started), or (3) the A1C level is very close to goal (within 0.5% of goal) at the time of diagnosis and the patient is motivated to make appropriate lifestyle interventions. Metformin reduces hepatic glucose production, is weight neutral, and does not increase the risk of hypoglycemia when used as monotherapy. It is a cost-effective agent for glycemic control and has been shown in the UKPDS to reduce mortality in obese patients. However, it is associated with dose limiting gastrointestinal side effects and should be avoided in any patient at risk of lactic acidosis (serum creatinine ≥1.4 ng/dL for females and ≥1.5 ng/dL for male, or heart failure exacerbation), patients receiving contrast dyes, or those with significant hepatic dysfunction. Most patients can tolerate the gastrointestinal side effects if they take metformin with meals, and the dose is started at 500 mg once or twice daily. After a few weeks, it should be titrated up to the maximum effective dose, which is 1000 mg twice daily, for the maximum benefit of lowering A1C.[9,10,11]

Advancing to Dual Therapy

If monotherapy with the maximized dose of metformin fails to achieve the desired A1C goal within about 3 months, the following actions can be taken: (1) add a second oral agent, (2) add a glucagon-like peptide 1 (GLP-1) receptor agonist (injection), or (3) add basal insulin. However, the choice of next oral agent to add with metformin is unclear. The choice should be individualized according to efficacy in A1C lowering, unique benefits, dosing frequency, side effect profiles, and cost. In general, the A1C lowering capacity is greatest for metformin and sulfonylureas (average 1–2%), next greatest for GLP-1 agonists and thiazolidinediones (average 1–1.5%), and least for meglitinides, dipeptidyl peptidase 4 (DPP-4) inhibitors, alpha-glucosidase inhibitors (AGIs), and colesevelam (average 0.5–1%). The mechanisms of action, A1C lowering, and advantages and disadvantages of each diabetes medication can be found in Table 11-1.[9,10,11]

However, in context of adding on any of the above oral agents to metformin, the efficacy of lowering the A1C further is only about 1%. If the patient is a "nonresponder" to an adequate trial of the additional agent (no clinically meaningful reduction in A1C), that agent should be discontinued and an

Table 11-1. Medications for Treatment of Diabetes

Class/Medications	Primary Physiologic Action/A1C Lowering Capacity	Advantages/Disadvantages
Biguanides Metformin	↓ hepatic glucose production/ ↓ A1C 1–2%	• No weight gain or hypoglycemia • ↓ CVD events in overweight patients (per UKPDS study) • Side effects include gastrointestinal and lactic acidosis risk
DPP-4 Inhibitors Linagliptin Saxagliptin Sitagliptin	↑ And ↓ glucose-dependent insulin and glucagon secretion, respectively / ↓ A1C 0.8%	• No hypoglycemia; weight neutral • Well-tolerated oral formulation • Modest A1C lowering
GLP-1 Receptor Agonists Exenatide Liraglutide Bydureon	↑ And ↓ glucose-dependent insulin and glucagon secretion, respectively; slows gastric emptying; ↑ satiety /↓ A1C 0.8–1.5%	• No hypoglycemia; weight reduction • Gastrointestinal side effects (less with Bydureon) • Possible acute pancreatitis • Medullary thyroid tumors (animals) • Injection-only; expensive
α-Glucosidase Inhibitors	Slows intestinal carbohydrate absorption / ↓ A1C 0.5–1 %	• Specific for ↓ postprandial glucose • Significant gastrointestinal side effects • Frequent dosing schedule • Modest A1C lowering
Insulin Human NPH Human Regular Lispro Aspart Glulisine Glargine Detemir Premixed	↑ Glucose uptake into cells ↓ A1C variable	• Best efficacy for A1C lowering • Hypoglycemia; weight gain • Injection-only • Expense can be variable • OTC and prescription only • Can have "stigma" for patients
Meglitinides Repaglinide Nateglinide	↑ Insulin secretion / ↓ A1C 0.4–0.6 %	• ↓ Postprandial glucose • Hypoglycemia; weight gain • Modest A1C lowering
Sulfonylureas Glyburide Glipizide Glimepiride	↑ Insulin secretion / ↓ A1C 1–2 %	• Extensive experience • Very effective • Inexpensive • Hypoglycemia; weight gain
Thiazolidinediones Pioglitazone	↑ Insulin sensitivity / ↓ A1C 1–1.5 %	• No hypoglycemia • Weight gain; edema

alternative agent added to metformin. Achieving optimal glycemic control should be the focus to alleviate the risk of complications, and therapy should be advanced methodically to achieve this goal.[9,10,11]

Advancing to Triple Therapy

Some studies have demonstrated efficacy of achieving glycemic control when a third oral agent is added to two-medication therapy. The most likely patient would be one who needs a 1% or less reduction in A1C to meet glycemic goals and does not wish to start insulin. Patients should be counseled thoroughly regarding possible side effects and likelihood of achieving target goals. As discussed with dual therapy, patients should not be allowed to linger with an extended trial of triple combination therapy if efficacy is not achieved within a reasonable time frame. When considering the progression from dual oral therapy, most patients should be transitioned to insulin therapy if the degree of hyperglycemia remains elevated with a two-drug regimen (e.g., A1C $\geq 8.5\%$, for those with a goal of <7%).[9,10,11]

Transitioning to Insulin

Although many patients are reluctant to start insulin therapy, thorough counseling, encouragement, support, and even use of motivational interviewing tools can assist in the transition. A basal insulin is usually begun at a low dose, such as 0.1–0.2 units per kg per day. For example, glargine (10 units) is typically started for many patients. Larger amounts of basal insulin (0.3–0.4 units per kg per day) are reasonable starting doses for patients who have very poor glycemic control.

At this time, oral regimens should be evaluated for continuation with insulin initiation. Continuing metformin is usually reasonable and effective for most patients. However, oral agents that enhance insulin secretion (i.e., sulfonylureas and meglitinides) are usually stopped, or the dose decreased, to eliminate increased risk of hypoglycemia. If postprandial blood glucose levels are elevated, bolus insulin (or a GLP-1 agonist as an alternative) could be started prior to meals. The class of TZDs could increase weight gain in combination with insulin and are usually avoided when starting injections as well.

The most common way to titrate insulin is to increase 10–20% of the total daily dose. Thus, basal insulin could be titrated 1–3 units with the intent of achieving a significant reduction in blood glucose levels. Titration should be individualized based on how sensitive or resistant the patient is to insulin. For example, insulin-resistant patients with poor glycemic control may need 5 units or more increase in insulin. Patients also could be given (and instructed on the use of) bolus insulin, with corrective insulin given based on each blood glucose reading. The average of corrective insulin needed for a particular meal over time could be added to the basal dose of insulin.[9,10,11]

As basal insulin is titrated, it is essential that patients perform effective self-monitoring of their blood glucose. The ADA recommends that self-monitoring should occur three or more times daily if patients are using multiple insulin injections. Self-monitoring is still a useful tool when less frequent daily injections are used. Thus, a typical self-monitoring program would consist of patients checking blood glucose levels before breakfast, before lunch, before their evening meal, and before bedtime. Also, patients could be encouraged to check blood glucose 2 hours after meals rather than before lunch and at bedtime.

An alternate method may be effective when used for short periods of time in patients who refuse to check frequently. For approximately a month, patients could check their blood glucose on the first day before breakfast and before their evening meals. On alternate days, they could check before lunch and before bedtime. This method will give the clinician adequate fasting blood glucose averages, as well as postprandial and bedtime averages. These averages can then be used to adjust basal and bolus insulin appropriately.

Use of bolus insulin before meals will become likely as the daily dose of basal insulin exceeds 0.5 units per kg per day. It can also be added to the regimen when the fasting blood glucose levels are within goal, but the A1C is still above goal after a 3–6 months trial of basal insulin alone. Bolus insulin given before meals is very effective at decreasing the postprandial blood glucose levels. For many patients, the blood glucose levels remain elevated for several hours after each meal—especially if the patient is eating heavier meals throughout the day. Also, use of daily peakless basal insulin and then bolus insulin before each meal most closely resembles normal physiology of insulin release. The pharmacist managing such patients through MTM services can be most helpful in dose adjustment of these insulin regimens. An example of this can be found in Table 11-2.[9,10,11]

Note that all of the information provided in this section is considered "general principles" of managing medication therapy. The specifics of the individualized situation, patient, and provider interactions will dictate what the pharmacist can and should do. Also, keep in mind that general principles for medication adjustment will change with the advancement of medication classes and research in diabetes management. The references in this chapter can also serve as a more thorough guide for those needing more nuances of medication adjustment in this area. Specific references that will be helpful include two position statements: one from the ADA and EASD for management of hyperglycemia in type 2 diabetes, and one from the AACE regarding an algorithm for glycemic control.[11,22]

■ CLINIC INITIATION

Preparing Yourself for Clinic

Ensuring that pharmacists involved in diabetes care services are adequately prepared for expanding pharmaceutical care services is vital to pharmacist confidence, practitioner buy-in, and patient adherence to program goals and appointments. Several credentialing options are available for pharmacists interested in initiating pharmacist services. The American Pharmacists Association offers a certificate training program entitled "The Pharmacist and Patient-Centered Diabetes Care" that provides comprehensive training on medication therapy, lifestyle modifications, and hands-on training for devices and physical assessments.[23] This program offers continuing education and a certificate for display and can help communicate additional training by the pharmacist to others.

Becoming a Certified Diabetes Educator (CDE) is perhaps the most recognized credential for health-care professionals participating in DSME. The National Certification Board for Diabetes Educators grants certification to health-care professionals, providing diabetes education through a written examination offered once yearly in December. Licensed clinical psychologists, registered nurses, occupational therapists, optometrists, pharmacists, physical therapists, physicians (MD or DO), and podiatrists are all eligible to sit for the CDE exam. Registered dieticians or health-care professionals with a master's degree or higher degree in social work are also eligible. Before applying for the CDE exam, pharmacists or other health-care professionals must have completed a minimum of exactly 2 years of professional practice experience and a minimum of 1000 hours of direct DSME experience (minimum of 40% of those hours accrued within the past 4 years). It is important to note that performing diabetes-related duties as part of one's job are not considered DSME for the purposes of the CDE exam. For example, a pharmacist could not include patient counseling for diabetes products, performed as part of normal dispensing duties, and as part of the DSME. After passing the CDE exam, pharmacists would be expected to document diabetes-related continuing education. Becoming a CDE would help with marketing of the services to other health-care practitioners because it is highly recognized and the requirements are well known that helps to communicate to others the level of training, knowledge, and experience. As will be discussed later, it can also be helpful in attaining site credentialing that can be instrumental in attaining payment for services.[24]

Board Certified-Advanced Diabetes Management Certification (BC-ADM) is another credentialing opportunity for registered nurses, registered dietitians, pharmacists, physician assistants, and physicians who communicate an advanced level of practice within the actual management of people with diabetes, as opposed to the education element of focus with the CDE credential. BC-ADM can be attained by written examination that is offered twice yearly. In order to qualify for the exam, pharmacists or other health-care

Table 11-2. Soap Note for Sample Insulin Adjustment Based on Average Blood Glucose Readings

S/O: JN is a 58-year-old man with type 2 diabetes for the past 15 years, with care transferred to medication therapy management (MTM) services for insulin initiation. Patient also has hypertension, heart failure, and hyperlipidemia. He has been taking metformin 1000 mg twice daily and glyburide 10 mg twice daily for the past 6 months. He also takes lisinopril 20 mg daily, carvedilol 25 mg twice daily, furosemide 20 mg daily, and atorvastatin 40 mg once daily. The physician sending the patient for MTM services notes that the patient has been instructed to start glargine 10 units once daily in the mornings. He also was instructed to bring in blood glucose levels that have been monitored four times daily, before meals, for the past 10 days. JN was instructed to stop glyburide and start insulin aspart according to the following sliding scale: for blood glucose levels <150 mg/dL, no insulin aspart; between 150 and 200 mg/dL, give 2 units; between 201 and 250 mg/dL, give 4 units; between 251 and 300 mg/dL, give 6 units; between 301 and 350 mg/dL, give 8 units; >350 units, give 10 units. The patient states that he has "felt low" twice over the past 10 days. During those times, he drank a "few" glasses of orange juice until the blood glucose increased and did not give any insulin until bedtime each of those days. His A1C 10 days ago was 9.4%. Today, he brings in the following record of blood glucose measurements.

Date	BF BG/SSI	Lunch BG/SSI	Dinner BG/SSI	Bedtime BG/SSI	Notes
7/1	212/4 units	234/missed	260/6 units	188/2 units	Skipped bedtime snack
7/2	138/–	198/2 units	280/6 units	200/2 units	Skipped snack again
7/3	102a/–	260/missed	290/missed	324/8 units	BF-felt jittery; drank OJ
7/4	238/4 units	164/2 units	178/2 units	134/–	"Light" dinner
7/5	156/2 units	178/2 units	202/4 units	160/2 units	
7/6	122/–	194/2 units	216/4 units	224/4 units	Skipped bedtime snack
7/7	118/–	168/2 units	184/2 units	160/2 units	"Light" dinner; no snack
7/8	96a/–	290/missed	320/missed	394/10 units	BF-felt jittery; drank OJ
7/9	202/4 units	198/2 units	355/10 units	224/4 units	Ate ice cream at lunch
7/10	180/2 units	208/4 units	168/2 units	182/2 units	

a Patient felt "symptoms" of low blood sugar and took action by drinking a "few" glasses of orange juice.

| Avg | 156.4 mg/dL | 209.2 mg/dL | 245.3 mg/dL | 219 mg/dL | |
| Avg | 1.6 units | 1.6 units | 3.6 units | 3.6 units | |

Insulin

A/P: JN's diabetes is not at goal with the most recent A1C 10 days ago at 9.4% (goal per ADA guidelines would be <7% for this patient). Although JN's blood glucose has begun to respond with the introduction of glargine, this needs to be titrated. Would suggest increasing glargine to 15 units QHS, instead of in the morning, and patient was instructed to continue taking the long-acting insulin regardless of "low blood sugar" because withholding glargine has resulted in escalation of blood glucose levels throughout the day. Patient instructed that if blood glucose levels are <70 mg/dL, it would be appropriate to administer three glucose tablets or half glass of orange juice (not "a few" glasses), recheck the blood glucose levels, and begin back with insulin when the hypoglycemia is resolved. Also, the number of units of the sliding scale are not able to reduce the next blood glucose measurement appropriately, so will "tighten" the sliding scale to the following: <150 mg/dL no insulin aspart; 151–180 mg/dL, 2 units;

(Continued)

Table 11-2.	Soap Note for Sample Insulin Adjustment Based on Average Blood Glucose Readings (*Continued*)

181–210 mg/dL, 4 units; 211–240 mg/dL, 6 units; 241–280 mg/dL, 8 units; 281–310 mg/dL, 9 units; 310–350 mg/dL, 10 units; >350 mg/dL, 12 units.

Patient counseled to continue to check blood glucose levels as instructed before and try not to "miss" taking his bolus insulin. Also, discussed dietary and exercise goals and only eating ice cream and other desserts with artificial sweeteners. Discussed not drinking "real" colas and substituting with those flavored with artificial sweeteners. Discussed with patient about initiating an exercise plan as well, starting with 10–15 minutes every other day walking because he is usually very sedentary. Patient stated that he would like to try to lose a pound per week, and would like to set this as his goal.

Patient verbalized understanding to all instructions. Plan for follow-up visit in 2 weeks and will proceed with plan to adjust insulin as needed at that time. Physician is also being notified of this note and instructions to the patient as well.

professionals must meet licensing requirements mentioned above and must have completed at least 500 clinical practice hours managing diabetes within the 48 months prior to the exam but after receipt of degree or license. BC-ADM also helps to communicate your level of expertise and experience managing the condition of diabetes to external stakeholders and patients. It is also helpful in attaining site certification.[25]

In addition to opportunities for credentialing, diabetes-related continuing education is vital for any pharmacist interested in diabetes pharmacy services. Breakthrough research in diabetes is dynamic and it is essential to read the literature available in major medical journals, as well as in mass media. It is not uncommon for patients to present to clinic with questions about a new FDA advisory or a new study seen on the morning news and pharmacists must be prepared to answer questions within the context of the research to make informed, individualized recommendations, and decisions. When trusting relationships with referring practitioners are built, physicians, nurse practitioners, or physician assistants may ask for the opinion of the pharmacist, especially when it is concerning new medication information.

Specific journals that pharmacists may want to frequent could include those published by the ADA such as *Diabetes, Diabetes Care* and *Clinical Diabetes*.[26] The journal specifically targeted for diabetes educators, entitled *The Diabetes Educator*, is a source for innovation and research regarding DSME.[27]

Preparing Your Clinic for Diabetes Services

When preparing for new pharmacy diabetes services, the level of service will determine the amount of preparation needed and the up front investment required. For example, if diabetes is to be included in existing MTM services, new brochures, handouts, models, and demonstration devices will be needed. If a collaborative practice agreement is to be pursued with area practitioners, the pharmacist will most likely need to perform some POC testing in order to make informed recommendations and decisions. For instance, if diabetes medications are to be initiated or dosing changes made, it will be important to be able to test A1C levels. If pharmacists intend to initiate statins for lipid lowering and cardiac benefits, the pharmacist should be able to assess lipid panels. It is extremely important that a plan for laboratory testing be made in order for adequate follow-up and therapeutic decisions to be made. This also helps improve continuity of care and collaboration among the diabetes management team.

If POC testing is considered, several safety concerns must be considered. Simple low risk tests that can be performed without regulatory oversight in clinic offices or other settings are defined by the Clinical

Laboratory Improvement Amendment of 1988 (CLIA) by level of complexity as waived, moderate complexity or high complexity. The devices used in most pharmacies for lipid testing, blood glucose testing, and A1C testing are considered waived.[28] When a pharmacy decides to include CLIA-waived testing, an application must be made to the appropriate State Agency office of the Centers for Medicare and Medicaid Services (CMS). The CLIA application form, CMS-116, is available from the CMS Web site and includes instructions and required fees for the certificate allowing the use of CLIA-waived devices.[29]

The Occupational Safety and Health Administration (OSHA) and other individual state requirements for work environments incorporating CLIA-waived devices should be consulted. The OSHA blood-borne pathogens standard applies to sites where employees may become exposed to blood or blood-borne illnesses. Requirements include having a written plan for control of exposure, the use of universal precautions with any human blood or body fluid, the use of safety needles, the use of gloves and protective equipment, the provision of hepatitis B immunization at no cost to the employee, and safety training on handling blood and disposal of biohazards.[28] Therefore, some initial start-up costs will be encountered if these have not already been addressed when initiating another service such as immunizations.

After safety concerns have been addressed, attention can be turned to selection of devices for the purpose of the new service. At a minimum, the clinic should be equipped with a blood pressure monitor (including several cuff sizes) and scale. As mentioned, monitoring A1C and lipid levels are most likely required for implementation of diabetes management via protocol. Pharmacists should consider the cost of the device itself, technical support, and the anticipated cost of each test. These devices may be a costly initial investment but can produce a return on investment with appropriate practitioner and patient buy-in because the cost per test is generally less than outside laboratory testing, usually offers results within minutes and allows the patient to have one stop for testing, management, and education.

Pharmaceutical sales representatives can be particularly helpful when stocking the patient care area because they can often provide demonstration devices, blood glucose meters, and injection cushions. Office supplies, some charting system (electronic or paper), a table, and chairs will be minimally expected to begin diabetes services.

Accreditation of diabetes education programs or sites can facilitate payment for services from third-party payers and Medicare. This may be a longer term goal for start-up programs because accreditation standards include evidence of the program's success and patient charts. It would be prudent to review application instructions and requirements to help initially structure the program if accreditation is an important goal. Becoming aware of the costs of accreditation applications and maintenance of accreditation once attained will help pharmacists to develop a long-term budget with appointment and reimbursement goals. Currently, CMS recognizes two national accrediting organizations and states that accreditation must be obtained in order to receive Medicare reimbursement for diabetes self-management training (DSMT). The DSMT benefit for Medicare beneficiaries has been historically underutilized.[30] The Diabetes Education Accreditation Program (DEAP) is offered through the American Association of Diabetes Educators[31] and the ADA also offers education recognition programs.[32]

Developing a Business Plan

Upon attainment of a sufficient level of knowledge regarding diabetes care plus seeking credentialing, if needed, the pharmacist should critically observe his/her resources, stakeholders, and potential for obtaining payment in order to build the optimal level of services provided for patients. The first aspect of developing the plan is to view the overall community and assess the need for a diabetes service.

Environmental Scan

The first place to begin, of course, would be to assess the needs of patients in the pharmacy. The pharmacist should determine what percentage of patients obtains refills for oral medications or insulin for diabetes.

Which patients obtain equipment for self-monitoring of blood glucose levels, such as monitors and strips, and which patients obtain insulin and needles—both through insurance and self-pay? Are many of the questions from the pharmacy's patrons regarding diabetes or ancillary aspects of this disease state? Of the top 10 diseases targeted by MTM programs in 2010 and the percentage of programs that targeted each disease, diabetes was the number one targeted disease state. Almost 97% of all MTM programs in 2010 targeted diabetes. If other pharmacies have not yet begun MTM services for diabetes in the community, the need for this service is potentially very high. Even if local services specifically for diabetes exist in the community, due to the high patient population with this disease state and the propensity of disease progression to lead to microvascular complications, there still may be great potential to market such a service to outside stakeholders and to clients already obtaining services from the pharmacy.[17] To evaluate the need further, other questions regarding those already using the pharmacy's services could be:

- What is the average number of medications for diabetes each person receives?
- Over time, have the doses and/or need for multiple medications increased?
- Over time, have patients added insulin therapy to their diabetes regimens?
- Are people frequently not obtaining their filled prescriptions or delaying purchase due to cost?
- Are the majority of prescriptions filled generally low-cost medications, or high-cost ones?
- Do most of the patients receiving medications for diabetes have adequate insurance coverage?
- Are diabetes supplies purchased in high volume at the pharmacy? If so, which ones?
- What percentage of patients with diabetes receives four or more prescriptions? Six or more prescriptions?
- What percentage of patients with diabetes is enrolled in Medicare programs?
- What percentage of patients with diabetes has other concomitant disease states that would meet the eligibility criteria for MTM programs (i.e., hypertension, heart failure, dyslipidemia, respiratory diseases such as asthma or chronic obstructive pulmonary disease, arthritis, or mental disorders such as depression, schizophrenia, or bipolar disorder)?
- Who are the prescribers for all of the patients with diabetes? Do certain prescribers tend to write higher priced prescriptions that the patients cannot purchase due to price?
- What percentage of patients with prescriptions for diabetes-related supplies and medications also obtain prescriptions for hypertension and dyslipidemia? What percentage of these patients receives six or more prescriptions?
- What percentage of patients with prescriptions for diabetes-related supplies and/or medications also smokes? Take aspirin?
- What percentage of these patients has presented discharge prescriptions from a local hospital within the past year?

These and other questions cover barriers that patients with diabetes have in filling their medications. They will give the pharmacist insight as to which direction he/she should go in enlisting outside stakeholders in the diabetes service, and what actual services should be provided.[17,33]

Support from External Stakeholders The successful pharmacist in the community already knows the importance of building and keeping good relationships with patients, physicians, and other health-care providers within the community. Long-standing patients with the pharmacy should already be supportive of MTM services that could be provided. They may have a need (either an actual need or perceived need) for various levels of services. The ones needing in-depth services are more likely the ones with whom the pharmacist has already spent much time answering questions. Alternatively, answering the questions above could also reveal the clients most likely to need these services.

Relationships already built with physicians and other health-care providers would be a reasonable starting point for marketing MTM services for patients with diabetes. If the pharmacy already has a collaborative practice agreement with physicians in some other aspect, such as with giving immunizations, this would be an optimal situation. If not, MTM services for patients with diabetes still are highly marketable for pharmacists. In the past, physicians may have been skeptical of pharmacist-based services due to the potential for competition. However, the prudent pharmacist will market his/her services by making it clear that a true collaboration is being sought with the physician. The aspect of being able to provide continuity of care could be lucrative to some physicians, especially if the physician expresses concern that not enough time is available to provide all the counseling and education that the patients need.[17,20]

A face-to-face discussion with the physician, preferably away from the clinic during a lunch or dinner, would be the most optimal way to pitch the potential MTM services. Concentrate the discussion on the services that could be provided and how the therapeutic goals for diabetes could be achieved (i.e., A1C to goal by concentrating on ADA recommendations, and decreasing the likelihood of patients developing microvascular complications). Many physicians are frustrated by their patient load and the fact that they usually do not have the amount of time to spend with each patient that they would like.[20] In addition to discussing potential medication management aspects, the pharmacist should discuss the counseling and education that they could offer to assist with behavioral modification efforts. The physician should be able to appreciate the amount of time that is needed with patients to assist them with proper education and behavioral modification for diabetes. Having a sample of patient-education handouts, computer monitoring programs, and how communication would take place with the physician (i.e., documentation system) about the patients would be helpful during the conversation. Be prepared to discuss recent and landmark studies (if the physician brings this up), ADA recommendations, and an example of MTM scenario. However, do not inundate the physician with vast, unnecessary information. Rather, keep the discussion focused and always make sure that he/she knows that you simply want to collaborate for the overall good of the patients' health. Also, keep in mind that physicians may be sensitive that medication changes will not be made just from a "cost" standpoint. Some may already feel that they have to field too many requests from pharmacists and third-party providers to change prescriptions to a lower cost alternative. They may feel that the alternatives are not as good of a therapeutic choice as the original prescription written. Finally, do not forget clinic support staff. Nurses could readily identify potential patients that need more intense instruction about diabetes, and could be a valuable resource as MTM services are being built.[20]

Some pharmacists new to providing MTM services have the impression that they must have all physicians in the community "on board" before services can be adequately provided. This is not true. Often, pharmacists find that if one physician will "buy-in" to the MTM concept and begin sending patients, early successes can lead to burgeoning MTM services. Remember the advertising adage that "word of mouth" is the best advertisement. This is true with providing valuable MTM services, because that physician will become a "champion" for the pharmacist. This will lead to enrolling more of that physician's patients, and other patients as well when word spreads to other providers in the community.

Levels of Services

The pharmacist should consider which level of service that will be offered upon the thorough needs analysis regarding the patient population of the clinic. Aspects that should be considered include the overall needs of current patients in the community and pharmacy, referral services through physicians and other health-care providers, ability to provide MTM services, and other considerations. Of course, multiple levels of services could be offered dependent on varying needs of potential patients. Services could take the form of intensive counseling sessions (individualized or group), sales of durable medical equipment (diabetes self-monitoring equipment) and related training, and MTM with or without collaborative practice agreements.

Table 11-3.	Cost = SAL + MAT + NDC + OHC[Rupp]

Legend Table 11-3
SAL: Salary of all personnel
MAT: Materials, supplies, equipment and variable costs
NDC: Non-salary direct fixed costs
OHC: Rent and non-rent overhead costs

Pricing Diabetes Services

As mentioned in other chapters, correct pricing of services helps ensure successful implementation of any pharmacy service. As mentioned in Chapter 5, direct cost of services offered can be calculated with the following formula (Table 11-3):

$$\text{Cost} = \text{SAL} + \text{MAT} = \text{NDC} + \text{OHC}^{34}$$

The most important difference in calculating the cost of providing diabetes services as opposed to asthma services is the cost of equipment that would be considered direct fixed costs. Examples of this include a Cholestech LDX cassette for assessing lipid panels, meter test strips, and A1C testing supplies. Because this testing is not required at every visit, pharmacists can consider marketing it as a separate fee from the diabetes management service. For example, if a patient is recently diagnosed or is discovered to have an elevated A1C at an office visit, it is important to communicate to referring practitioners and include the most recent lab results with the referral. This will prevent unnecessary retesting costs for the patient and can help the pharmacist have more informed ideas about medication recommendations or initiations before the patient arrives for the first appointment.

As with any business plan, it is important to recognize the price of diabetes services offered in other clinics, pharmacies, or surrounding institutions when deciding appropriate pricing strategies. It is not always necessary to undercut a competitor's price, but it is always necessary to differentiate a new service from what consumers already have available.

Marketing

Marketing of external stakeholders like local family medicine clinics or practitioners with established pharmacy relationships is the best first step when marketing a new service. Sometimes practitioners can be concerned that pharmacies offering POC testing can decrease patient visits to the practitioner or decrease lab revenue. It is crucial to correctly communicate through marketing and practitioner calls that pharmacist-provided services are collaborative and will not interfere with the practitioner–patient relationship. Be very clear about which POC testing will be offered, the benefits of it, and which laboratory testing will require a follow-up visit to the practitioner or lab. If collaborative practice agreements are developed, this needs to be clearly defined. Practitioners who are interested in a more traditional MTM relationship in which recommendations are offered and reviewed by the practitioner after each patient visit should also be targeted for marketing. If MTM is a newer concept, this marketing should occur as early in the process as possible to help ensure acceptance of recommendations and continued referrals.

Many times marketing of new pharmacy services can begin by scanning our own environment. Most pharmacies have return patients and it is important to make them feel important every time they walk through the pharmacy door. Patients who have had a specific question, needed help with a co-pay coupon, or just were not sure about a new medication until the pharmacist took the time to discuss it with them are prime targets for marketing of new services. Social media is becoming ever more important for all business. Encourage patients to "like" your business Facebook page or follow your Twitter account. Use this opportunity to advertise to your own patients about new diabetes services. More traditional marketing tools such as recorded messages that are played when a call is on hold, posters, and bag stuffers can be effective tools for marketing of a pharmacy's own patient base.

Having a "kick off" day or "grand opening" event for a new diabetes clinic is an excellent way to attract attention. Plan your event on a day mid-week when the pharmacy or clinic is adequately staffed to handle the normal workload. Sales representatives for blood glucose testing devices will often provide signage and bring meters for patients to trade in older models. Partnering with a school of pharmacy for student pharmacists to provide glucose and blood pressure screenings can help ensure that the event is accessible to a crowd. Often, student pharmacist organizations need service projects like these type of events or American Pharmacist Month projects and are willing to help local pharmacies while gaining patient care experience.

Methods of Payment

Diabetes costs Medicare a significant amount of money that makes it a targeted disease state for MTM. Some Medicare patients are eligible for MTM services through their Medicare Part D prescription drug plans. There are specific eligibility criteria including, but not limited to an amount spent on medications per year, number of medications, and number of disease states. Because there are many different Part D plans, eligibility also varies.[35] Each year Medicare sets standards for drug plan providers to adhere to in order to try and limit the variability between plans and allow for more patients to benefit from these services. Pharmacies can easily identify eligible patients by contracting with an MTM provider who refers patients to them based on location. Depending on the state, Medicaid and some third parties will pay for MTM services. Before setting up the appointment, discuss and review with the patient the possible price of service and hold them responsible for payment regardless if insurance will pay for services. An example of a form used to hold patients responsible for payment can be viewed in Fig. 11-1. The pharmacy or the patient should call the insurance company to find out their eligibility criteria and guidelines for reimbursement.

In some cases, state-specific Medicare Part B provides coverage for DSME. Requirements for coverage can vary but, in general, cover sessions provided by CDEs. These visits are billed in 30-minute increments and require referral by a provider specifying a patient's need for this type of service.[36] Medicare also covers diabetes-related supplies such as blood glucose meters strips, lancets, needles, pen needles, and diabetic shoes.

Pharmacists can also use a fee-for-service or sliding scale for payment. Using one of these methods allows the pharmacist or pharmacy to set fees and obtain payment without administration of insurance claims. Challenges with this method may include the patient's inability or resistance to pay out-of-pocket. Thoroughly explaining the benefit of this service and getting patient buy-in prior to the visit may be ways to overcome these issues. Pharmacists should thoroughly research what is available in the area and patient perception of the appropriate value of the service being provided.

Advocacy by pharmacy organizations and national health-care entities to increase recognition of pharmacists as a provider according to CMS is ongoing and improving.[37] In December 2011, the U.S. Public Service released a report called "Improving Patient and Health System Outcomes through Advanced Pharmacy Practice." This report provided evidence and examples of advanced pharmacy practice models that further promote the importance of pharmacists to be recognized as providers. It also discusses compensation and health-care reform that is necessary to continue advancing pharmacy. It is important for pharmacists to continue to demonstrate evidence of the value we bring to patient care and demonstrate the unique addition of a pharmacist's training especially in the care of patients with diabetes.[38,33]

Clinical Service Design and Collaborative Practice Agreements

Evaluation of the clinical service design should be developed synergistically with the collaborative practice agreement. Elements provided with the clinical service should be as cohesive as possible with the prescribers who will refer patients to the MTM service. The pharmacist should consider all aspects of an agreement for patient referral, how and for whom MTM services will be provided at the pharmacy, and the method of discharging patients from the MTM service. Even if a collaborative practice agreement is not implemented with a particular physician, the pharmacist can still make

ABC Pharmacy
123 Applewood Drive
Somecity, ST 12345

Name: _____

Profile Number: _____

NONCOVERED SERVICES WAIVER

If insurance does not pay for your Medication Therapy Management Visit, you may be required to pay. Insurances do not pay for all services, even some services that you or your health-care provider have good reason to think you need. We expect your insurance may not pay for the services as detailed below:

Service Description	Reason Insurer May Not Pay:	Estimated Cost:

ACTION(S) NECESSARY TO PROCEED:
- Read this entire waiver so you can make an informed decision about the care you desire or need.
- Ask us any questions, so that you may have a full understanding of what you have read.
- Choose an option below about whether or not to receive services.

OPTIONS: Please check only one box below. This decision is ENTIRELY up to you. (We cannot make the decision for you.)

☐ **OPTION 1.** I would like to still receive MTM services listed above. I understand that I may be required to pay in full at the time of service, but I also want my insurance company billed for an official decision on payment. I understand that if my insurance doesn't pay, I am responsible for payment.

☐ **OPTION 2.** I want MTM services listed above, but do not bill my insurance company. I understand that I may be required to pay in full at the time of service.

Additional Information:

Note: Official coverage decision is not final until insurance is processed (if you choose to do so). Signing below states that you understand this notice. You will receive a copy for your records.

Patient Signature   Date

ABC Pharmacy   Revised: 1-1-2008

Figure 11-1. Noncovered services waiver.

written and faxed recommendations regarding the discussion of lifestyle interventions with the patient and possible medication therapy adjustments. Ultimately, though, pursuing a collaborative practice agreement with physicians is advisable. Such an agreement formalizes the pharmacist–physician relationship and the fact that they are both part of the health-care team. It can serve as the foundation for a great clinical relationship with the physician. It also allows MTM to be performed within a certain scope of practice with which both pharmacist and physician are comfortable, and defines those activities within the MTM concept. An example of a collaborative practice agreement can be found in Figure 11-2.

Design of the service will depend on the level of service being provided and whether education will take place in an individual or group format. For example, sessions for single patients may take place at regularly scheduled visits and cover highly individualized counseling and medication management sessions to achieve therapeutic goals. In contrast, group diabetes counseling sessions could be conducted for a specifically identified group of patients, such as those newly diagnosed with diabetes or those needing escalation to insulin therapy. Alternatively, physicians could be encouraged to refer patients who continue to have poor glycemic control (e.g., >9 or 10%) for a year or more after starting treatment.

The group sessions could be mainly educational in nature with certain subjects discussed at each session. Group sessions are beneficial especially for those newly diagnosed with diabetes because initial education can be very similar. Also, patients have common questions and can learn from one another. Another advantage of group sessions is that patients develop a rapport with each other and provide support and accountability as they make behavioral changes in their diet and exercise regimen. An example of topics for different sessions of a continuous group program for patients newly diagnosed with diabetes could include an overview of diabetes, setting attainable short-term and long-term goals, the need for A1C measurements, blood glucose self-monitoring, diet and nutrition, starting an exercise regimen, how to take medications appropriately, and the need for follow-up with a diabetes care team.

A specific procedure should be developed for referral and provision of MTM services. When collaborating with a physician, there should be an understanding in writing (usually a protocol within a collaborative practice agreement) regarding how the patient will be referred for the MTM services and who will be the most likely candidates (e.g., patients with A1C >9%, newly diagnosed diabetes). An understanding between collaborators should be established regarding specific goals for the series of MTM visits, preferably with written goals at the time of the referral. The physician should also provide a thorough but pertinent history for the patient, including the present list of medications. A baseline A1C and most recent blood glucose levels as determined in clinic should be included in the referral, along with documentation of a diabetes diagnosis. The pharmacist should then take a thorough history, including the past medical history, family history, social history, medication use history, current disease presentation, and review of systems. The pharmacist should take basic physical assessment measurements, including vital signs and foot examination with monofilament testing. Laboratory monitoring should be conducted either through the patient's provider with appropriate communication to the pharmacist, or through POC testing. POC testing could be used to determine fasting blood glucose levels and A1C at the time of the MTM visit.

The pharmacist could be authorized to modify diabetes medications, depending on specific state laws and the scope of the collaborative practice agreement. The pharmacist should either contact the physician with specific recommendations or modify medications during the MTM visit. Communication is key regardless of the method of performing MTM, with proper documentation and consent by both the physician and the patient. If the pharmacist is allowed to alter medications, the physician entering into the collaborative practice agreement may be comfortable with allowing this to occur according to national guideline standards, or a certain protocol may be required.

Authority

As a physician of the Delta Family Medicine Clinic, I, James Goodfellow, MD, authorize Jonathan Upstart, PharmD, a clinical pharmacist with Delta Pharmacy and one who holds an active license from the State Board of Pharmacy, to manage patients of my clinic pursuant to my referral.

Scope of Practice

Pharmaceutical care services as part of this collaborative practice agreement include evaluation and management of the components of diabetes. Also, because of the cardiovascular implications of other disease states directly correlated with diabetes, this agreement includes the evaluation and management of hypertension, dyslipidemia, and smoking cessation.

Activities defined in this agreement include referral to medication therapy management (MTM) services, interviewing patients, patient education, limited physical assessment, initiation and modification of drug therapy, providing POC, documentation, and referral of patients to other needed health-care providers.

1. **Referral to the Delta Pharmacy**
   A formal document for referring the patient for MTM services from the Delta Family Medicine Clinic will include a statement of the diabetes diagnosis, a history including other disease states the patient has, a complete list of currently prescribed medications, and a history of all pertinent laboratory values and vital signs (e.g., HbA1c, fasting blood glucose levels, cholesterol measurements, and blood pressure measurements).

2. **Interview**
   At the initial visit for MTM services, information will be gathered from the patient including past medical history, social history, family history, medication use history (including nonprescription products), current disease presentation, and review of systems. At each follow-up visit, current disease presentation and review of systems will be gathered, and patients will be asked about possible changes in other parameters as listed above.

3. **Patient Education**
   At all visits, patients will be educated as appropriate about diabetes and other pertinent disease states. Self-management lifestyle techniques including diet, exercise, weight loss, and smoking cessation will be emphasized. Correct techniques for self-management of blood glucose will be reviewed with patients.

4. **Physical Assessment**
   Basic physical assessment, including vital signs and diabetic foot exam, will be performed. If additional physical assessment is needed, pharmacist will refer patient back to primary care provider for further evaluation.

5. **Initiation and Modification of Drug Therapy**
   Initiation and modification of drug therapy will be based on current nationally recognized treatment guidelines, including the American Diabetes Association Standards of Care, the 7th Report of the Joint Commission for the Prevention, Detection, Evaluation, and Treatment of High Blood Pressure, and the Third Report of the Expert Panel on Detection, Evaluation, and Treatment of High Blood Cholesterol in Adults. Initiation and modification of drug therapy will also reflect current FDA-approved labeling of medications and current medical literature.

   Prescription medication classes included in this protocol include oral hypoglycemic agents, injectable hypoglycemic agents (including insulin), antihypertensive medications, cholesterol medications, antiplatelet agents, neuropathy medications, and smoking cessation medications.

6. **Laboratory Tests and Point of Care**
   The pharmacist will notify the clinic of any laboratory tests that need to be completed for the patient, with the results released to the pharmacy for MTM records. The pharmacist will be authorized to use appropriate point of care testing, including HbA1c, blood glucose levels, and fasting cholesterol panel. The clinic will be notified of all point of care testing done during MTM services. The clinic also will be notified if other laboratory tests are needed beyond those for diabetes and cholesterol, such as appropriate monitoring for medication therapy.

7. **Documentation**
   The pharmacist will provide the clinic SOAP note documentation or other form of progress note for all MTM visits in a timely and confidential manner.

Figure 11-2. Example of a collaborative practice agreement for medication therapy management services in diabetes.

8. Referral
   Patients will be referred back to the clinic primary care provider for treatment of medical problems that were not part of the referral or other problems as previously indicated.

Agreement Review and Duration
This agreement shall be valid for a period not to exceed 1 year from the effective date of the original agreement or 1 year from the date of signed subsequent amendments. It may be reviewed and revised at any time at the request of the physician. This protocol is valid January 1, 20_ through December 31, 20_. Upon signature of pharmacists and physician, a copy will be provided to both and an additional copy will be mailed to the State Board of Pharmacy.

Withdrawal or Alteration of Agreement
The physician may withdraw from the agreement at any time or may override this agreement whenever he or she deems such action necessary or appropriate.

Agreement Signatures

Jonathan Upstart, PharmD   Date

James Goodfellow, MD   Date

Figure 11-2. (*Continued*)

The collaborative practice agreement should specify how documentation should be used. If the pharmacist is allowed authority to change doses of medications, this should be documented and sent to the physician in a timely manner. This is also true if the pharmacist is only allowed to make recommendations, of course. However, a clear understanding as described through the agreement should stress expediency with which this should occur—especially how recommendations should be implemented with the patient.

Finally, if the MTM services are individualized and not performed as a group education class only, the collaborative practice agreement should include the system of patient referral back to the provider. Remember that continuity of care is paramount. Ultimately, the provider does not want MTM services to replace his/her service, but rather they should be in addition to physician visits. Thus, the agreement should specify at what point the patient will be formally referred back to the physician for all services, and when the MTM services will be complete. Optimally, this referral will take place when the goals for A1C and other cardiovascular risk parameters (e.g., goal blood pressure and cholesterol panel) have been achieved through MTM services.

■ PUTTING IT ALL TOGETHER: PATIENT CASE

LU is a 47-year-old Caucasian man with type 2 diabetes who presents to clinic for initial diabetes management at the diabetes clinic. Patient was first diagnosed in 2004 after having blurry vision, increased thirst, and a random blood glucose of 400 mg/dL. LU has noticed increased fatigue and thirst over past 4–5 days. He has not been checking blood glucose very often in past 2–3 months. LU is currently taking metformin 500 mg twice daily, glimepiride 4 mg twice daily after meals, and HCTZ 25 mg daily. He reports tolerating all medications. LU is walking about twice per week for 30 minutes at a time. LU is aware his A1C is very high and asks if he will have to start insulin. He said that he wants his diabetes to be better controlled and is willing to do whatever it takes.

24-hour dietary recall:

Breakfast—1 cup of cheerios with milk, 1 large banana, 8 ounces of orange juice, 1 piece of toast with a teaspoon of jelly, coffee with sugar substitute

Lunch—1 turkey sandwich with cheese and mustard, small bag of baked lays, water

Snack—peanut butter crackers (2–3 crackers)

Supper—baked chicken breast, 2/3 cups of macaroni and cheese, small piece of cornbread, 1/2 cup peas, 8 ounces of sugar-sweetened soda

Lab data:

BP: 134/78 mm Hg

BMI: 34.7 (Wt: 256 lbs., Ht: 72 inches)

A1C: 10.7%

Fasting blood glucose: 220 mg/dL

Fasting lipid panel: TC 131, LDL 130, HDL 30, TG 178

SCr: 1.1 mg/dL

UACR: 200 mg/g

AST/ALT: WNL

What is this LU's goal A1C?

<7% (per ADA guidelines) **or** <6.5% (per ACE/AACE guidelines)

What changes would you recommend today?

- Start Lantus 20 units qhs due to extremely high A1C. In order to determine a starting dose of insulin, one method is to use weight-based dosing and estimate 0.2 units/kg for a patient with type 2 diabetes. When adding insulin you may reduce the dose of sulfonylurea in order to decrease chance for hypoglycemia. In this case, one may decrease glimepiride to 2 mg bid AC when adding Lantus.
- Increase metformin to 1000 mg bid.
- Add lisinopril 5 mg daily. May add an ACE inhibitor or ARB for renal protection due to (+) microalbuminuria and for blood pressure control (goal <140/80 mm Hg).
- Start atorvastatin 10 mg daily, since patient has diabetes, his LDL goal would be at least <100 mg/dL. For some patients, atorvastatin may not be covered well on insurance or the patient may not have prescription coverage. If this is the case, then pravastatin 40 mg qhs would be a great option for the patient.

What education would you give to LU today?

- Counsel him on taking glimepiride right before or with the first bite of food at breakfast and supper to decrease risk of hypoglycemia.
- Discuss dietary changes, such as eliminating sugary drinks (soda, orange juice) and switch to water, diet drinks, or other drinks with sugar substitute; also LU is eating too many carbohydrates at breakfast and supper (>100 g of carbohydrates at breakfast, and >90 at supper). As a general guide to counting carbohydrates, men should aim for 4–5 servings of carbohydrates per meal while women should aim for 3–4 servings. One serving of carbohydrates equals 15 g of carbohydrate, so LU should aim for 60–75 g per meal; however, his goal may be 45–60 g per meal if he is trying to achieve weight loss.
- Encourage patient to increase activity gradually to 5 days per week as tolerated.

■ SUMMARY POINTS

- Nearly 25.8 million people (8.3% of the U.S. population) have diabetes, of which nearly 7 million remain undiagnosed. Billions are spent yearly on health-care costs directly and indirectly attributable to diabetes and its complications, but studies such as the Ashville Project have reduced costs and optimized outcomes. Thus, pharmacists providing MTM services have considerable potential to attenuate the impact of diabetes on the patient population.
- Although the overall goal of diabetes management for most patients is to decrease the A1C to <7%, the pharmacist should try to achieve specific goals for concomitant disease states such as hypertension, dyslipidemia, and other cardiovascular diseases.

- Essential counseling points include action to take when experiencing hypoglycemia and hyperglycemia, medical nutrition therapy, exercise, medication use and adherence, self-management with checking blood glucose readings, sick day management, proper foot care, and insulin injection technique and storage (if applicable).
- Oral agents, starting with metformin, can be effective in reducing the A1C in most patients and can be advanced to dual or triple therapy if needed—except for those with a high baseline A1C who are not likely to achieve goal through oral medication therapy. In these cases, insulin therapy should be started and titrated to achieve A1C goals.
- For pharmacists wanting to start MTM services in diabetes, becoming credentialed as a CDE® or BC-ADM is helpful (especially for obtaining reimbursement for services), but not essential.
- When starting MTM services for patients with diabetes, factors that should be considered include developing a business plan, obtaining stakeholder support, deciding what level of services would be provided, how payment for services will be obtained, design of the service itself, and how collaborative practice agreements need to be implemented.

EXPERT INTERVIEW—DIABETES MANAGEMENT SERVICES

Elisa Greene, PharmD
Clinical Pharmacist
Assistant Professor, Pharmacy Practice
Belmont University College of Pharmacy
Nashville, TN

Siloam Family Health Center *is a faith-based, nonprofit clinic focused on providing affordable, whole person care to those in need. We serve uninsured patients in Middle Tennessee, over 80% of whom are immigrants or refugees. Siloam Family Health Center uses a multidisciplinary approach involving social work, behavioral health, pastoral care, and clinical pharmacy working along with physicians, nurses, and nurse practitioners to provide patients with quality care.*

What unique qualities do you believe pharmacists bring to a diabetes management team?

Pharmacists have extensive training in pharmacology, interpreting literature, and in managing patients with complex medication regimens. We are in a profession that generally enjoys collaboration and naturally seeks the patient's best interests. Additionally, we are conscious of the many barriers to patient adherence, and recognize that the best therapeutic option is one that the patient agrees to use. Because of these characteristics, diabetes management and pharmacy fit naturally together. A pharmacist in this position can often spend more time on patient education, and learning their needs, fears and beliefs, than would be possible in a typical office visit.

How is the clinic constructed in order to make recommendations?

We have worked out a system that suits the provider's preferences. It involves any recommendation being made in writing through the "task" function in the electronic medical record. This links the recommendation to a specific provider and patient, shows up in the providers "to do" list, but is not part of the permanent record. It also allows the providers to communicate back and forth, electronically, with any follow-up suggestions or questions. Per the request of the other health-care providers on my team, I always follow up a written recommendation with a face-to-face notification. This part may be brief or more in-depth, depending on the circumstances. Additionally, there are more formal consults that can be initiated by me or by another provider and involve documentation in the EMR, either in preset templates or free-text fields.

How is the clinic compensated for the pharmacist's time?

The clinic has a contract with Belmont University COP, which is my official employer and pays my salary. Since this site serves uninsured patients, funding comes largely from donors and grants, in addition to some governmental programs. There is no direct reimbursement or billing by the clinic for my services for these two reasons.

What barriers did you encounter in implementing diabetes services? How did you overcome them?

When I began at my clinic, very few, if any, of the other members of the health-care team had personal experience working with a clinical pharmacist. This in itself was a barrier, as I had to educate them on my background and training, what I hoped to implement, different models of providing interdisciplinary care, collaborative practice agreements, and how I, as a pharmacist, could help them provide quality patient care. Building relationships, accepting slow progress and small advances, and being willing to help wherever needed in the beginning went a long way in establishing myself as a valuable contributor. Another barrier was the limitation of physical space. Initially, a closet area was cleared out and renovated to provide workspace and a consultation area. However, it continues to be a high-traffic multipurpose area. We are working around this limitation by being flexible and accommodating in meeting with patients in exam rooms or the consultation area as needed. Other providers are also respectful of the shared space and recognize that on occasions when the door is closed, the situation calls for privacy. A third barrier involves working within an organizational structure; anytime there are changes, implementation is slow, and there are different perceptions of the best direction to take when working out the details. I have taken the approach that we are all working for the same goal—implementing focused diabetes services to better care for our patients—and have been willing to compromise on some of the details of my exact role and the timing when patient care will not be compromised.

What were your personal struggles when you first started diabetes management services?

I struggled with accepting that every practice is different, and what works at one clinic may not be the best model in another. I had to find a balance between what I had previously seen and been a part of versus acknowledging that there were many different ways we could reach the goal of improving patient care. Also, it was a difficult at first, as the "new kid on the block," to know when to push and when to compromise when barriers arose. Another struggle somewhat unique to my (or similar) sites was the language barrier present with non-English-speaking patients. I had to adjust my style to accommodate low levels of health literacy and interpreter services, which can really change the flow of an interaction.

What barriers did you experience while building relationships with providers?

I was blessed to come into a situation where the providers unanimously welcomed me. Some of the challenges came with educating them about what I was able to contribute, how they could best use my services, and incorporating me into the flow of the clinic. With everyone being stretched by their patient load and other responsibilities, there was not a copious amount of time for us to get to know each other initially. Over time, through many shorter conversations between meetings or patients, occasional shared lunches, identifying common interests or goals, and even beginning to socialize outside of clinic hours, our relationships have been strengthened. Being available and willing to help, taking the initiative to meet a need, and seeking feedback from them were also ways that I was able to win their trust.

How is quality assessed in your clinic?

For diabetes, quality is assessed by the percentage of patients meeting the standards of care for diabetes (A1C <7%, LDL <100 mg/dL, ASA if indicated, BP <130/80 mm Hg, annual retinopathy screen, on an ACE-i/ARB, if no contraindication). A previous assessment revealed that our clinic was in line with national averages for similar settings, which resulted in our push for improvement and implementation of more specific diabetes services (some of which are still in progress).

Were there any unexpected outcomes after initiating diabetes services?

Once providers realized how much time I could save them by providing diabetes services, especially with initial diagnosis, glucometer education, and insulin initiation, they began to seek me out more for these services. Additionally, they began to be creative with thinking of other ways to use my services in other areas as well. One component of my services is beginning to assess and document health literacy in our patients with diabetes. An unexpected outcome with this is that patients who have performed well on the health literacy assessment have often reported learning from weight watchers. This has prompted us to look into how we may be able to partner with them in using some of their materials in providing nutrition information to our patients.

What intangible benefits have you or your staff enjoyed from starting this service?

There is an enhanced sense of camaraderie and teamwork. Whether curbside or formal, consults are more frequent and well received. Having the vision of improving care in this specific area has helped unite us.

What tips can you give for someone who is planning to start diabetes management services?

Start with a plan and clear goals, know your population and your providers, be willing to compromise on unessential details, be open-minded, don't be discouraged if the going is slow, especially at first, be persistent with identifying particular patients who may be candidates for your services and volunteering, even in a small way, to contribute to their care.

STUDY QUESTIONS

1. Microvascular complications resulting from uncontrolled diabetes include all of the following **EXCEPT**:
   a. Arthropathy
   b. Neuropathy
   c. Retinopathy
   d. Nephropathy

2. When applying for the CDE® exam, which is true regarding eligibility:
   a. Applicant must have completed 3 years of professional practice
   b. A minimum of 1000 hours of direct DSME must be documented in the past 3 years
   c. Forty percent of the required hours for direct DSME must be accrued within the previous 2 years before sitting for the exam.
   d. Fifteen hours of diabetes-related continuing education must be documented within 2 years before taking the exam.

3. Which is *NOT* an avenue in which pharmacists may be reimbursed for services provided?
   a. Medicare Part D
   b. Fee-for-service
   c. Medicare Part A
   d. Third-party payers

4. A1C goal of <6.5% may be acceptable for an individual as long as which of these conditions is met?
   a. The patient is young, rarely has hypoglycemia, and was diagnosed with diabetes 2 years ago
   b. Hypoglycemic events only happen in the middle of the night from 12 am to 5 am
   c. The patient has advanced microvascular and macrovascular complications
   d. The patient has a limited life expectancy

5. Aspirin is recommended for patients with diabetes at an increased cardiovascular risk (10-year risk >10%) that would include most:
   a. Men ≥40 years of age or women ≥50 years of age with at least one major risk factor
   b. Men ≥50 years of age or women ≥60 years of age with at least one major risk factor
   c. Men ≥50 years of age or women ≥40 years of age with at least one major risk factor
   d. Men ≥60 years of age or women ≥50 years of age with at least one major risk factor

6. Which is a true statement about metformin?
   a. It should not be initiated unless the patient's A1C is >8%
   b. Avoid initiation in females with a serum creatinine ≥1.4
   c. It should be titrated to a maximum dose of 500 mg twice daily
   d. It has a high incidence of severe hypoglycemia

7. Which dose would be the most appropriate starting dose for a 100 kg male with an HbA1c of 8.5% starting insulin glargine?
   a. 50 units qhs
   b. 40 units qhs
   c. 10 units qhs
   d. 5 units qhs

BIBLIOGRAPHY

1. Centers for Disease Control and Prevention. National Diabetes Fact Sheet: national estimates and general information on diabetes and prediabetes in the United States, 2011. Atlanta, GA: U.S. Department of Health and Human Services, Centers for Disease Control and Prevention, 2011. http://www.cdc.gov/diabetes/pubs/pdf/ndfs_2011.pdf. Accessed July 9, 2012.
2. American Diabetes Association. Economic costs of diabetes in the U.S. in 2007. *Diabetes Care.* 2008;31:596-615.
3. Stratton IM, Adler AI, Neil HA, et al. Association of glycaemia with macrovascular and microvascular complications of type 2 diabetes (UKPDS 35): prospective observational study. *BMJ.* 2000;321(7258):405-412.
4. The Diabetes Control and Complications Trial Research Group. The effect of intensive treatment of diabetes on the development and progression of long-term complications in insulin-dependent diabetes mellitus. *N Engl J Med.* 1993;329(14):977-986.
5. Gilmer TP, O'Connor PJ, Manning WG, et al. The cost to health plans of poor glycemic control. *Diabetes Care.* 1997;20(12):1847-1853.
6. Boyle JP, Thompson TJ, Gregg EW, et al. Projection of the year 2050 burden of diabetes in the US adult population: dynamic modeling of incidence, mortality, and prediabetes prevalence. *Popul Health Metr.* 2010;8:29.
7. Cranor CW, Bunting BA, Christensen DB, et al. The Asheville Project: long-term clinical and economic outcomes of a community pharmacy diabetes care program. *J Am Pharm Assoc.* 2003;43:173-184.
8. Irons BK, Lenz RJ, Anderson SL, et al. A retrospective cohort analysis of the clinical effectiveness of a physician-pharmacist collaborative drug therapy management diabetes clinic. *Pharmacotherapy.* 2002;22(10):1294-1300.
9. American Diabetes Association. Standards of medical care in diabetes - 2013. *Diabetes Care.* 2013;36(Suppl 1):S11-S66.
10. Inzucchi SE, Bergenstal RM, Buse JM, et al. Management of hyperglycemia in type 2 diabetes: a patient-centered approach. *Diabetes Care.* 2012;35:1364-1379.
11. Handelsman Y, Mechanick JI, Blonde L, et al. American Association of Clinical Endocrinologists medical guidelines for clinical practice for developing a diabetes mellitus comprehensive care plan. *Endocr Pract.* 2011;17(Suppl 2):1-53.
12. Expert Panel on Detection E, and Treatment of High Blood Cholesterol in Adults. Executive summary of the third report of the National Cholesterol Education Program (NCEP) Expert Panel on Detection, Evaluation and Treatment of High Blood Cholesterol in Adults (Adult Treatment Panel III). *JAMA.* 2001;285:2486-2497.
13. Rizor H, Smith M, Thomas K, Harker J, Rich M. "Practical Nutrition: The Idaho Plate Method." *Pract Diabetol.* 1998;17:42-45.
14. Planning meals. http://www.diabetes.org/food-and-fitness/food/planning-meals/?loc=DropDownFF-mealplanning. Accessed July 6, 2012.
15. Ragucci KR, Fermo JD, Wessell AM, Chumney ECG. Effectiveness of pharmacist-administered diabetes mellitus education and management services. *Pharmacotherapy.* 2005;25(12):1809-1816.
16. Johannigman MJ, Leifheit M, Bellman N, Pierce T, Marriott A, Bishop C. Medication therapy management and condition care services in a community-based employer setting. *Am J Health Syst Pharm.* 2010;67:1362-1367.
17. Lewin Group. Medication therapy management services: a critical review. *J Am Pharm Assoc.* 2005;45(5):580-587.
18. Barnett MJ, Grank J, Wehring H, et al. Analysis of pharmacist-provided medication therapy management services in community pharmacies over 7 years. *J Manag Care Pharm.* 2009;15(1):18-31.
19. MacIntosh C, Weiser C, Wassimi A, et al. Attitudes toward and factors affecting implementation of medication therapy management services by community pharmacists. *J Am Pharm Assoc.* 2009;49(1):26-30.
20. Chawla S. Nontraditional or noncentralized models of diabetes care: medication therapy management services. *Fam Med.* 2011;60(Suppl 1):S12-S18.
21. Scott MA, Hitch WJ, Wilson CG, Lugo AM. Billing for pharmacists' cognitive services in physicians' offices. *J Am Pharm Assoc.* 2012;52(2):175-180.
22. Rodbard HW, Jellinger PS, Davidson JA, et al. Statement by an American Association of Clinical Endocrinologists/American College of Endocrinology consensus panel on type 2 diabetes mellitus: an algorithm for glycemic control. *Endocr Pract.* 2009;15:540-559.
23. The Pharmacist and Patient-Centered Diabetes Care. American Pharmacists Association. http://www.pharmacist.com/Content/NavigationMenu3/ContinuingEducation/CertificateTrainingProgram/PharmaceuticalCareforPatientswithDiabetes/Pharma_Care_Diabetes.htm. Accessed July 6, 2012.

24. National Certification Board for Diabetes Educators. http://www.ncbde.org/. Accessed July 6, 2012.
25. Board Certified-Advanced Diabetes Management Certification. American Association of Diabetes Educators. http://www.diabeteseducator.org/ProfessionalResources/Certification/BC-ADM/. Accessed July 6, 2012.
26. Diabetes Journals. American Diabetes Association. http://www.diabetesjournals.org/. Accessed July 6, 2012.
27. The Diabetes Educator. American Association of Diabetes Educators. http://www.diabeteseducator.org/ProfessionalResources/Periodicals/Educator/. Accessed July 6, 2012.
28. Howerton D, Anderson N, Bosse D, Granade S, Westbrook B. Good Laboratory Practices for Waived Testing Sites: Survey Findings from Testing Sites Holding a Certificate of Waiver Under the Clinical Laboratory Improvement Amendments of 1988 and Recommendations for Promoting Quality Testing. 11 Nov 2005. http://www.cdc.gov/mmwr/preview/mmwrhtml/rr5413a1.htm. Accessed July 6, 2012.
29. How to apply for a CLIA certificate, including international laboratories. April 30, 2012. http://www.cms.gov/Regulations-and-Guidance/Legislation/CLIA/How_to_Apply_for_a_CLIA_Certificate_International_Laboratories.html. Accessed July 6, 2012.
30. Diabetes Education. Reimbursement for Diabetes Self-Management Training (DSMT). Recognition News. Spring 2011. http://professional.diabetes.org/UserFiles/ERP/ERP%20News%20Archive/rec-news-spring-2011-2.pdf. Accessed July 6, 2012.
31. Applying for Accreditation. American Association of Diabetes Educators. http://www.diabeteseducator.org/ProfessionalResources/accred/Application.html. Accessed July 6, 2012.
32. Education Recognition Programs. American Diabetes Association. http://professional.diabetes.org/Recognition.aspx?typ=15&cid=84040. Accessed July 6, 2012.
33. Kliethermes MA, Brown TR. *Building a Successful Ambulatory Care Practice: A Complete Guide for Pharmacists.* Bethesda, MD: American Society of Health-System Pharmacists; 2012.
34. Rupp MT. Analyzing the costs to deliver medication therapy management services. *J Am Pharm Assoc.* 2011;51:e19-e27.
35. Centers for Medicare & Medicaid Services. Prescription Drug Benefit Manual: Chapter 7 – Medication Therapy Management and Quality Improvement Program. 2010; https://www.cms.gov/Medicare/Prescription-Drug-Coverage/PrescriptionDrugCovContra/downloads/Chapter7.pdf. Accessed July 12, 2012.
36. Centers for Medicare & Medicaid Services. Medicare Claims Processing Manual: Chapter 18- Preventive and Screening Services. Section 120. 2012; https://www.cms.gov/Regulations-and-Guidance/Guidance/Manuals/Downloads/clm104c18.pdf. Accessed July 10, 2012.
37. Centers for Medicare & Medicaid Services. Medicare Part D Medication Therapy Management (MTM) Programs-2011 Fact Sheet. 2011; https://www.cms.gov/Medicare/Prescription-Drug-Coverage/PrescriptionDrugCovContra/downloads/MTMFactSheet2011063011Final.pdf. Accessed July 12, 2012.
38. Giberson S, Yoder S, Lee MP. *Improving Patient and Health System Outcomes Through Advanced Pharmacy Practice. A Report to the U.S. Surgeon General.* Office of the Chief Pharmacist. U.S. Public Health Service; December 2011.

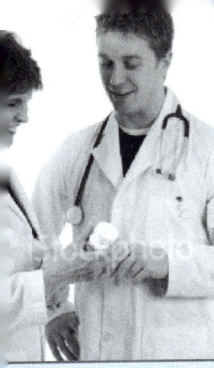

12

HYPERTENSION

Michelle Z. Farland

■ LEARNING OBJECTIVES

After reading this chapter, the student pharmacist, community practice resident, or pharmacist should be able to:

1. Accurately measure blood pressure (BP).
2. Appropriately classify severity of hypertension (HTN) by using the seventh report of the Joint National Committee on Prevention, Detection, Evaluation, and Treatment of High Blood Pressure (JNC 7) staging classification.
3. Identify compelling indications to assist with selection of appropriate pharmacotherapeutic agents for treatment of HTN.
4. Educate patients of the impact of lifestyle changes on BP control.
5. Develop pharmacotherapy treatment plans for patients with HTN, including those with compelling indications, difficult to treat HTN, and special populations.
6. Identify potential barriers to implementing services for patients with HTN in a community pharmacy.
7. Design workflow in a community pharmacy to establish and maintain services for patients with HTN.

BACKGROUND AND INTRODUCTION

Epidemiology of Hypertension in the United States

The 2011 Update on Heart Disease and Stroke Statistics indicates that 29% of adults (≥18 years) in the United States have high BP.[1] According to the most recent National Health and Nutrition Examination Survey (NHANES), 30.4% (66.9 million) of US adults (≥18 years) have HTN, defined as average BP ≥140/90 mm Hg, or currently using blood pressure lowering medication.[2]

HTN prevalence varies with age, sex, race, and ethnicity.[1,3] The prevalence of high BP is greater in men in the age group of 18–44 years. Women and men have equal prevalence from the age of 45–64 years. Women have a higher prevalence of high BP starting at age 65. Prevalence of HTN is greatest among black Americans. Black Americans have a higher average BP and develop HTN at an earlier age than white Americans. American Indians and Native Alaskans also have increased prevalence compared with white and Asian adults. Puerto Rican Americans have the highest rate of HTN-related deaths compared with other Hispanic populations. The rate of HTN-related mortality is similar between Hispanic and non-Hispanic whites. Being born outside the United States, speaking a non-English language at home, and fewer years of living in the United States are associated with decreased prevalence of HTN.

Among those with HTN, 69.9% have received pharmacological treatment between 2005 and 2008.[3] This was a slight increase compared with 1999–2002 when 60.3% of patients with HTN received pharmacological treatment. Patients without a usual source of medical care were the least likely to receive pharmacological treatment (19.7%). Overall disease control, defined as BP <140 mm Hg systolic and <90 mm Hg diastolic, in the United states was 53.5% between 2003 and 2010.[2] Of those with uncontrolled HTN, 39.4% were unaware they had elevated blood pressures, 15.8% were aware they had HTN but were not being treated with medications, and 44.8% were aware they had HTN and were being treated with medications. Hypertension unawareness had highest prevalence among those who did not receive health-care in the previous year, those without a usual source of health-care, adults aged 18-44 years, and those without health insurance. Hypertension awareness without treatment with medications had highest prevalence among those without a usual source of health-care, adults aged 18-44 years, those of Hispanic ethnicity other than Mexican-Americans, and those without health insurance. Uncontrolled HTN despite awareness and use of medications for treatment had highest prevalence among Medicare beneficiaries, those aged ≥65 years, and those who received medical care ≥ times in the previous year.[2]

Complications of Hypertension

HTN, along with dyslipidemia and smoking, is a leading modifiable risk factor for cardiovascular disease (CVD). Uncontrolled HTN may lead to end-organ damage such as myocardial infarction (MI), cerebrovascular accidents, and kidney failure. Other manifestations of uncontrolled HTN include retinopathy, angina, coronary revascularization, left ventricular hypertrophy, heart failure, nephrosclerosis, and peripheral artery disease. A linear relationship exists between BP and the risk of death from ischemic heart disease and stroke.[4] Risk of death from ischemic heart disease and stroke begins when BP is >115/75. The mortality risk doubles for every increase in BP of 20/10 mm Hg. Other reports have indicated that there is a twofold increase in relative risk of CVD in patients with BP of 130–135/85–89 mm Hg compared to those with BP <120/80 mm Hg.

Classification of Hypertension

The seventh report from the JNC 7 defines four stages of BP measurements (Table 12-1)[4] Lowering the BP can decrease the risk of complications related to HTN, but will not prevent all occurrences.

Hypertension Treatment Goals

One of the difficulties of determining BP control stems from the multiple different guideline statements available for HTN. Table 12-2 lists the BP treatment goals according to JNC 7, the American Heart Association (AHA), the National Kidney Foundation (NKF), and

Table 12-1. JNC 7 Definition of Hypertension

Stage	Systolic Blood Pressure	Diastolic Blood Pressure
Normal	<120	<80
Prehypertension	120–139	80–89
Stage 1 hypertension	140–159	90–99
Stage 2 hypertension	≥160	≥100

the American Diabetes Association (ADA).[4-7] The data to support the differences in the BP goals is lacking and primarily based on expert opinion and inferences made from observational studies. Future research should focus on the optimal BP goals for patients with CVD and CVD risk equivalents.

■ MEASURING BLOOD PRESSURE AND PULSE

The most important aspect of a clinical service for HTN is the accuracy of the measurement of BP. The most widely used method to measure BP is the auscultatory method. This method was first called the Korotkoff technique, which was developed nearly 100 years ago. The basis of the measurement is the occlusion of the brachial artery by a sphygmomanometer to above the systolic pressure. As the cuff is deflated, blood flow is reestablished and is accompanied with sounds that are detected by a stethoscope. The first appearance of sounds marks the systolic pressure. The diastolic pressure is measured when the sounds disappear. This process seems relatively simplistic; however, it is important that the patient is positioned properly, the correct cuff size is selected, the cuff is placed in the correct position, and the observer is properly trained.[8]

Patient Position

The most reliable position for the patient to be in to measure the BP is in the seated position with back and legs supported and the feet uncrossed resting on a firm surface. The arm should be bare to the shoulder. If the shirtsleeve was raised to expose the upper arm, it should be loose to ensure it does not alter the BP measurement. The arm should also be supported and raised to be in level with the heart (middle of sternum). Prior to measuring the BP, the patient should be resting in this position for at least 5 minutes. The patient should also avoid caffeine, smoking, and exercise 30 minutes prior to the measurement, as these will raise the BP. The patient should be asked to remain silent while taking the BP measurement.

Table 12-2. Blood Pressure Target Goals

Patient Description	JNC 7	AHA	NKF	ADA
General BP goal for most patients	<140/90 mm Hg	<140/90 mm Hg	No recommendation	No recommendation
Patients with diabetes mellitus, chronic kidney disease	<130/80 mm Hg	<130/80 mm Hg	<130/80 mm Hg	<140/90 mm Hg*
Patients with coronary artery disease, noncoronary atherosclerotic vascular disease, Framingham score ≥10%	No recommendation	<130/80 mm Hg	No recommendation	No recommendation
Patients with left ventricular dysfunction	No recommendation	<120/80 mm Hg	No recommendation	No recommendation
Patients with >1 g of proteinuria	No recommendation	No recommendation	<125/75 mm Hg	No recommendation

JNC 7, Seventh Report of the Joint National Committee; AHA, American Heart Association; NKF, National Kidney Foundation; ADA, American Diabetes Association.
*Specific to patients with diabetes mellitus and is not inclusive of patients with chronic kidney disease.

Table 12-3.	Cuff Size Selection Based on Arm Circumference[4,8]	
Arm Circumference (cm)	Cuff Measurement (cm)	Cuff Size
22–26	12 × 22	Adult small
27–34	16 × 30	Adult regular
35–44	16 × 36	Adult large
45–52	16 × 42	Adult thigh

Cuff Size Selection

For most adults, the cuff size will range from adult small to adult large. Some adults may require the use of a child cuff or a thigh cuff, so it is important to have multiple sizes available. The cuff should encircle at least 80% of the arm. The use of a cuff that is too small may result in overestimation of the BP, and a cuff that is too large may result in underestimation of the BP. Most cuffs are now marked with line indicators to assist with determining the appropriate size. When the cuff is wrapped around the patient's arm, the index line (runs along the edge of the cuff) should fall within the range lines (marked on the inside length of the cuff). If the index line does not fall within the range lines, a different sized cuff is needed. Table 12-3 lists the cuff size selection based on arm circumference.

Placement of the Equipment

The cuff should be placed 2 cm above the elbow crease. The midline of the bladder (usually marked on the cuff) should be placed over the brachial artery. The cuff should be tightly fitting when two fingers are underneath the cuff against the patient's arm. The manometer should be in place such that the person measuring the BP can view it straight on and is not more than 15 inches away. The bell of the stethoscope should be placed over the brachial artery (inner aspect of the upper arm). If the bell of the stethoscope is in contact with either the cuff or the patient's clothing, you will hear extraneous noises. To avoid these sounds, be sure the bell is only in contact with the patient's arm and not touching other objects.

Taking a Quality Measurement

Obtaining a quality BP measurement should be easy now that you have positioned the patient properly, selected the proper cuff size, and placed your equipment in the correct locations. At this point, you need to determine what pressure to inflate the cuff to. To do this, first put the stethoscope down. You will palpate the radial pulse (outer aspect of the wrist) while inflating the cuff. Note when the pulse disappears, then deflate the cuff and note when the pulse reappears. This is the obliteration pressure. This step helps to avoid under- or overestimating the BP in patients who have an auscultatory gap (an intermittent absence of sounds after they initially appeared). Patients with an auscultatory gap have potential to have their systolic BP underestimated or their diastolic BP overestimated.

To measure the BP, place the bell of the stethoscope on the brachial artery and inflate the cuff to 20–30 mm Hg above the obliteration pressure. Slowly deflate the cuff (2 mm Hg/second) and listen for the Korotkoff sounds. There are five phases of Korotkoff sounds. The two phases that are used for BP measurement are phase 1 (initial appearance of sounds) and phase 5 (disappearance of sounds). Phase 1 is the systolic BP measurement and phase 5 is the diastolic measurement. To avoid overestimation of the diastolic BP and underestimation of the systolic BP, it is recommended to continue to slowly deflate the cuff and listen for additional sounds for 10 mm Hg after you no longer hear sounds. This process will assist with identifying an auscultatory gap if one is present. An auscultatory gap occurs when there is a period when Korotkoff sounds can no longer be heard, but then reappear at a lower pressure measurement. The sounds heard during this time are indicative of systolic BP. If sounds reappear during this time, continue to slowly deflate the cuff until the sounds disappear again. It is also advised to document the patient has an auscultatory gap to assist with future measurements of the BP.

In the event if you obtain a different BP in each arm of the patient, it is recommended you use the arm with the higher measurement for future assessments.

Quantity of Measurements

JNC 7 recommends for the diagnosis of HTN that two measurements should be obtained on different days.[4] The AHA recommends obtaining at least two readings at least 1 minute apart in an outpatient clinical setting.[8] The readings are then averaged to determine the documented BP. If the two readings are more than 5 mm Hg different, additional readings (1–2) should be obtained, then average all readings to determine the documented BP.

The AHA recommends obtaining the BP in both arms on the first encounter with the patient.[8] This is due to the frequent occurrence of differences of BP between arms. If there is a consistent pattern of higher BP in one arm compared with the other, the AHA recommends using the results from the arm with the higher measurement as the documented BP.

A recent analysis was conducted to determine the certainty with which a BP measured using different strategies (home, clinic, research measurements) reflect the patient's true BP.[9] The study compared three methods of measuring BP based on location the measurement was taken (home, clinic, research center). The authors also examined the number of measurements and within patient variance. Results indicated that relying on only a single BP measurement in any of the three settings led to inappropriate classification of BP. Higher quantity of readings obtained from the patient increased the likelihood of properly classifying the patients' BP. The authors concluded that to obtain >80% certainty of correctly classifying the BP control, the average of several BP measurements (5–6) is needed. They also indicated that this is best done using home measurements, as obtaining several measurements only minutes apart from each other in a clinical setting does not capture the true variation in BP seen throughout the day.

Measuring Pulse

The two most commonplaces to measure the pulse is the radial artery on the outer aspect of the wrist and carotid artery on the neck. You should place two fingers over the artery to palpate, making sure you do not mistakenly feel your own pulse. In patients with a regular rhythm, you can measure the pulse for a short duration (10 or 15 seconds), then multiply to obtain the number of beats per minute (bpm). However, in patients with irregular rhythm it is recommended you measure the pulse for a full 60 seconds to determine the pulse rate.

Measuring Orthostatic Blood Pressures[10,11]

There are times when a patient will present with symptoms of orthostatic hypotension that require the measurement of orthostatic BPs. This requires being able to position the patient in two positions (supine and standing). It should be expected that the patient's diastolic BP will increase when transitioning between these positions. The patient should rest for 5 minutes in the supine position (lying down) prior to measuring BP and pulse. After lying still for 3 minutes, the patient should stand with an immediate repeat measurement of BP and pulse. Orthostatic hypotension is defined as a decrease in systolic BP of ≥ 20 mm Hg or diastolic BP of ≥ 10 mm Hg. The pulse may fluctuate during this time as well. A small change in pulse (<10 bpm) is indicative of baroreceptor reflex impairment. If the pulse increases >20 bpm, the patient is likely volume depleted. If the patient is not able to tolerate standing for 3 minutes, the patient should be referred for a tilt table test that simulates the same positional changes (supine to standing) without requiring the patient to rely on his/her own strength to transition between the positions.

■ LIFESTYLE INTERVENTIONS FOR HYPERTENSION

There are multiple different lifestyle modifications that will assist in reducing BP and assist with achieving BP treatment goals. Table 12-4 describes these modifications and anticipated systolic BP reduction that can be achieved. The lifestyle modification that has the greatest potential for improving BP control is weight loss. In order to achieve weight loss, it is important to educate patients on appropriate physical activity based on their current health status. For patients without restrictions on physical activity, the JNC 7 and AHA guidelines recommend moderate activity. The 2008

Table 12-4. Impact of Lifestyle Modifications on Blood Pressure Control[a]

Lifestyle Modification	Recommendation[b]	Approximate SBP Lowering (mm Hg)
Weight loss	10 kg reduction (goal to maintain healthy BMI 18.5–24.9)	5–20
DASH diet	Diet rich in fruits and vegetables (8–10 servings/day), low-fat dairy (2–3 servings/day). Reduce intake of saturated and total fat	8–14
Dietary sodium reduction	Reduce intake to <2.4 g/day sodium (6 g/day sodium chloride)	2–8
Dietary potassium intake	Increase potassium to 4.7 g/day-use caution in patients with chronic kidney disease, diabetes, severe heart failure, adrenal insufficiency, and medications known to increase potassium.	2–4
Physical activity	Regular moderate physical activity (i.e., brisk walking) 30 minutes/day most days/week	4–9
Moderate alcohol consumption (in those who consume more than the recommended amounts listed here)	Men: No more than 2 drinks daily (24 oz beer, 10 oz wine, 3 oz 80-proof liquor) Women: No more than 1 drink daily (12 oz beer, 5 oz wine, 1.5 oz 80-proof liquor)	2–4

SBP, systolic blood pressure; BMI, body mass index; DASH, dietary approaches to stop hypertension.
[a]Adapted from JNC 7[4] and AHA.[5,12]
[b]It is also recommended to quit smoking to assist with decreasing blood pressure and other cardiovascular risk factors.

Physical Activity Guidelines for Americans define moderate aerobic activity as working heard enough to raise your heart rate and sweat.[13] At this point, the patient should be able to talk, but should not be able to sing. Examples of moderate aerobic activity include brisk walking (3 miles/hour), water aerobics, bike riding (<10 miles/hour), ballroom dancing, and general gardening.

Food products have been linked with elevations in BP. The two most common are sodium and alcohol. The restrictions on consumption are listed in Table 12-4. Sodium restriction (<2.4 g/day) has shown to reduce systolic BP.[12] Patients with the following characteristics receive the greatest systolic BP reduction with sodium restriction: blacks, middle aged, elderly, diabetes, and chronic kidney disease (CKD). Foods with reduced sodium content typically have increased potassium content. Increasing potassium intake can also assist to reduce the BP, with the greatest impact on black patients. There is a dose-dependent relationship between alcohol intake and BP with significant increases above two drinks daily (1 drink is equal to 12 oz beer, 5 oz wine, 1.5 oz of 80-proof liquor). Effects of restricting alcohol consumption have been observed in patients with and without HTN. Licorice can also elevate BP. Most patients are unaware of this, so it is important to educate them to avoid licorice until more literature is available to determine safe amounts to consume.

Counseling Tips for Success with Lifestyle Modifications

Lifestyle modifications can be difficult to implement and maintain. The anticipated benefit of each specific lifestyle modification can assist you with prioritizing the changes to implement. In order to maintain lifestyle changes, patients are typically more successful when small changes are made in a progressive manner, while ensuring a patient can maintain the first change before moving to another change. It is also helpful to have the patient involved in selecting what behavior to change. This empowers the patient to want to be successful with the behavior change and increases the likelihood of maintaining the change. For example, if the behavior change is to increase physical activity, you would first ask what activity the patient enjoys doing, then ask them how much time they can comfortably spend doing the activity weekly. You can educate the patient that the ultimate goal is to complete a moderate aerobic activity 150 minutes weekly, but that you will agree to start with the time that is feasible to the patient with the intent to slowly increase to the goal time.

There are multiple ways to assist patients with reduction in sodium intake. These include (1) avoid frozen meals and prepackaged foods; (2) select fresh or frozen vegetables instead of canned vegetables; (3) if you buy canned vegetables, buy low sodium products, and rinse prior to cooking; (4) do not add salt to the food once it has been prepared (take the salt shaker off the table); (5) reduce number of times weekly that you eat out; and (6) read food labels for sodium content.

■ MEDICATION MANAGEMENT

There are multiple medication classes available to treat HTN. Most patients will require more than one medication to reach their BP goal. In patients whose BP is ≥20/10 mm Hg above the treatment goal, guidelines recommend to initiate two medications from different structural classes. All other patients should be initiated on one medication. Selection of medications to treat HTN is often based on patients' comorbid conditions. Both JNC 7 and the AHA detail recommendations on selection of medication class based on comorbid conditions. These recommendations are summarized in Table 12-5.

First-Line Treatment—Thiazide Diuretics

For patients with no compelling indications, diuretics are the medication class of choice. Thiazide diuretics are more effective at lowering the BP compared with loop diuretics. However, thiazide diuretics are not effective with impaired kidney function (estimated CrCl <30 mL/minute, as measured by the Cockroft–Gault equation), in which case the loop diuretics should be used.

The selection of a thiazide diuretic should be based on evidence-based improvement in patient outcomes. The two most commonly used diuretics in the United States are hydrochlorothiazide and chlorthalidone. There has been recent debate over the interchangeability of these agents.[14,15] There is little evidence that has directly compared the effectiveness of chlorthalidone with hydrochlorothiazide. It is also difficult to compare studies using either agent due to the differences in patient populations, study design, or medication combinations used. When comparing the evidence, stronger data supports the use of chlorthalidone in patients with HTN to prevent stroke, fatal, and nonfatal cardiovascular events. Of the trials published that used chlorthalidone, the two most notable are the Systolic Hypertension in the Elderly Program (SHEP)[16] and Antihypertensive and Lipid Lowering Treatment to Prevent Heart Attack (ALLHAT).[17,18] Chlorthalidone dose range studied in these trials was 12.5–25 mg/day.

The primary safety concern with thiazide diuretics is the risk of hypokalemia.[14] The risk of hypokalemia is dose dependent with increasing frequency at higher doses. Hydrochlorothiazide rose to favor when studies linked high doses of chlorthalidone (50 mg/day) with sudden death related to hypokalemia. Hydrochlorothiazide has also been widely studied with mixed results (positive, neutral, negative). One possible reason for the differences in patient outcomes observed when comparing these diuretics are differences in their pharmacokinetics. Chlorthalidone has a significantly longer half-life (45–60 hours) and duration of action

Table 12-5. Treatment Selection Based on Comorbid Conditions[a]

Comorbid Condition	Diuretic	Beta Blocker	ACE-I	ARB	D-CCB	ND-CCB	Aldosterone Antagonist	Comments
HF	1	1	1	2	3		1	BB of choice includes bisoprolol, carvedilol, metoprolol succinate ARB use in patients unable to tolerate ACE-I Aldosterone antagonists should be added to the regimen when NYHA class III or IV or LVEF <40% Use of ACE-I + ARB + aldosterone antagonist not recommended due to risk of hyperkalemia
MI		1	1	2			1	Select a BB without intrinsic sympathomimetic activity Aldosterone antagonists indicated post-MI with left ventricular dysfunction
Unstable angina		1	1	2	2	2		Select a BB without intrinsic sympathomimetic activity
Chronic stable angina	1	1	1	2	2	2		ND-CCB can be used in place of BB in absence of LV systolic dysfunction
DM	2	3	1	1	2	3		BB can mask symptoms of hypoglycemia except for sweating ND-CCB have more renal protective effects vs. D-CCB
CKD			1	1		2		
Recurrent ischemic stroke prevention	1		1					Combination of both thiazide diuretic + ACE-I has been shown to reduce rates of recurrent ischemic stroke
None of the above	1		1	2	1			ARB use in patients unable to tolerate ACEI

BB, beta-blocker; ACE-I, angiotensin-converting enzyme inhibitor; ARB, angiotensin receptor blocker; D-CCB, dihydropyridine calcium channel blocker; ND-CCB, nondihydropyridine calcium channel blocker; HF, heart failure; NYHA, New York Heart Association; LVEF, left ventricular ejection fraction; MI, myocardial infarction; DM, diabetes mellitus; CKD, chronic kidney disease; 1, drug of choice; 2, second-line recommendation; 3, third line recommendation.

[a]Adapted from JNC 7 and AHA guidelines.[4,5]

(48–72 hours) compared with hydrochlorothiazide (half-life 8–15 hours; duration of action 16–24 hours).[15] Unfortunately, a head-to-head comparison of these two agents has not been conducted to definitively document the superiority, inferiority, or equality to improve patient outcomes. The available evidence supports either of these agents as appropriate for first-line use in patients without compelling indications for different agents. The recommended dose range for hydrochlorothiazide is 12.5–50 mg daily and for chlorthalidone 6.25–25 mg daily.[15]

Additional adverse effects include hyperuricemia and hyponatremia. Uric acid and sodium levels should be monitored more closely in patients with history of gout and hyponatremia and in patients who are on other agents that increase uric acid or decrease sodium. Thiazide diuretics may also cause hyperglycemia at doses beyond what is considered usual care. It is not unreasonable to monitor blood glucose more closely in patients with diabetes mellitus. The thiazide diuretics also increase urinary frequency, especially upon initiation or dose increases. It is recommended that patients administer the medications in the morning to prevent nocturnal diuresis.

First-Line Treatment—ACE Inhibitors, Angiotensin Receptor Blockers, and Dihydropyridine Calcium Channel Blockers

Selection of the second medication class in patients without compelling indications should be based on efficacy and tolerability. Angiotensin-converting enzyme inhibitors (ACE-I), angiotensin receptor blockers (ARB), and dihydropyridine calcium channel blockers (D-CCB) should be considered. JNC 7 and the AHA guidelines recommend these classes of medications because of supporting evidence to reduce at least one HTN-related complication.

When discussing the ACE-I class, it is generally accepted that each medication will produce similar results (i.e., there is a class effect). Medications in the drug class have been studied extensively in patients with HTN. Studies comparing ACE-I with placebo have noted a reduction in cardiovascular death, MI, and stroke. Reduction in these end points is thought to be unrelated to the BP lowering achieved (average BP reduction 3–5/2–3.6 mm Hg).[5,16–18] Hyperkalemia is the most common adverse effect with ACE-Is. Hyperkalemia is more pronounced in patients with CKD or those taking other medications that increase potassium (ARBs, direct renin inhibitors, potassium-sparing diuretics, aldosterone antagonists). Dry cough is another common adverse effect that is caused by an increase in bradykinin. ACE-I-induced cough is sometimes confused with symptoms related to other disease states. It is advised that a detailed history of the onset of the cough is obtained prior to discontinuing the ACE-I. ACE-Is are contraindicated in patients with bilateral renal artery stenosis, as administration of an ACE-I in this patient population can induce acute kidney injury. A minimal raise in serum creatinine should be expected when ACE-I are initiation. However, if the serum creatinine increases >30% of the baseline value, the ACE-I should be discontinued. ACE-Is are FDA pregnancy category C in the first trimester and category D in the second and third trimesters. It is recommended that ACE-I should not be used in pregnancy. A rare, but serious adverse effect of ACE-I is angioedema (swelling of the tongue, mouth, throat). Patients with a history of angioedema should avoid ACE-I. If a patient experiences angioedema for the first time while taking an ACE-I, it should be discontinued immediately and the patient should not be rechallenged.

ARBs also exhibit a class effect related to reduction in cardiovascular end points. They are considered second-line therapy in patients who experience intolerable cough while taking an ACE-I. Results of studies have indicated ARBs reduce rates of ischemic heart disease, renal failure, and stroke. ARBs have a similar adverse effect profile as the ACE-I. Because the impact of ARBs is similar to that of the ACE-I, it is recommended to initiate an ARB in patients who are not able to tolerate an ACE-I due to cough. Based on mechanism of action, the ARBs do not increase levels of bradykinin, therefore are not likely to induce a cough. The risk of angioedema is also associated with ARB use, but less commonly than with ACE-I. In patients who experience ACE-I-induced angioedema, without history of hereditary angioedema, it is reasonable to consider a trial of an ARB for HTN treatment, particularly in patients with compelling indications. The approximate risk of the patient to have ARB-induced angioedema after experiencing angioedema while taking an ACE-I is 8%.[19] ARB use is also contraindicated in pregnancy with the same risk categories as ACE-I.

The D-CCB, amlodipine, was included in the ALLHAT analysis that showed no difference in the primary outcome (fatal CHD or nonfatal MI) when compared with chlorthalidone and lisinopril.[18] To maintain BP control, it is recommended to use the longer acting D-CCB agents (amlodipine, felodipine, sustained-release nicardipine, long acting nifedipine). Adverse effects of D-CCB include peripheral edema (dose related), headache, flushing, and tachycardia. Laboratory monitoring is not needed for these agents.

Beta-blockers (BB) have fallen out of favor as a first-line treatment option, unless compelling indications warrant their use. Reason for this is likely due to data presented in multiple meta-analyses that primarily included trials that used atenolol once daily. The half-life of atenolol is similar to that of carvedilol and metoprolol that are dosed twice daily as immediate-release products. The historical use of atenolol once daily may not be appropriate for maintaining steady state, resulting in inconsistent control of BP.

Combination Therapy

The majority of patients treated for HTN require more than one medication to achieve BP goals. Understanding the use of multiple antihypertensive agents allows the clinician to select the best possible combination to reduce the BP while minimizing the risk of adverse effects. Selection of combination therapy should be based on complementary (not similar) mechanisms of action. This will more effectively lower the BP without creating additive adverse effects. Two reviews have been published on selecting combination therapy.[20,21] Both reviews recommend the following medication combinations: thiazide diuretic plus either an ACE-I or an ARB or D-CCB or BB and D-CCB plus either an ACE-I or an ARB. These combinations have been shown to produce additive or synergistic BP lowering effects. The combination of ACE-I or ARB plus D-CCB seems to not only have an additive BP lowering effect, but also decreases frequency of peripheral edema caused by the D-CCB. It is recommended that a combination of thiazide diuretic plus BB is reserved for patients with angina or existing coronary heart disease, as this combination has led to a higher rate of new-onset diabetes mellitus compared with the combination of ARB plus D-CCB.

Assessing Safety and Efficacy of Treatment

Follow-up assessment time period should be individualized for each patient and his or her presenting comorbid conditions. Generally, to assess efficacy, follow-up should be scheduled 1 month following a change in medication therapy. In certain situations (elderly, CKD, orthostatic hypotension), follow-up should be scheduled within 1–2 weeks to assess the safety of the treatment changes (including symptoms and laboratory monitoring if necessary). Once the patient has reached their BP goal and is not experiencing medication adverse effects, it is reasonable to follow up with the patient every 6–12 months.

Special Patient Populations

Pregnancy

HTN is the most common medical problem during pregnancy. If left untreated, it can result in complications to the mother and child. Treatment goals of HTN during pregnancy are to extend the gestational age of the child while minimizing adverse effects from medication exposure. The Report of the National High Blood Pressure Education Program Working Group on High Blood Pressure in Pregnancy recommends initiation of medication therapy when the BP is ≥160/105 mm Hg.[22] The goal BP has not been established. The reason for pharmacotherapy initiation at higher BP levels during pregnancy is due to the lack of evidence to support reduced complications (preeclampsia, neonatal death, preterm birth, small for gestational age). BP also decreases during the first half of pregnancy. This helps to reduce or eliminate the need to use medications for treatment.

The drug of choice in pregnancy is methyldopa based on available evidence. However, methyldopa causes somnolence and may not be well tolerated. Labetalol is a good alternative to methyldopa, as there is clinical experience with the agent in pregnancy and is better tolerated than methyldopa. It is thought that use of other BB is generally safe. However, atenolol has been associated with growth restriction. Calcium channel blockers have been most frequently used late in pregnancy. Use of nifedipine starting in the second trimester did not result in harm or improved outcomes. Diuretics should not be considered first-line therapy, but can be safely continued if initiated prior to conception or initiated prior to mid-pregnancy. The reason for this is due to a theoretical concern of decreased plasma volume (which contributes to preeclampsia). It is recommended that the lowest possible dose of the diuretic be used during pregnancy. It should be noted that ACE-I and ARB are contraindicated in pregnancy due to risk of growth restriction, neonatal renal failure, and death.

Elderly

Prevalence of HTN increases with age. Patients ≥65 years are also more likely to have HTN-related complications such as CVD and renal insufficiency. The very elderly ≥80 years also have a significantly increased risk of developing isolated systolic HTN. However, few clinical studies have included this patient population. In 2011, the American College of Cardiology Foundation (ACCF) and AHA published a consensus document on treatment of HTN in the elderly.[23] Because of the lack of evidence, the consensus document is primarily based on expert opinion. They recommend four components to assessment of HTN in the elderly; "1) identify reversible/treatable causes of hypertension; 2) evaluate the patient for organ damage; 3) assess for CVD risk factors and comorbid conditions that affect the prognosis; 4) identify barriers to treatment adherence." BP treatment goals of <140/90 mm Hg are based on expert opinion in this patient population. However, it is important to pay close attention to the diastolic BP to ensure is does not fall below 50 mm Hg. It is recommended that treatment goals be individualized based on the current overall status of the patient.

The hypertension in the very elderly (HYVET) trial was the first to assess treatment of hypertension in patients ≥80 years.[24] The study randomized patients to receive placebo or indapamide ± perindopril to achieve a target BP of <150/80. The study was discontinued early due to the higher incidence of death (21%) in the placebo group. As a result of this study, it is recommended to continue to treat the very elderly patient population with pharmacotherapy.

Medication use needs to be individualized to the patients' comorbid conditions and concurrent medications. The risk of drug interactions and nonadherence increases with the number of medications the patient is taking. It is also recommended to start with lower doses, monitor more frequently, and titrate medications more slowly.

Resistant (Difficult-to-Treat) Hypertension

Resistant HTN is defined as uncontrolled BP despite use of three antihypertensive agents (at least one is a diuretic) at optimal doses.[25] Resistant HTN can also be misdiagnosed if patients present with medication nonadherence, white-coat HTN (BP elevations only in the clinical setting), or if BP was inappropriately measured. If medication nonadherence is suspected, a thorough medication history should be obtained to assess the reasons for nonadherence. In a patient with true resistant HTN, secondary causes should be considered. The most common causes of secondary HTN include obstructive sleep apnea, CKD, primary hyperaldosteronism, and drug-induced HTN.

Obstructive sleep apnea occurs most commonly in obese patients. Symptoms include snoring, not feeling well rested after sleep, witnessed episodes of apnea, and excessive daytime fatigue. Patients who present with these symptoms should be evaluated by a physician, as treatment of obstructive sleep apnea may be indicated and can significantly improve BP control.

CKD is an HTN-related complication, but can also worsen HTN. It is thought that treatment resistance is due to sodium and fluid retention with intravascular volume expansion. ACE-I or ARBs and diuretics should be initiated in this patient population with close monitoring of potassium and serum creatinine. Patients with CKD will also benefit from sodium restriction.

Primary hyperaldosteronism has recently been demonstrated to occur more frequently than previously thought. This condition is assessed by using a morning plasma aldosterone/renin ratio. A ratio of >20 or an aldosterone level >15 ng/dL is suggestive of primary hyperaldosteronism. It is recommended that the patient is referred to an HTN specialist or endocrinologist to confirm the diagnosis.[26] Once a diagnosis is made, treatment with an aldosterone antagonist (spironolactone or eplerenone) is preferred. In patients who experience gynecomastia while taking spironolactone, eplerenone is an appropriate alternative agent. In patients who cannot tolerate either of these agents, amiloride (an indirect aldosterone antagonist) is the treatment of choice. With all of these agents, it is important to monitor potassium and serum creatinine periodically.

Drug-induced HTN occurs with some commonly used medications. These include nonsteroidal anti-inflammatory agents, oral contraceptives (estrogen), sympathomimetics (cocaine, amphetamines, decongestants), and certain antidepressants (bupropion, tricyclic antidepressants, selective serotonin/norepinephrine reuptake inhibitors). Other agents that are less likely to cause HTN include corticosteroids, cyclosporine, tacrolimus, ergot alkaloids, erythropoietin, and monoamine oxidase inhibitors. Select herbal supplements can increase BP including ginseng, ephedra, ma huang, and bitter orange. A complete medication use history is important to identify these agents as the potential cause of resistant HTN.[26]

The other less common causes of secondary HTN include renal artery stenosis, pheochromocytoma, Cushing's disease, hyperparathyroidism, aortic coarctation, and intracranial tumor.

Hypertensive Urgency and Emergency

Hypertensive urgency (also referred to as severe asymptomatic HTN) is defined as BP ≥180/110 mm Hg without symptoms or signs of end-organ damage.[4,27] Hypertensive emergency is defined as elevated BP with symptoms or signs of end-organ damage (e.g., encephalopathy, intracranial hemorrhage, acute MI, unstable angina, acute left ventricular failure with pulmonary edema, and dissecting aortic aneurysm). Symptoms of these conditions may include but are not limited to chest pain, shortness of breath, weakness on one side of the body, slurred speech, visual changes, and severe headache. Treatment of these conditions can range from the addition of another antihypertensive agent to admission to the intensive care unit. Patients who present with hypertensive urgency should be referred to their primary care provider for assessment and treatment. Patients who present with hypertensive emergency should be immediately referred to the closest emergency department. It is important that the patient be instructed not to drive themselves to the emergency department, it is best to call 911.

■ SERVICE DEVELOPMENT

Developing Scope of Services

When developing the scope of services to provide at your practice, first consider the feasibility of implementing the services and determine if a collaborative practice agreement (CPA) is needed. When determining the feasibility of the service at your practice site, you need to consider the patient population you serve, the physical limitations of your clinical site, and the time required to implement the service (for both professional and nonprofessional staff). Many of these items have been addressed by Dr. Gross in the interview that follows in this chapter. She describes how a service for HTN was developed at her practice site. It was designed to work into an existing workflow with multiple staff members involved (both professional and nonprofessional). There was a clear indication for the need of the service based on local data indicating that patients in the region had poorly controlled HTN. You do not need to go out and perform an observational study to determine if there is a need in your area. There are national public access surveys that exist (with data available at the county level). One of such surveys is the Behavioral Risk Factor Surveillance System (BRFSS). This is a telephone survey conducted annually by the Centers for Disease Control and Prevention (CDC). Online access is available at http://www.cdc.gov/brfss/index.htm. There are questions available to assist with determining prevalence of diseases such as diabetes, asthma, CVD, and tobacco use. There is not a question specific to HTN; however, data is available on the prevalence of MI, coronary heart disease, and stroke. Survey results are available as national, state, county, or city data.

An additional method to obtain data is to utilize the prescription software at your site to determine the number of patients who take medications that are commonly used for HTN. This can give you an idea about the number of current patients in your pharmacy may be interested in the new clinical service. The final and most labor-intensive method to determine patient interest is to just ask! A short simple patient questionnaire can be developed to determine the needs and interests of the patient population you serve. Another strategy would be to develop contracts with self-insured employers, similar to the description that Dr. Gross provides in the interview.

Once you determine there is a need for a clinical service in HTN, you will need to develop the scope of the service. The scope of service describes the process/procedure of the service. For example, the service could include measuring BP/pulse/orthostatic BPs, providing patient education about lifestyle modifications, medications, and medication adherence; adjusting medication doses based on patient response; and ordering laboratory tests to monitor medication side effects.

You will also want to include a section for "what if's." What will you do when the patient's BP is considered hypertensive urgency or emergency; the patient has chest pain; the patient reports symptoms of orthostasis. Having a prearranged action plan will assist in the event of minor and major medical emergencies.

The scope of services that you select will depend on patient needs in your area, but will also be dependent on if the services require a CPA. A CPA is an agreement between a physician and (in this case) a pharmacist. The CPA defines the scope of services that can be conducted by a pharmacist under the supervision of the physician. You will need to check with your state board of pharmacy to determine if there are existing rules/regulations for CPA's in your state. Items of specific interest to include in a CPA for HTN services would be to define the physical exam you are able to conduct (BP, pulse, orthostatic BPs), the medications you are able to adjust, and the laboratory values you are able to order. It would also be important to define the process for the potential urgent or emergent medical situations that could develop in this patient population that are mentioned above. Selecting a physician to work with as the supervising physician for a CPA does not need to be difficult. The easiest person to approach first would be a local physician with whom you have an existing professional relationship. Look for someone who trusts you as an extension of his/her practice (someone who calls regularly to ask drug information questions or someone who frequently refers patients to your pharmacy). You will also need to determine if you will need multiple providers to serve as supervising physicians to the CPA or if you need medical professionals from multiple different disciplines (i.e., dietitian, physical therapy, and exercise physiologist).

Communicating with the Primary Care Provider

Once you establish a scope of practice and have completed a CPA (if needed), you also need to determine how you will communicate patient information you document with the patient's primary care provider. Without communication to the patient's primary care provider, you might as well not develop the service! Most physicians receive communication from patient appointments with specialists via facsimile. You also have the option to mail the documentation, or call the provider directly in the event of an urgent medical situation. When documenting care that you provide, it is important to use a documentation style the primary care provider is familiar with (SOAP format). When documenting recommended changes to the patient's medication regimen, it is important to also provide a succinct rationale for the changes. This will help to improve the acceptance rate of your recommendations.

Patient Education Materials

Developing a library of patient education materials can be very helpful when educating patients about lifestyle modifications and medication adherence. There are many premade materials developed for HTN available online from the National Heart, Lung and Blood Institute (available at: http://www.nhlbi.nih.gov) and from the AHA (available at: http://heart.org). Items of importance to keep on hand include information on the dietary approaches to stop hypertension (DASH) diet, reducing sodium consumption, physical activity, monitoring log for home BP measurements, and aids to improve medication adherence.

Incorporating a Hypertension Service into the Workflow of a Community Pharmacy

A service for HTN can be developed using several different methods. You may elect to have a block of time dedicated to the service for patient appointments, or you could offer a walk-in service. With either method, it is important that it does not disrupt your existing workflow too much. The benefits of a dedicated block of time are that you can plan for extra staffing needs, but it may not be convenient for your patients. A walk-in service has increased convenience for the patient, but can significantly disrupt other workflow of the pharmacy, as you are not able to anticipate increased staffing needs. At first, when the service is new and you are still recruiting patients to enroll in the service, a walk-in service may not significantly disrupt the pharmacy workflow, but as you become busier, you may need to revisit implementing scheduled appointments.

As with any service, it is important that you identify what patient care tasks can be delegated to non-professional staff. For example, you may be able to train the technicians to schedule appointments, call physician offices to obtain patient's most recent laboratory data, print the patients' medication profile and pull patient records prior to the appointment, check BP and pulse, and make copies of patient education materials and documentation forms. Delegating these types of tasks permits the pharmacist additional time to complete the patient interview and assessment, provide education, develop a treatment plan, document the care provided, and communicate with patient's primary care provider.

Marketing the Service

Many patients have been diagnosed with HTN, but since the disease has no symptoms, they may not understand the importance of controlling their BP. One marketing technique would be to use materials to educate patients on the complications of uncontrolled HTN. This will help the patient understand the need for the service. The most unique aspect of clinical pharmacist services in community pharmacies is the accessibility of the service to the patient. The patient is (hopefully) in the building at least monthly. Use this as a mechanism to let patients know one-on-one that they may benefit from a new service you are offering. The more personal your marketing technique, the more successful the method will be. The service may be able to be provided while the patient waits for his/her medications to be filled (i.e., measure the BP and provide education on the disease state, lifestyle modifications, and medications).

Marketing to physicians is only needed if you are going to rely on the physicians for referrals. If this is the case, you will want to take a cue from the pharmaceutical companies and implement relationship marketing. Schedule face-to-face time to meet with the physician to describe the service and how it can benefit patients in his/her practice. Be sure to indicate that you are not "taking patients away" from them, but working together to improve patient outcomes. A busy physician will appreciate the help, but be prepared for those who are not interested. You may want to try to anticipate all questions that could arise during your conversation with the physician so that you are able to answer them right away. If you are not able to schedule significant time to meet with the physician, have a shortened version of the description of the service ready to be able to run by the physician in 30 seconds (i.e., elevator speech). This version of the description of the service should be the highlights of the service with a focus on benefits to the patient and the physician's busy practice.

Developing a Business Plan

Components of a business plan that are specific to an HTN service include purchasing of the supplies needed to accurately measure the patients' BP and pulse, and space required to conduct the service (a quiet room is preferable). If you have included measurement of orthostatic BPs, you will also need an exam table that permits the patient to lie flat. These start-up costs are all fixed costs and once purchased will not regularly need to be replaced. There are only minor expenses needed to maintain a service for HTN beyond compensation for time of the personnel required to conduct the service. These expenses include copying or purchasing of replacement patient education materials, maintaining a method used for communication to the patients' primary care providers (facsimile, Internet, telephone), and training of new staff.

■ HYPERTENSION: PATIENT CASE

K. Cormier has come to the pharmacy today and has been seen by his physician (Dr. Stone) earlier this morning. The patient would like to discuss his desire to start an herbal weight loss medication. Dr. Stone, with whom the pharmacist has established medication therapy management (MTM) services, would also like the pharmacist to discuss any possible medication changes and counsel as needed for better BP control. K. Cormier's BP seems to be elevated this morning. In fact, it was so elevated that Dr. Stone gave the patient clonidine to decrease the BP a few minutes ago. The patient states, "I stopped one of my BP medications because it made me tired all the time. I need the energy to start exercising and losing weight."

Vital Signs (per patient records brought with him from his clinic visit)

BP	172/104 mm Hg (right arm, sitting; average of two measurements)
	138/86 mm Hg (right arm, sitting; recorded 40 minutes after 0.1 mg clonidine given)
	Recheck by MTM services by the pharmacist was 130/82 mm Hg (right arm, sitting)
T	98.6°F–37.0°C
RR	18 breaths/minute
HR	90 beats/minute
	Recheck by MTM services by the pharmacist was 84 beats/minute
WT	200 lbs
HT	5 ft 6 in
BMI	32
Name	Kurt Cormier
Age	50 years of age
Setting	Pharmacy (MTM services)
Appearance	Normal—experiencing no symptoms
Chief Complaint	"Can't I take another blood pressure medication that won't make me tired all the time? I need the energy to exercise and lose weight!"

History of Present Illness (obtained through appropriate questioning)

Dr. Jones started Mr. Cormier on a new BP medication called atenolol about 1 month ago, and the patient is at the clinic today for a follow-up visit (and now presenting to the pharmacist for

MTM services). However, Mr. Cormier stopped the new BP medication about a week ago because he was feeling "tired and lethargic since starting that medication." Mr. Cormier knows that his BP is pretty high today, so he has been afraid to tell Dr. Stone that he stopped the atenolol. Dr. Stone gave Mr. Cormier a pill called "clonidine" a few hours ago to help decrease the BP.

Also, Mr. Cormier wants to lose weight. He is now motivated because he received and started taking "Go-Phed," an herbal medicine, through the Internet about a week ago. Although Mr. Cormier did not tell Dr. Stone that he has started taking this herbal medicine, he shares this information with the pharmacist. Mr. Cormier hopes that the pharmacist will say that the herbal medicine is a good weight-loss drug.

Mr. Cormier states that his tiredness and sluggishness does not occur during a specific time of day. It has been "all the time after starting the medicine for my heart (atenolol)!"

The pharmacist decides to ask these further questions:

Did Dr. Stone do anything for his high BP already?
He gave me some pill called "clonidine" to get the BP down quickly.
Does he ever check his BP at home or at a pharmacy or store?
No
Does he ever have fluid buildup in his legs or feet?
No
Is he ever short of breath?
No
What about when he walks a long distance?
Only after a few miles, but I never usually walk that far.
How many pillows does he sleep on at night?
One
How is his diet?
Much better now; eating three small meals a day and a light snack at bedtime.
How often does he exercise?
None over the past month, but I have walked down my street and back twice a day over the past week.
Does he feel like he has more energy?
I do since starting Go-Phed a week ago.
How often does he check his sugar?
Twice a day, before breakfast and supper.
Does he keep a record of his sugar readings?
Yes, but I forgot my book.
Is his diabetes controlled?
Dr. Stone says that my A1C was under 7 last time it was checked.

Past Medical History

Disease states: Mr. Cormier has had high BP for 15 years, diabetes for 10 years, and heart failure for 1 year. Mr. Cormier would like to start exercising to keep his "sugars" under control, as they have become much better controlled since Dr. Stone started him on insulin. Mr. Cormier did have some shortness of breath and edema in his lower legs and feet related to his heart failure a year ago, but Dr. Stone started "that water pill" and it has been better ever since then.

Meds (all medications received from this pharmacy)

Valsartan 40 mg twice daily × 1 year
Furosemide 20 mg once daily × 1 year
Metformin 1000 mg twice daily × 10 years
Glargine 20 units injected once daily × 3 months
Atenolol 100 mg daily × 1 month (but stopped 1 week ago)
Herbal: Go-Phed (with ephedra, licorice, and ginseng on label) one capsule three times daily

Mr. Cormier has bottles for all of these medications. Mr. Cormier left his vial of insulin at home.

Mr. Cormier takes all the medications (except atenolol) just like they have been prescribed, and he hardly ever misses taking them. *Mr. Cormier stopped taking atenolol abruptly 1 week ago.*

Mr. Cormier has not had any side effects from any of the medications, as far as he knows.

Mr. Cormier has an allergy to ACE inhibitors (cough).

No history of heart attack or stroke.

No past surgeries.

Health Maintenance

Mr. Cormier has never been hospitalized. Mr. Cormier's last visit (besides today) to Dr. Stone was 1 month ago.

Nonsmoker. No alcohol use.

No illegal drug use.

Mr. Cormier feels like he has gotten much better control of his diet, although he admits to "splurging" occasionally.

Mr. Cormier would consider himself having only a moderate amount of stress. However, he is a little stressed trying to take off some of his "extra weight" to get back into the dating scene.

Family History

Mr. Cormier has both parents, still living in their 70s. His father is on medicine for diabetes, but otherwise both parents are in good health. He has an older brother who is healthy.

Social History

Mr. Cormier divorced his first spouse 10 years ago but is now "in a relationship" with someone.

He has a grown daughter from a previous spouse, but she doesn't come to visit often. He is a moderately successful writer of children's books.

Did Mr. Cormier have hypertensive urgency or emergency?
He displayed urgency because he did not have any symptoms of target organ damage that is associated with hypertensive emergency, such as acute chest pain, severe headache, confusion, dizziness, blurry vision, shortness of breath, or hemoptysis.

Did Dr. Stone treat the patient's hypertensive urgency appropriately?
Yes. Clonidine was given, and the BP was rechecked and the patient was not allowed to leave the clinic until the BP was reduced appropriately. Other possible medications that could have been given include labetalol or captopril due to their short onset of action.

A possible cause for the hypertensive urgency was not discussed. What would be the possible cause?
Actually, the patient has two possible reasons for the hypertensive crises. He stopped taking atenolol, and rebound HTN may result when stopping a BB abruptly. Also, the patient began taking an herbal medication with ephedra, which can increase BP (also, licorice has been known to increase BP, as well). Both of these events happened a week ago and could have contributed to the hypertensive crisis state.

What would be the best course of action for this patient at this time?
Mr. Cormier should be started on another BB (not atenolol) as indicated below and titrated up to the appropriate target dose for a patient with heart failure. Also, the patient should be instructed to stop the herbal medication and counseled on how such herbal medications could precipitate a hypertensive crisis.

Is he on appropriate antihypertensive medications for his concomitant disease states?
He is taking an appropriate ARB for his heart failure, as he has an intolerance to ACE-I. However, he should be taking either carvedilol or metoprolol succinate at appropriate target doses rather than atenolol. Atenolol is not indicated for use in patients with heart failure.

Are his concomitant disease states well controlled?
Both diabetes and heart failure seem to be well controlled. The patient has an HbA1c <7%, which is the goal according to the American Diabetes Association guidelines. He also does not have any symptoms associated with heart failure, such as lower extremity edema and increased shortness of breath or dyspnea on exertion.

IMPLEMENTING SERVICES FOR HYPERTENSION IN AN INDEPENDENT COMMUNITY PHARMACY—AN INTERVIEW

Brooke W. Gross, PharmD
Clinical Pharmacist; Clinical Management Concepts, Johnson City, TN

Q: Why did you decide to establish a service for HTN?
We decided to establish services for HTN based on the demographics of the patient population in the region we serve. There is a high incidence rate of HTN, with a high number of patients who have uncontrolled disease. The service also fits as part of an existing group of other disease states that were offered by the company to local employers including diabetes mellitus, dyslipidemia, tobacco cessation, asthma, and weight loss.

Q: How did you go about establishing a service for HTN?
The wellness team including clinical pharmacists and a registered nurse was conducting health risk assessments as part of an employer-based program. When developing relationships and contracts with the local employers, they are given the opportunity to select the clinical services they would like their employees (and family members) to receive. A medical director (local primary care physician) provides oversight for all clinical services provided. A protocol for the scope of practice was developed and agreed upon by the medical director and clinical pharmacists. The current protocol permits measuring of BP, educating patients about the disease state and medications, and ordering labs to monitor treatment. Recommendations for medication changes are sent to the patients' primary care provider. The program also provides a co-pay waiver for the medications specific to the disease state program in which they are enrolled. However, not all contracts elect to include the co-pay waiver as part of the benefit to their employees.

To prepare for a patient appointment, approximately 1 week prior to the appointment, the pharmacist (and student pharmacists) reviews the patient's chart to anticipate the focus of the appointment, as well as to determine if there is a need to obtain information from the patient's primary care provider prior to the appointment (e.g., labs, recent changes in health status). As a means for quality assurance, we have a pharmacist review patient charts following each appointment. The role of this review is to provide recommendations for the follow-up appointment that may be overlooked during the patient appointment due to other concerns the patient may have. In some situations, the recommendations left are urgent, in which case the patient is contacted immediately instead of waiting for a follow-up appointment to address the problem.

Q: What method do you use to communicate patient information to local physicians and mid-level providers?
Most of the local providers prefer communication via fax to send and receive information. We can obtain recent lab results from the primary care provider or send them the results of the tests that we ordered. We will also fax medication recommendations when we identify drug-related problems. Sometimes, with lower priority items, we encourage the patient to be proactive and communicate recommendations to the physician. This helps to encourage the patient to play an active role in their care.

Q: What references/resources did you find helpful when developing the service?
The most helpful reference materials were the current JNC7 guidelines, Diabetes Standards of Care, and information on the DASH diet. We also use resources from pharmaceutical companies for patient education materials.

Q: *How do you incorporate nonpharmacist staff to assist with the service?*

A: In addition to the four clinical pharmacist staff, we also have a registered nurse, dietician, and student pharmacists who assist with educating patients related to HTN. The nonprofessional staff are responsible for scheduling patient appointments and sending reminders to the patients about their appointments.

Q: *How do you go about marketing the service? Did you have any difficulty obtaining referrals from local employers?*

Marketing of the service is done as a bundle to local employers. In the past, this was done by a nonpharmacist staff member, but now is being conducted by the pharmacist clinical director and an additional pharmacist who dedicates a portion of his/her efforts to marketing. When marketing to local employers, there are multiple services discussed at one time that include clinical pharmacist services. We do not directly market our clinical services to patients or providers who are not part of the employer-based contracts.

Q: *How do you assess the success of the HTN service?*

We utilize quality improvement indicators such as BP and other disease markers of each patient enrolled in a chronic disease management program. These reports are generated quarterly to semiannually and are shared with the clinical pharmacist team and the employers. This data is also used internally to improve the care provided to patients. The data is used externally to maintain contracts with the local employers and for marketing to gain new employer contracts. The end points selected for reporting were first modeled after the Asheville Project, and then tailored to the disease states we expanded to include.

Q: *What barriers did you encounter in developing the HTN service?*

One of our biggest barriers is communicating with primary care providers. Since the provider did not refer the patient to the service, some view our recommendations and requests for patient information as unnecessary. Developing relationships with the patients in this region is also difficult. There are sometimes language, dialect, and cultural differences that interfere with appropriate communication with patients.

Q: *What benefits have been observed that you may not have anticipated from initiating services for HTN?*

We have noticed an increase in both over-the-counter and prescription volume at the pharmacy. This may be due to the waived co-payment for the medications for the disease state program the patients are enrolled in. However, most patients who live locally will use our pharmacy to obtain all of their medications. The patients who are enrolled in the program and do not take advantage of the waived co-pay program usually live a significant distance from our pharmacy.

Q: *Do you have any tips for other pharmacists interested in starting a similar service?*

A: We have had great success with establishing relationships with local employers as a means to grow these services. The key to the success of the program has been well-developed protocols and policies/procedures. I would recommend that these be in place prior to enrollment of your first patient in the program. Developing a sound flow sheet for patient care can help streamline a service. Don't forget to continuously update these materials. New information is always coming; therefore, it is vital to use new literature and guidelines to direct patient care and medication recommendations.

SUMMARY POINTS

- Thirty percent of Americans have HTN with increasing incidence with age.
- Uncontrolled HTN can lead to end-organ damage that includes cerebral vascular accidents, transient ischemic attacks, dementia, retinopathy, heart failure resulting from left ventricular hypertrophy, angina, MI, CKD, and peripheral vascular disease.
- Treatment goals vary among professional organizations that have developed treatment guidelines for HTN. JNC 7 recommends a goal BP of <140/90 for most patients, except for those with CKD and diabetes, in which the goal is <130/80. The AHA recommends the following treatment goals: (1) <120/80 for patients with left ventricular dysfunction; (2) <130/80 for patients with history of coronary artery disease, noncoronary atherosclerotic vascular disease, Framingham risk score of >10%, diabetes mellitus, CKD; (3) <140/90 for patients who do not meet the above recommendations.
- Proper measurement of BP is important to assessing treatment efficacy. It is important to ensure the proper cuff size and placement, patient position, and placement of the bell to listen for Korotkoff sounds.
- BP can be improved with implementation of lifestyle interventions. These changes include weight loss, DASH diet, salt restriction, and physical activity. On average, the systolic BP will be lowered 5–20 mm Hg with 10 kg weight loss, 8-14 mm Hg with DASH diet, 2-8 mm Hg with salt restriction (<2.4 g/day sodium), and 4-9 mm Hg with 30 minutes of physical activity per day most days of the week.
- First-line therapy for patients without a compelling indication for treatment of HTN is thiazide diuretics. However, the following comorbid conditions necessitate alternate treatment for HTN: systolic heart failure, history of MI, coronary artery disease, diabetes mellitus, CKD, and stroke (cerebral vascular accident or transient ischemic attack).
- Medication selection for initial therapy and for combination therapy should be tailored to the patients' age, race/ethnicity, and comorbid conditions. When using combination therapy, it is best to select medications with complementary (not similar) mechanisms of action to achieve improved outcomes.
- A well-developed service plan and workflow can help alleviate some potential barriers to implementing an HTN service. Some items to consider in the development plan include delegation of responsibilities to nonpharmacists to help improve the efficiency of the workflow; development of a CPA with local physicians; development of a well-defined scope of practice; predetermined communication methods with primary care providers; acquisition of appropriate references, resources, and patient education materials; marketing strategy to ensure success of the service; and a business plan to ensure sustainability of the service.

STUDY QUESTIONS

1. Uncontrolled HTN can lead to which of the following complications?
    a. Heart failure
    b. CKD
    c. MI
    d. Retinopathy
    e. All of the above

2. What is the goal BP for patients with CKD according to JNC 7 and the AHA?
    a. <160/100
    b. <140/90
    c. <130/80
    d. <125/75

3. Which of the following would result in underestimation of the BP?
   a. Using a cuff that is too small
   b. Using a cuff that is too large
   c. Consumption of caffeine within 30 minutes of BP measurement
   d. Exercise within 30 minutes of BP measurement

4. Which of the following would be a first-line drug of choice for a patient who has HTN and history of diabetes mellitus?
   a. Lisinopril
   b. Amlodipine
   c. Metoprolol
   d. Clonidine

5. When comparing the thiazide diuretics, which of the following statements is true?
   a. Hydrochlorothiazide has been included in more clinical trials than chlorthalidone; therefore, it is the drug of choice.
   b. Chlorthalidone has been included in more clinical trials than hydrochlorothiazide; therefore, it is the drug of choice.
   c. Chlorthalidone and hydrochlorothiazide are equipotent.
   d. Available evidence supports the use of either hydrochlorothiazide or chlorthalidone when used at appropriate doses.

6. Which of the following medication combinations is the most appropriate for treatment of HTN in a patient with no compelling indications?
   a. Lisinopril + atenolol
   b. Chlorthalidone + amlodipine
   c. Metoprolol + verapamil
   d. Hydralazine + hydrochlorothiazide

7. What is the goal BP in an elderly patient with isolated systolic HTN?
   a. Goal should be the same for this patient population as it is for others.
   b. Goal should be to control systolic BP without decreasing the diastolic BP below 80.
   c. Goal should be to control systolic BP without decreasing the diastolic BP below 50.
   d. Goal should be to lower the systolic pressure as low as possible without regard to the diastolic BP.

8. Which of the following disease states is considered a secondary cause of HTN?
   a. Heart failure
   b. Primary hyperaldosteronism
   c. Ischemic stroke
   d. MI

9. What is the drug of choice to treat HTN during pregnancy?
   a. Labetalol
   b. Hydrochlorothiazide
   c. Metoprolol
   d. Methyldopa

10. Which of the following tasks should NOT be delegated to nonpharmacist staff for a HTN service?
    a. Making appointment reminder telephone calls to patients
    b. Measuring BP and pulse
    c. Developing treatment plan recommendations
    d. Faxing documentation of the patient encounter to the patient's primary care provider
    e. Obtaining essential laboratory results from the patient's primary care provider

BIBLIOGRAPHY

1. Roger VL, Go AS, Lloyd-Jones DM, et al. Heart disease and stroke statistics 2011 update: a report from the American Heart Association. *Circulation.* 2011;123: e18-e209.
2. CDC. Vital signs: Awareness and treatment of uncontrolled hypertension among adults - United States, 2003-2010. *MMWR.* 2012;61:703-709.
3. CDC. Vital signs: prevalence, treatment, and control of hypertension – United States, 1999–2002 and 2005–2008. *MMWR Morb Mortal Wkly Rep.* 2011;60:103-108.
4. Chobanian AV, Bakris GL, Black HR, et al. Seventh report of the joint national committee on prevention, detection, evaluation, and treatment of high blood pressure. *Hypertension.* 2003;42:1206-1252.
5. Rosendorff C, Black HR, Cannon CP, et al. Treatment of hypertension in the prevention and management of ischemic heart disease: a scientific statement from the American Heart Association Council for high blood pressure research and the Councils on clinical cardiology and epidemiology and prevention. *Circulation.* 2007;115:2761-2788.
6. Levey AS, Rocco MV, Anderson S, et al. National Kidney Foundation K/DOQI clinical practice guidelines on hypertension and antihypertensive agents in chronic kidney disease. *Am J Kidney Dis.* 2004;43(5 Suppl 1): S1-S290.
7. American Diabetes Association. Standards of Medical Care in Diabetes - 2013. *Diabetes Care.* 2013; 36(Suppl 1):S11-S66.
8. Pickering TG, Hall JE, Appel LJ, et al. Recommendations for blood pressure measurement in humans and experimental animals: Part 1: blood pressure measurement in humans: a statement for professionals from the subcommittee of professional and public education of the American Heart Association Council for high blood pressure research. *Hypertension.* 2005;45:142-161.
9. Powers BJ, Olsen MK, Smith VA, et al. Measuring blood pressure for decision making and quality reporting: where and how many measures? *Ann Int Med.* 2011;154:781-788.
10. Sclater A, Alagiakrishan K. Orthostatic hypotension: a primary care primer for assessment and treatment. *Geriatrics.* 2004;59:22-27.
11. Lanier JB, Mote MB, Clay EC. Evaluation and management of orthostatic hypotension. *Am Fam Physician.* 2011;84:527-536.
12. Appel LJ, Brands MW, Daniels SR, et al. Dietary approaches to prevent and treat hypertension: a scientific statement from the American Heart Association. *Hypertension.* 2006;47:296-308.
13. U.S. Department of Health and Human Services. 2008 Physical activity guidelines for Americans. http://www.health.gov/paguidelines. Accessed September 25, 2011.
14. Neff KM, Nawarskas JJ. Hydrochlorothiazide versus chlorthalidone in the management of hypertension. *Cardiol Rev.* 2010;18:51-56.
15. Carter BL, Ernst ME, Cohen JD. Hydrochlorothiazide versus chlorthalidone: evidence supporting their interchangeability. *Hypertension.* 2004;43(1):4-9.
16. Perry HM, Davis BR, Price TR, et al. Effect of treating isolated systolic hypertension on the risk of developing various types and subtypes of stroke: the systolic hypertension in the elderly program (SHEP). *JAMA.* 2000;284:465-471.
17. Furberg CD, Wright JT, Davis BR, et al. Major cardiovascular events in hypertensive patients randomized to doxazosin vs chlorthalidone: the antihypertensive and lipid-lowering treatment to prevent heart attack trial (ALLHAT). *JAMA.* 2000;283:1967-1975.
18. Furberg CD, Wright JT, Davis BR, et al. Major outcomes in high-risk hypertensive patients randomized to angiotensin-converting enzyme inhibitor or calcium channel blocker vs diuretic: the antihypertensive and lipid-lowering treatment to prevent heart attack trial (ALLHAT). *JAMA.* 2002;288:2981-2997.
19. Cicardi M, Zingale LC, Bergamaschini L, et al. Angioedema associated with angiotensin-converting enzyme inhibitor use. *Arch Intern Med.* 2004;164: 910-913.
20. Sood N, Reinhart KM, Baker WL. Combination therapy for the management of hypertension: a review of the evidence. *Am J Health Syst Pharm.* 2010;67:885-894.
21. Frank J. Managing hypertension using combination therapy. *Am Fam Physician.* 2008;77:1279-1286.
22. Report of the national high blood pressure education program working group on high blood pressure in pregnancy. *Am J Obstet Gynecol.* 2000;183(1):S1-S22.
23. Aronow WS, Fleg JL, Pepine CJ, et al. ACCF/AHA 2011 expert consensus document on hypertension in the elderly: a report of the American College of Cardiology Foundation task force on clinical expert consensus documents. *Circulation.* 2011;123:2434-2506.

24. Beckett NS, Peters R, Fletcher AE, et al. Treatment of hypertension in patients 80 years of age or older. *N Engl J Med.* 2008;358:1887-1898.
25. Calhoun DA, Jones D, Textor S, et al. Resistant hypertension: diagnosis, evaluation, and treatment: a scientific statement from the American Heart Association Professional Education Committee of the Council for High Blood Pressure Research. *Hypertension.* 2008;51:1403-1419.
26. Viera AJ, Hinderliter AL. Evaluation and management of the patient with difficult-to-control or resistant hypertension. *Am Fam Physician.* 2009;79:863-869.
27. Kessler CS, Joudeh Y. Evaluation and treatment of severe asymptomatic hypertension. *Am Fam Physician.* 2010;81:470-476.

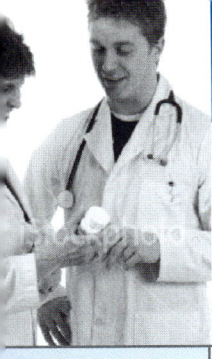

13

OSTEOPOROSIS

Lisa M. Lundquist and Liza G. Chapman

■ LEARNING OBJECTIVES

After reading this chapter, the pharmacy student, community practice resident, or pharmacist should be able to:

1. Utilize the current osteoporosis clinical guidelines to differentiate normal bone health, osteoporosis, and osteopenia.
2. Evaluate benefits and barriers of available bone densitometry devices and methods.
3. Develop osteoporosis screening services within a community pharmacy practice setting including marketing, primary care provider collaboration, and follow-up.
4. Recommend patient-specific over-the-counter (OTC) and prescription medication treatment regimens and lifestyle modifications.

BACKGROUND

Osteoporosis is a silent disease that is characterized by low bone mass, deterioration of bone architecture, and increase risk of fracture. According to the National Osteoporosis Foundation (NOF), osteoporosis is estimated to be a major health threat for Americans with 55% of people 50 years and older at risk.[1] Of the 43 million people at risk, 10 million have osteoporosis while the other 33 million suffer from low bone density of the hip, putting them at increased risk of osteoporosis.[1]

Osteoporosis exerts a large financial burden on the health system. In 2005, it was estimated that osteoporosis-related complications (such as fractures) cost an imposing $17 billion in the United States. With the aging population, this financial burden is expected to double or triple by the year 2040.[1] Not only is osteoporosis a costly disease, it is also a debilitating disease. Over 430,000 hospital admissions, 2.5 million physician visits, and 180,000 nursing home admissions each year can be attributed to fractures from osteoporosis.[2] Hip fractures are among the most common and debilitating of osteoporosis-related complications.[3] It is estimated that 50% of Caucasian women will experience a fracture related to osteoporosis at some point in their lifetime.[4] As a result of osteoporosis-related fractures, patients may experience a decreased quality of life because of acute and chronic back pain, disability, limited mobility, and loss of height that can all be deleterious results of a fracture.[5] Table 13-1 details nonmodifiable and modifiable risk factors for osteoporosis.

Currently the NOF, American Association of Clinical Endocrinologists (AACE), and International Society of Clinical Densitometry (ISCD) recommend bone mineral density (BMD) screening for all women aged 65 and greater regardless of risk factors, all postmenopausal women with a fracture, postmenopausal women younger than 65 years with one or more risk factors (other than fracture or low sex hormones), and any women who are considering therapy for osteoporosis.[1,6–8] The AACE also recommends testing women with increased risk factors for fractures.[6,7] In addition, ISCD recommends testing women with a disease or taking a medication associated with low bone mass or bone loss.[8] The United States Preventive Services Task Force (USPSTF) recommends routine screening beginning at age 60 for women at increased risk of fracture, and it makes no recommendations for or against routine osteoporosis screening in postmenopausal women who are younger than 60 years or who are not at increased fracture risk.[9]

Pharmacists have the opportunity to play an important role in increasing awareness of bone health and performing osteoporosis screenings. In the community setting, pharmacists are accessible to patients, have an established presence in the community, and have a direct relationship with patients and primary care providers, which provide an optimal setting for osteoporosis screenings.[2] In addition to patient-specific recommendations on prescription and OTC medications,

Table 13-1. Risk Factors for Osteoporosis

Nonmodifiable Risk Factors	Modifiable Risk Factors
• Caucasian or Asian race	• Low body weight
• Advanced age	• Low calcium intake/poor diet
• Female gender	• Alcohol abuse (3 or more drinks per day)
• Family history of fracture in a first-degree relative	• Cigarette smoking
• Personal history of an adult aged fracture	• Inactive lifestyle
• Certain diseases (such as rheumatoid arthritis or anorexia nervosa)	• Low levels of sex hormones

pharmacists can encourage dietary changes to increase calcium intake and promote adherence to osteoporosis-related medications to improve outcomes.

■ THERAPEUTIC GUIDELINES

Osteoporosis is defined by BMD at the hip or spine that is less than 2.5 standard deviations (SD) below the young normal mean reference population (T-score at or below −2.5). Low bone mass or osteopenia is defined as BMD between 1.0 and 2.5 SD below than that of a young normal adult (T-score between −1.0 and −2.5). The World Health Organization has established the following criteria based on BMD measurement at the spine, hip, or forearm by dual-energy x-ray absorptiometry (DXA) devices (Fig. 13-1).

- *Normal*: BMD is within 1 SD of a "young normal" adult (T-score at −1.0 and above).
- *Low bone mass* ("osteopenia"): BMD is between 1.0 and 2.5 SD below than that of a "young normal" adult (T-score between −1.0 and −2.5).

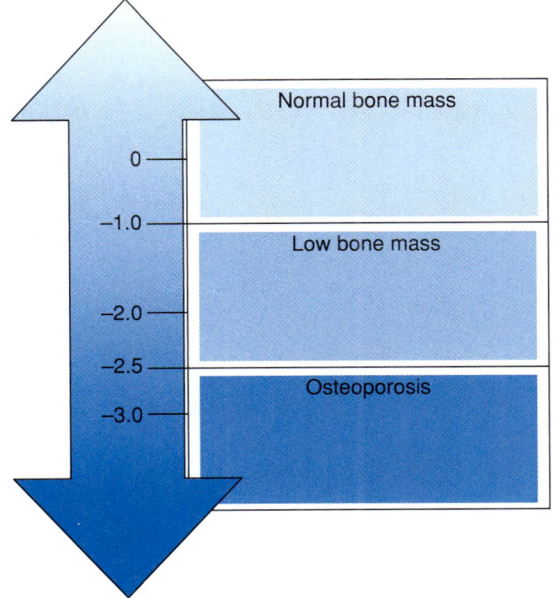

Figure 13-1. Definition Based on BMD Measurement.

- *Osteoporosis*: BMD is 2.5 SD or more below than that of a "young normal" adult (T-score at or below −2.5). Patients in this group who have already experienced one or more fractures are deemed to have severe or "established" osteoporosis.

All postmenopausal women and men over 50 years of age should be assessed for osteoporosis risk.[1] In addition to the modifiable and nonmodifiable risk factors, a number of medical conditions, disease states, and medications have been associated with an increased risk of osteoporosis. Some of the conditions and diseases that may cause bone loss and medications that contribute to an increased osteoporosis and fracture risk are detailed in Table 13-2.

Daily intake of calcium and vitamin D is a safe way to help reduce fracture risk. Adequate calcium intake throughout the lifespan is necessary for achieving sufficient bone mass and maintenance of bone health. Vitamin D plays an integral part in calcium absorption and bone health. The calcium and vitamin D recommendations for all patients defined by the NOF are outlined in Table 13-3.[1] Adults aged 50 years and older should have an intake of calcium of 1200 mg and 800–1000 international units of vitamin D every day from all sources, including food and supplements.[1] Increasing dietary calcium and vitamin D is the first-line approach; however, supplements should be used when an adequate dietary intake cannot be achieved.

There are many calcium-rich foods including milk, yogurt, cheese, broccoli, turnip greens, soy products, tofu, and calcium-fortified foods. Dietary sources of vitamin D include vitamin D-fortified milk and cereal, egg yolks, saltwater fish, and liver. Selected examples of approximate calcium amounts in food sources are:

Dairy foods

   Yogurt (1 cup)—350 mg
   Milk (1 cup)—300 mg
   Cheddar cheese (1 oz.)—200 mg

Table 13-2. Medical Conditions, Disease States, and Medications Associated with an Increased Risk of Osteoporosis

Medical Conditions and Disease States
- AIDS/HIV
- Blood and bone marrow disorders
- Breast cancer
- Chronic kidney disease
- Chronic obstructive pulmonary disease
- Cushing's syndrome
- Depression
- Diabetes
- Eating disorders, especially anorexia nervosa
- Female athlete triad (includes loss of menstrual periods, an eating disorder, and excessive exercise)
- Gastrectomy
- Gastrointestinal bypass procedures
- Hyperparathyroidism
- Hyperthyroidism
- Inflammatory bowel disease, including Crohn's disease and ulcerative colitis
- Liver disease, including biliary cirrhosis
- Lupus
- Lymphoma and leukemia
- Malabsorption syndromes, including celiac disease
- Multiple myeloma
- Multiple sclerosis
- Organ transplants
- Parkinson's disease
- Polio and post-polio syndrome
- Poor diet, including malnutrition
- Premature menopause
- Prostate cancer
- Rheumatoid arthritis
- Scoliosis
- Spinal cord injuries
- Stroke
- Thyrotoxicosis
- Weight loss

Medications
- Aluminum-containing antacids
- Aromatase inhibitors
- Chemotherapeutic drugs
- Cyclosporine A and tacrolimus
- Gonadotropin-releasing hormones
- Heparin
- Lithium
- Medroxyprogesterone acetate for contraception
- Methotrexate
- Phenytoin and phenobarbital
- Proton pump inhibitors
- Raloxifine (premenopausal use)
- Selective serotonin reuptake inhibitors
- Glucocorticosteroids
- Thiazolidinediones
- Thyroid hormones in excess

Table 13-3. National Osteoporosis Foundation's Calcium and Vitamin D Recommendations

Children & Adolescents	Calcium (Daily)	Vitamin D (Daily)
1–3 years	500 mg	400 IU[a]
4–8 years	800 mg	400 IU[a]
9–18 years	1300 mg	400 IU[a]
Adult Women & Men	**Calcium (Daily)**	**Vitamin D (Daily)**
19–49 years	1000 mg	400–800 IU
50 years and over	1200 mg	800–1000 IU
Pregnant & Breastfeeding Women	**Calcium (Daily)**	**Vitamin D (Daily)**
18 years and under	1300 mg	400–800 IU
19 years and over	1000 mg	400–800 IU

[a]NOF does not have specific vitamin D recommendations for these age groups. These are the recommendations of the American Academy of Pediatrics.

    Part-skim ricotta cheese (¼ cup)—170 mg
    Cottage cheese (1 cup)—150 mg

Nondairy foods

    Black beans (1 cup)—100 mg
    Broccoli (1 cup, cooked)—150 mg
    Orange juice, calcium-fortified (6 oz.)—350 mg
    Turnip greens, cooked (½ cup)—100 mg
    Pink salmon with bones, cooked (3 oz.)—180 mg

Soy products

    Soy milk, calcium-enriched (1 cup)—300 mg
    Soy yogurt, calcium-enriched (¾ cup)—300 mg
    Tofu, firm or extra firm (¼ cup)—250 mg

Calcium is available in several OTC supplement products including calcium carbonate (40% elemental calcium) and calcium citrate (21% elemental calcium). Calcium phosphate, calcium lactate, and calcium gluconate are not recommended for calcium supplementation because they have small amounts of elemental calcium. Calcium carbonate is the least expensive and has more elemental calcium; however, it must be taken with meals and needs an acidic environment for absorption. Calcium citrate is more expensive, but it is more easily absorbed and does not require an acidic environment for absorption. In addition, the frequency of the side effects of gas and constipation is more common with calcium carbonate than with calcium citrate. Patient's concomitant disease states and medications must be considered when making a calcium recommendation. For example, calcium carbonate products have decreased absorption with concomitant use of proton pump inhibitors; hyperthyroidism is associated with an increased excretion of calcium; fiber laxatives can decrease calcium absorption if given concurrently; alcohol intake can decrease calcium absorption.

Patients should be counseled to spread out the calcium intake from food and supplements throughout the day because no more than 500 mg of calcium can be absorbed at any one time. Since caffeine increases calcium loss in the urine, patients should limit caffeine intake to 1–2 cups of coffee or soda per day. In addition, products labeled "USP Verified" are guaranteed by the United States Pharmacopeia for identity, strength, purity, and quality and should be recommended whenever possible.

There are many medications that are Food and Drug Administration (FDA)-approved therapies for the prevention and treatment of osteoporosis. Table 13-4 provides details on each. Patient counseling regarding side effects and administration of these medications is very important. It is also essential to inquire about patient's adherence to the osteoporosis medication to reduce fracture risk.

Table 13-4. Medications Used for Osteoporosis Prevention and Treatment

Generic (Brand)	Therapeutic Category	Treatment	Prevention	Patient Information
Alendronate (Fosamax®)	Bisphosphonate	70 mg PO weekly or 10 mg PO daily	35 mg PO weekly or 5 mg PO daily	Take with a full glass of water 30 minutes before first food or beverage of the day. Remain sitting or standing for 30 minutes following administration to reduce potential for esophageal irritation.
Risedronate (Actonel®)	Bisphosphonate	35 mg PO weekly (delayed release) 5 mg PO daily, 35 mg PO weekly, or 150 mg PO monthly (immediate release)		Take with a full glass of water 60 minutes before first food or beverage of the day. Remain sitting or standing for 60 minutes following administration to reduce potential for esophageal irritation.
Ibandronate (Boniva®)	Bisphosphonate	2.5 mg PO daily or 150 mg PO monthly		Take with a full glass of water 30 minutes before first food or beverage of the day. Remain sitting or standing for 30 minutes following administration to reduce potential for esophageal irritation.
Zoledronic acid (Reclast®)	Bisphosphonate	5 mg IV infused over no less than 15 minutes yearly	5 mg IV infused over no less than 15 minutes every 2 years	Administered in primary care provider's office once yearly.
Raloxifene (Evista®)	Estrogen agonist/antagonist (formerly known as SERM)	60 mg PO daily	60 mg PO daily	May be administered any time of the day without regard to meals.
Calcitonin (Miacalcin®)	Hormone	200 international units (1 spray) intranasal daily		Alternate nostrils each day.
Estrogen hormone replacement therapy	Hormone		Use lowest effective dose for shortest duration to meet prevention goals.	Must consider risk versus benefit of pharmacotherapy with primary care provider.
Denosumab (Prolia®)	RANK ligand inhibitor	60 mg SC every 6 months		Keep in original container to protect from light. Do not shake injection.
Teriparatide (Forteo®)	Parathyroid hormone analog	20 µg SC daily		Inject into upper thigh or abdominal wall. Store in refrigerator.

SERM, selective estrogen receptor modulator; PO, by mouth; SC, subcutaneously; IV, intravenous.

BONE DENSITOMETRY DEVICES

Prior to establishing a community pharmacy-based BMD screening program, bone densitometry devices should be researched and compared on the basis of cost, portability, reliability, and ease of use. Pharmacists and other stakeholders should understand the scope of the selected device in the ability to provide screenings as opposed to diagnosis.[1] Screenings identify persons at risk that will require additional follow-up with a primary care provider to determine an assessment of osteopenia or osteoporosis. The following groups are identified as persons of risk to identify for BMD screening/testing:

- All women 65 years of age and older
- Postmenopausal women younger than 65 if they have one or more specific risk factors:
    - Current cigarette smoking status
    - Personal history of adult facture
    - Adult fracture in a first-degree relative
    - Low body weight (< 127 lb.)
- Postmenopausal women who present with factures
- Women considering therapy for osteoporosis
- Women who have been on hormone replacement therapy for prolonged periods of time

DXA is the gold standard to determine BMD, which can be either central or peripheral. Diagnosis of osteoporosis is only determined by central DXA, and screening may occur via peripheral DXA (pDXA).[1] Other means of screening are single-energy x-ray absorptiometry (SXA), radiographic absorptiometry, quantitative computed tomography (QCT), and quantitative ultrasound densitometry (QUS).[6] Identifying a screening device, either x-ray or ultrasound, that measures calcaneal bone (heel) will correlate with axial bone sites (hip and spine) and further determine the risk of future fracture.[2] Bone density instruments may range in price from $10,000 to $30,000.[2] It may not be cost-effective for pharmacies to purchase an expensive piece of equipment. However, operating costs of the screening devices are generally low and require the purchase of ultrasound gel, 70% isopropyl alcohol, and cleaning wipes. Creating a business plan will assist with determining the device necessary for completion of the osteoporosis screening services. Purchasing a device with high incidence of accuracy is necessary. Even though pharmacists are not diagnosing patients with osteoporosis, a reliable tool is needed to produce accurate results for use both by the patient and their primary care providers. Bone densitometry devices are detailed in Table 13-5.

Portability is an essential characteristic necessary for a BMD screening device. Having a mobile unit will allow pharmacists to transfer the unit from one pharmacy location to the next, conduct on-site screenings for employer groups, and partner with primary care providers in their offices. Having mobile equipment will strengthen the pharmacy and pharmacist's return on investment of the screening program. Mobility will also assist with marketing of the newly defined BMD services.

DEVELOPING SERVICES

Marketing is the key to making any screening service successful.[6] Materials should include patient education in order for customers to understand the need for osteoporosis screening services. Utilizing members of the pharmacy team to identify patients at risk, such as women over the age of 50 and patients taking medications that increase the risk of osteoporosis, is a very effective way to target marketing efforts. Examples of promotion materials include[6,10]:

- News releases
- Advertisements in local newspapers
- Store flyers
- Storefront banners
- Direct mail pieces to local businesses, fitness clubs, churches, and assisted/independent living facilities (see Appendix 13A)
- Social media
- Web site
- Shelf talkers
- Pharmacy receipts
- Live news segments on television

Table 13-5. Characteristics of Techniques for Measuring Bone Density

Technique	Bones Measured	Examination Time (Minutes)	Possible Accuracy Error (%)	Effective Radiation Dose (μSv)[a]
Dual energy x-ray absorptiometry (DXA) uses a double beam from an x-ray source	Spine, hip, total body	10–20	3–9	1
Dual photon absorptiometry (DPA) uses a double beam from a radioactive energy source	Spine, hip, total body	20–40	4–10	5
Quantitative computed tomography (QCT) uses a conventional CT scanner with specialized software	Spine	10–15	5–20	60[b]
Peripheral QCT (pQCT) is a special version of the QCT that measures only the bone density of the wrist	Wrist	10	4–8	3
Radiographic absorptiometry (RA) uses an x-ray of the hand and a small metal wedge to calculate bone density	Hand	1–3	4	1
Single energy x-ray absorptiometry (SXA) uses an x-ray source to measure bone	Wrist, heel	4	5	<1
Single photon absorptiometry (SPA) uses a single beam from an energy source passed through water	Wrist	15	4–6	<1
Quantitative ultrasound densitometry (QUS) is a nonionizing screening technique that provides information relating to bone density	Heel, tibia, patella	1–2		n/a

Data adapted from: National Osteoporosis Foundation. How strong are your bones? 1996.
[a]Effective dose refers to radiation that reaches internal organs. For comparison, one chest x-ray gives a radiation dose of about 50 μSv, a lateral spine x-ray 500–1000 μSv, an abdominal CT scan about 4000 μSv, and natural background radiation is about 2000–3000 μSv per year.
[b]Radiation dose may be up to 600 μSv on older CT scanners.

- Weekly pharmacy mailers
- Buttons to be worn by pharmacy staff
- Auxiliary labels
- Pharmacy refill messaging system
- Providing promotional screenings in medical providers offices

■ COMPENSATION/ REIMBURSEMENT

Compensation for BMD screenings in most cases is the responsibility of the patient and typically a nominal fee is charged to cover professional costs for providing the screening. When employer groups contract with community pharmacists to provide screenings, a flat fee or rate is generally established or a fee per employee or patient is established in advance of screening time. When determining a fee for each screening, consider the following costs: machine, supplies, hourly wage for pharmacist and technician, and transportation. Currently, pharmacists are not able to bill insurance companies, neither for medical or prescription benefits nor for osteoporosis screening opportunities. Some pharmacies have had success seeking reimbursement from Medicare.[10]

Setting aside funding for marketing will be beneficial and pay for itself as a result of increased participation in screening opportunities and awareness in the community. In addition to marketing of businesses and organizations, continuous detailing of primary care providers and follow-up will further strengthen services and partnerships. Primary care providers may assist with identifying those patients who are at risk based on the NOF guidelines. A simple example of a business plan to determine the profitability of starting an osteoporosis screening service is:

- Cost of the screening device: $15,000
- Suggested price of the screening per patient: $30
- Number of screenings to be completed in 1 year to cover cost of device: 500
- Number of screenings to be conducted per week: 10

Wages of a pharmacist and/or technician may also be considered as a cost determinant. Consider seeking grant opportunities or partnering with an employer group to assist with the cost of purchasing a screening device.

COMPONENTS OF SUCCESSFUL SCREENING SERVICES

Prior to completing a BMD screening, a pharmacist must obtain consent from the patient in order to conduct and complete the event (see Appendix 13B for an example of a screening consent forms). The process of completing the actual screening is very simple and noninvasive as with other health-care screenings. A prescreening questionnaire is recommended to establish if the patient has any risk factors of development of osteopenia or osteoporosis (see Appendix 13C). Determining which device being used, the screening generally involves having the patient place their heel in the unit for measurement. Some devices require ultrasound gel or alcohol to be applied to the bare area being measured where SXA and DXA units do not require any removal of clothing or hosiery to record the measurement. All screening devices display results in the form of a T-score and/or Z-score. The definition of T-score is the comparison of BMD screening results with those of typical, young, healthy people of the female sex. The T-score shows the amount your bones have weakened compared with a normal 20-year-old person. Z-score is defined as the comparison of bone quality to that of people of the same age and sex as the individual being screened.[1] One must familiarize self with the device manufacturers explanation of screening results in order to determine if a patient is at risk or not. All device companies do not follow the World Health Organization's definition of osteoporosis by BMD.[10]

Based on the screening results, the pharmacist will counsel the patient accordingly on lifestyle modifications, the need for calcium and Vitamin D supplementation, and primary care provider follow-up if necessary. See Table 13-6 for action plans based on T-score results and Appendices 13D and 13E for documentation forms. It is extremely important to communicate in a timely manner with primary care providers regarding the results of patients' screenings. This will improve patient care, encourage providers to refer others for pharmacist clinical services, and create consistency within the medical home. Follow-up with the patient via telephone is recommended to ensure the patient is seeking appropriate medical care with the primary care provider and adhering to lifestyle modifications, if needed.

Lifestyle modifications should include weight-bearing exercise, fall prevention and avoidance of

Table 13-6. Action Plans Based on T-Score Results

	T-Score ≥1.0	T-Score −1.0 to −2.5	T-Score ≤2.5
Fracture Risk	Low	Moderate	High
Patient education	Provide patient with educational materials about osteoporosis, health, and wellness.	Provide patient with educational materials about osteoporosis, health, and wellness. Provide treatment background information including therapy options.	Provide patient with educational materials about osteoporosis, health, and wellness. Provide treatment background information including therapy options.
Recommendations	Suggest that patient repeat BMD in 2 years unless they develop risk of fracture. Advise patient to maintain adequate calcium intake based on gender and age.	Provide patient with written information regarding their best next steps (e.g., increase calcium intake).	Suggest patient see primary care provider within next 90 days.
Actions	Obtain patient's consent to follow-up.	Obtain patient's consent to follow-up. Provide patient with referral to primary care provider. Inform patient about exercise regimens and other methods of reducing fracture risk.	Obtain patient's consent to follow-up. Provide patient with referral to primary care provider. Inform patient about exercise regimens and other methods of reducing fracture risk.
Follow-up	Contact patient in 1 year for another BMD if 2 or more risk factors.	Contact patient in 6 months to encourage primary care provider evaluation.	Contact patient in 9 months to encourage primary care provider evaluation and treatment.

tobacco use, and decrease in alcohol intake.[1] When counseling patients, recommend regular exercises that consist of muscle strengthening activities. Examples of weight-bearing exercises include:

- Walking
- Jogging
- Tai-chi
- Stair climbing
- Dancing
- Tennis
- Weight training
- Resistive exercises

Continuous exercise will strengthen core muscles to assist with fall prevention. Also, decreasing alcohol and tobacco intake and use will improve risk factors associated with the potential for future fractures.

The World Health Organization has developed the fracture risk algorithm (FRAX) to calculate the

10-year probability of a hip fracture and the 10-year probability of a major osteoporosis fracture (clinical spine, forearm, hip, or shoulder).[1] Fracture probabilities are calculated based on the number of risk factors for men and women over 50 years of age. A BMD of the femoral neck is needed; yet an estimated calculation can be made without a known BMD.

Levothyroxine 88 μg PO daily
Lisinopril 10 mg PO daily
Omeprazole 20 mg PO daily
Aspirin 81 mg PO daily
Calcium carbonate 600 mg 3 tablets with breakfast
Multivitamin PO daily

■ PATIENT CASE

BH is a 67-year-old Caucasian female who presents to the community pharmacy after seeing the Friendly Pharmacy's osteoporosis screening ad in Sunday's newspaper. BH consented to the osteoporosis screening. Below are her osteoporosis risk assessment form and screening results.

1. What is BH's level of osteoporosis risk (low, moderate, high)?
2. What is the most appropriate calcium choice for BH based on her medication profile?
3. What calcium-rich foods would you recommend for BH?
4. What lifestyle modifications would you recommend for BH?

Friendly Pharmacy

Osteoporosis Risk Assessment

Name: _B. H._ Ethnicity: _Caucasian_ DOB: _06/23/1944_
Height: _5'2"_ Weight: _115 lbs_ Gender: _female_

Please mark the appropriate answer for each question:	YES	NO	NOT SURE
1. Have you been diagnosed with osteoporosis? IF YES, PLEASE GO TO QUESTION 14		X	
2. Have you ever sustained a fracture as an adult (other than in a motor vehicle accident)?	X		
If yes, please indicate the skeletal site and age when the fracture occurred: _wrist, fell playing tennis_			
3. Do any of your close relatives suffer from osteoporosis? If yes, please indicate the relationship _mother_	X		
4. Do you currently smoke?		X	

	YES	NO	NOT SURE
5. If you are a woman, do you weigh less than 127 pounds?	X		
6. If you are a woman, have you gone through menopause?	X		
a. If yes, did it occur before age 45?		X	
b. If yes, are you currently on hormone replacement therapy?		X	
7. Have you had a hysterectomy? If yes, what year_____		X	
8. Is your diet low or lacking calcium (e.g., < 1000 mg/day of elemental calcium, low dairy food intake)?			X
9. Is your diet low or lacking vitamin D (e.g., < 200 IU/day of vitamin D, no sun exposure)?			X
10. Is your diet high in alcoholic beverages (4 or more alcoholic beverages a week)?		X	
11. Do you exercise less than 3 times a week? If yes, indicate type of activity(s) and duration (e.g., 15 minutes, 30 minutes) *play tennis twice a week*	X		
12. Is your diet high in caffeinated drinks (more than 2 cups/day)?	X		
13. Have you taken any of the following medications? Thyroid medications (e.g., Synthroid®)	X		
Dilantin® (long term)		X	
Cortisone®/prednisone (long term)		X	
Chemotherapy		X	
Heparin (long term)		X	
Aluminum containing antacids (long term)		X	
14. Are you currently taking any of the following medications? Calcium, if yes how much? *Caltrate 3 tablets in the AM*	X		
Hormone replacement therapy (oral/patches)		X	
Actonel®/ Fosamax®/ Boniva®		X	
Evista®		X	
Miacalcin®		X	
Forteo®/Reclast®/Prolia®		X	

Please note that:
- A "YES" answer to at least one of the questions from 2 to 12 indicates an increased risk of fracture.
- The medications listed in question 13 may potentially have a negative effect on bone; therefore, use of one or more of these medications may potentially increase the risk of fracture.
- The medications listed in question 14 are known to have a positive effect on bone. Therefore, use of one of these medications decreases the risk of fracture.

Friendly Pharmacy

How to Read Your Bone Density Report
(For the patient)

Name: _B.H_

Today's Date: _09/23/2011_

T-Score: _-1.5_

Z-Score: _0.2_

Fracture Risk*	T-Score (Standard Deviation)
Low	Greater than –1 SD
Medium	Between –1 SD and –2.5 SD
High	Less than –2.5 SD

*Fracture Risk ranges dependent on BMD screening device manufacturing guidelines.

Terms Defined
- A *standard deviation (SD)* is a measure of how widely values are dispersed from the average value (mean).
- *T-Score*—Comparison of your results with those of typical, young, healthy people of your sex. The T-score shows the amount your bones have weakened compared with a normal 20-year-old person of your sex. If your score is negative, then your bone quality is less than that of a healthy young adult. If your score is positive, your bone quality is greater than that of a healthy young adult (you are above average).
- *Z-Score*—Comparison of your bone quality to that of people of the same age and sex as you are. This score is likely to be higher than the T-score because it is age matched.

RECOMMENDATIONS

Recommended Calcium Intake	_1200 mg every day, divide doses of calcium citrate_
Recommend Vitamin D Intake	_800 IU daily_
Exercise	_Walking or any weight-bearing exercise at least 3 times per week_
Others	_Increase calcium-rich foods. Don't take calcium citrate at the same time as multiple vitamin._

Pharmacist: _Your Friendly Pharmacist_

INTERVIEW—OSTEOPOROSIS SCREENING SERVICES IN A COMMUNITY SETTING

Jonathan Marquess, PharmD, CDE, CPT
Owner
East Marietta Drugs and President
The Institute for Wellness and Education

- **What motivates you to provide osteoporosis screening services for your customers? Are there any intrinsic benefits for you, and do such services benefit your store as a whole?**

  Osteoporosis screenings increase the community's awareness of bone health and are a great way for pharmacists to give back to the community. From a marketing perspective, osteoporosis screenings can increase customer frequency in a community pharmacy and ancillary pharmacy sales.

- **As the owner and pharmacist in your store, what were the biggest barriers that you had to overcome to start osteoporosis screening services?**

  The cost of the BMD screening device initially is a substantial investment ($10,000–$30,000) for the community pharmacy. Formal certification for osteoporosis clinical services is currently not available; therefore training of pharmacists, residents, and technicians can be time consuming.

- **How does your staff help to provide osteoporosis screening services?**

  Depending on the location (at the pharmacy or off-site) and size of the screening event, technicians may be utilized to operate the BMD screening device. A pharmacist, resident, or student supervised by a pharmacist is required to counsel patients accordingly on screening result interpretation and provide patient education.

- **How do you define success for your osteoporosis screening services?**

  Patients have an increased knowledge of bone health and wellness and follow-up with their primary care provider to address screening results with additional tests or initiation pharmacotherapy. In addition, employer groups and patients have an increased awareness of additional clinical pharmacy services provided, which may lead to future opportunities.

- **Describe the reimbursement process for your osteoporosis screening services.**

  Depending on the location (at the pharmacy or off-site), the reimbursement process may vary. If the screening is at the pharmacy, patients are charged a nominal fee for professional services. If an employer group has contracted for osteoporosis screening services at an off-site event, the employer group negotiates a screening rate based on pharmacist's time or rate per patient.

- **Do your services translate directly into increased sales of OTC calcium and vitamin D products? Are there any other monetary benefits for providing such services?**

  Yes, calcium and vitamin D units sold increase, especially if the event is held at the pharmacy. Other ancillary sales may increase the day of the screening. In addition, patients may return to the pharmacy as new customers as a result of the positive interactions with the pharmacy staff during the screening.

- **Has it been difficult to get buy-in from the local primary care providers in town?**

  Primary care providers have been generally receptive to osteoporosis screening events. In fact, we have held screening events in local primary care provider offices in the area. We reinforce with the primary care providers that pharmacists are not diagnosing osteoporosis, and we are assessing risk.

- **What strategies do you use for follow-up with patients after an osteoporosis screening event?**

  At each screening event, patients are asked to consent to pharmacist follow-up at a predetermined time. Via a phone call, we inquire about primary care provider follow-up, lifestyle modifications, and calcium and vitamin D supplementation.

SUMMARY POINTS

- According to the NOF, 43 million people are at risk of osteoporosis. In 2005, it was estimated that osteoporosis-related complications (such as fractures) cost an imposing $17 billion in the United States.
- Osteoporosis is defined by a BMD at the hip or spine that is less than 2.5 SD below the young normal mean reference population (T-score at or below −2.5). Low bone mass (osteopenia) is a BMD between 1.0 and 2.5 SD below than that of a young normal adult (T-score between −1.0 and −2.5).
- BMD screenings should be recommended for all women aged 65 and older, all postmenopausal women with a fracture, postmenopausal women with one or more risk factors, and any other women who are considering therapy for osteoporosis.
- All patients 50 years of age or older should have a total intake (including food and supplements) of 1200 mg calcium and 800–1000 international units of vitamin D.
- DXA is the gold standard to determine BMD, which can be either central or peripheral. Diagnosis of osteoporosis is only determined by central DXA, and screening may occur via pDXA. Other means of screening are SXA, radiographic absorptiometry, QCT, and QUS.
- In the community setting, pharmacists are accessible to patients, have an established presence in the community, and have a direct relationship with patients and primary care providers, which provide an optimal setting for osteoporosis screenings.
- Patients who have had an osteoporosis screening should have recommendations based on the T-score and should include lifestyle modifications including weight-bearing exercise and smoking cessation, calcium and vitamin D recommendations, and encouragement to follow-up with a primary care provider to discuss the screening results.
- Initiation of osteoporosis screening services in a community setting involves marketing, developing a referral base of primary care providers in the area, networking with employer groups, development of appropriate documentation, and counseling forms.

STUDY QUESTIONS

1. Osteoporosis is responsible for approximately _____ in annual health-care costs in the United States:
   a. $17 billion
   b. $1 billion
   c. $100 million
   d. $20 million

2. Osteoporosis is defined as a T-score:
   a. More than −1.0
   b. Less than 1.0
   c. Between −1.0 and −2.5
   d. Less than −2.5

3. Which of the following calcium supplement products contains the highest amounts of elemental calcium?
   a. Calcium carbonate
   b. Calcium citrate
   c. Calcium phosphate
   d. Calcium bicarbonate

4. Which of the following bone densitometry devices is the gold standard for diagnosis of osteoporosis?
   a. DXA
   b. SXA
   c. QUS
   d. pQCT

5. Recommendations for whom osteoporosis screenings should be conducted on were developed by:
   a. Institute of Medicine
   b. National Institute of Health
   c. National Osteoporosis Foundation
   d. American Society of Endocrinology

6. According to the 2010 clinical guidelines, which of the following individuals should be tested for bone mineral density?
   a. All women 65 years of age and older
   b. Postmenopausal women with a fracture
   c. Women considering pharmacotherapy for osteoporosis
   d. All of the above

7. Which of the following are essential components for a successful osteoporosis screening in a community setting?
   a. Marketing plan
   b. Primary care provider or employer buy-in
   c. Trained staff
   d. All of the above

BIBLIOGRAPHY

1. National Osteoporosis Foundation. http://www.nof.org/professionals/pdfs/NOF_ClinicianGuide2009_v7.pdf. Accessed August 1, 2011.
2. Elliott ME, Meek PD, Kanous NL, et al. Osteoporosis screening by community pharmacists: use of National Osteoporosis Foundation resources. *J Am Pharm Assoc.* 2002;42(1):101-110.
3. Grabe DW, Cerulli J, Stroup JS, Kane MP. Comparison of the Achilles Express ultrasonometer with central dual-energy X-ray absorptiometry. *Ann Pharmacother.* 2006;40:830-835.
4. Hsieh C, Novielli KD, Diamond JJ, Cheruva D. Health beliefs and attitudes toward the prevention of osteoporosis in older women. *Menopause.* 2001;8(5):372-376.
5. Johnson JF, Koenigsfeld C, Hughell L, et al. Bone health screening, education, and referral project in northwest Iowa: creating a model for community pharmacies. *J Am Pharm Assoc.* 2008;48(3):379-387.
6. Goode JVK, Swiger K, Bluml BM. Regional osteoporosis screening, referral, and monitoring program in community pharmacies: findings from project ImPACT: osteoporosis. *J Am Pharm Assoc.* 2004;44(2):152-160.
7. AACE Task Force. Medical guidelines for clinical practice for the prevention and treatment of postmenopausal osteoporosis: 2001 edition with selected updates for 2003*. http://www.aace.com/pub/pdf/guidelines/osteoporosis2001Revised.pdf. Accessed August 1, 2011.
8. International Society for Clinical Densitometry. 2007 official positions. http://www.iscd.org/Visitors/pdfs/ISCD2007OfficialPositions-Adult.pdf. Accessed August 1, 2011.
9. U.S. Preventive Services Task Force. Screening for osteoporosis in postmenopausal women: recommendations and rationale. http://www.ahrq.gov/clinic/3rduspstf/osteoporosis/osteorr.htm. Accessed August 1, 2011.
10. Liu Y, Nevins J, Carruthers K, Doucette W, McDonough R, Pan X. Osteoporosis risk screening for women in a community pharmacy. *J Am Pharm Assoc.* 2007;47:521-526.

APPENDIX 13A. AN EXAMPLE OF DIRECT MAILING

Friendly Pharmacy

Date_____,

Dear Business Owner,

    My name is _____, and I am the pharmacist at _____Pharmacy in_____. Just recently, Friendly Pharmacy has begun to offer osteoporosis screenings for individual patients, churches, health clubs, and businesses throughout our community. The screening device that we are using is the _____ that measure the patient's T-score to determine if he or she is at risk for osteoporosis.

    At the time of screening, an osteoporosis risk assessment is completed along with education about the individual's bone health, explanation of the screening results, and answer questions regarding treatments and lifestyle changes to reduce the risk of potential fractures.

    If your company is interested in providing bone mineral density screenings services to employees, please contact me at _____ to schedule an event for our pharmacy team to come on site.

Sincerely,

Your Friendly Pharmacist
Friendly Pharmacy
Contact information

■ APPENDIX 13B. AN EXAMPLE OF SCREENING CONSENT FORM

Friendly Pharmacy

Bone Mineral Density (BMD) Consent Form

Patient Information

Name:_____ Phone #: _____

Address:_____ M ____ F ____ Age ____

City/State/Zip:_____ Date of Birth:_____

Primary Care Provider : _____ MD Phone #: _____

*Chronic Illnesses:*_____ *Drug Allergies:*_____

Consent/Release for BMD Screening:

I hereby consent to the clinical bone density screening for the purpose of bone densitometry, to determine my risk of osteoporosis utilizing the _____ osteoporosis screening system. In consideration of my interest, I hereby release Friendly Pharmacy and other organizations associated with this screening, their affiliates, directors, officers, employees, successors, and assigns, from any liability arising from or in any way connected with this BMD screening and its measurement or from any data derived therefrom. I understand that:

1. The data derived from my screening is considered preliminary only and does not constitute a diagnosis of osteopenia, osteoporosis, or any other medical condition.
2. If the results of my screening suggest osteopenia or osteoporosis, according to the NOF guidelines, I should contact my personal primary care provider for follow-up.
3. The responsibility for initiating a follow-up exam to confirm the results of this screening and obtain professional medical assistance is mine alone and not of any organization associated with this screening.
4. The screening is not diagnostic and it could fail to detect abnormalities which more definitive screening would detect. In addition, it is possible that apparent abnormalities would be found to be normal by a more definitive screening.
5. The written information that is given to me during this screening is to be used as guidelines and is not to be construed as policies of Friendly Pharmacy. Friendly Pharmacy specifically disclaims liability or responsibility for the results or consequences of any actions taken in reliance on the statements, opinions, or suggestions in the "Osteoporosis Risk Assessment" questionnaire and all other patient education material provided.
6. Participation in the screening is voluntary and the decision not to participate will not affect my future care or treatment from Friendly Pharmacy.
7. Friendly Pharmacy will keep the results of the screening confidential in accordance with applicable state and federal law.

Signature:_____ Date:_____

APPENDIX 13C. AN EXAMPLE OF RISK ASSESSMENT QUESTIONNAIRE

Friendly Pharmacy

Osteoporosis Risk Assessment

Name: _____ Ethnicity: _____ DOB: _____

Height: _____ Weight: _____ Gender: _____

Please mark the appropriate answer for each question:	YES	NO	NOT SURE
1. Have you been diagnosed with osteoporosis? IF YES, PLEASE GO TO QUESTION 14			
2. Have you ever sustained a fracture as an adult (other than in a motor vehicle accident)?			
If yes, please indicate the skeletal site and age when the fracture occurred:_____			
3. Do any of your close relatives suffer from osteoporosis? If yes, please indicate the relationship _____			
4. Do you currently smoke?			
5. If you are a woman, do you weigh less than 127 pounds?			
6. If you are a woman, have you gone through menopause?			
a. If yes, did it occur before age 45?			
b. If yes, are you currently on hormone replacement therapy?			
7. Have you had a hysterectomy? If yes, what year_____			

	YES	NO	NOT SURE
8. Is your diet low or lacking calcium (e.g., < 1000 mg/day of elemental calcium, low dairy food intake)?			
9. Is your diet low or lacking vitamin D (e.g., < 200 IU/day of vitamin D, no sun exposure)?			
10. Is your diet high in alcoholic beverages (4 or more alcoholic beverages a week)?			
11. Do you exercise less than 3 times a week? If yes, indicate type of activity(s) and duration (e.g., 15 minutes, 30 minutes)			
12. Is your diet high in caffeinated drinks (more than 2 cups/day)?			
13. Have you taken any of the following medications?			
Thyroid medications (e.g., Synthroid®)			
Dilantin® (long term)			
Cortisone®/prednisone (long term)			
Chemotherapy			
Heparin (long term)			
Aluminum containing antacids (long term)			
14. Are you currently taking any of the following medications?			
Calcium, if yes how much?			
Hormone replacement therapy (oral/patches)			
Actonel®/ Fosamax®/ Boniva®			
Evista®			
Miacalcin®			
Forteo®/Reclast®/Prolia®			

Please note that:
- A "YES" answer to at least one of the questions from 2 to 12 indicates an increased risk of fracture.
- The medications listed in question 13 may potentially have a negative effect on bone; therefore, use of one or more of these medications may potentially increase the risk of fracture.
- The medications listed in question 14 are known to have a positive effect on bone. Therefore, use of one of these medications decreases the risk of fracture.

APPENDIX 13D. AN EXAMPLE OF REPORTING RESULTS AND RECOMMENDATIONS TO PATIENT

Friendly Pharmacy

How to Read Your Bone Density Report
(For the patient)

Name: _____

Today's Date: _____

T-Score: _____

Z-Score: _____

Fracture Risk*	T-Score (Standard Deviation)
Low	Greater than –1 SD
Medium	Between –1 SD and –2.5 SD
High	Less than –2.5 SD

*Fracture Risk ranges dependent on BMD screening device manufacturing guidelines.

Terms Defined

- A *standard deviation (SD)* is a measure of how widely values are dispersed from the average value (mean).
- *T-Score*—Comparison of your results with those of typical, young, healthy people of your sex. The T-score shows the amount your bones have weakened compared with a normal 20-year-old person of your sex. If your score is negative, then your bone quality is less than that of a healthy young adult. If your score is positive, your bone quality is greater than that of a healthy young adult (you are above average).
- *Z-Score*—Comparison of your bone quality to that of people of the same age and sex as you are. This score is likely to be higher than the T-score because it is age matched.

RECOMMENDATIONS

Recommended Calcium Intake	
Recommend Vitamin D Intake	
Exercise	
Others	

Pharmacist: _____

APPENDIX 13E. AN EXAMPLE OF DOCUMENTATION FORM

Friendly Pharmacy

Date: _____

Dear Doctor _____:

Your patient, _____, was screened at our pharmacy for osteoporosis using the _____ osteoporosis screening device.

Screening results from the _____ osteoporosis screening device were as follows:

T-score _____ **Z-score** _____

Fracture Risk*:
___ Low (T-score > –1)
___ Moderate (T-score between –1 and –2.5)
___ High (T-score < –2.5)

*Fracture Risk ranges dependent upon BMD screening device manufacturing guidelines.

As a result of the above findings, the following information was provided to the patient:

___ *Educational brochure on osteoporosis*

___ *Recommendation for calcium supplementation of ____ mg/day*

___ *Education on the benefits of weight-bearing exercise and the need for primary care provider authorization prior to initiating any exercise regimen*

Please contact me if you have any questions

Sincerely,

_____
Pharmacist
Friendly Pharmacy
(777)777.7777

14

OBESITY—WEIGHT MANAGEMENT SERVICES

Katherine S. O'Neal

> ### ■ LEARNING OBJECTIVES
>
> After reading this chapter, the pharmacy student, community practice resident, or pharmacist should be able to:
>
> 1. List three variables contributing to the increased prevalence of obesity.
> 2. Calculate a patient's body mass index (BMI) when given a patient's height and weight.
> 3. Assess a patient's risk for other comorbid disease states.
> 4. Compare nonpharmacologic and pharmacologic treatment options/alternatives for patients, including contraindications and side effects, and formulate a treatment plan.
> 5. Identify various roles community pharmacists can have in weight management as well as the benefits and barriers for patients who want to participate in a community pharmacist managed weight management clinic.
> 6. Develop a business plan for implementing a weight management service.

INTRODUCTION

The problem of obesity is a nationwide crisis. The Centers for Disease Control and Prevention (CDC) reported that in 2009–2010, 35.7% or over 78 million adults were classified as obese.[1–5] This is a problem that extends into the pediatric/adolescent population with the 2004 overweight prevalence ranging from 5% for children aged 2–5 and 17.4% for adolescents up to 19 years of age and obese prevalence for 2009–2010 for adolescents aged 2–19 at 16.9%.[1,5] The prevalence of obesity is higher among certain ethnic groups. Figure 14-1 highlights some ethnic groups and their incidence of obesity.[3] Native American and Alaska natives are also ethnic groups that tend to have high obesity prevalence (32.4%).[3]

The economic impact of obesity is staggering. The CDC reported that the total medical costs of obesity in adults reached $147 billion in 2008 with people who are obese paying 42% more in health-care costs than normal-weight individuals.[1,3,6] These costs are attributed to the conditions and health risks associated with obesity and not the medications used for treating obesity.[7] Both Medicare and Medicaid pay about $1000–1700 more for obese patients than normal-weight patients.[3] In children, the costs are estimated to be $14.3 billion.[8] Other areas of impact include productivity, transportation, and human capital costs.[8] Studies have demonstrated the productivity loss for obesity-related "absenteeism" and "presenteeism" to be as high as $11 billion annually.[8] Productivity costs are also increased due to higher rates of disability costs and premature mortality.[8] Transportation costs are increased due to higher weight-based fuel needs. It is estimated that in 2000, the extra fuel costs for airlines due to higher numbers of obese passengers were about $275 million.[8] Major airlines such as Southwest Airlines and American Airlines now request customers of "certain size" to purchase two seats on the airplane. Studies have also shown that there is a link between education experience and obesity with obese students having increased absenteeism and in the end, lower income or education attainment.[8]

This problem is so severe and widespread that the CDC's Division of Nutrition, Physical Activity Program to Prevent Obesity and Other Chronic Disease States allots millions of dollars to assist states with funding to address this epidemic at the state and community level.[1,4] Their mission is to "lead strategic public health efforts to prevent and control obesity, chronic disease, and other health conditions through regular physical activity and good nutrition."[4] Target areas include increase in physical activity, increase in consumption of fruits and vegetables, decrease in consumption of sugar-sweetened beverages, increase in breastfeeding, and decrease in television viewing.[1]

The National Health and Nutrition Examination Survey (NHANES) is designed to assess the

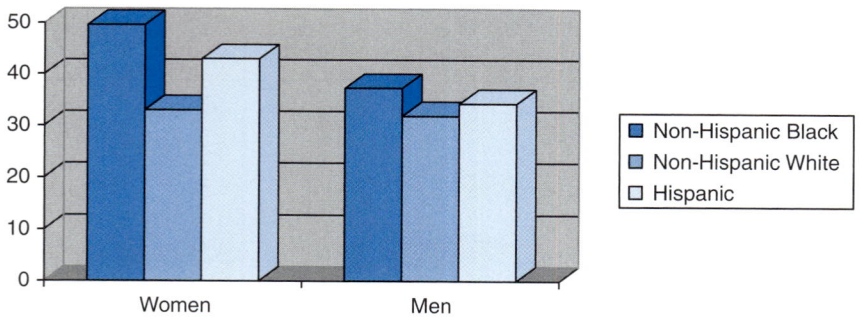

Figure 14-1. Incidence of Obesity by Ethnic Group/Gender

health and nutritional status of the United States. Data from the 1976–1980 and 2005–2006 surveys demonstrate a shift in BMI distribution from peaking around 20–25 to 24–30, respectively.[2] This shift implies that the population, as a whole, is heavier. In fact, in 1990, the majority of the states had a population in which 10–14% were in the obese category.[9] In 8 years, the majority of the states had populations in which >15% were obese.[9] Jumping to 2007, the majority of the states (36) had a population in which >25% were obese.[9] Now, all states have a >20% obesity prevalence.[9] Twelve states have a prevalence of 30% or more including Alabama, Arkansas, Kentucky, Louisiana, Michigan, Mississippi, Missouri, Oklahoma, South Carolina, Tennessee, Texas, and West Virginia.[4] The state with the highest prevalence in 2010 was Mississippi at 34%.[9] Oklahoma is expected to have the highest rate of obesity by 2018.[10]

Etiology

There are several factors that have contributed to the prevalence of obesity. The CDC summed it up well when they stated that "American society (is) 'obesogenic' characterized by environments that promote increased food intake, nonhealthful foods, and physical inactivity."[10] Some of these risk factors are easier to control than others. Genetics, for example, is a risk factor that one may find challenging.[11] Research has shown that there are genetic defects related to the development of obesity.[11] The cultural environment is a modifiable risk factor. In a society that is so focused on convenience and super-sized fast-food items, we have, essentially, put ourselves in this epidemic. It can be also argued that the economic state has a direct relationship with the prevalence of obesity. When families experience financial constraints, expensive and nutritious product is often replaced with unhealthy, high-calorie, cheaper fast-food alternatives. Time constraints also encourage fast-food alternatives.[12] These fast-food alternatives have a poor satiety value encouraging overconsumption.[12] Interestingly, the prices of several commodity-driven products has decreased from 1982 to 2008.[12] Sugar and sweets have decreased by 15%, fats and oil by 10%, and carbonated drinks by 34%.[12] The price of fresh fruits and vegetables increased by over 50%.[12] To add to this, energy consumption has increased by about 300 kcal/day during this same time while physical activity levels declined.[12] People are more sedentary now with televisions, computers, office jobs, and electronic games to keep them stationary and not moving.[12] Lack of physical inactivity is one of the biggest contributing factors to the obese state of our nation. Only 31% of US adults report routine physical activity (defined as at least 3 sessions/week lasting at least 20 minutes/session).[3]

Certain medications put a patient at risk of gaining weight.[13] Many antipsychotics and antidepressants have significant weight gain associated with them. Table 14-1 lists some common prescription medications and possible alternative choices that do not have weight gain associated with them or if they do, not as significant as the original medication prescribed.

In addition to medications, there are certain disease states that put a patient at increased risk of weight gain. These include hypothyroid, congestive heart failure, and Cushing syndrome.

Classification

Table 14-2 outlines the classifications of obesity.[14]

BMI is calculated by total body weight (kg)/height squared (m^2) or as weight (lbs) / height (in^2) × 703. It is the most common screening test for obesity and describes weight as a function of height and is strongly correlated with total body fat content.[14,15] Confounding factors can affect weight and the applicability of BMI classifications. These include edematous stages (e.g., congestive heart failure and pregnancy), extreme muscularity commonly seen in athletes, muscle wasting, short-stature, and Asian-Pacific ethnic background.[16] BMI does not distinguish between lean muscle and fat tissue. As a result, athletes may have a higher BMI.[16]

Table 14-1. Medications that Can Cause Weight Gain

Medication	Possible Alternative
Corticosteroids	NSAIDs, acetaminophen
Antidiabetics (sulfonylureas, insulin, meglitinides, thiazolidinedione)	Biguanides, dipeptidyl peptidase IV inhibitors, glucagon-like-peptide-1 receptor agonist
Antipsychotics (risperidone, clozapine, olanzapine)	Aripiprazole, quetiapine, ziprasidone
Antidepressants (TCAs: amitriptyline, imipramine, nortriptyline, SSRIs, MAOIs)	Venlafaxine, bupropion, nefazodone, desipramine
Anticonvulsants (gabapentin, carbamazepine, valproic acid)	Lamotrigine
Alpha-adrenergic blockers (clonidine, prazosin, terazosin)	Doxazosin
Antihistamine	Decongestants
Beta-adrenergic blockers (propranolol)	Angiotensin-converting enzyme inhibitors, angiotensin receptor, atenolol, calcium channel blockers
Hormonal contraceptives	Barrier methods

Increased Health Risks

Waist circumference is an independent predictor of cardiovascular risk factors and morbidity.[14] Studies have shown that people with larger waist circumferences are at increased cardiovascular risk.[16] In men, the cutoff is >40 inches and in women >35 inches.[14] Waist circumference is measured by

"locating the upper hip bone and the top of the right iliac crest. Place a measuring tape in a horizontal plane around the abdomen at the level of the iliac crest. Before reading the tape measure, ensure that the tape is snug, but does not compress the skin, and is parallel to the floor. The measurement is made at the end of a normal expiration"[16] (see Fig. 14-2).

The corresponding diseased risk in obese patients can be seen in Table 14-3. Waist-to-hip ratio can also identify cardiovascular risk (normal ratio for women ≤0.8 and men ≤0.9).[15] People that are overweight or obese have increased risk of certain disease states and health risks. Table 14-3 lists several of these disease states.[3,8,11,12,14,16]

Having existing comorbid diseases puts overweight and obese patients at increased risk of overall mortality and for further complications associated with their disease states.[14,17]

There are numerous examples in the literature demonstrating the health risk associated with obesity

Table 14-2. Classification of Overweight and Obesity

Classification	BMI (kg/m²)	Disease Risk[a]
Underweight	<18.5	
Normal	18.5–24.9	
Overweight	25–29.9	High
Obese		
Class I	30–34.9	Very high
Class II	35–39.9	Very high
Extreme obesity Class III	≥40	Extremely high

[a]Disease risk is for type 2 diabetes, hypertension, and CVD for men with waist circumference >40 inches and women >35 inches.

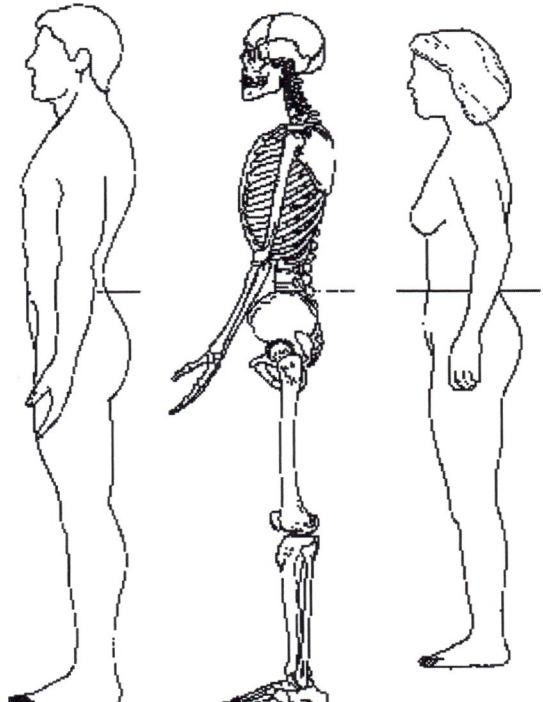

Figure 14-2. Waist circumference measurement.

Table 14-3.	Disease States and Health Risks Associated with Obesity
Type 2 diabetes	
Coronary heart disease	
Chronic kidney disease	
Dyslipidemia	
Depression	
Stroke	
Hypertension	
Gynecological abnormalities	
Nonalcoholic fatty liver disease	
Gallbladder disease	
Asthma	
Osteoarthritis	
Sleep apnea	
Cancers (breast, colorectal, endometrial, kidney)	
Pregnancy complications	
Menstrual irregularities	
Stress incontinence	
Varicose veins	
Infertility	
Sudden cardiac death	

as well as the positive effects of weight loss on comorbid disease states. With diabetes, for example, the risk of developing type 2 diabetes increases as BMI increases and is three to seven times more prevalent in people with BMI >35 kg/m^2. However, it has been demonstrated that a 5% weight loss can improve insulin action and decrease fasting blood glucose levels.[18] Intentional weight loss (reducing BMI from 33.5 to 27.7 kg/m^2) has been associated with a 25% reduction in mortality rates in overweight patients with diabetes.[11]

The risk of hypertension is 40% higher in obese individuals.[19] A 10-kg higher weight is associated with 3 mm Hg higher systolic and 2.3 mm Hg higher diastolic blood pressure.[11] Hypertension increases the risk of stroke and coronary heart disease.[11] The Trials of Hypertension Prevention Phase II study demonstrated that long-term reductions in blood pressure and reduced risk of hypertension can be achieved with weight loss.[20] The largest reductions in blood pressure were 7 mm Hg diastolic and 5 mm Hg systolic.[20] Weight reduction can lead to significant decreases in total cholesterol, low-density lipoprotein, and triglycerides and an increase in high-density lipoprotein.[21]

There is evidence that obesity also greatly increases the risk of various cancers. There is a 55% increased risk of colon cancer in men and 19% increased risk of pancreatic cancer in those with a higher BMI.[22] Obesity increases the risk of chronic kidney disease, which in turn, increases the risk of cardiovascular disease.[23]

It is also well documented that obesity negatively affects general quality of life and has increased generalized health complaints such as headaches, indigestion, constipation, joint pain, chronic fatigue, and bladder infections associated with it.[24,25]

TREATMENT

Goals of Treatment

The general goals for weight loss and management are (1) to prevent further weight gain, (2) to reduce body weight, and (3) to maintain a lower body weight over the long term.[14] The guidelines recommend targeting a weight-loss goal of 10% over 6 months or a weight loss of about 1–2 pounds/week.[14]

Initial assessment of a patient should include a thorough workup including history of weight gain, prescription and nonprescription medications, coexisting disease states, labs, previous approaches to weight loss, dietary habits, physical activity, readiness to change, goals, and available support system.[26] Patients are advised to weigh themselves on a weekly basis. However, this is controversial. Some studies promote daily weighing.[27,28] Other studies have found daily weighing can negate patient's motivation and self-confidence as daily weights will normally fluctuate.[29]

Treatment—Therapeutic Lifestyle and Behavioral Changes

The Health Belief Model and the Transtheoretical Model of Change provide the basis for lifestyle and behavioral counseling associated with successful weight management programs.[29] The Health Belief Model states that patients' willingness to adopt, change, or maintain a health-related behavior depends on whether they:

- Perceive themselves as susceptible to a particular health problem
- View the problem or its consequences as serious
- Are convinced that the recommended treatment or behavior will be effective, yet not be overly costly, inconvenient, or painful
- Are exposed to a cue to take a health action[29–32]

In other words, patients will be more likely to be successful with weight management programs if they have a coexisting condition exacerbated by obesity or at increased risk of other health conditions related to obesity. The Transtheoretical Model of Change involves five stages of progression that identify how ready a patient is to change.[29–32] These stages of change are precontemplation, contemplation, preparation, action, and maintenance. Patients will go through each stage several times before they succeed in their long-term goals.[29–32] Identifying which stage the patient is in can be helpful in forming the appropriate approach to their plan.

When initiated together, therapeutic lifestyle changes and behavioral counseling increase the chances of successful treatment. However, before any counseling takes place, it is important to assess why the patient wants to lose weight, what their goals are, and how confident they are.[16] The answers to these questions will help formulate the overall treatment plan. Their reasoning in starting a weight-loss program may be their motivating factor; this reason as well as new motivators that might be discovered throughout the course of the program should be visited continuously as a consistent reminder to the patient as to why they are doing this. The patient's goal may not be realistic, which can lead to overall frustration, drop in confidence and motivation, and ultimately, giving up on the program. Most patients have a dramatic difference between expectations and realistic goals;[29] therefore, it is important to address this from the very beginning. Key features of programs addressing behavioral changes include goal setting, self-monitoring, environmental modifications, cognitive restructuring, and prevention of relapse.[26]

Addressing barriers and learning about resources and basics of nutrition are critical components. These strategies provide patients with the skills and motivation it takes to succeed. This strategy is what Dr. Terry Forshee (see section "Expert Interview") follows in his weight management clinic, "Real change comes from the information the patient gets during the program combined with a readiness to change."

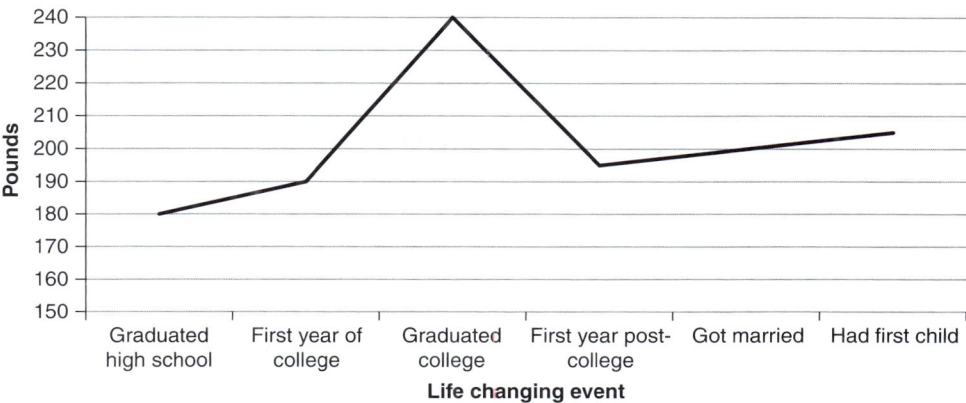

Figure 14-3. Weight time line.

A recommended method to identify barriers or triggers for weight gain is to have the patient draw out a time line of their weights over the years and then identify major life events that correspond to the various weights; these weight-changing events would vary for each person. Fig. 14-3 provides a fictional example.

Commonly, patterns will emerge that correlate periods of weight gain to major life events or stressors.[16] A method to evaluate physical activity is having the patient keep an activity journal similar in concept to blood sugar diaries for patients with diabetes or headache diaries for migraineurs.[16] It allows the patients to become more aware of their own habits and perhaps, barriers. Or, a straightforward question "what gets in the way or interferes with you consistently engaging in physical activity?" can help identify barriers that should be addressed.[16] On the opposite end of the spectrum, patients can identify activities they engage in that promote physical activity. Examples of additional assessment questions that can be asked to evaluate physical activity include:

- What is the most active thing you do in a typical day?
- What types of activities do you enjoy and how often do you engage in them?
- Do you enjoy doing activities alone/in private or with others/in public?
- How many hours each day do you spend in front of a television or computer?
- What types of exercise equipment or videos/DVD do you have at home?
- What is your attitude about exercise?
- What types of activities have you done in the past that you do not currently do?
- What hurts/aches during or after exercising?
- What type of gym shoes do you wear and how often do you replace them?
- What types of exercises would you like to learn how to do?
- When in your day do you have time to add in exercise?
- If you belonged to a health club, how many days per week did you go and what did you do when you were there?[14]

This same concept can be utilized with a food diary to evaluate food habits and behaviors. There are many approaches to keeping a food diary. Food diaries, at a minimum, should include information on all food eaten, including snacks, beverages consumes, serving sizes, and calorie total.[29] It is important to record every single food item eaten no matter how small the serving appears or how little the calories are. When calculating energy input, output, and deficit, unrecorded calories add up quickly.[29] Other items that should be recorded include the time of day the food was eaten; the location; whether the meal was eaten alone or with other people; and any emotions felt before, during, or after eating. This information is helpful in evaluating emotional, social, and environmental triggers to eating.[29] Studies have shown that the number of food records kept per week was the best predictor of weight loss during a weight management program.[29] Patients who kept food diaries with at least five entries lost twice as much weight as those who kept fewer records or no food diary at all.[29]

Dietary habits should be reviewed with the assistance of food logs, daily recall, or questionnaires.[16] Daily intake should be modified to create a daily caloric deficit of about 500–1000 kcal/day.[14] A 500 kcal deficit/day equates to about a 1 pound weight loss/week. In addition, education should be focused on making healthier food choices and reducing total fat intake to <30% of total daily calories.[14] Achieving caloric deficit can be obtained by a true low-calorie diet but can also be manageable with accompanying physical activity. The National Institutes of Health recommend 1000–1200 calories for women trying to lose weight and 1200–1800 for men.[14] A patient should always check with their primary care provider before starting an exercise routine or before limiting caloric intake. It is recommended that exercise should take place most days of the week for at least 30 minutes/day. Patients should be advised to start slow and gradually increase the duration and intensity of their exercise to achieve the goal of 30 minutes most days of the week.

If patients have tried other weight-loss programs, the patient should be probed for further information (e.g., how much weight was lost, reasons for stopping, and advantages/disadvantages of the program) to identify further barriers.[16] Some popular weight-loss programs are listed in Table 14-4. The patient's baseline knowledge of obesity, contributing factors and health risks associated with obesity, can also be used as a motivating factor once the patient is made aware of them.

Table 14-4. Popular Weight-Loss Programs

Program Name	Description
Atkin's Diet™	Low-carbohydrate diet
South Beach Diet®	Focuses on eliminating and reducing trans-fats and saturated fats for unsaturated fats and omega-3 fatty acids
WeightWatchers®	Point-based system and meetings
Nutrisystem®	Preselected meals delivered to the house
Slim Fast!	Meal replacement drinks and snacks with 3-2-1 plan™ (3100-calorie snacks, 2 shakes or meal bars, and 1500-calorie meal)
Jenny Craig	Preselected meals delivered to the house and meetings

There are special considerations for certain patient populations including geriatrics, pediatrics, and tobacco smokers. Assessing physical activity levels or barriers in the geriatric population should include questions addressing daily functioning skills to assess appropriateness of physical activity recommendations.[16] For example, a question such as, "do you lose your balance while walking?" would be important to know before recommending the patient incorporate a walking program. When working with the pediatric population, it is important to remember the caregivers' role and the dependence the patient has on the caregiver with both eating and exercise habits.[16] Assessment and treatment should be targeted at the entire family with questions like "How often does the family dine out for breakfast, lunch, or dinner in a typical week?" and "What is the most active think you do as a family and how often do you do it?"[16] For tobacco smokers, behavioral therapy should be incorporated and would include smoking cessation counseling to overcome barriers. These patients fear of weight gain when quitting. Weight gain with smoking cessation averages 4.5–7 pounds.[14] It is important to educate patients that this weight gain would actually affect their health positively compared with the effects from continued smoking.

Key to Success

Including all three of these factors (dietary modification, increased physical activity and behavioral interventions) in a weight management program lead to a more successful program and a higher likelihood of achieving long-term weight management.[14] It is well documented that patients will regain lost weight unless their weight management program consists of all three of these factors.[14]

Treatment—Pharmacologic

Pharmacologic treatment is not recommended unless patients have a (1) BMI ≥ 30 with no risk factors or comorbid disease states or (2) a BMI ≥ 27 with at least one risk factor or comorbid disease state (hypertension, dyslipidemia, coronary heart disease, type 2 diabetes, or sleep apnea).[14] Pharmacologic treatment should only be used as part of a comprehensive weight-loss program to augment lifestyle and behavioral changes.[14] The pharmacologic treatment options are limited as very few novel agents have been introduced and many have been removed from the market (e.g., sibutramine, fenfluramine, and dexfenfluramine) due to safety concerns. Table 14-5 lists the available treatment options and doses.[33]

The only lipase inhibitor available is orlistat, and it is available for long-term use. Its mechanism of action is a reversible inhibitor of gastric and pancreatic lipases, inhibiting absorption of dietary fats by up to 30% and achieving weight loss of 3–5.5 kg.[15,26,33] The side effects experienced with orlistat are GI related and are exacerbated by higher fat content foods but tend to subside with continued treatment.[33] A rare but serious side effect is liver injury.[33] These rare case reports prompted the FDA to make a labeling change warning about this risk.[33] It is recommended that patients taking orlistat should also supplement their diet with fat-soluble vitamins (A, D, E, and K) because of the decreased fat absorption.[33] Orlistat may decrease the serum concentrations of amiodarone, cyclosporine, and levothyroxine.[33] When evaluating the use of orlistat in obese individuals over a 4-year period, investigators found that those taking orlistat versus placebo over 4 years lost at least 5% of their initial body weight, and in those patients who had glucose intolerance, orlistat resulted in a 45% lower incidence of type 2 diabetes.[34] Orlistat is contraindicated in patients with chronic malabsorption syndrome or cholestasis.[33]

The available sympathomimetics include diethylpropion, phentermine, phendimetrazine, and benzphetamine, all of which are only for short-term use (few weeks). Diethylpropion and phentermine are both classified as Schedule IV-controlled substances and phendimetrazine and benzphetamine are Schedule III. Phendimetrazine and benzphetamine are rarely used. Diethylpropion and phentermine reduce appetite secondarily to the enhanced release of norepinephrine.[33] Evidence supporting the efficacy of phentermine is limited.[26] Weight reduction with this class is 3–4% more than placebo.[26] Studies have shown phentermine can have an average weight loss of 7.9 pounds compared with placebo and 6.6 pounds compared with placebo for diethylpropion.[35,36] The most serious side effects with these agents are cardiac related including tachycardia and palpitations and they are contraindicated in patients with severe hypertension, hyperthyroidism, history of drug abuse, and glaucoma.[33] Phentermine may lead to drug dependency with prolonged use.[33]

Qnexa is a new drug potentially coming down the pipeline. It is a combination of phentermine and topiramate. The new drug was initially rejected by the FDA in 2010 due to cardiovascular safety concerns. It was resubmitted in February 2012 and the FDA advisory committee voted almost unanimously to approve

Table 14-5. Pharmacologic Treatment Options Available in the United States

Class/Drug	Usual Dose	Common A/E
Lipase inhibitor		
Orlistat (OTC Alli, Xenical)	Alli: 60 mg three times daily with each fat containing meal. Xenical: 120 mg three times daily 1 hour after each fat containing meal	Headache, oily spotting, abdominal pain, flatus with discharge, fecal urgency, fatty/oily stool, oily evacuation, back pain, upper respiratory infection, influenza, menstrual irregularities, nausea, myalgia, hepatic failure, increased transaminases, acute kidney injury
Sympathomimetics		
Diethylpropion	25 mg three times daily 1 hour before meals or food; controlled-release 75 mg midmorning	Arrhythmia, anxiety, palpitation, alopecia, libido changes, menstrual irregularities, abdominal discomfort, impotence, tremor, dyspnea, bone marrow depression
Phentermine (Adipex-R)	15–37.5 mg/day given in 1–2 divided doses. Should be administered before or 1–2 hours after breakfast	Palpitations, tachycardia, dizziness, urticarial, constipation, impotence, tremor
Phendimetrazine (Bontril)	Capsule: 105 mg once daily before breakfast; Tablet: 17.5–35 mg 2–3 times daily 1 hour before meals	Flushing, hypertension, palpitations, constipation
Benzphetamine (Didrex)	25–50 mg one to three times daily	Hypertension, palpitation, tachycardia, depression

it. As of this writing, the drug is still waiting for FDA approval.

Treatment—Complementary and Alternative Medicine

There are several complementary and alternative medicine options that are used in weight management. These are listed in Table 14-6.[37] As with all complementary and alternative products (CAM), patients should be reminded of the lack of federal regulation as compared with prescription products. These products have unpredictable amounts of ingredients and unknown amounts of harmful ingredients. All patients should inform their health-care provider of any CAM products used to ensure there are no potential drug–drug interactions or drug–disease interactions.

Surgical Options

Surgical options are last-line and are typically reserved for patients with a BMI ≥ 40 or ≥ 35 with comorbid conditions or who have failed other options.[14,15] Options include laparoscopic gastric banding, sleeve gastrectomy, gastric bypass, and biliopancreatic division. These procedures can be successful but are not without risks and complications (e.g., nutritional deficiencies).[38,39]

Table 14-6. Complementary and Alternative Medicine

Herb	Dose	Effectiveness Rating	Common A/E
Chromium	None available for obesity, ranges from 200 to 1000 µg/day	Insufficient evidence	Headaches, diarrhea, mood changes, insomnia
Bitter orange	975 mg/day	Insufficient evidence	Increase in blood pressure, tachycardia, CV toxicity, QTc prolongation
St. John's wort	None available for obesity, ranges from 300 to 1200 mg/day	None available	GI discomfort, diarrhea, insomnia, anxiety
Pyruvate	6 g/day	Insufficient evidence	GI discomfort
Chitosan	1–5 g/day	Insufficient evidence	GI upset, nausea, flatulence, constipation
5-Hydroxytryptophan	None available, ranges from 150 to 300 mg/day	Insufficient evidence	GI upset, flatulence, belching, nausea, vomiting, diarrhea
Hoodia	No typical dosage	Insufficient evidence	None reported
Barley	No typical dosage	Insufficient evidence	Anaphylaxis in sensitive individuals
Blond psyllium	No typical dosage	Insufficient evidence	Flatulence, abdominal pain, diarrhea, constipation, dyspepsia, nausea

ROLE OF THE COMMUNITY PHARMACISTS

According to MarketData Enterprises, Inc., a market research company for the weight-loss industry, the meal replacement and diet pill market sales (small segment of the weight-loss industry) should reach roughly $3 billion by 2014.[40] They estimate that dieters will make about four weight-loss attempts/year.[40] This is essentially a fee-for-service program, which makes this a huge opportunity of untapped revenue for community pharmacies. Weight management services offered from a community pharmacy are not as common as, for example, diabetes education services. However, it is a service that is complimentary to almost every other clinical service for chronic disease management community pharmacists. As Dr. Terry Forshee has demonstrated (see section "Expert Interview"), an independent pharmacy can run a very successful weight management service for patients. An Australian study interviewed community pharmacists about weight management services and realized several themes that can be incorporated into any community pharmacy weight management service. The majority of pharmacists interviewed felt their accessibility, which is commonly cited in literature for reasons pharmacists should provide pharmaceutical care services, and existing knowledge facilitated the service.[41] The existing knowledge theme is echoed by Dr. Terry Forshee in his comment regarding barriers to implementing a weight management service.

There are several different models and considerations when providing weight management services. The length of the program can vary depending on the content of the program and the goal of the patient. The pharmacists in the Australian study agreed that the program needed to have a defined duration, 12 weeks, with a focus on lifestyle issues, and that it should be in collaboration with the patient's physician.[41] Ultimately, it should be up to the pharmacist and the goals of the patient as to the duration the patient should be enrolled in the program. Collaborating with physicians can provide an optimal environment for providing the patient with the care they need to be successful in their overall health. A collaborative partnership implies the pharmacist is working together with and/or under the license of the physician.

There are few examples in the literature of successful community pharmacy programs. Ahrens and colleagues evaluated an independent pharmacy providing two different methods of weight management services.[42] Patients were enrolled in one of two groups to evaluate using either a meal replacement program or a reduced calorie diet program.[42] The program duration was 22 weeks (13 visits) and both groups received counseling from a pharmacist.[42] The counseling included basic lifestyle modifications, proper nutrition principles, physical activity, and behavior modification as well as motivating and encouraging patients to stick with their plan.[42] The initial visit was 45 minutes in duration and the subsequent visits were 15 minutes long.[42] Each visit included a weight check, waist circumference measurement, blood pressure measurement, and survey.[42] A fasting lipid profile was obtained at weeks 12 and 22.[42] The investigators found that both groups lost weight (average of 5–6 kg) and were able to maintain the weight loss at a 10-week follow-up.[42] This study demonstrated two different models, both successful, of providing weight management services from the community pharmacy. Other proposed models follow the Transtheoretical Model and develop program sessions based off of the five stages: (1) assess obesity risk, (2) ask about readiness to change, (3) advise in designing a weight-control program, (4) assist in establishing appropriate intervention, and (5) arrange for follow-up.[43] These programs focus on counseling and guidance.

Table 14-7. Resources
The Centers for Disease Control and Prevention (http://www.cdc.gov/obesity/index.html)
The Obesity Society (http://www.obesity.org)
National Heart, Lung, and Blood Institute (NHLBI) Health Information Center Overweight and Obesity (http://www.nhlbi.nih.gov/health/dci/Diseases/obe/obe_whatare.html)
Clinical Guidelines on the Identification, Evaluation, and Treatment of Overweight and Obesity in Adults 1998 (http://www.nhlbi.nih.gov/guidelines/obesity/ob_home.htm)
American Pharmacists Association (www.pharmacist.com)
Healthfinder (www.healthfinder.gov)

In order to provide sustained services, there must be profit gained. There are few studies looking at patient's willingness to pay and participate in weight management services provided by a pharmacist. Larson evaluated patients' willingness to pay for pharmaceutical care services.[44] The study involved a mail survey to 2500 random adults.[44] The survey provided a description of pharmaceutical care services and asked questions such as the level of pharmaceutical care services received and willingness to pay. Fifty-six percent of the respondents were willing to pay.[44]

Table 14-7 lists additional resources that might be helpful for gathering background data on obesity and treatment guidelines.

Benefits and Perceived Barriers

When developing a new service the perceived benefits and barriers must be thoroughly evaluated from both the pharmacy and patient perspectives. Patients can present with a variety of barriers related to both personal weight loss and perceptions of the community pharmacist providing services. Patients will have barriers to the concept of physical activity. These can include not enough time to exercise; it is not convenient during their routine day; they do not enjoy it; they have no support; or they cannot afford it.[16] Patients may also have barriers due to perceived costs of the program, cost of maintaining a "healthier" lifestyle, time commitment involved, and their own self-confidence or motivation that they can be successful. In addition, the expanding roles of pharmacists are still fairly new concepts to some patients and will require some education/advertising to raise awareness. The pharmacy will need to evaluate time management, workflow, workforce shortages, and perceived perceptions from both patients and other health-care providers before starting a service.

Developing a Weight Management Service

Weight management services can be offered in a variety of different ways. Some examples include nutrition counseling, lifestyle education, and medication counseling/management.

The first step in developing and justifying a weight management service is to conduct a needs assessment, which is the collection of data to assess the need for a particular service or product within a defined population or community.[45–48] There are three basic questions to ask for a needs assessment:

- What is the patient need or problem to be addressed?
- How large is this problem, and what are the trends?
- How well is the patient need being addressed?[45]

This assessment can be done through patient surveys, physician surveys, and demographic trending research in both primary and secondary literature sources. Patient surveys can be simple, straightforward surveys asking whether or not the patient is interested in the service, if they would pay for the service, if they want the service from a pharmacist, or if they have used diet/weight-loss services or products within the last 6 months. The surveys can be mailed to the patients or the surveys can be made available in the pharmacy for the patient to complete. Timing of surveys should also be considered. For example, many people set a new year's resolution to lose weight and many people set goals to lose weight prior to the summer season. Secondary sources can be utilized to research demographic trends as well as industry information related to weight management services. To justify providing a weight management service, the pharmacist should always evaluate future goals of the pharmacy and patient interest implying growth potential.[45] A SWOT (strengths, weaknesses, opportunities, and threats) analysis should be conducted next to evaluate the existing ability of the pharmacy to expand or initiate new clinical services. The internal analysis focuses on strengths and weaknesses of the pharmacy. The strengths are factors that will help the pharmacy succeed in providing weight management services, whereas the weaknesses are factors that might create barriers. Examples of strengths might include competent staff and loyal customer base. Weaknesses might include lack of privacy space to conduct the service or lack of a computer software system to support the service (e.g., patient scheduling and documentation). The external analysis focuses on the opportunities that will allow the service to grow and threats that may put the service at risk of failing. Opportunities might include local physician groups supporting the weight management service, having an overweight/obese patient population, or having patients who have paid for other weight-loss services. Threats might include reimbursement challenges and patients' willingness to pay cash for these services. The Centers for Medicare and Medicaid Services, for example, recently issued a decision statement that Medicare beneficiaries under Part A or Part B with a BMI ≥ 30 kg/m^2 are eligible and covered to receive intensive behavioral therapy for obesity.[49]

Once the background research is completed, a business plan should be developed. The more detailed the business plan, the easier it will be to implement the service and the higher likelihood of success. The business plan should include several key components: mission and vision statement, description of the service, organizational structure, financial analysis and reimbursement method, practice agreements/scopes, documentation method, continuous quality improvement plan, and marketing plan.

The mission and vision statements provide focus for the service. The mission statement is a short statement defining the purpose of providing a weight management service.[45,46] An example of mission statement for providing weight management services might be "The weight management service's mission is to provide guidance and support to patients in their journey to improve their overall health." The vision statement is a motivating statement that defines the service's goal and directions for the future.[45,46] An example of vision statement might be "Our vision is that patients will gain the confidence and motivation to succeed in long-term weight management improving overall health and quality of life."

The description of the service should be clearly defined and include both operational and service descriptions. From the operational standpoint, there are several key areas that need to be addressed including hours/days the service will be provided, patient scheduling logistics, duration of patient visits, ancillary staff participation to help with workflow, supplies that are needed (e.g., weight scale, body fat analyzer, and nutrition guides), and location in the pharmacy the service will be provided. Having this information will better prepare the pharmacy to provide the service and minimize unexpected factors that may surface. The service description should include program-specific information such as program duration and what each visit will entail. For example, a weight management service could be designed to be 12 weeks in duration with one visit every month. The first visit may last 1 hour in duration due to initial patient workups (e.g., medication history, patient history, risk assessment, point-of-care labs, and patient goals/expectations) with subsequent visits lasting 15–30 minutes. Each visit may focus on a different topic to assist the patient in their journey. Example of topics for a 12-week program might include (1) behavior and support system; (2) nutritional components; (3) label reading; (4) vitamins, minerals and supplements; (5) eating heart-healthy diet; (6) self-image/confidence; (7) meal planning; (8) physical activity; (9) medications; (10) community resources; (11) eating out; and (12) overall health and maintaining a lifestyle change.[50]

Once the background research, physical layout and service descriptions are completed, the organizational structure should be developed. Ideally, the structure should maximize existing staff and be integrated into the existing pharmacy workflow. As Dr. Terry Forshee states, existing staff can be very helpful when providing weight management services allowing the pharmacist to use his/her time efficiently and giving the staff opportunities in providing "patient care." The cashier might be helpful in calling and reminding patients of their appointments or scheduling new appointments and checking the patient "out" after the visit. Technicians might be helpful in weighing the patient, rooming the patient, and providing them with any paperwork that needs to be completed prior to visiting with the pharmacist or making copies. However, the workflow design is established, it should be well communicated to the staff with clear expectations, and a clear reporting structure should be provided so staff know who they should report to if they have any difficulty or challenges.

The financial analysis provides baseline information on how the pharmacy is currently situated and how it expects to grow with the addition of the weight management service. Pharmacists should be paid for the services as a separate transaction from the prescription transaction.[45] In order to bill third-party payers for weight management services, the pharmacist must be recognized as a health-care provider and weight management services must be designated as reimbursable service from Medicare, Medicaid, and private insurers. As of this writing, weight management services are not reimbursable. A pharmacist may bill the patient directly for the services and provide the patient with the CMS-1500 form for them to submit to the insurance company for reimbursement. The industry standard rate for pharmacist services is $2–3/minute.[45] Pharmacists may also set up collaborative practice agreements with physicians to provide the service. While these agreements are not required, they may be beneficial in opening up opportunities to bill third-party companies for the service, in building collaborative relationships with the physicians, and possibly giving patients an opportunity to utilize their flexible spending accounts. A collaborative practice agreement is an agreement in which a physician authorizes a pharmacist to perform certain activities under his or her authority.[45] These agreements can be as broad or specific as they need to meet the goals of the pharmacist, physician, and patients. State pharmacy laws should be referenced when designing the agreements. The agreement, for a weight management service, might include details on point-of-care testing for dyslipidemia and diabetes and for obtaining vitals that are then forwarded to the physician for review. Pharmacist should review their respective state laws, regulations and health as well as organizational policies prior to implementing a collaborative practice agreement and reimbursement policy.

A documentation system is vital to the overall success of the service. Some Web-based documentation systems include Numera/Imetrikus (www.numerahealth.com), Chronic Disease Electronic Management System (www.cdems.com), and Medication Management System (www. medsmanagement.com). It does not only provide the pharmacy with legal support, "if you didn't document it, you didn't do it," but also provide patient documentation needed for third-party coverage for surgical intervention, for patient handouts, and for providing ongoing care/review.[45] It gives the pharmacist a "reminder" for what was being discussed or planned and where to pick up the next session with the patient. Proper documentation also allows professional and effective communication with the provider regarding patient updates or if agreed upon, lab measurements. Continuous communication between the pharmacist and the provider helps keep the service on the provider's radar, and it becomes part of the patient's primary medical record. It provides legal documentation support that is often required for reimbursement. Finally, it provides a method for the pharmacy to self-assess.[45] It is a source of information that can be used with continuous quality improvement evaluations and with justifying the service. The model often used to guide data collection is ECHO (*E*conomic, *C*linical, and *H*umanistic *O*utcomes).[45] Economic data will reinforce the financial stability of the service. Is there revenue being generated? What is the cost/benefit of the service? Is the pharmacist time being maximized? Clinical data would be related to the patient and health-related outcomes. Has the patient lost weight from the start of the program to the end? Has the patient's blood pressure improved? If they have diabetes, did their blood glucose improve? Did their lipid profile improve? Humanistic outcomes evaluate the patient's satisfaction with the program. Did their quality of life improve? Did they gain confidence in their ability to lose and/or maintain weight? Did they make positive behavioral changes that will benefit them in the long term? Are they able to maintain a lifestyle conducive to steady weight management?

Lastly, the marketing plan should be developed. Advertising is a critical component to increase awareness and build a customer base. Offering a well-developed service does not ensure demand. The purpose of advertising patient care services is to (1) create awareness of a product or service, (2) encourage patients or consumers to try something new, (3) enhance confidence in a product or service, (4) maintain market share by encouraging the continued purchase of a product or use of a service, and (5) encourage recommendations and word-of-mouth marketing.[48] There are several ways to advertise a weight management service. If a collaborative practice agreement is in place, fliers can be placed in the provider's office or physicians can refer patients to the service. Referral forms can be prewritten for the providers making the referral process easier. In addition, the pharmacy can create a Web page outlining the service and providing a link to a referral form patients can print and take to their provider. Other methods include television, radio, local newspapers, fliers, direct mail, pharmacy marquee, and, if available, weekly pharmacy advertisement mailings. Utilizing community health fairs is another great method to advertise the service, raise awareness, and recruit patients. BMI screenings can be a fairly easy service to set up for health fairs. Whatever the chosen method is, it is important to convey to the patient what the service is, what it costs, where it takes place, and who to contact.

Once the weight management service business plan is completed, it should be reviewed by key stakeholders (e.g., physicians and pharmacy managers/owners) to ensure it meets the goals, mission, and vision of the overarching pharmacy operations.

■ PATIENT CASE

A 35-year-old female visits you in the weight-management clinic for assistance in weight loss. She tells you that she has tried many times to lose weight over the past several years and has not been successful. She has even tried the South Beach Diet and the Atkins Diet. She states she is currently taking bitter orange daily and wants your thoughts on taking over-the-counter Alli. She currently weighs 244 pounds and is 5'4" tall. Her waist circumference is 44". Her past medical history is significant for depression and migraines.

Social history: She smokes one ppd and drinks wine and beer on the weekends; single, never married and never had children.

Family history: Her mother has type 2 diabetes and father had an MI at the age of 43.

Occupation: She works in the mall as a sales clerk in a local department store.

Dietary habits: She skips breakfast, and she eats fast food almost every day for lunch at the food court. Her dinners are usually picked up at fast-food restaurants on her way home from work.

Medications: Bitter orange 975 mg/day, amitriptyline 100 mg at bedtime for depression, and gabapentin 300 mg three times daily for migraine prophylaxis.

1. What is this patient's BMI and weight classification?

This patient's weight is 244 lbs, and her height is 64". Using the following equation:
[Weight (lbs)/height (inches^2)] divided by 703.
The patient's BMI is 41.9, classified as extreme obesity.

2. What level of risk does this patient have for other disease states?

With her BMI and waist circumference, this patient is at an extremely high risk for other disease states.

3. What recommendations can you make to her physician regarding current therapy and alternative options for weight loss?

There are several possibilities with this patient. This patient would benefit from dietary modifications, increased physical activity, and behavioral interventions. It would also be in the patient's best interest to discontinue the bitter orange. With a BMI of 41.9, this patient meets qualifications for pharmacologic treatment. However, it should be used in conjunction with lifestyle and behavioral coaching. Either class of medications could be prescribed (lipase inhibitor or sympathomimetics). An alternative option would be surgery. She has a BMI ≥ 40 and has "failed" other options. However, these procedures are not without risks and complications.

4. What would you counsel the patient on regarding her use of bitter orange?

The patient should be made aware that bitter orange has insufficient evidence to support its use for weight loss, and that the side effects can be serious (e.g., CV toxicity, increase in blood pressure, and QTc prolongation). In addition, complementary and alternative products are not regulated by the FDA to the extent of prescription products.

5. What behavioral and lifestyle strategies could the pharmacist recommend?

There are many areas in which the pharmacist can make an impact for this patient. Before even making a recommendation, however, the pharmacist should further evaluate the patient's past attempts at weight loss including duration of attempt, barriers, and goal with weight loss. Specific initial areas of intervention including counseling the patient on smoking cessation, possible concerns with weight gain associated with smoking cessation, and if she chooses to drink alcoholic beverages, drinking in moderation. The pharmacist can also review principles of healthy dietary habits and slowly incorporate physical activity. The patient should be encouraged to maintain a food diary along with a physical activity log. It would be important to maintain continuity in visits with this patient to help her reach her goals.

6. What counseling points could the pharmacist make about over-the-counter Alli?

   The patient should be counseled on the common side effects (e.g., oily spotting, abdominal pain, flatus with discharge, fecal urgency, fatty/oily stool, oily evacuation, and back pain) and increased risk of hepatic failure and acute kidney injury. In addition, a diet high in fat (fast food) would most likely exacerbate the side effects. This medication should be supplemented with fat-soluble vitamins (A, D, E, and K). The patient should also be made aware that typical weight loss associated with its use is 3-5.5 kg.

7. How should a patient be advised to take Alli?

   The patient should be instructed to take a 60 mg tablet with each fat-containing meal.

■ PUTTING IT ALL TOGETHER—SUMMARY POINTS

- The prevalence of obesity has increased from 1985 to 2010 with all states having an obesity rate >20%.
- Both BMI and waist circumference should be used to assess health risks.
- A reasonable and safe weight-loss goal is 10% over 6 months or 1–2 pounds/week.
- There are several health risks associated with obesity including type 2 diabetes, coronary heart disease, sleep apnea, and stroke.
- There are certain medications that cause weight gain and alternatives may be available that can help minimize this side effect.
- Therapeutic lifestyle and behavioral changes are the cornerstone of the treatment; including these with increased physical activity leads to a more successful weight-loss program.
- Prescription medications should only be used to supplement lifestyle and behavioral changes.
- Weight management services can be offered in a variety of different ways including nutrition counseling, lifestyle education, and medication counseling/management.
- To develop a successful weight management service, a detailed service business plan should be developed first.

EXPERT INTERVIEW—WEIGHT MANAGEMENT SERVICES IN AN INDEPENDENT COMMUNITY PHARMACY SITE

Dr. Terry Forshee, DPh, PD, CDE, is president and CEO of Take Charge Nutrition, LLC and owns Cherokee Pharmacies located in Cleveland, Tennessee, and Dalton, Georgia. He also owns Cherokee Medical Supply. Dr. Forshee has been practicing independent pharmacy for over 30 years. He has provided weight management services for 13 years and continues to provide them because of the "need" for education and the need to address the obesity epidemic our society is facing. Dr. Forshee's service has grown, in those 13 years, from 3–4 to 12–25 patients in a day. Dr. Forshee firmly believes he has a 100% success rate in educating patients and gages this by quizzes patients take at the end of each session. About 80% of his patients have made positive health-care changes.

Dr. Forshee incorporates the Take Charge Nutrition meal replacement shakes into his service with the ultimate *mission* being to "empower patients to get healthy." The program is "based on empowerment and education; teaching patients that there are alternatives . . . and rebuilding nutritional habits." He *values* education and "the more you learn, the less likely you are to rely on crutches to get results." In fact, the program is designed to offer the patients lessons focusing on different topics related to healthy lifestyle changes. He describes it as a "self-study course" with the pharmacist providing guidance and coaching. The program duration is about 6–12 months. Patients are currently self-paying for this service, but insurance reimbursements are in the foreseeable future for this service.

Dr. Forshee has a unique *workflow design* allowing the program to be a continued success and allow the pharmacist to "maximize his time" with the patient. He utilizes technicians to weigh patients, provide handouts, and administer/complete other necessary paperwork to get the patient ready to see the pharmacists. The first visit typically lasts 1 hour with subsequent visits lasting about 15 minutes. He has designed this specific service to be delivered on 1 day a week. However, occasional exceptions are made to accommodate patients. This lends itself to the existing pharmacy operations. He also involves the patients' physicians, keeping them up-to-date regarding the patient's progress with the program and any significant changes. He sends the physicians a "Health risk analysis" at the beginning and end of the program. As Dr. Forshee stated, weight loss and lifestyle changes can potentially impact medication doses requiring, for example, a diabetes-related medication to be titrated lower to avoid hypoglycemia. This *collaborative partnership* has been fruitful as physicians are now referring patients to the service!

When asked what he enjoys most about providing this service, Dr. Forshee states "seeing the light go on for patients . . . you've seen them change their lifestyle and gain confidence." A personal barrier that Dr. Forshee faced was having the confidence and what he thought was knowledge to provide the service. He didn't pursue additional training in weight management. He learned as he started providing the service, which as pharmacists, we already have the knowledge, and we have the ability to affect change. "We just need to believe in ourselves and in the words of Nike, 'just do it'! It isn't easy, (but it is the) most satisfying part of practicing pharmacy."

STUDY QUESTIONS

1. A patient who weighs 133 lbs and is 59 inches tall has a BMI and weight classification of:
   a. 24, normal weight
   b. 25, overweight
   c. 27, overweight
   d. 30, obese

2. All of the following variables contribute to the increasing prevalence of obesity EXCEPT:
   a. Decreased physical activity
   b. Genetic factors
   c. Increased energy consumption
   d. Increased health-care costs

3. A reasonable and safe weekly weight-loss goal for obese individuals is:
   a. 1–2 pounds
   b. 3–4 pounds
   c. 5–6 pounds
   d. 7–8 pounds

4. A successful weight management program should include which of the following services:
   a. Behavioral therapy
   b. Meal replacements drinks/shakes
   c. Physical therapy
   d. Supplemental energy drinks

5. All of the following herbals have been used for weight loss EXCEPT:
   a. Bitter orange
   b. Chromium
   c. Melatonin
   d. St John's Wort

6. Which of the following disease states are obese patients at increased risk of:
   a. Multiple sclerosis
   b. Osteoporosis
   c. Restless leg syndrome
   d. Sleep apnea

7. The first step to developing a weight management service is to develop the: _____ .
   a. Business plan
   b. Patient scheduling system
   c. Promotion schedule
   d. Workflow design

8. A SWOT analysis includes all of the following EXCEPT:
   a. Strengths
   b. Weaknesses
   c. Outcomes
   d. Threats

9. Which medication can cause weight gain?
   a. Amitriptyline
   b. Digoxin
   c. Effexor
   d. Metformin

10. Which of the following describes a role the community pharmacists can have in a weight management program?
    a. Educating patients on nutritional intake and health risks with obesity
    b. Identifying alternative medication options that do not cause weight gain
    c. Providing patients with behavioral and lifestyle coaching
    d. All of the above are roles community pharmacists can have

11. Which of the following should a patient be counseled on when taking Alli?
    a. Take in place of meals
    b. Supplement with a fat-soluble vitamin
    c. Take prior to eating meals and snacks
    d. Double the dose if fat content >7% of total calories

12. What is a perceived barrier preventing patients from being successful in a weight management program?

a. Cannot afford healthy foods
b. Too much time commitment
c. Unable to exercise
d. All of these are perceived barriers

BIBLIOGRAPHY

1. Centers for Disease Control and Prevention. U.S Obesity Trends. Trends by State 1985-2010. http://www.cdc.gov/obesity/data/trends.html. Accessed September 9, 2011.
2. Ogden CL, Carroll MD, Curtin LR, et al. Obesity among adults in the United States: No statistically significant change since 2003-2004. NCHS data brief no 1. Hyattsville, MD: National Center for Health Statistics; 2007.
3. Weight-Control Information Network. Overweight and obesity statistics. US Department of Health and Human Services. NIH Publication No. 04-4158. Updated February 2010. http://win.niddk.nih.gov/statistics/index.htm. Accessed September 24, 2011.
4. Centers for Disease Control and Prevention. Physical activity and good nutrition: Essential elements to prevent chronic diseases and obesity 2008. http://www.cdc.gov/nccdphp/dnpa. Accessed September 24, 2011.
5. Ogden CL, Carroll MD, Kit BK, Flegal KM. Prevalence of obesity in the United States, 2009-2010. NCH data brief, no. 82. Hyattsville, MD: National Center for Health Statistics; 2012.
6. Centers for Disease Control and Prevention. Adult obesity facts. http://www.cdc.gov/obesity/data/adult.html. Accessed June 10, 2012.
7. Finkelstein EA, Trogdon JG, Cohen JW, et al. Annual medical spending attributable to obesity: Payer-and service-specific estimates. *Health Affairs*. 2009;28(5): 822-831.
8. Hammond RA, Levine R. The economic impact of obesity in the United States. *Diabetes Metab Syndr Obes*. 2010;3:285-295.
9. BRFSS, Behavioral Risk Factor Surveillance System. Centers for Disease Control and Prevention. http://www.cdc.gov/brfss/. Accessed September 24, 2011.
10. Thorpe KE. Prevention takes center stage. *NC Med J*. 2010;71(1):48-51.
11. Poirier P, Giles TD, Bray GA, et al. Obesity and cardiovascular disease: pathophysiology, evaluation, and effect of weight loss. *Circulation*. 2006;113:898-918.
12. Ludwig DS, Pollack HA. Obesity and the economy: from crisis to opportunity. *JAMA*. 2009;301(5):533-535.
13. Malone M. Medications associated with weight gain. *Ann Pharmacother*. 2005;39(12):2046-2055.
14. National Institutes of Health. Clinical guidelines on the identification, evaluation, and treatment of overweight and obesity in adults: The evidence report. US Department of Health and Human Services. NIH Publication No. 98-4083. September 1998.
15. McTigue KM, Harris R, Hemphill B, et al. Screening and interventions for obesity in adults: summary of the evidence for the U.S. Preventative Services Task Force. *Ann Intern Med*. 2003;139:933-949.
16. Kushner RF, Blatner DJ. Risk assessment of the overweight and obese patient. *J Am Diet Assoc*. 2005;105: S53-S62.
17. Flegal KM, Graubard BI, Wiliamson DF, Gail MH. Cause-specific excess deaths associated with underweight, overweight, and obesity. *JAMA*. 2007;298(17): 2028-2037.
18. Klein A, Sheard NF, Pi-Sunyer X, et al. Weight management through lifestyle modification for the prevention and management of type 2 diabetes: rationale and strategies. *Diabetes Care*. 2004;27(8):2067-2073.
19. Kannan H, Thompson S, Bolge SC. Economic and humanistic outcomes associated with comorbid type 2 diabetes, high cholesterol, and hypertension among individuals who are overweight or obese. *J Occup Environ Med*. 2008;50:542-549.
20. Stevens VJ, Obarzanek E, Cook NR, et al. Long-term weight loss and changes in blood pressure: results of the trials of hypertension prevention, phase II. *Ann Intern Med*. 2001;134:1-11.
21. Dattilo AM, Kris-Etherton PM. Effects of weight reduction on blood lipids and lipoproteins: a meta-analysis. *Am J Clin Nutr*. 1992;56:320-328.
22. Giovannucci E, Michaud D. The role of obesity and related metabolic disturbances in cancers of the colon, prostate, and pancreas. *Gastroenterology*. 2007;132: 2208-2225.

23. Foster MC, Hwang SJ, Larson MG, et al. Overweight, obesity and the development of stage 3 CKD: the Framingham heart study. *Am J Kidney Dis.* 2008;52:39-48.
24. Patterson RE, Frank LL, Kristal AR, et al. A comprehensive examination of health conditions associated with obesity in older adults. *Am J Prev Med.* 2004;27(5):385-390.
25. Sullivan PW, Ghushchyan VH, Ben-Hoseph R. The impact of obesity on diabetes, hyperlipidemia, and hypertension in the United States. *Qual Life Res.* 2008;17:1063-1071.
26. Eckel RH. Nonsurgical management of obesity in adults. *N Engl J Med.* 2008;358:1941-1950.
27. VanWormer JJ, French SA, Pereira MA, Welsh EM. The impact of regular self-weighing on weight management: a systematic literature review. *Int J Behav Nutr Phys Act.* 2008;5:54-64.
28. O'Neil PM, Brown JD. Weighing the evidence: benefits of regular weight monitoring for weight control. *J Nutr Educ Behav.* 2005;37:319-322.
29. American Pharmacists Association. *Concepts in Comprehensive Weight Management: Monograph 2: Behavioral Strategies for Weight Management.* Washington, DC: American Pharmacists Association; 2007.
30. Elder JP, Ayala GX, Harris S. Theories and intervention approaches to health-behavior change in primary care. *Am J Prev Med.* 1999;17(4):275-284.
31. DiNoia J, Prochaska JO. Dietary stages of change and decisional balance: a meta-analytic review. *Am J Health Behav.* 2010;34(5):618-632.
32. Prochaska JO. Decision making in the transtheoretical model of behavior change. *Med Decis Making.* 2008;28:845-849.
33. Lexicomp Online. http://online.lexi.com/crlsql/servlet/crlonline. Accessed June 11, 2012.
34. Torgerson JS, Hauptman J, Boldrin MN, et al. Xenical in the prevention of diabetes in obese subjects (XENDOS) study: a randomized study of orlistat as an adjunct to lifestyle changes for the prevention of type 2 diabetes in obese patients. *Diabetes Care.* 2004;27(1):155-161
35. Haddock CK, Poston WS, Dill PL, et al. Pharmacotherapy for obesity: a quantitative analysis of four decades of published randomized clinical trials. *Int J Obes Relat Metab Disord.* 2002;26:262-273.
36. Li Z, Maglione M, Tu W, et al. Meta-analysis: pharmacologic treatment of obesity. *Ann Intern Med.* 2005;142:532-546.
37. Natural Medicines Comprehensive Database. Available at: http://naturaldatabase.therapeuticsresearch.com. Accessed September 27, 2011.
38. Pories WJ, Swanson MS, MacDonald KG, et al. Who would have thought? An operation proves to be the most effective therapy for adult-onset diabetes mellitus. *Ann Surg.* 1995;222:339–350.
39. Sardo P, Walker JH. Bariatric surgery: impact on medication management. *Hospital Pharmacy.* 2008;43:113-120.
40. MarketData Enterprises, Inc. (2011). Diet market worth $60.9 billion in U.S. last year, but growth is flat, due to the recession [Press release]. Retrieved from http://www.dietbusinesswatch.com/uploads/Diet_Mkt_2011_Press_Release.doc.
41. Um IS, Armour C, Krass I, et al. Managing obesity in pharmacy: the Australian experience. *Pharm World Sci.* 2010;32:711–720.
42. Ahrens RA, Hower M, Best AM. Effects of weight reduction interventions by community pharmacists. *J Am Pharm Assoc.* 2003;43:583–589.
43. Serdula MK, Khan LK, Dietz WH. Weight loss counseling revisited. *JAMA.* 2003;289(14):1747–1750.
44. Larson RA. Patients' willingness to pay for pharmaceutical care. *J Am Pharm Assoc.* 2000;40:618–624.
45. Stubbings J, Kliethermes MA. Justifying and planning patient care services. In: Chisholm-Burns MA, Vaillancourt AM, Shepherd M, eds. *Pharmacy Management, Leadership, Marketing and Finance.* Sudbury, MA: Jones and Bartlett Publishers; 2011.
46. Schumock GT, Wong G. Strategic planning in pharmacy operations. In: Desselle SP and Zgarrick DP, eds. *Pharmacy Management: Essentials for All Practice Settings.* 2nd ed. New York, NY: McGraw-Hill Medical; 2009.
47. Schumock GT, Stubbings J. *How to Develop a Business Plan for Pharmacy Services.* Lenexa, KS: American College of Clinical Pharmacy; 2007.
48. Oates, MB, Bhatt P. Advertising and Promotion. In: Chisholm-Burns MA, Vaillancourt AM, Shepherd M, eds. *Pharmacy Management, Leadership, Marketing and Finance.* Sudbury, MA: Jones and Bartlett Publishers; 2011.
49. Centers for Medicare and Medicaid Services. Decision memo for intensive behavioral therapy for obesity (CAG-00423N). US Department of Health and Human Services; 2011. http://www.cms.gov/medicare-coverage-database/details/nca-decision-memo.aspx?&NcaName=Intensive%20Behavioral%20Therapy%20for%20Obesity&bc=ACAAAAAAIAAA&NCAId=253
50. Pfizer. The newest vital sign: A new health literacy assessment tool for health care providers. http://www.pfizerhealthliteracy.com/physicians-providers/NewestVitalSign.aspx. Accessed February 24, 2012.

ANSWERS AND EXPLANATIONS FOR STUDY QUESTIONS

■ CHAPTER 1: PRACTICAL ASPECTS OF SERVICE IMPLEMENTATION

1. Answer c is correct. A quiet, partitioned room is the best location for MTM to be performed because access will be easy for the pharmacist and patient and will allow sufficient privacy during the patient consultation. Answer a is incorrect because this does not allow sufficient privacy during MTM services. Answers b and d are incorrect due to the access issue explained above.

2. Answer c is correct. Because patients often are only familiar with a pharmacist's dispensing responsibilities, they may not be aware of the type and depth of services that can be provided with MTM. Speaking to them face-to-face would be a better method of providing this information as opposed to any of the other answer choices.

3. Answer d is correct. Because when beginning the first MTM session with a patient, the pharmacist should start with a few general open-ended questions to review their current state of management. With this information, other problem areas could be identified, such as inaccurate use of insulin, not using blood glucose logs, or inadequately treating hypoglycemic episodes. Thus, answers a, b, and c are incorrect because they would not be the best counseling points to *begin* an MTM session.

4. Answer c is correct. Because the best way to handle prescribers who are nonresponders would be to continue to make recommendations and tell them that you are just doing your job. Answer a is incorrect because there is always a chance that even a nonresponder could eventually be influenced by your recommendations and become a participator. Having the patient take the recommendation to the prescriber or sending recommendations to another prescriber is not optimal because they do not deal with the prescriber in question directly. Answers b and d are incorrect because either answer b or d, respectively, could jeopardize the patient–prescriber relationship or any future relationship with the nonresponder from developing.

5. Answer d is correct. Because support staff could be used to schedule patients, create medication charts, and to take initial vital sign measurements.

6. Answer a is correct. Answer a is not only correct but also a better choice than answer b (incorrect) because providing MTM services for an employer with more employees increases the opportunities and potential revenue. However, the pharmacist providing MTM services is limited geographically in provision of quality services. Thus, answers c and d are incorrect.

7. Answer b is correct. Because each Medicare Part D plan must include an MTM program within the benefits package, whereas self-funded employer groups and self-pay patients are not required to participate in such services. Thus, answers a and c are incorrect. Answer d is incorrect because MTM can be performed within the community pharmacy setting.

8. Answer c is correct. The seven core chronic diseases that are mentioned as ones that must be targeted with MTM services include hypertension, diabetes, dyslipidemia, respiratory diseases (such as asthma), bone disease (such as osteoporosis), and mental health diseases (such as bipolar disorder). Thus, answer c is the correct answer, and answers a, b, and d are incorrect.

9. Answer c is correct. The Centers for Medicare and Medicaid Services state that plans "must offer

a comprehensive medication review by a pharmacist or other qualified health-care provider at least annually and perform quarterly medication reviews with follow-up interventions when necessary." Thus, answer c is correct, and answers a, b, and d are incorrect.

10. Answer c is correct. Because it is an example specifically of soft-dollar savings gained by saving a prescriber visit and costs associated with a bad clinical outcome. Answers a, b, and d all represent interventions that would lead to hard dollar savings.

CHAPTER 2: DOCUMENTATION

1. Answer b is correct. Patient counseling on its own does not fit the definition of documentation. All acts of documentation result in a record of activity that can be reviewed once an event has already taken place. A log, record, and signature all represent forms of documentation.

2. Answer d is correct. Explanation: There are many reasons to document all patient care activities. Federal and state laws require certain components of documentation. Proper documentation can enhance the continuity of care as it serves as a means of communication between health-care providers. In regards to professional liability, appropriate documentation practices are essential given the possible implications of inappropriate documentation.

3. Answer e is correct. A personal medication record (PMR) and medication action plan (MAP) are included in the current MTM practice guidelines as elements to be given to the patient at visit completion. An updated vaccination history may be reviewed with the patient, but is not a core element of MTM. While a physician consult letter is a core element, it is not routinely given to the patient, but is communicated directly to the physician.

4. Answer c is correct. Patient information cannot be shared with outside parties without documented permission from the patient. The PMR and MAP are forms of written communication with the patient. The physician consult letter is required, and serves as communication with the physician. Some elements of patient care documentation may be required by the patient's third-party payer, and this serves as communication on the care provided to ensure that the care provided meets certain standards.

5. Answer. Once a component has been identified to improve upon, the CQI plan should include a proposal for "Plan," "Do," "Act," and "Check." The improvement plan should include SMART (specific, measurable, achievable, realistic, time-bound) goals for implementation, evaluation, and resolution.

CHAPTER 3: COUNSELING AND MOTIVATIONAL INTERVIEWING

1. Answer a is correct. Within the Indian Health System model, the second prime question asks the patient, "How did your prescriber tell you to take this medication?" An appropriate follow-up question would be answer a. The other answers are incorrect because they reflect appropriate follow-up questions for the first prime question (answer b) or the third prime question (answers c and d).

2. Answer b is correct. From the example given in Table 3-1, a smoker in the contemplation stage of the Transtheoretical Model of Behavior Change would be intending to stop within the next 6 months. Thus, answer b is correct. In the precontemplation stage, the smoker is not intending to quit in the foreseeable future. In the preparation and action stages, the smoker is intending to quit within the next 30 days or is actively

applying overt modifications in his/her lifestyle, respectively. Thus, answer choices a, c, and d are incorrect.

3. Answer a is correct. Because personal or pharmacist-centered barriers could include not having enough confidence in oneself in the ability to communicate with patients. Patient-centered barriers are more likely to include language barriers and low health literacy. Environmental barriers deal mostly with problems inherent with having a prescription counter. Thus, answers b, c, and d are incorrect.

4. Answer c is correct. Because patients are most likely to believe nonverbal communication over verbal communication when the two are incongruent. For example, the pharmacist asks, "How may I help you?" However, if the pharmacist continues to type into the computer terminal rather than looking at the patient during the entire interaction, the patient is most likely to perceive that the pharmacist does *not* want to be of assistance. Thus, answers a, b, and d are incorrect.

5. Answer b is correct. Motivational interviewing is a patient-centered approach (answer a is incorrect). It is an approach where the provider avoids setting an agenda for the discussion (answer d is incorrect) and assesses the willingness of the patient to make behavior changes (answer c is incorrect). The pharmacist should be respectful of the patient's autonomy even when the patient chooses not to change his or her behavior (answer b is correct).

6. Answer d is correct. It is essential when using the motivational interviewing approach to ask the patient for permission before giving information in order to show respect for the patient's autonomy. He or she may not want to receive further information from the pharmacist. Although the pharmacist should give correct information, answer a is incorrect because this should be done regardless of whether one is using motivational interviewing. Answer b involves using closed-ended questions rather than open-ended ones (answer b is incorrect). While patients could be pointed toward articles to expand on information given, this is not as essential in motivational interviewing as it is to respect the patient's autonomy. Thus, answer c is incorrect.

7. Answer d is correct. Because this is the definition for change talk as defined within motivational interviewing. Patient-centered change encompasses the entire aspect of motivational interviewing rather than concentrating on statements made by the patient (answer a is incorrect). Developing discrepancy centers around helping the patient conclude that his or her actions are incongruent with the goals he or she has set (answer b is incorrect). Decisional balance involves discussing the "pros" and "cons" with the patient, and the patient concluding that the latter outweighs the former (answer c is incorrect).

8. Answer b is correct. See the above explanations for answer 7 for definitions of the other answer choices. Answer b is correct because this is the definition for developing discrepancy.

9. Answer a is correct. Rolling with resistance is when the pharmacist acknowledges the patient's statement but remains focused on the main topic rather than responding by arguing (answer a is correct). The pharmacist does not necessarily have to "agree" with the patient's statement but must respect the autonomy of the patient to make that statement (answer b is incorrect). Expressing empathy is not the same as rolling with resistance; thus, answer c is incorrect. Answer d is incorrect because this describes developing discrepancy.

10. Answer c is correct. Because the pharmacist is supporting the patient by congratulating him on the action that he is doing. All other answer choices either do not support the behavior, focus on the

patient rather than the patient's action, or advise the patient to do something incongruent with the behavior that is being supported.

CHAPTER 4: MEDICATION THERAPY MANAGEMENT SERVICES

1. Answer c is correct. Because it is an example of problems with the overall health-care system rather than being a patient-centered factor. Answers a, b, and d all denote patient-centered factors that contribute to medication use problems.

2. Answer a is correct. In pharmaceutical care, practitioners accept the responsibility to reduce medication-related morbidity and mortality. Pharmaceutical care is a patient-centered, rather than a pharmacist-centered, process (answer c is incorrect). It has only one patient care process (answer b is incorrect). Finally, a systematic approach is required (answer d is incorrect).

3. Answer b is correct. The five core elements as stated in answer b are correct. The following are not core elements of a MTM service: provider referral, personnel review, and payment plan (answer a is incorrect); intervention and adverse event monitoring (answer c is incorrect); and systematic provider contact (answer d is incorrect).

4. Answer d is correct. Because economic, humanistic, and clinical outcomes all have been demonstrated through the use of MTM services by pharmacists.

5. Answer c is correct. In New Mexico, the category of pharmacist clinician was established in 1993 under the Pharmacist Prescriptive Authority Act. In Mississippi, pharmacists could be paid for providing care for specific disease states (e.g., asthma, diabetes, hyperlipidemia, and anticoagulation therapy) if the pharmacist pursued credentialing by completing specific educational programs. Services were provided pursuant to a written referral from a provider. Thus, answer a is incorrect. In Minnesota, a pharmaceutical care implementation project was designed for the community pharmacy setting. The collective experience of researchers of this project helped to shape pharmaceutical care practice as defined by Cipolle, Strand, and Morley. Thus, answer b is incorrect.

6. Answer b is correct. Explained in answer 5.

7. Answer b is correct. One of the most often cited examples of MTM is the Ashville Project in North Carolina, which was initiated when two self-insured employer groups began offering payment for pharmacists' pharmaceutical care services for patients with diabetes. The Ten City Challenge replicated this community-based model across 10 other cities. Thus, answer b is correct. Answers c and d are incorrect, as defined in the explanation of answer 5. Clinical Pharmacy Demonstration Projects represent the first federal initiative to recognize MTM services and funded 18 demonstration projects across the country. This was similar to the Ashville Project, in that it focused primarily on diabetes; however, answer a is incorrect.

8. Answer d is correct. North Carolina (answer a is incorrect) developed the category of Clinical Pharmacist Practitioner in 2000, which can provide drug therapy management under supervision of a licensed physician under authority of the Boards of Pharmacy and Medicine. Drug therapy management includes controlled substances (answer b is incorrect), and a certificate program must be completed with the Board of Pharmacy (answer C is incorrect).

9. Answer b is correct. Because this is the definition of a patient-centered medical home. An accountable care organization brings together multiple providers in a risk-sharing arrangement (answer a is incorrect). Primary care initiated services and an evidence-based medicine approach are not discussed in the "Future Directions" section of the chapter (answers c and d are incorrect).

10. Answer a is correct. In contrast to a fee-for-service model, a performance-based model of reimbursement encourages providers to work in a collaborative care environment (answer a is correct). Answers b, c, and d all discuss disadvantages that are inherent in the fee-for-service model, and are incorrect.

CHAPTER 5: ASTHMA

1. Answer c is correct. According to Figure 5–2, adherence, environmental factors and comorbid conditions should be assessed before any changes to stepwise therapy.

2. Answer b is correct. Because pharmacists are medication experts, medication history and inhaler and device training are natural extensions of the pharmacist's role. Environmental trigger education is a vital part of asthma care education, but comprehensive physical exams are within the scope of practice of the referring practitioner.

3. Answer a is correct. This expense would be categorized as SAL and would be included with the salary of the amount of time the pharmacist or RN, in this case, would spend per week in appointments and conducting follow- up. This expense would not be considered materials and supplies, non-salary fixed costs, or rent/non-rent overhead costs.

4. Answer d is correct. Because answer d offers an assessment, its supporting information, a specific evidence-based recommendation (Step 4 of stepwise approach to therapy), and a plan for follow-up. Answer a is unprofessional and provides an unsupported conclusion. Answer b is more specific but is not specific enough for the provider to reply with a "yes" or "no." Answer c is also unsupported, offers no information to the provider on why Pulmicort® should be prescribed and offers no dosage.

5. Answer b is correct. Because answer b correctly explains that peak flow meters measure PEFR and spirometry measures FEV_1. Answer a is incorrect because while spirometry is more accurate than peak flow meters, they can be helpful in self-monitoring. Answer c is incorrect because both are highly dependent on patient effort. Answer d is incorrect because both measure different information and have evidence-based recommendations for use.

CHAPTER 6: IMMUNIZATION SERVICES

1. Answer c is correct. Because currently available data does suggest a possible association between Guillain–Barre syndrome and immunization with meningococcal vaccine (see Table 6-1). However, this risk is incredibly small, if it exists at all, with 26 cases reported with 6 weeks of immunization, after nearly *15 million* vaccines given. Large-scale studies have shown that no vaccine causes SIDs (answer a), autism (answer b), and that the hepatitis B vaccine does not cause multiple sclerosis (E). Furthermore, no vaccine contains antifreeze (answer d).

2. True. Please see Table 6-5. This information is current as of May 2012.

3. Answer a is correct. As of May 2012, Alabama was the only state that required a prescription for all vaccines in order for a pharmacist to administer them (i.e., a pharmacist could not vaccinate under a protocol or standing order) (see Table 6-5).

4. Answer e is correct. Based on the prescribing information for TIV products, anyone with a severe allergic reaction to egg protein should not be vaccinated (see Table 6-2). History of seizures (answer c) or minor illness (answer d) is often cited as reason not to be vaccinated, but are actually false contraindications. Children as young as 6 months old (answer a) and those with chronic medical conditions (answer b) should receive this vaccine.

5. Answer b is correct. Currently, every person should receive one dose of Tdap in a lifetime, and then get regular Td boosters (see Table 6-2).

6. Answer d is correct. The recommended series for HPV involves three doses at 0, 2, and 6 months (see Tables 6-2 and 6-3). This is now recommended as part of the routine adolescent vaccinations, but can be given anytime between the ages of 9 and 26.

7. Answer c is correct. Because the patient meets three criteria for revaccination: She is greater than 65 years of age, was vaccinated with PPSV more than 5 years ago, and was younger than 65 years at the time of her first dose (see Tables 6-2 and 6-3). Therefore, she should receive a second dose of PPSV at this time. No one less than 2 years old should receive PPSV (answer a). This boy (answer b) does not have any indications that would make him high risk and require vaccination beyond normal childhood vaccines. This old woman (answer d) is not greater than 65 years old, so does not need to be revaccinated yet, and this old man (answer e) received his first vaccine with PPSV after he turned 65 years old, so does not need revaccinating.

8. Answer c is correct. MMR (measles, mumps, and rubella) contains live virus, and cannot be given with blood products (see Table 6-3). All other vaccine products listed here are inactivated immunizations, and can be given without regard to timing with blood products.

9. Answer d is correct. The vaccine lot number (answer a) is required by VICP and MUST be documented. It is also wise to document the site of injection(s) (answer c), especially if more than one vaccine is being given, in case of an adverse reaction. Therefore, the correct answer is d. It is not necessary to document the patient co-payment (answer b). In fact, in many cases, there is no patient co-payment involved, so would be nothing to document.

10. Answer e is correct. Zoster is currently the only vaccine covered by Medicare Part D. Hepatitis B (high-risk) (answer a), influenza (answer b), and pneumococcal polysaccharide vaccine (answer d) are all covered by Medicare Part B.

CHAPTER 7: NONPRESCRIPTION AND SELF-CARE

1. Answer e is correct. Prescription medications via a collaborative practice agreement would not be considered self-care because it would require "seeking professional advice" that would not be sought when applying self-care principles.

2. False. Approximately 81% of consumers purchase an OTC product that their pharmacists recommend.

3. Answer f is correct. Open-ended questions combined with effective listening will lead to patients providing the most complete information. Directed and leading questions may lead to patients providing only the information pharmacists are seeking and leaving out important details. Validated survey tools would not be necessary to obtain a patient history but may be useful in assessing risk or other helpful clinical information.

4. Answer a is correct. This patient is describing the quality of pain. Descriptors of pain as burning, tingling and like "pins and needles" can help the pharmacist determine the cause of the pain and best determine a recommendation. Precipitating would be incorrect because the patient is not telling us what cause the pain to begin, relief is incorrect because there is not description of what cause the pain to feel better, and temporal factors such as how often it occurs are not described.

5. False. OTC consultations should be recorded via paper or electronic charting systems in order to maintain a complete medication record and are necessary to help facilitate payment for these services.

6. Answer a is correct. Cetirizine is the most closely related nonprescription, second generation antihistamine. Diphenhydramine and chlorpheniramine are both first-generation antihistamines that may increase the risk of drowsiness compared with

cetirizine. Ranitidine is an H_1 blocker use as an antacid as opposed to an antihistamine.

CHAPTER 8: LIPID DISORDERS

1. Answer d is correct. Based on STELLAR trial, LDL reduction among statins is highest with rosuvastatin at maximum doses.

2. Answer d is correct. Pharmacists are in a unique position to address multiple health-related barriers. Patient-specific counseling allows assessment of nonadherence, while medication utilization review gives a complete picture of drug-related interactions and adverse reactions.

3. Answer c is correct. Abdominal aortic aneurysm and peripheral artery disease (formerly known as peripheral vascular disease) are clearly risk equivalents. Ischemic stroke, particularly of carotid origin, is considered a risk equivalent in general; however, hemorrhagic stroke is not.

4. Answer e is correct. Trilipix is the first fibric acid derivative to have labeling information for use with statins. The primary reason is a lack of significant hepatic metabolism, and therefore lowers risk of statin–fibrate drug–drug interaction.

5. False. Non-fasting states will result in higher triglyceride levels. This is a critical concept since the Friedewald's equation is inaccurate in non-fasting states. While triglycerides are increased, LDL is falsely lowered.

CHAPTER 9: SMOKING CESSATION

1. Answer d is correct. Because nicotine does cause an increase in blood pressure, stroke volume, and cardiac output. Answers a and b are incorrect because nicotine causes the release of dopamine in the brain and nicotine crosses the blood–brain barrier quickly, respectively. Diabetic neuropathy is more likely for diabetic patients who smoke because carbon monoxide from cigarette smoke binds to hemoglobin and decreases the amount of oxygen that is transported to peripheral tissues. Thus, answer c is also incorrect.

2. Answer a is correct. For patients willing to quit, pharmacists can be of assistance by following the "five A's" as given in answer. Pharmacotherapy should be recommended for all patients willing to quit, except for pregnant patients, adolescents, and those with medical contraindications. Thus, answer c is incorrect. Answer d is incorrect because the "R" part of the START plan given in the chapter represents "Remove all tobacco products from the environment," not "Resist urges." Finally, answer b is incorrect because it is not productive to set a quit date for patients unwilling to quit, as these patients would not even be in the contemplation stage of the Transtheoretical Model of Behavioral Change.

3. Answer c is correct. Because she smokes approximately 30 cigarettes a day and will use an adequate number of scheduled times for nicotine gum. Answer a is incorrect because the number of cigarettes used per day determines the use of 2 mg (<25 cigarettes per day) or 4 mg (>25 cigarettes per day) nicotine gum. Answer b is incorrect because nicotine replacement therapy should not be recommended for pregnant patients, and answer d is incorrect because the smoker only wants prescription therapy (nicotine gum is OTC only, of course).

4. Answer d is correct. Answer a is incorrect because bupropion is not a partial nicotine agonist; that would be varenicline. Answer b is incorrect because it gives the wrong dose for varenicline, and neither bupropion nor varenicline should be started on the exact quit date. These smoking cessation medications should be started 1-2 weeks prior to the quit date in order to ensure an adequate blood concentration of the medications at

the time of smoking cessation. Answer d is a correct statement.

5. Answer e is correct. Because one smoking cessation medication that is effective for all smokers does not exist. All smoking cessation medications must be individualized.

6. Answer e is correct. All of the answers besides answer choice e represent important considerations for a pharmacist prior to setting up smoking cessation services. However, these should not be considered "significant" barriers, so answer e is correct.

7. Answer b is correct. Although the patient in this case could have been switched to other equally appropriate medications, answer b is the most plausible of the others given. It would be inappropriate to simply start a proton pump inhibitor in response to the adverse events (indigestion and heartburn) experienced in answer a. It would also be inappropriate to restart a medication that previously failed (Chantix), if the patient previously had given it an appropriate trial. Thus, answers a and c are incorrect. Although combination therapy would be a reasonable choice, answer d is also incorrect because a long-acting medication (either nicotine patch or bupropion) would have been more appropriate with prn nicotine lozenges.

8. Answer d is correct. Because it is the only true statement regarding the use of nicotine gum. This nicotine replacement therapy should be chewed until a "tingle" is experienced (after approximately 15 chews), and then it should be parked—rather than chewed continuously for 30 minutes. Thus, answer a is incorrect. Drinking acidic beverages could decrease the effectiveness of the nicotine gum (answer b is incorrect), and as monotherapy it should only be used as a scheduled medication (answer c is incorrect).

9. Answer d is correct. Because medication therapy for a smoking cessation attempt should not be recommended for patients who are pregnant, adolescents, and those with medical contraindications.

10. Answer a is correct. Regarding Chantix or bupropion, either should be started at least 1-2 weeks prior to the quit date set by the patient (answer b is incorrect). Stopping smoking and then starting either medication would delay the effectiveness of the medication being at a steady-state level, and would most likely result in a failed quit attempt (answer c is incorrect). Answer d is incorrect because the patient should be encouraged that a "slip" by smoking a cigarette or two should not preclude continuing the cessation medication and rededicating oneself to the quit attempt. Thus, only answer a is correct.

11. Answer d is correct. According to the guidelines *Treating Tobacco Use and Dependence*, women who are pregnant should be encouraged to stop nicotine use without cessation medications.

12. Answer b is correct. Answer b is the only answer listed that is a black box warning for Chantix. Specifically, the black box warning states that patients should be "monitored for serious neuropsychiatric events including behavior change, hostility, agitation, depression, and suicidality as well as worsening of preexisting psychiatric illness."

■ CHAPTER 10: ANTICOAGULATION SERVICES

1. Answer a is correct. A CLIA waiver certificate allows you to perform waived tests, such as POC monitors for testing INR. This is a biannual registration that states you will follow all of the manufacturer-recommended guidelines when performing tests utilizing their monitor.

2. Answer c is correct. A HIPPA form, signed by the patient, needs to be submitted to any provider with whom you request personal information. A copy of the signed form needs to be maintained in the patients file.

3. Answer a is correct. The ACCP evidence-based clinical practice guidelines are periodically updated with the most up-to-date information pertaining to appropriate INR goals for multiple disease states. Other publications will include INR goals, but for limited diseases; thus this is the best possible answer.

4. Answer d is correct. TTR is a widely accepted measure of quality within a practice setting.

5. Answer c is correct. $CHADS_2$ is a validated tool that is recommended to assess a patients stroke risk when they present with a-fib. Based on the overall score, recommendations are present as to whether or not initiate oral anticoagulation at a goal INR or to initiate aspirin.

CHAPTER 11: DIABETES

1. Answer a is correct. Arthropathy is pain in the joints, which would not be affected by microvascular damage. Neuropathy, retinopathy, and nephropathy (answer choices b, c, and d) are all complications resulting from microvascular damage.

2. Answer d is correct. Answer a is incorrect because the applicant must have completed 2 years of professional practice. Answer b is incorrect because a minimum of 1000 hours of direct DSME must be documented in past 4 years. Answer c is incorrect because the 40% of required hours of direct DSME must be accrued within the past year.

3. Answer c is correct. All the other avenues for reimbursement indicated in answers a, b, and d are available in some states, but Medicare Part A is only for hospital services, long-term care facilities, hospice, and some home health services.

4. Answer a is correct. A patient who is younger with a short duration of diabetes, long life expectancy, and no significant CVD may have a lower goal of <6.5%. Answer b is incorrect because hypoglycemia is a significant concern and the goal is to prevent this rather than trying to further lower the A1C to reach a more stringent goal. Answers c and d are incorrect because these are reasons one may set a slightly higher A1C goal of <8%.

5. Answer b is correct. Men ≥50 years of age or women ≥60 years of age with at least one major risk factor including hypertension, family history of CVD, smoking, dyslipidemia, or albuminuria or patients with a 10-year cardiovascular risk >10%.

6. Answer b is correct. One should avoid metformin in females with serum creatinine ≥1.4 or in males with serum creatinine ≥1.5. Answer a is incorrect because a patient can be started on metformin at any A1C level, even if the patient has prediabetes. Answer c is incorrect because the goal is to titrate the dose to 1000 mg twice daily if tolerated. Answer d is incorrect because metformin has a low risk of hypoglycemia.

7. Answer c is correct. One way of estimating starting doses is to either start 10 units qhs, or estimate based on weight by using 0.1–0.2 units/kg/day. This would give you an estimate between 10 and 20 units/day. Answer a is incorrect because 50 units would be 0.5 units/kg/day that is too high of a starting dose, and the patient would have a greater likelihood of having hypoglycemia. Answer b is incorrect because 40 units are still too high for this patient. This could possibly be an option if the patient's HbA1C was very high (>10%), but since this patient has an HbA1C of 8.5%, 40 units would not be the best answer. Answer d is incorrect because 5 units are too small of a dosage for this 100-kg patient.

CHAPTER 12: HYPERTENSION

1. Answer e is correct. End-organ damage, such as with myocardial infarction, CVA, and kidney failure can result from uncontrolled hypertension. Also, uncontrolled hypertension could lead to retinopathy, angina, coronary revascularization, left ventricular hypertrophy, heart failure,

nephrosclerosis, and peripheral artery disease. Thus, answer e is correct in that all of the answer choices listed could be complications.

2. Answer c is correct. Because patients with CKD, according to the JNC 7 and the American Heart Association, should try to achieve the goal blood pressure <130/80 mm Hg. Answer b is incorrect because it is the general blood pressure goal for most patients. Answer d is incorrect because it is the goal for patients with >1 g of proteinuria, according to the National Kidney Foundation. Answer a is not the goal for any condition.

3. Answer b is correct. Answer a is incorrect because using a cuff that is too small would overestimate blood pressure, while the reverse is true for a cuff that is too large. Answers c and d are incorrect because these actions would not result in over- or underestimation of blood pressure. However, answers c and d could result in an actual increase in the blood pressure measured.

4. Answer a is correct. Because an ACE inhibitor, such as lisinopril, is recommended as first-line drug of choice for a patient with hypertension and diabetes. Metoprolol is no longer recommended as a first-line choice unless the patient has a history of an MI (answer c is incorrect). Answer d is incorrect because clonidine is not a first-line antihypertensive choice. While amlodipine used first line could be reasonable, it is not the best choice above an ACE inhibitor for a patient with both hypertension and diabetes (answer b is incorrect).

5. Answer d is correct. Because little evidence directly compares hydrochlorothiazide and chlorthalidone for hypertension. It is also difficult to compare studies using either agent due to study differences (answer c is incorrect). Stronger data supports the use of chlorthalidone in patients with hypertension to prevent stroke, fatal CV events, and nonfatal CV events (answer a is incorrect). However, treatment choice should be individualized (answer b is incorrect).

6. Answer b is correct. Combination therapy should include a thiazide diuretic plus either an ACE inhibitor or ARB or D-CCB or BB. Answer b (correct) has both a thiazide diuretic and a D-CCB. Answers a and c are incorrect because a BB plus thiazide diuretic should be reserved for patients with angina or CHD (answer choices also do not include a thiazide diuretic). Hydralazine is not recommended as a first-line combination with a thiazide diuretic (answer d is incorrect).

7. Answer c is correct. For elderly patients with hypertension, expert opinion suggests that the goal for one with isolated systolic hypertension should be to control SBP without decreasing DBP below 50 mm Hg. Thus, answer c is correct, and answers a, b, and d are incorrect.

8. Answer b is correct. Secondary causes of hypertension include chronic kidney disease, pheochromocytoma, primary hyperaldosteronism, sleep apnea, thyroid disease, coarctation of the aorta, and Cushing syndrome, according to the JNC 7. Thus, answer b is correct, and answers a, c, and d are incorrect.

9. Answer d is correct. According to the JNC 7, methyldopa is the drug of choice to treat hypertension during pregnancy. Labetalol, while a good alternative, is not considered the drug of choice (answer a is incorrect). Although BB are considered generally to be safe in this population, metoprolol is not considered the drug of choice (answer c is incorrect). Diuretics are not considered first-line therapy in pregnancy because of the theoretical concern of decreased plasma volume, which could contribute to preeclampsia (answer b is incorrect).

10. Answer c is correct. A pharmacist should be the only personnel in the pharmacy developing treatment plan recommendations. All other answers (answers a, b, d, and e) are incorrect because they are reasonable responsibilities that can be delegated to a nonpharmacist staff member.

CHAPTER 13: OSTEOPOROSIS

1. Answer a is correct. In 2005, it was estimated that osteoporosis-related complications (such as fractures) cost $17 billion in the United States. With the aging population, this financial burden is expected to double or triple by the year 2040.

2. Answer d is correct. Osteoporosis: BMD is 2.5 SD or more below that of a "young normal" adult (T-score at or below −2.5).

3. Answer a is correct. Calcium is available in several over-the-counter supplement products including calcium carbonate (40% elemental calcium) and calcium citrate (21% elemental calcium). Calcium phosphate, calcium lactate, and calcium gluconate are not recommended for calcium supplementation because they have small amounts of elemental calcium.

4. Answer a is correct. Dual-energy x-ray absorptiometry (DXA) is the gold standard to determine BMD, which can be either central or peripheral. Diagnosis of osteoporosis is only determined by central DXA, and screening may occur via peripheral DXA (pDXA).

5. Answer c is correct. Currently the National Osteoporosis Foundation (NOF), American Association of Clinical Endocrinologists (AACE), and International Society of Clinical Densitometry (ISCD) recommend BMD screening.

6. Answer d is correct. BMD screening is recommended for all women aged 65 and greater regardless of risk factors, all postmenopausal women with a fracture, postmenopausal women younger than 65 years with one or more risk factors (other than fracture or low sex hormones), and any women who are considering therapy for osteoporosis.

7. Answer d is correct. Marketing is the key to making any screening service successful. Utilizing trained members of the pharmacy team to identify patients at risk, such as women over the age of 50 and patients taking medications that increase the risk of osteoporosis, is a very effective way to target marketing efforts. Gaining buy-in from the primary care providers can provide a referral base for osteoporosis risk assessments.

CHAPTER 14: OBESITY— WEIGHT MANAGEMENT SERVICES

1. Answer c is correct. The BMI formula is total body weight (kg)/height squared (m^2) or as weight (lbs)/height (in^2) × 703. So, 133 lbs/59 in^2 × 703 is equal to 26.8 rounded to 27. A BMI of 27 falls in the category of 25–29.9, which is overweight. While 24 is a normal weight BMI, 25 is an overweight BMI, and 30 is an obese BMI (a, b, and d), the patient's calculated BMI comes out to be 27.

2. Answer d is correct. Genetics and increased energy consumption coupled with decreased physical activity all contribute to the increasing prevalence of obesity (answers a, b, and c). All of the variables, in turn, contribute to increased health-care costs (answer d).

3. Answer a is correct. The National Institutes of Health Clinical Guidelines on the Identification, Evaluation, and Treatment of Overweight and Obesity in Adults recommends targeting a weight loss goal of 10% over 6 months or a weight loss of about 1-2 pounds per week.

4. Answer a is correct. The cornerstone of a weight management program should include three factors (dietary modification, increased physical activity, and behavioral interventions) to lead to a more successful program and a higher likelihood of achieving long-term weight management. It is well documented that patients will regain lost weight unless their weight management program

consists of all three of these factors. While meal replacement shakes, physical therapy, and supplemental energy drinks (answer b, c, and d) can be helpful, they are not factors that should be included in all weight management programs.

5. Answer c is correct. Melatonin is an herbal commonly used for insomnia, jet lag, and shift work sleep disorder. Bitter orange (answer a) is generally recognized as safe (GRAS) in the United States per the Natural Medicines Comprehensive Database. However, it has insufficient evidence when used for obesity. Chromium also has insufficient evidence for use in obesity (answer b). St John's wort is more commonly used for depression, but can also be used for weight loss (answer d). This also has insufficient evidence for use in weight loss.

6. Answer d is correct. Obesity puts people at risks for several chronic diseases including, but not limited to, diabetes, hypertension, dyslipidemia, infertility, and sleep apnea. Multiple sclerosis, osteoporosis, and restless leg syndrome are conditions that do not result from obesity (answers a, b, and c).

7. Answer a is correct. The first step in developing a weight management service should include the development of a business plan. The patient scheduling system, promotion schedule, and workflow design (answers b, c, and d) are all important considerations but are not the first step.

8. Answer c is correct. The letters in "SWOT" analysis stand for strengths (answer a), weaknesses (answer b), opportunities [not outcomes (answer c)], and threats (answer d).

9. Answer a is correct. A common side effect of amitriptyline is weight gain. The frequency is not defined. Digoxin (answer b) is more commonly associated with cardiovascular-related side effects. Effexor (answer c) is associated with anorexia (up to 17% incidence) and weight loss versus weight gain (up to 6% incidence). Metformin (answer d) is weight neutral and in some instances can be associated with weight loss versus weight gain.

10. Answer d is correct. Educating patients on nutritional intake and health risks associated with obesity (answer a), identifying alternative medication options that do not cause weight gain (answer b), and providing patients with behavioral and lifestyle coaching (answer c), which is a cornerstone treatment approach, are all roles community pharmacists can have in a weight management program (answer d). Pharmacists are in a great position to counsel patients regarding alternative choices for medications and educate and motivate patients on weight loss plans.

11. Answer b is correct. Alli® is commonly associated with gastrointestinal side effects (>10% incidence). Many patients will experience oily spotting, fecal urgency, fatty/oily stools, and increased defecation. These side effects can be attributed to the mechanism of action, which inhibits the absorption of dietary fats and fat-soluble vitamins. Patients should be counseled to supplement with fat-soluble vitamins (answer b) and to take it 2 hours before or after taking Alli. Alli should not be taken in place of meals (answer a). It should be taken up to 1 hour after eating a meal containing fat (answer c). There are only two strengths available: Alli OTC is labeled for 60 mg three times daily with meals containing fat. Xenical® prescription is labeled for 120 mg three times daily with meals containing fat.

12. Answer d is correct. All three choices are perceived barriers patients have that prevent them from being successful in a weight management program [cannot afford healthy foods (answer a), too much time commitment (b), and unable to exercise (answer c)]. These should all become areas for pharmacists to focus on during a weight management session when addressing behavioral interventions. There are several approaches available when working with patients and overcoming these barriers.

INDEX

Page numbers with f and t indicates figure and table.

A

Accountable care organizations (ACO), 57, 58
ACE-I-induced angioedema, 261
Adverse drug events (ADE), 50
Affordable Care Act (ACA), 57, 133
Alpha-glucosidase inhibitors (AGI), 230
American Association of Diabetes Educators, 236
American College of Clinical Pharmacy (ACCP), 53
American Diabetes Association (ADA), 225
American Heart Association (AHA), 254
American Pharmacists Association (APhA), 51–52, 132, 233
    core elements, 52–53
American Society of Internal Medicine, 121
Angiotensin-converting enzyme (ACE), 226
Angiotensin II receptor blockers (ARB), 226
Anticoagulation Service (AS), 198, 215
    billing strategy, 206
    case study, 206–207
    coumadin®, 222
    developing, 200–202
    goals and scope of service
        protocol development, 202–203
        quality control/quality assurance, 203
        resources needed, 203–205
    location, 205
    pharmacist value in, 200
    promotion plan, 205–206
    protocol, 215–222
    role of, 198
    target market, 202
Antihypertensive and Lipid Lowering Treatment to Prevent Heart Attack (ALLHAT), 259
Apolipoprotein (apo), 144
Asheville Project, 57, 66
Asthma
    action plan, 68f

    adult dosages
        for long-term medications, 94
        for quick-relief medications, 93
    assessment of, 65
    care education, 66
    case study, 79–80
    classification scheme, 89–90
    clinic initiation, 71–79, 78f
    definition of, 64–65
    follow-up workup, 88–89
    history workup, 87–88
    home treatment protocol, 95f
    inhaled corticosteroids for, 92
    management, 64–71, 85
        components, 65–71
        follow-up visit protocol, 86–87
        incorrect inhaler technique in, 64
        initial visit protocol, 85–86
    managing in adults, 90–91
    medication for, 67, 67t, 71
    monitoring of, 65
    referral form, 75f
    service cost, 73t
    SWOT analysis, 72
    symptoms, 65
        assessment questionnaires, 66t
    in youths
        managing, 69f
        severity and initiating treatment, 70f
Asthma and Allergy Foundation of America, 64
Atrial valve replacement (AVR), 199
Aversion therapy, for smoking cessation, 177

B

Behavioral modification strategies, in smoking cessation, 169–171. *See also* Smoking cessation
    practical changes to implement, 169–171, 170t
    recognizing and preventing triggers, 169
    self-observation, 169

Behavioral Risk Factor Surveillance System (BRFSS), 265
Beta-blockers (BB), 262
Bile acid sequestrants, role of, 148, 150
Board Certified-Advanced Diabetes Management Certification (BC-ADM), 233
Body mass index (BMI), 135, 147
Bolus insulin, for diabetes, 232–233
Bone densitometry devices, 283
    case, 287
    characteristics of, 284t
    compensation/reimbursement, 284–285
    components of, 285–287
    developing services, 283
    interview, 290
Bone mineral density (BMD), 278
    screening program, 283
Bronchial hyperresponsiveness (BHR), 64
Bupropion, 179

C

Calcium-rich foods, 279
Cardiovascular disease (CVD), 225, 254
    and type 2 diabetes, 226
Carotid intimal medial thickening (CIMT), 147
Centers for Disease Control and Prevention (CDC), 64, 100, 124, 302
Centers for Medicare and Medicaid Services (CMS), 5, 17, 123, 204, 236
Cerebral vascular disease (CVD), 146
Certified asthma educator (AE-C), 71
Certified Diabetes Educator (CDE®), 233
Cessation, benefits of, 163
CHADS$_2$
    scoring, 198t
    stroke risk, 199t
Chlorthalidone, 259
Chronic kidney disease (CKD), 147, 258
    defined, 147
Chronic obstructive pulmonary disease (COPD), 162
Chylomicrons, 144
Clinical Laboratory Improvement Amendment (CLIA), 204, 235–236
Clinical pharmacist practitioner (CPP), 56
Clinical Pharmacy Demonstration Projects (CPDP), 55
Cockroft–Gault equation, 259
Cold turkey, 173
Collaborative practice agreement (CPA), 68, 153, 264
    for asthma pharmacy services, 76–79, 77t
Combination therapy, 262
Community, anticoagulation services in, 198
    billing strategy, 206
    case study, 206–207
    developing, 200–202
    goals and scope of service
        protocol development, 202–203
        quality control/quality assurance, 203
        resources needed, 203–205
    location, 205
    oral anticoagulation, disease states requiring, 198–199
    pharmacist value in, 200
    promotion plan, 205–206
    target market, 202
Community pharmacy, 16
    lipid management services in
        business plan, 153
        collaborative practice agreement, 153
        documentation, communication, and reimbursement, 154
        patient visits, 154
        recruiting patients, 153–154
Comprehensive medication review (CMR), 5
Confidence interval (CI), 225
Continuous quality improvement (CQI), 27
Coronary artery calcium (CAC), 147
Coronary artery disease (CAD), 162
Coronary heart disease (CHD), 146
C-reactive protein (CRP), 147
Creatinine phosphokinase (CPK), 148
Current Procedural Terminology (CPT), 136, 206

D

D-CCB agents, 262
Deep vein thrombosis (DVT), 198
Diabetes, 224–225
    blindness and, 224
    bolus insulin for, 232–233
    case study, 244–245
    clinical service design and collaborative practice agreements, 240–244
    clinic initiation, 233–244, 241f
    concomitant disease state goals, 226–227
    cost of, 224
    diagnosis of, 225

goal of, 225–226
and hyperglycemia, 227–228
and hypoglycemia, 227–228
insulin therapy for, 232–233, 234t–235t
medical nutrition therapy and exercise, 228–229
medication therapy
   management services in, 243f–244f
   and principles of management, 230–233
primary counseling concepts, 227–229
services, 239t
therapeutic management of, 225–233
tobacco use and, 227
treatment of, 231t
triple therapy for, 232
Diabetes Control and Complications Trial (DCCT), 224
Diabetes Education Accreditation Program (DEAP), 236
Diabetes mellitus (DM), 146
  categories of, 225
  goals of, 225
Diabetes self-management education (DSME), 229
Diabetes self-management training (DSMT), 236
Diagnostic and Statistical Manual of Mental Disorders, 171
Dihydropyridine calcium channel blockers (D-CCB), 261
Dipeptidyl peptidase 4 (DPP-4) inhibitors, 230
Docosahexaenoic acid (DHA), 151
Documentation, for pharmacists
  components of, 17, 20–24
    drug therapy problems, 21t
    outcomes, 20–22
    reminders, 22–24
    SOAP note revisited, 22, 23f, 24f
  defined, 16
  importance of, 16–17
    continuity of care, 16
    professional liability, 17
    regulatory policy, 17
  purpose of
    continuous quality improvement, 27
    pharmacy's bottom line, implications on, 26–27
  resources, 24–26
    current situation, 24, 25f
    staff training, 26
    system, 24–26
  role of, 26–27
Dopamine, 162–163
Drug facts label, importance of, 132, 133
Drug-induced HTN, 264
Drug utilization review (DUR), 7
Dry powder inhalers (DPI), 64

E

Eicosapentaenoic acid (EPA), 151
Electronic health record (EHR), 16
Emerging Risk Factor Collaboration (EFRC), 147
Estimated cost avoidance (ECA), 20
European Association for the Study of Diabetes (EASD), 230
Expert Panel Report 3 (EPR3), 64
Ezetimibe, role of, 148

F

Fagerstrom test, of nicotine dependence, 165, 166t
Fenofibrate, 151
Fenofibric acid, 151
  adverse effects of, 151
Fibrates, 150t, 151
Food and Drug Administration (FDA), 150, 173, 230
Forced expiratory volume in the first second of expiration (FEV_1), 65
Forced vital capacity (FVC), 65
Framingham risk methods, 147

G

Gastroesophageal reflux disorder (GERD), 67
Gemfibrozil, 151
Glucagon-like peptide 1 (GLP-1), 230

H

Haemophilus influenzae type b, 122
Hard dollar savings, 7–8. *See also* Medication therapy management (MTM) services
Health-care practitioners (HCP), 215
Hemoglobin A_{1c} (HbA_{1c}), 54
High-density lipoprotein (HDL), 144, 226
Human immunodeficiency virus (HIV), 147
Hydrochlorothiazide, 259
Hydroxymethylglutaryl-CoA (HMG-CoA), 148
Hyperaldosteronism, primary, 264
Hyperglycemia. *See also* Diabetes
  and diabetes, 227–228
  symptoms of, 228
Hyperosmolar hyperglycemic nonketotic syndrome (HHNS), 228

Hypertension
  blood pressure and pulse measurements, 255
  classification, 254
  complications of, 251
  epidemiology of, 251
  interview, 270–271
  JNC 7 Definition, 255t
    cuff size selection, 256, 256t
    patient position, 255
  lifestyle interventions, 257–258, 258t
    counseling tips, 258–259
  medication management, 259
    comorbid conditions, 260t
    treatment, with thiazide diuretics 259
    treatment—ACE inhibitors, 261–262
  patient case, 267
  risk of, 303
  service development, 264–267
Hypertensive urgency and emergency, 264
Hypoglycemia. *See also* Diabetes
  and diabetes, 227–228

I

Immunization service, 119t
  adult, 101t–105t
  case study, 124–125
  documentation, 121–122
  marketing, 121
  pediatric, 106t–112t
  and pharmacists, 98
  planning
    business plan, 120–121
    facilities and resources, 116, 119
    legal issues, 100, 116
    physician collaborator, 121
    workflow, 119–120
  reimbursement, 122–123, 123t
  resource list, 123–124
  role of, 98
Incorrect inhaler technique, in asthma management, 64. *See also* Asthma
Indian Health Service Model, 30–31
Inhaled corticosteroid (ICS) inhalers, 64
Institute of Medicine (IOM), 50
Insulin therapy, for diabetes, 232–233, 234t–235t. *See also* Diabetes
Intermediate-density lipoprotein (IDL), 144

International normalized ratio (INR), 198
International Society of Clinical Densitometry (ISCD), 278
Ischemic stroke, risk factor for, 198

J

Joint Commission on Accreditation of Healthcare Organizations (JCAHO), 180
Journal of Asthma and Allergy Educators, 76

K

Ketoacidosis, 228
Korotkoff technique, 255

L

Lipase inhibitor, 309
Lipid disorders, 144
  case study, 154
  causes of, 145t
  definition, classification, characteristics, and general treatment of, 144t
  medication management, 152–153
    LDL-lowering agents, 148–151
    triglyceride-lowering agents, 151–152
  patient evaluation
    cardiovascular risk factors, 146t
    identification of risk, 146, 146t
    lipoprotein levels, classification of, 145
    risk factors, 146–147
    therapeutic dietary recommendations, 148t
    therapeutic lifestyle changes, 147
Lipid, management services in community pharmacy
  business plan, 153
  collaborative practice agreement, 153
  documentation, communication, and reimbursement, 154
  patient visits, 154
  recruiting patients, 153–154
Lipoproteins, 144
Low-density lipoprotein (LDL), 144, 226
  lowering agents, 148–151
    bile acid sequestrants, 148, 150
    ezetimibe, 148
    herbals, 150–151
    HMG-CoA, 148, 149t
    nicotinic acid, 150
Low molecular weight heparin (LMWH), 199–200, 215

M

Materials and supplies (MAT), 72
Measles, 98
   complications with, 98
   vaccine for, 98
Medical nutrition therapy (MNT)
   and diabetes, 228–229
Medicare Modernization Act of 2003, 5
Medicare Part B Reimbursement Codes, 123t
Medicare Prescription Drug Improvement and
      Modernization Act, 51, 56
Medication action plan (MAP), 25, 52
   adapted to CMS requirements, 18f
Medication therapy management (MTM) services, 2, 16,
      30, 133
   business pearls
      legalities, 6
      marketing, 6–7
      service mix, 6
   core elements of, 21t
   definition, 51–53
   for diabetes, 230–233, 243f–244f
   evolution of, 54–55
      Employer-Based Programs, 56–57
      Medicaid Programs, 56
      Medicare Part D, 56
      Minnesota Pharmaceutical Care Project, 55
      Mississippi Medicaid Disease Management Program, 55
      North Carolina and New Mexico Certified Pharmacy
         Practitioners, 56
   financial matters
      billing for services, 8–9
      financial issues, 9
      hard and soft dollar savings, 7–8
   future directions
      Accountable Care Organizations, 58
      patient-centered medical home, 57–58
   identification of, 4
      medicare part D plans, 5
      self-funded employer groups, 4
      self-pay patients, 5–6
   patient case, 10–11
   people involved in
      patient/caregiver, 2
      pharmacist, 2–3
      pharmacy students, 4
      prescriber, 3
      support staff, 3–4
   and pharmaceutical care, 50–51
      management system, 51
      patient care process, 51
      philosophy of practice, 51
   practice logo, 18f–20f
   providers, 53–54
   software, 9–10
Medication therapy review (MTR), 52
   defined, 52
   purpose of, 52
Meter dose inhalers (MDI), 64
Minnesota Pharmaceutical Care Project, 55
Minnesota Pharmacists Association, 76
Mississippi Medicaid Disease Management Program, 55
Mitral valve replacement (MVR), 199
Motivational interviewing (MI), 30
   barriers to communication
      environmental barriers, 34–35
      patient-centered barriers, 34
      personal barriers, 33–34
   case studies, 41–43
   components of, 36, 37t
   need for, 35–38
   in practice, 43–44
   principles, 39–40
      avoid argumentation, 40
      developing discrepancy, 40–41
      expressing empathy, 40
      supporting self-efficacy, 41
   usage of, 38–39

N

National Association of Chain Drug Stores (NACDS)
   core elements, 52–53
National Asthma Educator Certification Board, 71
National Certification Board for Diabetes Educators, 233
National Committee on Quality Assurance (NCQA), 57
National Council on Patient Information and Education
      (NCPIE), 132
National Health and Nutrition Examination Survey
      (NHANES), 254
National Health Interview Survey, 64
National High Blood Pressure Education Program, 262
National Kidney Foundation (NKF), 254
National Provider Identification (NPI), 122

Niacin, 150
Nicotine
    adverse effects of, 162–163
    dependence, Fagerstrom test of, 165, 166t
    gum, 177–178
    inhaler, 178–179
    lozenge, 178
    nasal spray, 178
    patch, 178
    use, impact of, 162
    withdrawal symptoms, 171
Nicotine replacement therapy (NRT), 171, 177
Nicotinic acid, 150
The Nonresponders, 3
Non-salary direct fixed costs (NDC), 72
North Carolina and New Mexico Certified Pharmacy Practitioners, 56

O

Obesity
    classification, 303, 304t
    disease states and health risks associated, 305t
    etiology, 303
    incidence of, 302f
    medications, 304t
    resources, 312
    role, 311
    treatment, 306–310, 310t
Obstructive sleep apnea (OSA), 147
Occupational Safety and Health Administration (OSHA), 116, 236
Omnibus Budget Reconciliation Act of 1990 (OBRA), 30–31
Qnexa, 309
Oral anticoagulation, disease states requiring, 198–199
Orthostatic blood pressures measurement, 257
Osteoporosis
    background, 278
    bone densitometry devices, 283
    developing services, 283
    medication for prevention and treatment, 282t
    recommendations, 281t
    risk factors, 278t
    therapeutic guidelines, 279
Overhead costs (OHC), 72
Over-the-counter (OTC), 5
    case study, 137
    consultations, documenting, 136
    as cost savings for patients, 136t, 137
    medication, 177–178
        history, 133
    medicines
        advantage of, 132
        categories of, 132
        importance of, 132
    nonprescription services, SWOT analysis for, 136t
    patient symptoms, assessment of, 133–134
        PQRSTA Mnemonic, 134
        SCHOLAR-MAC, 134
    pharmacist-provided clinics, 134–135
Oxycontin®, 16

P

The Participators, 3
Patient-centered medical home (PCMH), 57–58
Patient Centered Primary Care Collaborative (PCPCC), 58
Patient Safety and Clinical Pharmacy Services Collaborative (PSPC), 55
    defined, 55
Patient symptoms, assessment of, 133–134. *See also* Over-the-counter (OTC)
    PQRSTA Mnemonic, 134
    SCHOLAR-MAC, 134
Peak expiratory flow rate (PEFR), 66
Peripheral artery disease (PAD), 146
Personal medication record (PMR), 25, 52
    adapted to CMS requirements, 19f–20f
    defined, 52
    purpose of, 52
Pharmaceutical care
    defined, 50–51
    philosophy of, 51
    practice management system, 51
Pharmacist Immunization Center, 124
Pharmacist Prescriptive Authority Act, 56
Pharmacists
    in anticoagulation service, 200
    behavior changes discussing with patients
        readiness ruler, 32–33
        transtheoretical model, 31–32
    components of, 17, 20–24
        drug therapy problems, 21t
        outcomes, 20–22

reminders, 22–24
SOAP note revisited, 22, 23f, 24f
documentation for, 16–27
and immunizations, 98
importance of
continuity of care, 16
professional liability, 17
regulatory policy, 17
payment for services, 136–137
purpose of
continuous quality improvement, 27
pharmacy's bottom line, implications on, 26–27
resources
current situation, 24, 25f
staff training, 26
system, 24–26
The Physician Champions, 3
Pneumococcal polysaccharide vaccine (PPSV), 116
Point-of-care (POC), 203
monitors and supplies, 204
Prescriber. *See also* Medication therapy management (MTM) services
categories of, 3
role of, 3
Proactive prescribers, 6. *See also* Medication therapy management (MTM) services
Prosthetic valve (PV), 198
Pulmonary embolism (PE), 198

Q

Quantitative computed tomography (QCT), 283
Quantitative ultrasound densitometry (QUS), 283

R

Readiness ruler, role of, 32–33
Respiratory Health Conversation Maps®, 76

S

Salary of all personnel involved (SAL), 72
Self-care
defined, 132
role of, 132
Self-funded employer groups, 4. *See also* Medication therapy management (MTM) services
Short-acting beta-agonist (SABA), 71
Smoking cessation, 162
background, 162–165

behavioral change and level of dependence, 165
case study, 191–192
clinic/individual services
clinical service design, 183, 184t–185t, 185, 186t–190t, 190
enrolling participants, 183
initial decisions and overcoming barriers, 180–181, 182t
physical facilities, 181, 183
health-care providers, impact of, 164
medication management, 173, 177, 179–180
combination therapy, 180
nicotine replacement therapy, 177
OTC medications, 177–178
prescription medications, 178–179
quit attempt, 165–171
behavioral modification strategies, 169–171
components, 166–169, 168t
quit date and beyond, 172t
cravings, medications for, 171
nicotine withdrawal symptoms, 171
relapse prevention, 173, 175t–176t
slips *versus* slides, 173
stress management and cognitive techniques, 171, 173, 174t
TTM of behavior change in, 32t
Soft dollar savings, 7–8. *See also* Medication therapy management (MTM) services
Spirometry, usage of, 65
Stimulus control methods, 169
Sudden infant death syndrome (SIDS), 162
SWOT (Strengths, Weaknesses, Opportunities, Threats) analysis, 72. *See also* Asthma
for nonprescription services, 136t

T

Therapeutic lifestyle changes (TLC), 134, 147
Thiazide Diuretics, 259
Time in Therapeutic Range (TTR), 203
Transtheoretical Model (TTM), 31–32
stages of, 32t
Triglyceride-lowering agents, 151–152
fibrates, 150t, 151
n-3 polyunsaturated fatty acids, 151–152
Triglycerides (TG), 226
Trivalent influenza vaccine (TIV), 122
T-score, 285

U

United Kingdom Prospective Diabetes Study (UKPDS), 224
Utilization Review Accreditation Commission (URAC), 57

V

Vaccine Information Sheet (VIS), 122
Vaccine Injury Compensation Program (VICP), 121
Vaccines, 100
   clinics, 120
   concerns of, 99t–100t
   law, 117t–118t
   travel, 113t–115t
Vaccines for Children (VFC), 123, 124

Varenicline, 179
Venous thromboembolism (VTE), 198
   risk factors for, 199t
Very low-density lipoprotein (VLDL), 144

W

Waist circumference measurement, 305f.
Warfarin, 199–200
   clotting factor half-lives, 200t
   role of, 199
White-coat HTN, 263
World Health Organization (WHO), 198

Z

Z-score, 285